THE HUDSON RIVER ESTUARY

The Hudson River Estuary is a comprehensive look at the physical, chemical, biological, and environmental management issues that are important to our understanding of the Hudson River. Chapters cover the entire range of fields necessary to understanding the workings of the Hudson River estuary; the physics, bedrock geological setting and sedimentological processes of the estuary; ecosystem-level processes and biological interactions; and environmental issues such as fisheries, toxic substances, and the effect of nutrient input from densely populated areas. This book places special emphasis on important issues specific to the Hudson, such as the effect of power plants and high concentrations of PCBs. The chapters are written by specialists at a level that is accessible to students, teachers, and the interested layperson. The Hudson River Estuary is a unique scientific biography of a major estuary, with relevance to the study of any similar natural system in the world.

Jeffrey S. Levinton is Distinguished Professor of Ecology and Evolution at Stony Brook University and has worked for many years as a researcher in marine ecology and as a textbook writer in Marine Biology. He has been a Guggenheim Fellow, a Fulbright Senior Fellow and has done research and lectured at many institutions throughout the world. He is also the recipient of the State University of New York Chancellor's award for excellence in teaching.

John R. Waldman is Professor of Biology at Queens College of the City University of New York. He is a well-known fisheries scientist and is the author of a number of popular books in natural science. Before coming to Queens College, he worked for twenty years as a senior scientist of the Hudson River Foundation.

River, take me along,
In your sunshine, sing me a song
Ever moving and winding and free;
You rolling old river, you changing old river
Let's you and me, river, go down to the sea.

Bill Staines

The Hudson River Estuary

Edited by

Jeffrey S. Levinton
Stony Brook University

John R. Waldman
City University of New York

CAMBRIDGE
UNIVERSITY PRESS

CAMBRIDGE UNIVERSITY PRESS
Cambridge, New York, Melbourne, Madrid, Cape Town,
Singapore, São Paulo, Delhi, Tokyo, Mexico City

Cambridge University Press
32 Avenue of the Americas, New York, NY 10013-2473, USA

www.cambridge.org
Information on this title: www.cambridge.org/9780521207980

First published 2006
First paperback edition 2011

A catalog record for this publication is available from the British Library

Library of Congress Cataloging in Publication data

The Hudson River Estuary / edited by Jeffrey S. Levinton, John R. Waldman.
    p.   cm.
Includes bibliographical references.
ISBN 0-521-84478-9 (hardback)
1. Estuarine ecology – Hudson River Estuary (N.Y. and N.J.)   2. Estuarine pollution –
Environmental aspects – Hudson River Estuary (N.Y. and N.J.)   I. Levinton, Jeffrey S.
II. Waldman, John R.   III. Title.
QH104.5.H83H83   2005
577.7′86′097473 – dc22   2005011730

ISBN 978-0-521-84478-9 Hardback
ISBN 978-0-521-20798-0 Paperback

Additional resources for this publication at www.cambridge.org/9780521207980

Contents

The plates preceding Chapter 1 are available for download in color from
www.cambridge.org/9780521207980

Preface

The glorious Hudson! No river in the United States has been more loved, nurtured, ridiculed and defended, and more often written off for dead. The Hudson is replete with legends and lacks only one about a raft with Tom Sawyer and Huck Finn; but its own may be more fantastic. To native Americans it was the wondrous *Muhheakunnuk*, "great waters constantly in motion" or "the river that flows both ways." To the Dutch settlers of the valley it was a fertile wonderland, with many legends emerging from their lives and travels in the Hudson Valley and surrounding forests, fields, and mountains. Beneath the noisy bowlers that, according to legend, caused the thunderclaps atop Storm King Mountain, lay the sirenic fairies luring ships to the rocky shores of the Hudson Highlands, sending them to the deep watery grave of World's End. It is a river that held the key to the geographic unification of the nascent American revolutionary colonies and also the place where great environmental controversies led to a modern-day *sturm und drang*, giving birth to an era of environmental activism. If this is too burdensome a legacy to bear, the Hudson also gives us its lightness of being: A fall day in a kayak or a ferry ride, or a refreshing swim, or even a big fish to catch. The Hudson valley has produced the greatest school of landscape painting in America and a host of novels with a strong sense of place, from those of Washington Irving to T. C. Boyle.

Many of us have desperately wanted a book that could address a crucial and more concrete need. The many scientific faces of Hudson River research have never been gathered effectively in a single place. Some excellent volumes have captured the natural history of the Hudson and we especially have Robert Boyle to thank for his dedication to the Hudson in his 1969 volume "The Hudson River, A Natural and Unnatural History." Equally important is the more scientifically inclined treatment of Hudson River research compiled by Karin Limburg and others in 1986. This book set a high standard, but lacks many recent important findings.

With this background we sought to provide a comprehensive volume that covers a wide spectrum of topics, ranging from the physics of water movement, to the biology, to the current environmental problems created by human impacts on the Hudson. In 1998 I approached the Hudson River Foundation with such an idea, which was met with considerable enthusiasm and led to the pleasure of contacting a group of broad-thinking and highly competent colleagues who engaged the project with similar zeal. I later asked John Waldman to join me in editing this large and diverse array of contributions. Of the senior authors of the thirty chapters in this book, I can honestly say that virtually no one who was invited turned me down. All recognized the need for this book, but perhaps some had different schedules than others for completion. Hence, the invitations in 1999 were finally answered with the last typescripts in 2003. All but one were created de novo to fit the volume. The only exception is a very important paper (Baker et al., Chapter 24) describing the science behind the Polychlorinated Biehenyl (PCB) issue in the Hudson, which is reprinted here with slight modifications.

This book could not have been produced without the generous support of the Hudson River Foundation, which provided some support for me to design the scope of the volume and to contact prospective authors. I am especially grateful to the authors who so generously contributed their time and energy to producing the chapters that comprise the book. Clay Hiles and Dennis Suszkowski provided advice and support and provided crucial contacts and suggestions of chapter authors. We thank Susan

Detwiler and Peggy Rote for their preparation of the volume. Finally, we are very grateful to Kirk Jensen, formerly of Cambridge University Press, for his suggestions, support and encouragement and to Peter Gordon of Cambridge Press who completed the project.

I would especially like to thank John Waldman for joining me as an editor of this volume and we both are grateful to the patience and support of our families during the long time during which this book reached completion. I learned more and more every day I walked the shore with Cady.

Jeffrey Levinton
Stony Brook, New York
June 20, 2005

Contributors

Kenneth W. Able*, Rutgers University, Institute of Marine and Coastal Sciences, Marine Field Station, 800 Great Bay Blvd., Tuckerton, NJ 08087-2004, email: able@imcs.rutgers.edu

Michael Aucott, NJ Department of Environmental Protection, 401 East State Street, Trenton, NJ 08625-0409

Joel E. Baker*, Chesapeake Biological Laboratory, University of Maryland, Solomons, MD 20688, email: baker@cbl.umces.edu

Robin Bell*, Lamont-Doherty Earth Observatory, Palisades, NY 10964-8000, email: robinb@ldeo.columbia.edu

Elizabeth A. Blair, New York State Department of Environmental Conservation, Bard College Field Station, Annandale, NY 12504

W. Frank Bohlen, University of Connecticut, Department of Marine Sciences, 1080 Shennecossett Road, Groton, CT 06340, email: bohlen@uconnvm.uconn.edu

Henry Bokuniewicz*, Marine Sciences Research Center, Stony Brook University, Stony Brook, NY 11794-5000, email: hbokuniewicz@notes.cc.sunysb.edu

Richard F. Bopp*, Department of Earth and Environmental Sciences Rensselaer Polytechnic Institute, Troy, NY 12180, email: boppr@rpi.edu

Elizabeth W. Boyer, Department of Environmental Science, Policy, and Management, University of California, Berkeley, CA 94720, email: boyer@nature.berkeley.edu

Thomas M. Brosnan*, National Oceanic and Atmospheric Administration, 1305 East West Highway, Room 10355, Silver Spring, MD 20910, email: tom.brosnan@noaa.gov

Bruce Brownawell, Marine Sciences Research Center, Stony Brook University, Stony Brook, NY 11794, email: bbrownawell@notes.cc.sunysb.edu

Nina F. Caraco, Institute of Ecosystem Studies, 65 Sharon Turnpike, Millbrook, NY 12545, email: caracon@ecostudies.org

Suzanne Carbotte, Lamont-Doherty Earth Observatory, Palisades, NY 10964-8000, email: robinb@ldeo.columbia.edu

Robert M. Cerrato*, Marine Sciences Research Center, Stony Brook University, Stony Brook, NY 11794-5000, email: Robert.Cerrato@sunysb.edu

Damon A. Chaky, Lamont-Doherty Earth Observatory of Columbia University, Palisades, NY 10964, email: chakyd@ldeo.columbia.edu

Robert Chant, Institute of Marine and Coastal Sciences, Rutgers University, 71 Dudley Road, New Brunswick, NJ 08901, email: chant@imcs.rutgers.edu

Steven N. Chillrud, Lamont-Doherty Earth Observatory of Columbia University, Palisades, NY 10964, email: chilli@ldeo.columbia.edu

J. Kirk Cochran*, Marine Sciences Research Center, Stony Brook University, Stony Brook, NY 11794, email: kcochran@notes.cc.sunysb.edu

Jonathan J. Cole*, Institute of Ecosystem Studies, 65 Sharon Turnpike, Millbrook, NY 12545, email: colej@ecostudies.org

Tracy Collier, Northwest Fisheries Science Center, 2725 Montlake Blvd. East, Seattle, WA 98112-2097, email: Tracy.K.Collier@noaa.gov

Thomas F. Cooney, III, Hazen & Sawyer, 498 7th Ave, 11th Floor, New York, NY 10018, tel (212) 777-8400, email: tcooney@hazenandsawyer.com

Milene Cormier, Lamont-Doherty Earth Observatory, Palisades, NY 10964-8000, tel (845) 365-8827, fax (845) 365-8179

Christopher F. D'Elia, Environmental Science and Policy, University of South Florida, St. Petersburg, FL 33701, email: cdelia@spadmin.usf.edu

Jordi Dachs, 14 College Farm Rd., Rutgers University, New Brunswick, NJ 08901

Darin R. Damiani, U.S. Army Corps of Engineers New York District, Environmental Analysis Branch, Planning Division, 26 Federal Plaza, New York, NY 10278-0090, email: darin.r.damiani@usace.army.mil

Janet T. Duffy-Anderson, NOAA/National Marine Fisheries Service, Alaska Fisheries Science Center/RACE, 7600 Sand Point Way, NE, Bldg. 4 Seattle, WA 98115, email: Janet.Duffy-Anderson@noaa.gov

Stephen Eisenreich, 14 College Farm Rd., Rutgers University, New Brunswick, NJ 08901

Kevin J. Farley*, Environmental Engineering Department, Manhattan College, Riverdale, NY 10471, email: kevin.farley@manhattan.edu

Huan Feng, Dept. of Earth and Environmental Studies, Montclair State University, Upper Montclair, NJ 07043

Vicki Lynn Ferrini, Marine Sciences Research Center, State University of New York at Stony Brook, Stony Brook, NY 11794-5000

Stuart E. G. Findlay*, Institute of Ecosystem Studies, Box AB, Millbrook, NY 12545, email: FindlayS@ecostudies.org

Roger D. Flood, Marine Sciences Research Center, Stony Brook University, Stony Brook, NY 11794-5000, email: roger.flood@sunysb.edu

W. Rockwell Geyer*, Woods Hole Oceanographic Institution, 98 Water Street, MS #12, Woods Hole, MA 02571, email: rgeyer@whoi.edu

Cari L. Gigliotti, 14 College Farm Rd., Rutgers University, New Brunswick, NJ 08901

Anne L. Golden, Department of Community and Preventive Medicine, Mount Sinai School of Medicine, New York, NY 10029

Kathryn A. Hattala, Hudson River Fisheries Unit, New York State Department of Environmental Conservation, 21 South Putt Corners Road, New Paltz, NY 12561, email: kahattal@gw.dec.state.ny.us

Leo J. Hetling, Adjunct Professor, Environmental and Energy Engineering, Rensselaer Polytechnic Institute, 10 Gladwish Road, Delmar, NY 12054, email: lhetling@att.net

David J. Hirschberg, Marine Sciences Research Center, Stony Brook University, Stony Brook, NY 11794

Robert W. Howarth*, Department of Ecology and Evolutionary Biology, Cornell University, Ithaca, NY 14853, and The Ecosystems Center, Marine Biological Lab, Woods Hole, MA 02543

Andrew W. Kahnle, Hudson River Fisheries Unit, New York State Department of Environmental Conservation, 21 South Putt Corners Road, New Paltz, NY 12561-1620, email: awkahnle@gw.dec.state.ny.us

Erik Kiviat*, Hudsonia Ltd., P.O. Box 5000, Annandale, NY 12504-5000, email: kiviat@bard.edu

John W. Ladd, Hudson River National Estuarine Research Reserve, New York State Dept of Environmental Conservation, 43 Hudson Watch Drive, Ossining, NY 10562

Thomas R. Lake, New York State Department of Environmental Conservation, Hudson River Estuary Program, 21 S. Putt Corners Rd., New Paltz, NY 12561, email: trlake7@aol.com

Robin Landeck Miller*, HydroQual, Inc., 1200 MacArthur Boulevard, Mahwah, NJ 07430, email: rmiller@hydroqual.com

Phillip J. Landrigan*, Department of Community and Preventive Medicine, Mount Sinai School of Medicine, New York, NY 10029, email: phil.landrigan@mssm.edu

Jeffrey S. Levinton*, Department of Ecology and Evolution, Stony Brook University, Stony Brook, NY 11794-5245, tel (631) 632-8602, fax (631) 632-7626, email: levinton@life.bio.sunysb.edu

Karin E. Limburg*, State University of New York, College of Environmental Science Forestry, Syracuse, NY 13210, email: klimburg@esf.edu

Darcy J. Lonsdale, Marine Sciences Research Center, Stony Brook University, Stony Brook, NY 11794-5245, email: dlonsdale@notes.cc.sunysb.edu

Anne L. McElroy, Marine Sciences Research Center, Stony Brook, NY, 11794-5245, email: amcelroy@notes.cc.sunysb.edu

Cecilia McHugh, School of Earth and Environmental Sciences, Queens College, City University of New York, 65-30 Kissena Blvd., Flushing, NY 11367

Roxanne Marino, Department of Ecology and Evolutionary Biology, Cornell University, Ithaca, NY 14853, and The Ecosystems Center, Marine Biological Lab, Woods Hole, MA 02543

Steven G. Morgan*, Bodega Marine Laboratory, University of California at Davis, P. O. Box 247, Bodega Bay, CA 94923 USA, email: sgmorgan@ucdavis.edu

Rob Nairn, Baird & Associates, 627 Lyons Lane, Suite 200, Oakville, Ontario Canada L6J 5Z7, email: rnairn@baird.com

W. Charles Nieder, Hudson River NERR/New York State Department of Environmental Conservation, Annandale, NY 12504, email: wcnieder@gw.dec.state.ny.us

Michael L. Pace*, Institute of Ecosystem Studies, 65 Sharon Turnpike, Millbrook, NY 12545, email: pacem@ecostudies.org

Lisa Rosman, Coastal Protection and Restoration Division, NOAA, 290 Broadway, New York, NY 10007

William B. F. Ryan, Lamont-Doherty Earth Observatory, Palisades, NY 10964-8000

Robert E. Schmidt, Hudsonia Limited and Simon's Rock College, 84 Alford Rd., Great Barrington, MA 01230, email: schmidt@simons-rock.edu

Shu Yan, 14 College Farm Rd., Rutgers University, New Brunswick, NJ 08901

Edward L. Shuster, Department of Earth and Environmental Sciences Rensselaer Polytechnic Institute, Troy, NY 12180, email: shuste@rpi.edu

H. James Simpson*, Department of Earth and Environmental Sciences, Lamont-Doherty Earth Observatory of Columbia University, Palisades, NY 10964, email: simpsonj@ldeo.columbia.edu

Leslie Sirkin, deceased

John P. St. John, HydroQual, Inc., 1200 MacArthur Boulevard, Mahwah, NJ 07430

Andrew Stoddard, Dynamic Solutions, LLC, 112 Orchard Circle, Hamilton, VA, 20158-9734, email: StudyWQ@aol.com

David L. Strayer*, Institute of Ecosystem Studies, P.O. Box AB, Millbrook, NY 12545, email: strayerd@ecostudies.org

Dennis J. Suszkowski*, Hudson River Foundation, 17 Battery Place, New York, NY 10004, email: dennis@hudsonriver.org

Dennis P. Swaney, Department of Ecology and Evolutionary Biology, Cornell University, Ithaca, NY 14853

Joanne Thissen, Lamont-Doherty Earth Observatory, Palisades, NY 10964-8000, present address: Liberty Science Center, Liberty State Park, Jersey City, NJ 07305

Lisa A. Totten*, 14 College Farm Rd., Rutgers University, New Brunswick, NJ 08901, email: totten@envsci.rutgers.edu

Daryl A. VanRy, 14 College Farm Rd., Rutgers University, New Brunswick, NJ 08901

Roelof Versteeg, Lamont-Doherty Earth Observatory, Palisades, NY 10964-8000, present address: Idaho National Engineering and Environmental Laboratory, P.O. Box 1625, Idaho Falls, ID 83415

John R. Waldman*, Hudson River Foundation, 17 Battery Place, New York, NY 10004, present address: Department of Biology, Queens College, City University of New York, Flushing, NY 11367

James R. Wands, HydroQual, Inc., 1200 MacArthur Blvd., Mahwah, NJ 07430, email: jwands@hydroqual.com

Judith S. Weis, Department of Biological Sciences, Rutgers University, Newark, NJ 07102, email: jweis@andromeda.rutgers.edu

Cathleen Wigand, United States Environmental Protection Agency, Narragansett, RI 02882, email: wigand.cathleen@epamail.epa.gov

Isaac Wirgin*, Nelson Institute of Environmental Medicine, New York University School of Medicine, Tuxedo, NY 10987, email: wirgin@env.med.nyu.edu

THE HUDSON RIVER ESTUARY

View of the Hudson River from Olana (former home of artist Frederick Church), south of Hudson, New York. Photo by Heather Malcom.

Pickerel weed in flower, South Cove, with West Point in background.

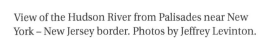

View of the Hudson River from Palisades near New York – New Jersey border. Photos by Jeffrey Levinton.

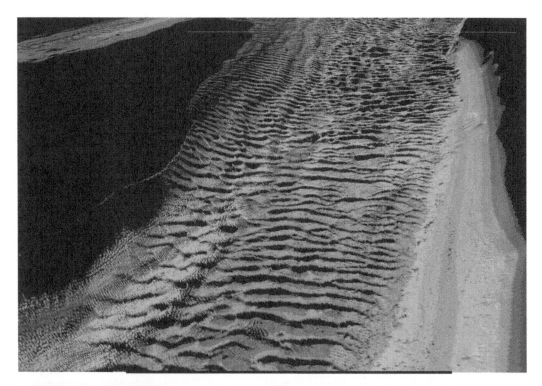

A great deal has been learned from a Hudson River survey using multi-beam scanning of the river bed (see Chapter 5). Top: a false-colored scan of the bottom showing large sand waves (scale at bottom in 300 m). Bottom: One of a number of wrecks discovered in the survey. Scans provided by Roger Flood.

Moodna Creek Marsh, Orange County, New York. Photo by Stuart Findlay.

Constitution Marsh, showing patch of expanding *Phragmites australis* among larger stands of cattails. Photo by Jeffrey Levinton.

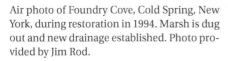

Air photo of Foundry Cove, Cold Spring, New York, during restoration in 1994. Marsh is dug out and new drainage established. Photo provided by Jim Rod.

Cattails, a dominant of freshwater tidal marshes. Photo by Jeffrey Levinton.

Muskrat lodge, Constitution Marsh. Photo by Eric Lind.

Left – Young-of-year menhaden (top) and gizzard shad. Right – White perch. Photos furnished by John Waldman.

Left – Marsh wren nest on cattails. Right – Sampling for benthic animals. Photos by Jeffrey Levinton.

Closeup of water chestnut, *Trapa natans*, bed; floating seed at lower left. Photos by Jeffrey Levinton.

Left: The zebra mussel, *Dreissena polymorpha*. Photo by Jeffrey Levinton. Right: Zebra mussels settled on a pipe, Foundry Cove. Photo by Jeffrey Levinton.

Left: A nesting female snapping turtle, *Chelydra serpentina* (shell length ca. 36 cm long). Right: Same turtle, about 200 feet above marsh in rear, from which she climbed up a steep slope to get to this nesting site. Photos by Jeffrey Levinton.

Returning a shortnose sturgeon, *Acipenser brevirostrum*, to the river. Photo by Kristin Marcell.

A shad bake, organized by Hudson River Foundation educator Christopher Letts. Photo by John Waldman.

Seining for fish in the shallows of Tivoli South Bay next to a water chestnut bed. Jeremy Frenzel (right) takes a sample with his father while working as a Polgar Fellow in the Hudson River Estuarine Sanctuary. Photo by Karin Limburg. Sadly, Jeremy died in 2005.

The blue claw crab, *Callinectes sapidus*. Photo by Gregg Kenney.

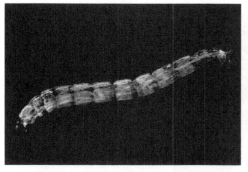

Chironomid larva. Photo by Eric Lind.

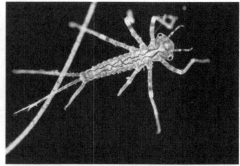

Damselfly larva. Photo by Eric Lind.

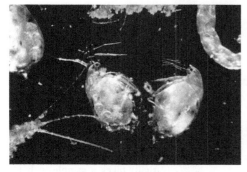

Daphnia sp. Photo by Eric Lind.

Gammarid amphipods. Photo by Eric Lind.

Bivalve, *Rangia cuneata*. Photo by Jeffrey Levinton.

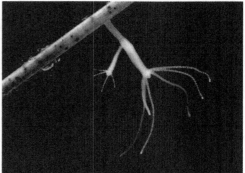

Hydra budding. Photo by Eric Lind.

1 The Hudson River Estuary: Executive Summary

Jeffrey S. Levinton and John R. Waldman

From the Tear of the Clouds to the Verrazano

The ecological and cultural importance of the Hudson is surely not revealed by its size. Its drainage basin is about 34,000 square kilometers (km) (13,000 square miles), which is less than one percent of the United States. In contrast, the Mississippi drains about half of the area of the lower 48 states. Compared to the mighty Mississippi's length of 3,700 km, the Hudson, originating in the Adirondacks and pulsing to the sea through the Verrazano Narrows, flows over a main course of only 500 km (ca. 300 miles).

Henry Hudson and his crew first saw the mouth of the Hudson in 1609, but it wasn't until the 1870s that its origin was declared, at tiny Lake Tear of the Clouds, near Mt. Marcy in the Adirondacks. The small rivers and streams flowing from Adirondack peaks over 1000 meters (m) in elevation descend to a lowland drainage usually less than 100 m above sea level. Below Troy the river is navigable to the Narrows entrance to the ocean.

The Terrane

The Hudson River drains New York, and parts of Vermont, Massachusetts, Connecticut, and New Jersey. The basin contains three subareas: the upper Hudson from Mt. Marcy to Troy, the Mohawk from Rome to Troy, and the lower Hudson from Troy to New York Bay (we try to stick to this terminology throughout the book, but some authors have failed us). The Hudson and Mohawk basins are fresh water; the lower Hudson is an estuary, with water greater than 1 practical salinity unit (psu) usually below West Point.

The drainage and flow pattern of the upper Hudson is complex and consists of a number of streams coursing through the Precambrian and early Paleozoic rocks of the Adirondacks (Chapter 2). By contrast, the lower Hudson takes a reasonably straight shot to its terminus (Figure 1.1a, b, c). The regional geological lineations seem oblivious to the Hudson's flow, which slices across a series of complex terranes. The mid-Hudson cuts through early and middle Paleozoic sedimentary rocks, with the Catskills to the west and the Taconics to the east. Most notably, the river then runs through the Hudson Highlands, early Paleozoic geological formations that trend directly east-west across the Hudson's flow path in the vicinity of West Point. The river's erosion simply cut downward through this cross-cutting terrane with no notice of its geological contrariness.

Below this region the river passes the Triassic volcanic cliffs of the Palisades and then moves past the New York group, a series of Proterozoic and early Paleozoic metamorphic rocks and then a series of terminal deposits of the last glacial epoch. Along the entire stretch of the lower Hudson, one is impressed by the steep banks and even cliffs along the shoreline. Most other estuaries in the United States meander to the sea along a broad low-relief flood plain. The Hudson clearly has cut down through a great deal of bedrock and yet, owing to its relative youthful erosional history, has not formed a large depositional plain near its mouth.

The Hudson's straight southerly course has cut through these disparate geological terranes and, during the time of the glacial ages, formed a classic U-shaped cross section, much like the glacial fjords of southwestern Norway. During the height of the most recent glacial advance during the Pleistocene Epoch, the glaciers scoured the Hudson to a depth of 150–200 m (488–650 feet). Then, as the glaciers retreated, the Hudson obtained the shape of a fjord, with a deep U-shaped valley. Glacially-derived sediment filled the now quiet-water Hudson so that today it is rarely more than 50 m deep, although

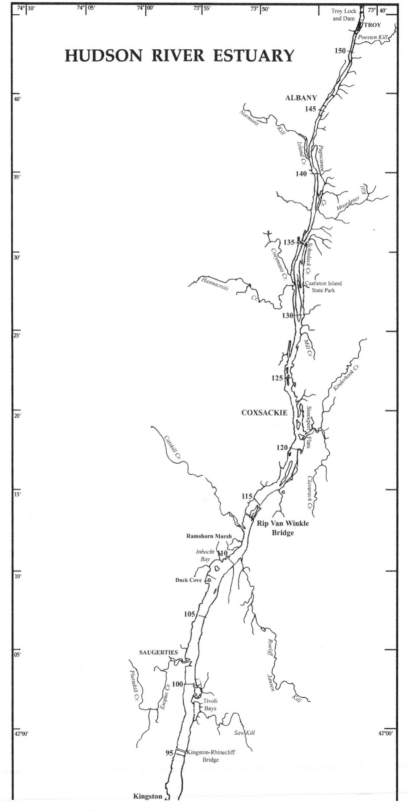

Figure 1.1. The Hudson River Estuary (*continued on next two pages*).

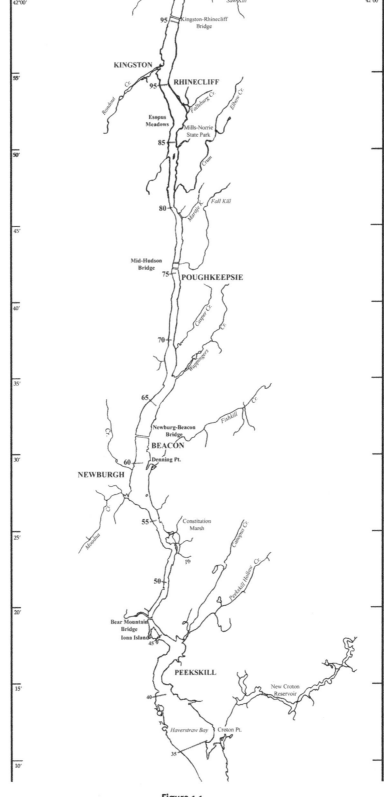

b

Figure 1.1.

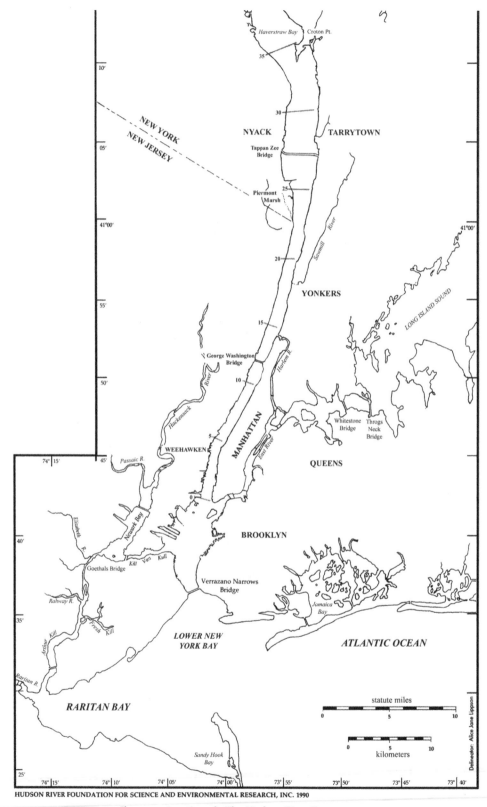

HUDSON RIVER FOUNDATION FOR SCIENCE AND ENVIRONMENTAL RESEARCH, INC. 1990

Figure 1.1 (*continued*). The Hudson River Estuary.

it reaches greater depths at World's End in the Highlands.

Thanks to the post glacial rise of sea level, the Hudson River Estuary is now a drowned river valley falling only 1.5 meters along the 240 km between Troy and the Battery. The estuary is maintained as a shipping channel, and dredged to a minimum depth of 9–11 m, although portions of the river are much deeper. Slightly more than half the estuary is fringed by marshes and wooded swamps; the remainder consists of mud flats that are flooded at high tide. Wetlands such as tidal marshes are in greatest abundance in the upper third of the estuary (Chapter 20).

The River That Flows Both Ways

The Hudson River is, in the parlance of estuarine scientists, a *partially mixed estuary*, which means that a distinct mixing occurs between the ocean and the freshwater river, leading to a layered structure. Higher salinity water is overlain by lower salinity water (Chapter 3) over a broad stretch of mixing between the river and the ocean. The estuary can be divided into four salinity zones: polyhaline (18.5–30 psu), mesohaline (5–18), oligohaline (0.3–5), and limnetic (<0.3). The location of these zones varies seasonally as well as daily depending on tidal and freshwater inputs. In New York Harbor, between the Verrazano Narrows and approximately the George Washington Bridge, the distinct two-layer vertical structure occurs, with a saline bottom layer overlain by a freshwater surface lens. Wind and tide mix the two layers so there is a vertical salinity gradient from fresh to saline, as one goes from the surface to bottom waters. At some point upstream the Hudson is fresh water from surface to bottom.

Although this basic salinity structure is always present, it varies radically with season and weather. After the spring freshet, when snows melt in the upper part of the watershed and spring rains increase freshwater flow downstream, the surface freshwater lens in the mixing zone extends much further down into New York Harbor. Thus, the three-dimensional distribution of salt is complex and dynamic. Water circulation also differs from bank to deepest depth to opposite bank and this also affects the distribution of salt in the river.

North and above the Federal Dam at Troy, the Hudson has a conventional river flow, with a series of rivers and streams feeding from eastern and western uplands into the main course of the river. Below the dam the river is tidal. It must be upsetting for a stranger to see the river flowing opposite ways, depending upon the movement of the tide. The surface of the river at Albany is not much more than a meter higher than at the narrows, 240 km downstream. Thus tidal currents propagate a surprisingly large distance upstream.

Tides are caused by the gravitational interaction of the sun, moon, and the waters of the earth. In our region, the rotation of the earth, combined with gravitational attraction, results in approximately two high and two low tides per day at the coast. In the transitional zone in New York Harbor, where fresh or very low-salinity water becomes salty, the tide exerts a major vertical mixing effect. During spring tides this mixing is nearly complete and the salinity in New York Harbor is relatively homogeneous from surface to bottom. During neap tides flow is more reduced and one sees a more distinct lower salinity later overlying a higher salinity bottom layer.

As the tide rises, a tidal current moves northward up the Hudson. The time taken for the propagation of this current results in a significant delay between the time of high tide at the Verrazano Narrows and points upstream. High tide at West Point is a full three hours later than at the Narrows. The propagation is so drawn out that it can be high tide at one part of the length of the Hudson while being dead low at another. This makes for complex flow patterns. Flow is further complicated by the changing width and depth. As the width decreases a greater volume of water is forced through a narrower channel, which increases the flow velocity. Thus water flow through the narrow throat adjacent to the Hudson Highlands is far greater than in the broad width of Haverstraw Bay in the vicinity of Indian Point Power Plant.

On the shortest time scale, tidal flow is the controlling factor of water motion. But over longer seasonal time scales, the inevitable flow of fresh water from uplands to the oceans creates a net movement of fresh water downstream. This flow varies strongly and is generally strongest during the late winter and spring. On the still longer decadal time scale, one encounters some years with far more fresh-water flow than others, with an inevitable shifting of fresh water downstream into New York Harbor.

A Dynamic Sedimentary Environment

The first impression one gets of the Hudson is its turbidity and the abundance of soft sediment. As a Secchi disk (the aquatic scientist's traditional in-dicator of turbidity) is dropped below the surface, one is impressed at how the disk quickly fades from view, usually only a half meter or so below the sur-face. As a large barge moves upriver, one imme-diately sees silt and mud stirred from the bottom adjacent to the shore. Both these phenomena com-bined indicate that the Hudson is dominated by suspended particles and is very dynamic as a sed-imentary environment. It is not unusual to find sites where 10–20 cm or more of sediment may be deposited in a matter of days, and where similar amounts can be eroded away.

The Hudson's load of suspended sediment de-rives principally from clays eroded from surficial glacial lake and glacial outwash deposits (Chap-ter 4). Otherwise, the main stem of the Hudson flows through relatively resistant rocky terrane, which does not supply a great deal of sedimentary material. While turbid along its entire main chan-nel, peaks of suspended sedimentary particles are found at the northerly extent of saline water and in the mid-Hudson. Because of the two-layered flow of the Hudson in the New York Harbor region, up-current flow in the deep layer transports sediment from the ocean to within the estuary.

The strong tidal mixing throughout the estuary results in strong current conditions at the bottom. Recently, a bottom survey using multibeam scan-ning sonar has detected a truly fantastic system of sand ripples with wave lengths of many meters and ripple amplitudes of a few meters (Chapter 5). The New York-New Jersey Harbor region is also a dy-namic sedimentary environment and water move-ment and sediment deposition is complicated by extensive dredge channels that are maintained for shipping traffic.

A River Contaminated

Sediments in the Hudson are repositories for a vast array of toxic substances, which have been discharged from industrial pipes, sewage treat-ment plants, and general runoff over many decades. Persistent contaminants include PCBs, dioxins, chlorinated hydrocarbon pesticides, and trace metals such as copper, lead, zinc, cadmium, chromium, and mercury (Chapters 7, 24, 25, 26). In recent years alkylphenol ethoxylate (APEO) metabolites have been found and are believed to act as endocrine disruptors. Most famous are the high concentrations of dioxins and other sub-stances in sites such as the Raritan River and high concentrations of PCBs in sediments above and be-low the Federal Dam in Troy. A 2001 EPA decision will result in the eventual dredging and disposal of PCB-laden materials. The Hudson River is the sec-ond most contaminated large estuary in the United States with metals, including mercury and copper.

In 1995, a Superfund cleanup removed cad-mium-laden sediments in Foundry Cove near Cold Spring (Chapter 30). Many areas, however, still have high concentrations of toxics and proposed New York Harbor dredging therefore raises the im-portant question of disposal. Extensive studies of dated sediment cores provide important evidence of contaminant deposition histories and insights into degradation processes (Chapters 25, 26).

A Rich Array of Habitats

The Hudson River Estuary is an ecologically het-erogeneous environment with a diverse array of habitat types (Table 1.1). It is essential to have an inventory of these habitats in order to under-stand their relative impacts on water characteris-tics of the Hudson and to develop management, conservation, and restoration plans. Most of the Hudson consists of deep water habitats that are dynamic hydrological and sedimentary environ-ments. We know far too little about these areas, which is a problem when considering deep-water populations, especially those of shortnose stur-geon and Atlantic sturgeon. Recent surveys using remote sensing and direct sediment coring have provided a complete sediment-habitat map of the freshwater part of the estuary (Chapter 5).

Among the most ecologically important and poorly understood habitats are tidal wetlands, which include freshwater and salt marshes (Chap-ter 20). Both are biologically diverse and are locations of sedimentation, which is strongly

Table 1.1. Habitat types of the Hudson River Estuary; Troy Dam to the Battery

Habitat type	Percent
Shallows	34
Tidal wetlands	9
Submerged attached vegetation	6
Floating vegetation	2
Non-vegetated bare bottom	17
Deep-water bottom >3m depth	66

Source: Courtesy of Elizabeth Blair, New York State Department of Environmental Conservation and Hudson River National Estuarine Sanctuary.

regulated by intertidal vegetation such as cattails (fresh water) and cord grasses of the genus *Spartina* (salt water). The vegetation harbors many animal species and also protects a series of channels, which are hotspots for aquatic animal diversity and often nursery grounds for juveniles of many fish species. Tidal marshes often dominate the large number of coves, whose hydrodynamics and overall ecology are strongly affected by the enclosing peninsulas created by railroad construction in the nineteenth century. The marshes may be sources of labile organic matter for the open Hudson River estuarine food web.

Shallow coves and bays are often covered by submarine attached vegetation, which includes at least twelve species, but is dominated by water celery. A number of coves have been successfully invaded by the floating water chestnut, a continuing source of annoyance to Hudson River residents. Despite this large amount of vegetation cover, most shallow areas consist of bare bottom and harbor a diverse benthic fauna (Chapter 19).

An extremely important but poorly understood habitat component of the Hudson River Estuary is the large suite of at least seventy-nine tributaries aside from the large Mohawk River, including rivers such as Indian Brook near Cold Spring and the Saw Mill River, which enters the river in Yonkers. The tributaries contribute approximately 20 percent of the water to the Hudson, a significant amount of particulate carbon and sedimentary material, and are crucial habitats for a wide variety of invertebrates and fishes. Alewifes use the tributaries extensively but we still do not know nearly enough about the importance of tributaries to the life cycles of a number of other fish species (Chapter 15). Interest in the Hudson's tributaries has heightened because urbanization has taken its toll on water quality and there is some evidence that the most urbanized tributaries contain greatly reduced fish populations.

The Base of the Food Web

Estuaries are among the most productive of marine environments, although food abundance does fluctuate greatly over space and time. This extraordinary productivity is a product of the large amounts of nutrients that enter the estuary seasonally and their extensive recycling between the overlying water and the biologically active sediments. The Hudson has some interesting complications that create exceptions to these generalizations. Most importantly, the Hudson bears a large sediment load, coming from its drainage system and consisting of materials ranging from clays derived from erosion of glacially derived deposits to organic particles derived from substances such as leaf litter. The combination of materials reduces light penetration in the water column, which in turn reduces photosynthesis of phytoplankton and restricts subaquatic attached vegetation to very shallow depths. The high particle concentration is complicated by strong vertical mixing, owing to tidal and wind mixing. Thus, phytoplankton cells spend much of their time in suboptimal light conditions.

Owing mainly to light limitation, the Hudson is not a river with high primary production in the water column (Chapter 9). Primary production is seasonal, with a peak in spring. Respiration, however, is a dominant process and little production is available for higher trophic levels in the Hudson. The freshwater phytoplankton are not limited by nutrients, but by light. In recent years the invasion of the zebra mussel has strongly reduced phytoplankton populations, which has further reduced the potential for oxygen production from photosynthesis. The respiration of the zebra mussels has lowered oxygen concentrations in the freshwater Hudson, which may be stressful to active organisms such as fish under some circumstances.

In the saline part of the Hudson in the vicinity of New York Harbor nutrient concentrations increase greatly as a result of dissolved sources from sewage. Nutrients are so concentrated that phytoplankton production is not limited by nutrients, but by light and temperature. Nutrient input in the saline part of the Hudson is among the highest of any coastal water body in America. Before the 1990s, organic matter input from untreated sewage resulted in anoxic or strongly hypoxic waters in New York Harbor. Since then, water quality has improved greatly, as has oxygen levels (Chapters 10, 23).

Zooplankton are abundant in both the freshwater and saline parts of the Hudson estuary, but in neither part of the estuary do they exert major grazing effects on the phytoplankton (Chapter 16). The zooplankton in the freshwater part of the Hudson are dominated by copepods, rotifers, and cladocera. Occasionally ciliates and flagellates are very abundant. While they may not be important in the cycling of nutrients, the zooplankton, nevertheless, are crucial food sources for larval and juvenile fish. It is notable, therefore, that the invasion of the zebra mussel resulted in strong decline of some zooplankton, particularly rotifers. It is not clear whether the decline was due to direct consumption by the mussels or by a shortage of phytoplankton food caused by zebra mussel feeding. In the saline portion of the Hudson, copepods dominate the zooplankton and feed mainly on phytoplankton.

Heartbeats in the Muck

The benthos of the Hudson is dominated by species capable of living in soft bottoms. In freshwater areas the benthos consists mainly of diminutive animal species such as larvae of chironomid flies, oligochaete worms who depend upon organic detritus and sediment microbes for food (Chapter 19). Predatory fly larvae and amphipods are also common. In the saline reaches of the estuary, these species are supplanted by abundant polychaete annelids, amphipods, and patchy occurrences of mollusks such as clams. Again, a dependence on particulate organic matter and sediment microbes is widespread (Chapter 18). These animal species form rich populations that burrow in the sediment and accelerate the breakdown of organic matter and recycling of this material back to the water column. A few invertebrate species are specialized and are confined to the low salinity (oligohaline

and mesohaline) parts of the Hudson and are neither common in open marine nor purely freshwater habitats.

Both the freshwater and saline parts of the Hudson Estuary were once far more dominated by native suspension-feeding bivalves. In the limnetic region, freshwater mussels (members of the bivalve family Unionidae) were common in both the tributaries and in the main course of the Hudson, but they have been decreasing for decades, probably owing to habitat alteration. The invasion of the zebra mussel has probably further accelerated the decline of this group. In the saline part of the estuary, oyster beds were once ubiquitous, and the Fresh Kills area of Staten Island was one of the most productive oyster grounds in the United States in the early part of the nineteenth century. Pollution and exploitation have taken their toll, however, and oysters remain uncommon in New York Harbor. Clams are still exploited in Raritan Bay but they have recently suffered from disease.

Fisheries, Past and Present

The Hudson River is blessed with high fish biodiversity for a temperate estuary, with more than 210 species recorded from its entire watershed (Chapters 13, 14). The Hudson once supported rich commercial fisheries throughout its tidal waters. American shad were landed along the entire river, even across from Manhattan. Today, nearly all of its native fishes survive – some in robust numbers – but its commercial fisheries are almost extinct, shut down in 1976 because of contamination with PCBs. Among finfish, only American shad (a species that spends most of its life outside the system) are still harvested for profit, albeit in limited numbers as both fish and fishermen dwindle. Blue crabs, at the very northern limit of their range, also are caught by commercial and recreational fishers alike.

Other formerly important commercial fishes are protected from any harvest or from commercial fishing alone. Shortnose sturgeon appear to have quadrupled in stock size since the 1970s, yet remain off limits to all fishing because of their listing as a federally endangered species. Atlantic sturgeon – the behemoth of the river, once reaching 12 feet and 800 pounds – have been protected from all harvest in U.S. waters since 1998. Striped bass, formerly a major commercial species, can only be legally taken by anglers. However, the Hudson's striped bass population has grown enormously over the past two decades and it now supports a regionally-important recreational fishery during springtime for large, spawning-size fish.

Resident freshwater fishes such as channel catfish, white catfish, brown bullhead, yellow perch, and white perch are fished recreationally despite consumption advisories. The two non-native black basses – largemouth and smallmouth bass – are also avidly sought in the Hudson, where they form the basis of catch-and-release tournament fisheries.

Electric generating stations that withdraw Hudson River water for cooling purposes have caused considerable mortality of young life stages of Hudson River fishes, but their eventual replacement with modern facilities which use far less water should reduce these effects. Long-term reductions in PCB levels should allow for greater enjoyment of the river's fish resources.

Invasion of Exotic Species

From the time of the settlement of the Dutch colony of New Amsterdam to the digging of the Erie Canal, New York Harbor and the Hudson estuary became a major focus of long-distance commerce, which has made this region a target for the introduction of exotic species (Chapter 21). The Hudson estuary has over 100 alien species in continuing residence, some of which have had major effects on structural habitats and ecosystem functioning. While some species were introduced purposefully, most arrived owing to the water-borne access to Great Lakes and New York Harbor shipping. In the nineteenth century, the use of solid ballast brought a number of aquatic plants to the region. In recent decades, solid ballast was replaced by water, but this has brought a new batch of alien species in the form of plankton and larvae of benthic species. Most alien species derived from Europe or from the interior of North America.

In some cases, the arrival of alien species has been perceived as desirable by residents of the region surrounding the estuary, as witnessed by the widespread black bass fishing tournaments. But in other cases, aliens are noticeable intruders. The water chestnut, a Eurasian native, was introduced

purposefully into a lake but soon escaped into the entire estuary. It produces a nearly impenetrable mat of vegetation, which often reduces oxygen in the waters beneath, enhances sedimentation, and impedes navigation by small boats. Its sharp spiny nut is a hazard to swimmers and barefoot walkers. In some shallow bays it has displaced native vegetation. Another notable example is the zebra mussel, which arrived in the estuary in 1989 and has spread throughout the entire freshwater portion of the estuary, colonizing shallow, subtidal hard surfaces. The planktivorous and rapidly dispersing plankton larval stage has facilitated its invasion of the river. Its high rate of suspension feeding has resulted in dramatic reductions of phytoplankton and its abundance and respiration resulted in sharp reductions of dissolved oxygen. Its clearance of particles, however, has had a slightly beneficial effect on shallow-water attached subaquatic vegetation, which can live at deeper depths owing to higher light penetration.

In the saline part of the estuary, a number of alien species have become very abundant. The green crab invaded our East Coast and spread in the early part of the last century but in recent years the Asiatic shore crab *Hemigrapsus sanguineus* has become dominant in the intertidal zone. Both species may be responsible for high mortality of juvenile mollusks, including young of harvestable shellfish species.

The Present and Future State of the River

Surely among the most predictable questions asked about the Hudson River are: what is its current state? And, given its historical reputation for being polluted, is it improving?

To provide answers, we face the question of which metrics to use, i.e., how do we establish a scoring system that reliably characterizes the Hudson's environmental condition and trajectory? This is not a trivial problem. The indicators chosen should represent the system in question and not geographically broader effects, should encompass its full breadth at numerous physical and biological levels, and should be sensitive to both gradual and episodic environmental impacts.

The New York-New Jersey Harbor Estuary Program tackled this issue with a report issued in 2003 that found nine of twenty-four proposed environmental indices showing improvement, including sediment loading, benthic community health, contaminant loadings, and the areal extent of shellfish beds. But meanwhile, harmful algal blooms were on the rise and abundances of some important resource species were on the decline. Other indicators, such as abundances of striped bass, forage fish, and winter flounder revealed no appreciable changes. On the whole, the weight of the evidence is positive, particularly indicators of toxic substances, but biological resources are still in need of upgrading.

Perhaps the most exciting results reported in this volume involve the great progress made in relating ecosystem processes to environmental change and human efforts at environmental restoration. The chapter on the benthic communities of New York Harbor (Chapter 18) shows a clear recovery over decades in response to reductions of contaminant inputs. The clean up of Foundry Cove has removed the major source of metal pollution to the Hudson, which will decrease trophic transfer of metals through food webs (Chapter 30). Follow through on current plans to dredge PCB hotspots should have similar effects for this contaminant (Chapters 24, 25), the limiting factor for unfettered consumption of Hudson River finfish.

Radically improved sewage treatment in the 1900s, particularly since the Clean Water Act of 1972, has led to major improvements in water quality throughout the estuary (Chapter 23). Indeed, a focus on this baseline issue has generated considerable new knowledge of how the system functions ecologically from nutrients upward to the watershed level (Chapters 9, 10). It may be argued that successes achieved in the water quality arena have allowed the recent focus in the estuary on habitat evaluation and restoration – an initiative that would not merit serious attention in the absence of adequate dissolved oxygen levels.

But all is not well and vigilance is required to prevent environmental backsliding. The recent invasion of zebra mussels (Chapter 21) has resulted in major declines in freshwater phytoplankton and noticeable decreases in oxygen. Much earlier misguided introductions of organisms such as water chestnut, common carp, and others (Chapter 21) have had profound effects in portions of the estuary and are reminders that such mistakes usually are irreversible. Pollution inputs have been lowered dramatically (Chapter 22), but intermittent episodes may still occur, such as oil spills. And nonpoint sources of contaminants still leach into the system.

Do we know all we need to know about the Hudson? No, although we've made great strides. Despite a volume filled with exciting progress and results, we still require more knowledge of the River's flow patterns and how they distribute sediments and contaminants. We still are in need of comprehensive modeling approaches to fisheries that relate physical variables and human impacts to fish production, and to how species abundances are affected by interactions with other species. We still know relatively little about the importance of tributaries to Hudson River fishes, sediment transport, and water quality. These and many other realms of study can only benefit from periodic syntheses, such as this one, of what we continue to learn about this great river, which will help steer future research efforts.

Geological, Physical, and Chemical Setting of the Hudson

2 The Hudson River Valley: Geological History, Landforms, and Resources

Les Sirkin[1] and Henry Bokuniewicz

ABSTRACT The course and character of the Hudson reflect its underlying geological structure and the modifications of Pleistocene glaciations. Radiating drainage out of the Adirondacks is transformed into a broad meandering pattern in its tidal reaches below Troy. The river's course then cuts through the Hudson Highlands in a fjord-like gorge. A broad curving path takes the river along the Triassic, Palisades Escarpment following the juncture with the older rocks of Manhattan. The bedrock foundation of the Hudson was established in three mountain-building episodes beginning over a billion years ago. Most recently, the entire region has been glaciated and the course of the Hudson takes it through relic beds of glacial lakes and several ice margin deposits of glacial sediment. After the deglaciation of the region, estuarine conditions were established in the Hudson beginning about 12,000 years ago. The Hudson briefly crosses the coastal plain breaching the Wisconsin terminal moraine at the Narrows. On the continental shelf, the course of the ancestral Hudson is marked by the Hudson Submarine Canyon.

Introduction

The source of the Hudson River was discovered in 1872 by the naturalist and surveyor, Verplanck Colvin. It is a pond on the western slope of Mt. Marcy, the highest peak in the Adirondacks at 1,629 m. Colvin, an ardent supporter of preserving the mountain forests and watershed, referred to the pond as 'tear of the clouds' (Schneider,

[1] Deceased

1997). He recognized that the many springs, ponds, bogs, swamps, and other wetlands provided the water flowing from the mountains to create the Hudson watershed. To Colvin and like-minded associates, these wetlands and their encompassing forests were a resource worth protecting. They lobbied the New York State Legislature to establish parkland for this purpose. By the late nineteenth century, the state began to set aside tracts of land and to preserve forested lands that otherwise would have reverted to the timber industry. Today these lands are the Adirondack Park.

During the colonization and growth of eastern and central New York, the Hudson River watershed supplied water for agriculture. A network of streams enabled lumbermen to drive logs from high mountain valleys to sawmills in the valleys beyond the Hudson gorge. Taking advantage of spring snow melt, water was stored in natural and manmade lakes in these tributaries and then released after the ice was out of the channel to drive rafts of logs down the river. The Hudson's water powered mill wheels, ore processing plants, and later, hydroelectric turbines. It provided potable water for communities on the river. Today, this watershed provides water for recreational boating as well as for snow making at ski resorts during the winter. Although the Hudson was not the true northwest passage sought by European entrepreneurs, the river made a major contribution in supplying water, timber, and mineral resources to the nation's economy and in opening up the routes of its westward expansion.

The Hudson River is over 500 km long from Lake Tear in the Clouds to the Narrows (between Brooklyn and Staten Island). The Hudson estuary is tidal and navigable upsteam for nearly 240 km to the dam in Troy and the locks that join the river to the barge canal system. In the Adirondacks, the watershed drains a region with 1,200 m peaks into a lowland less than 125 m above sea level. The Mohawk drains central New York into the Hudson. The watershed is also supplied by rivers that rise in southwestern Vermont. South of Albany, tributaries flow westward to the river from the Taconic mountain range and eastward from the Catskills Mountains (Fig. 3.1, Chapter 3). Many of the Catskill streams, such as Esopus, Neversink, and Rondout creeks, fill freshwater reservoirs for New York City.

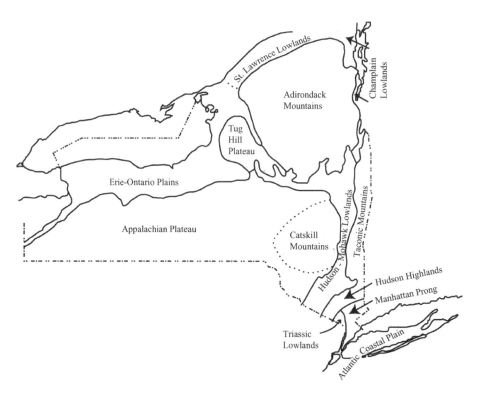

Figure 2.1. Principal physiographic provinces in the vicinity of the Hudson River (after Dineen, 1986).

The northern third of the Hudson's drainage radiates from the high peaks of the Adirondacks. Southward, the Hudson's tributaries appear rectangular, some following the trend of northeast to southwest faults and ridges, and others joining at right angles to the faults along joint planes. The river occupies its bedrock gorge, flowing over rock ledge rapids and coarse cobble point bars (from Mt. Marcy to Glens Falls), until partly blocked by mountains, it turns abruptly to the east through the Luzerne Mountain gorge. It then emerges onto glacial lake sediments and forms a broad, meandering pattern on lowlands underlain by shale for nearly 210 km (from Glens Falls southward to near Newburg).

From the Hudson's lowlands (70 km south of Glens Falls), the river is a tidal one (Fig. 2.1). For the final 240 km, it drops only about a meter to sea level, its course confined to a narrow meander band in this reach. Even though tidal, the Hudson behaves like any river at base level, depositing its bed load and some of its fine-grained suspended load in the form of sand bars.

Further southward, the river cuts laterally through the hard crystalline rocks of the Hudson Highlands (Fig. 2.1). Even here it has an entrenched meander pattern, shifting back and forth in its valley until it emerges from the mountains. Through the highlands the river exhibits characteristics typical of a fjord within towering rock walls. The river's course gently curves in front of the Palisades escarpment, which towers more than 100 m above the water's surface. At the Narrows, the Hudson has breached its final barrier, the terminal moraine of the last glaciation, before it reaches the Atlantic Ocean. On the continental shelf the ancestral course of the river is marked by a subsea canyon.

Geologic History

The Hudson Valley region has experienced three mountain-building episodes that punctuated prolonged intervals of subaerial erosion and periodic invasion by epicontinental seas (Seyfert and Sirkin, 1979). Late in this history, glacial erosion reshaped the peaks and ridges, and deepened valleys.

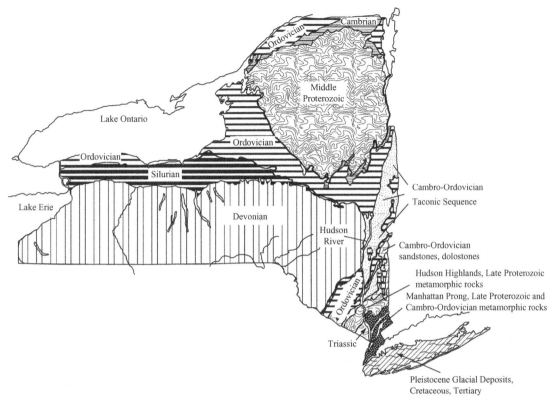

Figure 2.2. Generalized bedrock geology map of the New York State region. Modified after Geological Survey, New York State Museum, geological map, 1989.

The oldest bedrock in the Adirondack headwaters of the Hudson is an anorthosite of mid-Proterozoic age, dated at about 1.4 billion years (Fig. 2.2). Anorthosite originated as igneous rock intruded into sedimentary deposits, mainly sandstone and limestone. After mountain-building episodes, the sedimentary rock units were folded, faulted, and metamorphosed to quartzite, gneiss, and marble. The first major mountain building episode, the Grenville Orogeny, began around 1.2 billion years ago. This event affected a broad region along the margin of ancestral North America, from maritime Canada to northwestern Mexico. The mountain system created by the Grenville Orogeny is believed to have rivaled the Himalayas, driven by a collision in which Laurentia (North America) was overridden by Gondwana (Africa). The deep burial of Laurentia resulted in the first episode of metamorphism, partial melting of rock, and separation of light and dark minerals of the Adirondack gneisses. As the continents subsequently rifted in the late Proterozoic Period, basaltic volcanic rocks

were intruded into the mountains, cutting across the anorthosites and gneisses.

The Hudson Highlands gneisses and the lowest unit, the Fordham gneiss, of the New York Group rocks of the Manhattan Prong in southern New York (Fig. 2.2) are late Proterozoic in age. In both cases, the gneisses were probably derived from sedimentary rocks during the Grenville event. These gneisses have been dated at around one billion years, although the Highlands gneisses may be somewhat older and the Fordham somewhat younger. Long episodes of erosion of the Grenville mountains and subsequent crustal uplift have brought this once-deeply buried crust to the surface. Late in the Proterozoic, erosion of the Grenville mountains provided a source of thick sedimentary deposits that partly engulfed the upland, but while these deposits are found elsewhere in the Appalachians, almost all were removed from the Hudson Valley.

In the early Paleozoic, sand and gravel eroded from the mountains became basal sandstone and conglomerate (e.g., the Potsdam Sandstone of northern New York and the Lowerre Quartzite of the Hudson Highlands). As the epicontinental sea inundated the mountain region, a thick cover of marine limestone and shale was laid down in an elongated trough that formed on the continental margin where the mountains had once prevailed. Limestone was deposited in shallow water along the continental margin, and shale solidified from muds carried into the deeper, seaward part of the basin. The shale bedrock between Glens Falls and the Highlands is what remains of thousands of feet of sediment deposited in the trough. Limestone strata found north and west of the mid-Hudson valley represents the carbonate, platform deposits thought to be similar to the Modern Bahama Banks (Isachsen, Fisher, and Rickard, 1970).

In the late Cambrian Period (ca. 500 million years ago), Laurentia collided with the ancestrial core of Europe, Baltica and a large fragment of continental crust known as Avalonia. This mountain-building event, known as the Taconic Orogeny, lasted throughout the Ordovician Period and resulted in the new supercontinent called Laurasia. While much of the subduction, metamorphism, and volcanism took place well to the east, island arc volcanic structures (such as the Cortlandt Complex) have been identified in the vicinity of the Hudson Highlands. To the north and west in the mid-Hudson Valley, the sedimentary rocks were folded and faulted, with the trend of the folds parallel to the southwest to northeast Appalachian structures. Closer to the margin, thin sheets of rock were thrust dozens of kilometers westward, known as the Taconic thrusts. Fine-grained shales were crumpled and thrust into the narrow seaway west of the mountains. Blocks of limestone slid into the trough and were incorporated in the mélange of jumbled, shale masses. Today the river flows past the western edge of the thrusts and cuts into the mélange deposits.

Sandstone, limestone, and shale, similar in age to the mid-Hudson strata, and Proterozoic bedrock from the Highlands south and east in the Manhattan Prong, were deeply buried as the continent's margin was subducted near the zone of plate convergence. The rocks were partially melted and metamorphosed to gneiss, marble, and schist, and folded into the typical Appalachian alignment.

(The New York Group consists of the Proterozoic Fordham Gneiss and the early Paleozoic Lowerre Quartzite, Inwood Marble and Manhattan Schist; Isachsen and Fisher, 1970, Isachsen, 1980). Streams in the metamorphic lowlands follow valleys formed along fault lines or on the softer, more soluble marble layers. Metamorphosed oceanic crust borders the rocks of the New York Group to the east. Deep, ocean-basin volcanic and sedimentary sequences, that is, ophiolites, have been metamorphosed to greenstone schists, that is, serpentinites. Mafic mineral-rich metamorphic rock of the Hartland-Harrison Group represents the oceanic deposits.

Following the Taconic Orogeny, a long interval of erosion began the process of stripping away crustal overburden as the new continent was slowly uplifted by plate compression. As the upland was eroded, the epicontinental sea gradually inundated the Hudson Valley region from the low-lying continental interior to the west. During the Silurian Period and into the early Devonian, shallow seas covered the region, and tropical calcium carbonate-rich sediments were deposited. In the early Devonian, rivers flowed from the eastern uplands, carrying sediment westward into the sea to form layers of marine sandstone. At the shoreline, a large coastal delta formed over the marine beds. By the mid-Devonian an alluvial plan extended westward across the Catskill region; the shoreline had shifted to the west. At this time, thousands of meters of mid-Paleozoic sediment were piled over the Hudson Valley; continental red sandstones from the east interfingered with gray, marine sandstone to the west. The compressive force overturned folds to the northwest (Schunemunk Mountain along the New York State Thruway near Highland Mills is an example of folded early Devonian limestone and sandstone).

Renewed plate compression, and the resulting uplift of the eastern ranges, marks the beginning of the Acadian Orogeny. This mountain building episode was associated with collision of the North American continent, Laurasia, and the southern supercontinent, Gondwana. Acadian volcanic arcs and granitic intrusions of Devonian age were located east of the Hudson Valley near the continental margin. One granitic pluton, a possible volcanic arc remnant, was intruded just east of Peekskill (Isachsen, 1980).

By this time, the sea was retreating from east to west, exposing great thicknesses of sedimentary rocks from the Acadian Mountains across the Catskill Delta. The final compression of the converging Paleozoic Era continents, the Alleghenian Orogeny, began late in the Permian Period. All of earth's landmasses were now joined to form the supercontinent, Pangaea. Pulses of this orogeny had folded and uplifted the Paleozoic rocks of the Appalachians, forcing the epicontinental sea from the Catskills to the Pocono Plateau in northeastern Pennsylvania to western Pennsylvania. In the east, only relict marine embayments, like that in Rhode Island, persisted into late Paleozoic time when the sandstone, conglomerate, and coal deposits were metamorphosed.

Once above sea level, the Devonian strata of eastern New York were subjected to over 250 million years of subaerial erosion. At some point during this time span the drainage reoriented from west to southward aligning the ancestral Hudson River along a north-south trend. Perhaps this redirection of the drainage took place as the upslope edge of the deltaic beds on the east side were eroded from the mountain front during the late Paleozoic and early Mesozoic. Streams would have followed the tilt of the land and the resistant edge of the strata, both to the south, gradually capturing the headwaters of the west-flowing streams. As the bedrock was worn away, the boundary of the Paleozoic strata migrated westward so that only small outliers of mid-Paleozoic rock units would remain east of the Catskill Front. With the more resistant, metamorphic Taconic Mountains to the east and the Catskill Mountains to the west (Fig. 2.1), the river system in the mid-Hudson Valley worked its way down through softer sedimentary layers, leaving behind the slopes of the mid-Devonian Hamilton Shales and the limestone benches of the Onondaga and Helderberg formations, east of the Catskill Mountains, before reaching the Ordovician age Canajoharie Shale of the current bedrock surface (Isachsen and Fisher, 1970).

The break-up of Pangaea followed in the Triassic Period. Large rifts and grabens stretched from northeast to southwest. In the lower Hudson region, a Mesozoic rift basin known as the Newark Basin of the Triassic Lowlands (Fig. 2.2) covers much of southern New York south of the Hudson

Highlands, west of the river and continuing into east central New Jersey. This basin received thousands of meters of Hudson Valley sediment, much of it colored red by oxidized iron minerals from Proterozic and Paleozoic metamorphic rocks or re-deposited from the Catskill red beds. The Mesozoic red beds show flow patterns emanating from the Highlands as indicators of north to south drainage.

Concurrent with graben formation, basaltic magmas were intruded along fault lines and into the red beds of the basin between 200 and 190 million years ago. The magmas formed the Palisades Sill. Today, the more resistant Palisades stand as ridges above the softer red beds of the Newark Basin. The tabular Palisades Sill slopes to the west, and the eastern edge forms the escarpment, or 'palisade' of vertically jointed basaltic rock so recognizable from the New York side of the Hudson.

In late Mesozoic times, igneous intrusions were emplaced along a northwest to southwest trend across southern Canada and northern New England, and the mountains were uplifted. The linear trend of the intrusions aligns with a chain of younger seamounts, or subsea volcanoes, across the continental shelf and into the ocean basin, reaching as far as the mid-Atlantic rift. As the North American continent moved away the midocean ridge and over a source of high heat flow embedded in the earth's mantle, the hot spot generated intrusions and volcanoes. It may also have been responsible for uplifting the northern, or higher section of the Appalachian Mountains, thereby reactivating erosion in the mountains and doming up the Adirondack anorthosites. The lower-lying mountains of southern New York experienced uplift to a lesser degree, but the thick, overlying sedimentary cover was eroded to expose the deep-seated, high-temperature metamorphics of the Highlands and the New York groups.

Deposition in the Newark Basin ended in the early Jurassic Period. The Hudson became entrenched into its flood plain and began carving its gorge into the resistant gneisses of the Highlands and southern New York. Relict meanders of the channel may date from this time. With the widening of the Atlantic, river sediment was carried to the new continental margin to form the coastal plain and continental shelf. By late Cretaceous time, the eastern rivers were depositing alluvial and deltaic sediment over marine strata on the continent's margin from Long Island to Virginia. The Hudson drainage carried upland sediment to a new sea level close to the edge of the metamorphic upland, about twenty kilometers inland from the present shoreline.

Uplift of the Long Island platform and embayment in the Raritan region to the south, coupled with lower sea level, allowed deposition of the younger, Tertiary-age sediments on the seaward margin of the Cretaceous delta. Lower sea level may also have enabled the river to begin excavating the Hudson Canyon into the continental shelf both by subaerial erosion and turbidity currents below sea level (Shepard, 1963). In the late Tertiary Period, the river turned toward the southwest as a tributary to the Delaware River in central New Jersey (Stanford, 2000). This drainage carried fluvial sediments along the inner margin of the coastal plain, over Cretaceous strata in southern New Jersey, and into the Delmarva region (Owens and Minard, 1979; Owens and Denny, 1979). Tertiary fluvial sediments interfingered with marine strata in the coastal plains and the offshore shelf of New Jersey and the Delmarva Peninsula.

PLEISTOCENE GLACIATION

Although there is no definitive evidence of earlier Pleistocene glaciation, the Hudson River Valley was the arena for the last two advances of Laurentide glaciers, the older during the Illinoian glacial stage and between 140,000 and 200,000 years ago and the younger in the later part of the Wisconsinan stage ending 22,000 years ago. Regional topography enabled the glacier to form a lobate ice margin, as the ice thinned over the Catskill and Taconic uplands (Fig. 2.1) and thickened and expanded southward down the valley. The older drift on western Long Island appears to contain more rock debris from Highlands and Hartland gneisses and less material form the northwest side of the Valley. The lower, U-shaped tributary valleys and bedrock gorges may be related to the last ice advance and postglacial rivers, while more open upland topography might have originated during the earlier advance.

Pollen analysis and radiocarbon dating indicates much warmer conditions than the present during the last interglacial following the Illinoian glaciation. At that time, forests like those of the present, southeastern coastal plain grew in the Adirondacks

and as far north as Toronto (Muller et al., 1993). Sea level rose several meters higher than today's sea level. During the last advance glaciers expanded in the early Wisconsinan (60,000 years ago) as far as the St. Lawrence valley, and cold conditions, along with boreal forests, persisted in the northeast prior to 34,000 years ago when a warming trend began. This warm interval, called the Portwashingtonian warm interval, peaked around 28,000 years ago, at which time oak and hickory forests prevailed and sea levels rose from glacial lows around 100 meters below to within 20 meters of the present level (Sirkin and Stuckenrath, 1980; Sirkin, 1986). As cooling resumed, boreal forests migrated back into the region. By 26,000 years ago, the Laurentide Glacier covered the Ontario and St. Lawrence lowlands. Subsequently, an ice lobe advanced into the Champlain Valley and over the Adirondacks and Green Mountains. At the height of this glacial advance, the ice may have overtopped the High Peaks region by as much as 300 meters (Flint, 1971). The south-flowing glacier deepened the Hudson gorge guided by the softer, metamorphic rock, such as the marble on the west side of the Crane Mountain near Warrensburg.

South of Glens Falls, the ice deepened the channel of the river, and, at the Highlands, cut the fjord, leaving Storm King, Beacon and Bear mountains over 400 m high above the present water level and the river's thalweg over 250 m below sea level (Flint, 1971). With glacial sea level depressed over 100 m, the bedrock was lowered to over 80 m below present sea level near Manhattan and 60 m near the Verrazano Narrows as the river cut its way down to the lower base level. The pre-existing Hudson Canyon was also more deeply entrenched in its new subaerial reach by glacial meltwater flow, and, possibly, eroded below the glacial sea level to the continental rise by turbidity currents.

The Hudson-Champlain Lobe of the Laurentide Glacier reached its southerly boundary 22,000 years ago. The position is marked by the terminal moraine, which stretches from Long Island across Staten Island and New Jersey to Pennsylvania (Sirkin, 1986; Stanford, 2000). The terminal moraine of this lobe, known as the Harbor Hill Moraine (Fig. 2.3, after Long Island's Harbor Hill in Roslyn), impounded glacial meltwater resulting in large proglacial lakes, such as Lake Hackensack in New Jersey, Glacial Lake Hudson and Glacial Lake

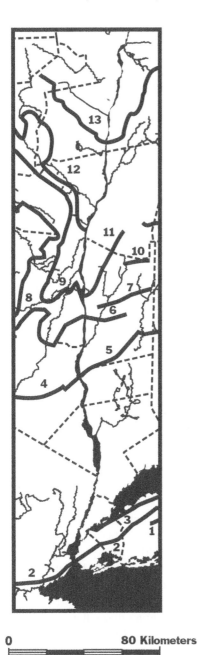

0   **80 Kilometers**

Figure 2.3. Major recessional ice margins. (1) Manetto Hills, (2) Harbor Hill Moraine, (3) Sands Point, (4) Pellets Island, (5) Shenandoah, (6) Poughkeepsie, (7) Hyde Park, (8) Wallkill, (9) Rosendale, (10) White Plains, (11) Red Hook, (12) Middleburg, and (13) Delmar. (After Cadwell, 1986; and Connally and Sirkin, 1986).

Connecticut whose basin is now occupied by Long Island Sound. Thick deposits of lake clay overlap bedrock along the Staten Island and Manhattan shorelines and into the low topography in mid-Manhattan (Cadwell and Pair, 1989). Meltwater drainage blocked by the moraine flowed eastward into the Glacial Lake Connecticut, in the current basin of the Long Island Sound.

Recession of the Late Wisconsinan Ice Sheet

Shortly after deposition of the terminal moraine, the ice front began to recede northward. In less than 2,000 years, Long Island and Staten Island were icefree. The ice front first receded from the terminal moraine to a new ice margin a few kilometers to the north. Here, a recessional moraine was deposited with a lineation of ice contact features, such as proglacial lakes and deltas, lateral meltwater channels, and kames. The ice front of the Hudson Lobe retreated northward from the Harbor Hill Moraine and formed the ground moraine terrain of the Oyster Bay Moraine. The ice stood long enough at the next northerly position, the Sands Point Moraine (Fig. 2.3), to develop an ice margin that cuts across the necks of western Long Island. This position is documented by the Sands Point and College deltas, the Kings Point bog, now dry land over thick peat deposits, and a lateral, west-to-east meltwater channel, that now separates Lloyd Neck and Eatons Neck from older glacial topography to the south.

As the ice front crossed the East River lowland, it deposited a minor recessional moraine at the City Island-South Bronx position, traceable at least to Central Park. By 19,000 years, the ice front reached the White Plains-Dobbs Ferry margin, where a delta of ice-contact sand, gravel, and till nearly 25 m thick was deposited into the eastern shore of Glacial Lake Hudson. Subsequently, the ice receded to a still stand along the present Croton River-Croton Reservoir Valley. Here, meltwater flowing into Lake Hudson deposited the prominent Croton Delta, a remnant of which still protrudes into the Hudson.

At the next ice margin, a delta, now concealed by downtown Peekskill, completes the northward recession of the ice to the southern edge of the Hudson Highlands and the opening of the fjord (Sirkin et al., 1989; Sirkin, 1999). Here, the ice simultaneously downwasted over the mountains and through the gap to establish an ice margin and a moraine, the Shenandoah Recessional Moraine, along the northern edge of the Highlands (Fig. 2.3; Connally and Sirkin, 1986). As the ice withdrew, further Glacial Lake Hudson expanded northward through the fjord to become Glacial Lake Albany.

The pattern of formation of ice margins, recessional moraines, and deltas continued into the mid-Hudson Valley where deltas were deposited into both sides of the lake (at Cold Spring, Moodna Creek, Marlboro, Milton, Hyde Park, Rhinebeck and Red Hook). About 17,200 years ago, the receding glacier stood long enough to build the Walkill-Poughkeepsie Moraine (Fig. 2.3) and then the Hyde Park, Pine Plains, and Red Hook moraines (Fig. 2.3), and the Rhinebeck and Red Hook deltas at an elevation of 60 m. Identification of ice margin position on the west side of the valley corresponding to the Red Hook stand is complicated by the first reversal in the trend of recession, the Rosendale readvance. The ice readvanced several kilometers, deforming lakebeds and depositing till around 16,100 years ago.

Glacial Lake Albany continued to expand and deepen behind the ice, leaving lake clays and shoreline deposits at elevations around 100 m (Dineen, 1986), although the stagnating glaciers in Catskill valleys dammed meltwater as high as 400 m. Ice margins formed at Woodstock, Cairo, and Middleburg (Fig. 2.3) before a second readvance of the glacier, around 15,500 years ago, overrode minor recessional moraines to form drumlins. The higher lakes drained into Lake Albany at an elevation of 100 m through a succession of tunnels in the stagnant ice; the meltwater depositing esker-like ridges (LaFleur, 1979). Later, ice margins developed at Ravena and Altamont before a final readvance in the Albany basin that overrode and deformed lakebeds near Delmar. At the next stand at the Schenectady ice margin, with the lake level at about 95 m, a delta nearly 20 m high was deposited from the west by the Mohawk River drainage. In all, up to 100 m of laminated lake silts and clays now fill the basin of Lake Albany (Cadwell and Dineen, 1987).

As the ice front receded and Lake Albany expanded northward toward present day Lake George, melt water was impounded in tributary valleys of the Adirondack foothills by both ice and moraines (Connally and Sirkin, 1971). Proglacial lake sediments and morainal segments cut across the valley and occur along several tributaries of the Hudson north and west of Warrensburg.

Postglacial Environments

Sediment cores taken from several bogs between Long Island and the Champlain Valley recorded the northward migration of eastern forests following the shrub-tundra and park tundra zones over deglacial terrain (Sirkin, 1977). In the vicinity of the terminal moraine, spruce forests replaced tundra around 18,000 years ago, as climate changed from very cold to cold and moist. Spruce forests reached the mid-Hudson Valley only 2,000 years after the ice left, the northern Hudson Valley less than 1,000 years after the ice, and the Champlain Valley only a few hundred years later. Between 11,000 and 9,000 years ago, warm and dry conditions favored the succession of pine forests. Spruce species migrated northward and into higher and wetter habitats, while pine colonized the well-drained outwash and lake plains of the valley. From 9,000 to 7,000 years ago, oak forests associated variously with pine, hemlock, and hickory overtook the pine-dominated forests as climate cooled.

Sea level rose to establish estuarine conditions in the Hudson. Around 12,000 years ago, the sea flooded into the Hudson Valley through a gap eroded into the terminal moraine across Long Island and Staten Island. The post-Lake Albany lakes in the Champlain Valley must have drained between 12,000 and 11,000 years ago. The river was tidal to Peekskill by 12,000 years before present and estuarine conditions reached Manhattan by 10,280. Salt marsh deposits in the Hudson estuary date from around 11,000 years ago (Newman, 1977), about the same time the sea flooded the Champlain and St. Lawrence valleys.

The estuary retreated slightly around 9,000 years ago but by 7,000 years before present estuarine conditions had reached as far north as Nyack. The estuary reached its maximum northern extent at Peekskill about 6,000 years ago. It has been receding since, perhaps due to sedimentation or continued climate change.

Postglacial Geologic Processes

After the Laurentide ice receded north of the St. Lawrence lowland over 12,500 years ago and local ice melted out of the cirques, very cold conditions, along with high winds and permafrost, persisted in the northern Hudson region. Ice still gripped the glacial soils and wedged into joints in the bedrock, loosening shed-sized angular blocks. The homogeneous, anorthosite domes developed curved sheets of rock decimeters thick at the surface. The sheets cracked into large angular plates along joint planes perpendicular to the surface, in a process known as exfoliation. The rock slabs continue to be prime candidates for sudden rockslides, and the ground-level bases of the domes are surrounded by this very coarse debris strewn over the talus slopes.

Ice-wedging is a common cause but earthquakes are also causative factors in debris slides, and they may be connected to groundwater problems. Earthquakes occur along ancient faultlines and trigger failure of unstable slopes and slumping of coastal plain sediments far from any earthquake's epicenter. Renewed movement and seismic activity in recent times has been linked to postglacial rebound in which stresses in the differentially rising crust are relieved along faults. In addition, industrial and suburban development along fault lines has led to increased use of groundwater and disposal of wastewater into the ground, as well as destabilization of slopes and excavation of bedrock for superhighways and residential and industrial construction sites. All of these factors can have a negative impact on fault line stability and lead to increased activity.

Rock and Mineral Resources

For over 250 years, the Valley has been exploited for earth materials, dating from the incipient iron industry of the early 1700s in the Hudson Highlands to the present need for aggregate and building materials (Hartnagel, 1927).

Of the metallic minerals, iron was the first to be mined from early scrapings of bog iron in wetlands to exploiting concentrations of magnetite, found mainly in veins cutting through the Proterozoic metamorphic rocks of the Hudson Highlands (Hurlibut, 1965). Iron was important to the Colonial economy as early as the 1750s. During the Revolutionary War, iron mines like the Sterling mine in Orange County supplied the forges of the American Army with the raw material for cannon

and ball, as well as the links for a chain to span the Hudson at West Point and block British naval advances (Isachsen, 1980). The emery is used for abrasives, and pyrite, an important source of sulphur, came from mines in the lenses and veins in the mafic Cortlandt complex rocks near Peekskill.

Magnetite mines opened in the Adirondacks in the early 1800s (Schneider, 1997). The northern mines became major sources of iron and titanium derived from magnetite and illmenite deposits. While magnetite supplied the steel for heavy industry, illmenite, limonite and other iron compounds were used mainly for paint pigment. Limonite, found as an iron oxide crust, was mined in Dutchess and Columbia counties early in the 1700s.

Other minerals associated with metamorphic rocks are graphite, garnet, and zircon. Graphite is mined in the Adirondacks near Ticonderoga and is used in making 'lead' pencils. Real lead is found in disseminated masses in sedimentary rocks in the Shawangunk Mountains southeast of the Catskills.

Garnet has been mined since the nineteenth century from the mountains bordering the Hudson gorge near North Creek in the Adirondack Town of Johnsburg (The Editorial Committee, 1994). It occurs as large, attractive, dark reddish-purple crystals accented by a halo of white feldspar in a matrix of black hornblende schist. While enticing in their size and color, the crystals are generally fractured, and only occasionally are gem-caliber specimens encountered. Garnet has been quarried for use in industrial abrasives. Zircon of gem quality is found in Orange County mines.

A great variety of whole rock products have been exploited in the Hudson watershed, taken from the earth where found or wherever convenient. Granite and gneiss have been quarried in the Highlands and Adirondacks, and anorthosite in the northern mountains. Quarried blocks were used as riprap on steep slopes, and glacial boulders support earthen walls and line roadways. Stonewalls were built of cobbles hauled from cornfields, while crushed rock is used for road fill and in gabions. Large-sized crystals of feldspar and mica have been taken from coarse-grained pegmatite dikes that cut across the metamorphic rocks of the Highlands: the feldspar is used in insulators and the mica formed the 'isinglass' windows in furnace doors. Crushed basaltic rock, mainly from quarries in the Palisades and the

Cortlandt Complex rocks, is the 'trap rock' in most railroad beds, selected for its crushing strength and durability. The product continues to be in demand.

Of the metamorphic rocks, the Inwood Marble and the Fordham Gneiss were quarried in Westchester County for facing stone to adorn high-rise buildings in Manhattan. White marble also comes from the marble belt east of Albany. Lower grades of marble wind up in sacks of ground and slaked lime for lawns and agriculture soil enrichment. The slate belt of eastern New York's Taconic range parallels the marble trend in Washington County. European slate miners crafted an enduring industry in slate products for roofing, walkways, and floor tiles.

Sandstone slabs and blocks are derived from beds of the Cambrian Period, Potsdam Sandstone, that border the Adirondacks. Taking advantage of the natural rectangular jointing of the bedrock, sandstone could be readily worked into facing and foundation stone. Red sandstone from the Newark Basin also shows up in older structures in the southern part of the valley, and crushed red sandstone gravel decorates creative gardens and driveways. Devonian-age flagstone, a uniformly fine-grained gray sandstone (a variety of which is the Catskill 'bluestone') was quarried and split into thin slabs for the sidewalks of northeastern cities.

While many mineral mines have closed, the sand and gravel and limestone-marble quarries prevail. The limestone formations, the Ordovician Trenton limestone, Silurian-Devonian Helderberg Formation, and the Devonian Onondaga limestone of the escarpments of the mid-Hudson region (Isachsen et al., 1970) became the walls of many colonial homes, such as the Huguenot cottages near New Paltz. The chemical nature of the Silurian-Devonian rock provided a basis for the Portland cement industry that flourished in the valley. Coal was not available as a local commodity. Colonial iron had been concentrated with charcoal because the thin coal seams in the Catskill delta, evidence of small Devonian swamps, were not enough to sustain smelting. Similarly, peat was not a major energy source.

Special use sediment of different grades supplied other building industries. Fine sands were used for molds, pure quartz for glass, and clay for bricks and ceramics. The brick industry throve in scores of factories turning clay, from the Cretaceous-age Raritan clays of Staten Island to Glacial Lake Hudson and Albany clays all the way to Glens Falls, into stone-hard building blocks.

All of these rocks and minerals, are, or have been, essential to the economy, but mining of earth materials has created a number of environmental hazards ranging from the variety of excavations – gaping and hidden holes in the ground, hollowed-out mountains, and forgotten subsurface rooms – to waste products, such as mine tailings, slag dumps, acid waters, acid rain, and air pollution, as well as sediment clogged streams. It was not until the 1970s that State and Federal environmental agencies began to require mine restoration and clean up and closure plans. But by then, many mines were grandfathered or abandoned, went out of business, or were converted into landfills. Today, the New York State Department of Environmental Conservation issues mining permits and monitors development, changing use, and closure plans.

REFERENCES

Cadwell, D. H. 1986. "Introduction," *The Wisconsinan Stage of the First Geological District, Eastern New York*. D. H. Cadwell, (ed.). Albany, NY: New York State Museum Bulletin No. 455: 1–5.

Cadwell, D. H., and Dineen, R. J. (eds.). 1987. Surficial Geologic Map of New York, Hudson-Mohawk Sheet. Albany, NY: New York State Geological Survey.

Cadwell, D. H., and Pair, D. L. 1989. Surficial Geologic Map of New York, Adirondack Sheet. Albany, NY: New York State Geological Survey.

Connally, G. G., and Sirkin, L. A. 1971. *Luzerne readvance near Glens Falls, New York*. Boulder, CO. Geological Society of America Bulletin 82: 989–1008.

Connally, G. G., and Sirkin, L. 1986. "Woodfordian ice margins, recessional events, and pollen stratigraphy of the mid-Hudson valley," in *The Wisconsinan Stage of the First Geological District, Eastern New York*, D. H. Cadwell (ed.). Albany, NY: New York State Museum Bulletin 455: 50–72.

Dineen, R. J. 1986. "Deglaciation of the Hudson Valley between Hyde Park and Albany, NY," in *The Wisconsinan Stage of the First Geological District, Eastern New York*. D. H. Cadwell, (ed.). Albany, NY: New York State Museum Bulletin No. 455: 89–108.

Editorial Committee, The 1994. *River, Rails, and Ski Trails*. The Johnsburg Historical Society, Johnsburg, NY.

Flint, R. F. 1971. *Glacial and Quaternary Geology*. New York: John Wiley.

Hartnagel, C. A. 1927. The mining and quarrying industries in New York from 1919–1924. New York State Museum Bulletin No. 273, 101 pp. Albany, NY.

Hurlbut, Jr., C. S. 1965. *Dana's Manual of Mineralogy*, 17th ed., New York: John Wiley.

Isachsen, Y. W., and Fisher, D. W. (eds.). 1970. Geologic Map of New York, Adirondack Sheet. Albany, NY: New York State Geological Survey.

Isachsen, Y. W., Fisher, D. W., and Rickard, L. V. (eds.). 1970. Geologic Map of New York, Hudson-Mohawk Sheet. Albany, NY: New York State Geological Survey.

Isachsen, Y. W. 1980. Continental collisions and ancient volcanoes. Albany, NY: New York State Museum Educational Leaflet 24.

LaFleur, R. G. 1979. Deglacial events on the eastern Mohawk-Northern Hudson lowland, in G. M. Friedman (ed.), *New York State Geological Association Guidebook*, 51st Annual Meeting, Rensselaer Polytechnic Institute, Troy, NY, pp. 326–50.

Muller, E. H., Sirkin, L., and Craft, J. L. 1993. Stratigraphic evidence of a pre-Wisconsinan interglaciation in the Adirondack Mountains New York, *Quaternary Research* **40**: 163–8.

Newman, W. S. 1977. "Late Quaternary paleoenvironmental reconstruction: some contradictions from northwestern Long Island, New York," in W. S. Newman and B. Salwen (eds.), Amerinds and Their Paleoenvironments in Northeastern North America. *Annals of The New York Academy of Sciences*, Volume **288**: 545–70.

Owens, J. P., and Denny, C. S. 1979. Upper Cenozoic deposits of the central Delmarva Peninsula, Maryland and Delaware. United States Geological Survey Professional Paper 1067-A.

Owens, J. P., and Minard, J. P. 1979. Upper Cenozoic sediments of the lower Delaware valley and the northern Delmarva Peninsula, New Jersey, Pennsylvania, Delaware, and Maryland. United States Geological Survey Professional Paper 1067-D.

Schneider, P. 1997. *The Adirondacks: A History of America's First Wilderness*. New York: Henry Holt.

Seyfert, C. K., and Sirkin, L. A. 1979. *Earth History and Plate Tectonics*, 2nd ed. New York: Harper and Row.

Shepard, F. P. 1963. *Submarine Geology*, 2nd ed. New York: Harper and Row.

Sirkin, L. 1977. "Late Pleistocene vegetation and environments in the middle Atlantic region," in W. S. Newman and B. Salwen (eds.), Amerinds and Their Paleoenvironments in Northeastern North America. *Annals of the New York Academy of Sciences*, Volume **288**: 206–217.

1986. "Pleistocene stratigraphy of Long Island, New York," in D. H. Cadwell (ed.), *The Wisconsinan Stage of the First Geological District, Eastern New York*. Albany, NY: New York State Museum Bulletin 455: 6–21.

1999. The Hudson-Champlain Lobe of the Laurentide ice sheet and the moraines of western Long Island, pp. 44–5. Long Island Geologists Programs with Abstracts, Sixth Annual Conference, State University of New York, Stony Brook, NY.

Sirkin, L., Cadwell, D. H., and Connally, G. G. 1989. Pleistocene geology of the eastern, lower Hudson valley, New York, in D. Weiss (ed.), *New York State Geological Association Field Trip Guidebook*, 61st Annual Meeting, Middletown, NY, pp. 231–40.

Sirkin, L., and Stuckenrath, R. 1980. The Portwashingtonian Warm Interval in the Northern Atlantic Coastal Plain. Geological Society of America Bulletin 91: 332–6.

Stanford, S. D. 2000. Plicene-Pleistocene discharge of the Hudson to the New York Bight: the view from the land. Geological Society of America Abstracts with Programs 32: A-76, Boulder, CO.

3 The Physical Oceanography Processes in the Hudson River Estuary

W. Rockwell Geyer and Robert Chant

ABSTRACT The Hudson River has the attributes of a typical, partially mixed estuary – a moderate salinity gradient, significant vertical stratification, and a vigorous, two-layer circulation regime. Yet it also displays considerable variability, both in space and in time. In its northern reaches, the estuary becomes a tidal river, with no trace of oceanic salt but vigorous tidal currents. The salinity intrusion extends 100 kilometers (km) into the estuary during low discharge conditions, but it retreats to within 25 km of New York Harbor during the high river flows of the spring freshet. Fortnightly variations of tidal amplitude also result in pronounced variations in the estuarine regime, becoming well-mixed during strong spring tides and highly stratified during the weakest neaps. At the mouth of the Hudson is a complex network of tidal channels that link the estuarine regime of the Hudson to Long Island Sound, Newark Bay, and the Atlantic Ocean. The influence of the Hudson extends into the Mid-Atlantic Bight in the form of a low-salinity plume, which forms a coastal current and flows south along the New Jersey shore during favorable wind-forcing conditions.

Introduction

The Hudson River is one of the major watercourses of the United States East Coast. It originates on the slopes of Mt. Marcy in the Adirondack Mountains, extending nearly 600 km to New York City. Over this distance the Hudson's character changes dramatically, starting as a mountain stream, descending to become a lowland river, and then turning into a peculiar tidal river, slowly increasing in salinity to become an estuary, and finally joining the ocean as a complex network of tidal channels and bays bisecting the New York metropolitan area. These different environments are shaped by the interplay of a variety of physical processes with one element in common: the river flow. Runoff from the hillslopes coalesces to form the lakes and streams in the Adirondack highlands. The action of gravity on the accumulating water provides the driving force for this flow through the upper Hudson valley. South of Albany, the motion of the river becomes complicated by the influence of tides, which can be witnessed a remarkable 250 km from the sea. Although the tidal river flows both north and south, the net southerly river flow persists and provides the freshwater input that creates the Hudson estuary. This freshwater source is a dominant contributor to the physical regime of the estuary and harbor, as it controls the salinity structure, the vertical stratification, and the exchange of properties between the estuary, the ocean, and the atmosphere.

The Hudson River Watershed

The Hudson River watershed has two main branches, the Upper Hudson River and the Mohawk River (Fig. 3.1). The Upper Hudson extends 160 miles from Lake Tear of the Clouds in the Adirondacks to the Federal Dam at Troy. The upper Hudson is a steep-gradient river with numerous rapids, flowing through the rough terrain of the Adirondacks. Just north of the Federal Dam at Troy, the Mohawk River joins the Hudson from the west. The Mohawk follows a gentler gradient than the upper Hudson, draining the farm country between the Catskills and the Adirondacks. Although it flows through very different terrain, it contributes nearly the same discharge as the upper Hudson and comparable sediment loads.

The upper Hudson is unusual among rivers in the heavily industrialized eastern United States in that it is nearly unimpeded by dams. Although there are several dams along its course, their reservoirs are small, representing relatively little storage compared to the magnitude of the flow. Thus the seasonal flow characteristics of the river are close to their natural state.

A freshet occurs during the spring, when snowmelt from the Adirondack and Catskill Mountains

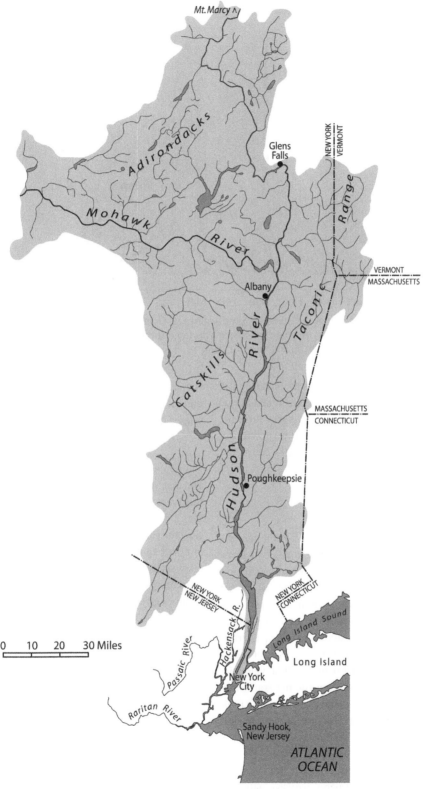

Figure 3.1. The Hudson River watershed. The length of the river, from Lake Tear of the Clouds to the Battery, is 725 km, and the area of its drainage basin is 34,700 km^2 (Howells, 1972).

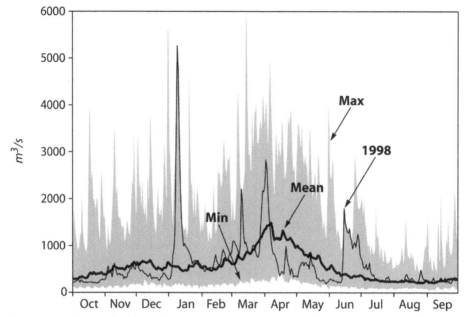

Figure 3.2. Hydrograph of the Hudson River discharge (at Green Island Dam, Troy, NY). The bold line is the mean discharge; the shaded area spans the range from minimum to maximum observed daily values; the thin line is the discharge for 1998.

combines with spring rains. This produces a peak flow of around 2,000 m³ s⁻¹, usually in late March or early April (Fig. 3.2). Big storms can raise the discharge to similar levels at other times of year, but typically the discharge decreases to 100–200 m³ s⁻¹ during the summer months.

The Tidal River

Below the dam at Troy, river flow is no longer the dominant agent of motion of the Hudson River. Owing to the particular suite of geological processes that have sculpted the landscape of the Hudson Valley, the river's shores in Albany are virtually the same elevation as those at the mouth. As a consequence, the tide extends 250 km up the river to the dam at Troy. River flow produces a net southward motion in the tidal river, but tidal velocities are usually much higher than the net southward motion due to river flow. Thus, in all but the most extreme outflow conditions, this part of the river flows in both directions, following the influence of the tides.

Through most of the length of the tidal Hudson, the tide propagates as a progressive wave, with high tide occurring later as it proceeds up the river. The speed of propagation of the tidal wave is approximated by the "long wave" speed c, which is approximated by the "long wave" equation

$$c = (gh)^{1/2}$$

where $g = 9.8$ m s⁻² is the acceleration of gravity and h is the average water depth. In the Hudson the average depth is about 10 meters (m), so $c \sim$ 10 m s⁻¹ (approximately 20 knots). Frictional effects slow the tide down by about 20 percent to 8 m s⁻¹ or about 16 knots (DiLorenzo et al., 1999). Thus it takes six hours for the high tide to propagate from the Battery to Catskill, 185 km to the north. (Fig. 3.3).

Although the tide propagates upriver at an appreciable speed, tidal currents are considerably slower. They are approximated by

$$u_L = \frac{1}{2} \frac{h_T}{h} c$$

where h_T is the tidal range and h is the water depth. Typical tidal range on the Hudson is 1.5 m, producing average tidal currents of 0.7 m s⁻¹. The currents are stronger in the middle of the channel and near the surface, averaging closer to 1 m s⁻¹ or 2 knots. The tidal currents are considerably stronger than the velocity due to the freshwater outflow in the tidal river, which is on the order of 0.01 m s⁻¹ during

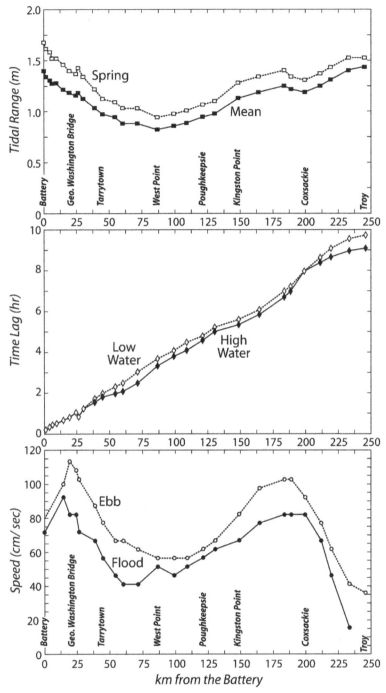

Figure 3.3. Tidal propagation conditions in the tidal portion of the Hudson River (adapted from DiLorenzo et al., 1999). The tidal wave is essentially a progressive wave, as indicated by the time delay as it propagates up the river. Tidal currents are quite energetic through most of the length of the tidal river.

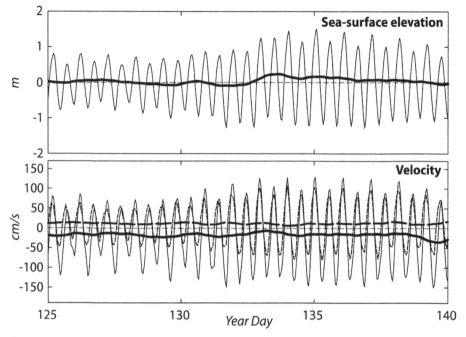

Figure 3.4. Time series of tidal elevation and currents in the lower estuary (near the Battery) in the spring of 1999. The upper panel indicates the tidal (thin line) and low-frequency (thick line) variations of sea level. The lower panel shows near-surface (solid) and near-bottom (dashed) currents, again indicating tidal (thin lines) and low-frequency (thick lines).

the dry summer months and reaches 0.2–0.5 m s^{-1} during the spring freshet. Thus, the tides provide most of the energy and fluid transport within the river below the dam at Troy.

The progressive wave character of the tide in the Hudson has an interesting influence on the phase of the currents relative to tidal height. In most tidal environments, slack water occurs close to high and low tide. However, in tidal rivers like the Hudson, maximum flood occurs within an hour of high tide, and the flood continues for the first two hours of the falling tide. As the tidal wave in the Hudson approaches the dam at Troy, it becomes more like a standing wave due to the reflection of the tidal wave at the head of tide.

The tidal forcing varies due to changes in the phase of the moon as well as other variations in the relative positions of the earth, moon, and sun. The most prominent of these occur at fortnightly and monthly time scales. These variations cause the tidal range at the Battery to vary from 1.2 m during small neap tides to almost 3 m during large spring tides (Fig. 3.4). The variations in currents

are more complicated, due to changes in vertical structure of the flow as well as the influence of the salinity structure. Near-surface currents vary from around 0.7 m s^{-1} during neap tides to 1.3 m s^{-1} during the strongest spring tides. Near-bottom currents are considerably weaker, due to the frictional effects of the bottom boundary layer. These spring-neap variations in tidal flow have a profound influence on the estuarine regime, and likewise the estuarine circulation affects the strength of the currents, as explained in the next section.

The Estuary

The Hudson River estuary is an unusual hybrid of estuarine types, with elements of fjord, salt-wedge, and coastal plain estuaries. Glacial scouring of the Hudson Valley during the Pleistocene Epoch yielded a long, deep trough, which became a series of lakes dammed by glacial moraines during the retreat of the glaciers. When those moraines collapsed and sea level rose, the Hudson valley became a fjord, with depths of possibly as much as 200 m in the vicinity of the Hudson Highlands, where the bedrock was deeply gouged by ice (Worzel and Drake, 1959). Seawater filled the deep basin, and the freshwater outflow was confined to the surface layer. Tidal currents within the estuary were weaker than at present because of its great depth. This fjord environment was a nearly perfect trap for sediment, because neither the river outflow nor the tidal currents provided adequate energy to move sediment after it settled to the bottom from the turbid, surface layer. Sedimentation over the last 10,000 years has filled this glacial trough, and now the Hudson has depths of 10–15 m, more typical of coastal plain estuaries than fjords.

As the Hudson estuary got shallower, its hydrodynamics were significantly altered. Tidal currents became stronger, finally reaching their present values of around 1 m s^{-1}. As the tidal currents increased, the mixing between the freshwater outflow and the seawater increased. No longer could sea water penetrate far into the Hudson valley, due to the combination of tide-induced mixing and freshwater outflow. The present regime in the lower Hudson is a partially mixed estuary, with vigorous, tide-induced mixing between fresh and salt waters. The seawater is progressively diluted by river water as it extends up the estuary, and even during low flow conditions the water is nearly fresh at Peekskill, 70 km to the north of the harbor.

THE INFLUENCE OF FRESH WATER

The position of the salt front varies mainly due to variations in freshwater outflow (Abood, 1974). During high discharge periods in the spring (discharge exceeding 1,500 m^3 s^{-1}), the salt front is pushed south past Tappan Zee, roughly 30 km north of the Battery (Fig. 3.5). At the summertime minimum flow of around 100 m^3 s^{-1}, the salinity intrusion extends more than 90 km north to the vicinity of Newburgh. Because Poughkeepsie, at km 120, draws its drinking water from the Hudson, the upstream intrusion of salt provides a potential threat to its water supply. Twice in the last fifty years, during severe droughts in 1964 and 1995, the intrusion of salt water has come close enough to Poughkeepsie to influence its sodium content. The human health ramifications of the salinity intrusion have motivated numerous studies, including an ongoing

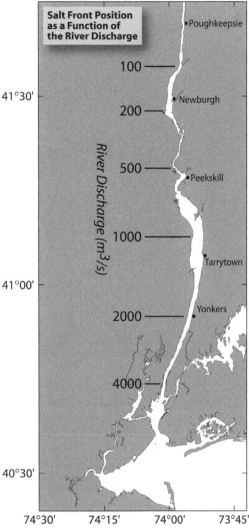

Figure 3.5. Map of the Hudson estuary showing the location of the salt front (approximately 1 psu) during different discharge conditions (adapted from Abood 1974). Discharge of 100 m^3/s typically occurs during dry summer months, whereas the typical freshet discharge is around 2,000 m^3/s. The highest observed discharge is slightly more than 4,000 m^3/s.

monitoring program by the U.S. Geological Survey that documents salinity at points between Hastings and Poughkeepsie.

Although the river flow is modest relative to the tides, it has a dramatic influence on the estuary by providing a density contrast with the oceanic water. Ocean water contains about 3 percent salt by weight (or 30 parts per thousand, referred to by

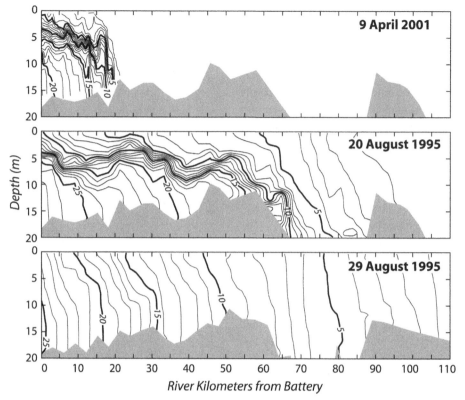

Figure 3.6. Salinity cross-sections in the Hudson estuary during different discharge and tidal conditions. Upper panel: high discharge (2,000 m³/s) spring tide; middle panel: low discharge (100 m³/s), neap tide; lower panel: low discharge (100 m³/s), spring tide. (adapted from Geyer et al., 2000).

oceanographers as practical salinity units or psu), which renders salt water about 3 percent more dense than fresh water. This density contrast causes the fresh water to flow over the salt water and vice versa, leading to an estuarine "salt wedge" (Fig. 3.6). Salt wedges are most evident at the mouths of rivers with weak tidal currents relative to the river flow, such as the Mississippi. The Hudson estuary is notable in that it exhibits a salt wedge structure during neap tides, when velocities are at their fortnightly minimum, but it goes through a remarkable transition to almost well-mixed conditions during spring tides (Fig. 3.6). Other estuaries exhibit this spring-neap change in stratification – it was first noted by Haas (1977) in the Rappahannock Estuary in Chesapeake Bay. However, the Hudson exhibits a more extreme range of stratification between neap and spring tides than any estuary in which this phenomenon has been observed (Geyer, Trowbridge, and Bowen, 2000).

THE ESTUARINE CIRCULATION

Although the vertical salinity gradient varies considerably between neap and spring tides, there is always a strong horizontal salinity gradient along the estuary. This salinity gradient causes a horizontal density gradient (due to the difference in density between fresh and salt water), which in turn induces a depth-varying, or "baroclinic" pressure gradient in the estuary. The baroclinic pressure gradient drives the deep water landward, and a compensating tilt of the water surface drives the surface water seaward (Fig. 3.7). This vertically varying motion is called the estuarine circulation (Pritchard, 1952). The estuarine circulation has the strange property that, at the bottom, is directed toward land against the direction of the river flow. This tendency is counterintuitive, particularly because the estuarine circulation owes its origin to the forcing by the freshwater outflow. The explanation for this is the forcing by the

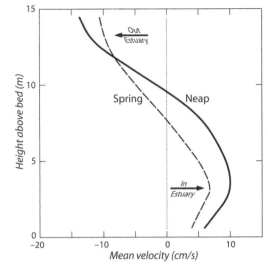

Figure 3.7. Vertical profiles of net estuarine velocity, during neap and spring tides, observed at the Battery in the spring of 1999 (from data presented in Geyer et al., 2001). Stronger estuarine currents occur during neap tides, when tidal mixing is weaker.

density contrast between seawater and fresh water, which yields a landward-directed force at the bottom of the estuary. The tilt of the water surface toward the sea provides a driving force for the surface outflow, but the density gradient is strong enough to reverse the direction of that force at the bottom.

The estuarine circulation is the mechanism that transports salt into the estuary against the outward motion of the river flow. This is accomplished by carrying high-salinity water in at the bottom and carrying out low-salinity water at the surface, resulting in a net inward motion of salt. The estuarine circulation is driven by the density gradient between fresh and salt water, thus the stronger the gradient, the stronger the estuarine circulation. The salinity distribution along the estuary is like a spring: when it is compressed during high river-flow conditions (Fig. 3.5), it exerts a greater force, driving a more vigorous estuarine circulation (Fig. 3.8). During high flow conditions, the seaward transport of salt due to the river is greater; thus a stronger estuarine circulation is required to keep salt in the estuary. When the river flow decreases, the spring relaxes, and the forcing of the estuarine circulation decreases.

STRATIFICATION

The estuarine circulation is not the only factor responsible for the salt transport in the estuary; the vertical salinity stratification is also key. The amount of salt that is transported by the two-way flow depends on the salinity difference between the surface and bottom waters. As that salinity difference increases, the amount of salt that is transported increases proportionately. Perhaps more importantly, the stratification is closely related to the amount of vertical mixing that occurs in the estuary, which in turn regulates not only most of the physical exchange processes in the estuary but also its ecology and biogeochemistry. Thus, stratification is generally considered the most important variable for the classification of estuaries.

Stratification originates from the interaction of the estuarine circulation and salinity gradient. The estuarine circulation always increases the salinity of the deep water and decreases the salinity of the surface water due to horizontal advection (Figs. 3.6 and 3.7). If there were no mixing, eventually the near-bottom water would be purely ocean water and the near-surface water just riverine, with a very strong *halocline*, or salinity gradient, between the two layers. Vertical mixing, due mainly to tidal currents, partially counteracts the stratifying tendency of the estuarine circulation. As tidal currents increase, there is greater vertical mixing and less stratification for a given amount of estuarine circulation (Fig. 3.8). Tidal mixing also has a direct influence on estuarine circulation by increasing the momentum exchange (or drag) between the incoming and outgoing water. Thus, tidal mixing affects the stratification directly, by producing vertical exchange between the upper and lower layers, and indirectly, by influencing the strength of the estuarine circulation (Fig. 3.8), which provides the source of stratification.

THE SPRING-NEAP CYCLE

The sensitive dependence of the stratification on the tides leads to large spring-neap changes in stratification in the Hudson (Figs. 3.6 and 3.8). These changes in stratification indicate large variations in vertical exchange in the estuary. Whereas stratification provides an indicator of the amount of vertical mixing, it also exerts a direct dynamical influence on turbulent motions. The vertical

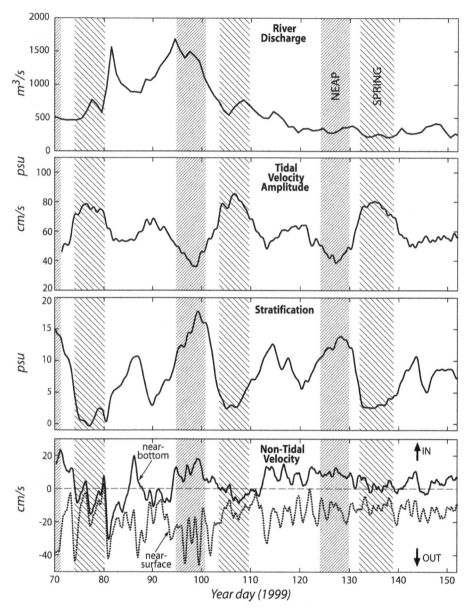

Figure 3.8. Time-series of discharge (top panel), tidal velocity amplitude (2nd panel), stratification (3rd panel), and estuarine circulation (bottom panel) from observations near the Battery in 1999 (from Geyer et al., 2001). Stratification reaches its maximum value during neap tides and its minimum during springs. The estuarine circulation also varies with the spring-neap cycle, but not as distinctly as stratification. Note that the freshwater inflow only has a modest influence on stratification.

density gradient (due to salinity stratification) acts to suppress turbulence, thus preventing the influence of tide-induced mixing from reaching the upper part of the water column during neap tides. This vertical barrier of stratification that occurs during neap tides affects the vertical transport of

nutrients and oxygen, with important ecological implications.

These spring-neap variations in stratification also have important implications for horizontal transport of salt. During neap tides, vertical gradients are strong, and there is minimal vertical

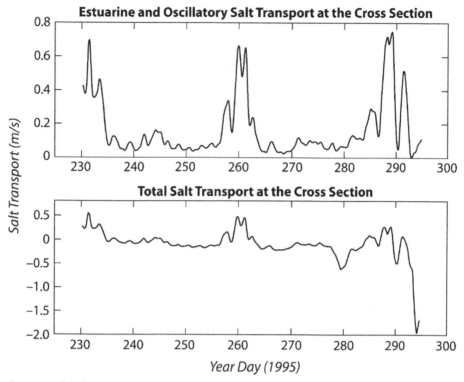

Figure 3.9. Salt flux in the Hudson estuary, during observations in 1995 (from Bowen and Geyer, 2003). The upper panel shows the landward salt flux due to the sum of the estuarine and tidal pumping transport. The lower panel indicates the net transport, including the river outflow and all of the other contributors. Large peaks in landward salt transport occur during weak neap tides, when stratification is maximal. Strong river outflow at the end of the observation period is responsible for the large negative value in the total transport.

exchange of either momentum or salt between the upper and lower layers. Thus, both the estuarine circulation and the stratification are enhanced, and the salt transport due to the estuarine circulation is maximal (Fig. 3.9). This causes salt to advance into the estuary during neap tides and to retreat during spring tides. Whereas the large variation in horizontal salt transport due to the spring-neap cycle is clearly evident, the changes in position of the salinity intrusion are not as obvious. The salinity intrusion is usually long enough that these spring-neap changes in salinity are small relative to the total length of the salt intrusion (Bowen and Geyer, 2003). In addition, variations in stratification may overwhelm the signal of the changes in the horizontal position of the salt front.

TIDAL DISPERSION

It is surprising that the estuarine circulation and river flow would have such important effects on the Hudson estuary, when the tidal currents are so much stronger. The energy provided by the tides far exceeds that provided by any other source in the estuary, and the velocities due to the tides are 5 to 10 times as great as the estuarine circulation and as much as 100 times as great as the river flow. The reason the tides do not totally dominate over these other motions with respect to the salt balance and exchange within the estuary is because of the oscillatory nature of the tidal flow. The *tidal excursion* is the distance that a parcel of water is transported by the tide in one-half cycle. It is calculated by the formula

$$L_T = \frac{T}{\pi} u_T$$

where T is the tidal period (in seconds) and u_T is the magnitude of the tidal velocity. For the tidal currents in the Hudson of 0.7–1 m s^{-1}, the excursion is 10–14 km. The reason that tides are not dominant in

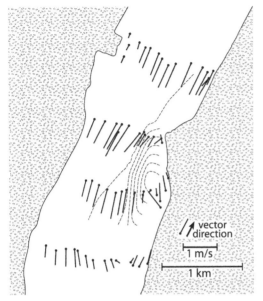

Figure 3.10. An eddy in the tidal stream due to deflection of the ebbing flow by the headland at the George Washington Bridge (from Chant and Wilson, 1997). The sticks indicate the direction and magnitude of the depth-averaged current (with dots at the origin). The eddy results in a salinity anomaly of 3 psu due to trapping in the core of the eddy.

the horizontal exchange in the estuary is that in the other half of the tidal cycle, the water parcel will be transported back roughly the same distance. What makes tides important is their net influence over a tidal cycle, which is due to nonlinearities (i.e., processes that depend on u_T^2).

Tidal dispersion is the net transport accomplished by the asymmetry between the flood and ebb motions that results in net displacement of water parcels over a tidal cycle. Tidal dispersion arises from a number of different mechanisms, most of which are associated with differences in the strength of the tidal current across the estuary. These processes can collectively be regarded as shear dispersion. Shear dispersion occurs both due to lateral and vertical variations in tidal velocity. Its magnitude is dependent not only on the cross-sectional variations of velocity; it is also dependent on the rate of mixing either in the vertical or transverse direction. The flow around headlands can produce eddies that enhance the transverse shears and thus increase the tidal dispersion (Fig. 3.10). Rarely, however, does tidal shear dispersion reach

the magnitude of exchange induced by the estuarine circulation (Zimmerman, 1986).

Other, more complicated types of dispersion can occur due to interactions between the tides and the estuarine circulation. The estuarine circulation and its associated salt flux are defined based on tidal averages of the flow and the salinity, but there can be correlation between variations in velocity and salinity that lead to net salt transport. In regions of irregular topography, these transports can exceed the strength of the estuarine circulation (Geyer and Nepf, 1996).

TIDE-INDUCED MIXING

As discussed in context with the estuarine circulation, one of the most important nonlinear processes accomplished by the tides is the generation of turbulence. The generation of turbulence at the bottom of the estuary is well understood: the flow over the rough bottom produces eddies that diffuse momentum and water properties in the vertical dimension. The turbulence problem becomes more complicated farther up in the water column, where stratification is stronger. Stratification tends to suppress turbulence associated with bottom-generated turbulence, but as that turbulence is suppressed, the shears tend to increase. Once the shears get high enough relative to the strength of the stratification, a new source of turbulence, shear instability, can start mixing within the stratified water column (Peters, 1997). Shear-induced mixing is important in the Hudson during neap tides and times of high flow, when stratification is strong. The complex interactions between tidal currents, shear-induced mixing, and internal waves are not yet fully understood, and these interactions represent an important aspect of estuarine dynamics that limits our ability to model estuarine physical processes.

NEW YORK HARBOR

The character of the estuary changes at the Battery, where the Hudson River joins the East River at New York Harbor. In contrast to the simple morphology of the Hudson, the Harbor has a complex geometry, with interconnections between several adjacent embayments through a series of tidal straits (Fig. 3.11). The flow in these straits, among the swiftest in the harbor complex, are driven primarily

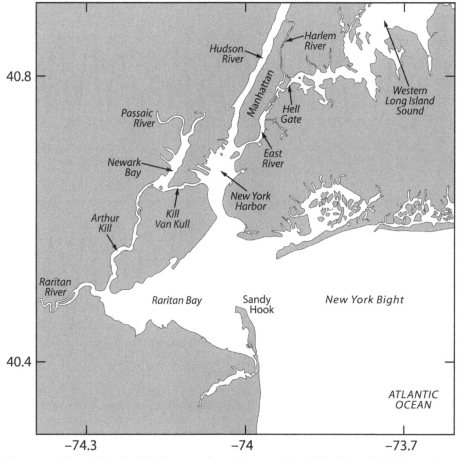

Figure 3.11. Map of New York Harbor complex and western Long Island Sound. The Battery is at the southern tip of Manhattan.

by sea level differences between different water bodies due to tidal and meteorological forcing. Weaker, but persistent two-layer flow is also driven by a salinity difference at the ends of the straits and by non-linear tidal dynamics.

THE EAST RIVER

Despite its name, the East River is not a river but rather a tidal strait, for it has no significant natural direct source of fresh water (in fact sewage outflows are the largest direct source of "fresh water" to the East River). Tidal currents in the East River are among the strongest in the region because of a remarkable difference in the amplitude and timing of the tide between Long Island Sound and New York Harbor. Tides in western Long Island are nearly 70 percent larger than those in the Harbor, and the time of high and low water occurs over

3 hours later in western Long Island Sound than in the Harbor (Fig. 3.12). This oscillating sea level slope drives 2 m s^{-1} tidal currents in the East River, and the notorious tidal currents at Hell Gate (at the junction of the East and Harlem Rivers) can exceed 3 m s^{-1}.

Weaker but lower frequency flows in the East River are also driven by sea level slopes set up by a difference in the wind-driven response of the Harbor and Western Long Island Sound (Wilson, Wong, and Filadelfo, 1985). These flows fluctuate with winds that typically vary at a 2–5 day time scale. While these flows are an order of magnitude weaker than the tidal currents, they are more persistent and may significantly contribute to the exchange between the Sound and the Harbor.

A mean salinity gradient exists along the East River with bottom waters in Western Long Island

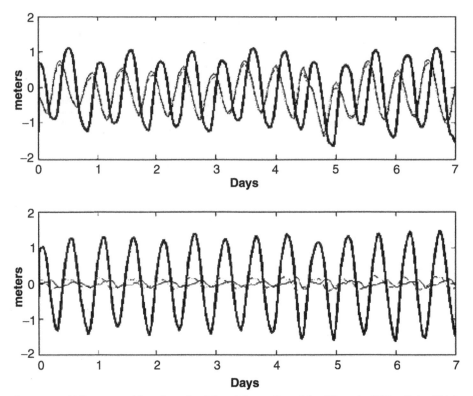

Figure 3.12. A) Upper panel, hourly sea level from Western Long Island Sound at Willets Point (thick line), The Battery (dashed line), Sandy Hook (dotted line) and the western Kill Van Kull at Bayonne (thin line). B) Lower panel, Sea level difference between the Battery and Willets Point (thick line), Sandy Hook and the Battery (dashed-dotted line), and Bayonne and the Battery (thin line).

Sound on average 4 psu more saline than those in the Harbor (Blumberg and Pritchard, 1997). Strong tidal currents in the lower East River maintains a well-mixed water column, while salinity stratification in the upper portions of the strait near Willets Point tends to be about 2 psu in the vertical dimension (Blumberg and Pritchard, 1997). Mixing is strong enough that the mean flow tends to be unidirectional throughout the water column. Yet there is debate on both the magnitude and even the direction of the mean flow. A number of investigators (Blumberg, Khan, and St. John, 1999; Blumberg and Pritchard, 1997; Jay and Bowman, 1975) estimate a mean flow of about 300 m^3 s^{-1} from the Sound into the Harbor. However, Filadelfo, Wilson, and Gomez-Reyes (1991) report persistent flow in the opposite direction.

THE KILLS, NEWARK BAY AND RARITAN BAY

Like the East River, the Kill Van Kull and Arthur Kill are tidal straits. Maximum tidal currents reach 0.75 m s^{-1} in the narrowest reaches of these straits and attenuate to less than 0.5 m s^{-1} in Newark Bay. Tidal excursions in the Kill Van Kull are greater than the length of the channel, thus tidal motion is effective in mixing water between Newark Bay and New York Harbor, particularly during spring tides. In contrast, tidal excursions in the Arthur Kill are significantly shorter than the length of the tidal strait; thus, tides are an ineffective agent driving exchange between Newark Bay and Raritan Bay.

The Raritan River and Passaic River are the major direct sources of fresh water to Raritan and Newark Bays, respectively – both with mean annual discharges of 50 m^3 s^{-1}, with peak flows in the spring of 100–300 m^3 s^{-1}. This fresh water drives a two-layer exchange in the tidal straits and Newark Bay. Salinity stratification and two layer exchange is persistent in the southern reaches of the Arthur Kill.

Meteorological forcing drives flow through the Kills both by the direct action of the wind on the water's surface and by producing a difference in the water levels at the ends of the tidal straits. Similar to what occurred in the East River, these meteorologically forced flows tend to last for several days, and potentially are an effective means to exchange water fluid between Newark Bay and Raritan Bay (Blumberg et al., 1999; Chant, 2002).

The New York Bight and the Coastal Current

In total, the Harbor system discharges annual mean flow amounting to over 700 m^3 s^{-1} of fresh water to the New York Bight. Approximately 600 m^3 s^{-1} of this is from the Hudson, Raritan, and Passaic Rivers, with an additional 100 m^3 s^{-1} from sewage outflows. In addition, the estimated 300 m^3 s^{-1} transported through the East River augments this flow and yields a mean volume transport leaving the Harbor complex through the Sandy Hook-Rockaway transect of approximately 1,000 m^3 s^{-1} – nearly double the discharge of the Hudson.

The flow through the Sandy Hook-Rockaway transect, like the flow throughout much of the Harbor system is two layered, with the surface layer flowing seaward and the lower layer flowing landward. Thus, the transport of fluid in the upper layer must also compensate for the inflow in the lower layer. Based on salt conservation at the Sandy Hook-Rockaway transect, an annual mean outflow of approximately 3,500 m^3 s^{-1} of estuarine water enters the New York Bight, with approximately 2,500 m^3 s^{-1} of saline waters from the Bight entering into the Harbor. These transports significantly vary at weekly, monthly, seasonal, and interannual time scales.

Once past the Sandy Hook–Rockaway transect, the estuarine water from New York Harbor forms a coastal current that flows south along the New Jersey shore. The tendency for the current to head southward is due to the effect of the earth's rotation, or the "Coriolis effect," which turns the fluid to the right in the absence of other forces. Winds also play a major role in defining the structure and direction of the outflow. Southerly winds (winds *from* the south) spread the plume offshore causing it to thin and may arrest its southward flow. Northerly winds compress the plume against the coast and augment its flow to the south. As the plume is transported south along the New Jersey coast it continuously mixes with the more saline shelf waters in the coastal ocean. The mixing is primarily wind driven, while the weak tidal currents, that tend to be less than 15 cm/s along the New Jersey inner shelf, play a secondary role. The Hudson's coastal current has been observed along southern New Jersey near Cape May, more than 150 km south of the Battery (Yankovsky et al., 2002). Eventually, the signature of the Hudson's freshwater flow is lost south of Cape May, New Jersey, where its plume becomes obscured when it mixes with waters from Delaware Bay.

Acknowledgments

Support was provided by the Hudson River Foundation and the National Science Foundation. Jayne Doucette provided the final figures. Sue Stasiowski provided editing and chapter preparation.

REFERENCES

Abood, K. A. 1974. Circulation in the Hudson estuary. *Annals of the New York Academy of Sciences* **250**:39–111.

Blumberg, A. F., and D. W., Pritchard 1997. Estimates of the transport through the East River, New York. *Journal of Geophysical Research* **102**(C3):5685–704.

Blumberg, A. F., Khan, L. A., and St. John, J. P. 1999. Three-Dimensional Hydrodynamic Model of New York Harbor Region. *Journal of Hydraulic Engineering* **125**:799–816.

Bowen, M. M., and Geyer, W. R. 2003. Salt transport and the time-dependent salt balance of a partially stratified estuary. *Journal of Geophysical Research* **108**(C5):3158.

Chant, R. J., and Wilson, R. E. 1997. Secondary circulation in a highly stratified estuary. *Journal of Geophysical Research* **102**(C10):23207–16.

Chant, R. J. 2002. Secondary circulation in a region of flow curvature: relationship with tidal forcing and river discharge. *Journal of Geophysical Research* **107**(C9):3131.

DiLorenzo, J. L., Huang, P., Ulman, D., and Najarian, T. O. 1999. Hydrologic and anthropogenic controls on the salinity distribution of the middle Hudson River estuary. Final Report prepared for the Hudson River Foundation.

Filadelfo, R., Wilson, R. E., and Gomez-Reyes, E. 1991. Subtidal Eulerian currents in the upper and lower East River tidal strait: Spring 1981. *Journal of Geophysical Research* **96**(C8):15217–26.

Geyer, W. R., and Nepf, H. M. 1996. Tidal pumping of salt in a moderately stratified estuary. *Coastal and Estuarine Studies* **53**:213–26.

Geyer, W. R., Trowbridge, J. H., and Bowen, M. 2000. The Dynamics of a Partially Mixed Estuary. *Journal of Physical Oceanography* **30**(8):2035–48.

Geyer, W. R., Woodruff, J. D., and Traykovski, P. 2001. Sediment Transport and Trapping in the Hudson River Estuary. *Estuaries* **24**(5):670–9.

Hass, L. W. 1977. The effect of the spring-neap tidal cycle on the vertical structure of the James, York and Rappahannock Rivers, Virginia, U.S.A. *Estuarine Coastal Marine Science* **5**:485–96.

Howells, G. P. 1972. The estuary of the Hudson River, U.S.A. *Proceedings of the Royal Society of London B* **180**:521–34.

Jay, D. A., and Bowman, M. J. 1975. The physical oceanography and water quality of New York Harbor and western Long Island Sound. Technical Report. 23:71. Marine Science Research Center State University of New York Stony Brook, Stony Brook, NY.

Peters, H. 1997. Observations of Stratified Turbulent Mixing in an Estuary: Neap-to-spring Variations During High River Flow. *Estuarine, Coastal and Shelf Science* **45**:69–88.

Pritchard, D. W. 1952. Salinity distribution and circulation in the Chesapeake Bay estuarine system. *Journal of Marine Research* **XI**(2):106–123.

Wilson, R. E., Wong, K. C., and Filadelfo, R. 1985. Low frequency sea level variability in the vicinity of the East River tidal strait. *Journal of Geophysical Research* **90**:954–60.

Worzel, J. L. and Drake, C. L. 1959. Structure Section Across the Hudson River at Nyack, New York, From Seismic Observations. *Annals of the New York Academy of Sciences* **80**:1092–1105.

Yankovsky, A. E., Garvine, R. W., and Münchow, A. 2000. Meso-scale currents on the inner New Jersey shelf driven by the interaction of buoyancy and wind forcing. *Journal of Physical Oceanography* **30**:2214–30.

Zimmerman, J. T. F. 1986. The tidal whirlpool: A review of horizontal dispersion by tidal and residual currents. *Netherlands Journal of Sea Research* **20**(2/3):133–54.

4 Sedimentary Processes in the Hudson River Estuary

Henry Bokuniewicz

ABSTRACT The Hudson River estuary is narrowly confined in its rocky valley. Unconsolidated sediments available to the estuary are primarily glacial till and glacial lake deposits. Estimates of sediment sources to the estuary range between 365,000 and 1.02 million metric tons (MT) y^{-1} at the head of tide with an additional amount to be added along the tidal estuary of between 80,000 and 390,000 MT y^{-1}. Tidal resuspension and transport is important throughout the estuary but fine-grained sediment transport associated with the recirculation of salt water is confined to the lower reaches. A substantial marine source of sediment is likely, but of uncertain magnitude. Two turbidity maxima appear to be generated by different mechanisms. One is formed near the head of salt and migrates down the estuary during times of high freshwater discharge. The other arises in mid-estuary. It is generated by tidally modulated and geomorphically controlled salinity fronts. A marine source of sediment is likely to be substantial.

Introduction

The Hudson River estuary, or the lower Hudson as it is sometimes called, begins where the tidal influence is first felt at Troy, New York, 240 kilometers (km) north of the Battery. From this point, the combined discharge of the upper Hudson and Mohawk rivers collects additional water from the drainage basins of twenty other, smaller tributaries. The intrusion of salt water is limited to the lower reaches and can extend 120 km above the Battery at times of low freshwater discharge.

The estuary acts as a machine for transporting sediment with two special, estuarine features. The first of these is the reversing tidal current. The Native American name for the Hudson is roughly translated as the "river that flows both ways." This tidal influence reaches all the way to the dam at Troy. Sediment introduced to the estuary is transported by tidal currents. Sand is usually moved near the estuary floor and sand transport can be recognized by the occurrence of ripples, or larger sand waves on the bottom. Because of the tidal conditions, sand is sometimes moved up the estuary and sometimes down.

The second distinguishing character of the estuarine sedimentary system is its relationship to the geochemical estuary, that is, the region of circulation of salty water. More dense, more saline water flows into the estuary at the sea floor while fresher, less dense surface water flows out to the sea. Within the geochemical estuary, fine-grained, suspended sediment is redistributed into turbidity maxima; that is, a region from which the concentration of suspended sediment decreases both upstream and downstream. Because of the landward circulation of bottom water, a marine source of sediment is likely. Fine-grained sediment is transported as suspended load in the estuary and deposited, resuspended, and redeposited many times before it is permanently buried in sediment deposits or exported to the sea. The deposition of fine-grained sediment is rapid in dredged navigation channels creating the need for continued maintenance.

The processes by which this transport occurs are extremely variable and cannot be predicted with certainty. Some measurements are available to document the general characterization of these processes, but there is little information concerning their variability in time and space. These processes are considered below.

Background

The Hudson and Mohawk Rivers transverse predominantly erosion-resistant uplands, although the valley itself occupies a terrain of erosion-susceptible shale. The lower Hudson crosses six geologic terrains. From Troy to Cornwall, the river runs through a valley in the Appalachian Ridge and Valley Province. This area is underlain by gently folded and tilted siltstones, shales, and carbonate rocks (Sanders, 1974). From Cornwall-on-Hudson southward to Peekskill, the river cuts through the Hudson Highlands, a band of resistant, Precambrian crystalline rocks. Below Peekskill, the west bank of the river skirts the rocks of the Newark Basin. These are predominantly Triassic and Jurassic Period sandstones, shales, and volcanic rocks (Sanders, 1974) and include the Palisades escarpment. The east bank is formed of high-grade metamorphic rocks of the Manhattan Prong of the New England Uplands: Precambrian and Lower Paleozoic Era schists, marble, quartzite, and gneiss. The Hudson discharges into the Upper and Lower bays on New York Harbor spilling out across the unconsolidated sediments of the Coastal Plain to the Atlantic Ocean.

All these rocks constrain the river in a resistant foundation wherein sediment sources are largely confined to a veneer of glacial deposits. Glacial tills, drift, and outwash sands blanket the entire drainage area. Most valleys of the tributaries are lined with unconsolidated silts and clays originally deposited in glacial lakes during the retreat of the Wisconsin glaciation. Ground moraine tends to be relatively resistant to erosion but can supply a wide range of grain sizes to the river. Sand enters the system from local concentrations of glacial sand bodies, while silt and clay can be provided from the reworking of glaciolacustrine deposits. In the lower reaches of the river, these sources are supplemented by a supply of sediment up-estuary from the sea. Sand from the Coastal Plain can migrate into the river under tidal influences and fine-grained, marine sediments are recycled into the Hudson by a characteristic, estuarine circulation.

Most of the lower Hudson drainage basin (57 percent) is forested, however anthropogenic influences permeate the entire estuary. Dredged areas comprise about 8 percent of the area of the estuary or some 23 km² out of a total surface area of 282 square kilometers above the Battery (Ellsworth, 1986). The banks of the estuary have been extensively stabilized by bulkheads and "rip-rap," or railroad beds, which run up the shore on both sides of the estuary. About 2 percent of the west shore and 21 percent of the east shore is stabilized by the railroad (Ellsworth, 1986). Rocky shoreline or stabilized shoreline accounts for approximately 43 percent of the total shoreline. The main stem of the estuary is dammed at Troy. Tributaries below Troy may be dammed or otherwise restricted by causeways supporting the railroads along the shores.

Important Processes

SEDIMENT INPUT

The amount of sediment delivered to the Hudson estuary is an important, but elusive number. The most direct measurements are made by periodically sampling the river water, determining the amount of suspended sediment per liter of water, and multiplying that by the discharge around the time of sampling. It can only be done easily above the tidal influence. Because it is an engaging task, it is not done all the time nor has it been done on every tributary. In addition, the sediment delivery is discontinuous; almost all the sediment supplied in a given year may be introduced over a few days during floods, exactly the time when measurements are most difficult to make. The sediment delivery can also vary widely from year to year. In the absence of direct measurements, sediment input may be calculated from estimates of the loss of soil from the land surface, but this isn't any easier or more certain.

As a result of such difficulties, estimates for the fluvially derived sediment input to the Lower Hudson Basin are scarce. Dole and Stabler (1909) put the total sediment discharge at Troy as 365,000 metric tons per year, ($MT y^{-1}$) while Panuzio (1965) places it at 750,000 MT y^{-1} at kilometer 120. For 1977, 1.02 million MT were supplied to the lower Hudson at Troy (Olsen, 1979), and 920,000 MT y^{-1}, on average, over thirty years (1947–77). Additional sediment is supplied by the tributaries entering the tidal portion of the river below the dam at Troy; these values must be added to the sediment load entering at Troy. Based on the relative areas of the drainage basin (Olsen, 1979), the river-borne sediment input from the lower Hudson provides 310,000 MT y^{-1} for 1977, and 280,000 MT y^{-1} for the thirty-year average. A different estimate can be made using the data from the United States Department of Agriculture, Soil Conservation Service to obtain a delivery ratio. In this way, the suspended sediment yield for each square kilometer was estimated to be between 25 MT $km^{-2} y^{-1}$ and 32 MT $km^{-2} y^{-1}$ (Ellsworth, 1986). Correspondingly, the calculation for the entire lower Hudson drainage basin, which has an area of 1.2 million hectares, is between 300,000 MT y^{-1} and 390,000 MT y^{-1}. A third estimate (Howarth, Fruci, and Sherman, 1991) was calculated by applying a generalized watershed loading model to the Hudson River drainage basin. The model result gave a three-year average (1983–86) fluvial sediment input for the lower Hudson of 260,000 MT y^{-1}.

Yet another model, the Hydrologic Simulation Program Fortran, was used for the quantification of the terrestrial source of sediment from the tributaries below Troy (Lodge, 1997). Twenty tributaries comprising the lower Hudson drainage basin were found to supply 80,000 and 100,000 MT y^{-1}, for 1992 and 1993, respectively. The combined discharge of the Catskill, Kinderhook, Normans Kill, and Wallkill creeks alone contributed 60 percent of the sediment load. New material was calculated to have a residence time of 22 days in the estuary (Lodge, 1997).

The sources of fine-grained sediment are diverse and distributed over 34,000 square kilometers. Little is supplied directly by erosion of the river banks (Ellsworth, 1986). The abundance of sand in the Hudson north of Kingston (Coch, 1986) is supplied by the local tributaries and, in part, by scouring of the channel floor.

MARINE SOURCES

The landward (i.e, up-estuary) transport of sediment seems common at the mouths of estuaries, and a marine supply can be substantial in some estuaries (Biggs, 1970; Bokuniewicz, Gebert, and Gordon, 1976; Meade, 1969; Hobbs et al., 1992; Turner, Millward, and Tyler, 1994). In Chesapeake Bay, for example, flood-dominated channels transport sand into the estuary mouth (Ludwick, 1974). This situation also seems to exist at the mouth of the Lower New York Bay (Swift and Ludwick, 1976). Large sandwaves have been found on the floor of the Ambrose Channel with asymmetry indicating landward transport. In the Hudson itself, the coarsening of sediments from the Hudson Highlands to the Battery has been attributed in part to the up-estuary transport of sand from the Coastal Plain (Coch, 1976).

Many estuaries are sinks for sediments (e.g., Nichols, 1977; Yarbo et al., 1983; Hobbs et al., 1992). The Hudson River Estuary also appears to be an effective trap for fine-grained sediment that

is capable of absorbing not only fine-grained sediment supplied by its rivers but also a substantial ocean source (Bokuniewicz and Coch, 1986; Olsen et al., 1984; Ellsworth, 1986). Such behavior seems common, especially in partially mixed estuaries like the Hudson. It has been explained by the superposition of characteristic estuarine circulation on the suspended sediment distribution (Schubel and Carter, 1984) in conjunction with rapid particle settling speeds due to agglomeration. In general, the estuarine, density-driven circulation drives saline bottom water landward into the estuary while fresher surface water flows out. Higher concentrations of suspended sediment tend to be found near the estuary floor both because particles tend to sink to the bottom and because sediment on the seafloor can be resuspended by waves and tidal currents. Higher concentrations of suspended sediment in the bottom waters are, therefore, imported by the estuarine circulation.

The import of fine-grained, marine sediment into estuaries along the east coast has often been proposed. In the Hudson, the geochemical signature of silts and clays provided evidence that 30 percent of the fine-grained sediment being deposited in the estuary entered at its mouth (Olsen et al., 1984) and, an attempted sediment budget for the Hudson River estuary (Ellsworth, 1986) needed to invoke a marine source to balance the sources and sinks. At the Battery, the estimated input from the sea was between 139,000 and 734,000 MT y^{-1} (with a fluvial input at Troy estimated at 870,000 MT y^{-1}; Ellsworth, 1986). In addition, grain size analysis of bottom sediments suggests that the bottom sediments in the lower estuary are composed of one component of sand from the ocean and another of particles in flocs (Gibbs, Jha, and Chakrapani, 1994; Coch, 1976).

There is little information concerning the production of sediment particles (opal) in situ. Production rates have been estimated to correspond 135,000 MT y^{-1} over the entire area of the estuary (Ellsworth, 1986).

SUSPENDED SEDIMENT CONCENTRATION

Early measurements of the ambient suspended sediment concentrations in the upper reaches of the estuary report an average concentration of 17 mg L^{-1} (at kilometer 190; Dole and Stabler, 1909) and 33 mg L^{-1} (at kilometer 120; Panuzio, 1965). A

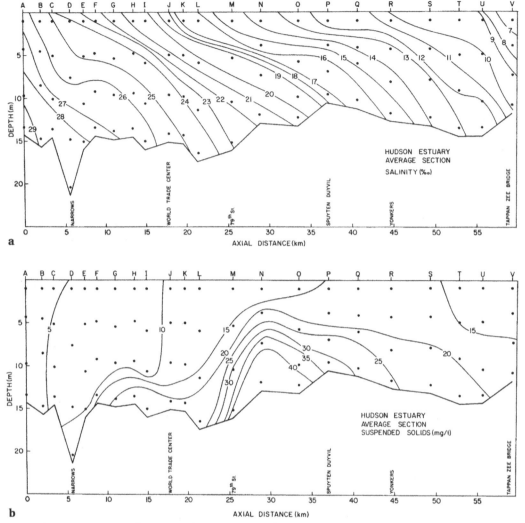

Figure 4.1. Average salinity (a) and average, suspended sediment concentrations (b) along the axis of the Hudson (from nine sections between November, 1980 and September, 1981; Hirschberg and Bokuniewicz, 1991).

value of 33 mg L^{-1} was also obtained from measurements at kilometer 30 over a tidal cycle (Olsen, 1979). Seasonal sampling along the axis of the estuary yielded an average concentration of 35 mg L^{-1} with mean values of 25 mg L^{-1} at the surface and 46 mg L^{-1} near the estuary floor (Arnold, 1982). Suspended particles appear in two dominant modes; those less than 4.65 μm in diameter and those greater than 22.1 μm (Menon, Gibbs, and Phillips, 1998).

Tidal cycle variations may range over a factor of 3 or 4 (at kilometer 30; Olsen, 1979) and seasonal variation from 17 to 45 mg L^{-1} in the upper reaches

and 23 to 26 mg L^{-1} in the lower reaches (Arnold, 1982). In the upper reaches, the variation of suspended sediment load is expected to be due to changes in the delivery of sediment past Troy over the seasons, while in the lower reaches the variations seem to be controlled more by tidal resuspension (Arnold, 1982).

TURBIDITY MAXIMA

The Hudson River Estuary appears to have two turbidity maxima formed by different mechanisms. One is associated with the landward limit of sea salt. It is apparently formed by the estuarine circulation,

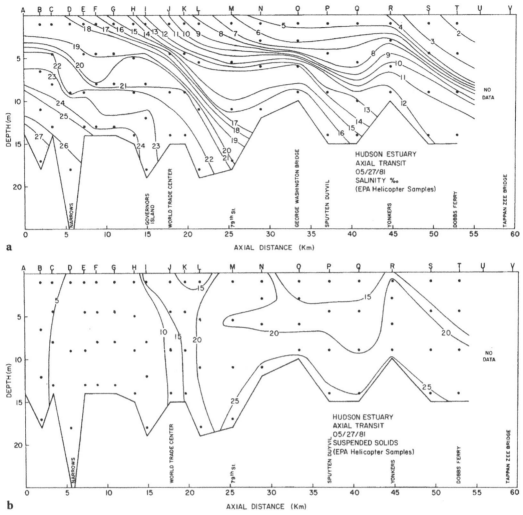

Figure 4.2. Near-synoptic, axial sections of salinity (a) and suspended sediment concentrations (b; 27 May, 1981).

although its location may be modified by bathymetric influence in the deepest parts of the estuary (the gorge). The second is formed at mid-estuary by the tidally modulated and geomorphically controlled formation and migration of salt fronts into the estuary. Secondary, mid-estuary turbidity maxima are sometimes seen, but these may be residuals from the previous tide.

Evidence for a turbidity maximum in a relatively limited reach of the estuary along the Manhattan shore below the George Washington Bridge was documented in a series of vertical distributions of water temperature, salinity, and suspended sediment concentrations measured along the axis of the Hudson River Estuary nine times between

November 1980 and September 1981 (Hirschberg and Bokuniewicz, 1991). The average salinity section and the average section of suspended sediment concentration are shown in Figure 4.1. The observations did not extend to the limit of sea salt, but a strong turbidity maximum was found at the estuary floor between 79th Street and the Spuyten Duyvil (approximately at the position of Grant's Tomb at 122nd Street). Suspended sediment concentrations reached levels over 100 mg L^{-1} and the highest recorded value was 447 mg L^{-1}. This turbidity maximum, however, was not present in all the individual transects. On 27 May 1981, a nearly synoptic section was done from a helicopter (Fig. 4.2). Although there was well-developed

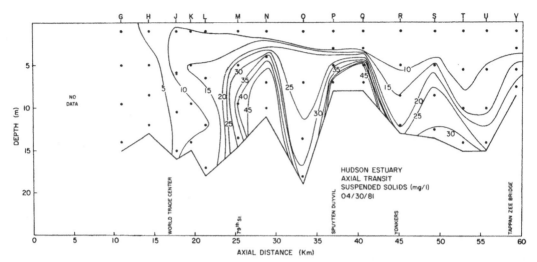

Figure 4.3. Axial section of the suspended sediment concentration showing two, mid-estuary turbidity maxima (30 April, 1981).

salinity stratification, no strong turbidity maximum was found. At another time (30 April 1981; Fig. 4.3), two turbidity maxima were found. This region of elevated turbidity was not associated with a local permanent or quasi-permanent salt front as one might expect in light of the conventional wisdom concerning the formation of estuarine turbidity maxima.

The turbidity maximum (Fig. 4.1) was located in the vicinity of the average position of the strong salinity gradients. Observations of this turbidity maximum showed near-bottom suspended sediment concentrations of 100 to 200 mg L^{-1} in the summer of 1992 increasing to between 100 to 400 mg L^{-1} during high discharge in 1993 (Geyer, 1995), although maximum concentrations reached 800 mg L^{-1} (Geyer, 1995). In the turbidity maximum, the concentration of the finest grained particles (less than 4.65 μm in diameter) increases about 50 percent over ambient levels to where it comprises 55 percent to 60 percent of the suspended load (Menon et al., 1998).

DEPOSITION

Fine-grained sediment may ultimately be deposited in wetlands, in dredged channels or in undredged areas of the estuary floors. Bridge borings disclosed a layer of estuarine sediment as much as 61 m thick in the Hudson (Newman et al., 1969). If we assume that estuarine conditions were established by 12,000 years B.P., the long-term

accumulation rate is something less than 0.5 cm y^{-1} Direct measurements of deposition rates using radiometric techniques vary from 1 to 5 cm y^{-1} in undredged areas south of the George Washington Bridge, 1 to 3 cm y^{-1} in marginal zones and 0.1 to 0.3 cm y^{-1} on the estuary floor north of the George Washington Bridge (Olsen, 1979).

The conventional wisdom is that marshes accumulate to keep pace with sea level rise. Indeed they must if they are going to maintain their position over thousands of years. At the Battery, sea level is rising at an average rate of about 3 mm y^{-1}. Combining this with an estimate of marsh sediment composition, Ellsworth (1986) calculated a total deposition of 12,000 MT y^{-1} over the 22.8 km^2 of marshland. In the lower Hudson, measured rates are more rapid. Measurements of sedimentation rates at five marshes (Piermont, Iona, Tivoli Bay North, Tivoli Bay South, and Stockport Flats) yielded rates from 2 mm y^{-1} to greater than 11 mm y^{-1} (Peller, 1985; Robideau, 1997). With an average rate of 6 mm y^{-1} the rates tended to be slightly higher in the north and slightly lower in the south. On the average, this would raise the total marshland deposition to 24,000 MTy^{-1}.

The lower 18 kilometers of the estuary has been extensively dredged. Ninety-five percent of the total annual dredged sediment is removed from this area (Ellsworth, 1986). In the decade between 1966 and 1976, 705,990 m^3 of sediment were removed (Conner et al., 1979). Deposition rates in dredged areas, therefore, may average 14 cm y^{-1}. The deposition rate is not uniform. Recently in the estuary along the Manhattan shore, observations show that 15 cm or more could be deposited in a single freshet (Woodruff, 1999).

RESUSPENSION

Resuspension rates may be determined directly by testing undisturbed sediment samples in a flume or by monitoring conditions at the sea floor closely over time. Flume tests have not been done on Hudson sediment but the importance of resuspension has been calculated from measurements of changes in the near-bottom suspended sediment concentration (Geyer, Woodruff, and Traykouski, 2001) at locations in the lower estuary along the Manhattan shoreline. Within the turbidity maximum, concentrations of suspended sediment were observed to decrease to low levels during slack tides from levels of several hundred milligrams per liter (Geyer, 1995). Although this tidally modulated deposition suggests that subsequent tidal resuspension is necessary to maintain the turbidity maximum, Geyer (1995) did not find a correlation between the suspended load and water velocity, suggesting that advection was the predominant control of concentrations.

Alternatively, resuspension rates may be estimated by assessing the vertical flux of settling sediment particles. The downward vertical flux of particles to the seafloor is often found to be much larger than the net, long-term deposition rate. As a result, the vertical flux to the seafloor is balanced to a first approximation by resuspension. One way to determine the vertical flux is from near-bottom sediment traps. These devices are designed to intercept the flux of sediment to the seafloor. Measurements of the vertical particle flux in the vicinity of the turbidity maximum ranged from 106 g cm^{-2} y^{-1} to 586 g cm^{-2} y^{-1} (Achman, Brownawell, and Zhang, 1996), which are three orders of magnitude greater than the long-term accumulation rate. Assuming that this is the rate at which sediment reaches the seafloor, this is also the resuspension rate.

Few measurements are available in the estuary and these were not taken for the purposes of determining the flux at the seafloor. Estimates can also be made from a combination of settling velocity and concentration. If 0.04 cm s^{-1} is taken as the settling velocity (Arnold, 1982) and 30 mg L^{-1} taken as a typical concentration away from the turbidity maximum, the vertical settling flux becomes 1.2×10^{-6} or 38 g cm^{-2} s^{-1}. This is lower than the sediment trap results but still much higher than the long term accumulation rate. As a result, it may be considered an estimate of resuspension.

SANDWAVES

Sandwaves are large ripples or underwater dunes that indicate the movement of sand along the estuary floor by currents. They may be active, with particles being moved continuously by the river flow or alternatively by the tides, or they may be relic, inactive fractures formed by unusual past events such as floods or exceptionally strong tides. They are often asymmetric in cross-sectional form with a steeper face in the direction of net transport. As has already been mentioned, asymmetric sandwaves in the mouth of New York Harbor indicate a net transport of sand up-estuary.

In the Hudson River Estuary, patches of asymmetric sandwaves are found as, for example, near Saugerties (Fig. 4.4; Bell et al., 2000). These usually show evidence of down-estuary transport of sand under the influence of the freshwater discharge and the ebbing tide. Where the estuary is divided into two channels, however, by a median shoal or island, one channel will show evidence of up-estuary transport under flooding tides while its partner will be dominated by down-estuary transport.

Discussion: Mechanism for a Mid-Estuary Turbidity Maximum

The reach of the estuary in the vicinity of the George Washington Bridge is characterized by large fractional changes in channel cross section area, in maximum channel depth, and in width. The channel cross-sectional area varies from approximately 11,000 m^2 to 177,000 m^2 (R. Wilson, 1999 Marine Sciences Research Center, personal communication). Preliminary observation in 1992, using a 200 KHZ echo sounder to visualize the halocline, and an AMS CTD showed the existence of large, quasi-stationary undulations in the halocline during maximum ebb as well as bottom salinity fronts situated in the vicinity of channel expansions. Hydraulically influenced, intratidal

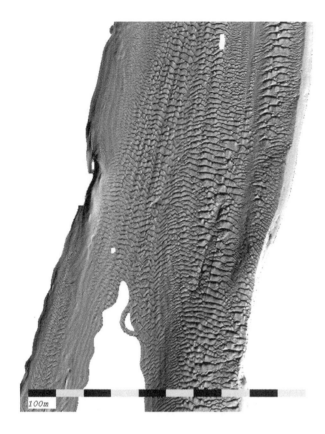

Figure 4.4. Sandwaves as shown by a multi-beam survey in the vicinity of Saugerties. Bedforms in the left-hand (west) side appear to be migrating up-estuary while those in the right hand (east) side are migrating down-estuary (courtesy of R. Flood and V. Ferrini, Marine Sciences Research Center, Stony Brook University, Stony Brook, NY).

halocline behavior could lead to advection of bottom fronts, which would influence particles trapping the area.

Evidence suggests the following mechanism for the formation of the mid-estuarine turbidity maximum (Bokuniewicz and Ullman, 1995). During an ebbing tide, a salt front is found downstream of the George Washington Bridge as a result of the downstream expansion of the channel below the construction at the Bridge. This front is characterized by strong salinity gradients that intersect the bottom and a strong halocline. Suspended particles settling through the halocline become trapped in the lower water layer. As the ebb tide wanes and the flood begins, the salt wedge moves northward into the estuary gravitationally. Additional sediment is resuspended as it transgresses and this sediment is trapped behind the front under the halocline. The front's progress seems to be arrested on the bathymetry south of the George Washington Bridge even as the flood continues as evidenced by a rise in the halocline. During the flood, suspended sediment apparently is also transported laterally to the west side of the river (Geyer, 1995). As the flood tide ends and the ebb begins, the salinity gradients become unstable and the front breaks down. This event apparently can strand turbid water near the northernmost position of penetration of the salt wedge while a new front is generated further downstream to begin the process again. I would suggest that the second mid-estuary turbidity maximum, which is sometimes seen north of the first, may be turbid water formed on the previous tide and stranded as the next ebb began.

The occurrence of these turbidity maxima are influenced, as expected, by the freshwater discharge. The mid-estuary maximum tends to remain fixed in the vicinity of Grant's Tomb and seems to be found as long as the freshwater discharge allows saltwater penetration to that location. The maximum at the head of salt migrates down the estuary at times of high discharge and up-estuary at low. The freshwater discharge to the estuary averages 550 m^3 s^{-1} (Olsen, 1979). Figure 4.5 shows the axial distribution of salt and suspended sediment in May 1994, when the discharge was 2,690 m^3 s^{-1}.

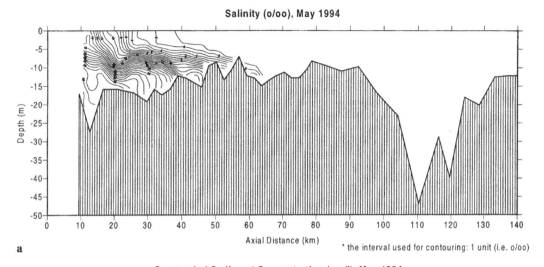

a

* the interval used for contouring: 1 unit (i.e. o/oo)

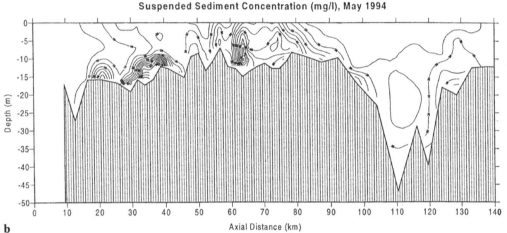

b

Figure 4.5. Axial distribution of salt (a) and suspended sediment (b) under high discharge (May, 1994). The salinity contour interval is one part per thousand; the suspended sediment concentration contour interval is 10 mg L^{-1}. The Battery is at kilometer 31 on this scale.

Three turbidity maxima were seen. One at the limit of sea salt, a second south of its expected position near Grant's Tomb and a third south of the Battery. By contrast, the summer of 1995 was a drought. The discharge in September 1995 was 255 m^3 s^{-1} and the axial distribution of salinity and suspended sediment is shown in Figure 4.6. The estuary is well mixed and two distinct turbidity maxima are seen; one at the head of salt, and one near Grant's Tomb.

Important Unsolved Problems

Available observations provide us with information about all the major processes occurring in the estuary. The Hudson, however, is both spatially diverse

and temporally variable so without adequate spatial and temporal observations, the integrated behavior of sediment in the estuary remains elusive. As a result, managers often find answers to their questions unsatisfying and inadequate. For example, a sediment budget for the estuary requires deposition rates in the various substrates on the estuary floor. These facies have not been mapped in detail, although a current effort by the New York State Department of Environmental Conservation is moving in that direction (see chapter by Bell et al., this volume). Even when they are, deposition rates have been determined in only a few locations, so large uncertainties will remain in the amount of sediment deposited.

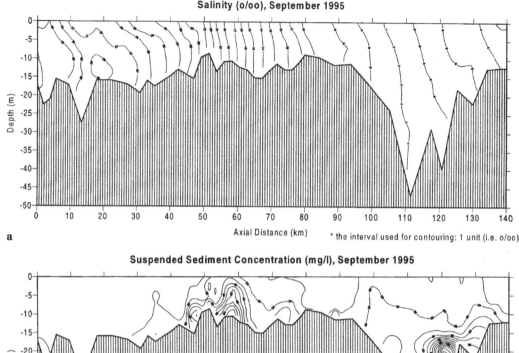

Figure 4.6. Axial distribution of salt (a) and suspended sediment (b) under low discharge (September, 1995). The salinity contour interval is one part per thousand; the suspended sediment concentration contour interval is 10 mg L^{-1}. The Battery is at kilometer 31 on this scale.

As we have seen, even straightforward questions, like how much sediment is brought into the estuary by rivers, are answered only within fairly broad ranges. Monitoring has not been continuous. Storm events are hostile to any measurement program and easy to miss. Most of the tributaries are not monitored, forcing reliance on indirect calculations.

The amount of resuspension poses similar difficulties. Because of the wide variety of variables that influence resuspension rates, the only way to know them are to measure them directly (Bokuniewicz, McTiernan, and Davis, 1991). Very few measurements have been made and no attempt has been made to measure spatial or temporal variability. As a result, resuspension can only be quantified in the most general terms. An oceanic source also seems likely, but what is its magnitude? How does it vary with changes in discharge? Could it be that the oceanic source buffers the system? Even without increases in the fluvial sources, increased dredging may result in an increased deposition of sediments of marine origin.

Likewise, the broad outlines for the estuarine turbidity structure in the Hudson are known but many questions remain concerning the mechanisms and dynamics. Predictive models of the suspended sediment transport will remain elusive. An important question on the road to these answers are the degree and mechanism of lateral transport in the estuary. Some work has been done on this issue but its significance remains to be integrated into a more comprehensive conceptual model of the estuarine sedimentary system.

In the future of estuarine research, in general, there needs to be attention given to comparisons between estuaries. Thirty years ago, Emery and Uchupi (1972) pointed out that far more effort has gone into making detailed studies of sediments of individual estuaries than into either comparing results from a variety of estuaries with similar physical or geological characteristics, or into critical evaluation of processes. Their observation still holds true today. Schemes for classifying the hydraulic regimes of estuaries have been developed and widely used but little effort has been devoted to comparing estuarine sedimentary systems. Holistic comparative studies are needed to better understand those sedimentary processes that characterize estuaries. The Hudson-Raritan estuarine system invites comparisons with a wide variety of other local systems such as Narrangansett Bay, Long Island Sound, Peconic Bay, and the Connecticut River estuary. Of these, the Hudson system is probably the most heavily impacted by human activities. Anthropogenic effects add an additional complicating factor that is not present in less urbanized estuaries.

REFERENCES

Achman, D. R., Brownawell, B. J., and Zhang, L. 1996. Exchange of Polychlorinated Biphenyls between Sediment and Water in the Hudson River Estuary, *Estuaries* **19**: 950–65.

Arnold, C. A. 1982. "Modes of Fine-grained Suspended Sediment Occurrences in the Hudson River Estuary." Marine Sciences Research Center, State University of New York at Stony Brook, Stony Brook, NY. Master's Thesis; 102 pp.

Bell, R. E., Flood, R. D., Carbotte, S. M., Ryan, W. B. F., McHugh, C., Cornier, M., Versteeg, R., Chayes, D., Bokuniewicz, H., Ferrini, V., and Thissen, J. 2000. Hudson River Estuary Program Benthic Mapping Project Final Report. NY State Department of Environmental Conservation, Albany, NY.

Biggs, R. B. 1970. Sources and distribution of suspended sediment in Northern Chesapeake Bay, *Marine Geology* **9**: 187–201.

Bokuniewicz, H. J. 1996. *Building the Turbidity Maximum in the Hudson River Estuary.* Marine Sciences Research Center, State University of New York at Stony Brook, Stony Brook, NY. Special Report 115. 35 pp.

Bokuniewicz, H. J., and Coch, N. K. 1986. Some management implications of sedimentation in the Hudson-Raritan estuarine system. *Northeastern Geology and Environmental Sciences* **8**: 165–70.

Bokuniewicz, H. J., Gebert, J., and Gordon, R. B. 1976. Sediment mass balance of a large estuary: Long Island Sound. *Estuarine, Coastal and Shelf Science*, **4**: 523–36.

Bokuniewicz, H., McTiernan, L., and Davis, W. 1991. Measurement of sediment resuspension rates in Long Island Sound. *Geo-Marine Letters* **11**: 159–61.

Bokuniewicz, H. J., and Ullman, D. 1995. *Turbidity Distribution in the Hudson River Estuary.* Marine Sciences Research Center, State University of New York at Stony Brook, Stony Brook, NY. Special Report 109. 12 pp.

Coch, N. K. 1976. Temporal and aerial variations in same Hudson River Estuary sediments, March – October, 1974: Geological Society of America, Northeastern Section, Abstract with Programs 8: 153, Boulder, CO.

1986. Sediment characteristics and facies distribution in the Hudson System. *Northeastern Geology and Environmental Sciences* **8**: 109–29.

Conner, W. G., Aurand, D., Leslie, M., Slaughter, J., Amr, A., and Ravenscroft, F. I. 1979. Disposal of dredged material within the NY District Vol. 1 – Present Practices and Candidate Alternatives, MITRE Corporation, McLean, VA: 362 pp.

Dole, R. B., and Stabler, H. 1909. Denudation. U.S. Geological Survey. Water Supply Paper No. 234: 78–93.

Ellsworth, J. M. 1986. Sources and Sinks for fine-grained sediment in the Lower Hudson River, *Northeastern Geology and Environmental Sciences* **8**: 141–55.

Emery, K. A., and Uchupi, E. 1972. Western Atlantic Ocean: Topography, rocks, structure, water, life and sediments. Amer. Assoc. of Petrol. Geol. Mem., 17. 532 pp.

Geyer, W. R. 1995. *Final Report: Particle Trapping in the Lower Hudson Estuary.* Hudson River Foundation, New York. 30 pp.

Geyer, W. R., Woodruff, J. P., and Traykouski, P. 2001. Sediment Transport and Trapping in the Hudson Estuary. *Estuaries* **24**: 670–79.

Gibbs, R. J., Jha, P. K., and Chakrapani, G. J. 1994. Sediment Particle Size in the Hudson River Estuary, *Sedimentology* **41**: 1063–68.

Hirschberg, D., and Bokuniewicz, H. J. 1991. Measurements of water temperature, salinity and suspended sediment concentrations along the axis of the Hudson River estuary 1980–1981. Marine Sciences Research Center, State University of New York at Stony Brook, Stony Brook, NY. Special Data Report No. 11: 30.

Hobbs, C. H., Halka, J. P., Kerkin, P. T., and Carron, M. J. 1992. Chesapeake Bay sediment budget. *Journal of Coastal Research* **8**: 292–300.

Howarth, R. W., Fruci, J. R., and Sherman, D. 1991. Inputs of sediment and carbon to an estuarine ecosystem: Influence of land use. *Ecological Applications* **1**: 27–39.

Lodge, J. M. 1997. "A model of tributary sediment input to the tidal Hudson River." Marine Sciences Research Center, State University of New York at Stony Brook, Stony Brook, NY. Master's thesis. 143 pp.

Ludwick, J. C. 1974. Tidal currents and zig-zag shoals in a wide estuary entrance. Boulder, CO: Geological Society of America, Bulletin 85: 717–26.

Meade, R. H. 1969. Landward transport of bottom sediments in estuaries of the Atlantic Coastal Plain. *Journal of Sedimentary Petrology* **14**: 22–34.

Menon, M. G., Gibbs, R. J., and Phillips, A. 1998. Accumulation of muds and metals in the Hudson River estuary turbidity maximum. *Environmental Geology* **34**: 214–22.

Newman, W. S., Thurber, D. H., Zeiss, H. S., Rokach, A., and Musich, L. 1969. Late Quarternary geology of the Hudson River estuary: A preliminary report. *Transactions of the New York Academy of Sciences: Series II.* **31**: 548–70.

Nichols, M. M. 1977. Response and recovery of an estuary following a river flood. *Journal of Sedimentary Petrology* **47**: 1171–86.

Olsen, C. R. 1979. Radionuclides, sedimentation and accumulation of pollutants in the Hudson Estuary. Columbia University, New York, NY. Ph.D. Thesis, 343 pp.

Olsen, C. R., Larsen, I. L., Brewster, R. H., Cutshall, N. H., Bopp, R. F., and Simpson, H. J. 1984. A geochemical assessment of sedimentation and contaminant distribution in the Hudson-Raritan Estuary. NOAA. Technical. Report. NOS OMS 2: 101p.

Panuzio, F. L. 1965. Lower Hudson siltation. In *Proceedings of the Federal Inter-Agency Sedimentation Conference*, 1963. Miscellaneous Publication No. 970. Agriculture Research Service: 512–50.

Peller, P. 1985. Recent sediment and pollutant accumulation in the Hudson River National Estuary Sanctuary. In Cooper, J. C. (ed) Polgar Fellowship Reports, Hudson River Foundation, New York, NY.

Robideau, R. M. 1997. "Sedimentation rates in Hudson River marshes determined by radionuclide dating techniques." Rensselaer Polytechnic Institute, Troy, NY. Master's thesis, 115 p.

Sanders, J. E. 1974. Geomorphology of the Hudson Estuary. *Annals of the New York Academy of Science* **250**: 5–38.

Schubel, J. R., and Carter, H. H. 1984. Suspended sediment budget for Chesapeake Bay. In M. L. Wiley (ed). *Estuarine Processes*, New York: Academic Press, pp. 48–62.

Swift, D. J. P., and Ludwick, J. 1976. Substrate response to hydraulic processes. Grain size frequency distributions and bedforms. In Stanley, D. J. and D. J. P. Swift (eds.). *Marine Sediment Transport and Environmental Management*, New York: John Wiley and Sons. pp. 159–96.

Turner, A., Millward, G. E., and Tyler, A. O. 1994. The distribution and chemical composition of particles in a macrotidal estuary. *Estuarine, Coastal and Shelf Science* **38**: 1–17.

Woodruff, J. D. 1999. Sediment deposition in the Lower Hudson River estuary. Masters Thesis, Massachusetts Institute of Technology Woods Hole Oceanographic Institution.

Yarbo, L. A., Carlson, P. R., Fisher, T. R., Chanton, J. P., and Kemp, W. M. 1983. A sediment budget for the Choptank River estuary in Maryland USA. *Estuarine, Coastal and Shelf Science* **17**: 555–70.

5 Benthic Habitat Mapping in the Hudson River Estuary

Robin E. Bell, Roger D. Flood,
Suzanne Carbotte, William B. F. Ryan,
Cecilia McHugh, Milene Cormier,
Roelof Versteeg, Henry Bokuniewicz,
Vicki Lynn Ferrini, Joanne Thissen,
John W. Ladd, and Elizabeth A. Blair

ABSTRACT Successful management of underwater lands requires detailed knowledge of the terrain and the interrelationships between landscape and habitat characteristics. While optical techniques can be used where the water is shallow or clear, other techniques are needed where the water is deeper or where optical transmission is limited by water clarity. Marine geophysical techniques provide quantitative measures of the nature of the estuary floor that can provide constraints on the distribution and movement of contaminated sediments as well as the nature of benthic habitats. The Benthic Mapping Program, supported by the Hudson River Estuary Program of the New York State Department of Environmental Conservation (NYSDEC) and the Hudson River Action Project, is being conducted in the Hudson River to characterize the river bed from the Verrazano Narrows in New York Harbor to the Federal Dam at Troy, New York. The study is using a range of acoustic and sampling techniques to gain new information on the river bed. The first phase of the Benthic Mapping Program, which occurred from 1998 to 2000, focused on four areas (about 40 river miles; 65 km). The products from the study have been incorporated into a GIS data management system for NYSDEC (see http://benthic.info for the DEC Benthic Mapper web site, an online version of the GIS database). This effort, supplemented by studies of benthic fauna and bathymetric change, is being continued under NYSDEC support for the remainder of the Hudson River. The second phase of the program worked in four areas in 2001 and 2002 (about 35 river miles; 57 km) and we completed the study by working in three areas in 2003 (about 66 river miles; 121 km).

Introduction

Successful land management requires detailed knowledge of the terrain and the interrelationships between landscape and habitat characteristics. For terrestrial areas, much information can be gathered about a region through analysis of topographic maps and aerial photographs as well as through direct inspection and study. When lands to be managed are underwater, other techniques need to be employed to understand the landscape. While optical techniques can be used where the water is shallow or clear, other techniques are needed where the water is deeper or where optical transmission is limited by water clarity. Marine geophysical techniques provide quantitative measures of the nature of the estuary floor that can provide constraints on the distribution and movement of contaminated sediments as well as the nature of benthic habitats.

The Benthic Mapping Program, supported by the Hudson River Estuary Program of the New York State Department of Environmental Conservation (NYSDEC) and the Hudson River Estuary Action Plan, is being conducted in the Hudson River to characterize the river bed from the Battery to the Federal Dam at Troy. The study is using a range of acoustic and sampling techniques to gain new information of the river bed. This report summarizes the first phase of the Benthic Mapping Program which occurred from 1998 to 2000 and focused on four areas (covering about 40 river miles (65 km), Fig. 5.1) of the river, including details of the data acquisition and reduction and a discussion of results from one of the study areas. The products from the study have been incorporated into a GIS data management system for NYSDEC. This effort, supplemented by studies of benthic fauna and bathymetric change is being continued under NYSDEC support for the remainder of the Hudson River from the Battery to the Federal Dam at Troy. About 35 river miles (57 km) were studied in 2001 and 2002 and the mapping phase was completed after studying about 66 river miles (121 km) in early 2003.

Major Findings

Major findings of the project include:

1. Broad bands of oyster beds, once active in the Tappan Zee, have been located. Dated oyster

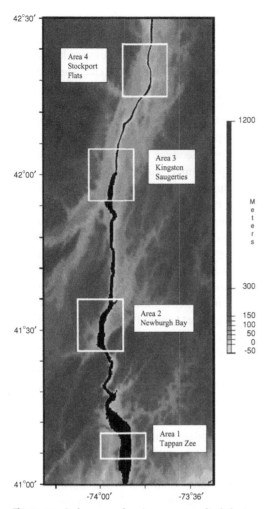

Figure 5.1. Index map showing areas studied during the first phase of the Hudson River Benthic Mapping program (1998–1999).

shells are 1,000 to 5,500 years old, but live oysters were found in the Tappan Zee and Haverstraw Bay during sampling in 2001.

2. Anthropogenic deposits are common in the Hudson River, and include numerous obstacles (some of which are ship wrecks), debris fields, Revolutionary War battlements, partially to fully infilled cable crossings and dredged channels, and linear bands of scour and deposition associated with bridge footings.

3. Sediment waves from 5 cm to 3 m high characterize the channel. Sand waves are dominant in the Kingston-Saugerties and Stockport Flats areas. The largest sand waves are found

in the river channel off Tivoli Bay. All sand waves in the tidal Hudson River are affected by tidal flow and many sand waves show downstream migration. However, sand waves in some areas show net upriver migration – demonstrating locally varying flow conditions. We estimate the rate of sand wave migration in some areas to in excess of 10 my^{-1}. Sediment waves also characterize several areas of overall muddy sediment, especially in the Tappan Zee and near Newburgh.

4. Most tributaries to the Hudson River have distinctive, generally elongated coarse-grained deposits at their mouths which extend both north and south, indicating that sediment deposition has been modified by tidal flow. These deposits can extend over five kilometers (km) along the river margin, as is the case for the Moodna and Wappinger Creeks.

5. Within the Tappan Zee region recent sediment accumulation is restricted to an abandoned dredge channel, tributary mouths, and the channel bend.

6. Although live zebra mussels are found in many of the sediment samples in the Kingston-Saugerties and Stockport Flats regions, they are concentrated at the mouths of tributaries and close to bedrock outcrops. No live mussels are recovered from areas of sand waves where the riverbed is more mobile.

Study Areas

The four segments of the river (Area 1 to Area 4; Fig. 5.1) mapped in the first phase of this Benthic Mapping Program include four distinct portions of the estuary.

Area 1 – The Tappan Zee Region: The Tappan Zee region extends 9.25 km from 1.8 km north of the Tappan Zee Bridge to the southern tip of Croton Point (41° 05′ N to 41° 10′ N). This wide region has a narrow, deep central channel cut into broad, shallow flats, and the water is saline through most of the year. Recent sedimentation, associated with potentially contaminated sediments, is limited to deposition in regions dredged near Nyack in the early 1900s, small tributary mouths, and the inside channel bend. A number of relict oyster beds were identified in this area.

Area 2 – The Newburgh Bay Region: The 18.5 km Newburgh Bay segment extends from Storm King Mountain in the south to Wappingers Creek in the north (41° 26′ N to 41° 36′ N). In this reach river morphology changes from the narrow, deep channel associated with the Hudson Highlands, to the open expanse of Newburgh Bay, to narrow again north of Danskammer Point. The river in this area alternates between saline and freshwater flow during the year. The region is dominated by human activities, and the effects of bridge construction, the path of a cable crossing, and numerous dump sites are clearly imaged in the data. Recent deposition is closely associated with flow obstructions by natural (e.g., Diamond Reef) and man-made (e.g., Beacon-Newburgh Bridge) features. The southern portion of this region appears to be less impacted by recent human activities and contains Revolutionary War structures and records of ancient storms.

Area 3 – Kingston – Saugerties Region: This 18.5 km region extends from Kingston at Esopus Creek to Saugerties at Rondout Creek (41° 55′ N to 42° 05′ N). The river is freshwater here, and is dredged in some stretches. This region has been affected by large sediment inputs from Esopus Creek and Rondout Creek, which drain east from the Catskill Mountains. A large coarse sediment influx may be, in part, responsible for the numerous large sand waves imaged in the area (color plate 2). Much of the modern hydrodynamics and the distribution of recent sediments may be linked to deepening of the western channel. This portion of the river includes Tivoli Bays, a component of the Hudson River Reserve (part of the National Estuarine Research Reserve System). As part of our study a pilot program in shallow water geophysics which included ground penetrating radar was carried out within Tivoli Bay.

Area 4 – Stockport Flats Region: The 18.5 km Stockport Flats survey area extends from the City of Hudson in the south to the town of New Baltimore in the north (42° 15′ N to 42° 25′ N). The section is tidal fresh water, and also includes the Stockport Flats National Estuarine Research Reserve site. This segment of the river has been impacted by 150 years of dredging, disposal of dredge spoils and the

Figure 5.2. Cartoon showing the operation of a multibeam echosounder. Sound is transmitted in a swath across the ship track, and the returning sound is analyzed to provide a series of water depths across the profile. Figure from Konsgburg-Simrad, Inc.

building of dredge spoil islands such as the Stockport Middle Ground. Much of the deeper channel is characterized by large sand waves. The present flow regime inferred from channel morphology and bedform distribution appears to be largely controlled by dredging.

Methods

The three major types of geophysical data acquired during the Hudson River Benthic Mapping Program were multibeam bathymetry, side scan sonar, and Chirp sub-bottom seismic data. These acoustic methods were supplemented by an extensive program of cores and grab sampling. A shallow-water geophysics program comparing Chirp sub-bottom seismic profiles and ground-penetrating radar was also conducted.

(1) **Multibeam Bathymetry:** Bathymetry provides basic information on riverbed morphology including the variations in channel structure that control sediment transport through the estuarine system (Hughes Clarke, Mayer, and Wells, 1996; Gardner et al., 1998; Flood, 2002; Fig. 5.2). Multibeam bathymetry can be presented as contoured maps (usually with 1 m contours) or as sun-illuminated maps that show smaller-scale relief as it would be revealed by shining a synthetic sun across the riverbed. Multibeam bathymetry

provides high-resolution imaging of the riverbed and shows the locations and dimensions of riverbed features, including rock outcrops and sediment bedforms (Fig. 5.3) as well as smaller features such as anchor drag scars, cable crossings, and other anthropogenic features.

We used the Simrad EM 3000 multibeam system to map with 100 percent coverage the portion of the river deeper than 5 m (ca. 15 feet) where this technique is most appropriate. The EM 3000 system transmits at 300 kHz in a fan-shaped pattern perpendicular to the survey track imaging a band or swath of the riverbed about four times water depth. Bottom depths are measured at up to 125 points across the swath, each beam nominally 1.5° wide and spaced 0.9° apart. The maximum ping rate is 25 times a second, decreasing to 13 times a second as water depth increases to 10 m. In water depths of 10 m and at a ship speed of 8 knots (kts) (4 m/s), depth measurements are acquired at about 30 cm intervals along and across track with a vertical accuracy of 5–10 cm. The amplitude of the reflected sound (which is converted into backscatter) is also measured at these points.

Multibeam bathymetry requires accurate navigation and orientation information. This information was provided by a TSS POS/MV model 320 v2 which uses three accelerometers and three gyroscopes to correct the multibeam data for heading, roll, pitch, and heave, and includes a differential GPS system (supplemented by inertial navigation; also part of the POS/MV system) to determine position to about 1 m. The real time differential GPS corrections were provided by Omnistar because we were generally out of range of the U.S. Coast Guard (USCG) station at Sandy Hook, New Jersey that transmits differential corrections. Other system components include: a separate display to guide the boat along precise survey lines; a CTD for determining the sound velocity profile; tide gauges for determining local sea level during a survey; Sun and SGI computers for logging, storing, processing, and displaying the data; and multibeam processing software. Near-final survey products can be generated within a short time after the survey is completed, and the resulting products generally meet hydrographic mapping standards. Seabed elevations were calculated relative to the NAVD88 geoid through the

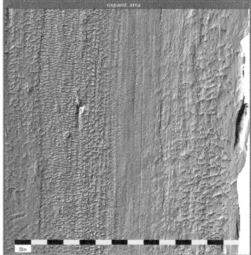

Figure 5.3. Upper: Multibeam backscatter data from the channel of the Hudson River (lighter areas have higher backscatter). There is a zone of higher backscatter from the center of the channel axis with variable (and generally lower) backscatter both east and west). North is up, bar shows scale. Lower: Multibeam bathymetry (viewed as sun-illuminated bathymetry) for the same area as the upper image. The channel axis (area of higher backscatter) is generally smooth but with some drag marks. Sediment waves of a variety of scales are imaged both east and west of the channel axis. Also visible are at least two debris deposits, several obstacles and one possible sunken barge. The trough on the eastern edge of the image is part of a dredged channel to the former GM plant in Tarrytown. The backscatter image shows that this is a region of low backscatter.

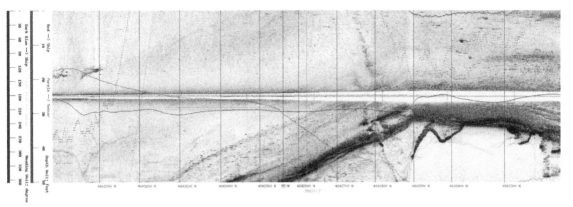

Figure 5.4. Example side-scan sonar record from the Hudson River. The ship track is in the center, and areas of higher backscatter are darker. This record shows the river bank (observed from underwater) on the right-hand side.

use of tide gauges. The NAVD88 datum is about 30 cm below mean sea level in the Hudson River. The EM 3000 multibeam system was mounted on the *R/V Onrust*, a research vessel operated by the State University of New York at Stony Brook. The multibeam data was processed using the SwathEd software toolkit developed at the University of New Brunswick (http://www.omg.unb.ca/omg/research/swath_sonar_analysis_software.html).

(2) Side-scan Sonar and Multibeam Backscatter: Backscatter is related to the amplitude of an acoustic signal scattered off the riverbed back toward the sound transducer (Nitsche et al., 2001). As part of the Hudson River Benthic Mapping Project these data were collected both with a dual frequency sidescan sonar system and with the multibeam bathymetry system. Backscatter data are ideally suited for distinguishing among sediment types based on differing acoustic properties. Properties which can be distinguished include fine versus coarse grained sediments and hard versus soft bottom. Side-scan sonar systems are effective in all water depths, including in water shallower than 5 m where multibeam systems are not efficient, and can be used to map the shoreline from underwater.

For this study the side-scan sonar study was conducted from the *R/V Walford* operated by the New Jersey Marine Consortium. We used the Edge Tech DF-1000 dual frequency side-scan sonar simultaneously operating at 384 kHz and 100 kHz (Fig. 5.4). The 1.8 m side-scan sonar tow fish was

deployed from a boom off the bow of the ship to place the system in quiet water for optimal instrument performance. The fish was towed at a depth of 2 m. The fish has transducers and receivers on either side of it, and the transducers transmit and receive both frequencies simultaneously. The acoustic signals are digitized in the tow fish and sent to the shipboard acquisition system through a high-speed digital uplink. A swath width of 200 m was used so that together a total width of 400 m of riverbed was surveyed with a single survey track. Full saturation of the riverbed for the side-scan sonar was accomplished in two directions using track lines with an approximate 85 m lateral spacing in a north-south orientation and with a 185 m lateral spacing east to west (Fig. 5.5). Orthogonal coverage was obtained in order to investigate the acoustic response of the riverbed as a function of look direction of the imaging sonar source.

The data acquisition topside unit was the ISIS system from Triton Elics. Side-scan data were time tagged in the ISIS system and recorded to hard disk. The Triton Elics system also recorded several auxiliary data streams including the ship's compass heading, single beam bathymetry and navigation. The Lamont – Doherty Earth Observatory (LDEO) ship compass was mounted in a magnetically quiet location amidships. The depth sounder used was the *R/V Walford*'s Raytheon DE-719C with a hull-mounted transducer. The transducer (Raytheon model 200TSHAD) operates at 208 kHz, with 8° beam width at half power points. The DE-719C system produces an analog

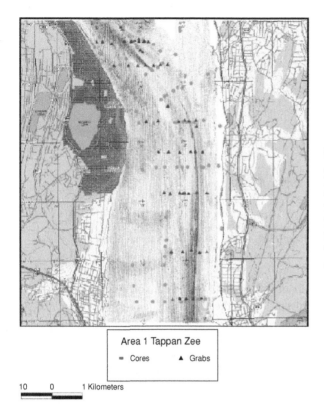

Figure 5.5. Side-scan sonar mosaic from Area 1 north of the Tappan Zee bridge. Note the east-west zones of high backscatter (old oyster reefs) and the zone of higher backscatter in the channel axis. The zone of lower backscatter in the channel appears to be a region of recent sediment deposition. The dots and triangles show the locations of core and grab samples, respectively.

Area 1 Tappan Zee

▪ Cores   ▲ Grabs

10   0   1 Kilometers

output and was interfaced with an "Odom Digi-trace" system. The transducer was mounted amid-ships and a bar check was performed daily to determine system offsets. The navigation data recorded in the ISIS system were DGPS positions from an Ashtech Z-12 receiver. The Ashtech Z-12 is a 12 channel dual-frequency, geodetic caliber GPS receiver. The real time corrections were provided by Omnistar and received by a Trimble AgGPS-132 unit. The Trimble unit was selected to enable the flexibility of using either the satellite broadcast corrections or the real time correction transmitted by the U.S. Coast Guard. During operations, only the satellite broadcast corrections were used to prevent the introduction of offsets between the two corrections.

(3) **Sub-bottom Chirp Data:** Sub-bottom or seismic profiles are made by recording acoustic energy reflected from sediment layers and other structures beneath the riverbed (Carbotte et al., 2001). The sub-bottom profile data reveal the relative age relationships between different sedimentary layers and can be used to study the erosion and deposition of sediments through time (Fig. 5.6).

Sub-bottom data were acquired simultaneously with the side-scan sonar data using an EdgeTech X-Star topside data acquisition unit and SB 4_24 tow fish. This is a Chirp or swept frequency sonar system, which emits a broadband FM source pulse with low frequencies providing depth penetration into the sub-bottom and higher frequencies providing high vertical resolution. The X-Star acquisition unit controls all data transmission, recording, and signal processing including Analogue to Digital (A to D) conversion, compression of the FM pulse, and spherical divergence correction. The recorded signal is the output of the correlation filter used for pulse compression and is stored in SEG-Y format. Data were acquired at a transmission rate of 5–6 pings s^{-1}. At survey speeds of 5 knots these transmission rates provide one trace for each 0.83 m of ship motion. Transmit pulse length was 10 m s^{-1}. Pulse power was set at 50–60 percent of maximum available output in order to avoid ringing and generation of cross-talk interference with the side-scan sonar data. The SB 4_24 tow vehicle offers the ability to transmit a variety of pulses with a frequency range from 4 to 24 kHz. After

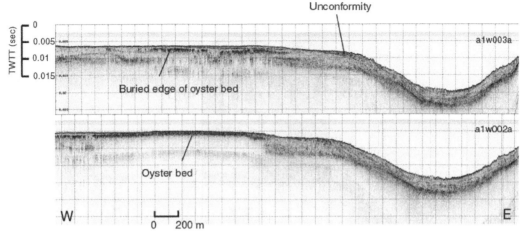

Figure 5.6. Example of Chirp sub-bottom profiles from north of the Tappan Zee Bridge. The upper profile shows a buried oyster bed (the high-amplitude sub-bottom layer on the left-hand side of the profile) as well as the unconformity produced where sediments deposited in the channel lie on top of older channel margin sediments. In the lower profile the oyster bed is at the sediment surface in some places. The identifications of the surficial and buried oyster beds have been confirmed by sampling.

comparison of data quality obtained with the range of pulse options, we chose the lowest frequency sweep pulse (4 to 16 KHz) to obtain maximum possible penetration with this fish.

All processing was carried out using a combination of in-house code for reading the raw data files and the Seismic Unix package maintained by the Colorado School of Mines (Stockwell, 1999). The raw data were combined and scaled during initial processing to output the envelope amplitude for each sample. SEG-Y data files were written for each profile and a gif image was produced to allow immediate assessment of data quality. The Chirp fish was towed from the stern of the boat.

(4) Sediment Cores and Grab Samples: An extensive suite of core and grab samples were collected to ground truth the geophysical data sets (McHugh et al., 2001; Fig. 5.7). Cores provide a key link with the sub-bottom data and are useful in regions of fine grained sediments (Fig. 5.8). The grabs provide ground truth information in the coarser grained and bedrock portions of the river where the coring device could not penetrate. Both sediment cores and grab samples were recovered from the Tappan Zee, Newburgh Bay, and Kingston-Saugerties Areas (Areas 1, 2, and 3). Only grab samples were obtained from the Stockport Flats Area (Area 4) where

sediment was sand dominated and poor core recovery was expected.

A gravity corer with a weight of 750 lbs. was used to penetrate the sediment. The core liners were 4 inches in inside diameter, providing more sediment volume for sampling than the traditional 2.5-inch diameter cores. The longest core recovered was 180 cm and the average length was 100 cm. The grab samples were collected with a Shipeck or Smith-MacIntyre grab. All cores and grab samples are being curated at the LDEO Core Laboratory under the support of the National Science Foundation. The processing of the cores included the following steps. Physical properties were measured on the unsplit cores including magnetic susceptibility, bulk density, and p-wave velocity. Cores were then split, photographed and described, grain size analysis of the core tops was carried out, and the cores were archived within the Lamont Core Archive. Grab samples were described and the presence of major components (e.g., slag: zebra mussels: oysters: and wood) was noted. For the grab samples, grain size analysis of the sand fraction was done by sonic sifter at MSRC, and, where present, the silt/clay fraction was analyzed by sedigraph at Wesleyan College.

Bottom photographs of the sediment-water interface were taken in Areas 1 to 3 using a sediment

Figure 5.7. Shipboard crews collecting grab samples (upper) and gravity cores (lower).

profile imagery (SPI) camera system (Rhoads and Germano, 1982; Iocco, Wilbur, and Diaz, 2000; Fig. 5.9). This system uses a prism inserted in the sediment to photograph a vertical profile or cross-section of about the upper 10 cm of the sediment to show sedimentary features such as ripples as well as any large animals living in the sediments or on the sediment surface. SPI images also show the depth of the oxygenated layer, the nature of and number of burrows, and sediment structures. SPI images were collected from the *R/V Onrust* through a collaborative program with the NOAA Coastal Services Center.

In 2001, we began a pilot study in which sediment samples from different bottom types in Areas 1 and 3 are being analyzed to determine invertebrate animal populations. This kind of interaction between biologists, geophysicists, geologists, and geochemists is important to be able to use our acoustic images to map benthic habitats.

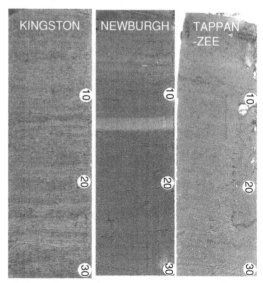

Figure 5.8. Photographs of split cores from the Hudson River. The cores show finer layering (perhaps a layer every few years) plus some thicker layers. The thicker layers may represent storm deposits.

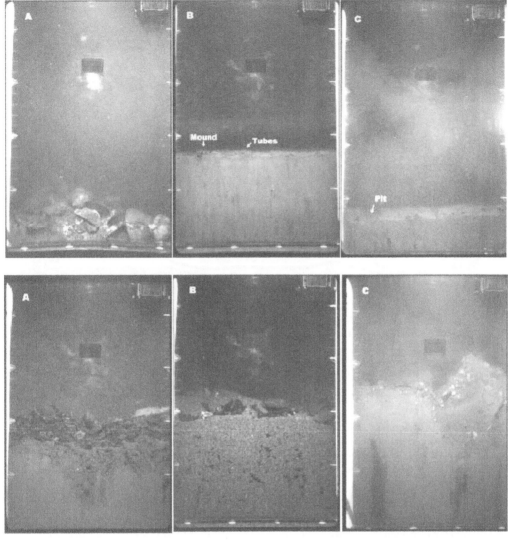

Figure 5.9. Example of SPI images from the Hudson River. Upper, left to right: oyster shells and shell hash, worm burrows and a thin oxidized layer, a thicker and pitted oxidized layer. Lower, left to right: wood and detritus, coal on a sandy surface, and a brick (from Iocco et al., 2000).

(5) Shallow Water Geophysics – Radar and Chirp: Significant portions of the Hudson River are shallower (<3 m) than can be mapped with the large boats used for the majority of this program. In April 1999, as part of this program, radar and chirp sonar sub-bottom data were collected in collaboration with the USGS Water Resources Division from a freshwater marsh in Area 3 (Haeni et al., 1999). An Edge Tech Xstar topside system with the SB216-S fish was used to acquire the Chirp sonar data. For the radar acquisition a Mala Geoscience radar system comprised of a pair of 200 MHz unshielded antennas was used. Radar data were acquired with a sampling frequency of 2,012 MHz. Other radar acquisition parameters were adjusted accordingly with water depth, and varied between 8 and 16 fold stack, and 600–1,500 samples. Radar triggering was done on time, and varied between 5 and 10 traces s^{-1} (roughly corresponding to a spatial distance of 10–20 cm between traces). The goal of this pilot effort was to assess the imaging capability of radar versus sonar methods within shallow freshwater settings. Results of this study indicate that radar methods provide better penetration and resolution

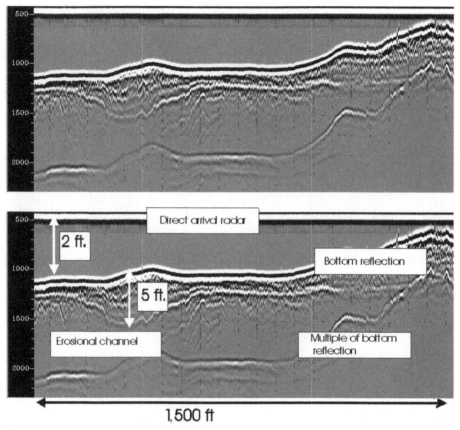

Figure 5.10. Example of ground penetrating radar (GPR) record from a shallow-water section of the freshwater Hudson River. Upper: original record. Lower: labeled record. This record, collected from water less than two feet (0.6 m) deep, shows the location and shape of an earlier channel about 5 feet (1.5 m) deep as well as layering within the sediment sequence. The record is 1,500 feet (460 m) long.

than sonar systems in the freshwater portion of the river for water depths shallower than 5 m (Fig. 5.10). The majority of the radar data showed significant sub-bottom structure, while only 35 percent of the coincident Chirp data provided any sub-bottom penetration. This difference in penetration arises because sound penetration is hindered by both gas and sand in the sediment, whereas neither of these properties affect radar penetration.

Sedimentary Features

The geophysical data along with the core and grab samples were analyzed to classify the river bed deposits. The sediment classification scheme included classes based on the major morphologic features, grain size, and sediment bedforms. Additionally, we identified exposed bedrock and anthropogenic deposits. Preliminary results for Area 1 are

presented here (Fig. 5.11). Similar results are available from NYSDEC for all four areas. From combined analysis of the benthic mapping data sets we have classified the Tappan Zee study area into four major deposits: channel axis, channel bank, marginal flat, and anthropogenic deposits. In addition, sites of recent sediment accumulation are identified.

CHANNEL AXIS DEPOSIT

The channel axis is broadest at the northern and southern ends of the study region, narrowing and shoaling within the channel axis bend south of Croton Point. A field of muddy sediment waves is present within the channel axis deposit at the southern end of the area. This field is 300–400 m wide, 3.3 km long and extends onto the western channel bank. The western half of the channel axis

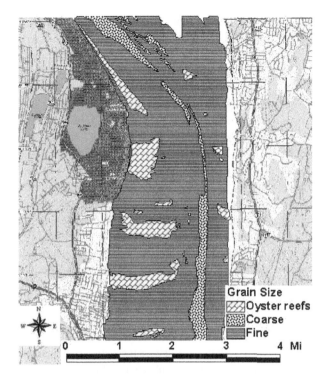

Figure 5.11. Summary map of the Area 1 showing the distribution of oyster reefs and areas of finer and coarser sediment. The coarser sediments are generally restricted to the channel while the oyster reefs are primarily on the margins.

corresponds with a 100–300 m wide region of moderate to high backscatter. Sub-bottom data show that sediment layers which are truncated at the riverbed coincide with this high backscatter zone, indicating active erosion within this portion of the channel axis. South of the channel bend, the eastern half of the channel axis is covered with a linear band of low backscatter sediments which may be redeposited sandy silts from the east channel bank. Finer grained sediments are also present within the channel bend where they appear to cover coarser channel axis sediments.

CHANNEL BANK DEPOSIT

The eastern and western banks of the channel are markedly different in morphology, surficial sediments, and subsurface structure. For much of the survey area, the eastern channel bank is narrow and steep whereas the western bank is broad and gently sloping. A field of irregular sediment waves covers much of the western channel bank, whereas sediment waves are found within only a narrow strip along the eastern channel bank in the southern half of the area. Elsewhere the eastern channel margin deposits are comprised of sandy silt with no discernable bedforms and moderate to

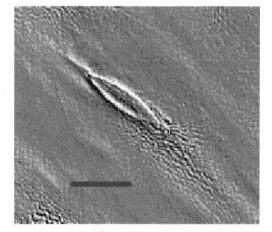

Figure 5.12. Sun-illuminated image of the hull of a sunken ship (probably a Hudson River Sloop) found in the Hudson River during this study. Scale bar is 25 m long, and the small-scale pattern to the lower left of the hull outline is an artifact. A number of shipwrecks and other items of possible historical significance have been discovered as part of this mapping program, and suitable steps need to be taken to inventory, identify, and preserve these features.

low backscatter. Adjacent to Croton Point, a field of irregular pinnacles is found with prominent channel-parallel sediment wave trains developed on their southern side. These pinnacles appear to be erosional remnants of the eastern marginal flat deposits, or they may be built of debris of anthropogenic origin.

The sub-bottom data reveal a distinct sediment package associated with each channel bank. Beneath the east channel bank, sediment layers typically are parallel to the riverbed, dipping west into the channel. In places, east bank sediments overlay channel deposits, possibly due to slumping along this channel wall. North of the channel bend, sediment layers can be traced uninterrupted from the western channel bank to beneath the axial deposits to form a nearly continuous depositional unit. South of the channel bend, these dipping sediment layers are truncated at the riverbed. At the channel bend a series of dipping layers, bounded by unconformities, document a history of prograding depositional layers terminated by erosional events. Channel bank deposits on both margins unconformably overlay the marginal flats deposits, indicating that the entire package of channel axis and channel bank sediments are younger than the marginal flats deposits.

MARGINAL FLAT DEPOSIT

A series of prominent east-west trending oyster beds are found within the marginal flat deposits of the Tappan Zee. These oyster beds are presumably associated with the oyster population once abundant along the river from Sandy Hook to Croton Point and harvested by Native American populations in prehistoric times. Oyster beds are evident in the side-scan sonar imagery as a series of linear, moderate backscatter regions that extend to the channel banks. In the sub-bottom data the beds correspond with strong, often irregular reflections that, within the main parts of the beds, do not permit penetration of sound energy. Oyster shells found within sediment cores and visible in sediment profile image (SPI) photography collected by NOAA confirm our interpretation of oyster beds from the geophysical data. The oyster beds are also evident in the bathymetric data as local regions elevated ~50 cm above surrounding terrain. The oyster beds are now exposed at the river bed along both the eastern and western marginal flats and older oyster beds exist as distinct deposits buried by up to 10 m of sediment. Portions of each exposed oyster bed extend to the channel bank

where a steep scarp is developed. Erosional remnants of the beds are found beyond the eastern edge of two of the centrally located beds, embedded within the west channel bank deposits. These remnants form prominent irregular mounds that are partially buried by sediments. A narrow sliver of oyster bed is found along the western edge of the river near Hook Mountain. This bed is bounded by a steep, linear scarp with up to 5 m of relief. Away from the oyster beds, the marginal flat deposits are low backscatter sediments with little internal stratification evident in the sub-bottom data. Sediment cores indicate that these sediments are higher in density than cores recovered from the channel axis and channel banks implying that the marginal sediments are somewhat older than the channel sediments.

Radiocarbon age dating of oyster shells from the marginal flats reveals that oysters at the river bed are ~1,000 years old (Carbotte et al., 2001). Oysters up to 5,500 years old were recovered from near the base of a 10 m core collected offshore at Nyack. Although our data set is limited, it appears that oysters thrived within this region during two distinct time periods from ~5,500 yrs B.P. to 4,500 yrs B.P. and during the more recent time period of 2,500 to ~1,000 yrs B.P. Small live oysters have been recovered during our sampling program.

ANTHROPOGENIC DEPOSITS

Numerous anthropogenic features and deposits were imaged, including cable crossings, anchor drags, old piers, debris fields, and several obstacles, some of which are clearly imaged shipwrecks (Fig. 5.12 and color plate 2). The wrecks appear to be most easily located on the multibeam data because there is often a topographic anomaly such as a moat or sediment drift created by flow around the obstacle. The existence and images of the shipwrecks in the river provides some new challenges. Publishing maps that reveal wreck locations is prohibited until they can be given an appropriate protective status. Additional studies are now underway to inventory, identify, and protect these submerged artifacts. A major debris field is found adjacent to Hook Mountain, close to the old Rockland Ice Pier, which may be rock debris dumped offshore during construction of the Hook Mountain ice chute in the early 1800s. The Rockland Ice Company provided ice for places as far away as Florida through the late 1800s. This debris field overlays the west channel bank sediments. This field is comprised of a series of doughnut-shaped structures, some of which form linear chains. These structures are 35–45 m in diameter and rise to 50 cm above the riverbed. The field extends for over 2.5 km along the channel margin and is ~500 m wide. A series of five narrow (<5 m) linear mounds ~350 m long that extend at oblique angles to the channel margin are found south of the major debris field. Anchor drags are imaged within the southern portion of the channel axis along the northwestern edge of the channel margin. Cable crossings are imaged off Nyack as three undulating low-backscatter lineations that extend diagonally across the western marginal flats toward Tarrytown. Mooring fields associated with Peterson's Boat Yard and the Nyack Boat Club are also identified.

RECENT SEDIMENT ACCUMULATION IN THE TAPPAN ZEE REGION

Recent sediment accumulation within the Tappan Zee region appears to be limited to a few local sites of anthropogenic disturbance and to the western wall of the channel bend off of Hook Mountain. These sites of recent accumulation are readily identified in backscatter data as regions of very low backscatter and in the sub-bottom data as thin sediment layers that unconformably overlay older sediments. The sites of recent sedimentation include a linear band of very low backscatter up to 50 cm thick which extends 2 km into the river from Nyack and which appears to be the recent fill of a dredged channel, maintained in the late nineteenth and early twentieth centuries, to the coal-to-tar plant in Nyack. Low density sediments are also found in a dredged area off Tarrytown near the site of the former GM plant. Recent sediments are also found in the western channel bend between Croton Point and Hook Mountain. This generally arcuate-shaped region of low backscatter stratigraphically overlays the channel axis and channel bank deposits, and is up to 25 cm thick. A small deposit from Nyack Creek imaged in the side-scan data also appears to be recent. These recent deposits contain the only occurrence of wedge clams (*Rangia cuneata*) recovered in the study. Sediment cores in regions of low backscatter reveal low-density muds,

and radionuclide dating confirms the presence of sediments deposited since the 1950s within the areas identified as recent sediments on the basis of geophysical data.

Directions for Further Study

High-resolution geophysical imaging, sediment and benthic sampling, and the creation of GIS-based products that are widely available are providing important new insights into the nature of the terrain and the interrelationships between landscape and habitat characteristics in the Hudson River Estuary. Initial evaluation of the detailed mapping results from the length of the Hudson River Estuary suggests that estuarine sedimentary environments and sediments can be highly variable, but that habitat characteristics appear to be consistent over much larger areas. Our results raise many new questions about the nature and faunal structure of benthic habitats and the temporal and spatial variability of sedimentary environments and their relationship to physical forcing and sediment supply. These results and increase the likelihood of recovering long-term and high-resolution climate records from the river in order to understand the evolution of this complex environment. We have also learned that the Hudson River Estuary contains an extensive record of cultural resources that need to be understood as well as protected. These kinds of insights help to provide a scientific basis for the management of this large and heavily used natural resource, to increase our understanding of natural processes in estuarine settings, and to provide a resource to a wide range of investigations into the structure and dynamics of the Hudson River Estuary.

Acknowledgments

New York State Department of Environmental Conservation provided funding for this project from the Environmental Protection Fund through the Hudson River Estuary Program. Additional expertise and facilities have been provided by the USGS Water Resources Division (ground penetrating radar) and by the NOAA Coastal Services Center (SPI). Contribution number 1301 of the Marine Sciences Research Center and contribution of the Lamont-Doherty Earth Observatory.

REFERENCES

Carbotte, S., Bell, R. E., McHugh, C., Rubenstone, J. L., Ryan, W. B. F., Nitsche, F., Chillrud, S., and Slagle, A. 2001. Recent evolution of the Hudson Estuary within the Tappan Zee (abstract). Geological Society of America Abstracts with Programs, 33: 453.

Carbotte, S. M., Bell, R. E., Ryan, W. B. F., McHugh, C., Slagle, A., Nitsche, F. O., and Rubenstone, J. 2004. Environmental change and oyster colonization within the Hudson River estuary linked to Holocene climate. *Geo-Marine Letters*, **24**(4): 212–24.

Flood, R. D. 2002. Complex circulation patterns in the Hudson River Estuary as revealed by bed form patterns (abstract). AGU Fall Meeting, Abstracts and Programs, San Francisco, CA.

Gardner, J. V., Butman, P. B., Mayer, L. A., and Clarke, J. H. 1998. Mapping US continental shelves, *Sea Technology*, **39**(6): 10–17.

Haeni, F. P., Powers, C. J., White, E. A., and Versteeg, R. 1999. Continuous seismic-reflection and ground-penetrating radar methods for subsurface mapping in water-covered glaciated areas (abstract). Geological Society of America Abstracts with Programs, 31: 142.

Hughes Clarke, J. E., Mayer, L. A., and Wells, D. E. 1996. Shallow-water imaging multibeam sonars: A new tool for investigating seafloor processes in the coastal zone and on the continental shelf. *Marine Geophysical Researches*, **18**: 607–29.

Iocco, L. E., Wilbur, P., and Diaz, R. J. 2000. Benthic Habitats of Selected Areas of the Hudson River, Based on Sediment Profile Imagery NY. Final Report, NOAA Coastal Services Center, Charleston, SC.

McHugh, C. M. G., Ryan, W. B. F., Pekar, S. F., Zheng, Y., Bell, R. E., Carbotte, S., Chillrud, S., and Rubenstone, J. L. 2001. Dynamic equilibrium of the Hudson Estuary revealed by the sedimentary record (abstract). Geological Society of America Abstracts with Programs, 33: 453.

McHugh, C. M., Pekar, S. F., Christie-Blick, N., Ryan, W. B. F., Carbotte, S., and Bell, R. E. 2004. Spatial variations in a condensed interval between estuarine and open-marine settings: Holocene Hudson River estuary and adjacent continental shelf. *Geology*, **32**(2): 169–72.

Nitsche, F. O., Bertinato, C., Carbotte, S., Ryan, B., and Bell, R. 2001. Comparison of different seabed classifiers based on different acoustic data in the Hudson River estuary (abstract). Geological Society of America Abstracts with Programs, **33**: 274–5.

Nitsche, F. O., Bell, R., Carbotte, S. M., Ryan, W. B. F., and Flood, R. 2004. Process-related classification of acoustic data from the Hudson River Estuary. *Marine Geology*, **209**: 131–45.

Rhoads, D. C., and Germano, J. D. 1982. Characterization of organism-sediment relations using sediment profile imaging; an efficient method of remote ecological monitoring of the seafloor (remote TM system). *Marine Ecology Progress Series*, **8**: 115–28.

Stockwell, J. W., Jr. 1999. The CWP/SU; Seismic Un*x package. *Computers & Geosciences*, **25**: 415–19.

6 Reconstructing Sediment Chronologies in the Hudson River Estuary

J. Kirk Cochran, David J. Hirschberg, and Huan Feng

ABSTRACT The sediments of the Hudson River Estuary record chronologies of the history of sediment and contaminant accumulation. The distribution of natural and anthropogenic radionuclides in the sediments provides a means of deciphering the sediment chronology because the rates of supply and decay of the radionuclides are known. Radionuclides that are useful in this context include naturally occurring ^{234}Th (Thorium), ^{7}Be (Beryllium), and ^{210}Pb (Lead), as well as anthropogenic ^{137}Cs (Cesium), input from atmospheric testing of atomic weapons and in association with the use of nuclear power. Sediment accumulation in the Hudson, as in many other estuaries, is controlled by a dynamic equilibrium among the processes responsible for transporting sediment. This equilibrium can shift seasonally, moderated by river discharge, tidal mixing, and other natural forces, or be shifted by human activities such as dredging or pier construction. Sediment chronologies of Hudson cores determined from natural radionuclides show that coves, marginal areas, and the inner harbor are areas of enhanced accumulation. Short-term storage of sediment is evident off Manhattan following the spring freshet, but these high rates of sediment accumulation are not sustained on longer, decadal time scales. Sediment chronologies also help to interpret the sediment record of particle-associated contaminants in the context of temporal changes of contaminant input and accumulation. To fully realize this application, it is necessary to build a long-term database of cores for which chronologies have been determined. Key stations should be recored over time to document trends in contaminant accumulation.

Introduction

The estuarine sediment record preserves a history of inputs of sediment to the estuary as well as of certain chemical species that strongly associate with particles. Reading the sediment record thus provides the opportunity to reconstruct events in the development of the estuary, including sediment transport events and inputs of contaminants to the system. Deciphering the sediment record is far from straightforward, however, and requires sorting out the effects of processes that perturb sediments after deposition. In the Hudson, these processes can include the effects of organisms living on or in the sediments and physical effects caused by river flow, as well as human-induced perturbations caused by dredging and shipping. One of the most powerful tools for determining rates of sediment accumulation in estuarine sediments is the use of natural and anthropogenic radioactive chemical species that are added to the estuary and become rapidly associated with sediments through a process referred to as 'scavenging'. Owing to their known rates of radioactive decay or varying rate of input to the estuary, these radionuclides serve as chronometers to estimate the time since they were present at the sediment-water interface and consequently the rate of sediment accumulation. Once the history of sediment deposition is determined at a given location, it can be applied to the estimation of inputs of particle-associated contaminants such as trace metals or Polychlorinated Biphenyls (PCBs). The purpose of this chapter is to review the primary methods used to determine sediment chronologies in the Hudson River and to describe the results.

Chronometers for Sediment Accumulation

The use of radionuclides as chronometers to reconstruct estuarine sediment history advanced significantly in the decade from 1975 to 1985. During that time, researchers from Scripps Institution of Oceanography, Yale University, Lamont-Doherty Geological Observatory and elsewhere measured distributions of natural and anthropogenic radionuclides in Chesapeake Bay, Narragansett Bay, Long Island Sound, and the Hudson River in an effort to determine sediment chronologies and contaminant histories (e.g., Goldberg et al., 1977, 1978; Thomson, Turekian, and McCaffrey, 1975; Benninger et al., 1979; Turekian et al., 1980; Bopp et al., 1982; Olsen, Simpson, and Trier, 1981b). Broadly speaking, the radionuclides that can be used as sediment chronometers fall into two groups: Those that are continuously supplied to the estuarine waters and those that arrive in discrete events or pulses. The former group includes the natural radionuclides such as those of the uranium and thorium decay series while the latter comprises anthropogenic radionuclides such as ^{137}Cs and Pu (Plutonium) isotopes that are added to the estuary from global fallout associated with atmospheric testing of atomic weapons, or, in the case of the Hudson, supplied by releases from nuclear power facilities.

In deciding which radionuclide(s) to use for sediment chronometry, an important consideration is the half-life. This parameter, indicating the time required for a given population of radioactive atoms to decrease to one-half its original value, can be matched to the time scale of sediment history being considered. Thus, a radionuclide such as ^{210}Pb, which has a half-life of 22 years, is appropriate for considering deposition over multi-decadal time scales (e.g., the past ~100 years) and is useful in looking at sediment deposition over the period of intense industrialization and human perturbation of an urban estuary such as the Hudson River.

The sediment geochemist's 'tool kit' includes chronometers with half-lives ranging from twenty-four days to thousands of years. The shorter-lived nuclides are useful for measuring short-term rates of deposition or the mixing effects of organisms on the sediment record, while the longer-lived ones can be used to look at long-term deposition rates. The natural radionuclides constitute one of the most important groups of sediment chronometers and comprise those produced in the atmosphere by the interactions of cosmic rays with atmospheric gases (and thus termed 'cosmogenic') and those in the uranium and thorium decay series. In order of increasing half-life this group includes:

- ^{234}Th (half-life = 24.1 days): ^{234}Th is produced from decay of dissolved ^{238}U (Uranium) in the water column and is rapidly scavenged to sediments. Early work in Long Island Sound by Aller

and Cochran (1976), subsequently confirmed by many researchers studying other estuaries, showed that ^{234}Th is scavenged extremely rapidly (time scales of hours to days) in the shallow estuarine environment. ^{234}Th scavenged from the overlying water column to the bottom sediments is referred to as "excess" ^{234}Th to differentiate it from ^{234}Th that is supported by ^{238}U contained in the constituent minerals of the sediments. In practice, excess ^{234}Th is calculated by subtracting the ^{238}U activity from the measured ^{234}Th activity. The short half-life of ^{234}Th makes it suitable for determining particle mixing rates in estuarine sediments and it is typically confined to the upper few centimeters of the sediment column. A complication in the use of ^{234}Th in estuaries is the fact that its source, dissolved ^{238}U, increases with salinity and thus is not constant throughout the estuary. Indeed, ^{234}Th is a useful tracer of particle transport across salinity regimes in a partially mixed estuary such as the Hudson (Feng, Cochran, and Hirschberg, 1999a, b).

- ^{7}Be (half-life = 53 days): ^{7}Be is produced naturally in the atmosphere from nuclear reactions of cosmic rays with atmospheric gases. It is added to the estuary by precipitation (wet and dry) and, like ^{234}Th, is rapidly scavenged onto particles. Its distribution in the sediments is similar to that of ^{234}Th and it also a useful tracer of particle mixing rate and sediment accumulation rates in areas where deposition rates are rapid.

- ^{210}Pb (half-life = 22.3 years): ^{210}Pb is produced in the atmosphere from decay of ^{222}Rn (Radon) gas that has emanated from rocks and soils. An important source of ^{210}Pb to many estuaries is direct deposition from the atmosphere and this radionuclide is often used to determine accumulation rates of estuarine sediments. This application is complicated by the fact that excess activity of ^{210}Pb (relative to its grandparent ^{226}Ra (Radium)) is often confined to the upper 15–20 cm, a zone in which particle mixing by organisms is likely to be important.

- ^{14}C (Carbon) (half-life = 5,730 years): Radiocarbon is added to the estuary by rivers, gas exchange of CO_2 with the atmosphere, and mixing of waters from the open ocean as well as in association with terrestrial organic matter. It is produced naturally in the atmosphere, but has

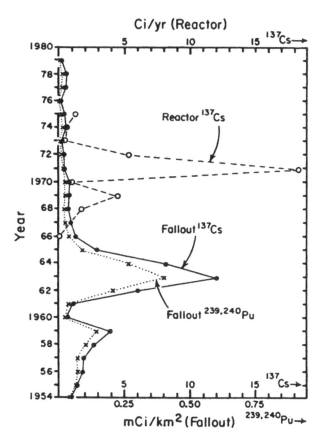

Figure 6.1. Releases of ^{137}Cs and Pu isotopes to the Hudson River estuary. These anthropogenic radionuclides have been added from the atmosphere and watershed as a consequence of atmospheric testing of atomic weapons. Such testing and the fallout flux decreased markedly after the Nuclear Test Ban Treaty (1963). ^{137}Cs also has been added by releases from the nuclear power plant at Indian Point. These inputs provide 'marker horizons' in sediment cores and enable sediment accumulation rates to be determined (from Bopp et al., 1982).

also been produced in association with atmospheric testing of atomic weapons. Radiocarbon is present in both sedimentary organic carbon and calcium carbonate shells of organisms, and by relating the radiocarbon content of a sample to that of a pre-industrial, pre-bomb standard, it is possible to determine the radiocarbon age of the sample. These ages may be offset from the true age by the 'age' of carbon in the reservoir from which the sample carbon was derived, but comparison of radiocarbon ages at several depth horizons in a sediment core often produces reliable indications of the accumulation history of the sediment (e.g., Benoit, Turekian, and Benninger, 1979).

Among the group of anthropogenic radionuclides, the one most extensively applied to Hudson River sediments is ^{137}Cs (half-life $= 30$ y). The input of this radionuclide to the Hudson is from several sources (Chillrud, 1996): atmospheric fallout from the global atmospheric testing of atomic weapons

augmented by discharges from the Knolls Atomic Power Laboratory and the Indian Point Nuclear Power Station. The ^{137}Cs signal from global fallout first appeared in the sediment record around 1954. While global fallout of ^{137}Cs peaked in 1963–64, releases from Indian Point were at a maximum in 1971 (Fig. 6.1). ^{137}Cs inputs associated with the nuclear power industry may be distinguished from those of global fallout by the presence of additional short-lived radionuclides (e.g., ^{60}Co (Cobalt) and ^{134}Cs) produced in reactors. However the half-lives of ^{60}Co and ^{134}Cs preclude their being detected in sediments older than about thirty years.

Determining sediment chronologies using natural radionuclides requires use of the gradient of the radionuclide with depth in the sediment. In the ideal case, the sediment-water interface has the highest radioactivity because it has recently been supplied with particles containing freshly scavenged radionuclide. Penetration of the radionuclide to depth in the sediments is a function of the half-life and sediment accumulation rate. Because radioactivity decreases exponentially with time, the familiar decay equation can be applied to sediments by assuming that depth in the sediment column is related to time via the sediment accumulation rate (S):

$$A = A_o \exp\left(-\lambda \frac{x}{S}\right) \qquad (1)$$

where A is the radioactivity (or simply activity) at depth x, A_o is the activity at the sediment-water interface and λ is the decay constant (= 0.693/half-life). Sediment accumulation rates can be determined by plotting ln(activity) vs. depth; the slope of the resulting line is $-\lambda/S$. In practice, plots of activity versus depth often show scatter related to variations in accumulation rate or A_o with time or to other processes such as physical or biological disruptions to the sediment column that are not represented in equation (1). These complications must be evaluated for each site (see below).

In contrast to the more-or-less continuous supply of natural radionuclides to the accumulating sediments, anthropogenic radionuclides such as ^{137}Cs are added sporadically depending on their source and are used to indicate specific time horizons in the sediment associated with inputs of these radionuclides to the system. For example, the 1963–64 peak arising from global fallout is a principal time horizon in applications of ^{137}Cs or [239,240]Pu to sediment chronologies (Bopp et al., 1982; Fig. 6.1). One caveat associated with the use of ^{137}Cs as a chronometer is that this radionuclide is subject to release or desorption from particles as they are transported from regions of low to high salinity through the estuary. Indeed, mass balances of anthropogenic radionuclides ([238]Pu, [239,240]Pu, [134]Cs, ^{60}Co and ^{137}Cs) in the Hudson River estuary have shown that nearly all of Pu was trapped in the estuary, but only 10–30 percent of ^{137}Cs, [134]Cs and ^{60}Co were retained on the fine particles and trapped in the estuary (Olsen et al., 1981b; Chillrud, 1996). The distribution patterns of sediment inventories of these radionuclides are influenced strongly by the transport of fine particles, variations in sediment accumulation rates and desorption (of Cs and Co) from particles as they encounter higher salinities (Olsen et al., 1981b). [137]Cs also may be mobile in the sediment column in the more saline reaches of the estuary, although the effect of Cs mobility

on ^{137}Cs profiles is less important in areas of rapid sediment accumulation (Olsen et al., 1981a).

An important consideration in application of natural or anthropogenic radionuclide chronometers to estuarine sediments is the characterization of the effects of other processes on the profiles. As indicated above, these can include post-depositional physical disturbances (ranging from the influence of waves and tidal currents to dredging and shipping) and biological mixing of the sediment by organisms. The measurement of multiple radionuclides on a single core can help sort out the effects of these processes, but it is also desirable to consider the radionuclide data in the context of other information such as sediment grain size or mineralogy, water content, benthic faunal data, bottom morphology, and sediment structure as revealed by X-radiography of cores. Indeed, as we shall see, X-radiography of a sediment core often reveals information on benthic faunal activities as well as sediment structure and composition.

Patterns of Sediment Accumulation in the Hudson River Estuary

An important conceptual advance in our understanding of the controls on sediment and contaminant deposition in estuaries arose with the articulation of the 'equilibrium surface' concept by Curtis Olsen and his colleagues (Olsen et al., 1993). Based on a large amount of data from the Hudson River estuary and elsewhere, they argued that sediment accumulation in estuaries is governed by a dynamic equilibrium among the processes responsible for transporting sediment, including river discharge, tidal mixing, and waves. Sediments accumulate until a balance among the various physical and biological transport processes is attained, after which little net accumulation takes place. Thus estuaries may have areas that are naturally in or out of equilibrium as a consequence of morphologic changes or seasonal variations in physical processes (tides, storms, river flow) that are unique to each estuary. Areas that are out of equilibrium can be characterized by rapid accumulation of fine-grained sediments and associated contaminants.

The Hudson River estuary presents a classic example of the application of the dynamic equilibrium concept of sediment and contaminant accumulation. The flow of the Hudson River changes dramatically over the course of the year, with strong flows occurring during the spring freshet. Variations in tidal currents as well as the occurrence of storms also can change the equilibrium of the system. Dredging is also a major factor affecting the equilibrium of the Hudson system with respect to sediment accumulation. Areas that have been dredged show large net rates of accumulation until a new equilibrium is established. Piers and other marginal structures have a similar perturbing effect on the dynamic equilibrium existing among the processes that transport sediment, and high rates of sediment accumulation are often found in such areas.

The large numbers of ^{137}Cs measurements made in Hudson River sediment cores since 1975 by C. Olsen, J. Simpson, R. Bopp, S. Chillrud and colleagues at the Lamont-Doherty Earth Observatory permit broad patterns of sediment accumulation to be ascertained. In general, the ^{137}Cs depth distributions and inventories (total amount of ^{137}Cs in the core) show that there is little accumulation in the main navigation channel and in areas such as Haverstraw Bay (Olsen et al., 1984). In contrast, broad shallow areas in coves and other marginal areas show distributions of ^{137}Cs to greater depths, suggesting enhanced sediment accumulation (Fig. 6.2). The lower estuary, including the western margin off Manhattan and especially the inner harbor, shows ^{137}Cs distributed to depths of 1–2 m in the sediment, indicating rapid rates of sediment accumulation. However, localized rates may be quite variable in such areas, ranging from 1 to 5 cm y^{-1} (with an average of about 3 cm y^{-1}) in non-dredged areas and 4 to 70 cm y^{-1} (with an average of about 9 cm y^{-1}) in dredged areas (Fig. 6.3; Olsen et al., 1981b, 1984).

Our research characterizing distributions of the natural radionuclides ^{234}Th, ^{7}Be and ^{210}Pb supports the high degree of spatial as well as temporal variability in the dynamic equilibrium governing sediment accumulation in the Hudson system (Hirschberg et al., 1996; Feng, et al., 1998). For example, collection of a localized set of cores in a non-dredged portion of the estuary off Manhattan (km point ~10) shows low activities of all three radionuclides in surface sediments in a transition area between the western margin of the estuary and the main channel (Fig. 6.4). The absence of the short-lived radionuclides ^{234}Th and ^{7}Be is particularly striking in that these radionuclides tag sediment that has recently been in contact with the overlying water column. In contrast activities of all three radionuclides are greater in cores taken in the western margin area, although there is significant spatial variability even in the relatively small area sampled. Sediment accumulation rates calculated from the ^{7}Be profiles range from ~6 to 26 cm y^{-1} (Fig. 6.5). Longer term patterns of accumulation are indicated by excess ^{210}Pb profiles to depths of ~50 cm and show that the rapid rates of accumulation indicated by ^{7}Be are not sustained over time intervals much greater than a year. Indeed, the equilibrium governing sediment accumulation in this area likely changes seasonally in response to river flow. The collected cores were taken several months after the spring freshet, which typically takes place in April/May of each year. Large variations in river flow and suspended sediment transport occur with these events, perturbing the equilibrium governing sediment accumulation. Thus, in this portion of the estuary, short-term, rapid sediment accumulation occurs along the western margin but longer term accumulation is prevented by annual changes in river flow as well as seasonal changes in tidal flow.

These results are reinforced by the recent work of Rocky Geyer, Jonathan Woodruff and colleagues from the Woods Hole Oceanographic Institution. Woodruff et al. (2001) used changes in sediment properties, X-radiography and ^{7}Be distributions to show that sediment was deposited in the lower estuary during the spring freshet, but was transported and redeposited upriver, in the vicinity of the estuarine turbidity maximum, several months later. Woodruff et al. (2001) also argued that the high rates of sediment accumulation in this area were not sustained on the long term (decadally).

Sediment can provide information about accumulation history through the use of other techniques in conjunction with radioactive dating. Cores of fine-grained sediment, composed of especially small grains of clay and silt, often contain subtle variations in the arrangement of the grains that can be interpreted by geologists to reveal the conditions under which the particles settled from the overlying river water. This is often referred to as the fabric of the sediment: small structures, often

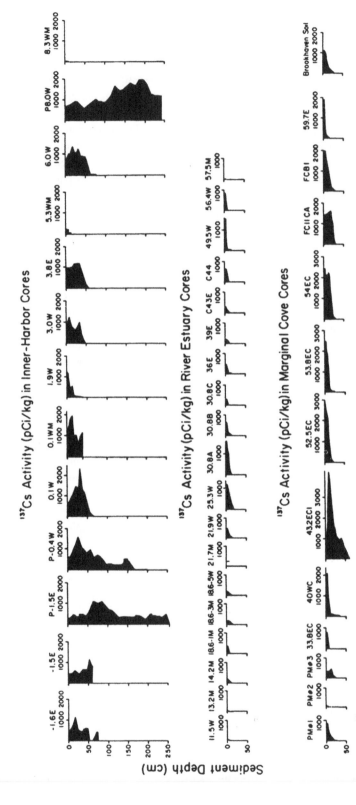

Figure 6.2. ^{137}Cs distributions in sediment cores collected in the Hudson River estuary and New York Harbor. Deeper penetration of ^{137}Cs into the sediment can be taken to indicate areas of enhanced sediment accumulation (from Olsen et al., 1984).

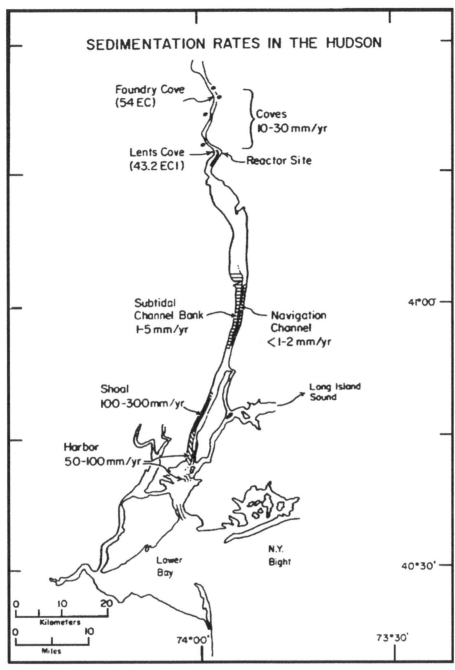

Figure 6.3. Patterns of sediment accumulation in the Hudson determined from ^{137}Cs distributions such as those shown in Fig. 6.2. Marginal areas of the estuary (especially the western margin off mid-Manhattan), coves and the inner harbor, are sites of rapid accumulation of sediment (from Olsen et al., 1981).

invisible to the naked eye, that are created by the interaction of the bottom sediment with the water above. X-radiography of sediment cores, often using portable medical X-ray equipment, is a sensitive technique for visualizing this sedimentary fabric. Like the human body, recently deposited sediment contains mostly water. The dense mineral grains that make up the relatively uncompacted sediment

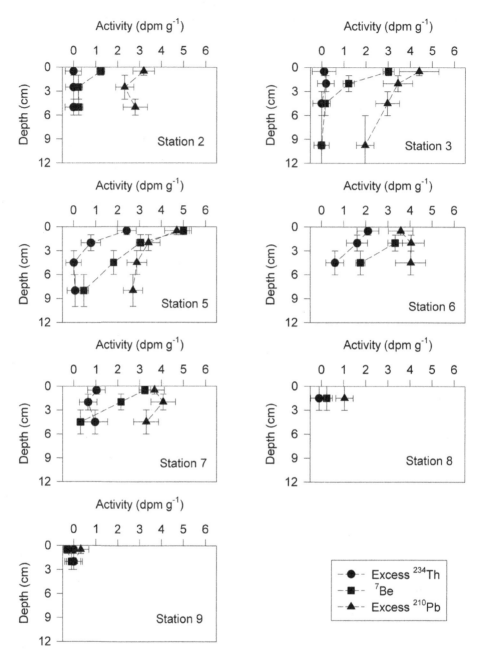

Figure 6.4. Profiles of natural radionuclides in sediment cores collected off Manhattan (~km point 10). The activities and penetration depths of the short-lived radionuclides ^{234}Th and ^{7}Be are greater in the western margin of the estuary (cores 2, 3, 5, 6 and 7) than in a transition area leading to the main channel (cores 8 and 9), where little accumulation takes place (from Feng et al., 1998).

absorb X rays strongly and are separated from one another by water, which blocks X rays much less effectively, providing a sharp contrast that can produce extremely sensitive images. Often a sediment core that appears featureless to the naked eye is revealed by X-radiography to contain striking features that can help in understanding the conditions under which it was deposited.

Sediment cores obtained by us from the western margin of the Hudson River, across from 79th

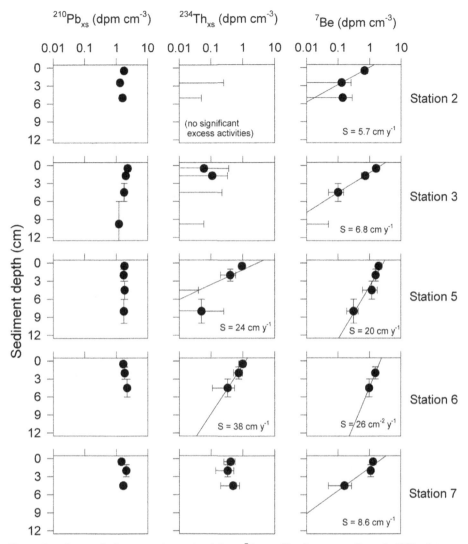

Figure 6.5. Accumulation rates determined from [7]Be profiles in cores collected off Manhattan (Fig. 6.4). The rates are determined by fitting a line to the log(activity) vs. depth profiles (see equation 1 in the text; from Feng et al., 1998).

Street in Manhattan, illustrate this well (Hirschberg et al., 1996; Feng et al., 1998). On visual observation the cores appeared to be composed of a feature-less, highly liquid mud that is easily stirred up into the overlying water. X-radiography of the cores (Fig. 6.6) revealed that this apparently featureless deposit is in fact highly structured, with numer-ous alternating bands of sediment of varying den-sity in the upper part of the core. Such bands are called laminations, and are indicative of sed-iment deposited from rapidly flowing water. They result from the alignment of the individual min-eral grains by the current flow. In the Hudson, most of the very muddy sediment is composed of clay minerals, which tend to have a flat or planar struc-ture and become aligned in a parallel fashion by the current flow, much like bricks. The more closely aligned grains have less space, and hence less wa-ter, between them, and therefore absorb X rays more strongly, resulting in a lighter band on the X-ray film. The degree of alignment is partially con-trolled by the strength of the current flow, so lami-nations indicate that this sediment was deposited from water with strong and variable currents. That

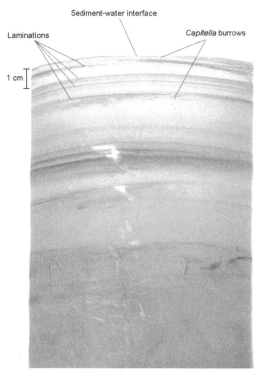

Laminations

Sediment-water interface

Capitella burrows

1 cm

Core 79W6

Figure 6.6. X-radiograph of a sediment core collected on the western margin of the Hudson River estuary off Manhattan (~km point 10). Laminations evident in the X-rays constrain interpretations of sediment accumulation and the importance of physical or biological mixing on the sediment. Small relict burrows of the opportunistic polychaete *Capitella* are evident and are truncated by erosion events.

much (at least) is obvious, since we know that the Hudson River here is strongly tidal, with the current reversing itself on ebb and flood twice daily. It is the scale of the laminations, their number, and the distance between them that may provide us with some new information about sediment deposition processes at this site.

As noted above, radioactive dating of these laminated sediments using the short half-life natural radionuclides ^{7}Be and ^{234}Th indicates that the laminations have been deposited over a period of less than a few months. The number of laminations is therefore too few to have been produced by individual ebb and flood currents, which occur twice daily. Instead the laminations are more consistent with another, longer term variation in the strength of the tidal currents, the neap and spring

tide cycle in tide height caused by the phases of the moon. During spring tides, the times of the month with the strongest tides, the tidal currents become significantly greater and the laminations may reflect this monthly cycle. The observed pattern of laminations is not that simple, however, as closer inspection of the X-radiographs shows. Some of the laminations show faint, dark (less dense) streaks originating at the bottom of the individual laminations and extending upward into the next lamination above. These are burrows made by a small marine worm (*Capitella* sp.) that lives near the surface of muddy sediment and feeds by ingesting deposited sediment. The burrow interior is filled with watery sediment and is less dense than the surrounding mud. Some of the *Capitella* burrows are abruptly truncated, especially at the interface between laminations (Fig. 6.6). This could indicate that in addition to sediment deposition, erosion or removal of sediment is also taking place.

Natural changes in the estuarine 'equilibrium' are complemented by those caused by human activities. In particular, changes in bottom morphology caused by dredging or sand mining shift the equilibrium strongly in favor of sediment accumulation. A clear example of this is seen in the lower harbor where excavation of coarse-grained sediments in the 1960s caused a series of 'borrow' pits to be created. The natural bottom in this area is sand and little mud is deposited, yet following the creation of the borrow pits, they began to accumulate fine-grained sediment. Measurement of ^{7}Be and ^{210}Pb profiles in one such pit (Fig. 6.7; Sneed, 1985) shows that on the short term (<1 y) indicated by ^{7}Be, sediments are accumulating at rates of ~7 cm y^{-1}. On the time scale of the half-life of ^{210}Pb, however, rates are ~4 cm y^{-1}. This is consistent with the long-term average rate of accumulation in the pit, based on the thickness of mud accumulated since the pit was created. X-radiography of the cores indicates that they are not disturbed by mixing by a benthic fauna. Thus, differences in accumulation rates on different time scales are likely related to aperiodic high-energy events such as storms that can erode sediment from the pits. These studies suggest that the estuarine equilibrium surface is truly dynamic on annual to multiannual time scales in the Hudson River/New

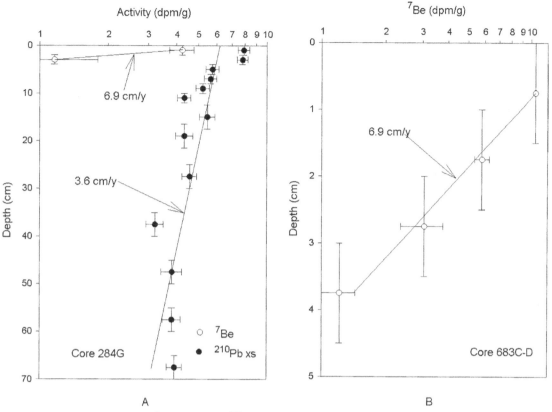

Figure 6.7. Profiles of ^{7}Be and excess ^{210}Pb in two sediment cores collected from a 'borrow' pit in New York Harbor. Such pits were created by sand mining in the 1960s and are now sites of fine-grained sediment accumulation. The decreases in the natural radionuclides with depth give indicators of the sediment accumulation rate (equation 1 in the text). No biological mixing is occurring in these deposits and the ^{7}Be results from cores collected in June 1983 (Fig. 6.7b) and February 1984 (Fig. 6.7a) show that short-term rates are $\sim$7 cm y^{-1}. Accumulation on the longer term, indicated by excess ^{210}Pb, is slower, presumably due to erosion of material from the pits by storms (data from Sneed 1985).

York Harbor system, causing large variations in patterns of sediment accumulation.

Chronologies of Contaminant Input to the Hudson River Estuary

How can sediment cores be used to evaluate contaminant input and deposition in the Hudson River system? First and foremost is the requirement of finding a site where deposition is rapid and a long (at least multidecadal) record is preserved. Such sites offer the opportunity to determine trends in contaminant input as well as to assess the relative importance of multiple sources. As noted above, the Hudson has such sites and cores can be dated using a variety of natural and anthropogenic radionuclides. In a study focussed on characterizing contaminant histories in the Hudson, Richard Bopp and James Simpson of Lamont-Doherty Earth Observatory used ^{137}Cs, Pu isotopes, ^{60}Co and ^{7}Be to date a suite of cores collected at key locations in the upper and lower Hudson from 1975 to 1986 (Bopp and Simpson, 1989; see Chapter 26 in this volume for further information). Several types of contaminants were measured:

- Polychlorinated Biphenyls (PCBs) – These organic compounds are noted for their insulating properties and have been released to the Hudson from a variety of sources. A principal source upriver has been the inputs from capacitor plants operated by the General Electric Company. PCBs that have been used commercially contain mixtures of nearly identical compounds (termed congeners) that differ in the number and arrangement of chlorine atoms. The cores analyzed by Bopp and Simpson (1989) show peaks in PCB deposition in the early to mid-1970s that were attributed to the removal of a dam in 1973. PCB-contaminated sediments were transported downriver following removal of the dam. Although the maximum PCB concentration occurs in cores throughout the estuary at about the same date, the PCB concentrations decrease from high values upriver to lower values in New York Harbor. The mix of PCB congeners in the latter sediments suggests both a source from upriver and from the New York metropolitan area. As the PCB-contaminated sediments have been buried, the upriver sources have become progressively less important in supplying these contaminants to the lower estuary. More recent profiles of PCB concentrations in Hudson sediments were examined by Steven Chillrud as part of his doctoral work at Columbia University (Chillrud, 1996). These results show continuing decreases in sediment PCB concentration through the 1980s (Bopp and Simpson, 1989; Chillrud, 1996).

• Pesticides – Bopp and Simpson (1989) also measured the chronologies of accumulation of the chlorinated hydrocarbon pesticides DDT and chlordane in Hudson sediments. In the cases of these contaminants, the New York metropolitan area is the dominant source, and the downriver increases in concentrations reflect this fact. The accumulation of both pesticides peaked in the 1970s, consistent with the timing of bans in their use (1972 for DDT; 1975 for chlordane).

• Concentrations of the trace metals copper and lead showed some declines in the cores studied by Bopp and Simpson (1989), but not to the extent that might be expected from efforts to reduce the concentrations of these metals in wastewater entering the system. A similar decline in zinc concentrations since the 1970s also was documented by Chillrud (1996). Lead has both significant atmospheric and watershed sources to coastal waters in New York (Cochran et al., 1998; Chillrud et al., 1999), although the

decrease in the use of leaded gasoline has diminished the atmospheric source of this heavy metal. It is possible that continuing inputs of trace metals from the Hudson River watershed have moderated declines in input from urban point sources.

Long-term Trends

One of the principal reasons for constructing sediment chronologies of particle-associated contaminants is to ascertain whether strategies for reducing contaminant inputs to an estuary are effective. Decreases in contaminant concentration in recently deposited sediments suggest that, although recent inputs may have declined, there remains a reservoir of contaminated sediment that is buried in the sediments. With increasing depth of burial, this material is less likely to be exposed to the fauna of the system. However, it is also possible that large scale, aperiodic events such as major storms can tilt the estuarine dynamic equilibrium in favor of large-scale erosion and transport of the contaminated sediment. The possibility of such large-scale sediment transport events has been recognized recently by Robin Bell of Lamont-Doherty Earth Observatory, Roger Flood of the Marine Sciences Research Center, and their colleagues (Chapter 5). Their work on long sediment cores, combined with a mapping of the sub-bottom morphology using acoustic approaches, indicates that the sediments of the Hudson preserve the record of disruptive events such as major storms that are able to mobilize large quantities of sediment. Such considerations are important in deciding how to handle reservoirs of contaminated sediment that may be buried but ultimately exposed if the estuarine equilibrium shifts.

A critical need in deciding between different courses of action with respect to contaminated sediment in the Hudson is an adequate database of dated sediment cores on which contaminant concentrations have been measured. Unfortunately, this is not a one-time effort but must be done repeatedly (perhaps decadally) over time to ascertain trends in sediment contaminants. The effort can be simplified by locating areas in the estuary where sediment deposition is rapid and using these as reference sites for the developing record of contaminant deposition. Such long-term databases of sediment and contaminant chronologies are critical to effective management of the Hudson River Estuary.

Acknowldgments

The authors' research in the Hudson River Estuary has been generously supported by the Hudson River Foundation. We are grateful to our colleagues R. Aller, H. Bokuniewicz, R. Flood, R. Wilson, R. Geyer, and G. Kineke for discussions and to M. Wiggins, K. Roberts, and E. Goldsmith for their support in the field and laboratory.

REFERENCES

Aller, R. C., and Cochran, J. K. 1976. ^{234}Th/^{238}U disequilibrium in nearshore sediment: Particle reworking and diagenetic time scales. *Earth and Planetary Science Letters* **29**:37–50.

Benninger, L. K., Aller, R. C., Cochran, J. K., and Turekian, K. K. 1979. Effects of biological sediment mixing on the ^{210}Pb chronology and trace metal distribution in a Long Island Sound sediment core. *Earth and Planetary Science Letters* **43**:241–59.

Benoit, G. J., Turekian, K. K., and Benninger, L. K. 1979. Radiocarbon dating of a core from Long Island Sound. *Estuarine and Coastal Marine Science* **9**:171–80.

Bopp, R. F., and Simpson, H. J. 1989. Contamination of the Hudson River – The Sediment Record, in *Contaminated Marine Sediments: Assessment and Remediation*. Washington, DC: National Academies Press, pp. 401–416.

Bopp, R. F., Simpson, H. J., Olsen, C. R., and Kostyk, N. 1982. Chlorinated hydrocarbons and radionuclide chronologies in sediments of the Hudson River and estuary, New York. *Environmental Science and Technology* **15**:210–216.

Chillrud, S. N. 1996. Transport and fate of particle associated contaminants in the Hudson River basin. Ph.D. Thesis, Columbia University, New York, NY.

Chillrud, S. N., Bopp, R. F., Simpson, H. J., Ross, J., Shuster, E. L., Chaky, D. A., Walsh, D. C., Choy, C. C., Tolley, L. R., and Yarme, A. 1999. Twentieth century metal fluxes into Central Park Lake, New York City. *Environmental Science and Technology* **33**:657–62.

Cochran, J. K., Hirschberg, D. J., Wang, J., and Dere, C. 1998. Atmospheric deposition of metals to coastal waters (Long Island Sound, New York, USA): Evidence from salt marsh deposits. *Estuarine, Coastal and Shelf Science*: **46**:503–522.

Feng, H., Cochran, J. K., Hirschberg, D. J., and Wilson, R. E. 1998. Small-scale spatial variations of natural radionuclide and trace metal distributions in sediments from the Hudson River estuary. *Estuaries* **21**:263–80.

Feng, H., Cochran, J. K., and Hirschberg, D. J. 1999a. ^{234}Th and ^{7}Be as tracers for the transport and dynamics of suspended particles in a partially mixed estuary. *Geochimica et Cosmochimica Acta* **63**: 2487–2505.

Feng, H., Cochran, J. K., and Hirschberg, D. J. 1999b. ^{234}Th and ^{7}Be as tracers for the sources of particles to the turbidity maximum of the Hudson River Estuary. *Estuarine, Coastal and Shelf Science* **49**:629–45.

Goldberg, E. D., Gamble, E., Griffin, J. J., and Koide, M. 1977. Pollution history of Narragansett Bay as recorded in its sediments. *Estuarine, Coastal and Marine Science* **5**:549–61.

Goldberg, E. D., Hodge, V., Koide, M., Griffin, J., Gamble, E., Bricker, O. P., Matisoff, G., Holdren, Jr., G. R., and R. Braun, R. 1978. A pollution history of Chesapeake Bay. *Geochimica et Cosmochimica Acta* **42**:1413–1425.

Hirschberg, D. J., Chin, P., Feng, H., and Cochran, J. K. 1996. Dynamics of sediment and contaminant transport in the Hudson River estuary: Evidence from sediment distributions of naturally occurring radionuclides. *Estuaries* **19**:931–49.

Olsen, C. R., Larsen, I. L., Brewster, R. H., Cutshall, N. H., Bopp, R. F., and Simpson, H. J. 1984. A geochemical assessment of sedimentation and contaminant distributions in the Hudson-Raritan Estuary. National Oceanic and Atmospheric Administration Technical Report OMS NOS 2, Rockville, MD.

Olsen, C. R., Larsen, I. L., Mulholland, P. J., Von Damm, K. L., Grebmeier, J. M., Schaffner, L. C., Diaz, R. J., and Nichols, M. M. 1993. The concept of an equilibrium surface applied to particle sources and contaminant distributions in estuarine sediments. *Estuaries* **16**:683–96.

Olsen, C. R., Simpson, H. J., Peng, T.-H., Bopp, R. F., and Trier, R. M. 1981a. Sediment mixing and accumulation rate effects on radionuclide depth profiles in Hudson estuary sediments. *Journal of Geophysical Research* **86**:11020–11028.

Olsen, C. R., Simpson, H. J., and Trier., R. M. 1981b. Plutonium, radiocesium and radiocobalt in sediments of the Hudson River estuary. *Earth and Planetary Science Letters* **55**:377–92.

Sneed, S. B. 1985. Sediment chronologies in New York Harbor borrow pits. Master's Thesis, State University of New York, Stony Brook, NY.

Thomson, J., Turekian, K. K., and McCaffrey, R. J. 1975. The accumulation of metals in and release from sediments of Long Island Sound, in L. E. Cronin (ed.), *Estuarine Research*, Vol 1. New York: Academic Press, pp. 28–44.

Turekian, K. K., Cochran, J. K., Benninger, L. K., and Aller, R. C. 1980. The sources and sinks of nuclides in Long Island Sound, in B. Saltzman, (ed.), *Advances in Geophysics*, Vol. 22, *Estuarine Physics and Chemistry: Studies in Long Island Sound*. New York: Academic Press, pp. 129–64.

Woodruff, J. D., Geyer, W. R., Sommerfield, C. K., and Driscoll, N. W. 2001. Seasonal variation of sediment deposition in the Hudson River estuary. *Marine Geology* **179**:105–119.

7 Major Ion Geochemistry and Drinking Water Supply Issues in the Hudson River Basin

H. James Simpson*, Steven N. Chillrud, Richard F. Bopp, Edward Shuster, and Damon A. Chaky

ABSTRACT This chapter uses data from a few representative sampling sites in the Hudson basin to understand variations in major ion concentrations, which are used as one simple proxy of gross drinking water quality. Other water supply issues, including potential implications of dissolved organic carbon concentrations on drinking water quality, are also discussed. The major ion content of surface waters is largely determined by precipitation chemistry, dry deposition from the atmosphere, chemical weathering of rock and soil minerals, and anthropogenic loadings, and then modified by biogeochemical reactions that take place within the system. (1) Based on data reported for West Point, New York by the National Atmospheric Deposition Program (NADP), precipitation chemistry in the Hudson River basin is similar to that in much of the northeastern United States. As a result of upwind and regional fossil fuel combustion, sulfate and nitrate are the most abundant anions and hydrogen is the most abundant cation (i.e., dilute solutions of sulfuric and nitric acids). Ammonium, chloride, and sodium have lower concentrations, with the latter two derived mostly from marine aerosols. Chloride appears to have an additional, nonmarine, source accounting for at least 25 percent of wet deposition of this ion at West Point. (2) Major element chemistry of surface waters in the Hudson River basin strongly reflects bedrock geology of tributary catchments. Adirondack and Catskill Mountain and Hudson Highland streams have low total dissolved solids (TDS) typical of ancient crystalline, metamorphic, or previously weathered coarse silicic sedimentary formations. In contrast, the significantly higher TDS of the Mohawk River reflect drainage from large areas of sedimentary rocks including limestones, carbonate-rich shales, and evaporite minerals. Anthropogenic influxes are an additional contributing factor to Mohawk TDS. (3) Hudson River dissolved ion concentrations downstream of the confluence with the Mohawk are similar to the global average for riverine flux to the ocean. Suspended particle concentrations are generally an order of magnitude lower than the global average for all rivers. (4) Essentially all surface waters in non-urban portions of the Hudson basin, including the tidal freshwater reach of the Hudson River, have sufficiently low TDS to serve as sources of relatively high quality raw water for municipal supplies, at least with respect to major ions. (5) Water quality in the basin following treatment by chlorination is more complex, however, due to relatively high concentrations of dissolved organic carbon (DOC) in the freshwater tidal Hudson River and the Croton River catchment of the NYC municipal supply. Chlorination of these waters can yield substantially more chlorination byproducts, including trihalomethanes (THMs), than occurs for low DOC Catskill and Delaware watershed sources. As permissible levels of total THMs in treated municipal supplies have been reduced from 100 ppb to 80 ppb, management of surface waters for public supplies in the Hudson basin has become more complicated.

Introduction

Surface runoff from the Hudson River basin (Fig. 7.1) is currently diverted in large amounts for public water supplies, including about half of that supplying the New York City (NYC) municipal system, the largest in the nation. Many aspects of water quality in the Hudson basin are quite favorable for public water supplies. A major fraction of the NYC metropolitan area population resides in or near the downstream end of the basin. Population densities upstream of NYC are relatively low. Much of the uplands are forested and have very low population densities, especially in the Adirondack and Catskill Mountains, with the latter (including runoff from both the East and West Branch of the Delaware River) providing most of the municipal supply for NYC. The main stem of the tidal freshwater Hudson River, although of lower quality than upland streams in the Catskills, remains a valuable resource for public water supplies. This source is used for smaller cities such as Poughkeepsie, as well as the primary drought emergency supply for NYC through pumping from a station at Chelsea, New York (103 km upstream of the Battery).

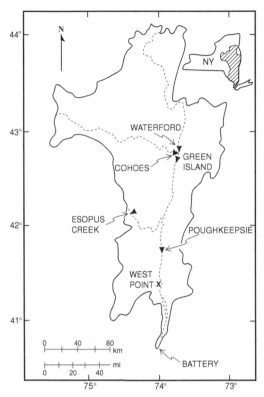

Figure 7.1. Hudson River drainage basin with selected discharge gauging (triangles) and precipitation chemistry (X) monitoring locations indicated.

The major ion content of surface waters is largely determined by inputs provided by precipitation, dry deposition from the atmosphere chemical weathering of rock and soil minerals, and anthropogenic loadings, and then also by biogeochemical reactions that take place within the system. Examination of major ion composition in precipitation and surface waters can provide information on these sources and biogeochemical reactions occurring within the basin. Furthermore, it allows us to understand basin-wide variations in major ion content, which can be thought of as one simple proxy of gross drinking water quality.

Precipitation chemistry in the Hudson River basin is similar to that found in much of the northeastern (NE) United States (Sisterson et al., 1991). Regional combustion of fossil fuels generates large quantities of acidic gases, resulting in rain and snow being, to the first approximation, dilute solutions of sulfuric and nitric acids. A few aspects of Hudson

River basin precipitation chemistry are outlined here, based on monitoring data from a National Atmospheric Deposition Program (NADP) station at West Point, New York.

Some general features of Hudson River basin water chemistry are briefly summarized here, based on monitoring data collected by the U.S. Geological Survey (USGS) at five surface water stations (Fig. 7.1) over the past four decades, as well as on observations obtained during several university research projects. Major element chemistry data are described as primarily indicative of chemical weathering processes in the basin. Dissolved organic carbon is discussed as a source of chlorination byproducts generated during treatment of raw water supplies from several regional sources.

Selected Data on Inputs of Dissolved Ions

MEAN ANNUAL PRECIPITATION CHEMISTRY AT WEST POINT, NEW YORK

Weekly composite samples of precipitation (wet-only deposition) have been collected at West Point since June 1979 as one of the NADP monitoring stations. The site initially occupied (NY51) was terminated in October 1984 for logistical reasons, while a second station (NY99), about one km away, was initiated in September 1983. Here we discuss a few aspects of mean annual precipitation chemistry from West Point (NY99) for the period from 1984–99. Chemical data from weekly samples have been aggregated by NADP as amount-weighted concentrations for various periods. Values compiled in Table 7.1 are calendar year amount-weighted means. Note that since the primary data are from weekly composites (samples collected on Tuesdays), annual means can represent periods a few days less than or greater than 365 days. Mean annual precipitation amount for this sixteen-year period was 128 cm yr^{-1}.

The most abundant anions for the period 1984–99, in rank order (μEq l^{-1}), were: SO$_4{}^{2-}$ (44), NO$_3{}^-$ (24) and Cl$^-$ (12). The most abundant cations in rank order (μEq l^{-1}) were: H$^+$ (49), NH$_4{}^+$ (12) and Na$^+$ (8). There appear to have been systematic decreases in mean annual [SO$_4{}^{2-}$], [NO$_3{}^-$] and [H$^+$] over this period, indicating that total annual

Table 7.1. National Atmospheric Deposition Program data from NY99, West Point, NY[a]

Year[b] Jan–Dec	Ppt cm	SO$_4^{2-}$ µEq l^{-1}	NO$_3^-$ µEq l^{-1}	Cl$^-$ µEq l^{-1}	Lab pH	Lab H$^+$ µEq l^{-1}	NH$_4^+$ µEq l^{-1}	Ca^{2+} µEq l^{-1}	Mg^{2+} µEq l^{-1}	K$^+$ µEq l^{-1}	Na$^+$ µEq l^{-1}	Cl$^-$/Na$^+$[c]	cat/an[d]	Field H$^+$ µEq l^{-1}	Lab EC µS cm^{-1}
1984	137.6	43.9	24.3	11.9	4.32	47.8	9.3	5.2	3.9	0.9	9.4	1.27	0.95		26.1
1985	108.1	53.1	30.5	9.7	4.21	61.0	12.2	4.9	3.6	0.4	6.3	1.54	0.95		31.5
1986	123.1	57.1	32.9	10.2	4.21	61.0	11.2	4.6	3.0	0.4	6.2	1.65	0.86		31.7
1987	128.3	47.6	24.4	10.8	4.27	54.0	8.5	3.5	2.7	0.5	7.4	1.46	0.93	58.7	27.5
1988	108.6	49.6	24.8	9.6	4.26	55.0	7.2	4.8	2.5	0.3	6.4	1.49	0.91	59.7	26.8
1989	144.7	46.8	27.3	11.6	4.27	54.0	12.9	3.1	2.4	0.6	7.0	1.67	0.93	58.2	28.2
1990	148.0	46.5	23.3	13.9	4.29	51.9	11.8	3.3	3.0	0.4	9.8	1.41	0.96	51.9	27.4
1991	121.1	52.2	25.6	8.9	4.24	56.9	12.1	5.5	2.1	1.1	5.6	1.60	0.96	57.7	29.5
1992	117.3	48.2	26.4	13.3	4.26	54.5	13.0	3.5	2.5	0.5	7.8	1.71	0.93	62.4	28.8
1993	120.0	44.9	24.0	14.8	4.31	48.6	10.6	3.4	3.2	1.9	10.2	1.45	0.93	53.7	26.5
1994	124.9	44.4	26.4	10.0	4.29	50.8	12.9	4.1	2.0	1.0	5.7	1.73	0.95	50.9	27.4
1995	110.6	30.4	20.4	16.3	4.45	35.1	10.4	3.4	3.2	0.7	13.0	1.25	0.98	38.4	20.7
1996	182.4	33.5	22.3	14.7	4.40	39.6	11.8	3.2	3.0	1.0	10.8	1.36	0.98	41.8	22.5
1997	109.0	37.8	21.1	8.3	4.37	42.9	11.6	2.9	1.7	0.6	5.0	1.66	0.96	46.2	22.8
1998	118.8	37.0	19.6	8.3	4.43	37.0	19.5	4.0	1.7	2.0	4.7	1.78	1.06	43.9	21.7
1999	137.4	32.4	16.2	15.7	4.47	33.7	8.3	3.3	3.0	0.5	12.0	1.32	0.94	38.5	20.3
Average values[e] µEq/L		44.1	24.3	11.7	4.31	49.0	11.5	3.9	2.7	0.8	7.9	1.48	0.95		26.2
µM		22.0	24.3	11.7		49.0	11.5	2.0	1.3	0.8	7.9				
ppm		2.12	1.51	0.42	0.05		0.21	0.08	0.03	0.03	0.18	Σ =	TDS =	4.6	ppm

[a] Obtained 3/8/2001 from NADP web site: http://nadp.sws.uiuc.edu/nadpdata/annualReq.asp?site=NY99

[b] Calendar year.

[c] Sea water ratio of Cl/Na: 0.55 M kg^{-1} to 0.47 M kg^{-1} = 1.17

[d] A charge balance of cations including lab pH vs. anions.

[e] Averages are unweighted means of annual values for NY99: '84–'99

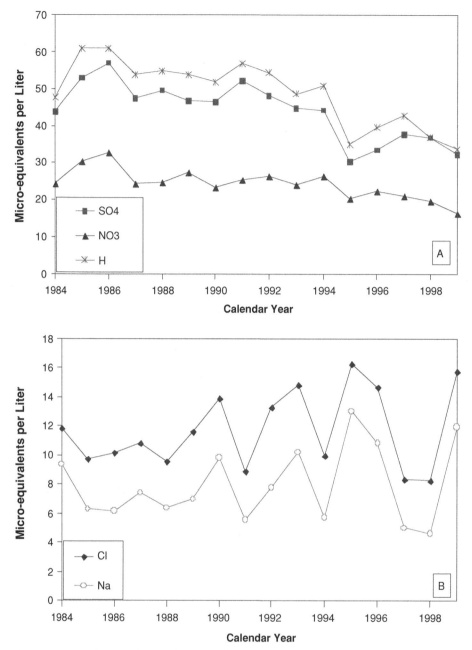

Figure 7.2. Annual mean (flux-weighted) wet deposition at West Point, NY, National Atmospheric Deposition Program: (A) $[SO_4^{2-}]$, $[NO_3^-]$ and $[H^+]$; (B) $[Cl^-]$ and $[Na^+]$.

delivery of acids via precipitation declined appreciably at NY99 since the early 1980s (Fig. 7.2A). Similar temporal trends for other areas of the Hudson River basin are likely, reflecting reductions in acidic gas emissions from electricity generating stations within and upwind of the region. Data from West Point suggest an increase in mean annual pH from about 4.2 in the mid 1980s to about 4.4 in the late 1990s.

The largest source of Na^+ and Cl^- to West Point wet deposition is marine aerosols. Precipitation episodes that entrain primarily marine air, more common during the winter half of the year, tend to have higher concentrations of both these

Table 7.2. Hudson River basin selected gauging locations and drainage areas

Station number	Station name	Hydrol Unit Code (HUC)	Latitude	Longitude	Drain area mi²	Drain area km²	Basin area%	Water quality data[a]
1335770	Hudson River near Waterford Lock 1	2020003	424945	734000	4611	11942	34%	1969–97
1357500	Mohawk River at Cohoes	2020004	424707	734229	3450	8936	26%	1978–98
	Ungaged above Green Island				29	75	0.22%	
1358000	Hudson River at Green Island	2020006	424508	734122	8090	20953	61%	1973–98
1362198	Esopus Creek at Shandaken	2020006	420659	742320	60	155	0.45%	1963–92
1372043	Hudson River near Poughkeepsie	2020008	414318	735628	11733	30390	88%	1973–94
	Hudson River at Battery				13367	34620	100%	

[a] Dates for which USGS Water-Quality Monitoring Networks (WQN) data is available.

ions, and lesser concentrations of sulfate and nitrate. Mean annual concentrations in NY99 precipitation of both Na^+ and Cl^- were often greater during the 1990s than the 1980s (Fig. 7.2B). Mean annual concentrations of both ions tended to vary together ($r^2 = 0.93$), consistent with their dominant sources being from marine aerosols. Increased frequency and/or intensity of marine air precipitation episodes during the latter half of the monitoring period (1984–99) could have also contributed to lower mean annual concentrations of sulfuric and nitric acids. Thus, trends in mean annual precipitation ionic concentrations over the period 1984–99 may reflect a higher proportion of marine-source precipitation episodes, as well as regional changes in acidic gas emission rates.

The molar ratio of Cl^- to Na^+ in amount-weighted precipitation for each year from 1984–99 (range: 1.25–1.78) was always greater than the seawater molar ratio ($Cl^-/Na^+ = 1.17$). Assuming marine aerosols are the only significant source of Na^+ in these samples, then there must be significant source(s) of Cl^- in addition to marine aerosols. Using mean equivalence values of Cl^- and Na^+ for this sixteen-year period (Table 7.1), the nonmarine aerosol source of Cl^- represents about 26 percent of total Cl^- in precipitation ($Cl^-/Na^+ = 1.48$; compared to Cl^-/Na^+ in seawater $= 1.17$). In an analysis

of rainfall over the United States from July 1955 to June 1956 none of the more than 60 stations had average Cl^-/Na^+ ratios in excess of that in seawater (Junge and Werby, 1958). However, Junge (1963) cited studies of precipitation chemistry in Europe from that same period where excess Cl^- was found in precipitation samples from urban and industrial areas. The release of HCl during combustion of coal was suggested as the probable source.

Precipitation for much of the Hudson basin would be expected to have somewhat lower concentrations of Cl^- and Na^+ than West Point, due to longer transport pathways for air from marine aerosol sources (Junge and Werby, 1958). Thus data from NY99 should provide an upper limit to likely contributions of wet deposition Cl^- to surface waters in most of the basin. Dry deposition of aerosols and gases from the atmosphere can also deliver significant inputs of dissolved ions to surface waters in the Hudson basin.

MAJOR ELEMENT STREAM CHEMISTRY DATA: MEDIAN VALUES

Data on water quality parameters and daily mean water discharge from five USGS monitoring stations were obtained from web sites and from correspondence with USGS personnel. The stations examined (Table 7.2) were selected as representative of important components of the Hudson River basin. Stations at Waterford and Cohoes include discharge from the upper Hudson River (including the Adirondacks) and Mohawk River, respectively, together including runoff from about 60 percent of total basin area. Monitoring data at Green Island should yield the combined influx to the northern end of the tidal Hudson, which is about 250 kilometers upstream of the Battery. All three of these stations have reported daily mean water discharge for a significant fraction or all of the period of water quality monitoring data. Poughkeepsie, situated approximately midway through the tidal reach of the Hudson (116 km upstream of the Battery), has more than 85 percent of basin area upstream of the site. Direct freshwater discharge gauging data based on stage measurements at Poughkeepsie are not available due to the tidal nature of the Hudson at this site. Saline intrusions are not reflected in the monitoring data at Poughkeepsie discussed here; however, during major droughts the salt front has reached that far upstream. USGS monitoring during the recent drought watch (February 2002) placed the salt front near Wappingers Falls (15 km south of Poughkeepsie). A significant fraction of natural runoff from western tributaries of the tidal Hudson upstream of Poughkeepsie are stored in reservoirs and diverted through the Catskill and Delaware Aqueducts to NYC, and thus do not influence water chemistry at this station. Water from the NYC municipal supply is returned after use to the downstream estuarine portion of the Hudson via a number of large wastewater treatment facilities in the NYC metropolitan area. Finally, data for Esopus Creek are discussed as representative of surface water quality entering NYC municipal storage reservoirs in the Catskill Mountains.

Data from each of these five monitoring stations were compiled and pruned here to eliminate samples for which relatively complete major element chemistry data were not available. Periods of monitoring varied significantly among the stations, and there were often substantial intervals with little or no data. The total number of individual samples with relatively complete major element chemistry data (Table 7.3) ranged from 37 (Poughkeepsie) to 204 (Esopus Creek). During high discharge episodes, more frequent samples were sometimes

collected. For purposes of comparison among stations, median values for each of the five monitoring stations are examined (Table 7.3). Median and mean concentrations were generally similar for most chemical species.

Median total dissolved solids (excluding SiO_2) was lowest for Esopus Creek (33 mg l^{-1}), and highest for the Mohawk River at Cohoes (192 mg l^{-1}). Green Island (124 mg l^{-1}) and Poughkeepsie (131 mg l^{-1}) TDS values were similar to each other and intermediate between Cohoes and Waterford (88 mg l^{-1}), as would be expected. Thus, the range of median TDS values for these five stations was about a factor of six. A similar, relatively large range of median concentrations was also observed for HCO_3^-, Cl^-, Ca^{2+}, Mg^{2+}, and Na^+. In contrast, the range of median SiO_2 concentrations (2.6 to 4.6 mg l^{-1}) was much smaller. The above data suggest that chemical weathering rates involving silicate minerals appear to be more uniformly distributed in the basin relative to weathering of formations with appreciable carbonate and evaporite minerals, which show much greater geographical variability.

[HCO_3^-] can be used as a first order index of inputs of major ions derived from carbonate and silicate weathering (Drever and Zobrist, 1993). At the five monitoring sites, [SO_4^{2-}] increased in the same order as [HCO_3^-] (Fig. 7.3A; Esopus < Waterford < Green Island < Poughkeepsie < Cohoes), but the last four showed less of a range in [SO_4^{2-}] than in [HCO_3^-]. Potential inputs of [SO_4^{2-}] include wet and dry deposition, chemical weathering of sulfides and gypsum, as well as direct anthropogenic sources. The Esopus sampling point has low [HCO_3^-] and [SO_4^{2-}], reflecting the lack of easily weathered carbonates, sulfides, or evaporite minerals in the central Catskills. Using the same approach comparing [Cl^-] and [HCO_3^-] (Fig. 7.3B), the Cohoes median [Cl^-] was substantially higher than for all of the other sites. These data suggest that the Mohawk River basin experiences greater chemical weathering of carbonates, and perhaps halite, than any other large area of the Hudson basin. Moreover, anthropogenic sources of [Cl^-] probably contribute significantly to the Mohawk at Cohoes (Phillips, 1994). The importance of chloride influxes in the Mohawk basin compared to the other regions of the Hudson basin is further illustrated by the high ratio of [Cl^-] to [SO_4^{2-}] (Fig. 7.3C). The relatively

Table 7.3. Hudson River basin selected monitoring data (USGS) summary

	Samples (n)	Q daily ft³ s⁻¹	Q daily m³ s⁻¹	HCO₃⁻ µEq l⁻¹	SO₄²⁻ µEq l⁻¹	Cl⁻ µEq l⁻¹	F⁻ µEq l⁻¹	Ca²⁺ µEq l⁻¹	Mg²⁺ µEq l⁻¹	Na⁺ µEq l⁻¹	K⁺ µEq l⁻¹	SiO₂ µM	TDSᵃ mg l⁻¹	SiO₂ mg l⁻¹
Median (Gl)	125	11200	317	999	354	310	5.3	1098	329	339	26	70	124	4.2
Median (Po)	37	15191	430	1059	396	310	5.3	1148	362	300	28	62	131	3.7
Median (Es)	204	83	2.4	218	158	92	2.6	259	99	87	8	43	33	2.6
Median (Wf)	136	6250	177	633	312	275	5.3	699	230	265	18	77	88	4.6
Median (Co)	99	4120	117	1682	416	508	2.6	1597	461	522	33	62	192	3.7
Average (Gl)	125	15536	440	996	367	332	5.5	1075	324	338	26	67	116	4.0
Average (Po)	37	22985	651	1042	392	389	7.8	1121	355	378	30	46	123	2.7
Average (Es)	204	131	3.7	230	162	99	3.5	272	99	96	9	43	32	2.6
Average (Wf)	136	9136	259	623	328	301	5.7	720	237	283	18	76	82	4.6
Average (Co)	99	8770	248	1657	404	546	4.1	1576	458	542	35	58	177	3.5

Green Island (Gl), Poughkeepsie (Po), Esopus Creek (Es), Waterford (Wf), Cohoes (Co)
ᵃ TDS Excluding SiO2

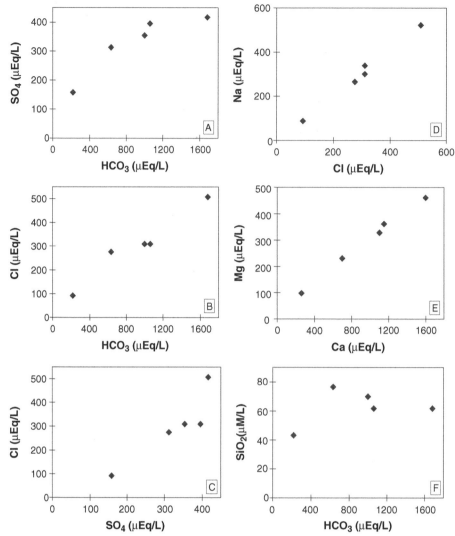

Figure 7.3. Hudson River basin stream gauge (five locations) median water concentrations: (A) $[SO_4^{2-}]$ vs $[HCO_3^-]$; (B) $[Cl^-]$ vs $[HCO_3^-]$; (C) $[Cl^-]$ vs $[SO_4^{2-}]$; (D) $[Na^+]$ vs $[Cl^-]$; (E) $[Mg^{2+}]$ vs $[Ca^{2+}]$; (F) $[SiO_2]$ vs $[HCO_3^-]$.

constant ratio of $[Na^+]$ to $[Cl^-]$ at all five gauging points is consistent with NaCl as the primary source of Na^+ in surface waters of the basin (Fig. 7.3D). Road salt, sewage effluent, and atmospheric deposition of sea salt are likely significant sources. Although dissolution of natural halite cannot be ruled out, the lack of identifiable surface deposits in the basin suggests that this source is relatively small. A scatter plot of $[Mg^{2+}]$ to $[Ca^{2+}]$ (Fig. 7.3E) suggests relatively uniform flux ratios of Mg^{2+} to Ca^{2+} carbonate weathering in much of the basin. Dissolved $Si(OH)_4$, reported as

$[SiO_2]$, however, were similar at all four stations representing large discharges, indicating that, to the first approximation, chemical weathering of silicates was not significantly higher in the Mohawk system compared to the upper Hudson or tidal Hudson tributaries (Fig. 7.3F).

MAJOR ELEMENT STREAM CHEMISTRY DATA: INDIVIDUAL STATION VALUES

The most abundant anion and cation at each of the five monitoring stations (Table 7.3) were HCO_3^- and Ca^{2+}, respectively. Plots of $[Ca^{2+}]$ vs $[HCO_3^-]$

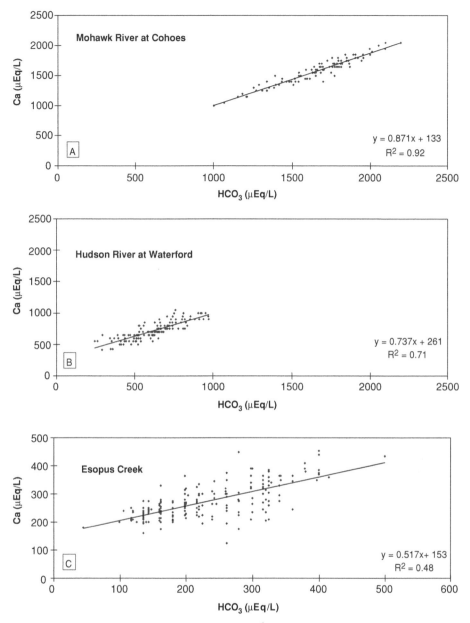

Figure 7.4. Hudson River basin stream gauge water $[Ca^{2+}]$ vs $[HCO_3^-]$ concentrations: (A) Cohoes; (B) Waterford; (C) Esopus Creek.

in $\mu Eq\ l^{-1}$ reveal several general features of the major ion chemistry. Absolute concentrations decrease from Cohoes (Fig. 7.4A) to Waterford (Fig. 7.4B) to Esopus (Fig. 7.4C). This observation indicates that stream chemistry in the Catskills is less buffered by soil and bedrock carbonate minerals against acid precipitation impacts than the Mohawk and downstream portions of the upper Hudson. The correlation of $[Ca^{2+}]$ with $[HCO_3^-]$ at Cohoes (Fig. 7.4A) was quite high ($r^2 = 0.92$), consistent with weathering of carbonate minerals being the primary source of Ca^{2+}.

Deviations of the slope from unity provide a measure of the relative importance of carbonate and silicate weathering inputs of the other major

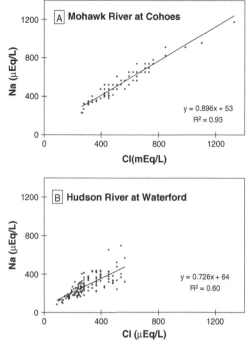

Figure 7.5. Hudson River basin stream gauge median [Na$^+$] vs [Cl$^-$] concentrations: (A) Cohoes; (B) Waterford.

cations. The other major cations were most significant at Esopus (slope = 0.52) and least important at Cohoes (slope = 0.87). The positive intercepts reflect the importance of other major anions, especially SO$_4^{2-}$. Although dissolution of gypsum cannot be ruled out, the lack of identifiable gypsum deposits in the Hudson-Mohawk basin focuses attention on two other sources of sulfate. Atmospheric deposition and oxidative weathering of iron sulfide minerals (pyrite) deliver sulfate as sulfuric acid. Whether the strong acid reacts with bicarbonate in solution or chemically weathers carbonates or silicates, the net effect on the water chemistry is the same – an increase in the relative importance of SO$_4^{2-}$ as a major anion. Atmospheric deposition of sulfate appears to dominate inputs to Esopus (see below). Iron sulfide mineral weathering as a source of sulfate has been described in detail for groundwaters of the Mohawk basin (Bator, 1997).

The correlation of [Na$^+$] with [Cl$^-$] at Cohoes (Fig. 7.5A) was quite high (r^2 = 0.93), consistent with the dominant fraction of Cl$^-$ influx to the Mohawk

being derived from halite dissolution, including both natural and anthropogenic sources (Phillips, 1994). The slope of [Na$^+$] vs [Cl$^-$] at Waterford (Fig. 7.5B) is appreciably lower than at Cohoes, with a moderate degree of overlap in the scatter plot distributions. This trend is also evident for Esopus Creek, with far lower concentrations of both ions than observed for Waterford, suggesting that other processes influence Cl$^-$ concentrations in this Catskills catchment. Atmospheric sources related to coal combustion could plausibly provide a significant fraction of Cl$^-$ transported in streams of this area.

Stream concentrations of major ions at Cohoes (Fig. 7.6A), Waterford (Fig. 7.6B) and Esopus Creek (Fig. 7.6C), all are systematically lower at higher discharge rates (Q), but the proportional decrease at higher Q was greater at the Catskills site than for the Mohawk and upper Hudson. (Note the large range of observed concentrations at relatively low stream discharge rates for each site. Aggregating all chemical monitoring data as a function of only stream discharge rate is likely to obscure some contributing processes to the observed range of values, and should be viewed with caution.) A scatter plot of [Ca^{2+}] vs Q-daily values for Cohoes (Fig. 7.6A) indicates that a relatively large fraction of the total pool of samples were collected when discharge rates were quite low. The distribution of samples as a function of discharge was significantly different for Waterford (Fig. 7.6B).

WET DEPOSITION INFLUXES TO HUDSON BASIN STREAM CHEMISTRY

The variation in mean annual precipitation (1951–80) in the Hudson basin is not large, ranging from >1,270 mm yr^{-1} in the Adirondack, Green, and Catskill Mountains to <965 mm yr^{-1} in the lowlands (Randall, 1996). The area–weighted annual precipitation for the entire basin is 1,080 mm yr^{-1}, about 15 percent less than for the West Point station (1,275 mm yr^{-1}) during the period of precipitation chemistry monitoring discussed here (1984–99).

The total area of the Hudson drainage basin is 34,620 km^2 (Table 7.2), while the total watershed area of the NYC municipal water supply is about 5,066 km^2, 53 percent of which lies within the Hudson basin (Table 7.4). The total influx of

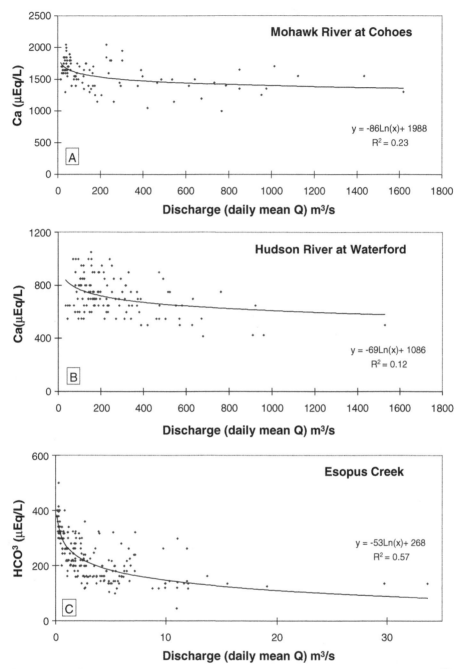

Figure 7.6. Hudson River basin gauging location major ions vs discharge rate: (A) Cohoes $[Ca^{2+}]$ vs Q; (B) Waterford $[Ca^{2+}]$ vs Q; (C) Esopus $[HCO_3{}^-]$ vs Q.

precipitation (P) to the basin, including the Catskill and Croton catchments of the NYC municipal supply, is about 37.4 km^3 yr^{-1} (Table 7.5).

Our estimate of mean annual discharge of the Hudson at the Battery (NYC), exclusive of inputs of wastewaters derived from NYC area water supplies, is 545 m^3 s^{-1} (Hammond, 1975). Adding the contribution of the NYC supply from the Catskill and Croton drainage areas, total "natural" discharge at the Battery would be 18.3 km^3 yr^{-1}, resulting

Table 7.4. Descriptive data on New York City municipal water system

	Reservoirs (Largest)	Area km²	Capacity 10^{+6} m³	Elevation Crest (m)
Delaware Basin				
Delaware, West Branch	Cannonsville	1166	362	351
Delaware, East Branch	Pepacton	963	531	390
Neversink	Neversink	241	132	439
Catskill area watersheds				
Schoharie	Schoharie	813	67	344
Esopus	Ashokan	666	465	179
Rondout[a]	Rondout	246	188	256
Croton System	New Croton	971	328	60
Delaware Basin		2370	1025	
Catskill + Croton		2696	1048	
Total Three Sources		5066	2073	

[a] Note that Rondout Reservoir is connected to the Delaware Aqueduct and thus usually reported as part of the Delaware System

in a first order runoff ratio (Q/P) of 49 percent (Table 7.5). The ratio of mean Q/P based on another compilation of water budget parameters (Table 7.5; Darmer, 1987) is 56 percent, due to differences in both Q and P between the two sets of estimates. Since about half of annual precipitation influx is returned to the atmosphere through evaporation and transpiration, the minimum expected median annual surface water concentration of a conservative ion (e.g., chloride) derived from wet deposition would be approximately twice that observed in precipitation.

In addition to wet deposition (rain and snow), there is appreciable dry deposition to the watershed from aerosol impaction on vegetation plus gas phase reactions (Likens et al., 1990). We estimate for

Table 7.5. Hudson River basin water budget[a]

	Units	Compiled here	Based on Darmer[d] estimates
Hudson basin area total	km²	34620	34618
Catskill and Croton drainage area (NYC muni supply)	km²	2696	2702
Mean annual basin precip	m yr⁻¹	1.08	1.02
Total annual basin precip influx (P)	km³ yr⁻¹	37.4	35.3
Mean annual Hudson discharge at Battery (Q)[b]	m³ s⁻¹	545	598
Mean annual Hudson discharge at Battery (Q)[c]	m³ s⁻¹	580	633
Mean annual Hudson discharge at Battery (Q)[c]	km³ yr⁻¹	18.3	19.9
Runoff ratio (Q/P)	%	49	56

[a] All budget terms exclude runoff to the NYC municipal water supply from Delaware drainage
[b] Hammond 1975 (1946–68?); Darmer 1987 (1946–85) (excludes all NYC muni runoff)
[c] Includes runoff captured by the NYC muni supply from the Catskills and Croton drainage; Identical Catskill and Croton watershed influxes of 35 m³ s⁻¹ were used for both compilations
[d] Derived primarily from data reported in Darmer 1987 (1946–85)

Table 7.6. Hudson River basin precipitation, surface water and world average river chemistry

Species	Precip Average[a] mg l^{-1}	Catskills (Es) Median[a] mg l^{-1}	Hudson (Wf) Median[a] mg l^{-1}	Mohawk (Co) Median[a] mg l^{-1}	Hudson (GI) Median[a] mg l^{-1}	Hudson (Po) Median[a] mg l^{-1}	World R. Actual[b] mg l^{-1}	World R. Natural[c] mg l^{-1}
HCO_3^-		13	39	103	61	65	53.0	52.0
SO_4^{2-}	2.12	7.6	15	20	17	19	11.5	8.3
Cl^-	0.42	3.3	10	18	11	11	8.3	5.8
F^-		0.05	0.1	0.05	0.1	0.1		
NO_3^-	1.51							
Ca_2^+	0.08	5.2	14	32	22	23	14.7	13.4
Mg_2^+	0.03	1.2	2.8	5.6	4.0	4.4	3.7	3.4
Na^+	0.18	2.0	6.1	12	7.8	6.9	7.2	5.2
K^+	0.03	0.3	0.7	1.3	1.0	1.1	1.4	1.3
NH_4^+	0.21							
SiO_2		2.6	4.6	3.7	4.2	3.7	10.4	10.4
TDS	4.6	35	92	196	128	134	110	100
pH	4.3							

[a] See Tables 7.1 and 7.2 for years included in each data set; Green Island (GI), Poughkeepsie (Po), Esopus Creek (Es), Waterford (Wf), Cohoes (Co).
[b] Discharge-weighted average including pollution (Meybeck, 1979).
[c] Discharge-weighted average corrected for pollution (Berner and Berner, 1996).

SO_4^{2-} and Cl^-, based on our research at Black Rock Forest (unpublished), that regional dry deposition inputs are similar in magnitude to wet deposition. If this is accurate, the minimum expected surface water $[SO_4^{2-}]$ or $[Cl^-]$, assuming no contribution from chemical weathering or pollution and no loss of SO_4^{2-} in soils, would be about four times that of precipitation.

The Esopus Creek gauging station in the Catskills (Table 7.6) has the lowest TDS value (median = 35 ppm) of the stream stations discussed here. The median value for SO_4^{2-} (7.6 mg l^{-1}) is slightly less than a factor of four greater than the amount–weighted average for West Point precipitation (2.1 mg l^{-1}; Table 7.1). These data are consistent with atmospheric sources (wet plus dry deposition) providing much of the inputs of SO_4^{2-} in Catskill streams. Chloride median concentration at Esopus Creek is about a factor of eight greater than West Point wet deposition (Table 7.1), indicating that about half of stream $[Cl^-]$ probably came from either chemical weathering or pollution influxes, such as road salting. The ratio of $[Na^+]$ in Esopus Creek to $[Na^+]$ in West Point precipitation is similar to that for $[Cl^-]$, also consistent with a halite source

for both ions beyond that provided by atmospheric deposition.

CHEMICAL WEATHERING INFLUXES TO HUDSON BASIN STREAM CHEMISTRY

For the other four stream stations, the contribution of wet and dry deposition is much less important to stream chemistry than for Esopus Creek. The Mohawk River at Cohoes has TDS (median = 196 ppm) about a factor of six greater than Esopus Creek (Table 7.6). Here, chemical weathering of carbonates and possibly evaporite minerals (plus anthropogenic inputs) appear to dominate the inputs of major ions (Fisher, Isachsen, and Rickard, 1971; Garvey, 1990). Although subject to biological regulation via diatom growth and shell dissolution (Clark et al., 1992), relatively low dissolved silica levels at all five of the gauging points indicate that chemical weathering of primary silicate minerals provides only a modest contribution to stream chemistry in the Hudson basin.

Hudson River median TDS at Green Island (128 ppm) and Poughkeepsie (134 ppm) are similar, and should be reasonably representative of mean freshwater discharge composition of the Hudson at the

Battery, exclusive of influxes of large amounts of wastewater in the NYC area. The main stem of the Hudson has a median composition similar to that calculated for the global flux-weighted "average" of all rivers (Meybeck, 1979; Berner and Berner, 1996). Compared to the global average river (TDS = 110 ppm), the Hudson River has about 20 percent greater TDS, with higher values for HCO_3^-, SO_4^{2-}, Cl^- and Ca^{2+}, and significantly lower concentrations of SiO_2. These data are consistent with chemical weathering of carbonates (and possibly evaporites) slightly greater per unit volume of surface water discharge than would be representative for global weathering of all continental areas, but appreciably less than average continental weathering of primary silicate minerals. Thus the Hudson River, draining a relatively small area (3.46×10^4 km^2), has a distribution of rock types available for chemical weathering that results in stream chemistry in the main stem of the tidal Hudson which is surprisingly similar for most ion concentrations to the flux-weighted global river average.

The chemical flux of dissolved ions from the Hudson River basin is approximately 70 T (km^2)$^{-1}$ yr^{-1}, compared to a global average estimated for natural conditions of 42 T (km^2)$^{-1}$ yr^{-1} (Berner and Berner, 1996). There is a large range of riverine chemical flux rates per unit area, depending upon the dominant types of rocks within a particular basin. At the low end are crystalline igneous and metamorphic rocks, and silica rich sediments [18 T (km^2)$^{-1}$ yr^{-1}], while carbonates (100 T (km^2)$^{-1}$ yr^{-1}) and evaporites (420 T (km^2)$^{-1}$ yr^{-1}) generate much higher chemical weathering fluxes by rivers (Meybeck, 1987). Thus, relatively small areas of the latter two types of rocks can have significant influence on the chemical composition of a given river.

The global mean flux per unit area of riverine suspended particles is 226 T (km^2)$^{-1}$ yr^{-1} (Berner and Berner, 1996), a factor of 5.4 greater than the chemical flux. The total downstream transport of fine suspended particles to the Hudson estuary appears to be about one million tons, similar to the long-term annual average of dredging of fine-grained sediments from NY Harbor (Olsen, 1979; Olsen et al., 1984–1985; Chillrud, 1996). This translates into a net fine particle flux of about 29 T (km^2)$^{-1}$ yr^{-1}, about a factor of eight less than the global average for all rivers. The ratio of chemical flux to particle flux by the Hudson River is about 2.4, while for the global average riverine flux this ratio is about 0.2. Relatively low suspended particle transport by the Hudson probably reflects the large proportion of forested basin area (Phillips and Hanchar, 1996), moderate topography, and uniform average monthly precipitation rate through the year. From the viewpoint of surface water management in the basin, low riverine transport of suspended particles is a major advantage, resulting in relatively low rates of silt accumulation in water-storage reservoirs and harbors, compared to high suspended particle flux rivers. Low suspended particle levels also reduce water treatment complexity and costs for municipal water supplies. Surface waters in the Hudson basin, especially in forested upland areas such as the Catskill Mountains, generally represent high quality raw water sources for municipal supplies.

GENERAL FEATURES OF NEW YORK CITY MUNICIPAL WATER SUPPLY

The municipal water system of New York City has been one of the great assets of the metropolitan region for more than 150 years. Following a sequence of water-related crises in the first third of the nineteenth century, including cholera epidemics and fires (e.g., 1832 and 1835, respectively), major investments for physical infrastructure were made to collect and transport surface water from low population density areas north of the city. The quality and stability of NYC municipal supply made a major advance with arrival of water from the first Croton Reservoir in Westchester County during the summer of 1842. Dramatic expansion of watershed area, storage reservoirs, and aqueducts continued over the next century, resulting in the elaborate network which currently supplies NYC with water of generally high quality.

Four distinct components of the NYC water supply discussed here (all derived from surface waters) include Delaware, Catskill, Croton, and Hudson (used only during drought emergencies). Each of these has features that significantly affect current management practices and water quality. Of the total base supply (derived from an area of about 5.1×10^3 km^2), upper Delaware River tributaries provide almost half of the watershed area (47 percent). This network, in the western Catskill region, was the most recently constructed and has generally high raw water quality. However, the West Branch, East Branch, and Neversink are tributaries of the Delaware River (Table 7.4) resulting in releases from NYC storage reservoirs being subject to regulations by an independent commission which must balance other municipal supply (primarily Philadelphia) and environmental needs with those of NYC. During an extended drought, when NYC has greatest need for diversion of water from Delaware tributaries, withdrawal limitations from storage due to competition with other demands in the Delaware basin are likely to be the most stringent. The Catskill drainage, with 34 percent of total watershed area, has similar raw water quality advantages as the upper Delaware basin for NYC, and is primarily dedicated to NYC demands. Its most significant limitation is size. There is not sufficient area to provide all of NYC water demand. The Croton System (19 percent of total watershed area), closest to consumers and earliest in construction, has lower raw water quality than the two components derived from the Catskill area. Situated in a region immediately north of NYC, pollutants associated with relatively high population density and extensive transportation corridors, the Croton watershed presents a more difficult challenge for NYC in terms of water quality management. The Hudson River is used as a source of water during drought emergencies, when water is pumped into the aqueduct system near Chelsea, following addition of chlorine and alum. Quality of Hudson River water, as reflected by a long history of persistent toxic influxes (Bopp et al., 1982; Bopp and Simpson, 1989), is appreciably lower than for most NYC watershed runoff. This situation presents a clear conflict between maintaining total supply quantity and quality during drought emergencies, resulting from blending of Hudson River water with the two major delivery flows derived from the Catskill Mountains.

CHLORINATION BYPRODUCT POTENTIAL IN COMPONENTS OF THE NYC MUNICIPAL WATER SUPPLY

One illustration of some potential water quality issues for treated water derived from different components of the NYC municipal supply can be

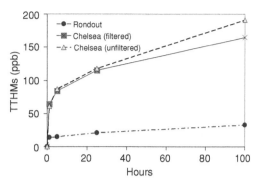

Figure 7.7. Laboratory chlorination experiments: total trihalomethane concentration vs time, with raw water from Rondout Reservoir (unfiltered); Hudson River at Chelsea (unfiltered and filtered).

gained by considering results of laboratory chlorination experiments using raw water from two of those components (Bopp et al., 1990). Total trihalomethane (TTHMs) concentrations (the most abundant trihalomethane treatment byproduct is chloroform), following chlorination of raw water derived from Rondout Reservoir, increased from 0 to 33 parts per billion (ppb) in 100 hours (Fig. 7.7). Parallel experiments, using unfiltered and filtered Hudson River water from Chelsea, at the point of withdrawal for the NYC system, resulted in TTHM concentrations of 191 and 165 ppb, respectively, after 100 hours, a factor of about five to six times greater (Fig. 7.7). Thus if Rondout water and Hudson River water were blended in proportions of 90 percent and 10 percent, the resultant TTHM concentration in laboratory experiments would be about 40 percent higher than if the raw water supply were 100 percent Rondout water. Although these simple experiments should not be considered as accurate simulations of THM levels within the actual distribution system following chlorination, they do provide insights about relative potential chlorination byproduct levels for different raw water components of the NYC municipal supply. One tentative conclusion is that addition of only modest proportions of Hudson River water to the treated flows into the delivery system could potentially have a substantial impact on chlorination byproducts in the blended water. Similar experiments illustrate the TTHM potential of Croton System water (Bopp et al., 1990; unpublished data). Laboratory chlorination of samples from three reservoirs produced an average of 173 ppb

TTHM, after seventy-two hours. A sample of mixed Catskill and Delaware System water under the same experimental conditions produced 73 ppb. Furthermore, THMs should also be considered as indicators of formation of other chlorination byproducts, such as di- and trichloroacetic acids.

Dissolved organic carbon (DOC) from both natural and anthropogenic sources provides precursor compounds that lead to formation of chlorination byproducts in treated water supplies (including di- and trichloroacetic acids as well as THMs). The three Croton System samples had DOC levels of 4.29, 4.53, and 4.65 mg l^{-1} and yielded 153, 173 and 193 ppb TTHM, respectively. DOC concentrations of eight samples from Chelsea and five samples from other Hudson locations (1985) averaged 5.45 mg l^{-1}, while five samples from Delaware System reservoirs averaged 2.31 mg l^{-1} in [DOC] (Bopp et al., 1990). Surveys of DOC during 1988–89 in the tidal Hudson suggest lower values during spring high discharge, but no appreciable variation along the axis of the river, and mean values of about 4 mg l^{-1} (Findlay, Pace, and Lints, 1991). There appears to be sufficient DOC in the tidal freshwater Hudson during most periods to result in formation of substantially higher concentrations of chlorination byproducts than from most Catskill area surface waters.

Samples of Hudson River water were collected from the NYC distribution system immediately after chlorine had been added at Chelsea on two separate occasions during the drought emergency of 1985 (Bopp et al., 1990) when pumping of water from the Hudson occurred from July 10th to December 11th. These stored samples from the NYC system had elevated TTHM concentrations, quite comparable to those from our laboratory chlorination experiments. The highest levels observed (Fig. 7.8) were 236 ppb (10/29/85) and 189 ppb (11/26/85), well above the current permissible level of 80 ppb for TTHMs.

Serious consideration has previously been given to the concept of operation of some reservoirs in the Catskill Mountains for both municipal water storage and pumped-storage hydroelectricity generation. This would permit additional supplies of electricity during peak demand hours by transfer through turbines of water from higher elevation to lower elevation reservoirs. During low demand pe-

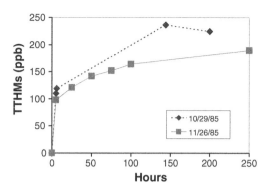

Figure 7.8. Total trihalomethanes vs time, in samples collected from the NYC municipal system on two dates, of treated (chlorinated) water withdrawn from the Hudson at Chelsea and stored in the laboratory.

riods (night), water would be pumped from lower to higher elevation reservoirs with electricity from base load facilities elsewhere (nuclear and fossil fuel generating stations). Construction of a new, higher elevation, reservoir near Schoharie Reservoir (Catskill System) was proposed for a number of years. Such a pair of coupled reservoirs is in operation at Blenheim-Gilboa on Schoharie Creek, just downstream of the NYC municipal supply watershed. DOC concentrations in water from these two pumped storage reservoirs averaged about 35 percent higher than in Schoharie Reservoir, although the sources of runoff were very similar in both cases (Simpson, Bopp, and Deck, 1981; Bopp et al., 1990). Since DOC concentrations are one of the major factors influencing chlorination byproduct levels in treated water, conjunctive operation of municipal water storage reservoirs with pumped-storage generation of electricity could potentially have negative consequences on some aspects of NYC water quality following treatment. Additional DOC in raw water supplies, from whatever source, should probably be minimized whenever possible.

Discussion

For most dissolved major ions in the main stem of the Hudson, atmospheric influxes and chemical weathering of soils and rocks dominates observed concentrations. For Cl^-, however, the situation appears to be more complex. The Mohawk River median $[Cl^-]$ of 18 mg l^{-1} is more than 40 times that of West Point precipitation $[Cl^-]$ of 0.42 mg l^{-1}. Taking into account inputs of dry deposition of

Cl⁻ and effects of evapotranspiration water losses of about 50 percent, approximately 90 percent of Mohawk [Cl⁻] appears to be derived from non-atmospheric sources. Plausible additional sources include: (1) natural evaporite mineral weathering, (2) wastewater treatment plant effluents, and (3) road salting. If the contribution of natural halite weathering could be better documented, the magnitude of the latter two types of anthropogenic influxes could be estimated. Chloride fluxes, as a conservative ion in surface waters, could then be used as an important constraint on integrated influxes of other, non conservative contaminants from wastewaters and transportation corridors.

Further studies of DOC and chlorination byproduct formation within the Hudson basin could provide important background information relevant to future water supply options in the region. Given the previous history of Hudson withdrawals by NYC during extended droughts, and proposals for large diversions from the tidal freshwater Hudson during high spring discharges, it is plausible that chlorination byproducts and other associated water quality issues may become important public policy considerations in future water supply decisions in the Hudson basin.

Acknowledgments

We thank the USGS-Troy, New York for providing surface water monitoring data discussed here. Support for our research on the Hudson has been provided by several previous grants from the Hudson River Foundation for Science and Environmental Research. The Black Rock Forest Consortium provided support for our examination of precipitation chemistry data at West Point. Additional support has been provided to the authors by the National Institute of Environmental Health Science through grants to the Mailman School of Public Health of Columbia University (P30 ES09089) and to Mount Sinai School of Medicine of New York University (P42 ES07384). This is LDEO contribution number 6445.

REFERENCES

Bator, S. J. 1997. Sulfate geochemistry of groundwater: A comparison of the Canajoharie and Clifton Park aquifers, Masters thesis, Department of Earth and Environmental Sciences, Rensselaer Polytechnic Institute, Troy, NY.

Berner, E. K., and Berner, R. A. 1996. Global Environment, Water, Air and Geochemical Cycles, Prentice Hall, NJ.

Bopp, R. F., Deck, B. L., Simpson, H. J., and Warren, S. D. 1990. Chlorinated hydrocarbons and water quality issues in the New York City municipal supply, in R. J. Jolley et al. (eds.), *Water Chlorination: Chemistry, Environmental Impact and Health Effects*, Volume 6, Chelsea, MI: Lewis Publishers, Inc., pp. 61–74.

Bopp, R. F., Simpson, H. J., Olsen, C. R., Trier, R. M., and Kostyk, N. 1982. Chlorinated hydrocarbons and radionuclide chronologies in sediments of the Hudson River and estuary, New York. *Environmental Science and Technology* **16**:666–76.

Bopp, R. F., and Simpson, H. J. 1989. Contamination of the Hudson River, the sediment record. In *Contaminated Marine Sediments – Assessment and Remediation*, Washington, D.C.: National Academy of Sciences Press, pp. 401–416.

Chillrud, S. N. 1996. Transport and fate of particle associated contaminants in the Hudson River basin, Ph.D dissertation, Columbia University, New York, NY.

Clark, J. F., Simpson, H. J., Bopp, R. F., and Deck, B. L. 1992. Geochemistry and loading history of phosphate and silicate in the Hudson Estuary. *Estuarine, Coastal and Shelf Science* **34**:213–33.

Darmer, K. I. 1987. Overview of Hudson River hydrology. Final Report to the Hudson River Foundation for Science and Environmental Research, Inc, New York.

Drever, J. I., and Zobrist, J. 1993. Chemical weathering of silicate rocks as a function of elevation in the southern Swiss Alps. *Geochimica et Cosmochimica Acta* **56**:3209–3216.

Findlay, S., Pace, M., and Lints, D. 1991. Variability and transport of suspended sediment, particulate and dissolved organic carbon in the tidal freshwater Hudson River. *Biogeochemistry* **12**: 149–69.

Fisher, D. W., Isachsen, Y. W., and Rickard, L. V. 1971. Geologic Map of New York State: Sheets 1,2,3, Chart No. 15, New York State Geological Survey, Albany, NY.

Garvey, E. A. 1990. The geochemistry of inorganic carbon in the Hudson estuary, Ph.D dissertation, Columbia University, New York, NY.

Hammond, D. E. 1975. Dissolved gases and kinetic processes in the Hudson River estuary, Ph.D dissertation, Columbia University, New York, NY.

Junge, C. E. 1963. *Air Chemistry and Radioactivity*, New York: Academic Press.

Junge, C. E. and Werby, R. T. 1958. The concentration of chloride, sodium, potassium, calcium and sulfate in rainwater over the United States. *Journal of Meteorology* **15**:417–425.

Likens, G. E., Bormann, F. H., Hedin, L. O., Driscoll, C. T., and Eaton, J. E. 1990. Dry deposition of sulfur: a 23 year record for the Hubbard Brook Forest ecosystem. *Tellus* **42**B:319–29.

Meybeck, M. 1979. Concentrations des eaus fluviales in elements majeurs et apports en solution aux ocean, *Revue de Geologie Dynamique et de Geographie Physique* **21**(3): 215–46.

Meybeck, M. 1987. Global chemical weathering of surficial rocks estimated from river dissolved loads. *American Journal of Science* **287**:401–428.

Olsen, C. R. 1979. Radionuclides, sedimentation and the accumulation of pollutants in the Hudson estuary, Ph.D dissertation, Columbia University, New York, NY.

Olsen, C. R., Cutshall, N. H., Larsen, I. L., Simpson, H. J., Trier, R. M., and Bopp, R. F. 1984–85. An estuarine fine-particle budget determined from radionuclide tracers. *Geo-Marine Letters* **4**: 157–60.

Phillips, P. J. 1994. Chloride concentrations as indicators of point source sewage discharges in the Hudson River Basin, New York (abstract). *EOS Transactions*, American Geophysical Union, 1994 Fall Meeting Supplement **75** (44): 229.

Phillips, P. J., and Hanchar, D. W. 1996. Water-quality assessment of the Hudson River Basin in New York and adjacent states – Analysis of nutrient, pesticide, volatile organic compound, and suspended sediment data, 1970–1990, *USGS Water Resources Investigations Report* 96–4065.

Randall, A. D. 1996. Mean annual runoff, precipitation and evapotranspiration in the glaciated northeastern United States, 1951–80, USGS Open-File Report 96–395.

Simpson, H. J., Bopp, R. F., and Deck., B. L. 1981 (July). Evaluation of the potential impacts of the proposed Prattsville pumped-storage project on drinking water quality in New York City, Report to Department of Environmental Protection, City of New York.

Sisterson, D. L., Bowersox, V. C., Olsen, A. R., and Simpson, J. C. 1991. Wet deposition of atmospheric pollutants, 6–41 to 6–78. In P. M. Irving (ed.), *Acidic Deposition: State of Science and Technology, Volume 1, Emissions, Atmospheric Processes and Deposition*. Washington, D.C.: U.S. National Acid Precipitation Assessment Program.

Primary Production, Microbial Dynamics, and Nutrient Dynamics of the Hudson

8 Bacterial Abundance, Growth, and Metabolism in the Tidal Freshwater Hudson River

Stuart E. G. Findlay

ABSTRACT Free-living, planktonic heterotrophic bacteria comprise a major portion of the living biomass of organisms in the Hudson River. Mean densities of bacteria are $>5 \times 10^9$ cells/L and abundances generally decrease in a downstream pattern. Bacterial growth is rapid with cells doubling about once per day during the warmer months. Demand for carbon is high and consequently the contribution of bacteria to ecosystem respiration is large, particularly in the mid-Hudson where phytoplankton respiration is low. The high demand for carbon and lack of strong correlation with phytoplankton abundance suggests bacteria are largely reliant on allochthonous carbon delivered from the watershed. Dissolved organic carbon (DOC) dominates the load from the watershed and bacteria have demonstrated roughly equal ability to grow on DOC derived from several different sources and tributaries. Bacterial abundance increased following the zebra mussel invasion in the early 1990s probably due to zebra mussel removal of important grazers on bacteria.

Introduction

In the past twenty years, heterotrophic microorganisms have become widely recognized as integral parts of aquatic ecosystems that play important roles in food webs, nutrient transformations, and organic carbon budgets. Planktonic bacteria can serve as effective links in food webs from dissolved organic matter to larger organisms, although the degree of efficiency varies greatly among aquatic systems (del Giorgio and Cole, 2000).

Microbes growing on particulate and dissolved carbon can also act as significant sinks for inorganic nutrients derived from the water column (Caraco et al., 1998). In large river systems where primary production is low relative to external loadings (see chapters by Howarth, and Cole and Caraco) one would predict that the microbial loop (Pomeroy, 1974) would be significant relative to the traditional macro-grazing food web. Dissolved organic carbon is the largest term in the organic carbon budget for the Hudson and links between this input, heterotrophic bacteria, and higher organisms in the food web could represent a significant energy basis for the system. In the tidal freshwater Hudson River we have documented moderately high abundances and rates of secondary production for the planktonic bacteria and estimated their contribution to organic matter metabolism. This chapter provides an overview of their abundance, spatial and temporal distributions, and metabolic processes. The greatest amount of information is available for the reach of the Hudson River from northern Haverstraw Bay (River km–RKM 64) to Castleton (RKM 228). Sampling there is restricted to the ice-free season (usually April through December). This chapter deals with the free-living, planktonic heterotrophic bacteria in the main channel. The microbial ecology of tidal marshes is covered by the chapter by Kiviat et al. Issues of human pathogens or sewage-derived indicator microorganisms are covered in the chapter by Brosnan et al.

Abundance and Distribution

CELL DENSITIES

Based on fifteen years of spatially extensive sampling, the grand mean bacterial abundance over the river reach examined is 7.6×10^9 cells/L and the distribution of observations shows quartiles of 4.6 and 9.5×10^9 cells/L. These abundances are in the upper portion of the range reported for estuaries in Ducklow and Shiah (1993). Not surprisingly, there is a strong seasonality to bacterial abundance (Fig. 8.1), the mean abundance in summer months (June through September) is about 50% higher than in spring (before June) or autumn (after September). There also is a significant positive correlation between bacterial abundance and

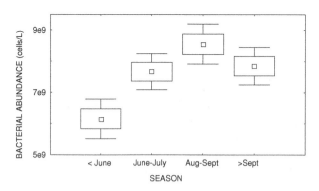

Figure 8.1. Seasonal mean abundance of planktonic bacteria averaged over twelve years (1988 through 2000) and six stations ranging from Haverstraw Bay to Castleton. Seasonal means differ significantly p < 0.001.

temperature (p < 0.05; r = 0.15) although it must be recognized that many other factors including river discharge and primary production co-vary with temperature. Superimposed on the expected seasonal changes in bacterial abundance have been interannual increases in abundance following the zebra mussel invasion (Findlay, Pace, and Fischer, 1998a) and these are discussed below.

Spatial variability shows a very consistent pattern with abundances about 25 percent higher in stations upriver of RKM 150 (Fig. 8.2). The range in spatial variability is only somewhat smaller than the range in seasonal variability, suggesting that whatever process, factor, or combination is responsible is equal with temperature in affecting bacterial numbers. The spatial pattern, although present in all seasons, varies over time with much smaller upriver-downriver contrasts (range = 23 percent of downriver mean) in spring (before June) than in mid-summer (range = 33 percent of downriver mean for Aug-Sept), implying the pattern may be related to residence time rather than simply loading and removal.

The reasonably high bacterial abundance multiplied by our estimate of cell carbon content yields values for bacterial biomass of 70 μg C/L, which is substantially larger than planktonic metazoan biomass (Findlay, Pace, and Fischer, 1996). The relative biomass of bacteria and phytoplankton has changed dramatically since the zebra mussel invasion (Strayer et al., 1999) with pre-zebra mussel ratios (bacterial/algal biomass) of less than 0.5 while post-zebra mussel values are typically 2.0 or higher (Findlay et al., 1998a).

BACTERIAL GROWTH

Bacterial production has been estimated from the rate of thymidine (TdR) incorporation into DNA (Findlay et al., 1991). For purposes of examining temporal and spatial patterns we use the actual rate of TdR incorporation while for carbon budgeting purposes we apply an empirically-derived conversion factor to arrive at a rate of carbon production (Findlay et al., 1991). As for bacterial abundance, thymidine incorporation is strongly seasonal (Fig. 8.3) with greater than two-fold variation from spring to summer and a strong positive

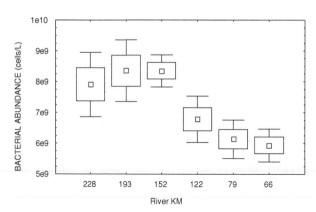

Figure 8.2. Spatial variability in planktonic bacterial abundance for six stations ranging from Castleton in the north (228 km north of the Battery) to the upper end of Haverstraw Bay in the south (66 km north of the Battery). Station means are significantly different (p < 0.0001).

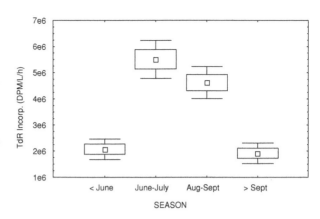

Figure 8.3. Seasonal mean growth rates (DPM of thymidine incorporation /L/h) for planktonic bacteria averaged over twelve years (1988 through 2000) and six stations ranging from Haverstraw Bay to Castleton. Seasonal means are significantly different ($p < 0.001$).

($p < 0.05; r = 0.51$) correlation with water temperature. The spatial pattern in growth mirrors abundance with upriver stations showing rates roughly double the growth rates, relative to downriver stations (Fig. 8.4). Given these patterns, it is not surprising that there is a significant positive correlation ($p < 0.05; r = 0.3$) between abundance and growth.

In a number of estuarine systems, bacterial abundance, growth and metabolic activity have been shown to vary dramatically with particle abundances, particularly in and near the turbidity maximum (e.g., Hollibaugh and Wong, 1999; Crump and Baross, 1996). For the lower Hudson River, bacterial abundance and growth were positively associated with salinity with no obvious increase in the zone of the turbidity maximum (Sañudo-Wilhelmy and Taylor, 1999). In the tidal freshwater Hudson River there was no correlation between bacterial abundance or thymidine incorporation and total suspended matter ($p > 0.05; r = -0.1$ and -0.04, respectively). Potential

limitation of bacterial growth by inorganic nutrients has been shown for a variety of aquatic ecosystems (e.g., Brett et al., 1999) although such limitation seems unlikely given the relatively high concentrations of dissolved inorganic nitrogen and phosphorus in the tidal freshwater Hudson (Lampman, Caraco, and Cole, 1999). Despite the apparent surplus of inorganic nutrients, Roland and Cole (1999) observed a significant stimulation of bacterial growth and respiration following the addition of nitrogen and/or phosphorus in bioassays. Moreover, assays of phosphatase in the mainstem Hudson show reasonably high values in spite of the apparently high availability of soluble reactive phosphorus (SRP) in the water column. These observations taken in concert suggest a more complex interaction of inorganic nutrients and bacterial dynamics than is usually suggested simply from ambient nutrient availability.

In absolute terms, bacterial secondary production is large relative to other components of

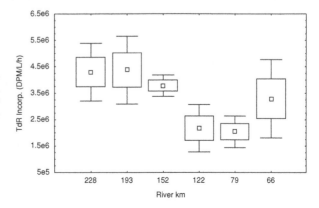

Figure 8.4. Spatial variability in bacterial growth rates for six stations ranging from Castleton to the upper end of Haverstraw Bay in the south. Stations differ significantly at $p = 0.002$.

secondary production within the tidal freshwater Hudson. The grand mean thymidine incorporation translates to a carbon production of 216 μgC/L/h using conversion factors detailed in Findlay et al. (1991). The rates of growth and abundance estimates yield bacterial turnover times ranging from as long as 3.4 days in autumn to about once per day during summer. Although marginally significant (p = 0.06), there is a pattern of shorter turnover times in the upriver stations with values above RKM 150 ranging from 1.3 to 1.8 days, while downriver sites were 2.3 to 2.6 days (data not shown). This pattern of shorter turnover is due to the more rapid decline of growth with distance downriver relative to the decline in abundance.

Bacterial Processes

Heterotrophic planktonic bacteria represent a reasonably large proportion of the living particulate organic matter in the Hudson River and so might be a significant food resource for some consumers. The debate over whether microbes are "links" versus "sinks" for organic carbon depends to a large extent on bacterial growth efficiencies but will also be a function of the particle-harvesting abilities of the microconsumers in an ecosystem. In the Hudson, as in many other aquatic systems, small heterotrophic flagellates are the predominant consumers of free-living bacteria (Vaqué et al., 1992) and these flagellates are themselves potential prey for larger zooplankton (see Chapter 16). Given the rapid turnover times for bacterial biomass there must be large consumption or other losses, otherwise the cell accumulations would be much greater than the ~50 percent seasonal changes in abundance actually observed. While zebra mussels have proven capable of filtering a large proportion of the river volume per day (Strayer et al., 1999), they do not capture natural bacterial cells efficiently and in fact the abundance of bacteria has increased post-zebra mussel (Findlay et al., 1998a) particularly in the upriver stations where zebra mussels are most numerous. These observations together with experiments designed to examine zebra mussel clearance of various grazers suggests zebra mussels have been released from flagellate control because zebra mussels can very effectively clear natural flagellates from the Hudson River's water column (Findlay et al., 1998a). This change implies that HR planktonic bacteria may be under less grazer control currently than pre- zebra mussel and perhaps their contribution to higher trophic levels has declined since the early 1990s.

Carbon inputs to the Hudson are overwhelmingly dominated by loads of dissolved organic carbon (DOC) and particulate organic carbon (POC) from the catchment. Mean annual inputs are on the order of 600 gC m^{-2} y^{-1} and this input is primarily from the upper Hudson drainage basin at a ratio of roughly 2/3 DOC and 1/3 POC (Howarth, Schneider, and Swaney, 1996). Tidal marshes (~4500 ha for entire river) are highly productive with NPP values commonly 1 or more kg carbon/m^2/yr and although the net export to the mainstem is uncertain, outwelling of particulate and dissolved organic carbon was estimated as 16 gC/m^2/yr (Howarth et al., 1996). Autochthonous carbon inputs include phytoplankton and submersed vegetation, which together currently make up about 20 gC m^{-2} y^{-1} (see Chapter 9).

Linking bacteria to potential carbon sources can be examined via correlational analyses and experimental manipulations. In the past, correlations have shown weak associations between bacterial abundance or growth and chlorophyll a (Chl a). Although some of the relationships using the full data set are statistically significant, they account for a small proportion of the variation in bacterial variables. For example, there is a positive association between bacterial production (BP) and Chl a (Fig. 8.5; p < 0.05; r = 0.34) but this might be covariation with temperature rather than evidence for phytoplankton as an important carbon source for planktonic bacterial production. There is no correlation between bacterial abundance and Chl a (p > 0.05; r = −0.06). Considering the nonliving carbon pools, there was no association between bulk DOC (the largest component) and bacterial growth (p > 0.05; r = 0.07). There was a significant positive relationship between DOC and bacterial abundance (p > 0.05; r = 0.37) but this was probably due to temporal covariation, as both cell density and DOC increase seasonally, which could generate a positive association between the

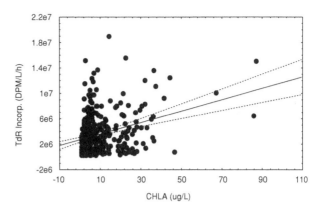

Figure 8.5. Correlation between bacterial growth and planktonic chlorophyll *a*. The relationship is significant (p < 0.0001) but only explains 32% of the variance in growth rate.

variables and should not be construed as cause and effect. There was no relationship between detrital POC (total POC minus the algal component) and either bacterial variable.

Experimental manipulations are commonly used to identify associations between presumptive resources and consumers. Large ecosystem manipulations are still fairly rare but in the Hudson the zebra mussel invasion provided an opportunity to examine the food web consequences of a major new filter-feeder capable of drastically reducing phytoplankton stocks. Prior to the zebra mussel invasion, correlational and budgetary analyses suggested that planktonic bacterial secondary production was, at best, weakly connected to carbon from phytoplankton (Findlay et al., 1991). The zebra mussel invasion provided a "natural" experiment to test the linkage and, in fact, bacterial abundance increased post-zebra mussel and production went up slightly (although not significantly). These observations confirm that these bacteria were not reliant on carbon fixed by phytoplankton, suggesting, by default, that growth may be linked to allochthonous carbon. Small scale bottle experiments (bacterial growth bioassays) have been used to examine use of POC and DOC from a number of specific plant materials and sources, such as wetland outwellings and tributaries (Findlay et al., 1992; Findlay et al., 1998b). These assays revealed that bacteria are able to grow at roughly equivalent rates on a wide range of sources including DOC from different submersed and emergent plants, various tributaries, and DOC exported by wetlands.

In order to metabolize the organic matter derived from these compositionally distinct sources,

the planktonic bacteria differentially allocate their extracellular enzymes resulting in different enzymatic "fingerprints" for bacteria growing on the various sources under experimental conditions. In the Hudson itself these "fingerprints" are not spatially isolated and enzyme patterns are fairly similar along a 150 km reach. This homogeneity in enzymes may be the result of (1) the overwhelming dominance of one source (the DOC load at head of tide is by far the largest single source) or (2) the longitudinal mixing in the river is sufficient to disperse all the separate "point sources" along the reach such that all inputs are available for metabolism across large areas. It appears that planktonic bacteria downriver of what we call the tidal freshwater portion (i.e., south of Newburgh) may rely to a much greater extent on phytoplankton-derived organic carbon than allochthonous sources. In a detailed transect conducted during spring high flows (Sañudo-Wilhelmy and Taylor, 1999), bacterial abundance and growth were strongly correlated with Chl *a* in marked contrast to the upriver pattern. Moreover, the relationship observed downriver was as strong as the cross-system correlation between planktonic bacteria and phytoplankton documented by Cole, Findlay, and Pace (1988). Even more striking is the apparent switch in the spatial pattern in bacterial abundance and growth observed in the lower river and New York Harbor. While we have documented a gradual decline in bacterial numbers and thymidine incorporation between RKM 220 and 64 (Figs. 8.2 and 8.4), Sañudo-Wilhelmy and Taylor (1999) describe manifold increases in abundance and production over the reach from roughly 90 km above Manhattan to Sandy Hook, in lower New York Bay.

These contrasting correlations and strong spatial patterns suggest a dramatic switching in carbon sources and regulation in planktonic bacteria in the more saline portions of the estuary. Rates of phytoplanktonic primary production in the mesohaline Hudson are very high relative to other regions of the River and even appear to have increased in recent years (see Chapter 10). This large increase in available autochthonous carbon could represent an important resource for heterotrophic bacteria and generate strong spatial patterns in bacterial abundance.

One logical scenario consistent with these patterns is dominance of the upriver carbon supply and metabolism by the large allochthonous load delivered at the head of tide (Findlay et al., 1998b) which apparently overwhelms all the "point sources" such as wetlands and other tributaries providing carbon in the tidal freshwater reach. Previous estimates of metabolic carbon demand (Findlay et al., 1992 and see below) imply there should be depletion of metabolizable carbon in the lower reaches and bulk DOC concentrations decline over this reach (Findlay et al., 1996). The downriver declines in abundance and growth would be consistent with a gradual winding down of an allochthonously-driven microbial loop. Perhaps in the more saline portions of the estuary, the microbial loop is revitalized by local inputs of phytoplankton-derived carbon and as nutrients are delivered to the estuary and water clarity improves moving seaward, the traditional phytoplankton-bacterioplankton trophic link assumes predominance.

The ability of bacteria in the tidal freshwater portion of the Hudson estuary to metabolize a significant portion of the allochthonous load has been suggested and verified by a number of lines of evidence. Firstly, bacteria grow in bioassay experiments receiving DOC derived from various tributaries (Findlay et al., 1998b) at rates equal or greater than in water from the mainstem Hudson. Separate and independent estimates of carbon metabolism (respiration) and net heterotrophy (Cole and Caraco, 2001; Raymond, Caraco, and Cole, 1997; Howarth et al., 1996) clearly require metabolism of a significant fraction of the allochthonous carbon load to drive observed patterns in dissolved oxygen and CO_2. Estimates of

in situ bacterial growth coupled with their relatively low growth efficiencies (Findlay et al., 1992; Roland and Cole, 1999), allow estimates of what proportion of the allochthonous load is needed to fuel growth. Median bacterial production estimated from thymidine incorporation is 153 µg $C L^{-1} d^{-1}$, which translates to 337 gC $m^{-2} y^{-1}$, assuming 200 days of growth per year and a mean depth of 11 m for this reach. This value is large relative to estimated allochthonous loading (650 gC $m^{-2} y^{-1}$; Howarth et al., 1996) and large relative to estimated system respiration 100–300 gC $m^{-2} y^{-1}$ (see the chapter by Cole and Caraco). Given the uncertainties in all components of the budget it is probably safe to state that: (1) planktonic bacteria are responsible for a major fraction of system respiration, and (2) this metabolism requires degradation of a substantial proportion of the allochthonous carbon load.

Degradation of allochthonous dissolved organic carbon in a range of large river-estuarine systems has been documented through a number of independent lines of evidence. The budgetary approach outlined here is supported by shifts in the apparent age of DOC in transit and marked changes in ^{14}C ages and δ ^{13}C strongly suggesting turnover of DOC components rather than simple conservative transport (Raymond and Bauer, 2001a and b). Aside from budgetary and tracer approaches, planktonic bacteria have shown rapid shifts in metabolism under changing carbon supply conditions with responses in extracellular enzymes as rapid as a few hours (Cunha, Almeida, and Alcântara, 2001) or days (Pinhassi et al., 1999). The capacity to rapidly shift degradative pathways implies that the diversity of carbon compounds entering estuaries (or produced at various points along estuaries) does not represent a fundamental obstacle to metabolism during transit. Bacterial communities can change in composition during downriver transport (Leff, 2000), providing a further opportunity to adjust degradative capacity. The relative contribution of allochthonous loading versus internal sources from phytoplankton production, floodplains (O'Connell et al., 2000), or wetland export will vary among river systems based on their relative abundance. Given reasonably long transit times (tens of days or more), planktonic bacteria via a number of mechanisms can access these carbon pools, which allows significant microbial growth and alteration of the DOC delivered to the oceans.

Studies of bacteria in the Hudson River revealed a large biomass linked to terrestrial carbon sources rather than the traditional dependence on phytoplankton-derived carbon. Their high growth rates and relatively low efficiency leads to bacterial respiration being a major fraction of organic matter mineralization. The broad capacity to acquire carbon from the diversity of sources entering the tidal Hudson allows high secondary production throughout the river and even a whole-system phytoplankton removal by zebra mussels, which did not depress bacterial growth. Spatial patterns of bacterial abundance and productivity suggest a switching from depleted terrestrially-derived carbon to a reliance on autochthonous primary production in the lower reaches of the Hudson River Estuary.

REFERENCES

Brett, M. T., Lubnow, F. S., Villar-Argaiz, M., Müller-Solger, A., and Goldman, C. R. 1999. Nutrient control of bacterioplankton and phytoplankton dynamics. *Aquatic Ecology* **33**:135–45.

Caraco, N. F., Lampman, G., Cole, J. J., Limburg, K. E., Pace, M. L., and Fischer, D. 1998. Microbial assimilation of DIN in a nitrogen rich estuary: implications for food quality and isotope studies. *Marine Ecology Progress Series* **167**:59–71.

Cole, J. J., and Caraco, N. F. 2001. Carbon in catchments: connecting terrestrial carbon losses with aquatic metabolism. *Marine & Freshwater Research* **52**:101–110.

Cole, J. J., Findlay, S., and Pace, M. L. 1988. Bacterial production in fresh and saltwater ecosystems: a cross-system overview. *Marine Ecology Progress Series* **43**:1–10.

Crump, B. C., and Baross, J. A. 1996. Particle-attached bacteria and heterotrophic plankton associated with Columbia River estuarine turbidity maxima. *Marine Ecology Progress Series* **138**:265–73.

Cunha, M. A., Almeida, M. A., and Alcântara, F. 2001. Short-term responses of the natural planktonic bacterial community to the changing water properties in an estuarine environment: ectoenzymatic activity, glucose incorporation, and biomass production. *Microbial Ecology* **42**:69–79.

del Giorgio, P. A., and Cole, J. J. 2000. Bacterial growth efficiency and energetics, in D. L. Kirchman (ed.),

Microbial Ecology of the Oceans. New York: Wiley-Liss, pp. 289–325.

Ducklow, H. W., and Shiah, F.-K. 1993. Bacterial productions in estuaries, in T. E. Ford (ed.), *Aquatic Microbiology: An Ecological Approach*. Boston, MA: Blackwell Scientific Publications, pp. 261–87.

Findlay, S., Pace, M. L., Lints, D., Cole, J. J., Caraco, N. F., and Peierls, B. 1991. Weak coupling of bacterial and algal production in a heterotrophic ecosystem, the Hudson Estuary. *Limnology and Oceanography* **36**:268–78.

Findlay, S., Pace, M. L., and Lints, D., and Howe, K. 1992. Bacterial metabolism of organic carbon in the tidal freshwater Hudson estuary. *Marine Ecology Progress Series* **89**:147–53.

Findlay, S., Pace, M. L., and Fischer, D. 1996. Spatial and temporal variability in the lower food web of the tidal freshwater Hudson River. *Estuaries* **19**:866–73.

Findlay, S., Pace, M. L., and Fischer, D. T. 1998a. Effect of the invasive zebra mussel (*Dreissena polymorpha*) on the microbial food web in the tidal freshwater Hudson River. *Microbial Ecology* **36**:131–40.

Findlay, S., Sinsabaugh, R. L., Fischer, D. T., and Franchini, P. 1998b. Sources of dissolved organic carbon supporting planktonic bacterial production in the tidal freshwater Hudson River. *Ecosystems* **1**:227–39.

Hollibaugh, J. T., and Wong, P. S. 1999. Microbial processes in the San Francisco Bay estuarine turbidity maximum. *Estuaries* **22**:848–62.

Howarth, R. W., Schneider, R., and Swaney, D. 1996. Metabolism and organic carbon fluxes in the tidal freshwater Hudson River. *Estuaries* **19**:848–65.

Lampman, G., Caraco, N. F., and Cole, J. J. 1999. Spatial and temporal patterns of nutrient concentration and export in the tidal Hudson River. *Estuaries* **22**:285–96.

Leff, L. G. 2000. Longitudinal changes in microbial assemblages of the Ogeechee River. *Freshwater Biology* **43**:605–615.

O'Connell, M., Baldwin, D. S., Robertson, A. J., and Rees, G. 2000. Release and bioavailability of dissolved organic matter from floodplain litter: influence of origin and oxygen levels. *Freshwater Biology* **45**:333–42.

Pinhassi, J., Azam, F., Hemphälä, J., Long, R. A., Martinez, J., Zweifel, U. L., and Hagström, Å. 1999. Coupling between bacterioplankton species composition, population dynamics, and organic matter degradation. *Aquatic Microbial Ecology* **17**:13–26.

Pomeroy, L. R. 1974. The ocean's food web, a changing paradigm. *Bioscience* **24**:499–504.

Raymond, P. A., and Bauer, J. E. 2001a. DOC cycling in a temperate estuary: a mass balance approach using natural ^{14}C and ^{13}C isotopes. *Limnology and Oceanography* **46**:655–67.

Raymond, P. A., and Bauer, J. E. 2001b. Riverine export of aged terrestrial organic matter to the North Atlantic Ocean. *Nature* **409**:497–99.

Raymond, P. A., Caraco, N. F., and Cole, J. J. 1997. CO_2 concentration and atmospheric flux in the Hudson River. *Estuaries* **20**:381–90.

Roland, F., and Cole, J. J. 1999. Regulation of bacterial growth efficiency in a large turbid estuary. *Aquatic Microbial Ecology* **20**:31–8.

Sañudo-Wilhelmy, S. A., and Taylor, G. T. 1999. Bacterioplankton dynamics and organic carbon partitioning in the lower Hudson River estuary. *Marine Ecology Progress Series* **182**:17–27.

Strayer, D. L., Caraco, N. F., Cole, J. J., Findlay, S., and Pace, M. L. 1999. Transformation of freshwater ecosystems by bivalves: a case study of zebra mussels in the Hudson River. *BioScience* **49**:19–27.

Vaqué, D., Pace, M. L., Findlay, S., and Lints, D. 1992. Fate of bacterial production in a heterotrophic ecosystem: grazing by protozoans and metazoans in the Hudson Estuary. *Marine Ecology Progress Series* **89**:155–63.

9 Primary Production and Its Regulation in the Tidal-Freshwater Hudson River

Jonathan J. Cole and Nina F. Caraco

ABSTRACT Photosynthesis is the main process by which new organic matter is synthesized. In many aquatic ecosystems, phytoplankton are the major photosynthetic organisms and are responsible for most of the organic C input. In the tidal-freshwater Hudson, primary production by phytoplankton is maintained at relatively low values by a combination of high turbidity and deep mixing (which lowers light availability), advective losses downstream and consumption by grazers. Limitation by nitrogen or phosphorus, the most common plant limiting nutrients, is not an important regulatory factor in the tidal-freshwater Hudson. Respiration by the phytoplankton themselves is the major fate of phytoplankton-derived organic matter (gross primary production), leaving relatively small amounts available to higher trophic levels. Thus, small increases in grazing pressure could have large impacts on phytoplankton. Phytoplankton biomass and gross primary production were dramatically reduced by the 1992 invasion of the zebra mussel, and phytoplankton have not yet recovered to pre-invasion levels. We estimate that phytoplankton gross primary production was $331 \, g \, C \, m^{-2} \, y^{-1}$ in the years prior to the zebra mussel invasion and $82 \, g \, C \, m^{-2} \, y^{-1}$ in the years following. This is from about one-half to one-eighth as large as the input of terrestrial organic C from the watershed.

Introduction

Primary production is the formation of organic compounds from inorganic building blocks. The energy required to synthesize these organic products may come from sunlight (photosynthesis); from chemical reactions, (chemosynthesis, e.g., ammonia or sulfide oxidation); or a mixture of the two as in some types of an oxygenic bacterial photosynthesis (Brock, 1979).

In the Hudson River, as in most aerobic aquatic environments, oxygenic photosynthesis is by far the major pathway of primary production. In the tidal-freshwater portion of the Hudson River this photosynthesis is carried out by several functionally different groups of organisms: phytoplankton (small, often single celled, eukaryotic algae and cyanobacteria suspended in the water column), periphyton (algae attached to various surfaces), submergent macrophytes (higher plants such as *Valisneria* [water celery] that grow attached to the bottom with leaves that remain within the water column), and floating or emergent macrophytes (higher plants such as *Trapa* [water chestnut] whose leaves are partially or completely exposed to the air). These differing groups of plants have different consumer organisms, different sets of regulation and constraints and different effects on dissolved gas dynamics in the river.

This chapter focuses on primary production by phytoplankton and its regulation, in the tidal, freshwater portion of the Hudson from Albany south to Newburgh, New York. Further, we compare phytoplankton production in this section of the river into the context of the entire river and other groups of primary producers and compare phytoplankton production in the Hudson to other rivers and estuaries of the world.

Why consider primary production in part of a large riverine estuary? First, the conditions in the tidal, freshwater river are substantially different from those in the saline part of the lower estuary. Thus, phytoplankton experience different regulatory factors in these two sections. Second, the invasion of the zebra mussel in the tidal-freshwater section had dramatic effects on the phytoplankton and provided a great deal of insight into how phytoplankton were regulated. Third, the investigative approaches have differed between the lower estuary and tidal-freshwater river. The lower estuary is covered in the chapter by Howarth et al. (Chapter 10).

MEASUREMENT AND TERMINOLOGY

To discuss primary production and its measurement, we need to introduce a few terms.

- Gross Primary Production (GPP) is total photosynthesis, including the portion respired by the autotrophs themselves.
- Respiration (R) is the respiration by all organisms. R is the sum of respiration by autotrophs (R_a) and heterotrophs (R_h).
- Net Primary Production (NPP) is GPP – R_a. NPP is the amount of organic matter available to consumer organisms. That is, NPP is the primary production left after plant respiration has removed that needed to sustain the plants themselves. While NPP is usually ≥ 0, it need not be. When NPP is <0, the biomass of autotrophs must actually be declining over time. That is, phytoplankton are respiring their stored biomass, in excess of new photosynthesis. This condition sometimes occurs for phytoplankton in Hudson River (below).

GPP, or R, or NPP can be studied for a group of organisms (e.g., phytoplankton, macrophytes, etc.) or for an entire community ecosystem. This chapter focuses on these quantities for phytoplankton.

In aquatic systems primary production is usually measured indirectly through changes in dissolved oxygen or dissolved inorganic C (DIC) or, most often, by labeling the DIC pool with ^{14}C and measuring the incorporation of label into phytoplankton or plant tissue. The various methods do not measure exactly the same quantities (see Williams, Raine, and Bryan, 1979; Williams and Robertson, 1991). From the changes in O_2 in paired light and dark bottles containing river water, one can measure total planktonic respiration ($R_a + R_h$ in the dark) and the rate of pelagic NPP in the light. By assuming that R in the dark and light are equivalent we can calculate GPP and R. With the oxygen method, there is no direct way to estimate R_a and therefore no direct way to estimate NPP. The ^{14}C method gives, in the light, something between GPP and NPP depending on the length of the incubation, the growth rate of the phytoplankton and the degree of C recycling (Williams et al., 1979). With the ^{14}C method there is no direct way to estimate any of the components of R. The ^{14}C method, because of its high sensitivity, is most widely used and

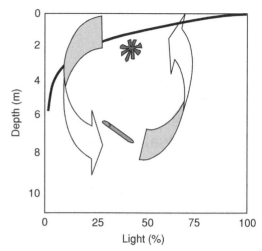

Figure 9.1. Phytoplankton in the Hudson River are well-mixed vertically and are often swept to depths with light conditions unfavorable for photosynthesis.

usually reported as "NPP." Typically results are integrated over depth and during daylight hours, excluding both nighttime and depths with light too low to sustain photosynthesis. To make clear what is, and is not, included, we will call this type of estimation Net Daylight Photic Zone Production (NDPZP; Cole, Caraco, and Peierls, 1992) to distinguish it from true NPP.

The Environment for Primary Production in the Tidal-freshwater Hudson

Riverine environments like the Hudson present certain challenges to photosynthetic organisms (Cloern, 1987; Alpine and Cloern, 1988). The water column of the tidal-freshwater Hudson is well mixed and turbid. The suspended particles absorb light; the full water-column mixing ensures that organisms suspended in the water are rarely in the surface where light is highest (Fig. 9.1). At the average depth (9 m) and light penetration for the Hudson, the average phytoplankton spends from 18 to 22 hours in light too dim for net positive photosynthesis to proceed (Cole et al., 1992). The situation differs in the saline parts of the estuary and harbor where the water column is stratified, at least some of the time, leading to shallower mixing depths (Swaney, Howarth, and Butler, 1999), and concomitantly higher rates of primary production (Chapter 10). Nevertheless, low light is still a major growth-limiting factor in the lower estuary as well (Garside et al., 1976; Malone, 1977).

Attached to the bottom, macrophytes and periphyton are restricted to extremely shallow water (<1 m) due to low light. On the other hand, these attached plants are less affected by advective loss than are phytoplankton. While the net freshwater flow of the Hudson is not very rapid, photosynthesis of suspended organisms needs to exceed the advective losses if biomass is to increase at a given site. During the growing season a typical residence time for water in the tidal-freshwater river is about 30 to 50 d, or 2 to 3 percent per day. To simply sustain biomass at a given location then, net growth, after respiratory and predatory losses are subtracted, must be at least this large.

In many aquatic environments the supply of essential nutrients for plant growth, typically phosphorus (P) or nitrogen (N), and some trace metals (iron, selenium e, etc.) limits the net growth of phytoplankton. In some rivers and most estuaries, since trace metals are generally high, N and P are the likely limiting nutrients (Howarth, 1988; Fisher et al., 1992). Such is not the case in the Hudson. In the tidal-freshwater river, for example, NH_4 depletes from winter values near 10 μM to fairly low values in mid summer (~2 μM). NO_3 varies seasonally between wintertime highs of near 50 μM and summertime "lows" above 30 μM. PO_4 values are lowest in spring (0.4 to 0.5 μM) and increase in late summer (at the peak of phytoplankton biomass) to as much as 0.8 to 1 μM (Fig. 9.2; Lampman, Caraco, and Cole, 1999). If either PO_4 or NO_3 were limiting one would expect a negative correlation with phytoplankton biomass, which is not seen at all in the Hudson.

Composition of Phytoplankton

The Hudson River contains a diverse array of phytoplankton, but diatoms (Baciliariophycea) are the numerical and biomass dominants and account for the majority of the species identified from the river (Marshall, 1988; Smith et al., 1998). Working in the tidal-freshwater river, Marshall (1988) identified 137 species of phytoplankton of which 43 percent were diatoms, 27 percent were Cholorophyceae, and 15.3 percent were Cyanobacteria. Other major groups (Cryptophyceae, Chrysophyceae,

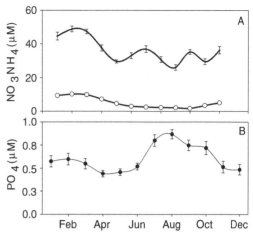

Figure 9.2. Twelve years of nutrient concentrations near Kingston, New York (river km 144). Shown are the means, by month (with SD for that month among years) for weekly to bi-weekly data for 14 years 1986–2000. The upper panel shows inorganic N; open circles are NH_4; x's are NO_3. The lower panel shows PO_4. These data are a summary of nutrient analysis from more than 500 individual dates sampled.

and Pyrrhophyceae) are represented in the river but with fewer species and much less biomass (Smith et al., 1998). Earlier work on the taxonomic structure of Hudson River phytoplankton reveals broadly similar conclusions, a dominance of diatoms and the presence of many other groups (Frederick et al., 1976; Sirois and Frederick, 1978; Howells and Weaver, 1969). Chapter 19 by Strayer reviews some of the factors that may regulate the difference in phytoplankton community structure in the Hudson (Caraco et al., 1997; Smith et al., 1998). We have not seen picoplankton (cells <3 μM) in the samples we have counted in the tidal-freshwater portion of the river and know of no published data suggesting that picoplankton are an important component of the Hudson River phytoplankton. Picoplankton have been reported as an important component of other coastal rivers (Kobayashi, Williams, and Kotlash, 2000).

Biomass of Phytoplankton

Phytoplankton biomass is usually reported as the concentration of standing stock of chlorophyll-*a*, a pigment that all phytoplankton have in common. Weekly to bi-weekly measurements of the

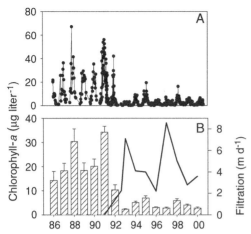

Figure 9.3. The biomass of phytoplankton in the mid-Hudson region. Shown in A are weekly to bi-weekly data for chlorophyll-*a* near Kingston, New York (river km 144). In B we show means for the May-October period for each year (hatched bars, errors are SD). The solid line (right-hand Y-axis) shows the water filtration rate of the zebra mussel (Caraco et al., 1997; Strayer, this volume). The filtration rate is expressed as volume per area per time (m^3 m^{-2} d^{-1}), which is the same as m d^{-1}.

concentration of chlorophyll-*a* near Kingston, New York (rkm 144–147) reveal several key features at several time scales about the magnitude and variation of phytoplankton in the Hudson (Fig. 9.3A).

First, there is an obvious seasonal cycle with peak biomass generally occurring in late spring. While the peak values can be quite high (20 to 50 µg liter^{-1}), the average level is moderate or low compared to other rivers and estuaries (discussed below). In many estuaries and lakes rapid phytoplankton growth occurs early in the season leading to a "spring bloom" in February to April. In the Hudson River, the bloom is substantially delayed and rarely, if ever, occurs in the spring. Among all years the mean day of peak phytoplankton biomass would be August 14. The earliest peak we have observed was in 1999 (May 12) and the latest in 2000 (October 25). In most years the peak occurs in mid July (Fig. 9.3A). There is high variance among years of the timing of the rapid growth phase. The day-of-year of peak chlorophyll-*a* is negatively correlated to the average amount of suspended load in the river (r^2 = 0.39; p = 0.01). Suspended load is the major factor controlling light extinction in the river. This correlation, however, explains only a fraction

of the variance in the timing of the peak, so other factors are clearly involved.

Second, there are very obvious interannual differences in the magnitude of chlorophyll-*a* in the Hudson (Fig. 9.3B). The largest is the change from moderately high values to low values before and after 1992, the year the zebra mussel first became established at high numbers in the river (Caraco et al., 1997; Strayer et al., 1999; Strayer, this volume). Prior to 1992 mean growing season (May–October), chlorophyll-*a* at Kingston averaged 22.1 ± 5.9 µg liter^{-1}. From 1993–2000 the mean was 4.4 = 1.2 µg liter^{-1}. This 80 percent decline in phytoplankton biomass is consistent with the dramatic increase in water filtration brought about by the zebra mussel (Caraco et al., 1997). Prior to the zebra mussel invasion biological filtration of the tidal, freshwater Hudson occurred about once in 50 d, and was largely the result of suspension feeding by cladocerans such as *Bosmina* and copepods (Caraco et al., 1997; Strayer et al., 1999; Pace and Lonsdale, this volume). The zebra mussel increased biological filtration so that the entire water column turnover time was as short as 1 to 3 d depending on the year (Fig. 9.3B).

As in San Francisco Bay, some of the interannual differences in the Hudson's phytoplankton biomass are related to variation in freshwater discharge among years, which controls the advective loss of phytoplankton (Cloern et al., 1985). Discharge during the growing season varies about three-fold in the Hudson from 100 to nearly 400 m^3 s^{-1} among years. Thus, the residence time of water within the tidal-freshwater region varies with this discharge from about 100 to 25 days. Discharge was negatively correlated to chlorophyll-*a* during the pre-zebra mussel period (Fig. 9.4; p = 0.002). During the post-zebra mussel period, this relationship has the same trend, but is not significant (Fig. 9.4; p = 0.19). Prior to the zebra mussel invasion, the advective loss term was of comparable magnitude to biological filtration; following the invasion biological filtration greatly exceeds the advective loss term.

Biomass over Space

The variation in phytoplankton biomass over the length of the river is as large as the seasonal

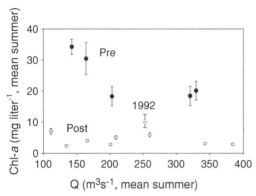

Figure 9.4. Relationship between phytoplankton biomass (as chlorophyll-*a*) and freshwater discharge, both averaged for the period from May 15 through October 1; error bar is SD. The solid circles are for the period from 1986–1991, prior to the introduction of the zebra mussel ("Pre"). The open circles are for the period 1993–2000 ("Post") and the open triangle is for 1992, the transitional year (see text).

variation at a single site (Fig. 9.5). The spatial structure is complex and has changed dramatically in response to the zebra mussel invasion, as we saw for the seasonal cycle. Even following the invasion, however, there is intriguing spatial structure that we do not fully understand. Clearly a primary determinant is water column depth. Within the tidal-freshwater portion, which is well mixed, the shallower reaches tend to have the highest volumetric biomass. Deeper water column depth causes cells to spend more time in the dark. Depth at a given reach interacts with other factors such as input from upstream and advective losses. A model that includes these factors along with grazing rates and phytoplankton growth rates is able to reproduce the major features of the chlorophyll pattern along the length of the river both before and the first few years after the zebra mussel invasion (Caraco et al., 1997).

Rates of Phytoplankton Primary Production

By varying light in a series of short-term incubations we can see the functional relationship between phytoplankton photosynthesis and irradiance (Fig. 9.6). The data from the Hudson, as with most other systems, fit a hyperbolic tangent function (Fig. 9.6). To compare to other sys-

tems, the photosynthetic parameters are normalized to the amount of biomass (expressed in terms of chlorophyll-*a*). Thus, P^b_{max} is the biomass specific rate of photosynthesis at optimum light and α_b is the biomass-specific initial slope in Figure 9.6. I_k is the value of light at which P^b_{max} is first reached. In very clear water systems photosynthesis can be inhibited at high light; in the turbid waters of the Hudson light inhibition is not an important consideration.

P^b_{max} in the tidal-freshwater Hudson is comparable to values found in other estuarine systems and in the lower Hudson as well (e.g., Cote and Platt, 1983; Shaw and Purdie, 2001). I_k is moderately high (and α_b moderately low) compared to many systems. In chronically low light environments phytoplankton are often adapted to low light by having low I_k and high α_b, that is, a high affinity for light. The Hudson phytoplankton are not strongly adapted to low light, but are able to grow as rapidly as phytoplankton in other systems at optimum light. In the well-mixed water column it is perhaps more reasonable to see the Hudson plankton as adapted to varying light, taking advantage of high light when they are mixed near the surface (see Cole et al., 1992).

Instantaneous photosynthesis is the product of algal biomass, the photosynthetic parameters and light. Light varies over depth according to light extinction and varies with season and time of day. Algal biomass and the photosynthetic parameters

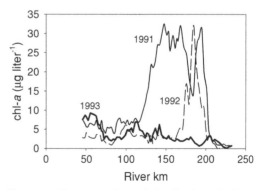

Figure 9.5. Representative variation in phytoplankton biomass over the length of the tidal-freshwater Hudson. Shown are transects from the Tappan Zee Bridge (river km 40) to Albany (river km 240) taken in August of three different years (labeled). River km are km north of the southern tip of Manhattan (river km 0).

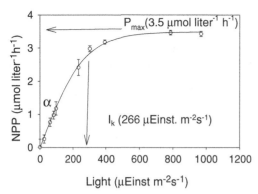

Figure 9.6. Result of a primary production versus irradiance measurement for the tidal-freshwater Hudson River. The Y-axis shows primary production measured as the assimilation of ^{14}C-HCO_3 into organic matter as a function of light (X-axis). In this example the organic matter includes both particulate and dissolved components (POC plus DOC). The actual data points, with SE, are shown as open circles and the line represents the fit hyperbolic tangent function fit to these data. The photosynthetic parameters (P_{max}, α, and I_k) are derived from the equation for the fitted line (see text). These data are for Hudson, New York, on September 12, 1998.

vary, as we have seen with season, flow, temperature, and the species shift induced by the zebra mussel invasion (Cole et al., 1992; Caraco et al., 1997; Caraco et al., 2000). We can put these pieces together and look at phytoplankton primary production.

Daytime Photic Zone Primary Production

Traditionally phytoplankton production (NPP, see introduction) is measured by the ^{14}C method and is integrated over the daylight period and to the depth of the photic zone, and does not consider respiration. Thus, these values are NDPZP (see introduction). For these calculations we computed primary production for each 0.1-m slice of the water column for each half hour during daylight, for each week for which we have chlorophyll-a data. Potential irradiance was calculated from the equations of Iqbal (1983) using an albedo of 10 percent and the average degree of cloudiness for the region 40 percent reduction in potential radiation (IES 2001). NDPZP ranges from extremely low values in winter ($\sim$1 mmol C m^{-2} d^{-1}) to values as

high as 300 mmol C m^{-2} d^{-1} during summer bloom conditions (Fig. 9.7). The seasonal pattern mirrors that of chlorophyll-a and shows the dramatic reduction following the invasion of the zebra mussel (Fig. 9.7).

Since NPP, based on ^{14}C measurements, does not include an estimate of algal respiration, NPP in daylight is potentially smaller than algal GPP by algal respiration in the light. In the dark part of the water column, and at night, algal respiration consumes algal C that is not accounted for at all (Banse, 1976). Using the approach outlined in Caraco et al. (1997) if we assume that algal R is proportional to P_{max}^b

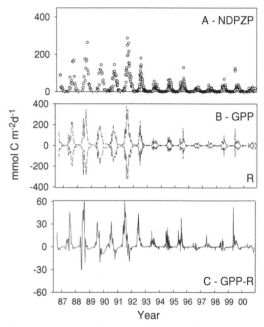

Figure 9.7. Phytoplankton primary production over time at Kingston, New York. From weekly measures of chlorophyll-a and the photosynthetic parameters three aspects of phytoplankton primary production were calculated. In A, we show photosynthesis, integrated over the entire daylight period and integrated to the depth that below no photosynthesis occurs. This is daytime net photic zone primary production. In B, we applied a biomass-specific value of phytoplankton respiration (R; see text) and calculated both phytoplankton respiration (plotted as a negative value to simplify the figure) gross primary production. In C, we plot GPP-R, or true 24 h net phytoplankton production integrated for the entire depth of the water column. Note that expressed this way, NPP is occasionally negative and is much smaller than GPP or NDPZP.

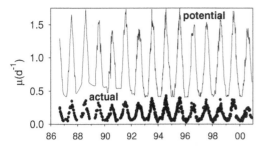

Figure 9.8. Growth rate of phytoplankton in the tidal-freshwater Hudson. The solid circles labeled "actual" show the growth rate calculated from GPP (Fig. 9.7) and biomass. The thin line shows the growth rate at optimum light ("potential"), with no light limitation. In this scenario the light level was 1000 μ Einst. m^{-2} s^{-1} throughout the water column for 12 h each day.

and the ^{14}C measures net phytoplankton production (GPP-R$_a$) in the light, we can provide an estimate of algal R and GPP (Fig. 9.7). In this scenario, we assumed that R$_a$ was constant at 7 percent of P$^b_{max}$. Actual estimates of phytoplankton R range from 5 to 25 percent of P$^b_{max}$ (Falkowski, Dubinsky, and Santostefano, 1985; Geider and Osborne, 1989; Raven and Beardall, 1981).

GPP is useful to know because we can compute the phytoplankton growth rate from GPP and algal biomass (Fig. 9.8). In the Hudson this growth rate (μ) ranges from about 0.05 to 0.4 d^{-1} and is much slower than these taxa are capable of. If we compute the growth rate the phytoplankton would have without light limitation (growth at P$^b_{max}$) we see the μ_{max} is much higher than μ ranging from 0.4 to more than 1.75 d^{-1}, about as fast as these organisms grow in culture. Averaged over the entire data set μ_{max} is 5.9 times faster than actual μ. Looking closely at the plot of actual μ we generally see slightly faster growth rates in the post zebra mussel years than in the pre-zebra mussel years, at least during the summer. Presumably the high filtration rate of the zebra mussel selects for phytoplankton species that are faster growing. We have seen a significant change in species composition of the phytoplankton in response to the invasion (Smith et al., 1998), perhaps reflecting this grazing pressure.

From GPP and R we can also estimate phytoplankton net production (GPP-R), which is an interesting quantity since it is the C available to be consumed or exported. Note that NPP is much smaller than either GPP or ^{14}C-based estimates of primary production (NDPZP), rarely exceeding 30 mmol m^{-2} d^{-1}, and is occasionally negative (algal R > GPP). On an annual basis, GPP-R is about ten times smaller larger than measured ^{14}C primary production. Had we assumed that ^{14}C in the light measured gross rather than net production, or had we used higher values for algal respiration, GPP-R would be even smaller (Cole et al., 1992). The very large difference between GPP-R and net daytime photic zone primary production is due to the deeply mixed water column. In the Hudson, phytoplankton spend a great deal of time in the dark. For the deeper-water parts of the river, Poughkeepsie for example, algal R would frequently exceed GPP (Cole et al., 1992). The inference is that phytoplankton, as they pass through these deeper regions, must lose biomass due in part to their own respiration. This is consistent with the observed pattern of less algal biomass in the deeper regions of the river, as long the water column is well mixed (Fig. 9.5). We do not know the actual rate of algal R, so these calculations are only illustrative of what is likely. However, it is unlikely that algal R is much lower than 7 percent of P$^b_{max}$ (Beardall and Raven, 1990; Geider and Osborne, 1989). It is also possible that R is neither constant nor always proportional to P$^b_{max}$. (e.g., Laws, 1975; Stone and Ganf, 1981). The major point here is that in the well-mixed and dimly lit water column of the Hudson River, algal respiration is a large and important fate of algal gross primary production. This condition is likely true in other well-mixed turbid rivers and estuaries but has only been considered in a few of them (Peterson and Festa, 1984).

Since the net production of phytoplankton (GPP-R$_a$) and growth rates of the Hudson River phytoplankton are low, a small change in a loss term (advection, predation, etc.) can be extremely significant. Even without considering the respiration of phytoplankton, the growth rate of phytoplankton based on GPP is only 0.3 d^{-1} at its peak. The biological filtration of the water column by zebra mussels is about this magnitude, 30 percent of the water column filtered each day. If R$_a$ is proportional to P$^b_{max}$, as we have modeled it, phytoplankton respiration consumes on the order of 80 to 90 percent of Gpp. Thus a change in removal rates of on the order of 5 to 10 percent of the water column per day would still significantly impact the phytoplankton of the tidal-freshwater Hudson. The major crash in phytoplankton biomass in response to the zebra mussel invasion is indeed consistent with this reasoning (Caraco et al., 1997).

The Tidal-freshwater Hudson in Comparison to Other Systems

In comparison to rivers and estuaries of the world, the tidal-freshwater Hudson, depending on the location, was fairly eutrophic prior to the invasion of the zebra mussel in 1992. That is, mean growing season chlorophyll-*a* at Kingston, New York, was higher than more than 75 percent of the rivers and estuaries for which we have data. Similarly, the Kingston region had high chlorophyll in comparison to downriver sites within the Hudson. Following 1992, (post-) chlorophyll-*a* in the mid Hudson would be considered moderately low in comparison to other river or estuarine systems (Fig. 9.9A).

As we pointed out, GPP is rarely measured in most systems, making comparison limited. However, we can compare our estimates of phytoplankton GPP to estimates of GPP made on the saline part of the Hudson River Estuary, many of which are reviewed in Chapter 10 and Swaney et al. (1999). GPP for the mid 1990s is about 850 g C m^{-2} y^{-1} in the saline part of the estuary and 450 g C m^{-2} y^{-1} for the oligohaline section. Both estimates are considerably higher than we estimate for the freshwater portion of the river of 330 g C m^{-2} y^{-1} for the pre-zebra mussel period and 82 g C m^{-2} y^{-1} post zebra mussel. On the other hand, the estimates reported by Howarth et al. (Chapter 10) for the mid 1990s are roughly 2 to 4 times higher than prior estimates from the 1970s for the saline and mesohaline sections, respectively. So, prior to the zebra mussel, GPP in the tidal-freshwater portion of the estuary was somewhat lower than for the oligohaline region and less than half that for the saline portion. Following the invasion, GPP in the tidal freshwater was only about 25 percent of that in the oligohaline region and roughly one-tenth the estimates for the saline portion.

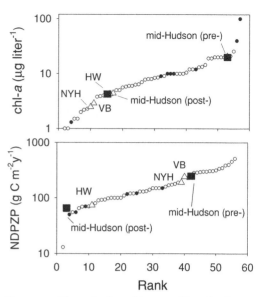

Figure 9.9. Phytoplankton biomass (A) and primary production (B) in comparison to other rivers (filled circles) and estuaries (open circles). Each point is for a different riverine or estuarine system, and the systems are ordered by chlorophyll values from low to high. Biomass is mean chlorophyll-*a* for the growing season. For the tidal-freshwater Hudson this is given for both prior to the zebra mussel invasion ("pre-") and following it ("post-"). Several other sites for the saline estuary are also shown. These are NYH – New York Harbor (Malone, 1975; Malone, 1977), and HW – Haverstraw Bay and VB – Verrazano Bridge (both from G. Taylor, personal communication) and are data from the mid-1990s.

For primary production values are net daytime photic zone production for the mid Hudson. For other systems we assumed the "NPP" was equivalent to our NDPZP. Values are expressed as daily means for the entire year. Non Hudson data are from Cadee and Hegeman, 1974; Cloern, 1984; Cloern, et al., 1985; Cole and Cloern, 1984; Bonnetto, 1983; Frey et al., 1984; Cadee, 1986; Ertl, 1985; Fisher et al., 1982; Flint et al., 1986; Gopinathan et al., 1984; Harding et al., 1986; Levasseur et al., 1984; Pennock and Sharp, 1986; Scott, 1978; Sinada and Karim, 1984; Shehata and Bader, 1985; Stockner and Cliff, 1979; Turner et al., 1979; Baker and Baker, 1979; Flemer, 1970; Furnas et al., 1976; Gilmartin, 1964; Haines and Dunstant, 1975; Keller, 1988; Kuparinen, 1987; Randall and Day, 1987.

In order to compare planktonic primary production in the tidal-freshwater Hudson more broadly to the saline parts of the estuary and New York Harbor, as well as to other estuaries and rivers, we need to revert to our estimate of NDPZP, which is akin to what most researchers report as "NPP."

Table 9.1. Phytoplankton primary production in the context of the organic C budget of the tidal, freshwater Hudson River

Primary producers	$g\,Cm^{-2}\,y^{-1}$ pre 1992			$g\,Cm^{-2}\,y^{-1}$ post 1992		
	GPP	R_a	NPP	GPP	R_a	NPP
phytoplankton	331	281	50	82	70	12
macrophytes (1)			30			41
periphyton (2)			2			2
TOTAL NPP			82			55
WATERSHED INPUTS (3)			650			650
Net inputs			732			705
Heterotrophic R		R_h			R_h	
pelagic bacteria (4)		116			116	
zebra mussel (5)		0			83	
other benthos (6)		9			9	
TOTAL R_h		125			208	
GPP-R (ECOSYSTEM) (7)			−43			−153
Net advective outputs (8)			607			497

The phytoplankton values here are derived from measurements near Kingston-Rhinecliff, New York, and do not take into account spatial variation in biomass and parameters in the freshwater river as a whole, and thus, are not identical to estimates in other papers (see Caraco et al., 1997; 2000). The values of GPP, R_a and NPP for the phytoplankton are explained in the text.

(1) Values for macrophytes from Cole and Caraco, 2001; Caraco et al., 2000; Harley and Findlay 1994. We assumed that the values for daily macrophyte net production in Caraco et al., 2000 apply to a 100-d season; we cannot estimate macrophyte gross production or respiration from this approach.

(2) Periphyton values are approximate and based on biomass data in Bianchi et al., 1993 assuming the same biomass-based photosynthesis as phytoplankton. This is likely an overestimate.

(3) Watershed inputs are based on Howarth et al., 1996.

(4,5,6) These values come from averages from several sources (Findlay et al., 1998; Roland and Cole, 1999; Caraco et al., 2000; Cole and Caraco, 2001), and are explained in those sources. Values should be considered approximate only.

(7) This is the difference of GPP and R in this table.

(8) Net advective outputs are estimated as difference between all inputs (GPP + watershed inputs) − R. In some cases we were able to estimate values both prior to the zebra mussel invasion and following it; where we did not have a separate estimate for both periods we used the existing value for both periods.

In the years prior to the zebra mussel invasion, annual NDPZP for the mid Hudson region averaged 243 ± 40 g C m^{-2} y^{-1}, among years (with 95 percent CI) a value close to that reported by Malone (1977) for New York Harbor and measured recently at the Verrazano Narrows by Taylor et al. (G. Taylor, personal communication). (Fig. 9.9B). In comparison to other rivers primary production in the tidal-freshwater Hudson was moderately high. Following the zebra mussel invasion (1993–2000) NDPZP for the mid Hudson region averaged 61 ± 8.3 g C m^{-2} y^{-1}, which groups the Hudson during this period with systems with the lowest reported planktonic primary production for rivers and estuaries in general.

Phytoplankton Primary Production in Context of the Hudson River Organic C Balance

In Table 9.1 we show estimates of the major inputs and outputs of organic C to the tidal-freshwater portion of the Hudson River based on the work of many investigators. The C balance of the lower estuary is discussed in the chapter by Howarth et al. (Chapter 10). The balance here is shown for both the pre-zebra mussel period (prior to 1992) and the post-zebra mussel period because of the major impact these bivalves have had on phytoplankton and because they have become an important component of respiration in the system. Unlike a number of large estuaries, phytoplankton production in the

Table 9.2. Net ecosystem heterotrophy (system GPP – system R) for the tidal-freshwater Hudson from several different approaches

Approach	Net Ecosystem Heterotrophy g Cm^{-2} y^{-1}		Reference
	pre 1992	post 1992	
Component GPP and R	43	153	This study
Annual O$_2$ influx	44	127	Caraco et al., 2000
Annual CO$_2$ influx	–	100–190	Raymond et al., 1997
Longitudinal DOC Profile	–	85–185	Cole and Caraco, 2001
Diel O$_2$	(293)		Howarth et al., 1996
Mean	44	161	

Each approach estimates the difference between annual GPP and annual R and is a minimum estimate of the amount of terrestrially derived organic C that must be respired within the river. The approaches and their limitations are explained in the references. See also Findlay et al., 1998. The diel O$_2$ from Howarth et al., 1996 includes some data in the post-zebra mussel period. It is not included in the mean.

tidal-freshwater river is not the dominant source of organic matter. Further, respiration of phytoplankton themselves greatly reduces the amount of organic C of phytoplankton origin that is available to consumers (Table 9.1). In the post-zebra mussel period primary production from aquatic macrophytes is comparable to that of phytoplankton, especially if we consider the net input (GPP-plant respiration). In both periods, loading of dissolved and particulate organic matter from the watershed is by far the dominant input, and advective losses downstream the dominant output. The net balance shows that the respiration of the known components in the river exceeds primary production, and this difference is more pronounced during the zebra mussel period. Thus, during the pre-1992 period, respiration exceeded GPP by about 43 g C m^{-2} y^{-1} and by about three times this amount (153 g C m^{-2} y^{-1}) post 1992. The R in excess of GPP must be supported by the respiration of some of the vast amount of organic material loaded from the watershed.

If it is true that the sum of the components of heterotrophic respiration exceed net primary production, we should be able to measure this net heterotrophy at the ecosystem scale. For example, if R exceeds GPP, the system will be undersaturated in dissolved O$_2$, and O$_2$ will invade from the atmosphere. Similarly the system will be supersaturated in CO$_2$ and CO$_2$ will evade to the atmosphere. Both these conditions are true for the

Hudson (Raymond, Caraco, and Cole, 1997; Caraco et al., 2000; Cole and Caraco, 2001). Estimates of these net gas balances are shown in Table 9.2 and show at least broad agreement to the balance of the known components. While there is a good deal of uncertainty in each individual estimate, all of them indicate that the tidal, freshwater Hudson is net heterotrophic and magnitude is not extremely far from that based on the sum of the components that we outlined in Table 9.1.

Future Research

The ecosystem balance concurs with the budget of the components that the respiration of heterotrophic organisms exceeds the input from phytoplankton production. The budget implies that some key heterotrophic organisms must utilize organic matter that was produced outside of the river. For example, the estimate of zebra mussel respiration alone is greater than the net input of organic matter from phytoplankton plus periphyton plus macrophytes. This is also true for pelagic bacteria. Clearly, organic matter of terrestrial origin is an important subsidy for the Hudson River food web. On the other hand, this balance does not imply that phytoplankton are unimportant. In fact, phytoplankton are likely a major resource for some components of the pelagic food web that lead to the production of some fish. In systems, like the Hudson, with multiple types of organic inputs and multiple primary producers, it is often difficult to tease apart the key pathways that lead to the production of important resource species. Stable C isotopes, which offer a hopeful approach in some ecosystems, are not a viable approach in the Hudson because the signals of the phytoplankton terrestrial inputs are nearly identical (see Caraco et al., 1998). Radiocarbon (^{14}C) appears to be a more useful tracer since it was discovered recently that much of the terrestrial input is quite old (500 to 1,500 years before present; Raymond and Bauer, 2001; Cole and Caraco, 2001), but much work remains to be done. Current research, which traces the production of unique fatty acids from either phytoplankton or bacteria into consumers, has revealed that copepods and some larval pelagic fish are tightly coupled to phytoplankton rather than to terrestrial detritus (K. Limburg and N. Caraco, unpublished data). The decline in some benthic filter-feeding invertebrates in conjunction with the phytoplankton decline brought about by the zebra mussel is also consistent with the idea that phytoplankton were a key element of their nutrition. Future work needs to seek ways to further unravel the importance of phytoplankton to the food web and to key resource species.

Implications for Management

To control eutrophication, reducing nutrient load is a key goal of ecosystem management. In systems in which the phytoplankton are strongly nutrient limited, the loading of nutrients (typically N and P) lead to large and often undesirable blooms of phytoplankton (Howarth, 1988). The sinking and decomposition of these blooms can lead to oxygen depletion in the sediments and bottom waters in systems in which the water column is physically stratified. The tidal-freshwater Hudson is neither stratified nor nutrient limited. Nutrient concentrations are high, but phytoplankton are limited by the other factors we have discussed here: light; deep mixing; and grazing. Thus lowering the input of these nutrients will not greatly affect phytoplankton or oxygen in this part of the river. On the other hand, if one were to try to manage the Hudson for water clarity by reducing the input of silts and clays, dramatic increases in phytoplankton would be expected (Caraco et al., 1997). If the

Hudson River lacked the suspended matter that now absorbs light, phytoplankton would be able to use much of the pools of inorganic N and P that are now exported downstream. In a simulation model of this effect, Caraco et al. (1997) suggested that summertime chlorophyll-a would be as high as 70 to 80 µg liter^{-1} (about 20 times the present values) before self shading or P-limitation further limited bloom formation in the mid-Hudson region. Thus while the abatement of turbidity might seem desirable to improve the river aesthetically and for swimming, it is likely to also lead to dramatic increases in eutrophication.

REFERENCES

Alpine, A. E., and Cloern, J. E. 1988, Phytoplankton growth rates in a light-limited environment, San Francisco Bay. *Marine Ecology Progress Series.* **44**:167–73.

Baker, A. L., and Baker, K. K. 1979. Effects of temperature and current discharge on the concentration and photosynthetic activity of the phytoplankton in the upper Mississippi River. *Freshwater Biology.* **9**:191–98.

Banse, K. 1976. Rates of growth, respiration and photosynthesis of unicellular algae as related to cell size: A review. *Journal of Phycology.* **12**:135–40.

Beardall, J., and Raven, J. A. 1990. Pathways and mechanisms of respiration in microalgae. *Marine Microbial Food Webs.* **4**:7–30.

Bianchi, T., Findlay, S., and Dawson, R. 1993. Organic matter sources in the water column and sediments of the Hudson River Estuary: the use of plant pigments as tracers. *Estuarine and Coastal Shelf Science.* **36**:359–76.

Bonnetto, C. A. 1983. Fitoplancton y produccion primaria del Parana Medio. *Ecosur.* **10**:79–102.

Brock, T. D. 1979. *Biology of microorganisms*, 3rd edition. Englewood Cliffs, NJ: Prentice-Hall, 802 pp.

Cadee, G. C. 1986. Increased phytoplankton primary production in the Marsdiep Area (Western Dutch Wadden Sea). *Netherlands Journal of Sea Research.* **20**:285–90.

Cadee, G. C., and Hegman, J. 1974. Primary production of phytoplankton in the Dutch Waddeen Sea. *Netherlands Journal of Sea Research.* **8**:240–59.

Caraco, N. F., Cole, J. J., Raymond, P. A., Strayer, D. L., Pace, M. L., Findlay, S., and Fischer, D. T. 1997. Zebra mussel invasion in a large turbid river: Phytoplankton response to increased grazing. *Ecology.* **78**:602.

Caraco, N. F., Lampman, G. G., Cole, J. J., Limburg, K. E., Pace, M. L., and Fischer, D. 1998. Microbial assimilation of DIN in a nitrogen rich estuary: implications for food quality and isotope studies. *Marine Ecology Progress Series*. **167**: 59–71.

Caraco, N. F., Cole, J. J., Findlay, S. E. G., Fischer, D., Lampman, G. G., Pace, M. L., and Strayer, D. L. 2000. Dissolved oxygen declines in the Hudson River associated with the invasion of the zebra mussel (*Dreissena polymorpha*). *Environmental Science and Technology*. **34**:1204–1210.

Cloern, J. E. 1984. Does the benthos control phytoplankton biomass in south San Francisco Bay. *Marine Ecology Progress Series*. **9**:191–202.

Cloern, J. E. 1987. Turbidity as a control on phytoplankton biomass and productivity in estuaries. *Continental Shelf Research*. **7**:1367–81.

Cloern, J. E., Cole, B. E., Wong, R. L. G., and Alpine, A. E. 1985. Temporal dynamics of estuarine phytoplankton: A case study of San Francisco Bay. *Hydrobiologia*. **129**:153–76.

Cole, B. E., and Cloern, J. E. 1984. Significance of biomass and light availability to phytoplankton productivity in San Francisco Bay. *Marine Ecology Progress Series*. **17**:15–24.

Cole, J. J., Caraco, N. F., and Peierls, B. 1992. Can phytoplankton maintain a positive balance in a turbid, freshwater, tidal estuary? *Limnology and Oceanography*. **37**:1608–1617.

Cole, J. J., and Caraco, N. F. 2001. Carbon in catchments: Connecting terrestrial carbon losses with aquatic metabolism. *Marine and Freshwater Research*. **52**:101–110.

Cote, B., and Platt, T. 1983. Day to day variations in the spring-summer photosynthetic parameters of coastal marine phytoplankton. *Limnology and Oceanography*. **28**:320–44.

Ertl, M. 1985. The effects of the hydrological regime on primary production in the main stream and the side arms of the River Danube. *Archive für Hydrobiolia Supplement*. **68**:139–48.

Falkowski, P. G., Dubinsky, Z., and Santostefano, G. 1985. Light-enhanced dark respiration in phytoplankton. *Verhandlungen Internationale Vereinigung Limnologie*. **22**:2830–33.

Findlay, S. E. G., Sinsabaugh, R. L., Fischer, D. T., and Franchini, P. 1998. Sources of dissolved organic carbon supporting planktonic bacterial production in the tidal-freshwater Hudson River. *Ecosystems*. **1**:227–39.

Fisher, T. R., Carlson, P. A., and Barber, R. T. 1982. Carbon and nitrogen primary productivity in three North Carolina estuaries. *Estuarine and Coastal Shelf Science*. **15**:621–44.

Fisher, T. R., Peele, E. R., Ammerman, J. W., and Harding, Jr., L. W. 1992. Nutrient limitation of phytoplankton in Chesapeake Bay. *Marine Ecology Progress Series*. **82**:51–63.

Flemer, D. A. 1970. Primary production in the Chesapeake Bay. *Chesapeake Science*. **11**:117–29.

Flint, R. W., Powell, G. L., and Kalke, R. D. 1986. Ecological effects from the balance between new and recycled nitrogen in Texas coastal waters. *Estuaries*. **9**:284–94.

Frederick, S. W., Heffner, R. L., Packard, A. T., Eldridge, P. M., Eldridge, J. C., Schumacher, G. J., Eichorn, K. L., Currie, J. H., Richards, J. N., and Boody, O. C. I. 1976. Notes on phytoplankton distribution in the Hudson River Estuary. *Hudson River Ecology: Fourth Symposium*. Hudson River Environmental Society, Consolidated Edison Auditorium, New York, NY.

Frey, B. E., Small, L. F., and Lara-Lara, R. 1984. *Water column primary production in the Columbia River Estuary*. Columbia River Estuary Data Development Program, Astoria, Oregon.

Furnas, B. E., Hitchcock, G. L., and Smayda, T. J. 1976. Nutrient-phytoplankton relationships in Narragansett Bay during the summer bloom, in Wiley, M. (ed). *Estuarine Process*, Vol. 1. New York: Academic Press, pp. 118–133.

Garside, C., Malone, T. C., Roels, O. A., and Sharfstein, B. A. 1976. An evaluation of sewage derived nutrients and their influence on the Hudson River Estuary and New York Bight. *Estuarine and Coastal Shelf Science*. **4**:281–99.

Geider, R. J., and Osborne, B. A. 1989. Respiration and microalgal growth: a review of the quantitative relationship between dark respiration and growth. *New Phytologist*. **112**:327–41.

Gilmartin, M. 1964. The primary production of a British Columbia fjord. *Journal of Fisheries Research Board of Canada*. **21**:505–37.

Gopinathan, C. P., Nair, R., and Nair, A. K. K. 1984. Quantitative ecology of phytoplankton in the Cochlin Backwater. *Indian Journal of Fisheries*. **31**:325–36.

Haines, E. B., and Dunstant, W. M. 1975. The distribution and relation of particulate organic material and primary productivity in the Georgia Bight. *Estuarine and Coastal Shelf Science*. **3**:431–41.

Harding, L. W., Jr., Meeson, B. W., and Fisher, T. R. 1986. Phytoplankton production in two east coast estuaries: Photosynthesis light functions and patterns of carbon assimilation in Chesapeake and Delaware Bays. *Estuarine and Coastal Shelf Science*. **23**:773–806.

Harley, M., and Findlay, S. 1994. Photosynthesis-irradiance relationships for three species of submersed macrophytes in the tidal freshwater Hudson River. *Estuaries.* **17**:200–205.

Howarth, R. W. 1988. Nutrient limitation of primary production in marine ecosystems. *Annual Review of Ecology and Systematics.* **19**:89–110.

Howarth, R. W., Schneider, R., and Swaney, D. 1996. Metabolism and organic carbon fluxes in the tidal freshwater Hudson River. *Estuaries.* **19**:848–65.

Howarth, R. W., Marino, R., Swaney, D. P., and Boyer, E. W. (this volume). Wastewater and watershed influences on primary productivity and oxygen dynamics in the lower Hudson River estuary. In: J. S. Levinton and J. R. Waldman (eds.). *The Hudson River Estuary.* Cambridge University Press.

Howells, G. P., and Weaver, S. 1969. Studies on phytoplankton at Indian Point, in G. P. Howells and G. J. Lauer (eds.), *Hudson River Ecology: Proceeding of a symposium.* New York State Department of Environmental Conservation, pp. 231–61.

IES (Institute of Ecosystem Studies), Environmental Monitoring Program. 2001. Institute of Ecosystem Studies, Box AB, Millbrook, NY 12545, www.ecostudies.org.

Iqbal, M. 1983. *An Introduction to Solar Radiation.* New York: Academic Press, 153 pp.

Keller, A. 1988. Estimating phytoplankton productivity from light availability and biomass in the MERL mesocosms and Narragansett Bay. *Marine Ecology Progress Series.* **45**:159–69.

Kobayashi, T., Williams, S., and Kotlash, A. 2000. Autotrophic picoplankton in a regulated coastal river in New South Wales. *Proceedings of the Linnean Society of New South Wales.* **122**:79–88.

Kuparinen, J. 1987. Production and respiration of overall plankton and ultraplankton communities at the entrance to the Gulf of Finland in the Baltic Sea. *Marine Biology.* **93**:591–607.

Lampman, G. G., Caraco, N. F., and Cole, J. J. 1999. Spatial and temporal patterns of nutrient concentration and export in the tidal Hudson River. *Estuaries.* **22**:285–96.

Laws, E. A. 1975. The importance of respiration losses in controlling the size distribution of marine phytoplankton. *Ecology.* **56**:419–26.

Levasseur, M., Therriault, J. C., and Legendre, L. 1984. Hierarchical control of phytoplankton succession by physical factors. *Marine Ecology Progress Series.* **19**:211–22.

Malone, T. C. 1975. Phytoplankton productivity in the apex of the New York Bight: Environmental regulation of productivity/chlorophyll *a. Limnology and Oceanography Special Symposium.* 260–71.

Malone, T. C. 1977. Environmental regulation of phytoplankton productivity in the lower Hudson Estuary. *Estuarine and Coastal Shelf Science.* **5**:157–71.

Marshall, H. 1988. Seasonal phytoplankton composition and concentration patterns within the Hudson River. Technical Report 018/86b/011. Hudson River Foundation. New York, NY.

Pace, M. L., and Lonsdale, D. J. (this volume). Ecology of the Hudson River Zooplankton Community. In J. S. Levinton and J. R. Waldman (eds.). *The Hudson River Estuary.* Cambridge University Press.

Pennock, J. R., and Sharp, J. H. 1986. Phytoplankton production in the Delaware estuary: Temporal and spatial variability. *Marine Ecology Progress Series.* **34**:143–55.

Peterson, D. H., and Festa, J. F. 1984. Numerical simulation of phytoplankton productivity in partially mixed estuaries. *Estuarine and Coastal Shelf Science.* **19**:563–89.

Randall, J. M., and Day, Jr., J. W. 1987. Effects of river discharge and vertical circulation on aquatic primary production in a turbid Louisiana estuary. *Netherlands Journal of Sea Research.* **21**: 231–42.

Raven, J. A., and Beardall, J. 1981. Respiration and photorespiration. *Canadian Bulletin of Fisheries and Aquatic Science.* **210**:55–82.

Raymond, P. A., and Bauer, J. E. 2001. Riverine export of aged organic matter to the North Atlantic Ocean. *Nature* (London) **409**:497–500.

Raymond, P. A., Caraco, N. F., and Cole, J. J. 1997. CO_2 concentration and atmospheric flux in the Hudson River. *Estuaries.* **20**:381–90.

Roland, F., and Cole, J. J. 1999. Regulation of bacterial growth efficiency in a large turbid estuary. *Aquatic Microbial Ecology.* **20**:31–8.

Scott, B. D. 1978. Phytoplankton distribution and light attenuation in Port Hacking Estuary. *Australian Journal of Marine and Freshwater Research.* **29**: 31–44.

Shaw, P. J., and Purdie, D. A. 2001. Phytoplankton photosynthesis-irradiance parameters in the near-shore UK coastal waters of the North Sea: temporal variation and environmental control. *Marine Ecology Progress Series.* **216**:83–94.

Shehata, S. A., and Bader, S. A. 1985. Effect of Nile River water-quality on algal distribution at Cairo, Egypt. *Environment International.* **11**:465–74.

Sinada, F., and Karim, A. G. A. 1984. A Quantitative study of the phytoplankton in the Blue and White Niles at Khartoum. *Hydrobiologia.* **110**: 47–55.

Sirois, D. L., and Frederick, S. W. 1978. Phytoplankton and primary production in the lower Hudson River Estuary. *Estuarine and Coastal Shelf Science.* **7**:413–423.

Smith, T. E., Stevenson, R. J. Caraco, N. F., and Cole, J. J. 1998. Changes in phytoplankton community structure during the zebra mussel (*Dreissena polymorpha*) invasion of the Hudson River (New York). *Journal of Plankton Research*. **20**:1567–79.

Stockner, J. G., and Cliff, D. D. 1979. Phytoplankton ecology of Vancouver Harbor. *Journal of the Fisheries Research Board of Canada*. **36**:1–10.

Stone, S., and Ganf, G. 1981. The influence of previous light history on the respiration of four species of freshwater phytoplankton. *Archive für Hydrobiolia Supplement*. **91**:435–62.

Strayer, D. L. (this volume). Alien species in the Hudson River. In: J. S. Levinton and J. R. Waldman (eds.). *The Hudson River Estuary*. Cambridge University Press.

Strayer, D. L., Caraco, N. F., Cole, J. J., Findlay, S., and Pace, M. L. 1999. Transformation of freshwater ecosystems by bivalves: a case study of zebra mussels in the Hudson River. *Bioscience*. **49**:19–27.

Swaney, D., Howarth, R. W., and Butler, T. J. 1999. A novel approach for estimating ecosystem production and respiration in estuaries: Application to the oligohaline and mesohaline Hudson River. *Limnology and Oceanography*. **44** (6):1522–29.

Turner, R. E., Woo, S. W., and Jitts, H. R. 1979. Phytoplankton production in a turbid, temperate salt marsh estuary. *Estuarine and Coastal Shelf Science*. **9**:603–613.

Williams, P. J. le B., Raine, C. T., and Bryan, J. R. 1979. Agreement between the carbon-14 and oxygen methods of measuring phytoplankton production: reassessment of the photosynthetic quotient. *Oceanologica Acta*. **2**:411–416.

Williams, P. J. le B., and Robertson, J. E. 1991. Overall planktonic oxygen and carbon dioxide metabolism: the problem of reconciling observations and calculations of photosynthetic quotients. *Journal of Plankton Research*. **13**:153–69.

10 Wastewater and Watershed Influences on Primary Productivity and Oxygen Dynamics in the Lower Hudson River Estuary

Robert W. Howarth, Roxanne Marino, Dennis P. Swaney, and Elizabeth W. Boyer

ABSTRACT Primary productivity in the saline Hudson River estuary is strongly regulated by water residence times in the estuary. Nutrient loads and concentrations are very high, and when residence times are more than two days, production is extremely high. When water residence times are less than two days, production rates are low to moderate. Residence times are controlled both by freshwater discharge into the estuary and by tidal mixing, so residence times are longest and production is highest during neap tides when freshwater discharge is low. Freshwater discharge was generally high in the 1970s, which kept primary production low. In contrast, freshwater discharge rates were lower in the 1990s, and the estuary became hypereutrophic.

Nutrient loading per area of estuary to the saline portion of the Hudson is probably the highest for any major estuary in North America. As of the 1990s, approximately 58 percent of the nitrogen and 81 percent of the phosphorus came from wastewater effluent and other urban discharges in the New York City metropolitan area. Some 42 percent of the nitrogen and 19 percent of the phosphorus came from upriver tributary sources. For nitrogen, these tributary inputs are dominated by nonpoint sources, with atmospheric deposition from fossil fuel combustion and agricultural sources contributing equally. Human activity has probably increased nitrogen loading to the Hudson estuary twelve-fold and phosphorus loading fifty-fold or more since European settlement. Nitrogen and phosphorus loadings to the estuary have decreased somewhat since 1970 due to universal secondary treatment of dry-weather wastewater effluents and a ban on phosphates in detergents.

The Hudson estuary suffered from low dissolved oxygen concentrations over much of the twentieth century, but by the mid 1990s, all dry-weather discharges from sewage treatment plants in the New York City region received secondary treatment. This greatly reduced labile organic carbon (BOD) loadings, and resulted in dissolved oxygen concentrations that in most recent years have met New York State standards. Between the 1970s and the 1990s, the estuary switched from sewage as the primary input of labile organic matter to phytoplankton primary production as the major input. Further improvement in water quality is desirable, with the goal of reducing the tropic status of the estuary from hypereutrophic to moderately eutrophic. This will require upgrading of sewage treatment plants to nutrient reduction technology, at an estimated cost of $112 to $277 million per year, and a substantial reduction in nitrogen loading from combined sewer overflows and from nonpoint sources.

Introduction

Over the past twenty years, the primary concern of water quality management in estuaries has switched from control of discharges of toxic substances and organic matter which contributes to biological oxygen demand (BOD) to control of nutrient pollution and eutrophication (NRC, 1993, 2000). In part, this is because of great success in reducing problems with BOD and toxics over this period, in the Hudson estuary and elsewhere (NRC, 1993). In addition, problems from excess nutrient inputs – and particularly nitrogen – have grown dramatically, to the point where nutrients are now considered the greatest pollution threat to coastal marine ecosystems (NRC, 2000; Howarth and Anderson et al., 2000). Some two-thirds of the estuaries in the contiguous United States are now moderately to severely degraded from nutrient overenrichment (Bricker et al., 1999). Estuaries vary in their sensitivity to nutrient pollution, and the Hudson in the past has been considered to be relatively insensitive (Bricker et al., 1999). However, our recent research demonstrates that primary productivity by phytoplankton in the saline regions of the Hudson estuary increased dramatically in the 1990s relative to the 1970s, and the Hudson is now quite eutrophic (Howarth and Swaney et al., 2000).

The Hudson River Estuary is profoundly influenced both by its watershed and by enormous inputs of materials from municipal wastewater

Table 10.1. Physical characteristics of the saline Hudson estuary in comparison to other representative estuaries in the temperate zone. Data for all estuaries except the Hudson are from the LOICZ web site (http://data.ecology.su.se/mnode/index.htm). Only estuaries larger than 15 km² are included

	Area of estuary (km²)	Drainage basin area (km²)	Ratio of basin area to estuary area	Riverine discharge per basin area (m y^{-1})	Riverine discharge per area of estuary (m³ km^{-2} s^{-1})	Mean water residence time (days)
Saline Hudson	149	34,680	233	0.54	4.0	1
Gulf of Riga	16,330	134,000	8	0.27	0.09	825
Narragansett Bay	264	3,500	13	0.86	0.36	26
Chesapeake Bay	11,000	164,180	15	0.35	0.16	230
Tomales Bay	16	560	35	0.16	0.19	15
Mobile Bay	1,060	115,000	108	0.60	2.1	8
Rio de la Plata	22,000	3,000,000	136	0.23	1.0	44
Szczecin Lagoon	687	118,780	173	0.14	0.73	45
Apalachicola Bay	260	45,000	173	0.65	3.6	2
Inner Thermaikos	336	72,000	214	0.07	0.48	14
Yalujiang estuary	170	62,630	368	0.62	7.1	5
Hawkesbury-Nepean	34	22,000	647	0.02	0.44	9
Swan-Canning	33	141,000	4,273	0.01	1.3	17

treatment plants. The estuary receives runoff from a watershed having an area of 34,600 km^2 (USGS, 2002). The freshwater discharge from the watershed is similar to that in several other large estuaries, such as Delaware Bay, San Francisco Bay, and Long Island Sound (Limburg, Moran, and McDowell, 1986; Howarth and Swaney et al., 2000; http://data.ecology.su.se/MNODE/wmap.htm; http://cads.nos.noaa.gov). However, when compared to other well-known estuaries with large drainage basins which are part of the Land-Ocean Interactions in the Coastal Zone (LOICZ) project data set, the surface area of the Hudson River Estuary is fairly small, and thus the freshwater discharge per area of estuary is quite high (Table 10.1). This contributes to a rapid flushing of the estuary, with water residence times on the scale of 0.1 to 4 days (Howarth and Swaney et al., 2000). By comparison, the water residence times in Delaware Bay, Chesapeake Bay, and Long Island Sound are on the order of 60, 250, and 1,100 days, respectively (Nixon et al., 1996; http://data.ecology.su.se/MNODE/wmap.htm; http://cads.nos.noaa.gov). Rapid flushing, particularly when water residence times are less than one to two days, makes the Hudson less sensitive to nutrient pollution than other estuaries with longer water residence times (Howarth and Swaney et al., 2000).

Some 4.4 million people live in the watershed of the Hudson River upstream of the Battery in Manhattan (U.S. Census Bureau, 2002), giving an average population density of 128 individuals km^{-2}. The majority live in the New York City metropolitan area, with fewer living in the mostly forested basin upriver (Howarth, Fruci, and Sherman, 1991; Swaney, Sherman, and Howarth, 1996; Boyer et al., 2002). Note that the population for the entire New York City metropolitan area is substantially higher than 4.4 million, but many of these live in watersheds and sewersheds that do not flow into the Hudson, but rather into Long Island Sound, the Raritan, lower New York Harbor, Jamaica Bay, and other water bodies. The Hudson River Estuary receives a substantial amount of sewage from the New York City metropolitan area, and as a result, the nutrient loading per area or volume of estuary is the highest for any large estuary in the United States (Nixon and Pilson, 1983; NRC, 1993). BOD loading is also high. The first sewers in New York City were constructed in 1696, and the sewer system grew

steadily in collection capacity until the middle of the twentieth century (Brosnan and O'Shea, 1996). The first primary sewage treatment plants in the New York City metropolitan area were only built in the 1930s, and secondary treatment plants to reduce BOD loadings were not constructed until after such treatment was mandated by the Clean Water Act in 1972. Full secondary treatment of the waste stream was only achieved in the past decade (Brosnan and O'Shea, 1996). The result has been a dramatic increase in water quality, as measured by dissolved oxygen levels in the estuary (see chapter 23).

In this chapter, we discuss how freshwater discharge and nutrients affect primary productivity in the saline Hudson River estuary, how human activity has altered the inputs of nutrients and labile organic matter to the estuary over time, what regulates oxygen concentrations in the estuary, and what actions might be taken to further improve water quality in the Hudson in the future. Our focus is on the portion of the Hudson River which begins at the Battery at the southern tip of Manhattan and extends northward 66 km to the northern end of Haverstraw Bay (Fig. 10.1). So defined, the saline Hudson estuary has an area of 149 km^2 and a volume of 1.11 km^3 (estimated from NOAA navigational charts). The estuary can be divided into the saltier, mesohaline region from the Battery north 36 km and the less salty, oligohaline region from river km 36 north to river km 66, an area that includes the Tappan Zee and Haverstraw Bay.

Primary Productivity: Rates and Controls

Nutrient concentrations and loadings in the saline Hudson River estuary are very high, and primary productivity is regulated largely by physical factors (Malone, 1977; Howarth and Swaney et al., 2000). Perhaps the most important of these physical factors is water residence time. Most species of phytoplankton have maximum growth rates that result in a doubling of the population in roughly one day, with larger species having somewhat longer doubling times ranging from two to fifteen days (Banse, 1976; Malone, 1977, 1980; Chan, 2001). Given the short residence times, much of the time phytoplankton are flushed from the Hudson estuary about as rapidly as they grow, limiting the size of populations and keeping rates of primary productivity fairly low.

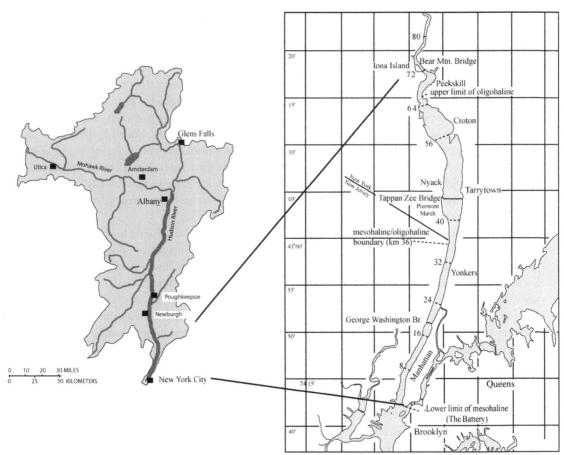

Figure 10.1. Hudson River basin and saline Hudson River estuary. As defined in this chapter, the Hudson River estuary begins at the Battery at the southern tip of Manhattan and runs north. The boundary between the mesohaline and oligohaline estuary varies with freshwater discharge but is generally near river kilometer 36. The oligohaline estuary boundaries also vary with salinity but generally fall between river kilometer 36 and 66. See text for further discussion.

Both the tidal cycle and freshwater discharge into the Hudson affect water residence times in the estuary. When freshwater discharge at the Green Island gauging station is greater than 300 m^3 sec^{-1}, water residence times in the photic zone are less than one day (Fig. 10.2A). At lower rates of discharge, water residence times vary greatly, with at least some of this variation related to the tidal cycle; shorter residence times are more prevalent during the spring-tide period of the month when tidal mixing is greater, and neap tides favor longer water residence times.

In a series of cruises in the mid 1990s, we found that rates of gross primary production (GPP) were always less than 2 g C m^{-2} d^{-1} and generally less than 1 g C m^{-2} d^{-1} when the freshwater

discharge (measured at Green Island) was greater than 300 m^3 sec^{-1}, leading to short water residence times (Fig. 10.2B). Substantially higher rates of production, up to 18 g C m^{-2} d^{-1}, were found during some neap tide cycles when freshwater discharge was low and water residence times in the photic zone exceeded two days. A similar effect of discharge on ^{14}C-production in the lower Hudson estuary during the 1990s has been reported by Taylor, Way, and Scranton (2003). In addition to increased water residence times, greater light penetration into the water column may have favored high rates of production during periods of low discharge and low tidal mixing (Fig. 10.2C). The greater light penetration likely resulted from lessened input of sediment from up river and decreased resuspension of

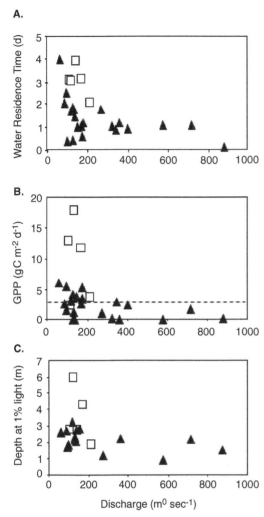

Figure 10.2. Relationship between freshwater discharge and water residence time (A), GPP (B), and light penetration (C) in the estuary during 25 cruises conducted during the spring, summer, and fall of 1994, 1995, and 1997. Open symbols represent times when tidal amplitude was <1.15 m; dark symbols represents tides greater than 1.15 m. The dashed line in (B) represents the approximate value for GPP above which an estuary is considered to be hypereutrophic. Discharge data are from the USGS monitoring station at Green Island and represent approximately two-thirds of the total discharge into the estuary. Reprinted from Howarth et al. (2000a).

bottom sediments. Estuaries have been classified as eutrophic when annual production ranges between 300 and 500 g C m^{-2} y^{-1}, and as hypereutrophic when annual production exceeds 500 g C m^{-2} y^{-1} (Nixon, 1995; NRC, 2000). This corresponds to a daily production rate of 2 to 3 g C m^{-2} d^{-1} on

average during the active growing season (NRC, 2000; Howarth and Swaney et al., 2000). Thus, the saline Hudson estuary would be considered hypereutrophic during neap tide periods when freshwater discharge is low, but not when discharge is high (Fig. 10.2B).

Prior to our measurements in the 1990s, the only published data on rates of primary productivity in the saline Hudson estuary were from studies in the early1970s. Then rates were generally less than 1 g C m^{-2} d^{-1} and were never higher than 2 g C m^{-2} d^{-1} (Malone, 1977; Sirois and Fredrick, 1978). These lower primary production values are consistent with our measurements during the 1990s for periods of high discharge, and in fact the decade of the 1970s was a wetter decade with generally higher rates of freshwater discharge (Fig. 10.3). Average summer discharge rates at Green Island exceeded 200 m^3 sec^{-1} in most of the years of the early to mid 1970s and exceeded 300 m^3 sec^{-1} in every year except 1972. The resulting high flushing and corresponding low rates of productivity during that period gave rise to the thought that the Hudson estuary is relatively insensitive to eutrophication despite the very high nutrient concentrations present (Garside et al., 1976; Malone, 1977; Bricker et al., 1999).

Different methods were used to measure productivity in the 1970s than in the 1990s, which can complicate direct comparison of the data sets. The measurements in the 1990s were made from in situ changes in dissolved oxygen concentrations over a diel cycle (Swaney et al., 1999), whereas the measurements in the 1970s were made by the ^{14}C method (O'Reilly et al., 1976; Malone, 1977) and by the light-dark bottle method (Sirois and Fredrick 1978). The in-situ oxygen technique would be expected to give a more reliable and most likely higher estimate of gross primary production (GPP) than the other two methods (Swaney, Howarth, and Butler, 1999; Howarth and Michaels, 2000). The ^{14}C method in particular would be expected to give a lower estimate, as it measures a rate of carbon fixation somewhere between net and gross primary production (Howarth and Michaels, 2000). Nonetheless, the apparent increase in production between the 1970s and the 1990s is probably real at least in part, as chlorophyll levels were also higher in the 1990s, while rates of production per

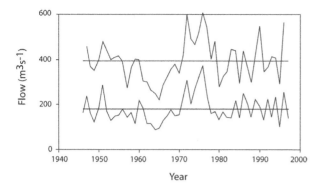

Figure 10.3. Average freshwater discharge to the Hudson at the USGS gauging station at Green Island, NY. Upper curve shows annual average flows, lower curve shows average summertime flows. Horizontal lines indicate mean values for annual and summertime discharge. Reprinted from Howarth et al. (2000a).

chlorophyll appear to be similar in both sets of studies (Howarth and Swaney et al., 2000). A conceptual model of how freshwater discharge down the Hudson River affects primary productivity in the Hudson estuary is presented in Figure 10.4.

Most of our data were collected between May and October, and we have not previously estimated an annual rate of production. However, for the six-month period from May through October over several years, we found GPP to range between 300 and 370 g C m^{-2} in the oligohaline estuary and 500 to 750 g C m^{-2} in the mesohaline estuary (Swaney et al., 1999, and our unpublished data). By comparison, for the May to October period for various studies in 1972–4, production was roughly 150 g C m^{-2} in the mesohaline estuary and 180 g C m^{-2} for the oligohaline estuary (Swaney et al., 1999, using data from Sirois and Fredrick, 1978 and Malone, 1977). Overall, it would appear that GPP in the 1990s was perhaps twice the rate of production reported for the 1970s in the oligohaline Hudson estuary and four times the rate reported for the mesohaline estuary. Annual productivity reported for the saline Hudson estuary in the 1970s was approximately

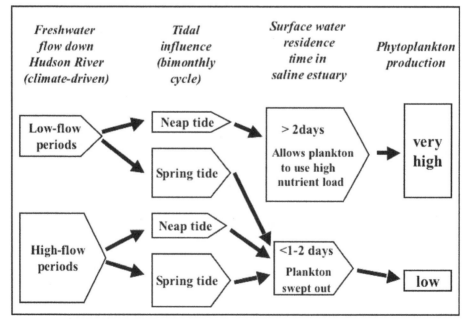

Figure 10.4. Conceptual model of how the freshwater flow down the Hudson River interacts with the bimonthly tidal cycle to regulate water residence times and rates of primary productivity in the saline Hudson River estuary. The estuary receives extremely high inputs of nutrients, but a rapid flushing of water from the estuary prevents phytoplankton blooms from occurring except when both freshwater flow and tidal mixing are low.

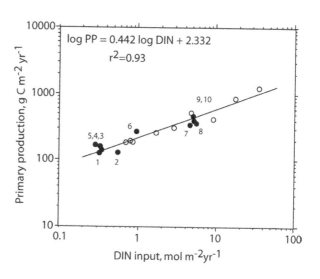

Figure 10.5. Primary productivity as function of the input of inorganic nitrogen per area for a variety of marine ecosystems. The open circles are from experimental mesocosm studies at the MERL facility. Dark circles represent natural ecosystems. Reprinted from Nixon et al. (1996).

1.3 times the rate measured over the May to June period in the 1970s (O'Reilly, Thomas, and Evans, 1976; Malone, 1977; Sirois and Fredrick, 1978; Limburg et al., 1986; Malone and Conley, 1996; Swaney et al., 1999). Assuming that this relationship holds for our data, mean annual rates of GPP in the Hudson during the 1990s can be estimated as 850 g C m^{-2} y^{-1} in the mesohaline estuary and 450 g C m^{-2} y^{-1} in the oligohaline estuary. The freshwater discharge during the 1990s is much more characteristic of the situation for the Hudson over the past six decades than is that of the 1970s (Fig. 10.3), so our estimates are a better reflection of long-term average rates of GPP in the saline Hudson. Future climate change may well lessen freshwater discharge from the Hudson during the summer, continuing a trend of high production (Howarth and Swaney et al., 2000; Scavia et al., 2002).

For many marine and estuarine ecosystems, the log-transformed rate of primary production (measured by the ^{14}C method) is a linear function of the log-transformed inorganic nitrogen loading rate (Fig. 10.5; Nixon et al., 1996). While primary productivity in many estuaries is less than predicted by the regression of Nixon et al. (1996) due to a variety of factors including rapid flushing and light limitation (NRC, 2000; Cloern, 2001), the regression sets a reasonable upper bound for the relationship between nutrient loading and production in estuaries if these physical factors were not limiting. Nitrogen (N) loading to the Hudson estuary is estimated as

43×10^3 tons N y^{-1} (Table 10.2, and discussion in section to follow in "Nutrient Loading in the Past 30 Years"), most of which is as inorganic nitrogen (Malone and Conley, 1996). This corresponds to an average loading per area of the estuary of 290 g N m^{-2} y^{-1}, although in fact the loading in the oligohaline estuary would be somewhat less, as most of the nutrient input enters directly into the mesohaline estuary near Manhattan and some of this N is exported from the estuary rather than being mixed into the oligohaline estuary. This level of nitrogen loading corresponds to a predicted value for ^{14}C primary production in the Hudson estuary of 820 g C m^{-2} y^{-1} (Fig. 10.5), which is remarkably close to our roughly estimated annual value of GPP in the mesohaline estuary (850 g C m^{-2} y^{-1}). While we might expect the maximum value of productivity predicted from nutrient loading to be higher than that measured in situ, ^{14}C productivity underestimates GPP. We tentatively conclude that the rates of GPP measured during the 1990s reflect the maximum rate that can be obtained in the Hudson under its current nutrient loading regime because of the constraint imposed by short water residence times from advection and tidal mixing.

Nutrient Loading over the Past Thirty Years

Nutrient inputs to the Hudson estuary are of interest both because they set an upper limit on rates of GPP there and because much of the nitrogen and phosphorus is exported from the Hudson to other

Table 10.2. Loadings of total nitrogen and phosphorus to the saline Hudson River estuary

	Early 1970s	Mid 1990s
Total nitrogen (10^3 tons y^{-1})	49	43
Contribution from wastewater plants effluent	61%	53%
Contribution from upriver tributaries	37%	42%
Contribution from CSOs and storm water	37% 2%	42% 5%
Phosphorus (10^3 tons y^{-1})	9.6	4.8
Contribution from wastewater plants effluent	88%	77%
Contribution from upriver tributaries	10%	19%
Contribution from CSOs and storm water	2%	4%

Note: the input from the ocean and downstream aquatic ecosystems are not included; see text for derivation of estimates.

parts of New York Harbor and to the coastal waters of the New York Bight. Primary production in lower New York Bay and in the plume of the Hudson River in the 1970s and 1980s was reported to be in the range of 600 to 800 g C m^{-2} y^{-1} (O'Reilly et al., 1976; Malone and Conley, 1996), indicating that these systems are quite eutrophic (Nixon, 1995; NRC, 2000). Chlorophyll concentrations in the plume of the Hudson River on the continental shelf range up to 20 µg l^{-1} (Malone and Conley, 1996), levels which also indicate a high degree of eutrophication (NRC, 1993). The apex of the New York Bight (an area of 1,250 km^2) becomes hypoxic every year, and a large region of the Bight became anoxic in 1976 (Mearns et al., 1982).

Nutrients enter the saline Hudson estuary from wastewater in the New York City metropolitan area, from combined sewer overflows and storm runoff in the metropolitan area, from the freshwater portion of the Hudson River (above river km 66), and from the salt water entering the estuary from the ocean. In this chapter, we only estimate the inputs from sources within the watershed, including the tributary sources coming down the Hudson River. While first-order estimates of nutrient exchange with the sea are possible under the assumption of steady state

(Gordon et al., 1996), this term is difficult to assess without detailed hydrodynamic modeling, and generally has not been estimated in nutrient budgets for other estuaries (Nixon et al., 1996; NRC, 2000). In the case of the Hudson, it may be large, as the salt water entering the estuary first passes through Raritan Bay and lower New York harbor, and these systems receive substantial nutrient inputs themselves.

The saline Hudson estuary receives a daily input of wastewater of approximately 3.4×10^6 m^3 d^{-1} (calculated from data in Clark et al., 1992), or one third of the total wastewater flux for the entire New York City metropolitan area, an estimated 10×10^6 m^3 d^{-1} (Clark et al., 1992; Brosnan and O'Shea, 1996). By the early 1990s, all of the dry-weather sewage discharges in the metropolitan area received secondary treatment (Brosnan and O'Shea, 1996; Hetling al., 2003; Chapter 23, this volume). The effluent from the average secondary sewage treatment plant in the United States has a total nitrogen concentration of 19 g N m^{-3} and a total phosphorus content of 3 g P m^{-3} (NRC, 1993). Assuming that these values apply to the treatment plants in the New York City metropolitan area, we estimate nitrogen and phosphorus loads to the saline Hudson estuary in the 1990s as 24×10^3 metric tons N y^{-1} and 3.7×10^3 metric tons P y^{-1} (Table 10.2). Other estimates of nutrient inputs from wastewater to this portion of the estuary can be made by scaling the estimates of Brosnan and O'Shea (1996) for the entire metropolitan waste flow to the percentage of the wastewater flow that enters the saline Hudson estuary (34 percent) and by similarly scaling the estimates of Hetling et al. (2003) and Brosnan et al. (Chapter 23, this volume), both of whom used the Verrazano Narrows as the lower limit of the Hudson estuary and therefore included a significantly greater urban watershed and population. The estimates for nitrogen input to the estuary calculated this way are all very similar to that estimated using the NRC, concentration data and wastewater flows (within 15 percent); however, the estimates for phosphorus input are only

2.1×10^3 to 2.5×10^3 tons P y^{-1}, values that are 30 percent to 40 percent lower.

For the entire metropolitan New York City area, Brosnan and O'Shea estimate that nitrogen and phosphorus inputs in combined sewer overflows (CSOs) and in storm water runoff are 4.1×10^3 tons N y^{-1} and 0.67×10^3 tons P y^{-1}. If we assume that the percentage of these inputs that go directly into the Hudson estuary is one third, as is true for wastewater effluent, then we can estimate these other urban inputs to the estuary as 1.4×10^3 tons N y^{-1} and 0.22×10^3 tons P y^{-1} (Table 10.2).

Lampman, Caraco, and Cole (1999) have estimated the flows of total nitrogen and phosphorus down the Hudson River as 18×10^3 tons N y^{-1} and 0.9×10^3 tons P y^{-1} at a point 125 km north of the Battery, or 60 km north of the beginning of the oligohaline estuary in Haverstraw Bay. This is a conservative estimate of the input of these nutrients to the saline estuary, as additional nitrogen and phosphorus enter the freshwater Hudson from tributaries over this 60 km stretch. Nonetheless, the estimates of Lampman et al. (1999) are the best available for total nutrient loading to the estuary from the upstream Hudson and its tributaries (Table 10.2).

These non-point source estimates of N and P input from the freshwater Hudson, combined with the total urban inputs (wastewater, CSOs and storm water runoff) result in an estimate of the total nutrient load to the saline Hudson estuary as of the mid 1990s of 43×10^3 tons N y^{-1} and 4.8×10^3 tons P y^{-1} (Table 10.2). For nitrogen, a similar but slightly smaller estimate (38×10^3 tons N y^{-1}) is obtained from the population density in the watershed and a regression model that relates population density to total nitrogen flux for large regions in the temperate zone (Howarth, 1998). Wastewater effluent plus CSOs and storm water runoff contribute 58 percent of the nitrogen and 81 percent of the phosphorus, while the upstream tributary sources contribute 42 percent of the nitrogen and 19 percent of the phosphorus (Table 10.2).

Nitrogen and phosphorus loading rates expressed per area of the saline Hudson are 290 g N m^{-2} y^{-1} and 32 g P m^{-2} y^{-1}. These are far higher than reported for any other large estuary in the United States (NRC, 1993). For comparison, total nitrogen and phosphorus loadings to Chesapeake Bay are estimated to be twenty to thirty-fold less than the Hudson (13 g N m^{-2} y^{-1} and 1 g P m^{-2} y^{-1}; Boynton et al., 1995), yet the Chesapeake is considered an ecosystem that is highly degraded from nutrient pollution (Bricker et al., 1999; NRC, 2000). Nitrogen loadings to Delaware Bay, Narragansett Bay, and Boston Harbor are also all substantially lower than to the saline Hudson, at 27, 27, 130 g N m^{-2} y^{-1}, respectively (Nixon et al., 1996). Total phosphorus loadings to these three systems are 5, 2.6, and 21 g P m^{-2} y^{-1}, respectively (Nixon et al., 1996). Even by European standards, the nutrient loading to the Hudson estuary is high. The highly polluted Scheldt estuary in Belgium has a nitrogen loading of 190 g N m^{-2} y^{-1} and a phosphorus loading of 33 g P m^{-2} y^{-1} (Billen et al., 1985).

Of the nutrients entering the estuary from upstream in the Hudson River, a substantial portion likely comes from non-point sources. Boyer et al. (2002) compared the nitrogen cycle of sixteen major watersheds in the northeastern United States, including the Mohawk River valley and the basin of the upper Hudson River (above river km 260 where the Mohawk joins the Hudson). Together, these two tributaries comprise 60 percent of the area of the entire Hudson River basin (Boyer et al., 2002) and contribute 65 percent of the total freshwater discharge of the Hudson River (Howarth, Schneider, and Swaney, 1996a). For the upper Hudson and Mohawk River valleys combined, nitrogen deposition from the atmosphere contributes 41 percent of the flux of nitrogen from the landscape into the rivers. Agriculture contributes another 39 percent of the flux, with 28 percent of the nitrogen in the rivers originating from nitrogen fixation by agricultural crops and 11 percent from nitrogen fertilizer (Table 10.3; Boyer et al., 2002). The total nitrogen flux from these two watersheds is 13×10^3 tons y^{-1} (Table 10.3; Boyer et al., 2002), as compared to an estimated flux of 18×10^3 tons y^{-1} for nitrogen further down the Hudson River at river km 125 (Lampman et al., 1999). We would expect the nutrient flux between river km 125 and 66 to be even greater than this, since the watersheds of the tributaries there are more disturbed. The watersheds of the Mohawk River and upper Hudson are 73 percent forested on average (Table 10.3; Boyer et al., 2002), while the lower Hudson is 57 percent forested (Swaney et al., 1996). Also, atmospheric

Table 10.3. Characteristics of the Mohawk and Upper Hudson River basins (data from Boyer et al., 2002)

	Mohawk River Basin	Upper Hudson River Basin	Combined Mohawk and Upper Hudson River Basins
Area (km²)	8,935	11,942	20,877
Population density (# km⁻²)	54	32	42
Land Use			
forested	63%	81%	73%
agriculture	28%	10%	18%
urban	5%	3%	4%
Nitrogen export (kg N km⁻² y⁻¹)	795	502	627
Nitrogen export (10³ tons y⁻¹)	7.1	6.0	13.1
N export from deposition	31%	52%	41%
N export from agriculture	48%	29%	39%
(% fertilizer)	(12%)	(10%)	(11%)
(% agricultural N fixation)	(36%)	(19%)	(28%)

deposition of nitrogen is much greater closer to urban sources (Holland et al., 1999; NRC, 2000). On the other hand, a significant fraction of the N entering the freshwater Hudson is not exported to the saline estuary, due to the in-river processes of denitrification and sedimentation (Lampman et al., 1999).

In the two decades between the 1970s and the 1990s, nutrient inputs from sewage decreased, due in part to improved sewage treatment (see Hetling et al., 2003 and Brosnan et al., Chapter 23, this volume, for further discussion). The improvements were designed to lower BOD loadings, and not nutrient levels, but nonetheless probably resulted in some reduction of nutrient loading. Population in the lower part of the Hudson watershed grew by only 2 percent between 1970 and 1990 (U.S. Census Bureau, 2002), and so total discharge of wastewater into the estuary likely remained almost unchanged over that time, at 3.4×10^6 m³ d⁻¹. While a major new treatment plant, the North River plant, was built and came on line in the 1980s, the total wastewater flow into the saline estuary was not increased; the plant simply replaced the wastewater volume of raw sewage from fifty individual outlets from Manhattan to the Hudson estuary with the same volume of secondary-treated sewage (Clark et al., 1992; Brosnan and O'Shea, 1996). As of the early 1970s, 38 percent of the wastewater discharge into the Hudson estuary was raw sewage,

15 percent received primary treatment, and 47 percent received secondary treatment (calculated from data in Clark et al., 1992). Using the average concentration of nutrients in effluents from plants receiving those different levels of sewage treatment in the United States (Table 10.4; NRC, 1993), we estimate that nutrient loads from wastewater plants would have been 30×10^3 tons N y⁻¹ in the early 1970s. Thus, the improved sewage treatment of the 1990s resulted in an estimated 25 percent decrease in N loadings to the saline estuary (Table 10.2). As noted above, our estimate for nitrogen loading from wastewater in the 1990s is in reasonable agreement with that derived from scaling down the estimates of Brosnan and O'Shea (1996), Hetling et al. (2003), and Brosnan et al. (Chapter 23, this volume). Similarly, scaling down the estimates of Hetling et al. (2003) and Brosnan et al. (Chapter 23, this volume) for the 1970s by the smaller effluent volume in the smaller watershed we are considering gives excellent agreement with our estimate. Considering all sources, we estimate that N loading to the Hudson River Estuary decreased by just over 10 percent, from 49×10^3 tons N y⁻¹, to 43×10^3 tons N y⁻¹, between the early 1970s and the mid 1990s (Table 10.2).

Phosphorus loadings to the Hudson estuary decreased substantially between the early 1970s and the mid 1990s not only because of some improvements in wastewater treatment but also because of

Table 10.4. Average effluent concentrations and costs for sewage treatment systems in the United States (data from NRC 1993)

Treatment System	BOD (g C m^{-3})	TN (g N m^{-3})	TP (g P m^{-3})	Operating costs ($ m^{-3})	Capital costs ($ m^{-3})	Total costs ($ m^{-3})
No treatment (Raw)	76	30	6	–	–	–
Primary	52	23	4	0.06	0.08	0.14
Secondary	6	19	3	0.14	0.14	0.28
Nutrient Removal	5.6	3	1.5	0.15	0.22	0.37

NRC (1993) refers to secondary treatment plants as "biological" plants. BOD loads are converted to units of labile organic carbon by assuming 1 mole of organic carbon oxidized for every mole of O_2 consumed. Costs are based on averages for facilities in the United States, assuming an 8% interest rate, 20 year design period, and facilities designed to handle $72.6 \times 10^3 m^3 d^{-1}$ of effluent. Land costs are not included. "Operating" costs include maintenance and operating costs. Note that costs are for cumulative level of treatment; secondary treatment includes primary treatment, and nutrient-reduction treatment includes both secondary and primary treatment.

a ban (as of 1973) in the use of phosphates in detergents (Hetling et al., 2003). Considering only the effects of wastewater treatment changes, and using data for average effluent streams in the United States (Table 10.4), we estimate that P loadings to the Hudson estuary from wastewater sources would have decreased from an estimated 5×10^3 tons P y^{-1} in the early 1970s to 3.7×10^3 tons P y^{-1} in the mid 1990s. The effect of the ban on phosphates in detergents was probably greater (Clark et al., 1992; Hetling et al., 2003; Brosnan et al., Chapter 23, this volume). If we take the estimates of Hetling et al. (2003) and Brosnan et al. (Chapter 23, this volume) and scale them to the smaller effluent released from the smaller watershed we are considering, an estimated 8.5×10^3 tons P y^{-1} were loaded to the Hudson River Estuary from wastewater treatment plants in the early 1970s (Table 10.2). This large decrease in P in the estuary is broadly consistent with a three-fold reduction in phosphorus loadings estimated by Clark et al. (1992) based on observations of soluble reactive phosphorus (SRP) in the estuary over time, the assumption that SRP is conservative within the estuary, and a transport model. Note, however, that the assumption that SRP is conservative in the Hudson estuary (Clark et al., 1992) may be less valid in the 1990s than in the 1970s, as increased GPP would have assimilated more SRP in the 1990s, and higher oxygen concentrations in the water column may have increased the phosphate adsorptive capacity of bottom sediments as well (Howarth et al., 1995). Considering all sources, we estimate that P loading to the Hudson

River Estuary decreased by a factor of two, from 9.6×10^3 tons P y^{-1} to 4.8×10^3 tons P y^{-1}, between the early 1970s and the mid 1990s (Table 10.2).

The upstream tributary sources of nitrogen have probably changed rather little in the Hudson basin since the 1970s (Jaworski, Howarth, and Hetling, 1997). We are aware of no data that would allow us to estimate how the upstream tributary inputs of phosphorus have changed since 1970. In any event, it seems likely that the wastewater sources were a greater percentage of the total nutrient input in the 1970s than in the 1990s.

Nutrient Loading and GPP in the Pristine Hudson Estuary

Even before European settlement, nutrient loading per area of the estuary was probably high in the Hudson River compared to most estuaries, because of the high ratio of watershed area to estuary area (Table 10.1). At the scale of large regions, the nitrogen flux into the North Atlantic Ocean per area of watershed in the temperate zone is a linear function of the net anthropogenic inputs of nitrogen per area to the region. The zero intercept of this relationship, corresponding to no human influence, gives an estimate of the riverine nitrogen export from the pristine landscape of approximately 100 kg N km^{-2} y^{-1} (Howarth et al., 1996b; NRC, 2000). This relationship holds well at a smaller scale, as seen for sixteen major watersheds in the northeastern United States, including the Mohawk River basin and the upper Hudson River basin

Table 10.5. Summary of nitrogen loading, estimated primary productivity, and inputs of organic matter from wastewater and upstream tributary sources over time

	TN loading[1] (g N m^{-2} y^{-1})	GPP[2] (g C m^{-2} y^{-1})	Organic matter from CSOs and wastewater[1] (g C m^{-2} y^{-1})	Total input of labile organic C (g C m^{-2} y^{-1})
Pre-European Settlement	23	270	–	270
Early 1970s	330	225	370	595
1990s	295	850	94	944
Potential future[3]	87	480	50	530

[1] TN and organic matter (BOD) loadings averaged over area of entire saline estuary.
[2] GPP estimates are for mesohaline estuary and are based on measured data for 1970s and 1990s and are estimated based on nutrient loading for pre-European settlement and potential future.
[3] Potential future assumes complete conversion to nutrient-reduction treatment for sewage treatment, elimination of CSO discharges, and a significant reduction in nitrogen loading from upriver tributaries. See text for further details on derivation of estimates.

(Fig. 10.6; Boyer et al., 2002). A nitrogen flux of 100 kg N km^{-2} y^{-1} from the landscape contributes a total load to the estuary of 3.5×10^3 tons N y^{-1} for a watershed the size of Hudson basin, suggesting that human activity up to the 1990s has increased nitrogen loading to the Hudson estuary twelve-fold (Tables 10.2, 10.5). Per area of estuary, the pristine nitrogen loading would have corresponded to an input of 23 g N m^{-2} y^{-1} (Table 10.5). Note that this estimated nitrogen loading to the Hudson estuary under pristine conditions is in fact higher than the current loading to Chesapeake Bay and is only slightly less than the current loading to Delaware and Narragansett Bays. Again, this reflects the very high ratio of watershed area to estuarine surface area for the Hudson in comparison to other large estuaries.

While the export of nitrogen from the landscape in the temperate zone can be well predicted from the net anthropogenic inputs of nitrogen, export of phosphorus is quite dependent upon the amount of phosphorus in the parent soil, which is highly variable across regions. As a result, there is no consistent estimate of a baseline flux of phosphorus from pristine watersheds, as there is for nitrogen (NRC, 2000). For the Hudson, we can estimate what the pre-European phosphorus input to the estuary may have been by evaluating changes in erosion. In the pristine landscape (i.e., 100 percent forested), most of the phosphorus input to the Hudson would likely have been bound to particles. Currently, inputs of sediment to the Hudson estuary from erosion in the watershed are ten-fold higher than if the basin were entirely forested (Swaney et al.,

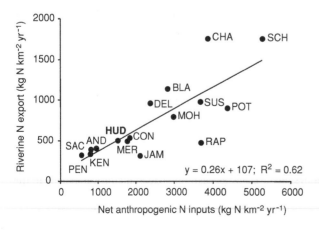

Figure 10.6. Export of nitrogen per area of watershed from large watersheds in the northeastern United States as a function of the net anthropogenic nitrogen inputs to the watersheds. Inputs include fertilizer use, nitrogen fixation in agricultural systems, deposition of NO$_y$ from the atmosphere, and the net import or export of nitrogen in food and animal feeds. "HUD" refers to the upper Hudson River basin, and "MOH" refers to the Mohawk River basin. Data are from Boyer et al. (2002).

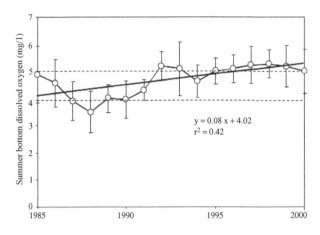

Figure 10.7. Mean oxygen concentrations in bottom waters of the saline Hudson River estuary during the summer, from 1985 to 2000. Bars represent 95% CI; dashed lines indicate the State of New York standards for secondary (4 mg l^{-1}) and primary contact recreation (5 mg l^{-1}). Reprinted from DEP (2001).

1996). Assuming that the phosphorus content of this eroded sediment has not changed over time, then the pre-European input of phosphorus to the estuary can be estimated as 10 percent of the current input from present upstream tributary sources (Table 10.2), or 0.09×10^3 tons P y^{-1}. The actual flux was likely less than this, both because the current input from upstream tributary sources includes some wastewater inputs from the tributaries and because the phosphorus content of the soils in the Hudson basin have probably increased from fertilization with phosphorus. In comparison to the estimated load for the 1990s (Table 10.2), human activity in the Hudson basin appears to have increased phosphorus loading to the estuary by at least fifty-fold. Note that phosphorus fluxes in the Hudson at the peak extent of deforestation in the nineteenth century may well have been greater than at present, due to very high rates of erosion (Swaney et al., 1996).

A pristine nitrogen loading of 23 g N m^{-2} y^{-1} would predict a rate of primary production of 270 g C m^{-2} y^{-1} (Fig. 10.5; Nixon et al., 1996) if the nitrogen loading were as inorganic nitrogen and if other factors such as short water residence times were not constraining GPP. As discussed in previous sections, GPP in the 1990s in the mesohaline estuary was roughly equal to the potential rate of ^{14}C production estimated from nitrogen loading (Fig. 10.5). Assuming this was true before European settlement, GPP can be estimated as 270 g C m^{-2} y^{-1}. The actual value was probably lower, because in fact, most of the nitrogen export from the pristine landscape was probably

as organic nitrogen (Howarth et al., 1996b; Lewis, 2002), of which the refractory component would be unavailable to phytoplankton, and short water residence times caused by spring tide mixing would have resulted in lower rates of primary production even during periods of low freshwater discharge. However, this exercise suggests that human activity has increased GPP in the mesohaline Hudson estuary by three-fold or more (Table 10.5).

Dissolved Oxygen: Historical Trends and Controls

The Hudson estuary is somewhat protected against low dissolved oxygen events both by the rapid flushing that removes organic wastes and by a rapid mixing over depth that can quickly replenish oxygen as it diffuses in from the atmosphere (Clark et al., 1995; Swaney et al., 1999). Nonetheless, the estuary has historically had problems with low oxygen (See Ch. 23). Much of this can be ascribed to organic loading from sewage effluents (BOD), and oxygen concentrations in the saline Hudson estuary have increased steadily in response to improved sewage treatment (Fig. 10.7; Suszkowski, 1990; Clark et al., 1995; Brosnan and O'Shea, 1996). The estuary is classified by the State of New York as Class I for water quality goals (secondary contact recreation, not primary contact), which sets a limit of 4 mg l^{-1} for minimum dissolved oxygen concentrations. As a result of reduced BOD loadings from upgrades to secondary sewage treatment throughout the New York City metropolitan area, this goal has been met most of the time since 1990 according to the data collected by the City of New York (Fig. 10.7; DEP, 2001). However, even in recent years the Hudson estuary would have difficulty meeting the state standard of 5 mg l^{-1} for primary contact recreation. In our cruises in 1998, 1999, and 2000, we found dissolved oxygen concentrations in the bottom waters of the estuary in early morning (when concentrations are lowest; Swaney et al., 1999) to be below 5 mg l^{-1} on roughly half the cruises and below 4 mg l^{-1} on two cruises (out of a total of twenty cruises), in August 1999 and July 2000 (our unpublished data).

In the saline Hudson estuary, the primary sources of organic matter that fuel respiration leading to oxygen depletion are BOD inputs from sewage and phytoplankton primary production. The estuary also received substantial inputs of organic matter from upriver, estimated as 50 × 10^3 tons C y^{-1} in the late 1980s (Howarth et al., 1996a). Much of the labile organic carbon that enters the freshwater Hudson is respired in situ (Howarth et al., 1996a), and as a result most of the organic C that is exported downstream is likely fairly refractory and has little influence on oxygen dynamics in the saline estuary. At the peak of agricultural activity in the Hudson River basin a century ago, the inputs of organic matter may have been 80 percent greater than at present due to higher erosion, and prior to European settlement in the basin, the flux may have been 40 percent of the current rate (Swaney et al., 1996).

By the early 1970s when the new environmental movement focused attention on water quality resulting in the Clean Water Act of 1972, the organic carbon inputs to the Hudson estuary were dominated by sewage. As discussed above, in the early 1970s, 38 percent of the wastewater discharge into the Hudson estuary was raw sewage, 15 percent received primary treatment, and 47 percent received secondary treatment (calculated from data in Clark et al., 1992). Using average values for the United States for the BOD load from treatment plants receiving various levels of treatments (Table 10.4), we estimate BOD loadings to the saline Hudson estuary in the early 1970s as 49 × 10^3 tons C y^{-1}. By the 1990s, virtually 100 percent of the wastewater inputs to the Hudson estuary during dry-weather conditions received secondary treatment (Brosnan and O'Shea, 1996). Using the same approach as for our 1970s estimate, we calculate that the complete

conversion to secondary level would have reduced the input of labile organic carbon from wastewater treatment plants to 7.5 × 10^3 tons C y^{-1} in the 1990s. Scaling the estimates of Brosnan and O'Shea (1996) for discharges from CSOs and storm water discharge for the entire metropolitan area to only the area of the saline Hudson estuary, as we did for nutrients above, suggests a further BOD loading of 6 × 10^3 tons C y^{-1}. If we assume that the CSO and storm runoff remained constant over the past several decades, then we estimate that the total BOD from wastewater effluent and other urban sources decreased by 75 percent between the early 1970s and the mid 1990s, from 55 × 10^3 tons C y^{-1} to 14 × 10^3 tons C y^{-1}.

At the same time as BOD loadings from wastewater treatment plants decreased, rates of GPP increased in the Hudson estuary, probably due to the longer water residence times resulting from the decrease in freshwater discharge between the 1970s and the 1990s. Given a rate of GPP of 200 to 250 g C m^{-2} y^{-1} in the early 1970s (O'Reilly et al., 1976; Malone, 1977; Sirois and Fredrick, 1978), phytoplankton production would have provided an input of 33 × 10^3 tons C y^{-1} of labile organic matter to the estuary. If we assume that in the 1990s, GPP was on average 850 g C m^{-2} y^{-1} in the mesohaline estuary and 450 g C m^{-2} y^{-1} in the oligohaline estuary, the total input of organic carbon from GPP to the saline estuary would be approximately 90 × 10^3 tons C y^{-1}. Despite the uncertainty in these estimates, the relative importance of sewage effluent and GPP clearly shifted between the early 1970s and the mid 1990s (Table 10.5; Fig. 10.8). BOD from sewage sources contributed over 60 percent of the labile carbon to the Hudson estuary in the early 1970s but only 10 percent in the 1990s. Surprisingly, the total input of labile organic matter to the estuary actually increased over those two decades due to the large increase in GPP (Table 10.5).

GPP by phytoplankton produces oxygen as well as labile carbon, and so given a comparable input of organic matter from GPP and BOD, the BOD loading will have a much greater negative impact on dissolved oxygen concentrations. However, excess GPP can lead to hypoxia and anoxia in estuaries, particularly when the water column is stratified (NRC, 1993, 2000). The saline Hudson estuary is generally stratified, yet significant mixing occurs

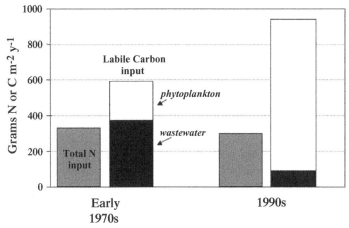

Figure 10.8. Comparison of inputs to the saline Hudson River estuary of total nitrogen and of labile organic matter (expressed as carbon) per area of estuary in the early 1970s and in the 1990s. Over this time period, improvements in wastewater treatment led to large decreases in organic carbon loads from sewage and smaller decreases in nitrogen loads. On the other hand, gross primary production by phytoplankton increased dramatically, as climatic changes resulted in lower flows of freshwater down the Hudson during some summers. The lower flows increased the residence time of surface waters in the saline estuary, and allowed phytoplankton to use the still high nitrogen loads to bloom. In the 1990s, the higher freshwater flows down the Hudson River kept residence times in the estuary short and, consequently, phytoplankton production low. Overall, the inputs of labile organic matter to the estuary actually increased between the 1970s and the 1990s.

across the pycnocline, and mixing is in fact rapid compared with gas exchange with the atmosphere (Clark et al., 1995; Swaney et al., 1999). Even in completely mixed water columns, high levels of GPP can lead to hypoxia, as was demonstrated experimentally in the Marine Ecosystems Research Laboratory (MERL) facility at nitrogen loadings comparable to those that occur in the Hudson estuary (Frithsen, Keller, and Pilson, 1985). Eutrophication leads to anoxic and hypoxic events in estuaries as a result of spatial and/or temporal separation of the production of oxygen associated with GPP and its consumption in respiration.

Freshwater discharge can dramatically affect oxygen concentrations in the saline Hudson estuary, with concentrations lower at times of lower discharge (Clark et al., 1995; Brosnan and O'Shea, 1996). This may result from the slower flushing that accompanies reduced discharges (Fig. 10.2B; Brosnan and O'Shea, 1996). The mesohaline Hudson estuary also becomes more stratified at times of lower freshwater discharge, in contrast to the general expectation that stratification lessens in estuaries as discharge decreases (Howarth and Swaney et al., 2000). This greater stratification may also

contribute to lowered oxygen concentrations. Thus, the lower discharge that increases GPP and so, in situ oxygen production, also makes the Hudson more sensitive to the effects of this organic loading on oxygen levels.

Further Improvements to Water Quality in the Hudson River Estuary

The upgrade of sewage treatment in the New York City metropolitan area to secondary treatment has resulted in marked improvement in water quality (Brosnan and O'Shea, 1996; DEP, 2001) and was highlighted by a 1993 report from the National Research Council as one of the greatest success stories in water quality management in estuaries over the past several decades (NRC, 1993). However, while oxygen concentrations in the Hudson estuary have improved and usually meet the New York State standard for secondary contact recreation (4 mg O_2 l^{-1}), they still do not reliably meet the standard for primary contact recreation (5 mg O_2 l^{-1}), as noted above. Our analysis shows that the Hudson estuary is often hypereutrophic, and despite fairly rapid flushing, is more sensitive to nutrient pollution than has been previously assumed. Further, water quality management in estuaries is moving beyond consideration just of dissolved oxygen levels, and must now consider other adverse effects of eutrophication, such as reduced biodiversity, increased incidences and duration of harmful algal blooms, and alteration in food web structure (NRC, 1993, 2000; Howarth and Anderson et al., 2000; EPA, 2001). Nutrient pollution from the Hudson estuary also contributes to eutrophication in downstream ecosystems, including the plume of the Hudson River on the continental shelf, where hypoxia is a regular event.

The nitrogen and phosphorus loads to the Hudson River Estuary and to the downstream ecosystems could be significantly reduced through improved sewage treatment. While the nitrogen in effluent from an average secondary sewage treatment plant in the United States contains $19 \, g \, N \, m^{-3}$, plants designed for nutrient removal on average discharge only $3 \, g \, N \, m^{-3}$; for phosphorus, nutrient removal technology results in an average effluent concentration of $1.5 \, g \, P \, m^{-3}$, as compared to $3 \, g \, P \, m^{-3}$ for secondary treatment (Table 10.4; NRC, 1993). If all the municipal wastewater plants that discharge into the saline Hudson estuary were to upgrade to this level of treatment, nitrogen loading from the sewage plants would be reduced from a current estimated 23×10^3 tons $N \, y^{-1}$ to 3.7×10^3 tons $N \, y^{-1}$. Assuming no change in discharges from CSOs and from storm sewers, and no change in the nitrogen coming down the Hudson River from upstream sources, total nitrogen loading to the estuary would be reduced to 24×10^3 tons y^{-1}, or $150 \, g \, N \, m^{-2} \, y^{-1}$ per area of estuary. Similarly, phosphorus loading from sewage plants upgraded to nutrient removal technology would be reduced from a current estimate of 3.7×10^3 tons y^{-1} to 1.9×10^3 tons y^{-1}, resulting in a total P loading to the saline estuary of 3×10^3 tons y^{-1} or $20 \, g \, P \, m^{-2} \, y^{-1}$.

The cost of building and maintaining sewage treatment plants that include nutrient-reduction technology in the United States is on average $0.37 per m^3 treated, compared to a cost of $0.28 per m^3 for only secondary sewage treatment (Table 10.4; NRC, 1993). Thus, if the New York metropolitan region had upgraded to nutrient removal technology rather than just to secondary over the past few

decades, the incremental cost would have been an estimated $0.09 per m^3 of effluent, or $112 million per year for the plants that discharge into the Hudson estuary. To build new nutrient reduction plants in the future would cost more, and if there were no capital savings from converting secondary plants to nutrient reduction plants, the capital cost would be an estimated $0.22 per m^3 and the increased operating costs over that for secondary plants would be $0.01 per m^3 of effluent (Table 10.4), or a total cost of $277 million per year. There probably is some saving of capital costs when converting secondary treatment to nutrient reduction treatment, so the actual cost of nutrient reduction technology for the Hudson estuary is probably between $112 and $277 million per year, or between $0.08 and $0.17 per person in the watershed per day, if national average costs apply. Note that these estimates are based on 1990 dollars and do not include land costs, but they are otherwise conservative as they are based on 8 percent interest rates and 20-year depreciation of plants (NRC, 1993).

The CSO and storm sewer discharges could in theory be eliminated as nitrogen sources to the Hudson estuary, and although the cost would be high, this would be desirable for other water quality reasons as well, such as reducing the pathogen load to the estuary. Most pathogens enter the Hudson estuary from CSOs (DEP, 2001). Ending CSO discharges should perhaps be a priority of rebuilding the urban infrastructure of the New York metropolitan area. Reducing the nitrogen from upstream tributaries would also be difficult, but a reduction of 50 percent or more seems possible through a combination of improved sewage treatment upstream, reduction in nitrogen deposition from fossil fuel pollution, improved farming practices, and other measures such as wetland creation (NRC, 2000). With this effort, it seems possible to reduce nitrogen loading to the Hudson estuary to 13×10^3 tons y^{-1}, or $87 \, g \, N \, m^{-2} \, y^{-1}$. The regression illustrated in Figure 10.5 indicates a maximum potential rate of primary production at this loading rate of $480 \, g \, C \, m^{-2} \, y^{-1}$. We conclude that, given sufficient public will and effort, the Hudson estuary can be restored to an ecosystem that is only moderately eutrophic rather than hypereutrophic, and where the risk of hypoxic events is greatly lessened (Table 10.5).

Acknowledgments

We thank Thomas Brosnan, Tom Butler, Jon Cole, and Gordon Taylor for their input and comments. Preparation of this manuscript was supported by an endowment given by David R. Atkinson to Cornell University. Additional support for our Hudson research has been provided by the Hudson River Foundation. The views expressed here are those of the authors and not of the Hudson River Foundation or Cornell.

REFERENCES

Banse, K. 1976. Rates of growth, respiration and photosynthesis of unicellular algae as related to cell size: a review. *Journal of Phycology* **12**: 135–40.

Billen, G., Somville, M., De Becker, E., and Servais, P. 1985. A nitrogen budget of the Scheldt hydrographical basin. *Netherlands Journal of Sea Research* **19**: 223–30.

Boyer, E. W., Goodale, C. L., Jaworski, N. A., and Howarth, R. W. 2002. Anthropogenic nitrogen sources and relationships to riverine nitrogen export in the northeastern USA. *Biogeochemistry* **57/58**: 137–69.

Boynton, W. R., Garber, J. H., Summers, R., and Kemp, W. M. 1995. Inputs, transformations, and transport of nitrogen and phosphorus in Chesapeake Bay and selected tributaries. *Estuaries* **18**: 285–314.

Bricker, S. B., Clement, C. G., Pirhalla, D. E., Orland, S. P., and Farrow, D. G. G. 1999. *National Estuarine Eutrophication Assessment: Effects of Nutrient Enrichment in the Nation's Estuaries*. Special Projects Office and the National Centers for Coastal Ocean Science, National Ocean Service, National Oceanic and Atmospheric Administration, Silver Spring, MD.

Brosnan, T. M. and O'Shea, M. L. 1996. Long-term improvements in water quality due to sewage abatement in the lower Hudson River. *Estuaries* **19**: 890–900.

Chan, F. A. 2001. "Ecological controls on planktonic nitrogen-fixation: the roles of grazing and cross-ecosystem patterns in phytoplankton mortality." Ph.D. thesis, Cornell University, Ithaca, NY.

Clark, J. F., Simpson, H. J., Bopp, R. F., and Deck, B. L. 1992. Geochemistry and loading history of phosphate and silicate in the Hudson estuary. *Estuarine and Coastal Shelf Science* **34**: 213–33.

1995. Dissolved oxygen in lower Hudson estuary: 1978–1993. *Journal of Environmental Engineering* **121**(10): 760–3.

Cloern, J. E. 2001. Our evolving conceptual model of the coastal eutrophication problem. *Marine Ecology Progress Series* **210**: 223–53.

DEP (Department of Environmental Protection). 2001. New York City 2000 Regional Harbor Survey. New York City Department of Environmental Protection, NY.

EPA (Environmental Protection Agency). 2001. *Nutrient Criteria Technical Guidance Manual: Estuarine and Coastal Marine Waters*. EPA-822-B-01-003, Office of Water, Washington, DC.

Frithsen, J. B., Keller, A. A., and Pilson, M. E. Q. 1985. *Effects of Inorganic Nutrient Additions in Coastal Areas: A Mesocosm Experiment Data Report*, Vol. 1. Marine Ecosystem Research Laboratory, Report 3, University of Rhode Island, Kingston, RI.

Garside, C., Malone, T. C., Roels, O. A., and Sharfstein, B. A. 1976. An evaluation of sewage-derived nutrients and their influence on the Hudson estuary and New York Bight. *Estuarine and Coastal Marine Science* **4**: 281–9.

Gordon, Jr., D. C., Boudreau, P. R., Mann, K. H., Ong, J.-E., Silvert, W. L., Smith, S. V., Wattayakorn, G., Wulff, F., and Yanagi, T. 1996. LOICZ Biogeochemical Modeling Guidelines. LOICZ Reports & Studies No 5, 1–96. IGBP, Stockholm.

Hetling, L. J., Stoddard, A., Brosnan, T. M., Hammerman, D. A., and Norris, T. M. 2003. Effect of water quality management efforts on wastewater loadings over the past center. *Water Environment Research* **75**: 30–8.

Holland, E. A., Dentener, F. J., Braswell, B. H., and Sulzman, J. M. 1999. Contemporary and pre-industrial global reactive nitrogen budgets. *Biogeochemistry* **46**: 7–43.

Howarth, R. W. 1998. An assessment of human influences on inputs of nitrogen to the estuaries and continental shelves of the North Atlantic Ocean. *Nutrient Cycling in Agroecosystems* **52**: 213–23.

Howarth, R. W., Anderson, D., Cloern, J., Elfring, C., Hopkinson, C., Lapointe, B., Malone, T., Marcus, N., McGlathery, K., Sharpley, A., and Walker, D. 2000. Nutrient pollution of coastal rivers, bays, and seas. *Issues in Ecology* **7**: 1–15.

Howarth, R. W., Billen, G., Swaney, D., Townsend, A., Jaworski, N., Lajtha, K., Downing, J. A., Elmgren, R., Caraco, N., Jordan, T., Berendse, F., Freney, J., Kuteyarov, V., Murdoch, P., and Zhao-liang, Zhu. 1996b. Riverine inputs of nitrogen to the North Atlantic Ocean: Fluxes and human influences. *Biogeochemistry* **35**: 75–139.

Howarth, R. W., Fruci, J. R., and Sherman, D. M. 1991. Inputs of sediment and carbon to an estuarine ecosystem: Influence of land use. *Ecological Applications* **1**: 27–39.

Howarth, R. W., Jensen, H., Marino, R., and Postma, H. 1995. Transport to and processing of P in nearshore and oceanic waters, in H. Tiessen (ed.), *Phosphorus in the Global Environment: Transfers, Cycles, and Management.* Chichester, UK: Wiley, pp. 323–45.

Howarth, R. W., and Michaels, A. F. 2000. The measurement of primary production in aquatic ecosystems, in O. Sala, R. Jackson, H. Mooney, and R. W. Howarth (eds.), *Methods in Ecosystem Science*, NY: Springer, pp. 72–85.

Howarth, R. W., Schneider, R., and Swaney, D. 1996a. Metabolism and organic carbon fluxes in the tidal, freshwater Hudson River. *Estuaries* **19**: 848–65.

Howarth, R. W., Swaney, D., Butler, T. J., and Marino, R. 2000. Climatic control on eutrophication of the Hudson River estuary. *Ecosystems* **3**: 210–215.

Jaworski, N. A., Howarth, R. W., and Hetling, L. J. 1997. Atmospheric deposition of nitrogen oxides onto the landscape contributes to coastal eutrophication in the northeast United States. *Environmental Science and Technology* **31**: 1995–2004.

Lampman, G. G., Caraco, N. F., and Cole, J. J. 1999. Spatial and temporal patterns of nutrient concentration and export in the tidal Hudson River. *Estuaries* **22**: 285–96.

Lewis, W. M. 2002. Yield of nitrogen from minimally disturbed watersheds in the United States. *Biogeochemistry* **57/58**: 375–85.

Limburg, K. E., Moran, A., and McDowell, W. H. 1986. *The Hudson River Ecosystem.* NY: Springer-Verlag.

Malone, T. C. 1977. Environmental regulation of phytoplankton productivity in the lower Hudson estuary. *Estuarine and Coastal Shelf Science* **5**: 157–71.

Malone, T. C. 1980. Algal size in I. Morris (ed.), *The Physiological Ecology of Phytoplankton.* Oxford, UK: Blackwell, pp. 433–63.

Malone, T. C., and Conley, D. J. 1996. Trends in nutrient loading and eutrophication: A comparison of the Chesapeake Bay and the Hudson River Estuarine Systems, in K. Sherman, N. A. Jaworski, and T. J. Smayda (eds.), *The Northeast Shelf Ecosystems: Assessment, Sustainability, and Management.* Oxford UK: Blackwell, pp. 327–49.

Mearns, A. J., Haines, E., Klepple, G. S., McGrath, R. A., McLaughlin, J. J. A., Segar, D. A., Sharp, J. H., Walsh, J. J., Word, J. Q., Young, D. K., and Young, M. W. 1982. Effects of nutrients and carbon loadings on communities and ecosystems, in G. F. Mayer (ed.), *Ecological Stress and the New York Bight: Science and Management.* Estuarine Research Federation, Columbia, SC. pp. 53–65.

Nixon, S. W. 1995. Coastal marine eutrophication: a definition, social causes, and future concerns. *Ophelia* **41**: 199–219.

Nixon, S. W., Ammerman, J. W., Atkinson, L. P., Berounsky, V. M., Billen, G., Boicourt, W. C., Boynton, W. R., Church, T. M., DiToro, D. M., Elmgren, R., Garber, J. H., Giblin, A. E., Jahnke, R. A., Owens, N. J. P., Pilson, M. E. Q., and Seitzinger, S. P. 1996. The fate of nitrogen and phosphorus at the land-sea margin of the North Atlantic Ocean. *Biogeochemistry* **35**: 141–80.

Nixon, S. W., and Pilson, M. E. Q. 1983. Nitrogen in estuarine and coastal marine ecosystems, in E. J. Carpenter, and D. G. Capone (eds.), *Nitrogen in the Marine Environment.* New York: Academic Press, pp. 565–648.

NRC (National Research Council). 1993. *Managing Wastewater in Coastal Urban Areas.* Washington, DC: National Academy of Sciences Press.

NRC (National Research Council). 2000. *Clean Coastal Waters: Understanding and Reducing the Effects of Nutrient Pollution.* Washington, DC: National Academy of Sciences Press.

O'Reilly, J. E., Thomas, J. P., and Evans, C. 1976. *Annual primary production (nanoplankton, netplankton, dissolved organic matter) in the lower New York Bay.* Paper #19 in Hudson River Ecology, 4th Symposium. Hudson River Environmental Society, Bronx, NY.

Scavia, D., Field, J. C., Boesch, Buddemeier, R., Burkett, V., Canyan, D., Fogarty, M., Harwell, M. A., Howarth, R. W., Mason, C., Reed, D. J., Royer, T. C., Sallenger, A. H., and Titus, J. G. 2002. Climate change impacts on US Coastal and marine ecosystems. *Estuaries* **25**: 149–64.

Sirois, D. L., and Fredrick, S. W. 1978. Phytoplankton and primary production in the lower Hudson River estuary. *Estuarine and Coastal Marine Science* **5**: 57–171.

Suszkowski D. J. 1990. Conditions in New York/New Jersey Harbor Estuary, in *Proceedings of Cleaning Up Our Coastal Waters: An Unfinished Agenda.* Manhattan College, Riverdale, NY, pp. 105–31.

Swaney, D. P., Howarth, R. W., and Butler, T. J. 1999. A novel approach for estimating ecosystem production and respiration in estuaries: application to the oligohaline and mesohaline Hudson River estuary. *Limnology and Oceanography* **44**: 1509–21.

Swaney, D. P., Sherman, D., and Howarth, R. W. 1996. Modeling water, sediment, and organic carbon discharges in the Hudson-Mohawk Basin: coupling to terrestrial sources. *Estuaries* **19**: 833–47.

Taylor, G. T., Way, J., and Scranton, M. I. 2003. Planktonic carbon cycling and transport in surface waters of the highly urbanized Hudson River estuary. *Limnology and Oceanography* **48**: 1779–95.

U.S. Census Bureau. 2002. *2000 Census of Population and Housing*. Economics and Statistics Administration, U. S. Department of Commerce. [online] url: http://www.census.gov/dmd/www/2khome.htm.

USGS (United States Geological Survey). 2002. National Water-Quality Assessment (NAWQA) Study-Unit Investigations in the conterminous United States: Watershed Boundaries. [online] url: http://water.usgs.gov/GIS/

11 Modeling Primary Production in the Lower Hudson River Estuary

Robin Landeck Miller and John P. St. John

ABSTRACT Mathematical models are useful tools for quantifying primary production. The evolution of mathematical modeling of eutrophication toward the understanding and management of nutrients and primary production includes successively more complex and sophisticated mathematical formulations which account for the interactions between light, nutrients, and phytoplankton. Application of modern eutrophication models to the management of the Hudson River Estuary requires linkage among the New York/New Jersey (NY/NJ) Harbor Estuary, the New York Bight, and Long Island Sound. The development and application of the System-Wide Eutrophication Model (SWEM) is an example of how primary production in the Hudson River Estuary can be studied from both a cause and effect and a systemwide perspective. SWEM results show that primary productivity in the Lower Hudson River Estuary and contiguous waterways, with the exception of western Long Island Sound and portions of Raritan Bay, is controlled by the availability of light and residence time rather than nutrients. SWEM results also show that both nitrogen and carbon contribute to dissolved oxygen deficit but the relative importance of each is quite dependent upon specific location and the interrelationship of a number of physical, chemical, and biological variables. It is due to these complexities that mathematical modeling becomes an effective technique in understanding the process of primary production in the Lower Hudson.

Introduction

The purpose of this chapter is to describe how mathematical models may be applied to increase the understanding of primary production. The main points of this chapter include:

1. An overview of primary production in natural water systems;
2. The utility of mathematical models for quantifying the causality of primary production;
3. The importance of eutrophication for the management of nutrients and primary production;
4. The evolution of mathematical models of eutrophication from simple calculations to state-of-the-science complex frameworks which can be applied to support management and regulatory decisions;
5. The complex interaction of the lower Hudson River Estuary with Long Island Sound and the New York Bight (requiring the analysis of primary production in the Hudson River Estuary on a systemwide basis); and
6. An illustration of the modeling of primary production in the Hudson-Sound-Bight system to address eutrophication in western Long Island Sound.

Primary Production

Primary production occurs through a complex process as shown schematically in Figure 11.1. As illustrated, primary production or algal growth is an ecosystem response to time-variable inputs of natural conditions such as river flows and man-made effects such as pollutant loadings. The primary production or ability of algae to grow is controlled by the availability of light (i.e., solar radiation), residence time and inorganic nutrients and is influenced by ambient water temperature. Additionally, the inputs are affected by the geophysical structure of the water body which influences the advective transport and, in the case of tidal estuaries, the dispersional transport of the pollutant loads. The distribution of materials in the natural system is also affected by various sources and sinks within the water body itself.

As shown schematically in Figure 11.1, the nutrient response to the inputs and natural water system effects characteristically produces bi-modal algal growth in marine waters, a late winter, early spring bloom, and another again in the summer. Dissolved oxygen in the water column may be increased

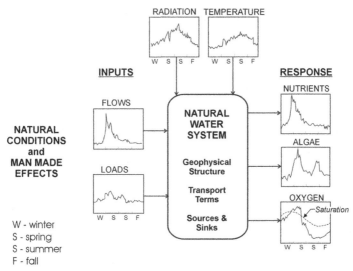

Figure 11.1. Schematic diagram of primary production: an ecosystem response to natural conditions and anthropogenic effects.

above the naturally occurring saturation value in winter by algal production, but may be significantly depressed below saturation in summer if the water column becomes vertically stratified by temperature and salinity.

The factors that control the supply of available light and inorganic nutrients are numerous and complex, particularly in a large urban estuarine system such as the Hudson. Factors controlling the availability of light to algae for growth include meteorological conditions such as cloud cover, the turbidity or amount of suspended matter within the water, the density of the algae already present (self-shading effect), and the amount of time the algae spend in the photic zone (i.e., residence time) which is a function of the hydrodynamic properties of the system. Factors controlling the availability of inorganic nutrients to algae for growth include the supply or loads of nutrients from natural and anthropogenic sources, the rates of recycle or conversion of organic nutrient forms to inorganic forms, and the hydrodynamic properties of the system which determine the fraction of the inorganic nutrients in the photic zone. Primary production on a net basis is also controlled by algal loss mechanisms such as respiration and predation. All of the factors or inputs controlling primary production act concurrently and vary over small temporal and spatial scales. Primary production as a response

may be measured in two ways, as algal biomass (i.e., by either carbon or chlorophyll-a) or as oxygen (i.e., by the difference between photosynthesis and respiration).

Modeling Primary Production

The primary production process schematically illustrated on Figure 11.1 is complex in nature but can be described in mathematical terms. Mass balance equations can be formulated for a natural water system by which the inputs in mass units can be modulated by the physics and transport characteristics of the system, along with inclusion of relevant instream source and sink mechanisms to produce response concentration values for nutrients, algae, oxygen and other relevant variables varying in time and space. The development of a predictive model based on these mathematical expressions allows for cause and effect mechanisms to be expressed and evaluated. The mathematical model can be tested against real world observations to assess whether the model and internal formulations are realistic and valid. If so, the model can then be used to assess the relative importance of pollutant loads and other factors contributing to water quality problems. The model can then serve as a management tool to test the effectiveness of various pollutant control actions.

The Eutrophication Process and Modeling Representation

EUTROPHICATION

In eutrophication of marine systems, nutrient loads contribute to excessive near-surface phytoplankton growth, resulting in algae blooms, which are both a source and sink of dissolved oxygen as the algae grow, settle, respire, die, and decompose. If vertical stratification of the water column is present due to variations in salinity and temperature, vertical oxygen transfer from the water surface is diminished. Algae become a net sink of dissolved oxygen in the lower layers of the water column, leading to hypoxia and possibly anoxia in extreme situations. Either condition can be lethal to marine life.

COMPONENTS OF EUTROPHICATION MODELING

Modern eutrophication models include three linked submodels: hydrodynamic, primary production, and sediment nutrient flux. The hydrodynamic sub-model calculates the water circulation and transport pattern that is passed to the primary production submodel and accounts for the movement and residence time of nutrients and algae through the water column as well as the vertical structure or stratification of the water column. The primary production submodel calculates the algal dynamics as a function of nutrient loadings, temperature, and light. The sediment nutrient flux submodel accounts for the exchange between the water column and sediment of nutrients and organic matter and diagenesis. Diagenesis is the process of chemical changes which take place in the sediment after materials are deposited from the water column and before decomposed or mineralized materials are returned to the water column by physical exchange mechanisms. Comprehensive interactive sediment models use fluxes of algae and detrital particulate organic matter from the water column to compute the fluxes of nutrients and oxygen demand resulting from the mineralization of organic matter (Di Toro and Fitzpatrick, 1993; Di Toro, 2001).

Inclusion of sediment interactions within eutrophication models necessitates the simulation of organic matter mineralization over time scales longer than one year. Over such a time scale, loadings of nutrients and carbon may vary dramatically as do physical conditions. For the models to accurately capture the dynamics of the algal populations, it is necessary to incorporate the variability in loadings and physical conditions. In the case of a large system such as the Hudson River Estuary, loadings include headwater tributary inputs, runoff from the land, effluent from large industries, wastewater treatment plants, and combined sewer overflows, deposition from the atmosphere, and oceanic inputs. The variability of these loadings is probably hourly, but the major signal may be captured on a daily basis. Similarly, the variability in physical conditions occurs with high frequency that must be incorporated into eutrophication models. The factors influencing light conditions are appropriately specified at time scales of one day to one hour.

In general, nutrients include nitrogen, phosphorus, and, for diatomaceous phytoplankton, silica. In the saline lower Hudson and other typical marine environments, observed nutrient concentrations and ratios of inorganic nutrients indicate that nitrogen is the nutrient that limits phytoplankton growth. For this reason, marine eutrophication models address management of nitrogen loads but all nutrients are included in the computations for completeness. Additionally, discharges of organic carbon can also adversely affect concentrations of dissolved oxygen and are included in modeling calculations. Management actions which reduce organic carbon loads are also therefore considered.

Available Tools for Primary Production Modeling

Figure 11.2 is a simplified diagrammatic representation of the principal eutrophication kinetics and water column-sediment interactions included in the primary production and sediment nutrient flux submodels of eutrophication models. Specifically, the kinetics shown in Figure 11.2 come from the model Row Column Aesop (RCA), a generalized, three-dimensional, time-varying water quality modeling program which has been described in detail (Di Toro, Lowe, and Fitzpatrick,

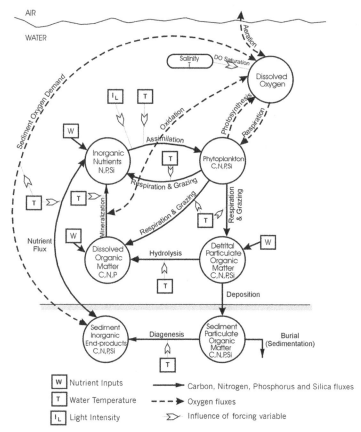

Figure 11.2. Principal kinetics and water column – sediment interactions included in the primary production and sediment nutrient flux submodels of modern eutrophication models.

2000; HydroQual, 1999b). Following an overview of the features of hydrodynamic submodels, brief descriptions of the key features of primary production and sediment nutrient flux submodels as shown in Figure 11.2 are presented.

a. Hydrodynamic transport. An example of a hydrodynamic transport submodel is ECOM3D which has been described in detail (Blumberg and Mellor, 1980 and 1987). ECOM3D and other similar hydrodynamic sub-models provide advection and dispersion terms and water temperatures needed for primary production and sediment nutrient flux submodels.

b. Available light. The light that algae can use for growth is modeled as a function of four dependencies: incident solar radiation, the photoperiod or fraction of daylight, the depth of the water column, and light extinction or attenuation. One modeling framework frequently used is an extension of a light curve analysis formulated by Steele (1962). The available light is important to primary production in the lower Hudson River Estuary.

c. Algal growth. Phytoplankton growth is modeled for two functional groups or assemblages: winter diatoms and summer flagellates. The reason phytoplankton are considered as two assemblages rather than as individual species is the growth rate of an individual population of phytoplankton in a natural environment is a complicated function of the species present and their differing reactions to solar radiation, temperature, and the balance between nutrient requirements and nutrient availability. The complex and often conflicting data pertinent to this problem have been reviewed exhaustively (Rhee, 1973; Hutchinson, 1967; Strickland, 1965; Lund, 1965; Raymont, 1963). The available information is not sufficiently detailed at present to specify the growth kinetics for individual algal species in a natural environment, but we can divide the assemblages into distinct functional groups, namely diatoms and flagellates.

d. Nutrient and organic carbon cycling. Five phosphorus, six nitrogen, two silica, and six organic carbon principal forms are included in the nutrient and carbon formulations in RCA as schematically shown in Figure 11.2. Starting with the phosphorus forms, inorganic phosphorus is utilized by phytoplankton for growth and is returned to various organic and inorganic forms via respiration and predation. A fraction of the phosphorus released during phytoplankton respiration and predation is in the inorganic form and is readily available for uptake by other viable phytoplankton. The remaining fraction released is in the dissolved and particulate organic forms. The organic phosphorus must undergo a mineralization or bacterial decomposition into inorganic phosphorus before it can be used by other viable phytoplankton.

During algal respiration and death, a fraction of the algal cellular nitrogen is returned to the inorganic pool in the form of ammonia. The remaining fraction is recycled to the dissolved and particulate organic nitrogen pools. Organic nitrogen undergoes a bacterial decomposition, the end product of which is ammonia. Ammonia nitrogen, in the presence of nitrifying bacteria and oxygen, is converted to nitrite nitrogen and subsequently nitrate nitrogen (nitrification). Both ammonia and nitrate are available for uptake and use in cell growth by phytoplankton; however, for physiological reasons, the preferred form is ammonia.

Two silica forms are considered. Available silica is dissolved and is utilized by diatoms during growth for their cell structure. Unavailable or particulate biogenic silica is produced from diatom respiration and diatom grazing by zooplankton. Particulate biogenic silica undergoes mineralization to available silica or settles to the sediment from the water column.

Pools of dissolved and particulate organic carbon are established on the basis of timescale for oxidation or decomposition. Zooplankton consume algae and take up and redistribute algal carbon to the organic carbon pools via grazing, assimilation, respiration, and excretion. Since zooplankton are not directly included in the kinetics, the redistribution of algal carbon to the organic carbon pools by zooplankton is simulated by empirical distribution coefficients. An additional term, representing the excretion of dissolved organic carbon by phytoplankton during photosynthesis, is included in the model. This algal exudate is very reactive. The decomposition of organic carbon is assumed to be temperature and bacterial biomass-mediated. Since bacterial biomass is not directly included within the model framework, phytoplankton biomass is used as a surrogate variable. An additional loss mechanism of particulate organic matter is that due to filtration by benthic bivalves. This loss is handled in the model kinetics by increasing the deposition of nonalgal particulate organic carbon from the water column to the sediment.

e. Sediment dynamics. The mass balance equations of the sediment submodel account for changes in particulate organic matter (carbon, nitrogen, phosphorus, and silica) in the sediments due to deposition from the overlying water column, sedimentation, and decay or diagenesis. The decay of particulate organic matter follows first-order kinetics as described by Berner (1964, 1974, and 1980). The end products of diagenesis or decay of the particulate organic matter include ammonia nitrogen, dissolved inorganic phosphorus, and dissolved inorganic silica. These end products can undergo additional biological, chemical, and physical processing within the sediment layer such as nitrification, sorption, and exchange with the overlying water column. Of particular importance to the overlying water column is the calculation of sediment oxygen demand (SOD). A more complete development of the sediment submodel theory is presented elsewhere (Di Toro and Fitzpatrick, 1993).

f. Dissolved oxygen balance. The dissolved oxygen balance includes both sources and sinks. Algal growth has two sources: the production of dissolved oxygen from photosynthetic carbon fixation and an additional source of oxygen from algal growth when nitrate rather than ammonia is utilized. Atmospheric reaeration is another source of dissolved oxygen. Sinks include algal respiration, nitrification, and oxidation of carbonaceous material.

g. Primary production. Primary production, an indirect measure of the depth integrated algal growth rate, is calculated in RCA. Both source and sink terms from the dissolved oxygen balance, photosynthetic carbon fixation and algal respiration, are used to calculate primary production in oxygen units.

Features of the Lower Hudson River Estuary

In order to apply the primary production modeling tools described above to the lower Hudson River Estuary, it is necessary to understand some of the physical characteristics of the system. Geographically, the lower Hudson River Estuary includes the saltwater portion of the Hudson River. Although the Hudson River is tidal as far north as the Federal Dam at Troy, New York, approximately 250 km (150 miles) north of the Battery (at the southern tip of Manhattan Island in New York City), salinity generally propagates up river only as far north as Poughkeepsie, New York, approximately eighty miles north of the Battery. Thus, for our purposes, the lower Hudson River Estuary refers to the eighty miles of the Hudson River north of the southern tip of Manhattan Island in New York City.

The lower Hudson River Estuary is the central water body in the larger urban estuary commonly referred to as New York/New Jersey Harbor Estuary. Water quality in the New York/New Jersey Harbor Estuary is influenced by numerous point (including more than 30 freshwater tributary inputs, 100 wastewater treatment plants (WWTPs) and 700 combined sewer outfalls (CSO) and nonpoint source discharges.

Consistent with the concentration of large point source discharges in the region, nutrient levels are high, in excess of what is required by the phytoplankton populations which the available light regime and residence time in the photic zone can support. Water quality in the lower Hudson River Estuary also includes a depression in dissolved oxygen of several mg/L below saturation, which is an integrated response to both nutrient and carbon loadings from all loading sources.

In addition to the loadings described above, water quality in the lower Hudson River Estuary is influenced by the ocean. Tidal exchange with the ocean through the Sandy Hook-Rockaway transect is an important sink of nutrients and organic carbon in New York/New Jersey Harbor and the lower Hudson River Estuary. In addition, the influence of the ocean is an important consideration for modeling water quality. An important requirement for numerical models of natural water systems which are to be used for predictive or diagnostic purposes, that is, to assign causality, is open boundary conditions which are not affected by internal loads. In estuarine systems this requirement for independent boundaries necessitates an open boundary located far out into the ocean. Conditions in the lower Hudson River Estuary are also influenced by conditions in Long Island Sound by exchanges through the East and Harlem Rivers. Therefore, the boundaries for a proper evaluation of the Hudson River Estuary must include the New York Bight and Long Island Sound.

The exchanges between the lower Hudson River, New York/New Jersey Harbor, the New York Bight and the Long Island Sound have been extensively studied. Jay and Bowman (1975) present a comprehensive literature review of regional hydrodynamics and water quality from 1848 to the early 1970s. It is appropriate to consider New York/New Jersey Harbor, New York Bight and the Long Island Sound as an integrated system. This integrated approach has been undertaken in the development of the System-wide Eutrophication Model (SWEM).

System-Wide Eutrophication Model (SWEM)

DEVELOPMENT OF SWEM

The System-Wide Eutrophication Model (SWEM) was developed for the New York City Department of Environmental Protection (NYCDEP) to assist in water quality management planning. SWEM is a comprehensive regional management tool which has the capability to diagnose the causative agents of dissolved oxygen deficit in New York/New Jersey Harbor and adjacent waterways. NYCDEP has utilized SWEM to predict likely improvements in dissolved oxygen resulting from specific management actions.

New York Harbor, New York Bight, and Long Island Sound have historically been modeled as independent system compartments. Historical modeling efforts of eutrophication in the individual system compartments include the Harbor Eutrophication Model (HEM) (HydroQual, 1999a), the New York Bight Model (HydroQual, 1989), and the Long Island Sound Model, version 3 (LIS3.0) (HydroQual, 1996). SWEM represents the first regional modeling effort to integrate the three major system compartments in a complex eutrophication framework. SWEM was constructed to be analogous in technical complexity to its predecessor models, HEM and LIS3.0. The New York Bight Model has much simpler and less sophisticated kinetics than HEM, LIS3.0, and SWEM. SWEM has several technical advantages over both HEM and LIS3.0.

SWEM SPATIAL DOMAIN

The spatial domain of SWEM includes the Hudson River from Albany to the Battery, the East River, the Harlem River, Long Island Sound, Upper and Lower New York Bay, Jamaica Bay, Raritan Bay, the Raritan River, Arthur Kill, Kill van Kull, Newark Bay, Hackensack River, Passaic River, and the New York Bight extending out into the Atlantic Ocean to the shelf break and to Cape May and Nantucket Shoals. The drainage area covered by SWEM is 57,800 km^2 (34,700 square miles). The drainage area of SWEM includes 11 major tributary basins, 325 municipal wastewater treatment plants, 750 combined sewer overflows, and a population of more than 26 million.

FIELD PROGRAM – CALIBRATION AND VALIDATION DATA

The calibration and validation of eutrophication models such as SWEM requires a synoptic database including hydrodynamic and water quality measurements for both the water column and sediment. Model calibration involves the comparison of model calculations to measured values. Model validation involves the further comparison of model calculations to measured values, but for a set of conditions different from calibration conditions. SWEM was calibrated to data collected during 1994–5 and validated for data collected in 1988–9.

The 1994–5 monitoring program conducted in support of SWEM included three components: loadings, hydrodynamics, and water and sediment quality. Monitoring of loadings involved sampling of thirty sewage treatment plants STPs and eleven tributaries eight times over the course of the year. In addition, eighteen CSO and fifteen stormwater locations were sampled three times and atmospheric deposition samples were collected at ten locations for seven precipitation events. Hydrodynamic monitoring included the deployment of eight moored instruments which continuously recorded temperature, salinity, currents, pressure, and meteorological conditions over twelve months. The water and sediment quality monitoring included more than 100 stations at two depths for nine synoptic events. The variables measured include physical parameters, plankton, nutrients, dissolved oxygen, and sediment fluxes.

Other data sources include NYCDEP Harbor Survey, monitoring by the Connecticut Department of Environmental Protection, Consolidated Edison monitoring of the Hudson River, and special studies performed by the Interstate Environmental Commission and HydroQual. The major source of data for model and data comparison under validation conditions is the database collected for the Long Island Sound Study for the development of LIS3.0 and the NYCDEP Harbor Survey.

SWEM CALIBRATION/VALIDATION

Calibration and validation of water quality models is essential to demonstrate the model's credibility and utility for use as a management tool. This process consists, in simplest terms, of inputting measured pollutant loads, river flows and other necessary inputs into the model calculations and computing the predicted concentration of the response variables (nutrients, algae, dissolved oxygen, etc.) in space and time. The calculated response outputs are then compared with observed data in the water column and bed sediments of the receiving waters.

SWEM contains a number of rate and distribution coefficients for various source and sink terms. Laboratory data and repeated application of these types of models in numerous water bodies has produced reasonable, first estimate values to be assigned initially in the calibration process. Selected parameter values as appropriate are then adjusted within limits to improve the model's reproduction of observed field data.

During the calibration procedure, parameter values are adjusted one at a time so that the consequences of, or the sensitivity of the model to, an assigned parameter value is well understood. For this reason, model calibration is a long and time consuming task. In the case of SWEM, more than 100 calibration simulations were performed.

An overall goal of model calibration is to avoid having a situation where small adjustments to a single unmeasured model input produce large changes in calculated model results. Such a situation rarely occurs with sophisticated models such as SWEM which essentially are closed mass balances. Less sophisticated models which are not closed mass balances (i.e., do not include linked sediment flux or hydrodynamic transport submodels) can suffer from this problem.

A control on the calibration procedure is the necessity to reproduce observed field data for many dependent water quality variables simultaneously. For example, parameter values cannot be adjusted to produce a satisfactory reproduction of measured chlorophyll unless a satisfactory reproduction of dissolved oxygen, nutrient, and light measurements is also achieved, demonstrating that an entire process is properly modeled and the parameter adjustment is not an exercise in curve fitting to a single parameter.

The starting point for calibration of SWEM for 1994–5 conditions was the parameters used in predecessor models, particularly LIS3.0 and HEM. Only minor modifications were made to the parameters applied from LIS3.0 and HEM for SWEM. The identical set of parameters for the final SWEM 1994–5 calibration was successfully carried over to the application of SWEM to 1988–9 conditions, proving that two distinctly different sets of conditions in New York/New Jersey Harbor could be modeled with a uniform set of equations and parameters. Further, essentially the same framework as SWEM has been applied to other systems such as Chesapeake Bay and mesocosms of Narragansett Bay with consistent and similar parameters (Di Toro et al., 2000). These results demonstrate that modern eutrophication models such as SWEM are valid and reproducible and can be used for predictive purposes.

The calibration and validation of the water quality model portion of SWEM included model and data comparisons both along spatial transects and over time at specific locations. Specifically, an individual SWEM calibration or validation simulation included model and data comparisons for approximately 2,600 spatial profiles and 650 temporal profiles. The calibration and validation of the SWEM benthic sediment model involved model and data comparisons for almost 500 temporal profiles per simulation. The major water quality variables of concern for SWEM calibration and validation included salinity, temperature, dissolved oxygen, chlorophyll-a, BOD-5, carbon, nitrogen, phosphorus, and silica.

Figures 11.3 and 11.4 present model and data comparisons for August 1995 for eighteen variables along a spatial transect that runs down the centerline of the Hudson River Estuary south from Poughkeepsie, New York through the Battery and the Narrows toward the apex of the New York Bight. For comparison purposes, a ten-day average of model results closest to the time period during which the data were collected is used.

SALINITY AND TEMPERATURE

On Figure 11.3, panels A and B show model and data comparisons for salinity and temperature. Comparisons are shown for both surface and bottom waters. The model results for salinity are presented by two sets of curves. The dashed lines show the salinity calculated by the hydrodynamic submodel. The solid and broken lines show the salinity used in the carbon production submodel. Temperature results as calculated by the hydrodynamic submodel are shown by solid (surface) and broken (bottom) lines. The general agreement between model results (ten-day averages) and the observed data for salinity and temperature (grab samples) is an indication that the physics and transport have been correctly calculated. Both model and data show that the Hudson is a vertically stratified system.

Total nitrogen. On Figure 11.3, panels F, G, H, and I show model and data comparisons for several organic and inorganic nitrogen forms (TON, NH_4, $NO_2 + NO_3$, TN). The model results shown by the solid and broken lines reproduce the data extremely well, capturing sharp gradients in all nitrogen forms. The increase in ammonia

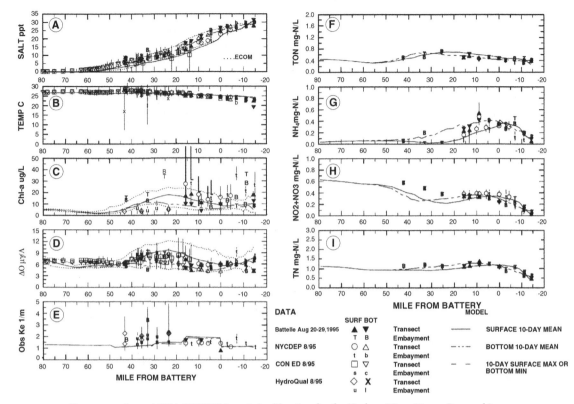

Figure 11.3. August 1994–95 SWEM spatial calibration for the Hudson River, Upper Bay, and Lower Bay for key parameters A – I.
Note: For Salt, results of the ECOM hydrodynamic model are also shown.

concentrations shown by both the model calculations and the data in the vicinity of mile 0, along the southern tip of Manhattan Island, is due to the high number of point source nitrogen discharges located in the lower Harbor.

Chlorophyll-a. On Figure 11.3, panel C shows model and data comparisons for chlorophyll-a (Chl-a). The model results are shown with four curves. The solid line is the model mean in the surface layer and the broken line is the model mean in the bottom layer. The dashed lines show the model maximum and model minimum. Notice that the model means reproduce well the monitoring data collected along the transect which are represented by the filled upwards and downwards pointing triangles, and the model maximum and minimum capture some of the variability in the observed data.

Organic carbon. On Figure 11.4, panel K shows model and data comparisons for particulate organic carbon (POC). POC, like chlorophyll, is also

a measure of algal biomass. For POC, the model results are shown by four curves as follows: The solid line is the model calculation in the surface layer. The broken line is the model calculation in the bottom layer. These two lines capture the magnitude of the observed data shown by the symbols. The two dotted lines show the algal fraction of the POC for both surface and bottom layers. In the Hudson River, almost all of the POC is algal POC. The model captures the POC peak concentration near milepoint 25 (Haverstraw Bay).

Biochemical oxygen demand (BOD). Panel L on Figure 11.4 shows model and data comparisons for BOD. The model results are shown as ten-day average concentrations in the surface layer (solid line) and in the bottom layer (broken line). Although measured BOD shows a high degree of variability, the ability of the model to calculate average BOD which falls within the range of the measurements indicates that the model correctly calculates the consumption of oxygen (i.e., the sinks of dissolved

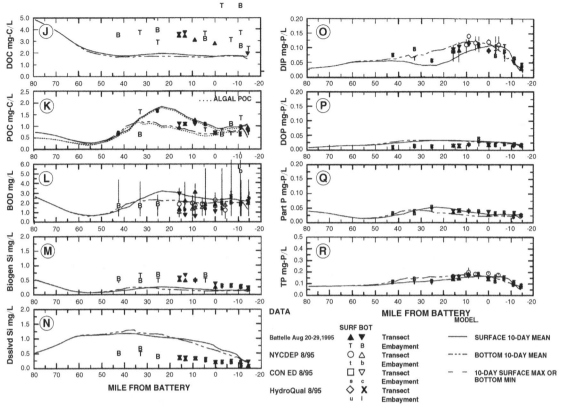

Figure 11.4. August 1994–95 SWEM spatial calibration for the Hudson River, Upper Bay, and Lower Bay for key parameters J – R.

oxygen). BOD is an important variable because it represents carbon, nitrogen, and oxygen kinetics simultaneously.

Dissolved oxygen. Panel D on Figure 11.3 shows model and data comparisons for dissolved oxygen (DO). The model results are shown as ten-day average concentrations in the surface layer (solid line) and in the bottom layer (broken line). Model results for surface maximum and bottom minimum are shown by the dashed lines. The model averages agree well with the mean observations, shown by various symbols, and the model maximums and minimums illustrate that the model is capturing the variability over time in the observed data.

Other variables. Figures 11.3 and 11.4 show model and data comparisons for other water quality variables including phosphorus (panels O through R), silica (panels M and N), and light extinction (panel E). The agreement between SWEM calcu-

lations and measurements of light extinction and additional nutrients simultaneously is further evidence that SWEM is useful for understanding the causality of primary production.

Primary productivity. A limited number of primary production measurements were collected for comparison to SWEM results. Primary productivity measurements were obtained by deploying a series of bottles containing surface water at various light levels and measuring dissolved oxygen production. Such a deployment measures net production as some of the oxygen that is being produced by algae within the bottles is also lost to respiration. By also deploying dark bottles, respiration could be estimated directly. A summation of light and dark bottle results yields gross primary production. Not enough primary production measurements were made to test the ability of the model to capture spatial gradients. Further, the data were difficult to interpret as dark bottle measurements showed oxygen production in some cases.

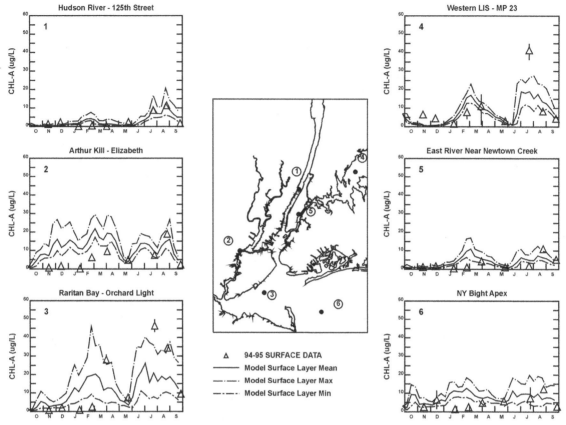

Figure 11.5. SWEM 1994–95 temporal calibration for primary production.

Figures 11.5 and 11.6 show summary model and data comparisons temporally over the course of a year for several locations as indicated on the map for chlorophyll and dissolved oxygen. These model and data comparisons demonstrate that primary production and eutrophication for the Hudson River Estuary and contiguous waterways is accurately calculated by SWEM. The model results and data at the locations shown are representative of both light/residence time limiting (i.e., Hudson River) and nutrient limiting (i.e., western Long Island Sound) conditions. The ability of SWEM to perform equally well under both conditions demonstrates model robustness and suitability for predictive purposes. The chlorophyll calibration represents modeled primary production in biomass units and is evidence that algal dynamics, nutrients, light, and physical conditions are all properly accounted for in the model. Further, dissolved oxygen (like chlorophyll) is an integrated system response. The dissolved oxygen calibration is a measure of the ability of the model to capture all features of primary production as well as additional source and sink terms in the dissolved oxygen balance including bacterially mediated decay processes. In this regard, dissolved oxygen may be viewed as the most important endpoint for calibration. Results on Figure 11.5 show that SWEM picks up much of the variability observed in near surface measurements. Results on Figure 11.6 show that SWEM captures observed vertical stratification.

Conclusions Drawn from SWEM

From SWEM projection work, two important generalizations can be drawn. First, primary production, as controlled by either the availability of nutrients, light, or residence time is location specific. For the Lower Hudson River Estuary and contiguous waterways, the areas for which primary production is controlled by the availability of nutrients include western Long Island Sound and New York Bight

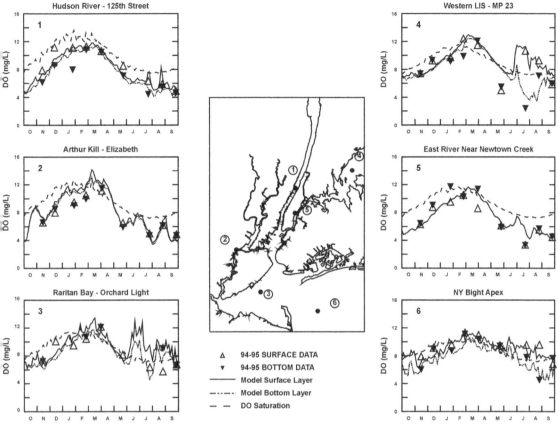

Figure 11.6. SWEM 1994–95 temporal calibration for dissolved oxygen.

and potentially portions of Raritan Bay. This conclusion is supported by measured data. Dissolved inorganic nitrogen measurements collected in New York/New Jersey Harbor during August 1995 have been separated into three groups: greater than 0.25 mg/l, between 0.25 mg/l and 0.05 mg/l, and less than 0.05 mg/l. Dissolved inorganic nitrogen measurements less than 0.05 mg/l, as observed in western Long Island Sound and New York Bight, indicate that nitrogen is limiting algal growth. Dissolved inorganic nitrogen measurements between 0.05 and 0.25, as observed in Raritan Bay, indicate that while nitrogen levels are low enough to contribute to less than maximum algal growth, the algal growth is being controlled more by light availability and residence time in the photic zone than by nitrogen availability. Dissolved inorganic nitrogen measurements greater than 0.25 mg/l, as observed throughout most of New York/New Jersey Harbor including the Hudson River Estuary, indicate that algal growth is not being limited by nitrogen, but

almost entirely by these other factors. Our results imply that:

1. increasing or decreasing the amount of nitrogen reaching western Long Island Sound and New York Bight will affect algal growth directly,
2. increasing or decreasing nitrogen will have a more limited effect on algal growth in Raritan Bay, and
3. increasing or decreasing nitrogen will have even less effect on algal growth in most areas of New York/New Jersey Harbor, including the Hudson River Estuary.

The second observation from SWEM projection work concerns the location-specific relative significance that nitrogen and carbon have on the resulting dissolved oxygen deficit. Model projection results show that the relative contributions of nitrogen and carbon to dissolved oxygen deficit vary significantly by location. For example, on a summer average basis, carbon accounts for 68 percent of the dissolved oxygen deficit and nitrogen accounts for 32 percent of the dissolved oxygen deficit at a location in the lower Hudson River Estuary along Manhattan Island. This is consistent with the fact that oxidation of allochthonous (that is, from point and nonpoint sources rather than from primary production) carbon is a large component of the dissolved oxygen budget in the lower Hudson River Estuary. Conversely, nitrogen accounts for 62 percent of the dissolved oxygen deficit and carbon accounts for 38 percent of the dissolved oxygen deficit at a given location in western Long Island Sound. This is consistent with western Long Island Sound being nutrient limited and algal processing of nitrogen (that is, primary production) dominating the dissolved oxygen balance.

The comprehensive and regional nature of models such as SWEM are useful to both the New York/New Jersey Harbor Estuary Program (HEP) and the Long Island Sound Study (LISS), as well as the City of New York. Since 1994, SWEM has undergone extensive technical review by panels of experts convened by both HEP and the LISS. A future application of SWEM may include the development of total maximum daily loads (TMDLs)/wasteload allocations (WLAs) for the Harbor, Bight, and Sound to the extent necessary to attain appropriate water uses and standards in the Lower Hudson River Estuary, the New York/New Jersey Harbor, and adjacent water bodies.

Unsolved Problems and Future Research

Future work in the area of primary production modeling of the Lower Hudson River Estuary is likely to center around three pressing needs arising in New York/New Jersey Harbor. These needs include:

1. The response of the local regulatory community to the U.S. Environmental Protection Agency's new marine dissolved oxygen criteria and nutrient criteria guidance documents,
2. Regulatory requirements for the development of total maximum daily loads (TMDLs) for nutrients and dissolved oxygen, and
3. The assessment of the impact of external chemical loadings to the New York/New Jersey Harbor ecosystem on water quality,

sediment quality, bottom dwelling organisms, and fish. The hydrodynamic transport and carbon production kinetics developed for primary productivity models are essential to a technically defensible modeling approach to address water quality, sediment, and food chain contaminant issues.

Acknowledgments

This work was supported by the New York City Department of Environmental Protection, and was performed under subcontract to Greeley and Hansen in association with Hazen and Sawyer, P. C., and Malcolm Pirnie, Inc.

REFERENCES

Berner, R. A. 1964. An idealized model of dissolved sulfate distributions in recent sediments. *Geochimica et Cosmochimica Acta (UK)* **28**:1497–1503.

———. 1974. Kinetic models for the early diagenesis of nitrogen, sulfur, phosphorus and silicon in anoxic marine sediments, in E. D. Goldberg (ed.), *The Sea*, Vol. 5, New York: Wiley, pp. 427–50.

———. 1980. *Early Diagenesis. A Theoretical Approach*. Princeton, NJ: Princeton University Press.

Blumberg, A. F., and Mellor, G. L. 1980. A coastal ocean numerical model, in J. Sundermann and K. P. Holz (eds.), *Mathematical Modeling of Estuarine Physics, Proceedings of an International Symposium*. Berlin: Springer-Verlag, pp. 202–219.

———. 1987. A description of a three-dimensional coastal ocean circulation model, in N. Heaps (ed.), *Three-Dimensional Coastal Ocean Models, Coastal and Estuarine Sciences*, Vol. 4. Washington, D.C.: American Geophysical Union, pp. 1–16.

Di Toro, D. M. 1980. The effect of phosphorus loadings on dissolved oxygen in Lake Erie, in R. C. Loehr, C. S. Martin, and W. Rast (eds.), *Phosphorus Management Strategies for Lakes*. Ann Arbor, MI: Ann Arbor Science, pp. 191–205.

Di Toro, D. M. and Fitzpatrick, J. J. 1993. *Chesapeake Bay sediment flux model*. Contract report EL-93-2. U.S. Army Corps of Engineers Waterways Experiment Station, Vicksburg, MS.

Di Toro, D. M. 2001. *Sediment Flux Modeling*. New York: John Wiley & Sons, Inc.

Di Toro, D. M., Lowe, S. A., and Fitzpatrick, J. J. Application of a water column-sediment eutrophication model to a mesocosm experiment. I. Calibration. In press.

Hutchinson, G. E. 1967. A treatise on limnology, in *Introduction to Lake Biology and Limnoplankton*, Vol. II, New York: Wiley, pp. 306–54.

HydroQual, Inc. 1989. *Assessment of pollutant fate in the New York Bight*. Prepared under contract with the Dynamac Corporation, Rockville, Maryland for the New York Bight Restoration Plan.

—— 1996. *Water quality modeling analysis of hypoxia in Long Island Sound using LIS3.0*. Report prepared for the New England Interstate Water Pollution Control Commission and the Management Committee of the Long Island Sound Estuary Study.

—— 1999a. *Newtown Creek WPCP Project East River Water Quality Plan, Task 9.0 – Harbor Eutrophication Model (HEM)*, Sub-tasks 9.1–9.7. Reports prepared under contract to Greeley and Hansen for the City of New York Department of Environmental Protection.

—— 1999b. *Newtown Creek WPCP Project East River Water Quality Plan, Task 10.0 – System-wide Eutrophication Model (SWEM)*, Sub-tasks 10.1–10.7. Reports prepared under contract to Greeley and Hansen for the City of New York Department of Environmental Protection.

Jay, D. A., and Bowman, M. J. 1975. *The physical oceanography and water quality of New York Harbor and western Long Island Sound*. Technical Report 23. Marine Sciences Research Center, State University of New York at Stony Brook, Stony Brook, NY.

Lund, J. W. G. 1965. The ecology of the freshwater phytoplankton. *Biological Reviews of the Cambridge Philosophical Society*. **40**:231–93.

Raymont, J. E. G. 1963. *Plankton and Productivity in the Oceans*. New York: Pergamon Press.

Rhee, G. Y. 1973. A continuous culture study of phosphate uptake, growth rate and polyphosphates in *Secendemus sp. Journal of Phycology* **9**: 495–506.

Steele, J. H. 1962. Environmental control of photosynthesis in the sea. *Limnology and Oceanography* **7**: 137–50.

Strickland, J. D. H. 1965. In J. P. Riley and G. Skivow (eds.), *Chemical Oceanography, Production of Organic Matter in Primary Stages of the Marine Food Chain*. Vol. 1, New York: Academic Press.

Hudson River Communities, Food Webs, and Fisheries

larvae are distributed and transported in the lower Hudson River Estuary.

12 Larval Migrations between the Hudson River Estuary and New York Bight

Steven G. Morgan

ABSTRACT Gaining insight into the causes of temporal and spatial variation in larval recruitment to estuaries is an important goal of fisheries biologists who ultimately aim to accurately predict year class strength of recreationally and commercially important species. I present essential information about the most abundant invertebrates and fishes that develop in the Hudson River Estuary and New York Bight during the summer and how their larvae migrate between these areas. This was accomplished by conducting an oceanographic research program that blended four approaches: 1) extensive larval surveys from the upper estuary to the edge of the continental shelf, 2) intensive hourly sampling of larvae over consecutive light-dark and tidal cycles and multiple depths, 3) a comparative hypothesis testing approach using passive eggs and swimming larvae, and 4) comparisons of larval production and settlement. Depending on the species, larvae remained in the estuary, migrated from the estuary to the continental shelf, or migrated from the shelf to the estuary. Interspecific differences in larval behavior enabled larvae to complete these different migration patterns. Moreover, the coupling of simple behaviors with conservative oceanographic features may have enabled larvae to reliably migrate between adult habitats and larval nursery areas regardless of how far larvae traveled. Thus, larvae undertake true migrations that may return them to natal populations more reliably than previously believed, which has important implications for the management of estuarine resources and the evolution of marine life histories. Additional research is needed to track larval movements, determine how postlarvae cross the continental shelf, and document how fish

Introduction

Estuaries provide essential habitat for many commercially and ecologically important animals during at least one phase of their life cycle. Most of these estuarine-dependent animals produce tremendous numbers of microscopic larvae that disperse away from parents before returning to suitable settlement sites. Because population dynamics of such organisms may be regulated by factors that affect either the larval or adult stages of their life histories, fluctuations in population sizes often may be great. Most mortality is believed to occur in the plankton because eggs and larvae have less control over their fates in this dynamic environment than do larger juveniles and adults that live on stable substrates. According to this line of thinking, few larvae survive long enough to settle into adult habitats except during years when favorable planktonic conditions prevail (Thorson, 1950; Morgan, 1995, 2001). The shear numbers of larvae produced, poor swimming capabilities of tiny larvae, and episodic settlement events have led to the belief that various sources of mortality overwhelm larvae.

Advection of larvae by currents may be one of the most important sources of mortality and may generate considerable variation in the timing and magnitude of recruitment. Indeed, one of the earliest mysteries that intrigued investigators throughout the twentieth century was how weakly swimming larvae avoid being flushed from estuaries and lost to the population (Young, 1990). Net flow in estuaries is seaward, which would seemingly sweep weakly swimming larvae out to sea. Once larvae are adrift in a vast ocean, the probability of them finding their way back into an estuary would seem to be small. At the very least, larvae should be transported downstream from the parental population, raising the question of how they return upstream to recruit to adult habitats. These sorts of problems have led many to believe that marine organisms play the lottery; they produce thousands or millions of larvae, increasing the odds that a few will return by chance. In contrast to this traditional view of marine life histories, mounting evidence suggests that larvae of estuarine-dependent animals

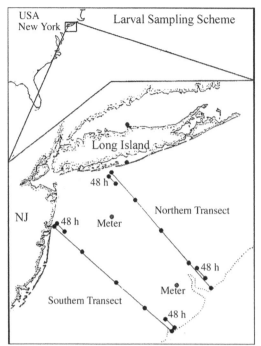

Figure 12.1. Sampling scheme consisting of three 48-hour stations in the upper Hudson River estuary sampled during spring and neap tides, multiple stations to map the location of the estuarine plume, a transect across the estuarine plume sampled for several days four times during spring and neap tides, two transects across the continental shelf sampled weekly for four months (June–Sept), two pairs of 48-hour stations on the inner shelf, two pairs of 48-hour stations on the outer shelf and two moorings with current meters on the inner and outer shelf between the transects. For each sampling scheme, the vertical and horizontal distributions of larvae relative to water column structure and current velocity were documented during two consecutive summers. The dotted line at the seaward end of the two transects represents the shelf break.

make true migrations between adult and larval habitats by exploiting predictable oceanographic features (Epifanio and Garvine, 2001, Strathmann et al., 2002).

Most of the previous research on larval transport in the Hudson River estuary has been conducted on commercially important species of anadromous fishes that spawn and develop in the upper reaches of the river. However, many other important species develop in the estuary and adjacent coastal waters and their larval distributions are barely known. With the help of my students and colleagues, I launched an oceanographic research program to

provide an initial understanding of how larvae are transported between the Hudson River Estuary and New York Bight. The research program consisted of three sampling schemes reaching from the upper estuary near the George Washington Bridge to the edge of the continental shelf (Fig. 12.1). The sampling program coupled extensive horizontal surveys of the study area with intensive vertical profiles of the water column to determine how this differential transport is accomplished.

The purpose of this chapter is to provide an overview of this comprehensive research program. I will highlight (1) larval transport patterns of species that spend at least part of their life cycle in the Hudson River Estuary, (2) the mechanisms enabling differential larval transport, (3) management implications of these transport patterns, and (4) directions for future research.

Migration between the Hudson and New York Bight

I begin this section by documenting differential transport between the Hudson River Estuary and New York Bight. Then, I present evidence that these transport patterns are maintained behaviorally. I discuss how larvae are (1) retained in the upper estuary, (2) exchanged between the estuary and shelf, and (3) transported on the continental shelf. Lastly, I suggest that larval migrations to the continental shelf are as reliable as migrations that are completed within the estuary.

LARVAL MIGRATIONS

Five larval migration patterns were documented for eighteen taxa: (1) larval retention in the Hudson River estuary by five taxa of invertebrates and two taxa of fishes, (2) retention in the estuarine plume by one taxon of crab, (3) larval migration from the estuary beyond the estuarine plume by three taxa of crabs, (4) larval migration from New York Bight into the estuary by one taxon of fish, and (5) larval retention on the shelf by one taxon of crab and five taxa of fishes (Fig. 12.2). Lastly, the larvae of the one taxon of crab and five taxa of fishes that live on the continental shelf largely remained there throughout development. A substantial body of work suggests that the same species-specific larval migration patterns occur along the Atlantic coast of the United States (Epifanio and Garvine, 2001).

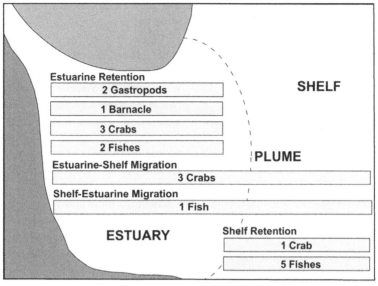

Figure 12.2. Larval migration patterns documented for the Hudson River Estuary and New York Bight. 1) Estuarine retention: eggs or larvae of two gastropods (periwinkle *Littorina littorea*, slipper shell *Crepidula fornicata*), one barnacle (*Balanus improvisus*), two mud crabs (*Rhithropanopeus harrisii, Dyspanopeus sayi*), spider crabs (*Libinia* spp.) and two fishes (bay anchovy *Anchoa mitchilli*, naked goby *Gobiosoma bosc*) were released in the estuary and larvae primarily remained there through development. 2) Estuarine-shelf migration: larvae of three crab taxa (lady crab *Ovalipes ocellatus*, fiddler crabs *Uca* spp., blue crab *Callinectes sapidus*) were released in the estuary, emigrated to the shelf and returned to the estuary as postlarvae. 3) Shelf-estuarine migration: bluefish (*Pomatomus saltatrix*) spawned on the shelf, larvae immigrated to the estuary and returned to the shelf as juveniles. 4) Shelf retention: larvae of rock crabs *Cancer* spp. and eggs of five fish taxa (Gulf Stream flounder *Citharichthys arctifrons*, fourspot flounder *Hippoglossina oblonga*, smallmouth flounder *Etropus microstomus*, Atlantic butterfish *Peprilus triacanthus*, searobins *Prionotus* spp.) were released on the shelf, and larvae mostly remained there through development.

An initial picture of differential larval migration emerged over the last quarter century by piecing together results of previous studies, which typically focused on only one species, larval habitat, or development stage. One of the strengths of the present study is that all larval stages of the dominant species of crabs and fishes were surveyed across the full range of larval habitats to definitively document inshore-offshore shifts in larval assemblages and stages of development. This comprehensive approach has yielded a more complete picture of the range of larval transport patterns than the simpler classification of retention and export (Strathmann, 1982). It is now clear that the dichotomy of retention and export really represents a continuum of larval migration by crab species, ranging from short migrations within different regions of the estuary to longer migrations between the lower estuary and different regions of the continental shelf (Fig. 12.3). This results in horizontal zonation of species in the plankton between the upper estuary and the edge of the continental shelf. Larval migration by fishes also results in a predictable spatial gradient with larvae either largely remaining in the estuary, remaining on the shelf or migrating from the shelf to the estuary. Thus, larvae of some species remain near parents either in the estuary or on the continental shelf, while others migrate between these environments. How was this differential transport accomplished?

BEHAVIORAL REGULATION OF LARVAL MIGRATIONS

Behavior must have been important because larvae migrated in opposite directions at the same time, i.e., different species move in opposite directions

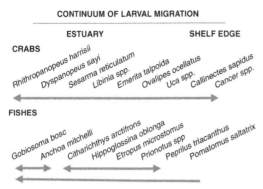

Figure 12.3. A continuum of larval migration by crab species results in horizontal zonation of species in the plankton between the upper estuary and the edge of the continental shelf: *Rhithropanopeus harrisii* larvae occur in the upper estuary, *Dyspanopeus sayi* larvae occur in the mid to lower estuary, *Libinia* spp. larvae occur in the lower estuary to the plume front, *Ovalipes ocellatus* and *Uca* spp. larvae occur from the upper, mid, or lower estuary (depending on the species) to the inner shelf, *Callinectes sapidus* larvae occur from the lower estuary to the outer shelf, and *Cancer* spp. larvae occur on the shelf. Larval migration by fishes also results in a predictable spatial gradient with larvae either largely remaining in the estuary, remaining on the shelf, or migrating from the shelf to the estuary: *Anchoa mitchelli* and *Gobiosoma bosc* larvae primarily occur in the estuary, *Pomatomus saltatrix* larvae occur on the shelf and enter the estuary as postlarvae, and nonestuarine-dependent species (*Citharichthys arctifrons*, *Hippoglossina oblonga*, *Etropus microstomus*, *Peprilus triacanthus*, *Prionotus* spp.) largely remain on the shelf.

at the same time, and different stages of the same species move in opposite directions at the same time. Therefore, currents alone cannot explain the observed horizontal distributions of larvae, and behavior must be regulating migrations between adult and larval nursery areas. The continuum of larval transport patterns was maintained by the behavioral exploitation of circulation patterns. This was determined by coupling repeated extensive horizontal surveys with intensive vertical surveys relative to tides, currents, winds, and stage of development. This approach showed a clear relationship between interspecific differences in horizontal and vertical distributions of larvae. The vertical distributions were shown to be largely under behavioral control by using a comparative hypothesis

testing approach that contrasted passive eggs with active larvae.

Upper estuary. Larvae remained within the upper Hudson River estuary (between the George Washington and Verrazano bridges) by exploiting typical two-layer flow. Residual flow was seaward at the surface, landward along the bottom and zero at 4–5 m depth at the shallowest site near the George Washington Bridge and 8–10 m depth at the deepest site near the Verrazano Bridge. At the shallow site, larvae remaining above 5 m would be swept downstream, those near 5 m would slosh back and forth over the tidal cycle without any net transport, and those at the bottom would be carried upstream. Larvae could use this two-layer flow as a conveyor belt to move up and down the estuary provided that they effectively regulated their vertical position. The problem is that the water column is very dynamic over the tidal cycle. During spring tides when tidal currents were strongest, the water column at the shallow site was thoroughly mixed by flood and ebb currents every six hours and was partially mixed at the deep site. Can larvae regulate their vertical positions under such dynamic conditions?

The ability of larvae to regulate depth was tested by comparing the vertical distributions of nonmotile eggs and swimming larvae (Fig. 12.4). Eggs were passively mixed throughout the water column by strong ebb and flood currents every six hours as expected. By contrast, larvae were not mixed like eggs, and instead, apparently regulated depth. For example, all four larval stages of both species of crabs remained near the depth of no net transport and stayed near adult populations (Fig. 12.5). All four larval stages of *R. harrisii* were present upstream and were rare downstream, clearly indicating that they did not travel far after hatching. Larvae of the second species of mud crab, *D. sayi*, occurred in higher salinity waters downstream, thereby replacing *R. harrisii* larvae. Thus, similar vertical distributions of larvae of the two crab species resulted in larval retention within the estuary.

Larvae of *R. harrisii* have been shown to remain in the upper reaches of two other estuaries by remaining near the level of no net motion (Bousfield, 1955, Cronin and Forward, 1986). Laboratory studies suggest that both *R. harrisii*

HYPOTHESES

H_0: Turbulent mixing overcomes larvae if vertical distributions of eggs and larvae are similar.

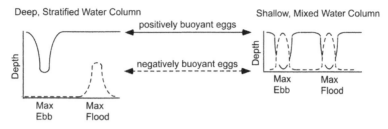

H_1: Larvae regulate depth if they remain at one depth or periodically change depth.

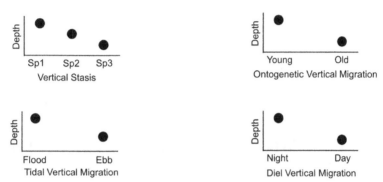

Figure 12.4. Upper panel: expected vertical distributions of eggs and larvae over the tidal cycle in deep and shallow portions of the estuary, provided that turbulent mixing overwhelms larval behavior. Lower panel: expected distributions of larvae if they regulate depth effectively. Larvae may remain at one depth or change depth during development, and they may periodically change depth relative to tidal or light-dark cycles.

and *D. sayi* larvae may remain at their preferred depth by swimming upward until they reached light intensities and hydrostatic pressures sufficient to cause them to sink to a lower depth, and they may fine tune their vertical distributions over the tidal cycle by responding to changes in temperature and salinity.

Tidal vertical migrations also may facilitate retention of crab larvae in the upper estuary. They were first described for *R. harrisii* larvae in the laboratory, but they were not detected in the present study nor were they evident in a previous field study (Cronin and Forward, 1986). It is possible that the amplitude of vertical migration about the level of no net motion is too slight to be detected without finely sampling the vertical distributions of larvae over the tidal cycle. Another possibility is that larvae are overwhelmed by the strong tidal currents at these sites, because tidal vertical migrations by

D. sayi larvae have been detected in a quiet backwater of Long Island Sound where turbulent mixing may be much reduced (Hovel and Morgan, 1997). Crab postlarvae also undertake tidal vertical migrations (Christy and Morgan, 1998). Both crabs metamorphose to postlarvae after ten to fourteen days, sink lower in the water column, and undertake tidal vertical migrations back upstream to adult habitats (Fig. 12.5).

As for crab larvae, the vertical distributions of anchovy and goby larvae differed from eggs, suggesting that they regulated depth. However, they regulated depth differently than did crab larvae. These fish larvae appeared to undertake both tidal and diel vertical migrations at the downstream site. Tidal vertical migrations should lead to the upstream transport of larvae. This was the first time that tidal migrations have been observed for either species, although upstream transport has

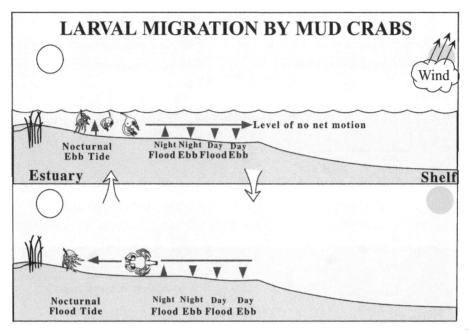

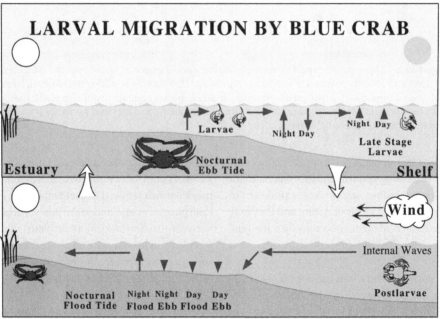

Figure 12.5. Larval migration by mud crabs (*Rhithropanopeus harrisii, Dyspanopeus sayi*) and blue crab (*Callinectes sapidus*) between the estuary and shelf, depicting changes in behaviors relative to physical transport processes.

been inferred from the horizontal distributions of eggs and larvae of both fishes before (Massman, Norcross, and Joseph, 1963; Schultz et al., 2000).

The vertical distributions of larvae of both fish species changed at the upstream site, and vertical migrations were no longer evident. However, larval distributions still differed from those of passively distributed eggs. Goby larvae occurred primarily in bottom waters throughout the tidal cycle, which would enable them to move slowly upstream. These larvae school near the bottom before settling in shallow oyster beds (Breitburg, 1989), but it remains unclear whether the changes in vertical distributions of anchovy larvae represent a behavioral switch in response to changing environmental conditions or whether larvae were simply overcome by strong mixing from ebbing surface currents. Anchovy larvae occurred in the upper water column near slack tides and appeared to be mixed throughout the water column near mid-flood and mid-ebb tides. An extensive study of anchovy larvae that was conducted upstream from the present study showed that this pattern was maintained throughout the uppermost region of the estuary (Schultz et al., 2000). Thus, anchovy larvae may have moved upstream by undertaking tidal vertical migrations until they reached the shallow uppermost estuary, whereupon they may have been overcome, slowing upstream transport.

Tidal vertical migrations apparently were not essential for crab and fish larvae to be retained in the upper estuary, despite expediting upstream transport. Maximal ebb currents occurred at the surface, so that if larvae maintained their position at mid-depth, they would not be transported as far downstream as they would be transported upstream by a velocity jet that formed beneath the pycnocline during flood tides. However, larvae were mixed throughout the water column by ebbing surface currents and may have spent some time near the surface in maximal ebb currents and some time near the bottom in minimal ebb currents. Therefore on average, larvae still would have been transported seaward more slowly during ebb tide than they would have been transported upstream by remaining near the velocity jet during flood tide.

In summary, larvae remained in the upper estuary by regulating depth. All larval stages were collected, the vertical distributions of larvae differed from nonmotile eggs over tidal cycles and were consistent with behaviors that would foster retention, and interspecific differences in vertical distributions of larvae were evident that would result in differential transport.

Estuarine plume. The first step in determining how larvae migrate between the Hudson River estuary and New York Bight was to map the location of the front that separates turbid, river water from clearer, shelf water. The plume is a dynamic feature that moves back and forth with the tides, winds,

and runoff, and therefore, it must be mapped continuously relative to larval distributions to determine how larvae are exchanged between estuarine and coastal waters. Surveying horizontal distributions across the plume front revealed an interspecific continuum of larval transport away from shore; larvae of some species occurred farther offshore than did others. At one end of the spectrum, *R. harrisii* larvae were absent, again indicating that these larvae were retained effectively in the upper estuary despite net seaward flow, and larvae of *D. sayi* remained almost exclusively (98 percent) in the mouth of the estuary. Larvae of spider and lady crabs mostly were released near the mouth of the estuary and moved farther offshore during development than did *D. sayi* larvae. The two larval stages of spider crab take only six to eight days to develop (Johns and Lang, 1977), enabling them to largely remain shoreward of the front while most postlarvae eventually were transported seaward of it. The lady crab has five larval stages, and late stage larvae of the lady crab were much more abundant seaward of the front than were late stage larvae of the spider crab. Few blue crab and fiddler crab larvae occurred in the estuary, and they became increasingly abundant farther offshore, indicating that they may have been transported into the study area from elsewhere.

The differential transport of larvae may have been facilitated by interspecific differences in the vertical distributions of larvae during development. *Dyspanopeus sayi* larvae were retained in the mouth of the estuary by remaining near the level of no net motion, as was evident in the upper estuary. Spider crab larvae were transported toward the plume front by occurring throughout the water column, and lady crab larvae were transported out to sea by primarily occurring in outwelling surface currents. Like lady crab larvae, blue crab larvae mostly occurred near the surface but apparently were carried in the opposite direction toward shore. Therefore, mean depth distributions alone may not entirely account for differential offshore-onshore transport.

Ontogenetic vertical migrations may have facilitated differential onshore-offshore transport. Spider and lady crab larvae both appeared to undertake classic ontogenetic vertical migrations, wherein early stage larvae occurred primarily in the neuston and late stage larvae or postlarvae occurred deeper in the water column. Therefore, early stage larvae of these species all may have been transported seaward by outwelling surface currents early in development, while seaward transport may have slowed or reversed late in development. In contrast, blue crab larvae appeared to undertake a reverse ontogenetic vertical migration (Fig. 12.5). By becoming increasingly more abundant in the neuston during development, blue crab larvae and especially postlarvae may have been transported into our study area from elsewhere.

The plume front was a persistent feature throughout the duration of sampling, but there was little evidence that larvae aggregated there, even though tremendous numbers of ctenophores and salps did. Gelatinous zooplanktons may have physically displaced larvae or they may have greatly reduced larval densities by predation. However, it may be even more likely that larvae did not aggregate at the front because most of them occurred beneath converging surface currents.

New York Bight. Of the four taxa that hatched in the estuary and were common in the estuarine plume, only lady and blue crab larvae were abundant on the open shelf. Fiddler crab larvae also were abundant on the shelf even though they were uncommon in the estuary and plume. First stage larvae of these three taxa were most abundant nearshore, and later larval stages were increasingly more abundant farther from shore during development. However, the distance that larvae traveled from shore differed among taxa. Fiddler crab larvae remained closest to shore and were most prevalent at stations 1 and 2 throughout development while rarely occurring beyond station 3 even late in development. Lady crab larvae also were most common at station 1 throughout the larval period but occurred in low concentrations as far offshore as station 4 beginning midway during development. Unlike larvae of these taxa, blue crab larvae were at least as common at stations 2 and 3 as they were at station 1, were common as far from shore as station 4 late in development, and even were collected at station 5 in low concentrations. Progressive seaward transport of larvae during development may have been due to Ekman transport by prevailing northeasterly winds, because larvae of all three taxa

frequented surface waters, especially at night during diel vertical migrations.

The distance that larvae were transported offshore may have depended more on the location of larval release and larval development time than on the time that larvae spent in surface waters. Fiddler crab larvae were not transported as far offshore as were lady crab larvae, even though most of them occurred in the neuston rather than in near surface waters (1 to 10 m deep) and the two taxa have the same number of larval stages (5) and similar development times (Williams, 1984). Rather, lady crab larvae had a head start; they hatched near the mouth of the estuary, whereas fiddler crab larvae hatched throughout the lower estuary (Williams, 1984). Blue crab larvae were transported farthest offshore, because they are released near the mouths of estuaries, have three more larval stages, and were most abundant in the neuston of the three taxa (Fig. 12.5).

Spending time near the surface may be imperative for larvae to remain near the parental estuary. When these crabs develop, prevailing subsurface currents in New York Bight flowed to the southwest, and winds blew in the opposite direction to the northeast generating a countercurrent mid-shelf. Therefore, larvae in the neuston may be transported northward against the prevailing subsurface flow. Northward transport clearly occurred for the surface-dwelling larvae of blue and fiddler crabs. Few first stage larvae of either species were collected in the Hudson River estuary, the estuarine plume or farther offshore, and later larval stages generally increased during development in New York Bight. Therefore, larvae likely were released elsewhere and transported into our study area. Larvae likely originated from southern populations, because they generally became increasingly more abundant all along the southern transect during development. The time required to travel northward from southern populations likely explains why late stage were more prevalent than were early stage larvae along the southern transect. By the time long-lived blue crab larvae metamorphosed to postlarvae, they again abounded along the northern transect, indicating that they traveled farther north than did fiddler crab larvae.

The proportion of lady crab larvae along the southern transect also increased during development, which again is consistent with northward transport. However, fewer of these slightly deeper dwelling larvae may have been transported northward than were larvae of the other taxa, because a lower proportion of them occurred along the southern than the northern transect. Furthermore, first stage larvae were abundant and larval density progressively declined during development, which is consistent with cumulative larval mortality without the extensive immigration shown by the other taxa. Thus, lady crab larvae largely appeared to be retained in New York Bight with some immigration from southern populations, and most blue and fiddler crab larvae in New York Bight likely originated to the south. Further evidence of northward transport was provided by the appearance of expatriate larvae of southern species that do not occur in New York Bight as adults, such as the box crab *Calappa flammea*.

Now that multiple studies of vertical migration by a single species are beginning to accumulate, it is becoming increasingly clear that the vertical migration behavior of larvae changes in space and time. Although lady crab larvae consistently appeared to undertake a classic ontogenetic vertical migration in the estuarine plume, in New York Bight and elsewhere in the Middle Atlantic Bight (Epifanio, 1988), blue crab larvae undertook a reverse ontogenetic vertical migration in the plume and a classic ontogenetic vertical migration farther offshore, elsewhere in the Middle Atlantic Bight (Epifanio, Valenti, and Pembroke, 1984; Epifanio, Little, and Rowe, 1988) and in the laboratory (Sulkin et al., 1980). Furthermore, fiddler crab larvae appeared to undertake a reverse vertical migration during our 48-hour study and in the laboratory (Anastasia, 1999), but they undertook classic ontogenetic vertical migrations elsewhere in the Middle Atlantic Bight (Epifanio et al., 1988). Moreover, a reverse tidal vertical migration was evident for lady crab larvae in New York Bight, but classic vertical migrations were apparent in the Hudson River plume. Finally, rock crab larvae appeared to undertake both classic and reverse ontogenetic and tidal vertical migrations, depending when and where larvae were sampled between the mouth of the Hudson River estuary to the edge of the shelf. This variation probably is not random noise but is under rhythmic behavioral control. This has been demonstrated by contrasting the timing of vertical swimming by blue crab postlarvae from onshore and offshore waters in the laboratory (Forward and Rittschof, 1994) and by fiddler crab larvae that were collected from different tidal regimes and observed under constant conditions in the laboratory (Anastasia, 1999). Plasticity in vertical migration behavior of larvae in response to changing oceanographic conditions may play an important role in facilitating cross-shelf migrations between adult habitats and larval nursery areas, and we need to increase our understanding of the underlying mechanisms generating plasticity in vertical migration.

We are just beginning to understand how larvae recruit back onshore, but they may have been transported shoreward by internal waves and directed onshore swimming (Fig. 12.5). Tidally generated internal waves propagate across the shelf transporting postlarvae that accumulate in surface convergences above the wave with them (Shanks, 1995). Onshore swimming may facilitate onshore migrations, because these postlarvae are able swimmers; blue crab larvae can swim about 10 cm/s (Luckenbach and Orth, 1992) and bluefish larvae swim even faster at 2–3 body lengths/s (Hunter, 1981). Recent evidence suggests that postlarvae may use chemical, auditory, and other cues to swim toward shore and locate estuaries (Kingsford et al., 2002). Crab and bluefish postlarvae remained at the surface after they crossed the estuarine plume front, but once inside estuaries, these chemical cues may initiate a change in behavior (Forward and Rittschof, 1994). All crab postlarvae investigated thus far undertake selective tidal migrations (Fig. 12.5) that transport them up estuary to adult habitats (Christy and Morgan, 1998).

Behavior ensures a steady supply of recruits, even though postlarvae of some species begin their journey from as far away as the edge of the continental shelf. Many investigators point to occasional large recruitment events as evidence that physical forcing rather than behavior controls larval supply. For example, downwelling winds episodically force blue crab postlarvae from nearshore coastal waters into the mouths of estuaries resulting in large recruitment events (Epifanio and Garvine, 2001). However in the absence of these wind events, they recruit regularly to estuaries. Winds are light throughout the peak recruitment season of blue

Table 12.1. Rank orders of Stage I larvae captured in plankton tows and postlarvae captured in the plankton or on settlement collectors in Flax Pond, New York

Flax Pond is a shallow embayment on the south shore of Long Island Sound. Larval production matched larval recruitment, regardless of whether larvae typically develop on the continental shelf or entirely within estuaries, except for *Ovalipes ocellatus* that did not recruit to the salt marsh. Larvae of two other crabs were present but were not included here because postlarvae were not reliably sampled (pinnotherids) or larvae were rare and the dispersal pattern is not well known (*Hemigrapsus sanguineus*).

Species	Larval habitat	Larval production	Larval recruitment
Uca spp.	Shelf	1	1
Dyspanopeus sayi	Estuary	2	2
Ovalipes ocellatus	Shelf	3	6
Sesarma reticulatum	Estuary	4	3
Libinia spp.	Shelf	5	4
Panopeus herbstii	Estuary	6	5

Adapted from Hovel and Morgan, 1997.

crabs along the north central Gulf Coast, and yet blue crabs recruited to Mobile Bay, Alabama, every two weeks during minimum amplitude tides throughout the six-month study period for two consecutive years (Morgan et al., 1996). Therefore, blue crab larvae may cross the continental shelf and enter estuaries by exploiting reliable physical transport mechanisms.

Cross-shelf mechanisms may be as reliable as much better understood estuarine mechanisms. This surprising conclusion was reached by measuring larval production and recruitment of estuarine crabs to determine whether species that developed on the shelf recruited to a salt marsh in Long Island Sound as reliably as did those that developed entirely within estuaries (Hovel and Morgan, 1997). Indeed they did; postlarvae recruited back proportionally to the numbers of larvae that were released regardless of whether larvae were retained or exported (Table 12.1). The one exception was for lady crab that may not recruit to salt marshes. The same result was obtained in both other estuaries (North Inlet, South Carolina; Mobile Bay, Alabama) where this comparison was made (Christy and Morgan, 1998; Morgan unpublished data). Thus, recruitment appears to be reliable whether larvae leave the estuary or not along the Atlantic and Gulf coasts, thereby calling into question the widely held belief that larvae that migrate far away on the continental shelf and that develop for a long time in the plankton recruit less reliably than do species that do not migrate far and spend little time in the plankton. This also suggests that recruitment probably may not be decoupled from local production, as is commonly thought.

Management Implications

Whether larvae settle near parental estuaries or disperse far away has important implications for the management of estuarine resources, as well as the evolution of estuarine life histories. From a management perspective, stocks in the Hudson River Estuary may be managed far more easily if local conditions regulate recruitment into adult populations than if many recruits originated from estuaries in neighboring states. Identifying the larval transport mechanisms is critical if we are to understand how variation in oceanographic and meteorological conditions affects the location, timing, and magnitude of recruitment. Ultimately, the aim is to understand the underlying causes of variation in larval recruitment in order to forecast harvests of commercially and recreationally important species and to model fundamental ecological processes that regulate the abundance of marine populations.

This study has provided an initial picture of larval transport patterns of species that recruit to the Hudson River Estuary and the underlying transport mechanisms that enable differential transport between the estuary and New York Bight. The coupling of simple behaviors with conservative oceanographic features may enable larvae to re-liably migrate between adult habitats and larval nursery areas. Understanding how larvae routinely accomplish these migrations is necessary before we can fully appreciate how episodic changes to pre-vailing oceanographic conditions affect larval re-cruitment to adult populations. Predictions of year class strength will be greatly improved by moni-toring the key physical variables that affect larval transport processes.

Monitoring river runoff may be especially im-portant to species that develop within estuaries. A nine-year record of settlement variation by bar-nacles in Narragansett Bay, Rhode Island, was explained by variation in runoff, which affected the number of larvae that were retained in the bay or flushed into coastal waters; settlement was low when flushing rates were high (Gaines and Bertness, 1992). Monitoring larval supply of estuarine-dependent species and correlating it with variation in river runoff would be the first step toward determining whether this potentially im-portant factor affects recruitment success. If it does, then the second step would be to determine how the larval transport mechanism weakened by con-ducting vertical and horizontal plankton surveys.

Monitoring internal wave formation and wind velocity may be particularly important to estuarine-dependent species that develop on the continental shelf. Concurrently monitoring both larval supply and postsettlement mortality is necessary to fully understand recruitment dynamics; only by doing so did it become apparent that early postsettlement mortality rather than larval supply was the bottleneck in blue crab populations, even though postlarvae had to cross the shelf to reach the estuary. Blue crabs prefer to settle in submerged vegetation, and packing more recruits into this limited area leads to very highly postsettlement mortality from cannibalization (Pile et al., 1996; Heck, Coen, and Morgan, 2001). The connection between larval transport, larval supply, settlement, and recruitment into adult populations will become clearer as concurrent monitoring of benthic and pelagic phases of the life cycle continue and our understanding of coastal transport processes improves.

The recruitment studies conducted in Long Is-land Sound and elsewhere along the Atlantic and Gulf coasts suggest that a high proportion of lar-vae may recruit back to parental estuaries. The proportion of larvae that return to the parental es-tuary cannot be known with certainty until we can effectively tag and recapture them. However, if self-recruitment eventually proves to be the case, then local conditions will have a greater impact on re-cruitment than conditions in neighboring estuar-ies. This knowledge of transport mechanisms is im-portant in understanding stock discreteness and size. Without such information, managers are lim-ited in their estimates of stock abundance. Armed with a model of transport mechanisms, predic-tions can be made about the timing and relative strength of recruitment events. Moreover, manage-ment practices implemented in the Hudson River Estuary will have a large effect on local species that do not migrate as adults between estuaries, even if managers in adjacent estuaries choose not to im-plement them. Thus, greater local control may be exerted over stocks in the Hudson River Estuary, rendering policy easier to enact and stocks easier to manage effectively.

Finally, monitoring plankton populations re-vealed surprisingly few larvae of several taxa, in-cluding fiddler, blue, and marsh (*Sesarma retic-ulatum*) crabs in the Hudson River estuary and estuarine plume, even though larvae of these species abounded in neighboring Long Island Sound (Hovel and Morgan, 1997) and bays and es-tuaries along the coast of Delaware (Epifanio et al., 1984, Epifanio et al., 1988). Destruction of inter-tidal adult habitat, perhaps compounded by pollu-tion may have greatly reduced the number of fiddler and marsh crab larvae in the Hudson River estuary. Dense breeding populations in Fire Island Inlet on the southern shore of Long Island, also virtually dis-appeared about a decade before this study was con-ducted (J. Ebert, Natural Resources Manager Fire Island, personal communication), perhaps due to pollution or localized disease. First stage blue crab larvae may have been uncommon, because New York Bight may be nearing the northern limit of the reproductive range of this subtidal crab (Williams, 1984). Rather than living there year-round, females migrate along the coast from farther south to re-lease larvae in late August and September (P. Briggs, New York Department of Environmental Conserva-tion, personal communication). The implications of the loss of the large input of crab larvae into estuarine and nearshore plankton communities during the summer when many fishes are feeding and developing there is unknown.

Future Research

It is difficult to evaluate the general well-being of animal populations in the Hudson River estuary and to manage them without knowing how this nursery area is used. This research has provided basic, crucial information about the most abundant species that develop in the Hudson River Estuary and New York Bight during the summer and how their larvae migrate between these areas. Detailed physical-behavioral models have been developed for larvae of each species that collectively show how differential migrations between adult and larval habitats are made. This was accomplished by blending four approaches: 1) a comparative hypothesis testing approach using eggs and larvae, 2) extensive horizontal surveys, 3) intensive hourly sampling over consecutive light-dark and tidal cycles and multiple depths, and 4) comparing larval production to settlement. This sampling strategy has yielded important new insights into the relative contributions of behavior and hydrodynamics to larval transport. Using eggs of different buoyancies as passive tracers indicated that larvae regulated their position in the water column. Contrasts among diverse species with different swimming capabilities and sites with different levels of mixing revealed considerable variation in the abilities of larvae to regulate depth. Comparing vertical migrations by larvae of the same species across the range of habitats encountered during their horizontal migrations revealed the first evidence of tidal vertical migrations and phenotypic plasticity in response to changing oceanographic conditions. Contrasting larval abundances and distributions across study sites with known adult distributions revealed the probable consequences of larval behavior, turbulent mixing, and advection to larval transport. Comparing larval production to recruitment revealed that larval export was as reliable as larval retention.

Although our sampling design was a significant advance in studying larval transport of estuarine-dependent species, it was not without its limitations. Two notable deficiencies were our inability to survey larvae and to monitor recruitment in the lower estuary. Daily monitoring of recruitment over several months is required to gain meaningful data, but it was not feasible to do so from our remote location. A much better understanding of the relationship between larval transport and recruitment could be gained by concurrently monitoring recruits, larval distributions, and physical variables. Our understanding of larval transport processes on the continental shelf also needs to be greatly improved, and I refer the reader to Shanks' (1995) review for an insightful discussion of how to tackle this difficult problem.

Perhaps the biggest gap in our knowledge is how fish larvae use the lower Hudson River Estuary. Even basic information on larval distributions and abundances is limited, making it difficult to foresee how the complex circulation of the lower bay affects the movements of fish larvae. However, it may be that 1) most larvae migrate to and from the Hudson River Estuary and Raritan Bay along main channels, 2) larvae found in Ambrose Channel likely will be flushed from the lower estuary unless they remain in landward flowing bottom waters, 3) tidal vertical migrations may not greatly facilitate retention or reinvasion over shoals and flanks because flow is seaward throughout the water column, 4) most larvae would recruit during neap tides due to enhanced stratification, 5) eddies may concentrate larvae in calm shoal areas, and 6) flux should be greatest along channels at openings to the lower estuary, depending on winds and tidal amplitude. These hypotheses can be addressed by concurrently describing the circulation, larval distributions, and larval behaviors to estimate larval retention and flux.

In conclusion, we have provided an initial understanding of the relative roles of these two processes in larval depth regulation and transport between the Hudson River Estuary and New York Bight that ultimately may lead to better predictions of year class strength of recreationally, commercially, and ecologically important species. However, an exhaustive sampling strategy should be coupled with promising new approaches, such as individual based models, larval behavior mimics (Wolcott, 1995) and larval tagging (Anastasia, Morgan, and Fisher, 1998; Thorrold et al., 2002), to fully resolve the roles of behavioral and physical processes in larval transport.

Acknowledgments

This research was a result of the collaborative efforts of my colleagues (Kamazima Lwiza, Bob Cowen), students (Holly Kunze, Andy Matthews, Karl Lobue, Jeff Schell, Jean Anastasia, Kevin Hovel) and the crew of the R/V Onrust (Brett Zielenski, Mark Wiggins). Lynn McMasters and Justin Neviackas assisted with figure preparation. Funding was provided by two grants from the Hudson River Foundation (01091A, 0993A) and one grant from the National Oceanographic and Atmospheric Administration (NA90AA-D-SG078) to the Research Foundation of the State University of New York for the New York Sea Grant Institute. The U. S. Government is authorized to produce and distribute reprints for governmental purposes notwithstanding any copyright notation that may appear hereon. The views expressed herein is the author's and do not necessarily reflect the views of NOAA or any of its subagencies. Contribution Number 2183 from the Bodega Marine Laboratory, University of California at Davis.

REFERENCES

Anastasia, J. C. 1999. Plasticity and the cost of dispersal by estuarine crab larvae. Doctoral dissertation. State University of New York, Stony Brook, New York.

Anastasia, J. C., Morgan, S. G., and Fisher, N. S. 1998. Tagging crustacean larvae: assimilation and retention of trace elements. *Limnology and Oceanography* **43**:362–8.

Bousfield, E. L. 1955. Ecological control of the occurrence of barnacles in the Miramichi estuary. *Bulletin of the National Museum of Canada* **137**:1–69.

Breitburg, D. L. 1989. Demersal schooling prior to settlement of larvae of the naked goby. *Environmental Biology of Fishes* **26**:97–103.

Christy, J. H., and Morgan, S. G. 1998. Estuarine immigration by crab postlarvae: mechanisms, reliability and adaptive significance. *Marine Ecology Progress Series* **174**:51–65.

Cronin, T. W., and Forward, Jr., R. B. 1986. Vertical migration cycles of crab larvae and their role in larval dispersal. *Bulletin of Marine Science* **39**: 192–201.

Epifanio, C. E. 1988. Dispersal strategies of two species of swimming crabs on the continental shelf adjacent to Delaware Bay. *Marine Ecology Progress Series* **49**:243–8.

Epifanio, C. E. and Garvine, R. W. 2001. Larval transport on the Atlantic continental shelf of North America: a review. *Estuarine Coastal and Shelf Science* **52**:51–77.

Epifanio, C. E., Little, K. T., and Rowe, P. M. 1988. Dispersal and recruitment of fiddler crab larvae in the Delaware river estuary. *Marine Ecology Progress Series* **43**:181–8.

Epifanio, C. E., Valenti, C. C., and Pembroke, A. E. 1984. Dispersal and recruitment of blue crab larvae in the Delaware Bay. *Estuarine Coastal and Shelf Science* **18**:1–12.

Forward, R. B., Jr., and Rittschof, D. 1994. Photoresponses of crab megalopae in offshore and estuarine waters: implications for transport. *Journal of Experimental Marine Biology and Ecology* **182**:183–92.

Gaines, S. D., and Bertness, M. D. 1992. Dispersal of juveniles and variable recruitment in sessile marine species. *Nature* **360**:579–80.

Heck, K. L, Jr., Coen, L. D., and Morgan, S. G. 2001. Pre- and post-settlement factors as determinants of juvenile blue crab (*Callinectes sapidus*) abundance: results from the north-central Gulf of Mexico. *Marine Ecology Progress Series* **222**:163–76.

Hovel, K. A., and Morgan, S. G. 1997. Planktivory as a selective force for reproductive synchrony and larval migration. *Marine Ecology Progress Series* **157**:79–95.

Hunter, J. R. 1981. Feeding ecology and predation of marine fish larvae, in R. Lasker (ed.), *Marine Fish Larvae: Morphology, Ecology and Relation to Fisheries*. Washington Sea Grant Program, University of Washington, Seattle, pp. 34–77.

Johns, D. M., and Lang, W. H. 1977. Larval development of the spider crab, *Libinia emarginata* (Majidae). *Fishery Bulletin* **75**:831–41.

Kingsford, M. J., Leis, J., Shanks, A., Lindeman, K., Morgan, S., and Pineda, J. 2002. Sensory environments, larval abilities and local self-recruitment. *Bulletin of Marine Science* **70**:309–40.

Luckenbach, M. W., and Orth, R. J. 1992. Swimming velocities and behavior of blue crab (*Callinectes sapidus* Rathbun) megalopae in still and flowing water. *Estuaries* **15**:186–92.

Massman, W. H., Norcross, J. J., and Joseph, E. B. 1963. Distribution of larvae of the naked goby, *Gobiosoma bosci*, in the York River. *Chesapeake Science* **4**:120–5.

Morgan, S. G. 1995. Life and death in the plankton: larval mortality and adaptation, in L. McEdward (ed.), *Ecology of Marine Invertebrate Larvae*. Boca Raton, FL: CRC Press, pp. 279–321.

2001. The larval ecology of marine communities, in M. Bertness, M. Hay, and S. D. Gaines (eds), *Marine Community Ecology*, Sunderland, MA: Sinauer Associates, pp. 158–81.

Morgan, S. G., Zimmer-Faust, R. K., Heck, Jr., K. L., and Coen, L. D. 1996. Population regulation of blue crabs, *Callinectes*, in the northern Gulf of Mexico: postlarval supply. *Marine Ecology Progress Series* **133**:73–88.

Pile, A. J., Lipcius, R. N., Van Morntfrans, J., and Orth, R. J. 1996. Density-dependent settler-recruit-juvenile relationships in blue crabs. *Ecological Monographs* **66**:277–300.

Schultz, E. T., Cowen, R. K., Lwiza, K. M. M., and Gospodarek, A. M. 2000. Explaining advection: do larval bay anchovy (*Anchoa mitchilli*) show selective tidal-stream transport? *ICES Journal of Marine Science* **57**:360–71.

Shanks, A. L. 1995. Mechanisms of cross-shelf dispersal of larval invertebrates and fishes, in L. McEdward (ed.), *Ecology of Marine Invertebrate Larvae*. Boca Raton, FL: CRC Press, pp. 323–67.

Strathmann, R. R. 1982. Selection for retention or export of larvae in estuaries, in V. Kennedy (ed.) *Estuarine Comparisons*. New York: Academic Press, pp. 521–36.

Strathmann, R. R., Hughes, T. P., Kuris, A. M., Lindeman, K. C., Morgan, S. G., Pandolfi, J. M., and Warner, R. R. 2002. Evolution of self-recruitment

and its consequences for marine populations. *Bulletin of Marine Science* **70**:377–96.

Sulkin. S. D., Van Heukelem, W., Kelly, P., and Van Heukelem, L. 1980. The behavioral basis of larval recruitment in the crab, *Callinectes sapidus* Rathbun: a laboratory investigation of the ontogenetic changes in geotaxis and barokinesis. *Biological Bulletin* **159**:402–417.

Thorrold, S. R., Burton, R. S., Jones, G. P., Hellberg, M. E., Swearer, S. E., Niegel, J. E., Morgan, S. G., and Warner, R. R. 2002. Quantifying larval retention and connectivity in marine populations with artificial and natural markers: can we do it right? *Bulletin of Marine Science* **70**: 273–90.

Thorson, G. 1950. Reproductive and larval ecology of marine bottom invertebrates. *Biological Review* **25**:1–45.

Williams, A. B. 1984. *Shrimps, Lobsters, and Crabs of the Atlantic Coast of the Eastern United States, Maine to Florida*. Smithsonian Institution, Washington, D.C.

Wolcott, T. G. 1995. New options in physiological and behavioural ecology through multichannel telemetry. *Marine Ecology Progress Series* **193**:257–75.

Young, C. M. 1990. Larval ecology of marine invertebrates: a sesquicentennial history. *Ophelia* **32**:1–48.

the power industry on the Hudson, a major user of river water and source of fish mortality, will be an important factor influencing fish abundance, including of the anadromous forms.

13 The Diadromous Fish Fauna of the Hudson River: Life Histories, Conservation Concerns, and Research Avenues

John R. Waldman

ABSTRACT The Hudson River hosts almost a dozen diadromous fishes – species that migrate between marine and fresh waters. Only one, American eel, is catadromous (spawn at sea); the remainder are anadromous (spawn in fresh water). American shad, Atlantic sturgeon, and striped bass have been subjected to large, long-term, commercial fisheries; striped bass also support an intensive recreational fishery. Because of protection afforded the coastal migratory mixed stock of striped bass, the Hudson's population is high at this time. Among Hudson River finfish, only American shad have low enough body burdens of polychlorinated biphenyls (PCBs) to allow commercial harvests today, but this stock has shown a long-term decline. Because of late twentieth century commercial overfishing of the Hudson River Atlantic sturgeon stock and the depleted status of most of its other populations, this species is being conserved under a fishing moratorium that may extend to 2038. The river's other acipenserid, shortnose sturgeon, was one of the original taxa listed under the 1973 U.S. Endangered Species Act; there is evidence that its abundance has multiplied four-fold since then. Marine-migrating blueback herring have colonized the Mohawk River – thus extending their distribution and increasing their abundance in the system. Two cold-water fishes at the southern margin of their ranges have become apparently extinct (rainbow smelt) or have shown declines (Atlantic tomcod) that may be related to warming. Recent studies have increased knowledge of the Hudson's diadromous ichthyofauna, but many questions remain, particularly concerning the effects of non-native species and shifting community compositions. Opportunities exist to mitigate some population declines through habitat enhancement. The future of

Introduction

Diadromous fishes are species that, as a routine phase of their life cycle, and for the vast majority of the population, migrate between marine and fresh waters. Of the diadromous fishes, anadromous species spawn in fresh water and catadromous forms spawn in salt water. The Hudson River hosts a diadromous ichthyofauna of almost a dozen species (Table 13.1). They range from large, commercially-valuable anadromous fishes such as Atlantic sturgeon and striped bass to small, largely ignored ones such as hickory shad. The only catadromous species in the Hudson is American eel. The Hudson is also home to euryhaline species that typically remain within the estuary (for example, white perch, gizzard shad). Two of these, shortnose sturgeon and Atlantic tomcod, make seasonal movements between fresh and marine waters to the degree that they often are considered to be anadromous. Diagnostic keys, morphological descriptions, and information on the basic biology of the diadromous fishes of the Hudson River are available in Smith (1985).

Populations of anadromous fishes in the Hudson River were established recently – within about 10,000 years – as the river was recolonized following deglaciation (Schmidt, 1986). Other rivers within the Hudson River Estuary complex, such as the Raritan, Passaic, Hackensack, and smaller tributaries supported or still support some diadromous species that run up the Hudson; the extent of reproductive interchange among these subpopulations remains unknown.

Several commercially-fished Hudson River species have experienced fluctuations in abundance in historical times due to anthropogenic effects. Commercial and recreational overharvest is primary among them. Entrainment and impingement mortality by electric-generating stations also has decreased the abundance of some diadromous fishes. Information on abundances of a variety of fish species is available from surveys conducted by the Hudson River electric generating companies (for example, Barnthouse et al., 1988).

Table 13.1. Life history mode, importance to humans, and status and trends of the Hudson River's diadromous fishes

Latin name	Common name	Life history mode	In-river fisheries		Abundance trend over last decade	Conservation status
			Historical	Present		
Petromyzon marinus	sea lamprey	Anad	None	None	Unknown	None
Acipenser oxyrinchus	Atlantic sturgeon	Anad	Major commercial	None	Possibly increasing	Declining, then 40-year range-wide moratorium since 1998
Acipenser brevirostrum	shortnose sturgeon	Anad	Commercial	None	Increasing	Federally endangered
Anguilla rostrata	American eel	Catad	Commercial	None	Declining range-wide	None
Alosa sapidissima	American shad	Anad	Major commercial	Minor commercial	Declining	Commercial restrictions
Alosa mediocris	hickory shad	Anad	None	None	Increasing range-wide	None
Alosa pseudoharengus	alewife	Anad	Minor commercial	Commercial (for bait)	Stable to declining	Commercial restrictions
Alosa aestivalis	blueback herring	Anad	Minor commercial	Commercial (for bait)	Stable	Commercial restrictions
Osmerus mordax	rainbow smelt	Anad	Recreational netting	None	Declining	None
Migrogadus tomcod	Atlantic tomcod	Anad	Minor angling	Minor angling	Declining	None
Morone saxatilis	striped bass	Anad	Major commercial	Major angling	Stable to increasing	Angling restrictions

Life history mode: Amph = amphidromous, Anad = anadromous, Catad = catadromous. Conservation status refers to special restrictions beyond consumption advisories.

Synopses about certain of the Hudson River's diadromous fishes can be found in Barnthouse et al. (1988), and Smith (1988; 1992). In this paper I briefly summarize the life histories of the Hudson's diadromous fishes, focusing on recent findings, conservation concerns, and status and trends. I also explore commonalities and differences among them and point to questions in their biology that would benefit from further research. The species are presented in phylogenetic order (Nelson, 1976) by family.

Life Histories and Recent Research Findings

PETROMYZONTIDAE

Petromyzon marinus sea lamprey. Sea lamprey is a large parasite with a complex life cycle (Beamish, 1980). Although sea lamprey spawn and are numerous in the two large systems that bracket the Hudson River, that is, the Connecticut and Delaware Rivers, adults are scarce in the Hudson. Greeley (1937) listed them as rare in the mainstem river. No directed studies of sea lamprey in the Hudson drainage have occurred but there have been reports that suggest some reproduction takes place in a few of the more than sixty tributaries to the tidal river. The system-wide survey by Greeley (1937) caught one larva in Rondout Creek and one adult in Catskill Creek; none were found in the Roeliff Jansen Kill or other tributaries sampled. However, Brussard, Collings-Hall, and Wright (1981) later electroshocked thirty-one ammocoetes from the Roeliff Jansen Kill. More recently, adult sea lamprey were observed near the confluence of Catskill and Kaaterskill creeks (R. Schmidt, Simon's Rock of Bard College, personal observation) and in the Roeliff Jansen Kill (J. Waldman and R. Schmidt, personal observation). Subadult sea lampreys are sometimes seen in the Hudson River attached to American shad (Greeley, 1937; HRA, 1998) and gizzard shad (HRA, 1998).

Why sea lamprey are abundant in the Delaware and Connecticut Rivers but not in the Hudson is not obvious but may be due to habitat limitations. Although sea lamprey have been documented to occur in at least 134 coastal rivers in North America, they do not reproduce in every river available range (Beamish, 1980). Sea lamprey construct nests of rock rubble, in sections of rivers with moderate flows. After hatching, larvae leave the nest and drift downstream to suitable silt beds (e.g., eddies, backwaters, behind obstructions) where the ammocoetes mature.

The main channel of the Hudson River clearly does not provide suitable spawning habitat for sea lamprey, nor are ammocoetes known to occupy tidal waters. Although some sea lamprey reproduction may occur in a few tributaries to the Hudson River, I believe it is limited by the generally small sizes of these systems, their short lengths below the fall line, and perhaps, their infrequent combinations of good spawning and nursery habitats.

ACIPENSERIDAE

Acipenser oxyrinchus oxyrinchus Atlantic sturgeon. Extant populations of the east coast subspecies occur from the St. Lawrence River to rivers in southern Georgia and, possibly, to the St. John River, Florida (Waldman and Wirgin, 1998). This sturgeon is known to exceed 300 kg in weight and 60 years in age.

Dovel and Berggren (1983) performed the first detailed studies of Atlantic sturgeon in the Hudson River. Sonic transmitters were used to describe movement patterns, which included delineation of spawning as occurring near the salt front (~km 55) in late May and moving upstream as far as Hyde Park later in the season. Growth of younger specimens was found to occur primarily between May and October and to slow after age three. Conventional tagging of immature Atlantic sturgeon showed that some leave the Hudson as early as their fifteenth month, but no later than age six. Specimens were recaptured in coastal waters as far north as Marblehead, Massachusetts, and south to Ocracoke, North Carolina. Most recaptures occurred in the Delaware River and Chesapeake Bay estuaries, and their pattern implied a northerly migration in spring and southerly movements in autumn. Dovel and Berggren estimated that the 1976 year class of Atlantic sturgeon in the Hudson River totaled about 25,000 in 1978.

A flourish of studies in the 1990s greatly extended knowledge of the life history of Atlantic sturgeon. Analysis of fin ray sections suggested that Hudson River-stock females reproduce on average every four years (Secor, Stevenson, and Houde, 1997).

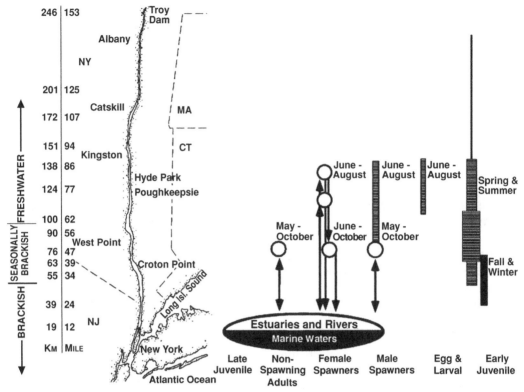

Figure 13.1. Seasonal movements of Atlantic sturgeon in the Hudson River by life stage, gender, and reproductive condition (developed by M. Bain, Cornell University).

VanEenennaam et al. (1996) could collect spawning specimens only at two historically important upriver fishing sites (Hyde Park and Catskill) and they argued that reproduction near the salt front was unlikely given the physiological requirements of the species' early life stages. Sonic tagging by Bain et al. (1998; 2000) showed that spawning occurs over a period of weeks at several sites between km 113 and 184. They also found that many subadults and adults (some believed to be post-spawners) aggregate midsummer through fall just upstream of the Bear Mountain Bridge, part of a complex seasonal phenology that varies by life stage, gender, and reproductive condition (Fig. 13.1).

Haley (1998) developed a gastric lavage technique to study sturgeon food habits without sacrificing them. When applied to twenty-third Atlantic sturgeon captured in the river between June and September 1996, major prey items were found to include polychaetes, isopods, and amphipods.

In October 1994, 4,929 hatchery-reared, six-month-old Atlantic sturgeon were stocked into the Hudson near km 90. Because these fish were marked, they were distinguishable from wild specimens from the same year class. Peterson, Bain, and Haley (2000) used this difference to perform a Peterson estimate of abundance of wild age-1 Atlantic sturgeon, which generated a value of 4,313 individuals, with a 95 percent confidence interval of 1,917–10,474. This estimate was about 80 percent lower than those obtained by Dovel and Berggren (1983) from the mid 1970s.

Atlantic sturgeon had been fished in the Hudson since prehistoric times (Brumbach, 1986) and in the late nineteenth and early twentieth centuries, they were skinned, sliced, and then sold under the name "Albany beef" (Greeley, 1937). However, the Hudson River's population appeared not to experience the magnitude of overfishing that occurred in the Delaware River during the caviar craze of the late nineteenth century (for example, Secor and Waldman, 1999).

But there was no evidence of a significant population change in Atlantic sturgeon in the

Hudson until the mid 1980s when numbers of juveniles observed in commercial fishing bycatch and utilities-sponsored monitoring programs decreased substantially (Bain et al., 1998). Moreover, as alternative species declined, some commercial fishermen inside and outside of the Hudson River began to focus on Atlantic sturgeon. Landings in New Jersey's coastal waters increased from 5,900 kg in 1988 to approximately 100,000 kg in 1990. And New York's coastal harvest rose from about 7,700 kg in 1993 to almost 16,000 kg in 1994 (Waldman, Hart, and Wirgin, 1996a). Mixed-stock analysis using mitochondrial DNA (mtDNA) markers indicated that 99 percent of the sturgeon in the New York Bight fisheries were of Hudson River origin (Waldman et al., 1996a). In response to this increase and to the overall scarcity of Atlantic sturgeon in other river systems (Waldman and Wirgin, 1998), a moratorium on commercial harvest in U.S. waters was enacted in 1998 that may extend for as much as 40 years. (Limburg et al., this volume).

Acipenser brevirostrum **shortnose sturgeon.** Shortnose sturgeon is a small, federally-endangered acipenserid which occurs in about twenty estuaries from New Brunswick to Florida (color plate 6). Many of its populations have been reduced and number only in the hundreds to thousands (ASMFC, 1998).

Shortnose sturgeon are long lived, reaching almost seventy years. Hudson River males don't mature until age three and females not until age six, or later (Bain, 1997). Early growth is rapid: yearlings may exceed 30 cm by their second summer (Dovel, Pekovitch, and Berggren, 1992). However, the rate of growth declines substantially as subadults and adults (Bain, 1997). Indeed, it may halt, based on the results of Bain et al. (1998) who recaptured nineteen individuals between 1993 and 1995 that were tagged by Dovel et al. (1992) in 1979 and 1980. Of these recaptures, seventeen were adults when tagged and on average had grown only 86 mm and some showed no increase in length.

There is limited information on the feeding habits of shortnose sturgeon in the Hudson River. Carlson and Simpson (1987) examined forty-two young-of-the-year and ten yearling specimens killed on the cooling water intake screens at a power plant at km 228. Predominant prey varied

seasonally but included midge larvae, amphipods, and isopods. Although Carlson and Simpson found little reliance on molluscs for young age classes, Bain et al. (1998) determined that shortnose sturgeon also eat the non-native zebra mussel *Dreissena polymorpha*. Haley (1998) found principal food items to include soft-bodied invertebrates (e.g., amphipods, chironomids, and isopods) and shelled organisms such as snails and zebra mussels.

Data syntheses (Geoghegan, Mattson, and Keppel, 1992) from three utilities-sponsored monitoring programs between 1983 and 1988 (excluding winter) showed that shortnose sturgeon from 10 to 120 cm TL were most common between Kingston and Croton Point. Dovel et al. (1992) and Bain (1997) demonstrated a complex seasonal pattern of movements for reproductively-mature adults that is dependent on whether individuals are spawning in a given year. The frequency of spawning for the St. John River population was estimated at between every third to fifth year for females, and every second year for males (Dadswell, 1979). However, these values may not apply to the Hudson River population inasmuch as Dovel et al. (1992) reported the occurrence of some tagged shortnose sturgeon on the spawning grounds in successive years.

Prespawning adults overwinter aggregated at a bend in the river near Esopus Meadows (Bain, 1997). They then reaggregate and spawn far up river from about km 190 to immediately downstream of the Federal Dam. Later, postspawners disperse widely, mixing with nonspawners, primarily in channels of the fresh- and brackish-water reaches. As winter approaches adults again segregate according to whether they will spawn the following year, with nonspawners wintering farther down river than spawners, between km 54 and 61 (Bain, 1997).

Recent work demonstrated stock differences between shortnose sturgeon from the Hudson and other populations. These included some morphometric features in comparison with specimens from the Kennebec and Androscoggin Rivers (Walsh et al., 2001) and mtDNA control region sequences in comparison with populations across the species' range (Grunwald et al., 2002).

There was no concerted commercial fishery for shortnose sturgeon in the Hudson River (where they were also known as "roundnosers"; Dovel et al.,

1992), although some individuals were harvested (Boyle, 1969; Dovel et al., 1992), particularly in the central river, where Greeley (1937) stated it was of "some commercial importance." Bain (personal communication, Cornell University) estimated the abundance of adult shortnose sturgeon in the Hudson during the late 1990s at about 61,000, a more than four-fold increase since the early 1980s (based on Dovel et al., 1992). Bain believes the Hudson's population may exceed the total of the approximately twenty other populations of the species. It may be that the shortnose sturgeon population of the Hudson River is recovered and is a candidate for de-listing under the 1973 U.S. Endangered Species Act. If de-listing should occur, it would be the first instance for a population segment of a fish species.

ANGUILLIDAE

***Anguilla rostrata* American eel.** This catadromous species spawns in the Sargasso Sea; afterwards its developing larvae (leptocephali) are advected toward North America (ASMFC, 2000). Leptocephali metamorphose into glass eels (transparent juveniles) in coastal habitats and are subsequently transported into estuaries. They become pigmented as they move farther inland. They are then called "yellow" eels, residing for upwards of 30 years before metamorphosing into "silver" eels and returning to the Sargasso Sea to spawn and die. Because of their random recruitment to river systems, American eels form one genetically panmictic population.

Eels have been little studied within the Hudson River estuary. They were known to move upstream past the Federal Dam as far as Saratoga Lake (Brumbach, 1986) and into several Adirondack lakes (Greeley and Bishop, 1933). Greeley (1937) found eels in numerous streams and lakes in the drainage of the lower Hudson River.

Peak immigration of elvers into the Hudson estuary occurs from mid-March through April (Mattes, 1989). Stomach analysis by Mattes (1989) of 468 eels trawled between Manhattan and Troy revealed a generalized feeding pattern with forty-eight prey species found. Important food items included crustaceans, molluscs, and fish.

The commercial fishery for yellow eels in the Hudson River has been closed since 1976 because of contamination with polychlorinated biphenyls (PCBs); specimens were found to have PCB levels of 50 to 75 ppm (Blake, 1982). U.S. landings of American eel together with estimates of eels passed at dams and taken in surveys indicate a substantial decline since 1979 (ASMFC, 2000). Although a significant glass eel fishery never developed in New York, in 1995 the state has imposed a minimum length limit for harvest in marine waters of 15 cm (ASMFC, 2000).

CLUPEIDAE

***Alosa sapidissima* American shad.** American shad is the largest North American alosine, reaching weights of 10 pounds or more. Populations occur in rivers from the St. Lawrence to the St. Johns. American shad has long been fished with nets for both its flesh and roe throughout the Hudson River and the New York bays (Fig. 13.2). Because its PCB body burdens meet federal standards, American shad is the only fin fish still legally harvestable in the Hudson by commercial fishermen.

American shad spawn in spring at water temperatures between 12° and 21°C, mostly between dusk and midnight. In the Hudson, American shad are main channel spawners (although I am aware of anecdotal reports of adult American shad occurring in the Croton and Rondout Rivers). Eggs of American shad have been collected from the Albany area to about km 83, but with highest densities in northern sections (Schmidt et al., 1988). Limburg (1996) performed a fine-scale study of growth and seaward migration of the 1990 year class of American shad in the Hudson River. She found this migration to be both size- and age-related, with upriver fish consistently smaller and younger than downriver specimens until late in the season. Otolith analysis showed that recruitment of juveniles from the 1990 year class was not spread proportionately across birth dates. Although most American shad spawning activity occurred in early to mid May, the year class was established mainly by individuals hatched in June; a discrepancy attributed to probable weather-related effects on food availability to larvae.

Juvenile American shad in the Hudson River prey primarily on epiphytic rather than benthic invertebrates, particularly chironomid larvae and formicid hymenopterans (Grabe, 1996). They often feed at the surface during afternoon and evening, consuming terrestrial insects.

Figure 13.2. Shad fishing in New York Bay using stake nets, circa 1867 (courtesy of the New York Public Library).

American shad range coastally from Labrador to Florida. They are long-distance but mainly in-shore migrators; during an average life span of five years at sea, an individual may travel 20,000 km (Dadswell et al., 1987). Dadswell et al. (1987) analyzed 1,837 returns from 11,579 American shad tagged in the Hudson River and New York Bight. Although more than 85 percent of recaptures occurred in the Hudson, recaptures from outside the river ranged from just south of Cape Hatteras to the upper reaches of the Bay of Fundy and to Halifax on Nova Scotia's east coast.

Leggett and Carscadden (1978) demonstrated that American shad show latitudinal variation in reproductive characteristics, including whether all individuals in a population died after first spawning (semelparity) or if repeat spawning occurred (iteroparity). Repeat spawning of American shad in the Hudson River appears to occur at a rate of more than 40 percent (ASMFC, 1998).

American shad population size in the Hudson declined from about 2.3 million in 1980 to 404,000 in 1996 (ASMFC, 1998). Inriver commercial landings fell from 2.6 million pounds in 1980 to less than 250,000 pounds in 1996. Although inriver fishing

mortality rates fell over that period, coastal fishing mortality rates ("intercept fishery") increased, and total fishing mortality rates have remained stable and independent of stock decline from 1980 to 1996. Moreover, recruitment has been high and relatively stable, yet adult stock size continued to decline to historic low levels. It may be that abiotic or biotic factors (possibly striped bass predation) rather than overfishing have caused the recent decrease in the Hudson's shad stock (ASMFC, 1998).

A number of genetic studies have shown significant differences among American shad stocks, including the Hudson River's (for example, Nolan, Grossfield, and Wirgin, 1991; Waldman et al., 1996b). Brown (1996) used genetic data to estimate the relative contributions of American shad stocks to coastal intercept fisheries. In New York Bight waters proximal to the Hudson River, the Hudson River stock was estimated to compose 21 percent of the 1994 catch and 22 percent of the 1995 catch.

Within-population variation of American shad has received little attention. Interesting differences in external characteristics were observed by commercial fishermen early in the 1900s (Greeley, 1937). Greeley reported that two types were seen: a form called the "blueback" and the much less common "yellowback." These types differed subtly in ground color, pigmentation pattern, and snout dimensions. Yellowbacks already were rare at the time of Greeley's survey.

***Alosa mediocris* hickory shad.** Hickory shad is a medium-sized alosine (max length ~60 cm) that ranges from the Bay of Fundy to the St. Johns River, Florida. Its life history remains largely undescribed. Adults often occur in inshore waters in the New York Bight and Long Island Sound, sometimes in high abundance, particularly near river mouths. Unlike the other North American shads, hickory shad is highly piscivorous, but it also consumes invertebrates.

Little is known of hickory shad within the Hudson River. Beebe and Savidge (1988) noted that it has been recorded from the Yonkers to Indian Point regions of the Hudson River. Smith (1985) reported that anglers occasionally take them in the Hudson. Bean (1903) stated that it was commonly caught at Gravesend Bay (at the mouth of the Hudson estuary) between September and November. Bean (1903) reported that the ascent of hickory shad precedes that of American shad in rivers where they co-occur. But although hickory shad have been caught in the Hudson River, there does not seem to be any conclusive evidence that they reproduce there.

I believe hickory shad abundance in the coastal waters of the New York Bight and Long Island Sound has increased substantially in the 1990s based on anecdotal reports in the angling literature and my personal observations, a trend that also has been noted in Connecticut and the Chesapeake Bay (ASMFC, 1999). If so, it is not clear whether this increase represents increased reproduction in the Hudson River or, more likely, immigration from other sources.

***Alosa pseudoharengus* alewife.** Alewife is a small alosine that occurs in rivers and coastal waters from Newfoundland to South Carolina. It differs from the other "river herring," the blueback, in several characteristics, most notably its greater body depth and pale, instead of dark, peritoneum.

Alewives co-occur with blueback herring in many drainages between New Brunswick and South Carolina. A maximum total length of 38 cm

has been attributed to both species (Loesch, 1987). Unlike blueback herring, the alewife landlocks readily, often in dwarf form. These populations are referred to as "sawbellies" and are widely used as bait for salmonids. Landlocked alewives exist in numerous reservoirs in the Hudson River drainage, including in the New York City Reservoir Supply System (e.g., Kensico Reservoir; Greeley, 1937).

Alewives begin spawning at between 5 and 10°C and prefer lakes and ponds or slow-flowing sections of streams. Fecundity is variable but is related to size and age, reaching as many as 467,000 eggs. First spawning of both river herrings occurs from ages three to six, but is dominated by age-four fish (Loesch, 1987). Fecundity appears to peak at age-six and declines afterward. Alewives return to sea after spawning but little is known of their marine migrations.

There has been little research on either river herring in the Hudson drainage, but some system-specific information has emerged. Schmidt, Klauda, and Bartels (1988) analyzed data from early life history surveys performed between 1976 and 1979. Juveniles appeared in seine collections from late June to early July, about a month later than American shad young. In the upper and middle estuary, seine catches declined in early July while they increased in offshore bottom trawls, signifying a movement from the shallows and mouths of streams to deeper waters. Summer catches showed a movement downriver, with numbers declining after August, presumably because of emigration. Juveniles were found downriver through mid December, but some may remain in the estuary all winter. Indeed, elemental composition analysis of small but spawning adult alewives from Coxsackie Creek indicated that some may remain within the Hudson River estuary for their entire life cycle (R. Schmidt, personal communication). Hudson juveniles feed primarily on chironomids and amphipods, with no diel differences in feeding activity (Grabe, 1996).

Lake and Schmidt (1997) surveyed fish usage during spring of a small Hudson River tributary, Quassaic Creek, located near Newburgh. In 1996, the first alewife specimens were seen on April 3, with only males caught until April 14. Peak spawning appeared to occur on April 19 at a water temperature of 9.4°C, with a secondary peak in mid-May, but spawning continued until early

June. The total adult spawning run in Quassaic Creek for 1996 was estimated at about 5,600 individuals. Lake and Schmidt (1998) investigated the alewife spawning run in Quassaic Creek more intensively in 1997. They found fecundity to range from 15,000 to 135,000 eggs and female total lengths of between 232 to 318 mm. Spawning activity was similarly bimodal to 1996 and the total number of eggs deposited in this single system was estimated at 162 million. In more extensive surveys in 1998 and 1999, Schmidt and Lake (2000) documented river herring (mainly alewife) runs in twenty-eight of the thirty-eight Hudson River tributaries they sampled. Although river herring are rarely sought for food from the Hudson River, they are harvested for bait (Vargo, 1995).

Alosa aestivalis **blueback herring.** Blueback herring range from Nova Scotia to Florida. Where they co-occur in spawning rivers with alewives, bluebacks achieve some niche separation by running later in the season (peak spawning lagged by two to three weeks) and by choosing relatively swiftly running sites to spawn in (Loesch, 1987).

Because they spawn later, recruitment of juvenile blueback herring in the Hudson system occurs after that of American shad and alewife (Schmidt et al., 1988). They also found that juvenile blueback herring numbers dwarfed other alosines in summer. Blueback herring are the most planktivorous of juvenile alosines and are most active during daylight (Schmidt et al., 1988; Grabe, 1996). Primary prey includes copepods, chironomids, and cladocerans.

In recent decades, blueback herring have become more abundant in the Hudson River system, but it appears that this increase is due mainly to an expansion of range. Daniels (1995) noted that Greeley (1937) found blueback herring at only 4 of 112 sites sampled; whereas in Daniels' own 1990 survey and in monitoring conducted in the 1970s and 1980s, blueback herring dominated summer catches at inshore sites. Surveys have shown that blueback herring are either absent or uncommon in most of the tributaries examined that enter the Hudson below the dam at Troy. In their 1998 and 1999 surveys, Schmidt and Lake (2000) found adult blueback herring in only 7 of the 28 tributaries in which river herring were encountered. Bluebacks were seen in the four northernmost tributaries,

which ranged to the Poesten Kill (km 241). The reason for the apparent increase in the population size of bluebacks in the Hudson system is that large numbers of spawners move up the mainstem tidal Hudson River to the Federal Dam and then pass through the hydroelectric turbines or the navigation lock. MacNeill (1998) believes they spawn near Rome, New York, at the highest elevation of the Mohawk corridor.

OSMERIDAE

Osmerus mordax **rainbow smelt.** Rainbow smelt is a slender, elongate fish that ranges from the Hudson River northward to the Arctic. Maximum size is about 30 cm. Little is known of their marine movements. Spawning occurs after individuals have passed two winters at sea. Rainbow smelt reproduce in early spring; egg fecundity ranges between 10^3–10^4 and eggs hatch in ten to thirty days. In salt waters smelt eat crustaceans, nereid worms, and fish. In fresh water they consume shrimp, amphipods, oligochaetes, and insect larvae.

In his 1936 survey, Greeley (1937) encountered young smelt at seven stations between Rhinecliff and Port Ewen. Rainbow smelt once ran into many Hudson River tributaries in early spring when the mainstem reached about 4°C (Boyle, 1969). These runs were actively fished in locations such as the Rondout River and Saugerties Creek (Greeley, 1937). They have also been observed in the Croton River (Boyle, 1969; Rose, 1993), Wappingers Creek, Columbiaville Creek, Roeliff-Jansen Kill, Black Creek, Crum Elbow Creek, Fishkill Creek, and Esopus Creek (Rose, 1993). The last significant tributary runs appear to have occurred in 1979 (Rose, 1993) and recreational net fisheries have since disappeared.

All indications are that rainbow smelt in the Hudson declined during the late 1900s and became extinct shortly before 2000. Between 1974 and 1980, annual catches in the Hudson River utilities nearshore survey ranged from 108 to 1,880 individuals (Daniels and Lawrence, 1991). But in 1981, the survey caught only forty-six, and just a single specimen was sampled between 1982 and 1989. In a 1988 survey of Hudson River tributaries, Schmidt and Limburg (1989) caught several smelt larvae in Catskill Creek but not in fifteen others (located between km 42 and 220). Schmidt and Lake (2000) caught a single smelt larva in the Moordener Kill in 1998.

Rose (1993) analyzed the Hudson River utilities survey data to describe spawning locations and abundance trends in the mainstem between 1974 and 1990. Although anecdotal accounts indicated that Hudson River tributary runs had dwindled to almost undetectable levels by the early 1980s, the Long River Survey did not show a decline in the Hudson River over that period, that is, high average densities of post-yolk sac larvae were seen in 1986, 1988, and 1990. However, Rose found that the center of abundance of these larvae had shifted since the 1970s from the lower river to the Catskill to Albany regions. Since 1995, rainbow smelt essentially disappeared from the Hudson River ichthyoplankton (Daniels et al., in press). Despite comparable levels of effort with earlier periods during which 10^3–10^4 post-yolk sac larvae were collected annually in the Long River Survey, between 1996 and 2000 only four individuals (during 1998) were found.

GADIDAE

Microgadus tomcod **Atlantic tomcod.** The Hudson River is the southern population limit of this small, boreal gadoid. In the Hudson, spawning occurs in early- to mid-winter, primarily between the Tappan Zee and Poughkeepsie reaches, and centered near West Point (Klauda, Moos, and Schmidt, 1988). Egg incubation lasts sixty-one to seventy days (Dew and Hecht, 1994). Larvae become distributed throughout the Hudson, but at highest densities downriver. Between April and November juveniles are most abundant in the Tappan Zee and West Point regions and south to Manhattan (Dew and Hecht, 1994). However, summer distributions appear to advance upriver with the salt front, with high monitoring catches being made in the Indian Point region (Klauda et al., 1988).

Juvenile Atlantic tomcod in the Hudson River were found to feed mainly on invertebrates, particularly calanoid copepods (McLaren et al., 1988). Adults displayed greater piscivory, but invertebrates still predominated, especially *Gammarus*, *Neomysis*, *Crangon*, and chironomid larvae. McLaren et al. (1988) identified three phases of first-year growth for Hudson River tomcod: a summer phase of little or no growth (because of

high temperature stress) separated rapid growth phases during spring and fall. Dew and Hecht (1994) estimated a decrease in weight gain from 2.9 percent d to 1.3 percent d as temperatures rose above 13°C in late May.

The Hudson River population has an unusual maturation schedule and age-structure. Both sexes begin to mature reproductively at nine months and are capable of spawning at eleven months. In early winter, these newly-mature individuals move upriver along with older tomcod to spawn. However, unlike in northern estuaries where they may live for several more years, only three age classes are known from the Hudson River, with individuals older than age-1 being rare. McLaren et al. (1988) found that among spawners collected during the winters of 1975–76 through 1979–80, age-1 fish comprised 92–99 percent of the annual totals, with age-2 individuals making up most of the remainder. Age-3 fish were extremely rare (<0.1 percent of total).

Because the tomcod population is composed almost completely of one age class, its annual abundance is unusually responsive to environmental conditions that influence recruitment and subsequent survival; thus, its abundances fluctuate widely. For example, winter spawning population estimates were 12.5 million in 1982–83, and 6.7 million, 2.1 million, 3.5 million, and 5.9 million in succeeding years (Mattson, Geoghegan, and Dunning, 1992).

Most Hudson River tomcod remain within the estuary for life. However, a few individuals tagged in the Hudson in the late 1970s were recaptured in lower New York Bay, the East River, and western Long Island Sound (Klauda et al., 1988), suggesting broader limits for this population.

Because it is bottom dwelling, dependent on benthic prey, has a lipid-rich liver, and tends to remain within its natal estuary, tomcod from highly polluted systems tend to accumulate unusually high concentrations of contaminants. In the Hudson River, these include PCBs and other chlorinated hydrocarbons (Courtenay et al., 1999). Tomcod from the Hudson exhibit biochemical responses and molecular damage not observed in those from cleaner estuaries (Wirgin et al., 1994) and a remarkably high prevalence of liver tumors (Dey et al., 1993).

MORONIDAE

***Morone saxatilis* striped bass.** This species appears to be the most popular sport fish in the Hudson River. It also was harvested commercially in the river until the fishery was closed in 1976 because of PCB contamination. The striped bass population of the Hudson River is the northernmost of the three main migratory stocks (together with Chesapeake Bay and Delaware River) that support the fishery along the northeast U.S. coastline.

Striped bass spawn in the Hudson from early May through early June. Between 1974 and 1979, maximum egg densities occurred at water temperatures of 12°–22°C and a spatial peak occurred between km 54 and 98 each year, although early life stages were encountered in all regions between Albany and Yonkers (Boreman and Klauda, 1988). However, the downriver limit of egg deposition is usually associated with the position of the salt front. Sample densities of juveniles peaked between km 38 and km 74. But juveniles may occur anywhere within the estuary and even into western Long Island Sound (LoBue and McKown, 1998). A high proportion of juveniles and yearlings winter in the lower river, particularly off Manhattan.

Several studies have described early life history processes of striped bass in the Hudson. Pace et al. (1993) examined relationships among abundances of life stages and temperature and flow conditions between 1974 and 1990. They concluded that temperature and river flow were not related to interannual variation in recruitment and, that there were no statistically significant relationships between the abundances of yolk-sac larvae, post yolk-sac larvae, and juveniles. They believe the absence of relationships among early life stages means that differences in mortality are less important than variability in egg numbers in determining larval abundance.

Limburg et al. (1997) tracked the abundance and food consumption of larval striped bass during 1994. The cladoceran *Bosmina longirostris* and large copepodites and adult copepods composed 97.4 percent of the diet. They found that larval cohorts extant before the zooplankton bloom had the least available food but also the lowest respiration costs. Postbloom cohorts had both high consumption rates and respiration rates due to increased temperatures. Cohorts coincident with the bloom had moderately high consumption rates and lower metabolic costs relative to late cohorts. The investigators concluded that larval cohorts coincident with the bloom possess an energetic advantage relative to early cohorts but not relative to late cohorts.

Hurst and Conover (1998) explored the possible effects of winter mortality stemming from bioenergetic stresses on striped bass recruitment in the Hudson. They found that age-1 abundance was negatively correlated with the severity of winter; however, numbers of age-0 fish were not correlated with abundance at age 1 – leading to the conclusion that winter mortality greatly modified year class strength. A progressive increase in the mean length of young-of-the-year fish, coupled with a decrease in the coefficient of variation in length, occurred during some winters. This, combined with laboratory experiments that showed that growth in length requires temperatures in excess of 10°C suggest that these changes result from a bias toward greater mortality of smaller specimens. Dunning et al. (1997) provided evidence that subadult striped bass in the lower Hudson River feed during winter at temperatures well below 10°C (although consumption was not compared with growth).

As part of the Hudson River Cooling Tower Settlement Agreement, the electric utilities were to operate a hatchery that would plant 600,000 young-of-the-year striped bass in the Hudson annually (Dunning et al., 1992). Hatchery-reared individuals were marked with coded magnetic-wire tags before stocking. In the course of trawl sampling for these individuals to estimate their contributions to the Hudson River stock, many wild specimens were caught and these were tagged with external tags to learn more about their movements and to monitor year class abundance. The goal of 600,000 hatchery-reared specimens per year never was met because of disease problems and the resultant contributions to the stock of the 1.3 million fish stocked from 1983 through 1987 were small (e.g., 0.1 percent to 1984 cohort, 3 percent to 1985 cohort). Moreover, the hatchery-reared striped bass showed more limited movements inside the Hudson River than did wild fish (Wells et al., 1991). For these reasons, the hatchery ceased operations in 1995.

Striped bass stockings in the Hudson River appear to have made little contribution to coastal waters. Waldman and Vecchio (1996) examined hatchery-reared specimens from Hudson River and Chesapeake Bay sources among more than 1,500 striped bass caught in haul seines in eastern Long Island in 1991 and 1992. Hatchery-reared specimens comprised 3.5 percent of the total catch in 1991 and 2.5 percent in 1992. Although only about twice as many marked individuals were stocked in Chesapeake Bay as in the Hudson River, the recapture ratio of Chesapeake Bay to Hudson specimens was 62:1 in 1991 and 37:2 in 1992 – a difference attributed to differences in relative survival or vagility. Hatchery-reared specimens from both stocks also showed a pronounced increase in the incidence of broken striping patterns, a phenomenon that remains unexplained (Waldman and Vecchio, 1996).

The increase in the abundance of the Hudson River striped bass stock that occurred since the late 1970s appears to have affected its coastal migratory range. Tagging studies performed between 1948 and 1952 concluded that the Hudson River stock limited its movements outside the river to western Long Island (Raney, Woolcott, and Mehring, 1954). McLaren et al. (1981), based on tagging done in 1976 and 1977 reported broader coastal movements, but only as far northward as Newburyport, Massachusetts, and an absence of a relationship between fish length and distance from the river. But tagging conducted in the Hudson River between 1984 and 1988 showed an expansion of range, with recoveries made northward as far as the Annapolis River, Nova Scotia (Waldman et al., 1990a). They also found a strong relationship between fish length and distance from the river, and interpreted the absence of such a relationship in the results of McLaren et al. (1981) as an artifact of size-dependent tag retention (Waldman, Dunning, and Mattson, 1990b).

Although the Hudson's striped bass stock makes coastal migrations, it was suspected that not all individuals participated and that some were residential in the freshwaters of the river (Raney et al., 1954) or did not move past the lower estuary (Clark, 1968). Secor (1999) used elemental analysis of otoliths to reconstruct the salinity history of individuals in relation to age. His work supported the notion of "contingents," finding evidence for resident Hudson River, New York Harbor, western Long Island Sound, and

coastal Atlantic components to the total Hudson River stock. Individuals of the Hudson-resident contingent (primarily males) showed elevated PCB levels consistent with greater lifetime exposure to PCB sources (Zlokovitz and Secor, 1999).

The relative contributions of the migratory striped bass stocks to coastal waters vary with their spawning success and subsequent conservation. Berggren and Lieberman (1978) analyzed striped bass caught in coastal waters in 1975 using morphological stock identification approaches and estimated that the Hudson population comprised only 7 percent of the stock mixture, with 90 percent originating from the Chesapeake Bay. VanWinkle, Kumar, and Vaughan (1988) reanalyzed these data on a year-class basis and found that the contribution of the Hudson stock approached 50 percent for some cohorts. Wirgin et al. (1993) applied a mtDNA-based approach to this question with a collection of specimens ($N = 112$) from eastern Long Island made in 1989, and estimated a Hudson component of 73 percent. A similar study (Wirgin et al., 1997) performed on a larger sample ($N = 362$) collected in 1991 and including nuclear DNA markers also showed a Hudson River stock contribution of about 52 percent. These later estimates of large contributions of the Hudson River population to coastal waters reflect both its increased abundance and the decline of the Chesapeake stock over this period.

Conservation Concerns and Research Avenues

Habitat. Changes to the habitat of the Hudson River estuary have diminished its runs of diadromous fishes. The southernmost dam on the river was constructed in 1832 near Troy (Brumbach, 1986). Prior to the building of this and other upstream dams, American shad and river herring ascended to at least the Battenkill River (Greeley and Bishop, 1933), Fish Creek (Brumbach, 1986), and possibly, Glens Falls (Boyle, 1969); eels penetrated considerably farther into the watershed (Greeley and Bishop, 1933). Today some fish pass upriver through the navigation locks or through the dam's hydroelectric turbines (at their peril – during their spawning migration wounded adult blueback herring often drift immediately downcurrent of these turbines), but these obstacles create a bottleneck for fish movements in the upper river.

South of the Federal Dam but north of Manhattan, about half of the approximately sixty tributaries surveyed have manmade barriers that impede or prohibit fish passage (Schmidt, 1996). Artificial obstacles are also found on most tributaries entering greater New York Harbor (Durkas, 1992). Also, the degree of urbanization was shown to correlate negatively with runs of river herring in Hudson River tributaries (Limburg and Schmidt, 1990). Larger tributaries capable of supporting diadromous fishes have also been compromised by contamination; the Passaic (Waldman, 1999) and Hackensack Rivers (Zeisel, 1995) once sustained runs of anadromous fishes.

It is reasonable to assume that the overall contraction of available habitat for diadromous fishes has resulted in a decrease in their abundance, albeit, one that is difficult to quantify. I am aware of only two locations in which available habitat has enlarged significantly in recent decades. One is the Mohawk River, which following improvements in water quality, now supports a large run of blueback herring which ascend from the Hudson River after moving past the Federal Dam. The other is the increase in water quality in the area of the Albany Pool, which suffered severe contamination and deoxygenation from industry and sewage disposal. It is likely that passage of the Clean Water Act in 1972 helped offset fish losses due to habitat restriction.

The most beneficial proactive improvement to habitat for diadromous fishes would be the removal of dams on tributaries and, where not feasible, the construction of fish passage facilities. An attractive location for a fish ladder is the Eddyville Dam near Kingston, which would open up seven miles on the Rondout River, potentially large enough to support American shad reproduction. Many additional sites have been identified (Schmidt, 1996; Schmidt and Lake, 2000).

Also, the Hudson River estuary lost the last of its vast oyster reefs approximately a century ago (Waldman, 1999). Oyster reefs are not only sources of human food but perhaps more importantly, nursery and feeding grounds for many estuarine fishes, including diadromous forms (Coen, Luckenbach, and Breitburg, 1999). Construction of artificial oyster reefs in the Hudson River estuary, as is actively occurring in the Chesapeake Bay, would be beneficial to the river's ichthyofauna.

Ecological interactions. A focus of research on the Hudson's diadromous fishes should be to achieve a better understanding of their ecological interactions with each other, with non-diadromous fishes, and with other organisms. Much of the work that has occurred on the diadromous fishes has been autecological and abundance- and mortality-based. Comparatively little attention has been given to the competitive and predatory connections among Hudson River fishes. For example, is the recent decline in white perch abundance partly attributable to the increase in striped bass? Have striped bass reduced the stock size of American shad and alewife? Did the protection afforded the river's shortnose sturgeon population provide them with a competitive advantage over Atlantic sturgeon? Young bluefish appear to prey heavily on juvenile striped bass (Juanes, Buckel, and Conover, 1994). How significant are bluefish in modulating recruitment of the Hudson's anadromous fishes? How important are sometimes abundant juvenile menhaden *Brevoortia tyrannus* in the lower estuary to subadult striped bass? What would application of Haley's (1998) gastric lavage approach to shortnose sturgeon and Atlantic sturgeon caught contemporaneously from the same river reaches tell us about their trophic niches?

Strikingly little attention has been paid to the fishes of the Hudson River on the community level (see Gladden et al., 1988 for one exception). Daniels (1995) stated that "Although the Hudson River is among the most-studied aquatic systems in North America, data necessary to confirm population trends in its fish assemblage are scant." Although some changes in the relative abundances of particular species can be explained, many cannot. Moreover, how a dynamic community composition affects its individual components is not often clear.

Some species behaviors and interactions pose interesting evolutionary questions. Is carrying capacity a factor in the abundances and behaviors of anadromous fishes? Why is it that shortnose sturgeon – the far more residential of the two sturgeons – appears to nearly stop growing at adulthood and at a small size for an acipenserid whereas the more marine Atlantic sturgeon continues to grow and to a potentially massive size? Is the shortnose sturgeon adapted to the finite resources of a highly discrete river system and the Atlantic sturgeon to the nearly infinite resources of a vast coastal range? Likewise, does the relative abundance of the marine-migrating contingent of striped bass increase with stock size as a means to exploit resources outside the river?

And how have the diadromous fishes responded to the many colonizations by non-native species? Do the now highly-abundant gizzard shad compete with alosines? How heavily do black bass compete with or prey on anadromous piscivores? What is the net effect on anadromous fish nursery habitats of the replacement in entire freshwater coves of native plants such as Vallisneria by the Asian water chestnut Trapa natans?

Fishing and fish mortality from power plants. Any complex fish community is affected by sharp changes in abundance or age structure generated by unnatural sources of mortality. Because of PCB contamination, the entire diadromous fish complex of the Hudson River is not subject to legal commercial harvest in the river, albeit at the price of any sublethal effects stemming from their PCB body burdens.

The effects of electric generation plants on the Hudson's anadromous fish stocks continue to be monitored but are not necessarily well understood. Much of the knowledge gained between 1963 and 1980 through studies conducted in the course of the controversies over the effects of existing and proposed power plants on the Hudson River was summarized in Barnthouse et al. (1988). However, comparatively little information learned over the next score of years has reached the peer-reviewed literature and much of it remains in narrowly distributed and thinly distilled reports. Although the Settlement Agreement included provisions to reduce power plant-mortality of anadromous fishes, fundamental issues persist, such as whether compensatory processes mitigate mortalities to significant degrees. The role of power plants in the population dynamics of Hudson River fishes is likely to remain unclear in the near-term future as a reshuffling of ownership because of deregulation of the power industry and the possible construction of a new generation of power plants that use less river water.

Climate change. Ashizawa and Cole (1994) analyzed long-term water temperature data from Poughkeepsie and found a statistically significant trend of a 0.12°C increase per decade from about 1920 to 1990, a change they believed was consistent with suggested rates of global increases. The biological effects of warming are becoming more apparent as the physical changes become more pronounced and as the time spans monitored become lengthier. Oglesby (1995) showed evidence of significantly earlier blooming of vegetation and spring arrivals of migratory birds in the Hudson Valley. However, he did not detect a change in the average arrival time of anadromous fish in the Hudson River, due, in part, to high interannual variances.

Nonetheless, the status of rainbow smelt at the limits of its southern distribution may be a bellwether. Decades ago smelt entered the Delaware River and its tributary, Brandywine Creek in Maryland; the last known capture in the Delaware system occurred in 1986 (Raasch and Altemus, 1991). Rainbow smelt now appear to be extinct in the Hudson River and, another cold-water species at the margin of its distribution, Atlantic tomcod, also may be thermally stressed and could become extinct in the Hudson River Estuary.

REFERENCES

Ashizawa, D., and Cole, J. J. 1994. Long-term temperature trends of the Hudson River: a study of the historical data. *Estuaries* **17**(IB):166–71.

ASMFC (Atlantic States Marine Fisheries Commission). 1998. Final recovery plan for the shortnose sturgeon *Acipenser brevirostrum*. Washington, D.C.

1999. 1999 review of the Atlantic States Marine Fisheries Commission Management Plan for shad and river herring (*Alosa* sp.). Washington, D.C.

2000. Interstate fishery management plan for American eel. Fishery Management Report 36. Washington, D.C.

Bain, M. B. 1997. Atlantic and shortnose sturgeons of the Hudson River: common and divergent life history attributes. *Environmental Biology of Fishes* **48**:347–58.

Bain, M., Arend, K., Haley, N., Hayes, S., Knight, J., Nack, S., Peterson, D., and Walsh, M. 1998.

Sturgeon of the Hudson River. Final Report to the Hudson River Foundation, New York, NY.

Bain, M., Haley, N., Peterson, D., Waldman, J. R., and Arend, K. 2000. Harvest and habitats of Atlantic sturgeon Acipenser oxyrinchus Mitchill, 1815 in the Hudson River estuary: lessons for sturgeon conservation. *Boletín. Instituto Español de Oceanografía* 16:43–53.

Barnthouse, L. W., Klauda, R. J., Vaughan, D. S., and Kendall, R. L. (eds.). 1988. Science, law, and Hudson River power plants: a case study in environmental impact assessment. *American Fisheries Society Monograph* 4.

Barse, A. M., and Secor, D. H. 1999. An exotic nematode parasite of the American eel. *Fisheries* 24(2):6–10.

Beamish, F. W. H. 1980. Biology of the North American anadromous sea lamprey, *Petromyzon marinus*. *Canadian Journal of Fisheries and Aquatic Sciences* 37:1924–43.

Bean, T. H. 1903. Catalogue of the fishes of New York. *New York State Museum Bulletin* 60, Zoology 9.

Beebe, C. A., and Savidge, I. R. 1988. Historical perspective on fish species composition and distribution in the Hudson River estuary. *American Fisheries Society Monograph* 4:25–36.

Berggren, T. J., and Lieberman, J. T. 1978. Relative contribution of Hudson, Chesapeake, and Roanoke striped bass, *Morone saxatilis*, stocks to the Atlantic coast fishery. *U. S. National Marine Fisheries Service Fishery Bulletin* 76:335–46.

Blake, L. M. 1982. Commercial fishing for eel in New York State, in K. Loftus (ed.), Proceedings of the 1980 North American eel conference. *Ontario Fisheries Technical Report Series* 4:39–41.

Boreman, J., and Klauda, R. J. 1988. Distributions of early life stages of striped bass in the Hudson River estuary, 1974–1979. *American Fisheries Society Monograph* 4:53–8.

Boyle, R. H. 1969. *The Hudson River: a natural and unnatural history*. New York: Norton.

Brown, B. L. 1996. Mixed-stock analysis of American shad in New Jersey's coastal intercept fishery. Final Report to the Hudson River Foundation, New York, NY.

Brumbach, H. J. 1986. Anadromous fish and fishing: a synthesis of data from the Hudson River drainage. *Man in the Northeast* 32:35–66.

Brussard, P. F., Collings-Hall, M., and Wright, J. 1981. Structure and affinities of freshwater sea lamprey (*Petromyzon marinus*) populations. *Canadian Journal of Fisheries and Aquatic Sciences* 38:1708–1714.

Carlson, D. M., and Simpson, K. W. 1987. Gut contents of juvenile shortnose sturgeon in the upper Hudson estuary. *Copeia* 1987:796–802.

Clark, J. R. 1968. Seasonal movements of striped bass contingents of Long Island Sound and the New York Bight. *Transactions of the American Fisheries Society* 97:320–43.

Coen, L. D., Luckenbach, M. W., and Breitburg, D. L. 1999. The role of oyster reefs as essential fish habitat: a review of current knowledge and some new perspectives. *American Fisheries Society Symposium* 22:438–54.

Courtenay, S., Grunwald, C., Kreamer, G.-L., Fairchild, W. L., Arsenault, J. T., Ikonomou, M., and Wirgin, I. 1999. A comparison of the dose and time response of cytochrome P4501A1 mRNA induction in chemically treated Atlantic tomcod from two populations. *Aquatic Toxicology* 47:43–69.

Dadswell, M. J. 1979. Biology and population characteristics of the shortnose sturgeon, *Acipenser brevirostrum* LeSueur 1818 (Osteichthyes: Acipenseridae), in the Saint John River estuary, New Brunswick, Canada. *Canadian Journal of Zoology* 57:2186–2210.

Dadswell, M. J., Melvin, G. D., Williams, P. J., and Themelis, D. E. 1987. Influences of origin, life history, and chance on the Atlantic coast migration of American shad. *American Fisheries Society Symposium* 1:313–330.

Daniels, R. A. 1995. Nearshore fish assemblage of the tidal Hudson River, in E. T. LaRoe, G. S. Farris, C. E. Puckett, P. D. Doran, and M. J. Mac (eds.), *Our Living Resources: A Report to the Nation on the Distribution, Abundance, and Health of U. S. Plants, Animals, and Ecosystems*. U.S. Department of the Interior, National Biological Service, Washington, DC, pp. 260–63.

Daniels, R. A., and Lawrence, T. 1991. *Stability of fish assemblages in the lower Hudson River*. Final Report to the Hudson River Foundation, New York, NY.

Daniels, R. A., Limburg, K. E., Schmidt, R. E., Strayer, D. L., and Chambers, R. C. In press. Changes in fish assemblages in the tidal Hudson River, New York. In Rinne, J. N., R. M. Hughes, and B. Calamusso (eds.). *Historical Changes in Large River Fish Assemblages of America. American Fisheries Society Monograph*.

Dew, C. B., and Hecht, J. H. 1994. Recruitment, growth, mortality, and biomass production of larval and early juvenile Atlantic tomcod in the Hudson River estuary. *Transactions of the American Fisheries Society* 123:681–702.

Dey, W. P., Peck, T. H., Smith, C. E., and Kreamer, G.-L. 1993. Epizoology of hepatic neoplasia in Atlantic tomcod (*Microgadus tomcod*) from the Hudson River estuary. *Canadian Journal of Fisheries and Aquatic Sciences* 50:1897–1907.

Dovel, W. L., and Berggren, T. J. 1983. Atlantic sturgeon of the Hudson estuary. *New York Fish and Game Journal* **30**(2):140–72.

Dovel, W. L., Pekovitch, A. W., and Berggren, T. J. 1992. Biology of the shortnose sturgeon (*Acipenser brevirostrum* Lesueur, 1818) in the Hudson River estuary, New York, in C. L. Smith (ed.), *Estuarine Research in the 1980's*. Albany, NY: State University of New York Press, pp. 187–216.

Dunning, D. J., Ross, Q. E., Kirk, W. L., Waldman, J. R., Heimbuch, D. G., and Mattson, M. T. 1992. Postjuvenile striped bass studies after the Settlement Agreement, in C. L. Smith (ed.), *Estuarine Research in the 1980's*. Albany, NY: State University of New York Press, pp. 339–47.

Dunning, D. J., Waldman, J. R., Ross, Q. E., and Mattson, M. T. 1997. Use of Atlantic tomcod and other prey by striped bass in the lower Hudson River estuary during winter. *Transactions of the American Fisheries Society* **126**:857–61.

Durkas, S. J. 1992. Impediments to the spawning success of anadromous fish in tributaries of the NY/NJ Harbor watershed. American Littoral Society, Highlands, New Jersey.

Geoghegan, P., Mattson, M. T., and Keppel, R. G. 1992. Distribution of the shortnose sturgeon in the Hudson River estuary, 1984–1988, in C. L. Smith (ed.), *Estuarine Research in the 1980's*. Albany, NY: State University of New York Press, pp. 217–41.

Gladden, J. B., Cantelmo, F. R., Croom, J. M., and Shapot, R. 1988. Evaluation of the Hudson River ecosystem in relation to the dynamics of fish populations. *American Fisheries Society Monograph* **4**:37–52.

Grabe, S. A. 1996. Feeding chronology and habits of *Alosa* spp. (Clupeidae) juveniles from the lower Hudson River estuary. *Environmental Biology of Fishes* **47**:321–6.

Greeley, J. R. 1937. Fishes of the area with an annotated list, in: *A Biological Survey of the Lower Hudson Watershed*. Supplemental to Twenty-sixth Annual Report, 1936. New York State Conservation Department, Albany, pp. 45–103.

Greeley, J. R., and Bishop, S. C. 1933. Fishes of the upper Hudson watershed with an annotated list, in: *A Biological Survey of the Lower Hudson Watershed*. Supplemental to Twenty-second Annual Report, 1932. New York State Conservation Department, Albany, pp. 64–101.

Grunwald, C., Stabile, J., Waldman, J. R., Gross, R., and Wirgin, I. I. 2002. Population genetics of shortnose sturgeon *Acipenser brevirostrum* based on mitochondrial DNA control region sequences. *Molecular Ecology* **11**:1885–98.

Haley, N. J. 1998. A gastric lavage technique for characterizing diets of sturgeons. *North American Journal of Fisheries Management* **18**:978–81.

Hoff, T. B., McLaren, J. B., and Cooper, J. C. 1988. Stock characteristics of Hudson River striped bass. *American Fisheries Society Monograph* **4**:59–68.

HRA (Hudson River Almanac). 1998. Volume IV, 1997–1998. Fleischmanns, NY: Purple Mountain Press.

Hurst, T. P., and Conover, D. O. 1998. Winter mortality of young-of-the-year Hudson River striped bass (*Morone saxatilis*): size-dependent patterns and effects on recruitment. *Canadian Journal of Fisheries and Aquatic Sciences* **55**:1122–30.

Juanes, F., Buckel, J. A., and Conover, D. O. 1994. Accelerating the onset of piscivory: interaction of predator and prey phenologies. *Journal of Fish Biology* **45**(Supplement A):41–54.

Klauda, R. J., Moos, R. E., and Schmidt, R. E. 1988. Life history of Atlantic tomcod, *Microgadus tomcod*, in the Hudson River estuary, with emphasis on spatio-temporal distribution and movements, in C. L. Smith (ed.), *Fisheries Research in the Hudson River*. Albany, NY: State University of New York Press, pp. 219–51.

Lake, T. R., and Schmidt, R. E. 1997. Seasonal presence and movement of fish populations in the tidal reach of Quassaic Creek, a Hudson River tributary (HRM 60): documentation of potamodromy, anadromy, and residential components. Section VII in W. C. Nieder and J. R. Waldman (eds.), *Final Reports of the Tibor T. Polgar Fellowship Program, 1996*. Hudson River Foundation, New York, NY.

1998. The relationship between fecundity of an alewife (*Alosa pseudoharengus*) spawning population and egg productivity in Quassaic Creek, a Hudson River tributary (HRM 60) in Orange County, New York. Section II in J. R. Waldman and W. C. Nieder (eds.), *Final Reports of the Tibor T. Polgar Fellowship Program, 1997*. Hudson River Foundation, New York, NY.

Leggett, W. C., and Carscadden, J. E. 1978. Latitudinal variation in reproductive characteristics of American shad (*Alosa sapidissima*): evidence for population specific life history strategies in fish. *Journal Fisheries Research Board of Canada* **35**:1469–78.

Limburg, K. E. 1996. Growth and migration of 0-year American shad (*Alosa sapidissima*) in the Hudson River estuary: otolith microstructural analysis. *Canadian Journal of Fisheries and Aquatic Sciences* **53**:220–38.

Limburg, K. E., Pace, M. L., Fischer, D., and Arend, K. E. 1997. Consumption, selectivity, and use of zooplankton by larval striped bass and white perch in a seasonally pulsed estuary. *Transactions of the American Fisheries Society* **126**:607–21.

Limburg, K. E., and Schmidt, R. E. 1990. Patterns of fish spawning in Hudson River tributaries: response to an urban gradient? *Ecology* **71**:1238–45.

LoBue, C., and McKown, K. A. 1998. A study of the striped bass in the Marine District of New York VII. Completion Report for P.L. 89-304, Project AFC 20, New York State Department of Environmental Conservation, Stony Brook, NY.

Loesch, J. G. 1987. Overview of life history aspects of anadromous alewife and blueback herring in freshwater habitats. *American Fisheries Society Symposium* **1**:89–103.

MacNeill, D. 1998. Research needs for the blueback herring: a new invader? *Dreissena* **9**(2):5–6, New York Sea Grant, SUNY College at Brockport, Brockport, NY.

Mattes, K. C. 1989. "The ecology of the American eel, *Anguilla rostrata* (Lesueur), in the Hudson River." Doctoral dissertation, Fordham University, New York.

Mattson, M. T., Geoghegan, P., and Dunning, D. J. 1992. Accuracy of catch per unit effort indices of Atlantic tomcod abundance in the Hudson River, in C. L. Smith (ed.), *Estuarine Research in the 1980's*. Albany, NY: State University of New York Press, pp. 323–38.

McLaren, J. B., Cooper J. C., Hoff T. B., and Lander V. 1981. Movements of Hudson River striped bass. *Transactions of the American Fisheries Society* **110**:158–67.

McLaren, J. B., Peck, T. H., Dey, W. P., and Gardinier, M. 1988. Biology of Atlantic tomcod in the Hudson River estuary. *American Fisheries Society Monograph* **4**:102–12.

Nelson, J. S. 1976. *Fishes of the World*. New York: John Wiley & Sons.

Nolan, K., Grossfield, J., and Wirgin, I. 1991. Discrimination among Atlantic coast populations of American shad (*Alosa sapidissima*) using mitochondrial DNA. *Canadian Journal of Fisheries and Aquatic Sciences* **48**:1724–34.

Oglesby, R. T. 1995. *Timing of Phenological Events and Climate Change in the Hudson River Corridor*. Final Report to the Hudson River Foundation, New York, NY.

Pace, M. L., Baines, S. B., Cyr, H., and Downing, J. A. 1993. Relationships among early life stages of *Morone americana* and *Morone saxatilis* from long-term monitoring of the Hudson River estuary. *Canadian Journal of Fisheries and Aquatic Sciences* **50**:1976–85.

Peterson, D. L., Bain, M. B., and Haley, N. 2000. Evidence of declining recruitment of Atlantic sturgeon in the Hudson River. *North American Journal of Fisheries Management* **20**:231–8.

Raasch, M. S., and Altemus, Sr, V. L. 1991. *Delaware's Freshwater and Brackish Water Fishes: A Popular Account*. Dover, DE: Dover Litho.

Raney, E. C., Woolcott, W. S., and Mehring, A. G., 1954. Migratory pattern and racial structure of Atlantic coast striped bass. *Transactions North American Wildlife Conference* **19**:376–96.

Rose, F. P. 1993. "Have all the smelt gone somewhere? Assessing changes in population size of the rainbow smelt (*Osmerus mordax*) in the Hudson River estuary." M. S. thesis, Bard College, New York.

Schmidt, R. E. 1996. *A catalog of barriers to upstream movements of migratory fishes in Hudson River tributaries*. Final Report to the Hudson River Foundation, New York, NY.

——— 1986. Zoogeography of the northern Appalachians, in C. H. Hocutt and E. O. Wiley (eds.), *The Zoogeography of North American Freshwater Fishes*. New York: John Wiley and Sons, pp. 137–159.

Schmidt, R. E., Klauda, R. J., and Bartels, J. M. 1988. Distributions and movements of the early life stages of three species of *Alosa* in the Hudson River, with comments on mechanisms to reduce interspecific competition, in C. L. Smith (ed.), *Fisheries Research in the Hudson River*. Albany, NY: State University of New York Press, pp. 193–215.

Schmidt, R. E., and Lake, T. R. 2000. *Alewives in Hudson River Tributaries, Two Years of Sampling*. Final Report to the Hudson River Foundation, New York, NY.

Schmidt, R. E., and Limburg, K. 1989. *Fishes Spawning in Non-tidal Portions of Hudson River Tributaries*. Final Report to the Hudson River Foundation, New York, NY.

Scott, W. B., and Crossman, E. J. 1973. *Freshwater Fishes of Canada*. Fisheries Research Board of Canada, Bulletin 184.

Secor, D. H. 1999. Specifying divergent migrations in the concept of stock: the contingent hypothesis. *Fisheries Research* **43**:13–34.

Secor, D. H., Stevenson, J. T., and Houde, E. D. 1997. *Age Structure and Life History Attributes of Atlantic Sturgeon* (Acipenser oxyrinchus) *in the Hudson River*. Final Report to the Hudson River Foundation, New York, NY.

Secor, D. H., and Waldman, J. R. 1999. Historical abundance of Delaware Bay Atlantic sturgeon and potential rate of recovery. *American Fisheries Society Symposium* **23**:203–216.

Smith, C. L. 1985. *The Inland Fishes of New York State*. New York State Department of Environmental Conservation, Albany, NY.

Smith, C. L. (ed.). 1988. *Fisheries Research in the Hudson River*. Albany, NY: State University of New York Press.

Smith, C. L. (ed.). 1992. *Estuarine Research in the 1980s.* Albany, NY: State University of New York.

Smith, T. I. J. 1985. The fishery, biology, and management of Atlantic sturgeon, *Acipenser oxyrhynchus,* in North America. *Environmental Biology of Fishes* **14**:61–72.

VanEenennaam, J. P., Doroshov, S. I., Moberg, G. P., Watson, J. G., Moore, D. S., and Linares, J. 1996. Reproductive conditions of the Atlantic sturgeon (*Acipenser oxyrhynchus*) in the Hudson River. *Estuaries* **19**:769–77.

VanWinkle, W., Kumar, K. D., and Vaughan, D. S. 1988. Relative contributions of Hudson River and Chesapeake Bay striped bass stocks to the Atlantic coast population. *American Fisheries Society Monograph* **4**:255–66.

Vargo, J. H. 1995. *Hudson River Stripers: The Guide.* Beacon, NY: Beacon Publishing Corporation.

Waldman, J. 1999. *Heartbeats in the Muck: The History, Sea Life, and Environment of New York Harbor.* New York, NY: Lyons Press.

Waldman, J. R., Dunning, D. J., and Mattson, M. T. 1990b. A morphological explanation for size-dependent anchor tag loss from striped bass. *Transactions of the American Fisheries Society* **119**:920–23.

Waldman, J. R., Dunning, D. J., Ross, Q. E., and Mattson, M. T., 1990a. Range dynamics of Hudson River striped bass along the Atlantic coast. *Transactions of the American Fisheries Society* **119**:910–19.

Waldman, J. R., Hart, J. T., and Wirgin, I. I., 1996a. Stock composition of the New York Bight Atlantic sturgeon fishery based on analysis of mitochondrial DNA. *Transactions of the American Fisheries Society* **125**:364–71.

Waldman, J. R., Nolan, K., Hart, J., and Wirgin, I. I. 1996b. Genetic differentiation of three key anadromous fish populations of the Hudson River. *Estuaries* **19**:759–68.

Waldman, J. R., and Vecchio, V. J. 1996. Selected biocharacteristics of hatchery-reared striped bass in New York ocean waters. *North American Journal of Fisheries Management* **16**:14–23.

Waldman, J. R., and Wirgin, I. I., 1998. Status and restoration options for Atlantic sturgeon in North America. *Conservation Biology* **12**:631–8.

Walsh, M. G., Bain, M. B., Squiers, Jr., T., Waldman, J. R., and Wirgin, I. 2001. Morphological and genetic variation among shortnose sturgeon *Acipenser brevirostrum* from adjacent and distant rivers. *Estuaries* **24**:41–8.

Wells, A. W., Randall, D. M., Dunning, D. J., and Young, J. R. 1991. Dispersal of young-of-the-year hatchery striped bass in the Hudson River. *North American Journal of Fisheries Management* **11**:381–92.

Wirgin, I. I., Grunwald, C., Courtenay, S., Kreamer, G.-L., Reichert, W. L., and Stein, J. 1994. A biomarker approach in assessing xenobiotic exposure in cancer-prone Atlantic tomcod from the North American Atlantic coast. *Environmental Health Perspectives* **102**:764–70.

Wirgin, I., Maceda, L., Waldman, J. R., and Crittenden, R. N. 1993. Use of mitochondrial DNA polymorphisms to estimate the relative contributions of the Hudson River and Chesapeake Bay stocks to the mixed fishery on the Atlantic coast. *Transactions of the American Fisheries Society* **122**: 669–84.

Wirgin, I. I., Waldman, J. R., Maceda, L., Stabile, J., and Vecchio, V. J. 1997. Mixed-stock analysis of Atlantic coast striped bass (*Morone saxatilis*) using nuclear DNA and mitochondrial DNA markers. *Canadian Journal of Fisheries and Aquatic Sciences* **54**:2814–26.

Zeisel, W. 1995. *Angling on a Changing Estuary: the Hudson River, 1609–1995.* Final Report to the Hudson River Foundation, New York, NY.

Zlokovitz, E. R., and Secor, D. H. 1999. Effect of habitat use on PCB body burden in Hudson River striped bass (*Morone saxatilis*). *Canadian Journal of Fisheries and Aquatic Sciences* **56**(Supplement 1): 86–93.

14 Fisheries of the Hudson River Estuary

Karin E. Limburg, Kathryn A. Hattala, Andrew W. Kahnle, and John R. Waldman

ABSTRACT Fisheries have been prosecuted in the Hudson since prehistoric times. Oysters, American shad, and sturgeon were important food fisheries into the twentieth century, although of these, only a dwindling commercial shad fishery persists. Striped bass, another formerly important commercial fishery, went into decline and subsequent recovery from management actions; today, it supports a major recreational fishery. Other important sport fishing includes largemouth and smallmouth bass, and American shad. Toxicants and power plants have been long-term threats to fisheries, and will continue to pose problems for the indefinite future.

Introduction

Of all the relationships humankind entertains with the Hudson River, perhaps none is so intimate as that of fishing. The harvest of fish and shellfish from the Hudson has endured for thousands of years, and connects us both with the river's productivity and with our cultural past.

Other chapters in this book describe the fish fauna and its use of various habitats within the system. Here, we concentrate on the fisheries themselves, focusing on key species within the commercial and sportfishing arenas. We also examine some of the factors that potentially have large effects on fisheries, namely, the impacts of power plants that withdraw water from the river, and the persistence of contaminants, especially PCBs.

Historical Importance of Hudson River Fisheries

FROM NATIVE TO COMMERCIAL FISHING

Before modern agriculture and globalization of products, the fisheries of the Hudson River were an important and diverse local source of protein. Native Americans harvested fish and shellfish long before the arrival of European settlers. Dating of the oyster middens at Croton Point Park show that humans fished there nearly six millennia ago (Anonymous, 2001). Middens at Tivoli Bays in the upper tidal Hudson bear evidence of the consumption of fish and even bland-tasting freshwater mussels (Funk, 1992). Adriean Van der Donck, one of the documenters of the first Dutch settlements, noted "this river is full of fishes" (Boyle, 1979). Settlers could feast on finfish, including American shad, sturgeons, and striped bass, as well as on blue crab, scallops, and the plentiful oysters that extended throughout New York Harbor, East and Harlem Rivers, and up the Hudson as far as Stony Point. Oysters from Gowanus Bay were the size of dinner plates and especially sought after (Waldman, 1999). The Hudson River beds produced well over 450,000 barrels (50,000 m³) of oysters per annum in the early nineteenth century (Boyle, 1979).

Commercial fishers in the eighteenth and nineteenth centuries harvested a wide variety of finfish species from the Hudson, many of which were documented by Mitchill (1815) who made numerous observations in the public markets. Among the species most heavily exploited in the nineteenth century were American shad and the two sturgeons. Sturgeons were valued for both their roe and flesh. Harvests were so great in the tidal Hudson that sturgeon was popularly known as "Albany beef," because it was shipped upriver to a hungry market. Shad could be taken in great numbers in the spring spawning runs by stake-nets or drift-nets, then salted for later consumption. In 1895, it was the number one inland fish harvested in the United States (Cheney, 1896), valued at almost $185,000 – equivalent to over $3,900,000 today.

Both American shad and sturgeons were overharvested in the late nineteenth century. Because of its life history characteristics of late maturation and nonannual spawning, coastwide

Number of shad licenses sold

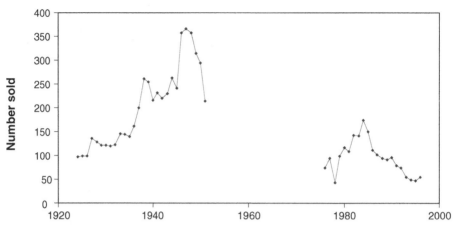

Figure 14.1. Numbers of shad licenses sold to Hudson River fishermen, 1924–96. Data from 1924–51 are from Talbot (1954) and from 1976–96, Hattala and Kahnle (1997). License records from intervening years were lost.

overharvesting of sturgeon was inevitable, given the level of effort. Overharvesting of shad peaked in the 1890s, with catches declining precipitously thereafter (Stevenson, 1899). Writing in 1916, Dr. C. M. Blackford declared,

... there is probably no fish on earth that surpasses the shad in all the qualities that go to make up an ideal food fish ... [*but it*] *is the one whose preservation has become a national problem.*

In the late 1800s, the U.S. Fish and Fisheries Commission took the radical step of artificial propagation, which was the state-of-the-art in U.S. fisheries management at the time. Indeed, in June 1871, Seth Green, then one of the top fish culturists in the country, steam-trained across the country with delicate shad fry held in milk cans, discharging them into the upper Sacramento River (recounted in Boyle, 1979). Shad became established on the Pacific coast, invading the Columbia River within 30 years (Ebbesmeyer and Hinrichsen, 1997) and constituting an important, if exotic, component of the ichthyofauna there today.

Concurrent with turn-of-the-century overharvesting problems, a growing and rapidly industrializing New York City created serious stress on New York Harbor, with dumping of soot and garbage and discharges of wastes an ever-increasing nuisance. The oyster fisheries were essentially gone by the 1920s (Franz, 1982), and the fouled water imparted an unpleasant flavor to most of the fishes

(NYSCD, 1964). Nevertheless, fisheries continued to constitute a livelihood, at least in part, for many upriver communities throughout much of the twentieth century (Fig. 14.1). With the enactment of the National Environmental Policy Act in 1970 and amended Clean Water Act in 1972, conventional pollution declined and in many aspects, the river recovered (Limburg, Moran, and McDowell, 1986). However, as a result of widespread PCB contamination, several of the important commercial fisheries are closed, and today commercial effort is at an all-time low (see Shapley, 2001 for a journalistic account or Hattala and Kahnle, 1997).

ANGLING

The Hudson River Estuary figures prominently in the history of American angling. Due in part to the high quality of fishing in its waters and to the many books and articles written about it, Zeisel (1990) considered New York City to have become the capital of American angling by 1850. Among the important angling writers were Frank Forester and Genio Scott. In his classic work, *Fishing in American Waters*, (Scott, 1875) wrote about angling in the Hudson River estuary in the vicinity of New York City. Several sections were devoted to striped bass angling, including trolling for them from skiffs in the "seething and hissing" waters of Hell Gate in the East River, a riptide where currents reached ten knots. Scott also described fishing for striped bass from rowboats near the hedges (fish weirs made from brush) in the Kill Van Kull and from bridges in the Harlem River. The Harlem River, although dammed for tidal mill power for the first half of the nineteenth century, was a major resource which offered excellent angling for striped bass, bluefish, weakfish, porgy, and flounder (Zeisel, 1995).

These species, and others, were fished all over New York Harbor from shore and from vessels. Zeisel (1995) quoted *Harper's Weekly* of August 4, 1877, which stated that "On almost any day of the year except when the ice makes fishing impossible, hundreds of men and boys may be seen on the river front engaged in angling." Zeisel (1990, 1995) also reported that in the mid-1800s, skiffs could be rented from various liveries and that during summer, hundreds of boats filled with anglers could be seen on the harbor's best spots.

Angling in New York Harbor during Scott's time included species almost never seen today. Scott provided instructions on exactly where and how to catch sheepshead near Jamaica Bay, an area where they were so abundant that farmers would fish them with hand-lines to supplement their income. Black drum, another twentieth century absentee, also were commonly landed during the previous century in Upper and New York Bays and the East and Harlem Rivers (Zeisel, 1995).

A surprising category of fish that were caught in Upper New York Bay and along the docks of lower Manhattan from 1760 to 1895 was sharks (Zeisel, 1990). Although their species identities remain unknown, large sharks were abundant in these inshore waters during that period, possibly drawn by large amounts of food refuse being disposed of in New York Harbor. Accounts exist (ca. 1815) of shark fishers catching as many as seven sharks at lengths of up to 14 feet at Manhattan's Catherine Market (Zeisel, 1990).

Fish along the shores of Manhattan began to taste contaminated from petroleum by the late 1800s, pushing anglers to more distant waters such as the "fishing banks" in the New York Bight (Zeisel, 1995). But angling farther upriver in the Hudson River developed more slowly. According to Zeisel (1995), fishing activity centered on wharves and docks at major landings such as the mouth of Rondout Creek in Kingston, and at Newburgh, Poughkeepsie, and Hudson. Both shad and sturgeon roe were commonly used baits

in the Hudson's freshwater reaches. Important species caught (mainly with hand-lines) included striped bass, white perch, American eel, and catfish. Tributaries of the Hudson River were also fished, particularly in spring for spawning runs of suckers and yellow perch. Many of these tributaries also supported trout, but this angling declined as they were fished out, with attention shifting to the black basses.

The endemicity in the Hudson River of one gamefish, Atlantic salmon, has been debated since Robert Juet – a member of Henry Hudson's exploratory expedition up the river – reported "many Salmons and Mullets and Rays very great." This notion was fueled by their occasional capture by net in the river throughout the nineteenth century. However, a number of scientists have concluded that the Hudson did not support a salmon population and that such appearances were probably strays from neighboring systems such as the Connecticut River. Nonetheless, Atlantic salmon eggs from Penobscot River specimens were stocked in the Hudson River in the 1880s (Zeisel, 1995). These stockings were sufficient to result in hundreds of commercial catches in the lower river and fewer via angling upriver, chiefly at Mechanicville (following collapse of a dam at Troy). However, there is no evidence that natural reproduction occurred and this fishery dwindled after stocking was halted. Given that Juet's observation was made in September in Lower New York Bay and because of its superficial salmonid resemblances, it is likely that he mistook weakfish for salmon.

Fishing clubs became numerous along the Hudson River beginning in the late 1800s (Zeisel, 1995). They led the fight against the Hudson fishing license, which was in effect from the 1930s to 1946. Inasmuch as it was instituted during the Depression and was costly, many people ignored it as they angled for sustenance. Game wardens were overwhelmed and judges dismissed cases against destitute offenders, which together with the fact that the river was not stocked by the state with fish, eventually led to its repeal.

Angling on the Hudson River estuary continued without fanfare during the early to mid-1900s. But because of its severe sewage and industrial contamination, the estuary appears to have reached a nadir in angling activity over that period.

The Current Regulatory Framework

Hudson River fisheries are managed by the New York State Department of Environmental Conservation (DEC). Regulatory capacity lies within the Division of Fish, Wildlife and Marine Resources. For anadromous fish species in the Hudson and in marine waters, state regulations for commercial and recreational fishing follow guidelines set by Interstate Fishery Management Plans developed through the Atlantic States Marine Fisheries Commission (ASMFC). The ASMFC is a Federal commission created to coordinate cooperative management of shared coastal resources for the fifteen coastal states from Maine to Florida, along with the two Federal resource agencies, the U.S. Fish and Wildlife Service (FWS) and the National Marine Fisheries Service (NMFS). As set forth in its mission statement (ASMFC, 2002),

With the recognition that fish do not adhere to political boundaries, the states formed an Interstate Compact, which was approved by the U.S. Congress. The states have found that their mutual interest in sustaining healthy coastal fishery resources is best achieved by working together cooperatively, in collaboration with the federal government. Through this approach, the states uphold their collective fisheries management responsibilities in a cost effective, timely, and responsive fashion.

A number of important laws underpin fishery management in the Hudson (see text box, "Milestones in Fisheries Legislation"). The Anadromous Fish Conservation Act provides authority and funding for preservation and restoration of anadromous fisheries, and was the impetus for much-needed research on biology, life history, population status, and characteristics of fisheries. The Fishery Conservation and Management Act of 1976, known as the Magnuson Act, created a 200-mile Exclusive Economic Zone (EEZ) along the U.S. coast, enabling controlled fishing in U.S. territorial waters. Fishing in the EEZ is regulated by regional management councils and NMFS. State jurisdiction is defined as zero to three miles, and is coordinated through the ASMFC. The Sustainable Fisheries Act and the Magnuson-Stevens Act of 1996 evolved from the Magnuson Act. In particular, Magnuson-Stevens changed emphasis to include protection of aquatic habitats, to focus on optimum sustained

Milestones in Fisheries Legislation	
1965	Anadromous Fish Conservation Act
1976	Fishery Conservation and Management Act (Magnuson Act)
1979	Emergency Striped Bass Study (sub-set of AFCA)
1984	Atlantic Striped Bass Act
1993	Atlantic Coastal Fisheries Cooperative Management Act
1996	Sustainable Fisheries Act
1996	Magnuson-Stevens Fishery Conservation and Management Act

yield that took account of "relevant social, economic, or ecological factor[s]," and mechanisms to reduce the risk of decision making by vested interests (Ross, 1997).

The Emergency Striped Bass Study (ESBS) of 1979 and the Atlantic Striped Bass Act (ASBA) of 1984 responded to dramatic declines in catches of striped bass, particularly in the Chesapeake Bay. The ESBS increased coastwide research and monitoring for striped bass stocks, and the ASBA, as a follow-on, required mandatory compliance with the Interstate Fishery Management Plan for striped bass. Finally, the Atlantic Coastal Fisheries Cooperative Management Act, modeled on the ASBA, provides a regulatory framework for all species managed through the ASFMC. A Fishery Management Plan (FMP) must be developed for each species, and fisheries must be monitored by each member state.

Profiles of Significant Hudson River Fisheries Stocks

In this section, we describe recent trends and status of the major commercial fishery species in the Hudson.

STRIPED BASS

Striped bass **live approximately 25 to 30 years**		
Sex	**Age at Maturity**	**Size**
Male	3 to 6 y	16 to 24 in (40 to 60 cm)
Female	6 to 8 y	27 to 32 in (68 to 80 cm)
Migratory range: Canada, New England, and mid-Atlantic coasts		

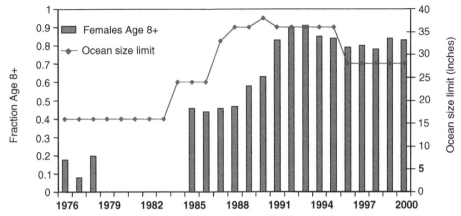

Figure 14.2. Changes in ocean size limits, and the proportion of female striped bass aged 8+ in the Hudson River spawning stock.

In the years prior to 1983, few restrictions governed the take of striped bass in state and coastal marine waters. Size limits were minimal. In New York waters, fish as small as 16 inches fork length (FL, equivalent to 40.6 cm enacted in 1939 by New York State) could be taken, there existed limited seasonal and gear restrictions, and there was no catch limit. The small size limits allowed few striped bass to reach maturity. Females begin to reach maturity at six years of age, with over 97 percent spawning by age eight. These fish are in the size range of 24 to 28 inches (61 to 71 cm; see text box).

In the Chesapeake Bay, the striped bass fishery focused on "pan rock" with fish as small as 12 to 14 inches (30.5 to 35.6 cm) making up most of the harvest. Over the course of roughly 15 years from the 1970s through the early 1980s, few adult spawners returned to the Bay. With the collapse of the Chesapeake stock in the mid 1970s, states realized that it would take a concerted, cooperative effort to restore the Chesapeake population. To achieve this goal, the Emergency Striped Bass Act (part of the Anadromous Fish Conservation Act) was passed by the U.S. Congress in 1979. This new Federal law required all coastal states that harvested striped bass to follow management regulations contained in the newly developed fishery management plan. Management would no longer be by voluntary agreement, but rather by enforced compliance. The enforcement for non-compliance is complete closure of an entire state's fishery for that species. The first striped bass fisheries management plan (FMP) was adopted by ASMFC in 1981.

Over the course of the next fifteen years, management regulations followed an adaptive process, and the FMP was amended six times. The most severe restrictions occurred in Maryland where a moratorium on striped bass fishing was implemented in Chesapeake Bay. Marine commercial fisheries were limited by severely reduced quotas to less than 20 percent of historical harvest levels, and season, size limits, and allowable gears were specified and enforced. Recreational fisheries were limited by size and bag limits, and by seasons. These regulations, especially size limits, were adjusted annually from 1984 until 1990, from 24 to up to 38 inches (61 to 96.5 cm), to protect the females from the 1982 year class (young fish produced) of the Chesapeake Bay until most of them spawned at age eight.

The effect of these regulations was startling, not only for the Chesapeake stock, but for other striped bass stocks along the coast. The coastal protective measures immediately protected immature fish of the Hudson spawning stock of striped bass. Hudson River striped bass may leave the estuary as early as age one to seasonally utilize the nearshore marine waters. Prior to adoption of the FMP, recreational and commercial fisheries alike exploited these immature bass. Once fish were no longer harvested at 16 inches, the increasing coastal size limits gave refuge to the Hudson's immature and mature population. The effect was the return of greater numbers of older, larger fish each year (Fig. 14.2), which in turn produced ever greater numbers of young.

By 1995, coastwide management targets were being met: striped bass were returning to the rivers to

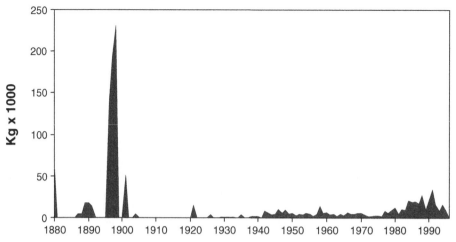

Figure 14.3. Historic commercial fishery landings of Atlantic sturgeon in the Hudson River Estuary, 1880–1995.

spawn, production estimates were up, and adult age structure was stabilized. It was then that the Chesapeake stock was declared restored. The state management agencies were not complacent about their success. Even with record numbers of fish, management restrictions were loosened slowly. Commercial harvest quotas were increased, and recreational size limits were lowered to 28 inches.

Annual tracking of mortality rate of the stock is still key. Harvest from all sources is compiled annually. Spawning stocks are monitored for age structure and survival. Young-of-year abundance estimates provide early warning of changes that may come.

ATLANTIC STURGEON

Atlantic sturgeon live approximately 60 to 80 years. Males mature by age 8 to 12 and 15 to 20 years for females. Females spawn every three years.

Migratory range: entire Atlantic coast, Canada to FL

Records of sturgeon harvest are available as far back as the 1880s, a time when harvest levels climbed to record highs. The high harvest level essentially clear-cut the once robust population. The Hudson's Atlantic sturgeon stock continued to remain severely depressed through the rest of the twentieth century (Fig. 14.3).

A vestigial fishery persisted in the river through the 1980s, made up of a small group of fishers taking a few fish each year for their caviar and meat. However, interest in this fishery began to change in the late 1980s. Elsewhere on the east coast, other Atlantic sturgeon stocks had already been overfished and harvest restricted or eliminated. The most important were those that targeted sturgeon produced in the rivers of North Carolina, South Carolina, and Georgia (Smith, 1985). These fisheries stimulated a market demand for smoked sturgeon products as the supply was eliminated through regulation of harvest. In ocean waters, interest rose in the late 1980s targeting the immature sturgeon for the smoked meat market, especially in New York and New Jersey (Waldman, Hart, and Wirgin, 1996).

This market shift occurred while the restrictions in striped bass management were taking hold along the Atlantic coast. Atlantic sturgeon was among the species that became fishing targets to make up for lost income. In addition, import restrictions from the Middle East (Iran was a source of much of the caviar available in the United States) greatly enhanced the value of any domestic source of caviar. Some of the Hudson's shad fishers began to experiment and eventually became very successful at capturing adult Atlantic sturgeon.

Based on the success of rebuilding the striped bass stocks, the Atlantic Coastal Fisheries Cooperative Management Act was passed in December

1993. This act gave the same stringent enforcement power to all FMPs developed under ASMFC. States, with New York in the lead, began to look with much scrutiny at the condition of the River's Atlantic sturgeon stock and the rate at which they were being fished.

With their long lifetime, older age at maturity, and irregular spawning schedules, Atlantic sturgeon are easily over-fished. Young individuals were being harvested in coastal waters as they left the Hudson at age three to seven to begin their long marine residence before they mature ten to fifteen years later. Few fish were surviving to return to the river, and even here a fishery targeted the spawning adults. In 1995, New York tried to implement controls in the fishery with season and area closures, followed in 1996 with the imposition of a quota system, limiting the total take. But by 1997, New York's stock assessment demonstrated that harvest and fishing rates were severely over the limit that the population could handle. A moratorium was put in place that year, and by 1998 the entire U.S. Atlantic coast was closed to harvest. The interstate management plan set a forty-year time limit for the coast-wide moratorium based on the life history of the animal. That is, within the next forty years, the current spawning population's young should be able to grow and mature to produce one more generation before examining the reopening of any fishery.

AMERICAN SHAD

> *American shad* in the Hudson River live 13 to 15 years. Males begin to spawn by age 3 to 5, females by age 5 to 7.
>
> **Migratory range of Hudson shad:** Atlantic coast, Canada to NC

At the turn of the twentieth century, the new immigrant population continued to swell the growing Atlantic coast cities, including New York. It amazed them to find that every spring fish returned to the Hudson by the thousands, an easy food supply to feed the hungry. Unfortunately for shad, it earned recognition as the second highest harvested fish on the east coast following Atlantic cod. Atlantic sturgeon came in third. The seemingly unlimited harvest, however, wore down the stock, and before

long shad suffered the same fate in the Hudson as in other Atlantic coast rivers.

The story of respite, rebuild, overharvest, and collapse occurred several times for the Hudson shad stock (Hattala and Kahnle, 1997). During periods of lowered fishing pressure, the stock rebuilt between collapses. However, the resiliency of this highly fecund species was slowly being eroded as the century wore on. The first collapse occurred prior to the known record. United States Fish Commission reports documented that in the 1870s the Hudson stock was "over-fished and in need of replenishment." Seth Green, then working for New York State, began a hatchery to stock shad in the spawning areas in the upper reaches of the tidal Hudson and even above the Troy Dam (Cheney, 1896). Fishing was not the only problem for the stock. Spawning areas were lost as the shallow bays behind the river's islands were slowly filled with dredge spoil from creation of a shipping channel to the Port of Albany. Nearly a third of the upper tidal Hudson was filled, almost all of it shad spawning habitat. Water quality in the spawning reach also suffered through much of the twentieth century (Faigenbaum, 1937; Burdick, 1954; Talbot, 1954; Boyle, 1979) until improvements to sewage treatment were made.

The gaps in the fishery landings records from the early 1900s (Fig. 14.4) are thought to be from lack of fishing activity. This lack of fishing would have allowed the shad stock to rebuild to a size necessary to produce the dramatically large harvest that occurred during the years leading up to World War II. Fishing this available food source became a valued trade during the war, so much so that fishing rules in the river were suspended. Each spring in the war period, hundreds of fishermen set their nets, and riverside communities took as many fish as the nets could bear.

In less than twelve years, the next stock collapse was underway: the greater the effort, the fewer the fish. In addition, water quality worsened. Sewage poured in and habitat suffered. In the summer, sections of the river, around Albany and the lower estuary, were completely devoid of oxygen. A few shad kept returning, but the overall stock size remained much reduced from its former status. This problem was not unique to the Hudson: for example, the Delaware River was so polluted between

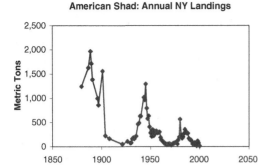

Figure 14.4. Catches of American shad in New York State. Most of the catches are from the Hudson. Top panel: trends since 1880. Bottom panel: trends since 1950. Note differences in scale. *Sources:* National Marine Fisheries Statistics, Walburg and Nichols (1967).

Trenton and Philadelphia that this entire segment went anoxic in the summer months, preventing any movement of fish, such as migrating shad (Chittenden, 1969).

Finally in the mid 1970s, the environmental movement gained momentum. With the passage of the much-strengthened amendments of the Clean Water Act in 1972, the sewage dumping eventually abated. The river slowly started to recover, along with its fisheries.

Humanity's influence again was felt, just as in the case of Atlantic sturgeon. During the recovery effort for striped bass, many near-shore ocean fishers shifted their focus to American shad. These "ocean intercept" fisheries directed their fishing pressure onto mixed assemblages of east coast shad stocks, including the Hudson's. Some stocks began to show declines, or no sign of recovery, despite restoration programs. Since 1991, the Hudson's shad stock began its latest decline, showing classic signs of overfishing. Individuals are smaller at any given age, and fewer older fish are returning to spawn.

A 40% reduction in effort of the directed ocean intercept fishery occurred in 2003 followed by a

complete closure on December 31, 2004. How effective will this measure be? At this point, it is unclear how quickly the stocks will respond to the reduced harvest. Directed fishing may come to an end, but in some cases, shad picked up in other fisheries may become discarded bycatch. Continued monitoring of this bycatch will be a key element in managing the coastwide restoration. In the Hudson River, it is still unknown whether further cutbacks will be required, for example, closure of more spawning area, or lengthening the lift (no fishing) period.

The Contemporary Sport Fishery

With the general upgrading of sewage treatment during the twentieth century and, particularly since passage of a New York State Bond Act in 1965 and the federal Clean Water Act amendments of 1972, the Hudson River and New York Harbor have seen recoveries of many fish populations (Waldman, 1999). The increased availability of fish and a growing perception that the Hudson River system has become cleaner has led to a pronounced increase in angling activity. However, this increase has not been well quantified due to the rarity and limited scope of angling surveys conducted, and to potential knowledge lost through consideration of the mainstem tidal Hudson River as an extension of the sea for which fishing licenses are not required. Moreover, despite this angling revival, its enjoyment is hindered by the continuing presence of PCBs and other contaminants in the river's finfish and shellfish and in resultant governmental restrictions and health advisories.

Boyle (1979) contrasted the intense angling effort for striped bass in the mid 1900s along the ocean coast with the dearth of striped bass anglers in the Hudson River, despite the species' high abundance in the river. Boyle wrote: "... only a relative handful of anglers, perhaps fifty at best, regularly take advantage of the striper fishing that is to be had in the Hudson." He also described the Albany Pool as being "so awesomely foul as to be a source of wonder to sanitary engineers" from raw sewage releases and that this caused the river to be essentially devoid of oxygen in summer for twenty to thirty miles south of the Federal Dam at Troy.

But in the last two decades of the twentieth century, as the Hudson River reached levels of purity not seen for decades to a century or more and the striped bass population continued to increase, angling over the length of the tidal river grew in popularity, with the area below the Federal Dam becoming especially attractive as striped bass and other anadromous fish aggregated there in large numbers (Lake, 1985; Zeisel, 1995). A snapshot of this emergent striped bass fishery in 1997 between the George Washington Bridge and the federal dam was provided by Peterson (1998). Using a combination of 37 aerial flights and 2,700 angler interviews from April through June, he estimated the striped bass fishery supported 619,132 angler-hours distributed over 145,842 angler-trips. Of these, the boat fishery was responsible for 71 percent of effort and 84 percent of catch. Total catch was estimated at 112,757 striped bass, of which only 12.5 percent were harvested. This low harvest was attributed to concerns over PCB contamination and to restrictive bag limits (one fish 18 inches or larger north of George Washington Bridge; one fish 28 inches or larger south of George Washington Bridge). This fishery in the Hudson River and New York Harbor became so popular that several, mainly springtime charter boat operations were launched (Vargo, 1995; Waldman, 1999), and annual tournaments are now held. Accounts of urban angling for striped bass in New York Harbor may be found in Waldman (1998, 1999).

Another fishery that has grown from one enjoyed by relatively few local residents in the mid 1970s to one that supports charter boats and tournaments that garner national publicity is for the two black basses of the river: largemouth and smallmouth bass (Nack et al., 1993). These species occur in freshwater and low salinity reaches of the river. Recruitment in the Hudson River is low for black basses but growth is rapid (the fastest in New York State; Green, Nack, and Forney, 1988), resulting in a fishery that is attractive because it provides a high percentage of large specimens despite low densities of adults (<2 largemouth bass per hectare; Carlson, 1992). Moreover, these fisheries are primarily catch-and-release, with considerable effort spent in tournaments or practicing for tournaments; Green and Jackson (1991) estimated that as of 1990, there were fifty to sixty black bass tournaments held annually in the river. This tournament activity is centered in Catskill (Green et al., 1993).

There is concern over the effects of tournaments on the Hudson River black bass population. Green et al. (1993) estimated that during 1989–91 at least 10 percent of the river's largemouth bass were weighed in during summer. Increased handling, especially during warm conditions, may lead to greater mortality (Cooke et al., 2002). Although cause and effect was not demonstrated, the estimated population size of largemouth bass (>280 mm) declined from 22,000 in 1989 to 14,000 in 1991. On the other hand, more recent estimates of populations indicate that largemouth were back up to 22,000 by 2000 (LMS, 2001). Smallmouth bass abundance was estimated at 5,000–6,000 (LMS, 2001). Tournament intensity was lower in 1999 and 2000 compared to surveys conducted in the late 1980s, and the catch rate for largemouth bass in 2000 was the highest on record (LMS, 2001).

Ironically, a new sport fishery has developed for American shad in the Hudson River as they continue their long-term decline there. Anglers have learned that in addition to below the Federal Dam where shad aggregate, they may also be found by targeting particular types of habitat and tidal stages throughout much of the tidal freshwater portion of the river (NYSDEC, 1982).

Several angling surveys have occurred that stemmed from health concerns about fish consumption but that nonetheless provided ancillary information on the nature of the fishery. Belton, Roundy, and Weinstein (1986) surveyed anglers in the lower Hudson River, Upper New York Bay, and Newark Bay between 1983 and 1985. Young-of-the-year bluefish made up 85 percent of the observed finfish catch, with larger bluefish, striped bass, summer flounder, and winter flounder also prominent. Blue crab was heavily fished and was the most frequent species consumed. Two-thirds of respondents who admitted eating their catches considered them to be totally safe to eat and about one-fifth viewed them as slightly polluted but not harmful, despite a New York State Department of Health advisory aimed at limiting human consumption of cadmium.

Another factor that contributed to a recent increase in angling activity in the Hudson River is the development of shoreline access. Many communities have opened shorelines, piers, and bulkheads to fishing with the help of directed funding such as the Hudson River Improvement Fund. New

Table 14.1. Current power plants along the tidal Hudson River.

Name of facility	Initial year of operation	Original operator	Current operator	Location (km from Battery)	Total gross rated capacity (Mwe)	Total cooling water flow (1,000 m³/d)	Fuel type
Albany Units 1–4	1952–1952	Niagara Mohawk		229	400	1,921	Fossil
Danskammer 1–4	1951–1967	Central Hudson	Dynegy	107	480	1,725	Fossil
Roseton 1 & 2	1974	Central Hudson	Dynegy	106	1,248	3,496	Fossil
Indian Point 2	1973	Con Edison	Entergy	69	906	4,746	Nuclear
Indian Point 3	1976	NY Power Auth.	Entergy	69	1,000	4,746	Nuclear
Lovett 1–5	1949–1969	Orange & Rockland	Mirant	68	496	1,725	Fossil
Bowline 1 & 2	1972–1974	Orange & Rockland	Mirant	60	1,244	4,189	Fossil
59th Street, NYC	1918	Con Edison	Entergy	8	132	917	Fossil

Data from Limburg et al. (1986) and updated.

York City has constructed piers for angling at several sites.

Conflicts with Fisheries

As seen throughout the pages of this book, the Hudson River is many things to many people. So far we have reviewed the conflict between the river as food production base and sewage recipient. We now discuss, briefly, two other anthropogenic activities potentially at odds with sustainable fisheries: power generation and toxicants. For more detail on background, see Limburg et al. (1986) and Chapter 25.

WATER WITHDRAWAL BY ELECTRIC POWER PLANTS

Until recently, a consortium of public utility companies (Consolidated Edison of New York, Orange and Rockland Utilities, Central Hudson Gas and Electric, New York Power Authority, and Niagara-Mohawk) owned and operated seven generating stations ranging from 59th Street on Manhattan to Albany (Table 14.1). The plants are under new ownership as a result of industry deregulation. All of the plants use Hudson River water as coolant, and recycle the water back to the river. These plants have a combined rating of 5,905 Mwe, but more relevant here, a combined total cooling water flow exceeding 23,465,000 m³ per day. This flow is on par with freshwater discharges measured at Green Island, where the average annual discharge (1918–1980) is 44 percent higher, but where mean August flows are 42 percent lower (Limburg et al., 1986).

Initial concern about potential impacts of power plants was that the heated effluent would cause harm to the biota, but it was soon seen that the larger potential threat was direct mortality due to two factors: entrainment, or the passage of small organisms, particularly fish larvae, through the plants and across the heated turbines; and impingement, or the trapping of fish on intake screens designed to keep large particles out of the cooling water inlets. Gradually, attention focused mostly on the potential impacts of the power plants on a few "representative and important species," but primarily on striped bass.

Between 1974 and 1980, a protracted series of hearings and litigations by a group of plaintiffs consisting of government agencies and environmental organizations examined the utilities' environmental impact statements. During these hearings, increasingly complex mathematical models were developed to describe the potential losses of key species, especially striped bass, as a result of entrainment and impingement. At the same time, data were collected in several major programs, all funded by the utilities and continuing today. These are the Long River Survey, designed to assess egg and larval densities; the Fall Shoals Survey, to assess juvenile densities offshore; and the Beach Seine Survey, designed to assess onshore fish communities and abundance. It was determined through statistical analysis of the data sets that the level of variation in the data obscured any clear forecasting of the impacts of the plants, and that it might take as long as fifty years of data collection to observe any clear trends (Limburg et al., 1986). With no foreseeable scientific determination, all the parties to the litigation entered into a negotiated settlement, lasting from 1980–90, that prescribed outage (period of reduced water use) schedules to reduce larval mortality, modifications of intake screens, and the establishment of an institution (The Hudson River Foundation) to provide secure funding for future Hudson River studies.

During the fifteen years since the Hudson River Settlement Agreement expired, the utility companies continued to monitor fish communities and produce annual reports. In addition, they prepared a new draft environmental impact statement (DEIS, 1999). In the meantime, the Federal government deregulated the power industry, and over the past few years all the utilities have been purchased by private corporations (Table 14.1). Additionally, approval has been sought for another five new-generation power plants along the Hudson. The new plants will use only a fraction of the water and will be closed-cycle, i.e., will use cooling towers rather than returning thermal effluent to the river.

The socioeconomic climate for operating utilities along the Hudson appears to have changed; deregulation's intent was to produce more competition, and a potential side effect is that the companies operating the existing plants are less concerned with environmental effects than the previous owners. However, the new owners inherited the environmental issues of operating the old plants, and these are still in need of resolution. Among the issues that will likely be contested in future hearings are whether or not fish populations (particularly striped bass) have "compensatory mortality," or the ability to rebound at low densities, as when depleted by power plant mortality; whether bay anchovy, an important estuarine forage species that suffers up to 50 percent year class removal by the plants, truly constitutes a Hudson River population or is part of a larger, offshore stock; and whether the power plants affect species that experience other environmental stresses, for instance, Atlantic tomcod that has been stressed due to a long-term warming trend in the river (Daniels et al., in press), which could severely affect this cold-adapted species.

Table 14.2. FDA guidelines on maximum allowable levels of selected contaminants in fish

Substance	Level	Food type
Aldrin, Dieldrin	0.3 ppm	all fish
Chlordane	0.3 ppm	all fish
DDT, TDE, DDE	5.0 ppm	all fish
Heptachlor	0.3 ppm	all fish
Mirex	0.1 ppm	all fish
PCBs	2.0 ppm	all fish
2,4-D	1.0 ppm	all fish
Arsenic	76 ppm	crustaceans
	86 ppm	molluscan bivalves
Cadmium	3 ppm	crustaceans
	4 ppm	molluscan bivalves
Chromium	12 ppm	crustaceans
	13 ppm	molluscan bivalves
Lead	1.5 ppm	crustaceans
	1.7 ppm	molluscan bivalves
Methyl mercury	1 ppm	all fish
Nickel	70 ppm	crustaceans
	80 ppm	molluscan bivalves

Source: FDA 1999.

PCBs AND OTHER TOXICANTS

Toxic substance contamination is widespread in the Hudson and is covered in other chapters. It has had a fundamental impact on fisheries here, as well as throughout New York State. Fish commonly angled in the Upper and Lower Hudson contain ten-fold greater levels of PCBs than Great Lakes fish, and these levels are two orders of magnitude greater than found in Chesapeake Bay (Baker et al., 2001).

The Food and Drug Administration (FDA) prohibits the interstate sale of contaminated products. FDA guidelines on selected toxic substances are given in Table 14.2. Note that for PCBs, the action level of 2 ppm is now considered by many to be too high, and many states are adopting more stringent guidelines. This has translated into the closure of commercial fisheries for striped bass since 1976, some of which do remain for many years in the Hudson and build up elevated body burdens of PCBs (Zlokovitz and Secor, 1999). Other species for which smaller commercial fisheries existed include eels, bullhead, and carp, all of which currently contain high levels of PCBs and other contaminants. According to data from Skinner et al. (1996, 1997), striped bass also exceed the action limits on mercury and dioxin, eels do so on PCBs, DDT, dioxin, and chlordane, and white perch has concentrations above the action limit for chlordane.

Although crustaceans bioaccumulate high levels of metals and organochlorines in their hepatopancreas, their muscle tissue is very low in contaminants, and hence fisheries persist with the caveat that hepatopancreas, or "tomalley," should be discarded. The only other commercial fisheries that persist are for American shad and river herring which as adults only return to the Hudson to spawn, and therefore have low contaminant burdens. River herring are sold as bait to striped bass sport fishers. Ironically, the increase of striped bass that cannot be kept and sold commercially has driven some of the few remaining commercial fishers to give up, because the nets become full with striped bass and must be laboriously picked out without profit.

Since the awareness of widespread contamination in the 1970s, the New York State Health Department and the DEC both issue annual health advisories against eating certain fish from particular waters, including many specific areas within the Hudson drainage. Nevertheless, angler surveys indicate that the message does not always get through to the fishers. A survey by Barclay (1993) interviewed anglers in 1991 and 1992 at twenty shorefront locations from Fort Edward to New York Harbor. Survey respondents were predominantly male (92 percent) and 84 percent were between the ages of 15 and 59. Two-thirds of the anglers were Caucasian, 21 percent were African American, and 10 percent were Hispanic (others were 2 percent). Barclay found that almost one-fifth (18 percent) of the anglers who eat their catch were trying to catch blue crabs, whereas another 23 percent indicated they were not targeting any particular species. Of those who eat their catches, only 48 percent were aware of health advisories. Fish consumption varied by ethnicity; 94 percent of Hispanic, 77 percent of African American, and 47 percent of Caucasian anglers ate their catches. During 1995 in a New Jersey portion of New York Harbor, Burger et al. (1999) found there were ethnic differences in consumption rates, sources of information about fishing, knowledge about the safety of the fish, awareness of fishing advisories, and knowledge about health risks.

Most recently, in 1996, NYSDOH (2000) surveyed shoreline-based anglers on the Hudson River between Hudson Falls and Tarrytown, New York; the protocol of this survey was similar to that of Barclay (1993). Three regions were defined: Area 1, from Hudson Falls to the Federal Dam at Troy; Area 2, from the Federal Dam to Catskill; and Area 3, from Catskill to Tarrytown. Because of high levels of PCB contamination, angling in Area 1 during 1996 was catch-and-release only. In both the Barclay (1993) and NYSDOH (2000) surveys, more than 90 percent of anglers said they were fishing primarily for recreation or other similar reasons, and only 6–7 percent said they were fishing primarily for food. In 1996, about one-third of anglers surveyed had kept at least some of the fish they caught from the river.

The most numerous catches were of white perch and blue crab, with striped bass, white catfish, and American eel also frequent (NYSDOH, 2000). But species most commonly kept (by total weight and in order) were white perch, white catfish, striped bass, and carp. Together with the two black basses, bluefish, and American eel, these eight species accounted for 83 percent by weight of the fish observed to have been harvested in this survey. NYSDOH (2000) concluded that numerous anglers in Area 3 remained unaware of health advisories for consumption of fish from the Hudson River. This is likely because anglers fishing the lower Hudson are not required to purchase licenses, and the health advisories are included in the state's fishery regulations booklet given out with the license.

A landmark decision by the U.S. Environmental Protection Agency in 2000, upheld by Director Whitman in August 2001 (Johnson, 2001), enforces a dredging order that will require sediments from a 10-mile (16 km) stretch of the upper Hudson to be removed. These contaminated sediments have been shown to be the greatest continuing source of PCB contamination for fish in the River and Estuary. As Baker et al. (2001) point out, such a massive project will require careful execution and monitoring, but the resultant lowering of PCB concentrations in fish should be rapid following project completion. This will have the immediate effect of permitting consumption of many currently inedible species.

The Future of Fisheries in the Hudson

It is difficult enough to forecast catches from one year to the next for a single species, and virtually impossible to predict the future of Hudson River multispecies fisheries over the long term with any sort of accuracy. Nevertheless, we can comment on some trends.

Commercial fishing is in long-term decline, in the Hudson and many other east coast estuaries. If the status quo were to remain, the future would not look optimistic. However, the restoration of striped bass through a concerted, interstate management program demonstrates that overexploited species can be brought back, and restoration programs are under way for American shad, river herring, and sturgeon in many of the same systems. Fishery management programs in the Hudson use a combination of regulatory instruments (closures, seasons, and limits on minimum size, numbers caught, etc.), focusing on regeneration of a natural stock rather than through hatchery supplementation, although these last are ongoing in a number of east coast states. Further, a number of interagency programs are working to remove toxicants from the river and reduce the inputs. Beside the EPA's PCB removal project in the upper Hudson, programs such as the Contaminant Assessment and Remediation Project, part of the New York-New Jersey Harbor Estuary Program, are identifying the fate and transport of contaminants in order to remove them. Although serious problems still exist in the Harbor region, improvements have been noted (Steinberg et al., 2001).

Whereas commercial fisheries have diminished in the River, recreational fishing has increased to unprecedented levels. The restoration of striped bass stimulated a wave of angling interest, and sport fishers throng the Hudson during the stripers' spawning season. The projected toxicant cleanups will benefit all users of the resources, including users of striped bass. However, the conflict between sport and commercial resource users of striped bass may widen, unless both can come to an understanding on how management allows sharing of this common resource, as it occurs in marine waters along the entire mid-Atlantic coast. Recreational angling contributes to local economies, but so do commercial fisheries to a lesser, and some think, unimportant degree. But there are noneconomic impacts of cultural value in preserving the heritage of commercial fisheries, as well as in promoting stewardship of the resource by all users.

Overlain on the patterns of human alteration of fish stocks and their habitats is the prospect of fundamental climate change, resulting in a warmer Hudson River. Already we may be seeing evidence of this. Rainbow smelt and Atlantic tomcod, both northern boreal species at the southern extent of their range in the Hudson, are disappearing. Smelt have not appeared in utilities' or state fisheries' surveys since the mid 1990s, and tomcod have declined dramatically and appear to be cycling between moderately and very low abundances (DEIS, 1999). On the other hand, gizzard shad, a species known from the Mississippi and southeastern drainages, appears to be increasing dramatically in the Hudson, and is also appearing in estuaries as far north as Maine. Gizzard shad has the potential to become a strong ecological actor in the Hudson fish community, because it can compete for zooplankton effectively, rapidly outgrow its "window of vulnerability" to predation, and can then subsist on detritus and thus not be food limited. How these and other changes in the dynamic fish community will affect fisheries is a research question, but clearly they will have an impact.

The long-term patterns seen in fisheries statistics, and especially the more intensive monitoring studies of the past twenty to thirty years, have taught us much about the dynamics of Hudson River fish stocks, what is possible to know (e.g., spawning stock characteristics such as age and size distributions) and what may never be possible to know precisely (e.g., absolute stock abundances). In many respects, we now have the tools available for sustainable fisheries management. The critical element needed to carry through is strong public and political commitment of resources for continued adaptive assessment and management.

Acknowledgment

We thank Michael Flaherty, New York State Department of Environmental Conservation, and John

Carnwright, Dynegy Corporation, for providing information on black bass tournaments and utility licensing issues, respectively.

REFERENCES

Anonymous. 2001. "Effort Launched to Protect History of Croton Point," *Half Moon Press Newsletter*. Croton-on-Hudson, NY: Half Moon Press, May 2001 issue.

ASMFC. 2002. Atlantic States Marine Fisheries Commission Mission Statement. Available online at www.asmfc.org (accessed May 2002).

Baker, J. E., Bohlen, W. F., Bopp, R., Brownawell, B., Collier, T. K., Farley, K. J., Geyer, W. R., and Nairn, R. 2001. *PCBs in the Upper Hudson River: The Science Behind the Dredging Controversy*. Report prepared for the Hudson River Foundation, New York, NY.

Barclay, B. 1993. Hudson River angler survey: a report on the adherence to fish consumption health advisories among Hudson River anglers. Hudson River Sloop Clearwater, Poughkeepsie, NY.

Belton, T., Roundy, R., and Weinstein, N. 1986. Urban fishermen: managing the risks of toxic exposure. *Environment* **28**(9): 18–20, 30–7.

Blackford, C. M. 1916. The shad – a national problem. *Transactions of the American Fisheries Society* **45**: 5–14.

Boyle, R. H. 1979. *The Hudson River: A Natural and Unnatural History*. 2nd Edition. New York: W.W. Norton & Co.

Burdick, G. E. 1954. An analysis of the factors, including pollution, having possible influence on the abundance of shad in the Hudson River. *New York Fish and Game Journal* **1**: 188–205.

Burger, J., Pflugh, K. K., Lurig, L., Von Hagen, L. A., and Von Hagen, S. 1999. Fishing in urban New Jersey: ethnicity affects information sources, perception, and compliance. *Risk Analysis* **19**:217–29.

Carlson, D. M. 1989. Preliminary estimates of survival and abundance of smallmouth bass. New York State Department of Environmental Conservation, Stamford, NY.

——— 1992. Importance of winter refugia to the largemouth bass fishery in the Hudson River estuary. *Journal of Freshwater Ecology* **7**:173–80.

Cheney, A. N. 1896. Shad of the Hudson River, in *First Annual Report of the Commissioners of Fisheries Game and Forests*. Albany, NY, pp. 125–34.

Chittenden, M. E., Jr. 1969. "Life history and ecology of the American shad, *Alosa sapidissima*, in the Delaware River." Ph.D. dissertation, Rutgers University, New Brunswick, NJ.

Cooke, S. J., Schreer, J. F., Wahl, D. H., and Philipp, D. P. 2002. Physiological impacts of catch-and-release angling practices on largemouth bass and smallmouth bass, in D. P. Philipp and M. S. Ridgway, (eds). *Black Bass: Ecology, Conservation, and Management*. American Fisheries Society Symposium 31. *American Fisheries Society*, Bethesda, MD, pp. 489–512.

Daniels, R. A., Limburg, K. E., Schmidt, R. E., Strayer, D. L., and Chambers, C. In Press. Changes in fish assemblages in the tidal Hudson River, New York. In J. N. Rinne, R. M. Hughes, and B. Calamusso (eds.). *Historical Change in Large River Fish Assemblage of America*. American Fisheries Society Monograph.

DEIS (Draft Environmental Impact Statement). 1999. Draft environmental impact statement for state pollutant discharge elimination system permits for Bowline Point 1 & 2, Indian Point 2 & 3, Roseton 1 & 2 steam electric generating stations. Produced by Central Hudson Gas & Electric Corp., Consolidated Edison of New York, Inc., New York Power Authority, and Southern Energy New York.

Ebbesmeyer, C., and Hinrichsen, R. 1997. Oceanography of the Pacific shad invasion. *The Shad Journal* **2**(1): 4–8.

Faigenbaum, H. M. 1937. Chemical investigation of the Lower Hudson area, in A Biological Survey of the Lower Hudson watershed. State of New York Conservation Department, Biological Survey No XI. Albany, NY: J. B. Lyon Co., pp. 147–216.

FDA 2001. Fish and Fisheries Products Hazards and Controls Guidance: Third Edition. U.S. Food & Drug Administration, Center for Food Safety and Applied Nutrition. Rockville, Maryland.

Franz, D. R. 1982. An historical perspective on mollusks in Lower New York Harbor, with emphasis on oysters, in G. F. Meyer, (ed.). *Ecological Stress and the New York Bight: Science and Management*, Estuarine Research Federation, Columbia, SC, pp. 181–197.

Funk, R. E. 1992. The Tivoli Bays as a middle-scale setting for cultural-ecological research. *The Hudson Valley Regional Review* **9**(1): 1–13.

Green, D. M., and Jackson, J. 1991. Characterization of angling activity on the Hudson River estuary, in E. A. Blair and J. R. Waldman (eds.). *Final Reports of the Tibor T. Polgar Fellowship Program, 1990*. Hudson River Foundation, New York, NY, pp. VII-1 to VII-52.

Green, D. M., Landsberger, S. E., Nack, S. B., Bunnell, D., and Forney, J. L. 1993. *Abundance and Winter*

Distribution of Hudson River Black Bass. Final Report to the Hudson River Foundation, New York, NY.

Green, D. M., Nack, S. B., and Forney, J. L. 1988. *Identification of Black Bass Spawning and Nursery Habitats in the Hudson River Estuary.* Final Report to the Hudson River Foundation, New York, NY.

Hattala, K. A., and Kahnle, A. W. 1997. *Stock Status and Definition of Over-fishing Rate for American Shad of the Hudson River Estuary. Report to the Atlantic States Marine Fisheries Commission.* New York State Department of Environmental Conservation, New Paltz, NY.

Johnson, K. 2001. "Whitman to issue order to dredge Hudson for PCB's." *The New York Times,* August 1, 2001.

Lake, T. 1985. Hudson River hotspot: Fishing the federal dam at Troy, New York. *Upland Fishing: Freshwater Fishing in New England and New York* 3:80–81, 189–193.

Limburg, K. E., Moran, M. A., and McDowell, W. H. 1986. *The Hudson River Ecosystem.* New York: Springer-Verlag.

LMS (Lawler, Matusky and Skelly Engineers, Inc.). 2001. *Hudson River Estuary black bass study.* March 1999–January 2001 Progress Report to the New York State Department of Environmental Conservation, Hudson River Estuary Program. Pearl River, NY.

Lossing, B. J. 1866. *The Hudson, from the Wilderness to the Sea.* New York: Virtue and Yorston.

Mitchill, S. L. 1815. The fishes of New-York, described and arranged. *Transactions of the Literary and Philosophical Society of New York* (1814) **1**: 355–492.

Nack, S. B., Bunnell, D., Green, D. M., and Forney, J. L. 1993. Spawning and nursery habitats of largemouth bass in the tidal Hudson River. *Transactions of the American Fisheries Society* **122**: 208–216.

NYSCD (New York State Conservation Department). 1964. *The Hudson: Fish and Wildlife.* A report on fish and wildlife resources in the Hudson River Valley, prepared for the Hudson River Valley Commission by the Division of Fish and Game of the New York State Conservation Department. Albany, NY.

NYSDEC (New York State Department of Environmental Conservation). 1982. *1982 guide to angling for Hudson River shad.* Flyer.

NYSDOH (New York State Department of Health). 2000. *Health Consultation: 1996 Survey of Hudson River Anglers.* Final Report, CERCLIS No. NYD980763841. Albany, NY.

Peterson, D. L. 1998. *Assessment of the Striped Bass Fishery of the Hudson River, 1997.* Final Report to the Hudson River Fishery Unit, New York State Department of Environmental Conservation, New Paltz, NY.

Ross, M. R. 1997. *Fisheries Conservation and Management.* Upper Saddle River, NJ: Prentice Hall.

Scott, G. 1875. *Fishing in American Waters.* New York: Harper and Brothers.

Shapley, D. 2001. "Valley fishing industry fading; interest flagging among the young." *Poughkeepsie Journal,* May 20, 2001.

Skinner, L. C., Jackling, S. J., Kimber, G., Waldman, J., Shastry, Jr., J., and Newell, A. J. 1996. *Chemical Residues in Fish, Bivalves, Crustaceans and a Cephalopod from the New York-New Jersey Harbor: PCB, Organochlorine Pesticides and Mercury.* New York State Department of Environmental Conservation.

Skinner, L. C., Prince, R., Waldman, J., Newell, A. J., and Shastry, Jr., J. 1997. *Chemical Residues in Fish, Bivalves, Crustaceans and a Cephalopod from the New York-New Jersey Harbor: Dioxins and Furans.* New York State Department of Environmental Conservation.

Smith, C. L. 1985. *The Inland Fishes of New York State.* New York State Department of Environmental Conservation, Albany, NY.

Steinberg, N., Way, J., Suszkowski, D. J., and Clark, L. 2001. *Harbor Health/Human Health: An Analysis of Environmental Indicators for the NY/ NJ Harbor Estuary.* New York/New Jersey Harbor Estuary Program. Published by the Hudson River Foundation, New York, NY.

Stevenson, C. H. 1899. The shad fisheries of the Atlantic coast of the United States, in *U.S. Commission of Fish and Fisheries, Part XXIV.* Report of the Commissioner for the year ending June 30, 1898. Government Printing Office, Washington, D.C., pp. 101–269.

Talbot, G. B. 1954. Factors associated with fluctuations in abundance of Hudson River shad. *United States Fish and Wildlife Service Fishery Bulletin* **56**: 373–413.

Vargo, J. H. 1995. *Hudson River Stripers: The Guide.* Yonkers, NY: Beacon Publishing Corporation.

Walburg, C. H., and Nichols., P. R. 1967. *Biology and Management of the American Shad and Status of the Fisheries, Atlantic Coast of the United States, 1960.* United States Department of the Interior, Fish and Wildlife Service. Special Scientific Report – Fisheries No. 550.

Waldman, J. 1998. *Stripers: An Angler's Anthology.* Camden, ME: Ragged Mountain Press.

1999. *Heartbeats in the Muck: The History, Sea Life, and Environment of New York Harbor.* New York: The Lyons Press.

Waldman, J. R., Hart, J. T., and Wirgin, I. I. 1996. Stock composition of the New York Bight Atlantic sturgeon fishery based on analysis of mitochondrial DNA. *Transactions of the American Fisheries Society* **125**: 364–71.

Zeisel, W. 1995. *Angling on a Changing Estuary: the Hudson River, 1609–1995.* Final Report to the Hudson River Foundation, New York, NY.

Zeisel, W. N., Jr. 1990. Shark!!! and other sport fish once abundant in New York Harbor. *Seaport (Autumn)*: 36–9.

Zlokovitz, E. R., and Secor, D. H. 1999. Effect of habitat use on PCB body burden in Hudson River striped bass (*Morone saxatilis*). *Canadian Journal of Fisheries and Aquatic Sciences* **56** (Suppl. 1): 86–93.

15 The Role of Tributaries in the Biology of Hudson River Fishes

Robert E. Schmidt and Thomas R. Lake

ABSTRACT The objectives of this chapter are to summarize our observations of fishes in Hudson River tributaries and to document the significance of tributaries to them. Currently alewife is the only anadromous fish that extensively uses Hudson River tributaries. Several potamodromous species depend on tributaries for reproduction (at least smallmouth bass and white sucker) or reproduce in several areas including tributaries (white perch). In many cases, the data available are not adequate to determine how significant tributary spawning is in these species. Young-of-year fishes present in tributary mouths are also abundant in other habitats in the tidal Hudson River, which is also true for those species considered resident in the tributary mouths. Too few tributaries have been examined thoroughly enough to determine whether tributaries are significant for either of these groups of fishes.

Introduction

The tidal Hudson River has at least seventy-nine small to large tributary streams in addition to the Upper Hudson and Mohawk Rivers, which enter the tidal Hudson at the Troy Dam, the upstream limit of tidal influence. There are also an unknown number of smaller, often ephemeral, streams that contribute water to the tidal Hudson River. These tributaries (other than the Upper Hudson/Mohawk) contribute about 20 percent of the freshwater input to the Hudson River (Cooper, Cantelmo, and Newton, 1988). Various researchers have considered these tributaries as sources of important materials such as carbon, sediments (Howarth et al.,

1991; Howarth, Schneider, and Swaney, 1996; Swaney, Sherman, and Howarth, 1996), and contaminants (Hirschberg et al., 1996). This is a reasonable view of the role of tributaries since anything dissolved, suspended, or entrained in tributary flow will end up in the tidal Hudson River. But it is not a complete picture of the role of tributaries in this ecosystem. Our observations over at least the last fifteen years have shown that there is an exchange of fishes between the tidal Hudson River and its tributaries in both directions that occurs over several time scales and that varies from critical to the fishes and ecosystems, to incidental. Our purpose in this chapter is to document what we have observed about this exchange of fishes between tributaries and the tidal Hudson River and to propose some hypotheses about the significance of this phenomenon.

In order to organize our observations, we have categorized the fishes we have seen in tributaries as anadromous, catadromous, potamodromous, resident, and other species. These categories overlap and are not necessarily mutually exclusive. We have chosen to ignore the movements of fishes between the Upper Hudson/Mohawk River and the tidal Hudson River (through the locks on the Troy Dam) not because they aren't significant, but because we think these movements are complex and poorly documented. We would have liked to characterize the tributaries to the tidal Hudson River on some scale of quality, but we visited many of these tributaries only briefly and we have thoroughly sampled only a few. We have also omitted presentation of methodologies in this chapter. Methods are described in detail in the various reports and publications we have cited and we therefore direct anyone interested to those sources.

Anadromous Fishes

The Hudson River hosts eight species of anadromous fishes (see Waldman, Chapter 13, this volume). Some of these species (Atlantic sturgeon, shortnose sturgeon, and American shad) are not usually seen in Hudson River tributaries. Today, only alewife (*Alosa pseudoharengus*) out of all the anadromous species present in the Hudson River spends a significant part of its life cycle in tributary streams. Tributary spawning may be critical to the maintenance of this population. Historically, rainbow smelt (*Osmerus mordax*) and, possibly, sea lamprey (*Petromyzon marinus*) were also much more common in tributaries, but their populations are now very low in the Hudson River.

Catadromous Fishes

The only catadromous species in the Hudson River is the American eel (*Anguilla rostrata*). This species has a unique but well known life cycle (Smith, 1985) involving migratory adults spawning in the Sargasso Sea and passive transport of small leptocephalus larvae by the Gulf Stream along the Atlantic coast. American eels enter the Hudson River as small unpigmented "glass eels" after transforming from the planktonic leptocephalus stage (Smith, 1989). Glass eels are passively transported up tidal rivers using selective tidal stream transport behavior and a circa-tidal endogenous clock (McCleave and Wippelhauser, 1987). In Hudson River tributaries, we see glass eels essentially at the end of this migratory phase when they are transforming into pigmented benthic elvers (juveniles). In this section, we will only present our observations on these small young-of-year (yoy) eels and we will discuss older elvers as part of the resident fish community.

Most of our observations of yoy eels are based on captures in drift nets and incidental encounters. Drift net captures cannot be considered a proper representative sampling of this species since drift nets are placed to catch fishes moving passively downstream while the yoy eels are actively moving upstream. We have collected yoy eels from mid-March through mid-June, which correlates well with the presence of glass eels at sea (Kleckner and McCleave, 1985), in Great Bay, New Jersey (Able and Fahay, 1998), and with quantitative data recently collected in two Hudson River tributaries (Schmidt and Lake, 2003).

Summary. Tidal creek mouths and streams further upland are critical habitat for American eel. The subadult freshwater stages have been relatively well studied, but we know very little about the glass eel stage in the Hudson River.

Potamodromous Fishes

Potamodromy has been defined as a reproductive migration within freshwater (Myers, 1949) which includes long distance migrations of riverine fishes and migration of lacustrine fishes into tributary streams (Lagler et al., 1977). We are also using this term to describe migratory movements of fishes from the tidal Hudson River into tributary streams for spawning. We have observed ten species that are or may be potamodromous in the Hudson River (Table 15.1). Our evidence for categorizing these species as potamodromous ranges from conclusive to dubious and represents reproduction of the entire Hudson River population or a small fraction of that population. Our observations of Hudson River tributaries have been limited to the warmer parts of the year. We wish to mention the possibility that some winter spawning species, for instance Atlantic tomcod (*Microgadus tomcod*), may be spawning in some tributaries during a time that has never been sampled.

White sucker (*Catostomus commersonii*). Spring spawning runs of white sucker are well documented phenomena throughout the species' range (Geen et al., 1966; Mansfield, 1984; Smith, 1985). White sucker prefer to spawn in moderate water velocities over a gravel or rocky substrate (Scott and Crossman, 1973), habitats that are rare in the tidal Hudson River but abundant in the tributaries.

We have collected eggs and/or larvae of white sucker in fifteen out of twenty-one tributaries sampled with drift nets (Schmidt and Lake, 2000; Schmidt and Limburg, 1989; Schmidt and Stillman, 1994) from the Pocantico River (RKM 45) to the Moordener Kill (RKM 221). We have observed spawning adults in many other tributaries (Schmidt and Cooper, 1996). We have collected white sucker eggs as early as March 24 (Fishkill Creek, RKM 95.5) and collected larvae as late as June 18 (Stockport Creek, RKM 194.5). These observations indicate a lengthy spawning season that occurs in tributaries to the Hudson River. Among tributaries, there is great variation in the numbers of early life stages or adults observed. Many of these tributaries also have resident white sucker populations, which complicates the issue.

Schmidt and Limburg (1989) suggested that white sucker in the tidal Hudson River depend on tributary spawning for maintenance of the population. We concur with this suggestion based on the relative scarcity of white sucker early life

Table 15.1. Degree of potamodromy exhibited by Hudson River fishes using tributaries for spawning

Species	Degree of potamodromy	Evidence
Catostomus commersonii White sucker	Complete	Large runs in most tributaries No early larvae in tidal river
Micropterus dolomieu Smallmouth bass	Complete	Schmidt and Stillman (1998) Movements of tagged adults No black fry in tidal river
Morone americana White perch	Partial Significant?	Large numbers of spawning adults and drifting early stages
Perca flavescens Yellow perch	Partial	Substantial runs and larval drift in some tributaries
Notropis hudsonius Spottail shiner	Partial Insignificant?	Runs historically large, small recently
Notemigonus crysoleucas Golden shiner	Partial Insignificant?	Adults seen in the spring, some drifting larvae
Cyprinus carpio Carp	Possible Insignificant	A few adults and some larvae seen
Dorosoma cepedianum Gizzard shad	Possible Significant?	Adults observed in spring
Esox lucius Northern pike	Possible	Adults observed in spring
Sander vitreus Walleye	Possible?	Adults observed in spring
Moxostoma macrolepidotum Shorthead redhorse	Possible	Adults seen in one river, spring, 2000–2001

stages taken in ichthyoplankton surveys in the tidal Hudson River compared to their abundance in the tributaries. From 1988–95, only fifty-six white suckers were collected in the ichthyoplankton surveys out of 10^7 individuals identified (J. Young, ASA Analysis & Communication, State College, PA, personal communication).

Concluding that tributaries are significant to white sucker is a relatively simple deduction from our observations, but determining whether white sucker are significant to the tidal Hudson River is considerably more difficult. Carlson (1986) reported that white sucker were as abundant as striped bass in the tidal Hudson north of RKM 169. White sucker are relatively large (47.6 cm TL individual from Coxsackie Creek, RKM 204.5), benthic carnivores feeding on small organisms (Yozzo, 1990; Schmidt, Chandler, and Strayer, 1995). An abundant large benthic carnivore could play a significant role in the tidal Hudson River, but white sucker is not the only species that would fit that description.

Smallmouth bass (*Micropterus dolomieu*). Some populations of smallmouth bass are known to be potamodromous (e.g., Robbins and MacCrimmon, 1977; Gerber and Haynes, 1988). Schmidt and Stillman (1998) provided evidence from their capture of drifting young that Hudson River smallmouth bass may be potamodromous, at least in Stockport Creek (RKM 194.5). Recent tracking of radio-tagged smallmouth bass adults showed a spring migration from the tidal Hudson River into Stockport Creek above the first barrier (J. Hecht, Lawler, Matusky, and Skelly Engineers, Pearl River, NY, personal communication). This observation substantiates the Schmidt and Stillman (1998) hypothesis.

We think that the Hudson River smallmouth bass population is entirely supported by potamodromy. There are three pieces of evidence for this supposition. First, we have never seen a smallmouth bass nesting in the tidal Hudson River, nor have we heard any reports of smallmouth bass nesting there. Researchers have looked in the Hudson for nesting bass and have documented largemouth bass (*M. salmoides*) nesting in tidal water (Nack and Cook, 1987).

Smallmouth bass spend the early stages of larval development in the nest and become free-swimming at about 8 mm TL (Meyer, 1970). These free-swimming individuals are called "black fry" because they are heavily pigmented with discrete black spots (Auer, 1982). Although we have collected yoy smallmouth bass in the tidal Hudson River, especially in recent years, we have never seen a black fry in the main Hudson River. The smallest smallmouth bass we have measured was 3.1 cm TL from Tivoli North Bay (RKM 159).

Our observations of Hudson River tributaries indicate that smallmouth bass are widespread and that potamodromous migrations occur throughout the Hudson River. We base this statement on observations of nesting adults in areas where they are not resident, presence of black fry in areas with easy access to the tidal Hudson River, and the presence of smallmouth bass in the spring in tributaries where they are not resident. Some Hudson River tributaries do have resident smallmouth bass populations that can complicate our interpretations as is true for white sucker.

Smallmouth bass are a valuable resource in the tidal Hudson River. Largemouth and smallmouth bass are heavily fished for sport and in tournaments (Green et al., 1993). Our observations suggest that adequate spawning habitat in the tributaries and potamodromy are critical phenomena for maintaining this population.

White perch (*Morone americana*). The biology of white perch in the Hudson River is well documented (Klauda et al., 1988) and they spawn throughout the tidal Hudson River from the Troy Dam to Yonkers. Some portion of the population is potamodromous (Waldman, 1981) and eggs and yolk-sac larvae are common in tributaries.

White perch appear in Hudson River tributaries early in the season (late March; Lake and Schmidt, 1997) and are one of the three (white sucker and yellow perch) early spring potamodromous species. We collected adults in the spring in all tributaries where we sampled for adult fishes, but we did not necessarily confirm spawning in all Hudson River tributaries. We did not collect early life stages in

the drift in Pocantico River (RKM 45), Sing Sing Brook (RKM 53), Peekskill Hollow Brook (RKM 71), and Lattintown Creek (RKM 111) although we collected adults in the latter tributary (Schmidt and Lake, 2000) and in Annsville and Sprout Creeks whose mouths are adjacent to Peekskill Hollow Brook (Schmidt and Cooper, 1996). Very few white perch early life stages were observed in Stockport Creek (RKM 194.5 – Schmidt and Stillman, 1994), but here adults may be barred from ascending the first rapids.

White perch eggs and larvae are the most to third most abundant fishes in the drift in Hudson River tributaries, median of second most abundant. Yolk-sac larvae are more abundant than eggs since the eggs are adhesive until hatching (Wang and Kernehan, 1979). White perch early life stages are present in the drift from mid-April through early June, which correlates well with their reported presence in the tidal Hudson River (Klauda et al., 1988). Spawning may continue until the end of June (Klauda et al., 1988) but we have usually stopped sampling larval drift before then.

No one has yet been able to estimate the relative contribution of tributary-spawned white perch to the egg and larval standing crop in the tidal Hudson River. This would be a Herculaean task given that white perch are spawning in most Hudson River tributaries for a rather extended period of time. We suspect, from our subjective observations, that this contribution is significant.

In addition to spawning in tributaries, TRL has observed white perch actively feeding on alewife eggs and glass eels in several Hudson River tributaries. Although many are potamodromous, there may be alternative reasons for a given individual white perch to be in a Hudson River tributary in the spring.

Yellow perch (*Perca flavescens*). As mentioned above, yellow perch is one of the three early spawning fishes to appear in Hudson River tributaries. Their spawning runs in tributaries are spatially erratic, being abundant in some tributaries and absent from others. Of the five tributaries we intensively sampled for adults, none were seen in Canterbury Brook (RKM 91.5) or the Moordener Kill (RKM 221), nine were collected in Quassaic Creek (RKM 96.5) and five in Lattintown Creek (RKM 111), and substantial numbers were seen in Coxsackie Creek (RKM 204.5). TRL observed many egg strands of yellow perch in Fishkill Creek (RKM 95.5) in 1998 and has collected many ripe females in Popolopen Brook (RKM 75.5) over the past ten years. We have collected adults in other tributaries but our spot samples, unless taken early in the season, would not necessarily detect their presence.

Drifting larvae were seen in eight of twenty-one rivers sampled (Schmidt and Limburg, 1989; Schmidt and Stillman, 1994; Lake and Schmidt, 1997; Schmidt and Lake, 2000). Larvae were collected usually in May except in two of the southern tributaries (Peekskill Hollow Brook, RKM 71 – April 15 and Pocantico River, RKM 45 – April 22) suggesting that spawning is earlier for this species along the southern tidal Hudson.

The most substantial yellow perch run that we observed occurred in Coxsackie Creek (RKM 204.5) in 1999. Adults were collected when we first began sampling on April 6 and were last seen on May 18. Most of the individuals were females (94.6 percent) and were rather small (average 22.0 cm TL, range 20.0–24.0). The males were smaller, however (average 16.7 cm TL, range 14.0–19.4). Yolk-sac and post-yolk-sac larvae were collected from April 17 through May 18, 1999, and yellow perch was the fourth most abundant species in the drift.

It is not possible for us to assess the value of tributary spawning for this species since we have no understanding of the population size in the tidal Hudson River nor do we know the magnitude of spawning that may occur in the tidal areas. The mature adults that we observed were all quite small compared to the yellow perch that support a small sport fishery (for instance in the mouth of Rondout Creek in the late fall and winter). We do not know where these larger individuals may be spawning.

Spottail shiner (*Notropis hudsonius*). Spottail shiner is one of the most abundant fishes in the tidal Hudson River. Some fraction of the spottail shiner population is potamodromous and we have observed spring and early summer spawning runs (Lake and Schmidt, 1997) in several tributaries. Spottail shiner larvae were the third most abundant species (after alewife and white perch) in the drift in tributaries in 1988 taking into account that many of the "unidentified minnow" specimens

reported by Schmidt and Limburg (1989) were spottail shiner in hindsight. Lake and Schmidt (1997) collected substantial numbers of adult spottail shiner in small mesh gill nets in Quassaic Creek (RKM 96.5) and estimated a run of 2,850 adults, almost twice as many as the potamodromous white perch.

Subsequent to the above studies, the picture of potamodromy in this species changed. We sampled Quassaic Creek in 1997 (Lake and Schmidt, 1998) using the same gill nets as in 1996 (Lake and Schmidt, 1997) and caught no spottail shiners. In fact, we have not seen a spottail shiner adult in small mesh gill nets in any tributary since (except a small catch in the mouth of the Roeliff Jansen Kill, RKM 178 – Coote, 2001). We still collect spottail shiner larvae in the drift (Lake and Schmidt, 1998; Schmidt and Lake, 2000) but in considerably smaller numbers than in the past. It may be that the large spottail shiners (average 11.2 cm TL; Lake and Schmidt, 1997) which would probably be 2+ years old (Schmidt, 1986) are no longer spawning in the tributaries. Spottail shiners aged 1+ (6–9 cm TL; Schmidt, 1986) which would not be taken in our gear could be the source of the drifting larvae.

Given that spottail shiner are abundant and ubiquitous in the tidal Hudson River, we doubt that tributary spawning makes a significant difference to the population. We do remain curious about the changes we observed in this species' behavior.

Golden shiner (*Notemigonus crysoleucas*). Golden shiner is a common ubiquitous species in the tidal Hudson River. Spawning occurs in association with submerged vascular plants and larvae are frequently seen around water chestnut (*Trapa natans*) beds (Anderson and Schmidt, 1989). We have collected mature golden shiner moving upstream into tributaries throughout the Hudson River, but never in large numbers. TRL has observed a robust annual spring run of golden shiner into Wappingers Creek (RKM 108.5), however. Golden shiner larvae are taken in drift nets, but again in low numbers. Although potamodromy is occurring in this species, compared to the numbers that we see in the tidal Hudson River, tributary spawning is probably not significant to the Hudson River population.

Carp (*Cyprinus carpio*). Carp is an abundant very large minnow in the tidal Hudson River. Most of the spawning of this species occurs in beds of vascular plants, particularly noticeable in water chestnut stands. Comparatively few individuals migrate into tributaries, but we have seen large carp moving upstream through rapids (Schmidt and Stillman, 1994) and we have collected carp larvae in the drift. The numbers of adults and larvae that we have seen in tributaries are very small compared to the population in the tidal Hudson River.

Gizzard shad (*Dorosoma cepedianum*). This large herring is a comparatively recent immigrant into the Hudson River and is still expanding its range in the Northeast. Gizzard shad is now becoming abundant in the tidal Hudson River and large individuals are often observed. Gizzard shad larvae have been reported from the tidal Hudson since at least 1989 (J. Young, ASA Analysis and Communication, personal communication) and their abundance in ichthyoplankton samples has been increasing since then.

In the last five years, we have encountered gizzard shad in several tributaries. We suspect they are spawning in those tributaries but we have not been in the right place with drift nets to collect early life stages. TRL has observed and anglers have reported large numbers of gizzard shad adults accumulating at the base of the Eddyville Dam on Rondout Creek (RKM 146.5). The gizzard shad population is still increasing in the Hudson River and we suspect that tributary spawning will become significant to this species in the future.

Northern pike (*Esox lucius*). This large piscivore is one of the targets for an early spring and late fall sport fishery in the northern end of the tidal Hudson River (also "tiger muskellunge," *E. lucius* X *E. masquinongy* and other fishes). Pike spawn over beds of submersed macrophytes in the early spring (Smith, 1985), a habitat that is unavailable in the tidal Hudson River.

RES collected two spawning pike (66 and 76 cm TL) in Coxsackie Creek (RKM 204.5) on April 16, 1999. The habitat was inappropriate for pike spawning, tidal with a rocky and silty bottom. This observation plus reports (G. Stevens, Hudsonia Ltd., Annandale, New York, personal communication) of anglers catching post spawning pike in the mouth of Mill Creek (RKM 206.5), suggests that pike are spawning in Hudson River tributaries. A few yoy pike are collected in the tidal Hudson River every year (K. Hattala, NYS DEC, New Paltz, New York, personal communication).

Walleye (*Sander vitreus*). Walleye has been stocked in Hudson River tributaries for quite a few years, and therefore it is not surprising to see individuals in the tidal Hudson River. Observations of adult walleye have become more frequent in the past five years. RES collected three in Murderers Creek (RKM 190), TRL collected one in Rondout Creek (RKM 146), and J. Hecht (LMS Engineers, personal communication) saw several in Stockport Creek (RKM 194.5). Also, a yoy walleye was reported from Norrie Point (W. Gilchrest, Norrie Point Environmental Laboratory, Staatsburg, New York, personal communication). We have a recent (2003) report of several hundred walleye in the Poesten Kill (RKM 241.5) in April.

We do not know if walleye are spawning in the Hudson River, but the most appropriate habitat (Smith, 1985) occurs mainly in the tributaries. Walleye larvae are difficult to distinguish from yellow perch larvae and they may have been collected but not noticed.

Shorthead redhorse (*Moxostoma macrolepidotum*). A small group (12–15) of shorthead redhorse was observed in the Poesten Kill (RKM 241.5) in early June, 2000. An individual was collected (R. Morse and D. Peterson, NYSM) and the identification confirmed. These fish were in breeding color with bright red pectorals, pelvics, and the lower caudal lobe. This is the first record of this species for the tidal Hudson River but their presence in the Poesten Kill and their life history (Smith, 1985) suggests that potamodromy is reasonable for this species. We were unable to confirm successful spawning. RES observed these fish in the Poesten Kill in 2001 and 2003.

Summary. Potamodromous use of tributaries in the Hudson River may be the most significant aspect of the relationship between fishes and tributary streams in this ecosystem. We suggest this because the number of potamodromous species is large (and may be increasing) and the number of individuals seen in tributaries is often large. Several of these species are acknowledged as having significant value for sport fishing as a major component of the ecosystem.

Resident Fishes

A fish that we would consider to be resident in a tributary mouth would be expected to be present throughout most of the year. Unfortunately, we have no studies available in which fishes have been sampled over most of a year in this habitat. Anderson (1988) did a cluster analysis (single linkage, Euclidean distance) on Smith's (1985) field data for the Hudson Valley and characterized a cluster as a tidal stream mouth assemblage. This cluster included American eel, banded killifish (*Fundulus diaphanus*), pumpkinseed (*Lepomis gibbosus*), and bluegill (*L. macrochirus*). We did a summer and early fall study on Quassaic Creek (RKM 96.5) and categorized a set of nine "resident" species that we consistently saw in the stream mouth (Lake and Schmidt, 1997). In addition to the fishes listed by Anderson (1988), we included fathead minnow (*Pimephales promelas*), fallfish (*Semotilus corporalis*), redfin pickerel (*Esox americanus*), redbreast sunfish (*Lepomis auritus*), and tessellated darter (*Etheostoma olmstedi*). Neither study had a long enough time span to categorize these fishes, other than hypothetically.

With the exception of fallfish, redfin pickerel, and fathead minnow, all the species listed as residents are widespread organisms in the tidal Hudson River and were listed as long term components of the freshwater tidal marsh community (Schmidt, 1986). Fallfish has been encountered in the mouths of several tributaries, notably RES observed (literally tripped over) a fallfish nest in the tidal Saw Kill (RKM 157.5). However, we doubt that they are widespread in Hudson River tributary mouths and same can be said for redfin pickerel. Fathead minnow is an introduced species that appears to be increasing in abundance and distribution in Hudson River tributaries. In recent years, we collected larvae and saw adults in several tributary mouths (Stockport Creek – RKM 194.5, Moordener Kill – RKM 221, Coxsackie Creek- RKM 204.5, and Lattintown Creek – RKM 111).

Therefore, there doesn't seem to be a community of fishes that is unique to the tidal mouth habitat in the Hudson River, but rather an assemblage consisting of American eel, widespread estuarine species, and, in some tributaries, species usually associated with upland habitats. From our observations of the resident fish fauna, we could best characterize the tidal tributary mouths as transitional zones between the tidal Hudson River and true riverine habitats. We would expect to see large variation in the species composition of the fish fauna of such an area when viewed over seasons and over years. We have no such observations to consider, however.

Two of the species that we commonly observe in the tidal tributary mouths are worth discussing briefly. Not surprisingly, seining or gill netting rarely produced American eels. However, in those instances where we have shocked in tributary mouths, we have seen many, often very large, eels. We suspect that the biomass of American eel in tributary mouths is very high and exceeds all other resident species combined. The freshwater subadult eels may reside in tributary mouths for up to perhaps fifteen years (Helfman et al., 1987). They are nocturnal scavengers and predators of fishes and invertebrates (Moriarty, 1978) but we do not know if they feed exclusively in the tributary mouths (in which case they would probably be a highly significant predator in the habitat) or if they venture out into the tidal Hudson River. TRL has observed American eel feeding on alewife eggs and has seen them aggressively interacting with ripe females (inducing them to release eggs?).

Tessellated darter (*Etheostoma olmstedi*) is common in Hudson River tributary mouths, as it is elsewhere in the Hudson River (Schmidt, 1986). Our seining efforts in Quassaic Creek (RKM 96.5; Lake and Schmidt, 1997) took them regularly and we frequently collected yolk-sac and post-yolk-sac larvae in the drift from most tributary streams (Schmidt and Lake, 2000). It is unclear whether tessellated darter have a pelagic larval stage or whether the larvae are simply washed down with the current; however, tessellated darter larvae are commonly taken in ichthyoplankton surveys in the main Hudson River (J. Young, ASA Analysis and Communication, personal communication).

Having larvae in the drift is reasonable for species whose presence in tributaries is likely to be brief (anadromous and potamodromous species) and where most of the ontogenetic development occurs in the tidal Hudson River. For a small, benthic, relatively sedentary species resident in tributary mouths (which we presume characterizes tessellated darter), drifting larvae could be considered a loss to the population. We do not know how far a given individual larva may drift, or, in fact, how far a captured individual may have drifted at the point of capture, so we have no evidence of whether the drifting darter larvae are leaving a given tributary or not. If these observed larvae are a significant loss to the population, one might expect that there is a mechanism is place that recruits individuals back into the population, one of which may be upstream migration of juveniles or adults. We have no evidence that such migrations may occur in this species.

Summary. We were able to identify few species of fishes resident in tidal tributary mouths. Those that we did consider as residents are also widespread in freshwater tidal marshes in the Hudson River. The tidal mouths of tributaries may be a very challenging habitat for fishes and we might expect the abiotic conditions to fluctuate dramatically, daily and tidally. Other that the American eel, little is known about the biology or population dynamics of these species in the Hudson River.

Other Species

In addition to the species mentioned above, we have encountered other fishes in Hudson River tributary mouths. Our observations of these species range from seeing certain life stages consistently but temporarily in tributary mouths to seeing an occasional individual.

We have already mentioned that some fishes may be feeding on alewife eggs during their spring spawning runs (e.g., white perch). We often see adult predatory fishes in tributary mouths in the spring and our hypothesis is that they are following anadromous and potamodromous species upstream to feed on them or their eggs. These species include striped bass (*Morone saxatilis*), catfishes (*Ameiurus catus, A. natalis, A. nebulosus, Ictalurus*

punctatus), chain pickerel (*Esox niger*), largemouth bass (*Micropterus salmoides*), and walleye (*Sander vitreus*). We have no information that would provide a test for this hypothesis. If we accept that we are observing a feeding migration, the concentration of forage fishes and eggs in a small area in the early season could be a significant nutritional supplement for these opportunistic predators.

After the spring concentration of migratory fishes subsides in Hudson River tributaries, there is a summer and fall occurrence of immature fishes. We have only examined one tributary thoroughly through this time period (Quassaic Creek – RKM 96.5, Lake and Schmidt, 1997) but incidental observations elsewhere suggest that our observations on Quassaic Creek are applicable to other tributaries.

These small herrings (*Alosa aestivalis, A. pseudoharengus, A. sapidissima*), white perch, striped bass, and spottail shiner are found throughout the Hudson estuary in large numbers and, although it is tempting to suggest that tributary mouths provide some valuable habitat for these fishes, they may be seen in tidal tributary mouths simply because they are widespread in tidal waters. Young-of-year bluefish (*Pomatomus saltatrix*), and crevalle jack (*Caranx hippos*) are regularly found in the vicinity of tributaries in Haverstraw Bay and southward (Juanes et al., 1993; McBride and Able, 1995) and have been observed at least in the Croton River (Wällhauser and Tashiro, 1989). Bay anchovy are similarly very abundant in the southern end of the estuary (Schmidt, 1992) and are often observed in tributary mouths.

We must mention that we have observed yoy and yearling blue crab (*Callinectes sapidus*) in tributary streams. RES collected them as far north as the Poesten Kill (RKM 241.5) and as far as 4 km (approximately) from the tidal Hudson River in Minisceongo Creek (RKM 64.5; Schmidt and Cooper, 1996). The presence of these animals in certain tributaries varies interannually. We have no information on what significance this behavior may have for blue crab or for the tributary mouth habitat.

Finally, there are a number of fishes that we have encountered occasionally in tributary mouths. The main habitats for these species are elsewhere in the watershed, either upland in lentic or lotic environments, or in the tidal Hudson River. The presence of these species enhances the diversity of the tributary mouth habitat, but our observations indicate that they are occasional wanderers and probably do not interact significantly with the other species mentioned above. Theoretically, any species in the watershed would probably show up in a tributary mouth and one could consider our observations as a small sample of that possibility. It is possible that some of these species might be more accurately classified in some other category of tributary use, but our sampling efforts were inadequate to document seasonal or interannual use of the tributaries.

There is a bias in our efforts to sample tributaries. The vast majority of our effort has been in tributaries in the freshwater portion of the Hudson River (roughly north of RKM 75). We expect that a number of euryhaline (for example, *Menidia* spp., *Microgadus tomcod*) and marine species (for example, *Pseudopleuronectes americanus*, *Cynoscion regalis*) would appear in tributary mouths in the vicinity of the higher salinity areas of the Hudson River, but we feel our sampling has been inadequate to document the presence of these species.

Summary. The young-of-year individuals and their predators that appear in Hudson River tributaries are an indicator of the dynamic nature of the fauna in tributary mouths and of the nursery function of the Hudson River in general. We have no information about whether tributaries are playing a significant role as nursery areas.

Discussion

Streams tributary to the Hudson River are significant habitats for some Hudson River fishes and may be significant for more species than we have been able to document. However, not all tributaries are equally valuable primarily due to variation in accessibility.

The distance of the Fall Line from the tidal Hudson River varies along the length of the Hudson. There are some areas, like in the Hudson Highlands, where tributary streams are naturally impassable for fishes because of very steep gradients at their mouths. These streams, like Highland Brook (RKM 82), Breakneck Brook (RKM 90), and Philipse Brook (RKM 85) have probably been inaccessible to Hudson River fishes since the

glacial lakes filling the Hudson Valley drained (ca. 12,000 years ago; Connelly and Sirkin, 1973).

Degraded water quality can limit access to tributary streams. Great progress has been made in the past several decades in reducing or eliminating municipal and industrial pollutants from Hudson River tributaries. Most of the fishes that enter tributaries do so in the spring when we can expect higher water volumes and reduction of pollution effects. There are still some Hudson River tributaries where we think water pollution limits fish use, however, so this task of cleaning up water is incomplete in the Hudson Valley. The worst case we observed was Mill Creek (Rensselaer – RKM 231.5).

Through the history of European settlement in the Hudson Valley, tributary streams often have been dammed. Dams have provided power to run mills, processing water for industry, drinking water for communities, and recreational opportunities. Currently, half of the tributaries to the Hudson River have dams (or other obstructions) that limit fishes' access to the streams. Depending on where the dams are placed, they have decreased or eliminated access to nontidal stream habitats. Recently, the first dam on Furnace Brook (RKM 62.5) washed out and TRL observed potamodromous fishes already using the newly available stream bed in spring 2000. We have seen anadromous and potamodromous fishes aggregating below dams, such as the Eddyville Dam on Rondout Creek (RKM 146.5). We have no doubt that fishes would use the stream habitat upstream of these dams if access were provided.

In the Hudson Valley, we have no facilities available for helping fishes gain access to aquatic habitat above dams. Some dams are so large, like the dam on Murderers Creek (RKM 190), that designing fish passage would be prohibitively expensive – thus that tributary is essentially extinct as far as Hudson River fishes are concerned. Other Hudson River tributaries have barriers that can be bypassed, breached, or removed. We think that providing access to tributary streams can only enhance the populations of Hudson River fishes.

Acknowledgments

Most of this work has been funded by the Hudson River Foundation, through research grants, the

Tibor T. Polgar Fellowship Program, and the Hudson River Improvement Fund. We greatly appreciate this support and the individual encouragement we have received from the people that make the Hudson River Foundation work.

We did not do this work by ourselves. Although we enjoy being out on the Hudson River and its tributaries, not all of the people that accompanied us shared our enthusiasm, but they persevered. Producing a list of people who have physically helped us in the fifteen to twenty years it has taken for us to form our ideas would inevitably leave people out, so we will not do so. You know who you are, and we deeply appreciate your help. Additionally, this book chapter does not signal an end to our involvement in the Hudson River or its tributaries. There is plenty of opportunity for you to accompany us again.

REFERENCES

Able, K. W., and Fahay, M. P. 1998. *The First Year in the Life of Estuarine Fishes in the Middle Atlantic Bight*. New Brunswick, NJ: Rutgers University Press.

Anderson, A. B. 1988. "A dendrogrammatic ichthyofauna classification of the tributaries of the lower Hudson River watershed." B.A. Thesis, Simon's Rock College of Bard, Great Barrington, MA.

Anderson, A. B., and Schmidt, R. E. 1989. A survey of larval and juvenile fish populations in waterchestnut (*Trapa natans*) beds in Tivoli South Bay, a Hudson River tidal marsh, in E. A. Blair and J. R. Waldman (eds.), *Polgar Fellowship Reports of the Hudson River National Estuarine Research Reserve Program, 1988*. New York State Department of Environmental Conservation and Hudson River Foundation, New York, NY, Section VI:1–34.

Auer, N. A. 1982. *Identification of Larval Fishes of the Great Lakes Basin with Emphasis on the Lake Michigan Drainage*. Great Lakes Fishery Commission, Special Publication 82–3.

Carlson, D. M. 1986. *Fish and Their Habitats in the Upper Hudson Estuary*. New York State Department of Environmental Conservation. Unclassified Report.

Connelly, G. G., and Sirkin, L. A. 1973. Wisconsin history of the Hudson-Champlain lobe, in R. F. Black, R. P. Goldthwait, and H. B. Williams (eds.), *The Wisconsin Stage*. Geological Society of America, Memoir 136, pp. 47–69.

Cooper, J. C., Cantelmo, F. R., and Newton, C. E. 1988. Overview of the Hudson River estuary. *American Fisheries Society Monograph* 4:11–24.

Coote, T. 2001. *Comparative Analysis of Fish Assemblages in Select Hudson River Tributaries*. Report to New York Sea Grant and the Hudson River National Estuarine Research Reserve.

Geen, G. H., Northcote, T. G., Hartmore, G. F., and Lindsey, C. C. 1966. Life histories of two species of catostomid fishes in Sixteenmile Lake, British Columbia, with particular reference to inlet spawning. *Journal of the Fisheries Research Board of Canada* 23:1761–88.

Gerber, G. P., and Haynes, J. M. 1988. Movements and behavior of smallmouth bass, *Micropterus dolomieui*, and rock bass, *Ambloplites rupestris*, in Southcentral Lake, Ontario, and two tributaries. *Journal of Freshwater Ecology* 4:425–40.

Green, D. M., Landsberger, S. E., Nack, S. B., Bunnell, D., and Forney, J. L. 1993. *Abundance and Winter Distribution of Hudson River Black Bass*. Report to the Hudson River Foundation, New York, NY.

Helfman, G. S., Facey, D. E., Hales, Jr., L. S., and Bozeman, Jr., E. L. 1987. Reproductive ecology of the American eel. *American Fisheries Society Symposium* 1:42–56.

Hirschberg, D. J., Chin, P., Feng, H., and Cochran, J. K. 1996. Dynamics of sediment and contaminant transport in the Hudson River estuary: Evidence from sediment distributions of naturally occurring radionuclides. *Estuaries* 19:931–49.

Howarth, R. W., Fruci, J. R., and Sherman, D. 1991. Inputs of sediment and carbon to an estuarine ecosystem: Influence of land use. *Ecological Applications* 1:27–39.

Howarth, R. W., Schneider, R., and Swaney, D. 1996. Metabolism and organic carbon fluxes in the tidal freshwater Hudson River. *Estuaries* 19:848–65.

Juanes, F., Marks, R. E., McKown, K. A., and Conover, D. O. 1993. Predation by age-0 bluefish on age-0 anadromous fishes in the Hudson River estuary. *Transactions of the American Fisheries Society* 122:348–56.

Klauda, R. J., McLaren, J. B., Schmidt, R. E., and Dey, W. P. 1988. Life history of the white perch in the Hudson River estuary. *American Fisheries Society Monograph* 4:69–88.

Kleckner, R. C., and McCleave, J. D. 1985. Spatial and temporal distribution of American eel larvae in relation to the North Atlantic Ocean current systems. *Dana* 4:67–92,

Lagler, K. F., Bardach, J. E., Miller, R. R., and Passino, D. R. M. 1977. *Ichthyology*. New York: John Wiley & Sons.

Lake, T. R., and Schmidt, R. E. 1997. Seasonal presence and movement of fish populations in the tidal reach of Quassaic Creek, a Hudson River tributary (HRM 60): Documentation of potamodromy, anadromy, and residential components, in W. C. Nieder and J. R. Waldman (eds.), *Final Reports of the Tibor T. Polgar Fellowship Program, 1996.* Hudson River Foundation, New York, NY, Section VII:1–36.

——— 1998. The relationship between fecundity of an alewife (*Alosa pseudoharengus*) spawning population and egg productivity in Quassaic Creek, a Hudson River tributary (HRM 60) in Orange County, New York, in J. R. Waldman and W. C. Nieder (eds.), *Final Reports of the Tibor T. Polgar Fellowship Program, 1997.* Hudson River Foundation, New York, NY, Section II:1–24.

Mansfield, P. J. 1984. Reproduction by Lake Michigan fishes in a tributary stream. *Transactions of the American Fisheries Society* **113**:231–7.

McBride, R. S., and Able, K. W. 1995. Perennial occurrence and growth rates by crevalle jacks (Carangidae: *Caranx hippos*) in the Hudson River estuary, in W. C. Nieder, J. R. Waldman, and E. A. Blair (eds.), *Final Reports of the Tibor T. Polgar Fellowship Program, 1994.* Hudson River Foundation, New York, NY, Section VI:1–34.

McCleave, J. D., and Wippelhauser, G. S. 1987. Behavioral aspects of selective tidal stream transport in juvenile American eels. *American Fisheries Society Symposium* **1**:138–50.

Meyer, F. A. 1970. Development of some larval centrarchids. *Progressive Fish-Culturist* **32**:130–6.

Moriarty, C. 1978. *Eels – A Natural and Unnatural History.* New York: Universe Books.

Myers, G. S. 1949. Usage of anadromous, catadromous and allied terms for migratory fishes. *Copeia* 1949:89–97.

Nack, S. B., and Cook, W. 1987. Characterization of spawning and nursery habitats of largemouth bass (*Micropterus salmoides*) in the Stockport component of the Hudson River National Estuarine Research Reserve, in E. A. Blair and J. C. Cooper (eds.), *Polgar Fellowship Reports of the Hudson River National Estuarine Research Reserve Program 1986,* New York, NY, Section IV:1–24.

Robbins, W. H., and MacCrimmon, H. R. 1977. Vital statistics and migratory patterns of a potamodromous stock of smallmouth bass, *Micropterus dolomieui. Journal of the Fisheries Research Board of Canada* **34**:142–7.

Schmidt, R. E. 1986. *Fish Community Structure in Tivoli North Bay, a Hudson River Freshwater Tidal Marsh.* National Oceanographic and Atmospheric Administration, Technical Report, Series OCRM/SPD.

——— 1992. Temporal and spatial distribution of bay anchovy eggs through adults in the Hudson River estuary, in C. L. Smith (ed.), *Estuarine Research in the 1980s.* The Hudson River Environmental Society, Seventh Symposium on Hudson River Ecology. Albany, NY: State University of New York Press, pp. 228–41.

Schmidt, R. E., Chandler, W. E., and Strayer, D. L. 1995. Fishes consuming zebra mussels in the tidal Hudson River, in W. C. Nieder, J. R. Waldman, and E. A. Blair (eds.), *Final Reports of the Tibor T. Polgar Fellowship Program, 1994.* Hudson River Foundation, New York, NY, Section IV:1–20.

Schmidt, R. E., and Cooper, S. 1996. *A Catalog of Barriers to Upstream Movement of Migratory Fishes in Hudson River Tributaries.* Report to the Hudson River Foundation, New York, NY.

Schmidt, R. E., and Lake, T. R. 2000. *Alewives in Hudson River Tributaries, Two Years of Sampling.* Report to the Hudson River Foundation, New York, NY.

——— 2003. *Young of Year American Eel* (Anguilla rostrata) *in Hudson River Tributaries; Year One.* Report to Hudson River Estuary Program, New York, NY.

Schmidt, R. E., and Limburg, K. E. 1989. *Fishes Spawning in Nontidal Portions of Hudson River Tributaries.* Report to the Hudson River Foundation, New York, NY.

Schmidt, R. E., and Stillman, T. 1994. *Drift of Early Life Stages of Fishes in Stockport Creek and Significance of the Phenomenon to the Hudson River Estuary.* Report to the Hudson River Foundation, New York, NY.

——— 1998. Evidence of potamodromy in an estuarine population of smallmouth bass (*Micropterus dolomieu*). *Journal of Freshwater Ecology* **13**: 155–63.

Scott, W. B., and Crossman, E. J. 1973. *Freshwater Fishes of Canada.* Fisheries Research Board of Canada, Bulletin 184.

Smith, C. L. 1985. *The Inland Fishes of New York State.* New York Department of Environmental Conservation, Albany, NY.

Smith, C. L., and Lake, T. R. 1990. Documentation of the Hudson River fish fauna. *American Museum Novitates* 2981, 17pp.

Smith, D. G. 1989. Family Anguillidae, in E. B. Böhlke (ed.), *Fishes of the Western North Atlantic, Part Nine, Volume One.* Memoir Sears Foundation for Marine Research, New Haven, CT, pp. 25–47.

Swaney, D. P., Sherman, D., and Howarth, R. W. 1996. Modeling water, sediment and organic carbon discharges in the Hudson-Mohawk basin: Coupling of terrestrial sources. *Estuaries* **19**: 833–47.

Waldman, J. R. 1981. White perch on the run. *Underwater Naturalist* **13**:22–3.

Wällhauser, I., and Tashiro, J. S. 1989. Studies of the life history and trophic connections of a population of *Palaemonetes pugio* in the Croton River, in E. A. Blair and J. R. Waldman (eds.), *Polgar Fellowship Reports of the Hudson River National Estuarine Research Reserve Program, 1988*. New York State Department of Environmental Conservation and Hudson River Foundation, New York, NY, Section V:1–40.

Wang, J. C. S., and Kernehan, R. J. 1979. *Fishes of the Delaware Estuaries, A Guide to the Early Life Histories*. EA Communications, Towson, MD.

Yozzo, D. J. 1990. "Fish predation on littoral microcrustacea associated with water chestnut (*Trapa natans*) in Tivoli South Bay, a Hudson River tidal freshwater wetland." M.S. Thesis, University of Virginia, Charlottesville, Virginia.

16 Ecology of the Hudson River Zooplankton Community

Michael L. Pace and Darcy J. Lonsdale

ABSTRACT Zooplankton in the Hudson River estuary include both freshwater and estuarine species and range in body lengths from microns to millimeters. Measurements of abundance and biomass as well as community rate processes indicate that zooplankton do not generally exert significant grazing pressure on phytoplankton. In addition, recycling of nutrients by zooplankton is not significant to primary producers because concentrations of dissolved nutrients are quite high in the Hudson and controlled by other processes. Zooplankton do provide an important linkage in the food web as they are key prey items for many young-of-year fish as well as fish that are primarily planktivorous throughout life. Long-term observations indicate many zooplankton populations undergo regular seasonal cycles in abundance, typically with increases during warm, low-flow periods of the year. The invasion of the zebra mussel into the Hudson had strong impacts on zooplankton in the freshwater section of the estuary. Microzooplankton such as rotifers declined dramatically. Cladocerans also declined in annual average abundance between pre- and post-zebra mussel periods when the effects of wet and dry years are taken into account. Zebra mussels, however, had little effect on larger zooplankton. Regulation of zooplankton appears to be a function of physical forces that affect population residence times as well as food and predators. Evidence for food limitation is mixed. Some species benefit from food supplements in experimental trials, but the reduction of phytoplankton biomass in association with the zebra mussel invasion had no effect on cladoceran egg production. There are a variety of potential predators, and calculations indicate fish exert high rates of mortality on zooplankton. Direct measures

of predatory mortality and a better understanding of benthic-pelagic interactions are important topics for future research. In addition, we raise the general question of how strongly zooplankton interactions with predators and prey are coupled in the food web. If interactions are weak, changes such as species invasions or large interannual variation in fish populations may not impact the zooplankton, and thereby, propagation of effects up and down the food web could be highly attenuated.

Introduction

Zooplankton are small animals that live suspended in water. This water column life-style requires coping with a number of distinct abiotic and biotic factors. Zooplankton movement is largely the consequence of currents and not directed swimming activities. The flow of the Hudson River pushes plankton continuously downstream. Tidal currents in the estuary retard this downstream movement, but populations must still contend with constant net displacement toward the sea with associated increases in salinity. Plankton in the Hudson are adapted to live in freshwater or moderate salinity conditions, and as a consequence there are two fairly distinct communities – freshwater plankton and those tolerant of salinity that we will call true estuarine plankton. In addition to adapting to the abiotic features of the Hudson, zooplankton must acquire food to support growth and reproduction. Appropriate food resources like algae are embedded in a mixture of organic and inorganic particles from which zooplankton must acquire energy. Hudson River zooplankton are also preyed on by many fishes and invertebrates that may be sufficiently abundant to regulate their prey populations.

There are many ways to organize a discussion of a community of organisms. Here, we describe the composition of the freshwater and estuarine zooplankton communities including their distribution and abundance at several temporal and spatial scales. Measurements of abundance allow us to assess the importance of zooplankton relative to other groups (for example, benthos) in the Hudson. Our main contention is that zooplankton are not particularly significant in the context of the overall flow of energy in the Hudson ecosystem. Zooplankton do not account for a large component of system biomass, respiration, or productivity, nor do they consume a large fraction of primary production. Nutrient recycling by zooplankton is also not important, because dissolved nutrients are in plentiful supply. Zooplankton, however, are key intermediaries in the food web. They are a major diet item for many fishes, particularly critical early life history stages. Thus, zooplankton consume phytoplankton, bacteria, detritus, and other small animals, and provide suitably-sized food for larger invertebrates and fish.

A second focus of the chapter concerns the changes of zooplankton communities in the Hudson as a consequence of human impacts. Major alterations to the ecosystem include the introduction of sewage treatment, changes in pollutant loadings, alterations of fisheries and fish populations, and invasions of exotic species. Ideally we could assess how each of these impacts affected zooplankton and their interactions with other components of the ecosystem. However, both general understanding and specific data are insufficient. Instead, we focus on one documented case – the invasion and spread of zebra mussels (see chapter on invasive species). These animals invaded the freshwater Hudson estuary in the early 1990s and by late 1992 established a large population (Strayer et al., 1999; Strayer, Chapter 21, this volume). Since 1993 the zebra mussel population has sustained high filtration rates with consequent impacts on phytoplankton (Caraco et al., 1997) and other components of the Hudson ecosystem (Strayer et al., 1999; Strayer and Smith, 2001). Zebra mussels have also had significant differential impacts on zooplankton (Pace, Findlay, and Fischer, 1998) that are important in assessing how changes imposed by the invasion may propagate to fish populations.

Our strategy for this chapter is not an exhaustive treatment of the ecology of the Hudson zooplankton or even a partial review of the ecological interactions affecting zooplankton in a riverine-estuarine system. For a more detailed treatment of life history, physiological ecology, evolutionary biology, predator-prey dynamics, and population processes, the reader should consult more comprehensive texts and reviews. We recommend Day et al. (1989) for a basic introduction to estuarine zooplankton, and for more advanced treatments of zooplankton, Kerfoot (1980) and Mauchline (1998).

Community Composition

Our discussion of zooplankton in this chapter includes both animal zooplankton and heterotrophic protists (also called protozoans). The principal planktonic microbial protists that feed on other organisms are ciliates and flagellates. Ciliates and flagellates are often not well characterized taxonomically, but they are important consumers that may be quite significant in rivers and estuaries both as grazers on phytoplankton as well as consumers of bacteria (Gasol and Vaqué, 1993).

Fresh water dominates much of the Hudson. Principal freshwater zooplankton include flagellates, ciliates, rotifers, and crustaceans. The latter group includes cladocerans and copepods – both are common in the Hudson. There are numerous species of flagellates that do not contain chloroplasts and are presumed to feed primarily on bacteria. Little is known about the species in this group. The ciliates are typical of planktonic forms, primarily composed of choreotrichs (inclusive of oligotrichs and tintinnids), a group distinguished by the lack of somatic ciliature but with complex ciliated structures associated with the feeding apparatus (Fig. 16.1). Rotifers are very small animals, with many of the species in the Hudson being less than 100 μm in maximum length. Two genera, *Keratella* and *Polyarthra*, are found in almost any freshwater sample taken from the Hudson. A variety of other genera are common, e.g., *Asplanchna, Ascomorpha, Brachionus, Collotheca, Filinia, Kellicotia, Notholca, Pleosoma*, and *Synchaeta*. Copepods include representatives of the three main groups: cyclopoids, calanoids, and harpacticoids. The latter are primarily benthic, although harpacticoid copepods are found in Hudson zooplankton samples. Two species of cyclopoid copepods, *Diacyclops bicuspidatus thomasi* and *Halicyclops sp.*, are common. The calanoid copepod, *Eurytemora affinis*, while more typically associated with low salinity conditions, also occurs in the freshwater Hudson. The most common cladoceran is *Bosmina freyi* (Fig. 16.1). Other cladoceran species of the genera *Daphnia, Diaphanosoma*, and *Ceriodaphnia* occur sporadically at low abundance. Additionally, the large, predatory cladoceran *Leptodora kindtii* is found in the Hudson where it feeds on a variety of prey including *Bosmina freyi*.

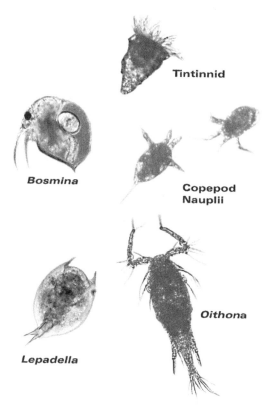

Tintinnid

Bosmina

**Copepod
Nauplii**

Oithona

Lepadella

Figure 16.1. Representative Hudson River zooplankton including a tintinnid, copepod nauplius, a rotifer, *Lepadella*, a cladoceran *Bosmina freyi*, and a cyclopoid copepod *Oithona* sp. Diagram is not to scale. Tintinnids, rotifers, and nauplii are small zooplankton in the size range of 50–200 μm. *Bosmina* are typically 200–400 μm, and *Oithona* >500 μm.

In saline sections of the Hudson, a true estuarine fauna occurs. Freshwater forms decline in the oligohaline sections and do not occur in the southern portion of the estuary. As in the freshwater Hudson, flagellates and ciliates can be abundant. Functionally the species resemble freshwater forms, but there is a greater diversity of ciliates, especially tintinnid species (Fig. 16.1). Estuarine rotifers and cladocera (i.e., *Evadne*) can occasionally be important (Lonsdale, Cosper, and Doall, 1996) as are a variety of larvae of benthic organisms (referred to as meroplankton) including those of polychaetes, barnacles, and crabs. Copepods, however, are the most abundant animals (Fig. 16.1). There are a variety of calanoid copepods that vary in salinity preferences and seasonal occurrence. The most common species include *Eurytemora affinis*, *Acartia tonsa*, and *A. hudsonica*. In addi-

tion, species of *Centropages*, *Pseudocalanus*, and *Temora* are found. *Oithona* is an important cyclopoid copepod. There are also larger, predatory zooplankton such as ctenophores (e.g., *Mnemiopsis leidyi*) and mysids (*Neomysis americana*). These zooplankton taxa are typical of temperate estuaries along the east coast of the United States (e.g., Narragansett Bay, Rhode Island, Long Island Sound, New York, and Chesapeake Bay, Maryland).

As water moves from the Hudson River to New York Harbor and offshore, the estuarine zooplankton community is replaced by a coastal zooplankton community (Stepien, Malone, and Chervin, 1981). Copepods of the genera *Eurytemora* and *Acartia* are emblematic of the estuarine-nearshore community, while further offshore, the New York Bight is characterized by *Calanus*, *Pseudocalanus*, *Centropages*, and *Temora*.

Another useful way of viewing the zooplankton community is based on size. Size is well related to metabolic activity, feeding rates, and predator-prey interactions. One convention is to organize the community into size classes. These are nano- (2–20 μm in maximum dimension), micro- (20–200 μm), meso- (200–2,000 μm), and macro- (>2,000 μm) plankton (Omori and Ikeda, 1984). Based on this organization, flagellates and some of the smaller ciliates constitute the nano- size class. Microzooplankton are principally ciliates, rotifers, copepod nauplii, some meroplankton, and some of the smaller cladocerans and copepods. Mesozooplankton are mostly crustaceans, especially postn400naupliar life stages of copepods and cladocerans. Finally, macrozooplankton are some of the largest copepods and various, largely predatory zooplankton such as *Leptodora*, ctenophores, mysids, and even fish larvae. This largest size class of organisms is much more capable of directed swimming, and so at some point these animals are better considered nekton, but there is no strict separation of the groups.

Distribution and Abundance

Variations in animal populations and community structure are inherently scale dependent. For Hudson zooplankton interesting scales of variation include the temporal scales of diel and tidal cycles as well as seasonal and interannual variation. These temporal scales might be measured in hours (diel and tidal), weeks (seasonal), and years (interannual). Some interesting spatial scales of variation include relatively small-scales that encompass replicate samples as well as the "patchiness" of zooplankton. These occur at scales of hundreds to thousands of liters. At the opposite end of the spectrum is the distribution and river-wide abundance of zooplankton along the north-south axis of the river (a length of >250 km).

Specific questions often dictate the scale of sampling and variance analysis. For example, studies of predation on zooplankton by fish need to consider the mean and variance of zooplankton at the foraging scale of the fish. If zooplankton are aggregated in space, fish might successfully forage from aggregation to aggregation if they have a means of detecting concentrated patches of zooplankton. The population consequences of such behavior for both zooplankton and fish require some means of "scaling-up" foraging interactions to assess their consequences for the respective populations. These types of scale-dependent and scale-translation issues are important problems in zooplankton research specifically, in ecological research generally, and represent an exciting frontier of research. Most zooplankton studies focus on samples taken at a single or a few stations. Whole-system estimates of abundance based on sampling across spatial and temporal scales are rarely made but are needed to effectively assess the possible ecosystem consequences of zooplankton dynamics. Here, we describe variation of zooplankton at several scales and an example of "scaling-up" to estimate riverwide abundances from temporal and spatial data.

At the scale of replicate samples (approximately 100–1,000 liters), the logarithm of the mean of a set of replicate samples is related to the logarithm of the variance, and the slope of this relationship is in the range of 1.4 to 1.9 (Pace, Findlay, and Lints, 1991). Variance is predictable, therefore, given an estimate of mean abundance. Sampling can be adjusted to achieve a desired precision. This is an important advantage in hypothesis testing as both the consequences of varying statistical significance level and power can be assessed as a function of expected differences in density and sample size (see Cyr et al., 1992 for an example).

Tides are a significant feature of the Hudson and may influence zooplankton variation at the scale of hours as the tide ebbs, slackens, and then floods. Tidal magnitude also varies over the monthly cycle of spring and neap tides. Significant variation associated with tidal dynamics has been observed in the Hudson (Pace, Findlay, and Lints, 1992). In estuarine systems plankton exploit tides for migration as well as maintenance of position in the estuary (e.g., Christy and Morgan, 1998). A study of larval transport in the Hudson estuary (Kunze, 1995) showed that the ability of swimming larvae (for example, a gastropod, *Littorina*, and a barnacle, *Balanus*) to maintain depth was highly dependent not only on their swimming capabilities but also the degree of tidal mixing. At the George Washington Bridge (river km (RKM) 19), larvae were mixed throughout the water column during mid-ebb and mid-flood of a spring tide. At the Verrazano Narrows (in New York Harbor), waters were less mixed because of greater salinity stratification. Here, larvae were able to regulate their depth in the water column, potentially reducing their loss from the estuary.

At seasonal time scales zooplankton exhibit consistent seasonal variation within the Hudson. Figure 16.2 illustrates the dynamics of rotifers, copepods, and cladocerans at a single station located near Kingston, New York (RKM 152), for two years: one prior to the establishment of large populations of the zebra mussel (1991) and a post-zebra mussel year (1999). Zooplankton are typically at low levels during winter and early spring when low temperatures reduce population growth and high inputs of fresh water result in short water residence times and increased advective losses. As temperature increases during spring, zooplankton become more abundant. For example, in 1991 rotifer abundances increased from about 10 l^{-1} in April to 1,000 l^{-1} by June and densities greater than 100 l^{-1} were sustained until late November. Rotifer dynamics were similar in 1999, but overall abundance was reduced due to zebra mussels (see next section). Copepods, principally cyclopoids, are persistently abundant with occasional summer increases to greater than 10 l^{-1} (Fig. 16.2). Cladocerans undergo a consistent seasonal cycle that features rapid increase to high densities in spring, sharp mid-summer decline, and moderate populations (1–10 l^{-1}) in late summer and fall. This is

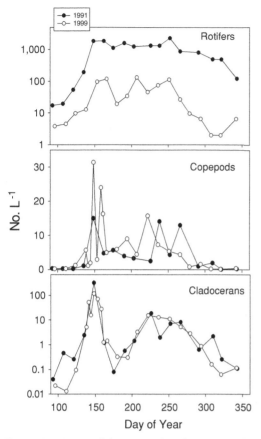

Figure 16.2. Seasonal dynamics of rotifers, copepods, and cladocerans for the years 1991 and 1999 at a freshwater station near Kingston, New York (river km 152).

the result of a single species, *Bosmina freyi*, and is remarkably consistent from year to year (Fig. 16.2 and Limburg et al., 1997).

Zooplankton also vary across the large spatial area of the Hudson ecosystem. For example, the early June increase in *Bosmina freyi* (Fig. 16.2) is not observed uniformly throughout the river. In 1992 for example, large increases in the population occurred primarily between river km 80 and 160 (Fig. 16.3). Below river km 50, *Bosmina* are rarely abundant in association with the transition from freshwater to oligohaline conditions. In contrast to the pattern for *Bosmina*, calanoid copepods are often most abundant toward the oligohaline end of the estuary (Fig. 16.3).

Spatial and temporal data on the period of high abundance ("bloom") of *Bosmina freyi* in 1992 can be used to project an estimate of the riverwide biomass and production. This projection is

significant not only for understanding zooplankton dynamics but also because the bloom of *Bosmina* overlaps with critical periods in the development of larval fishes in the Hudson (e.g., Limburg, Pace, and Arend, 1999). Assuming an average of 100 animals l^{-1} between river km 80 and 160 and a volume of 900 billion liters for this section of the river, the abundance of *Bosmina* was 90 trillion animals. An individual *Bosmina* weighs about 0.7 μg dry wt or 0.3 μg C. This translates to a total biomass of 27,000 kg C or 27 metric tons (mt). In 1992, as in most years, this biomass developed and disappeared over a two-week period. Specifically, densities were greater than 10 l^{-1} between May 26 and June 10, 1992, at the Kingston station (Fig. 16.3). Assuming a production-to-biomass ratio of 1 over this two-week time interval, secondary production was about 2 mt per day. While these calculations are approximate, they indicate that there is large productivity available for exploitation by fish and invertebrate predators. The calculations also indicate how spatial and temporal data are needed to assess riverwide abundance. Sampling conducted only at a station above, below, or within the bloom

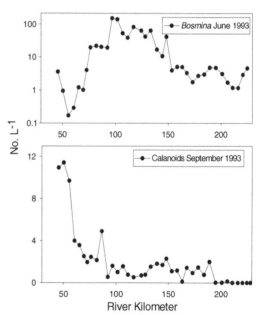

Figure 16.3. Abundance of *Bosmina freyi* on June 2–3, 1992, along a transect from river km 46 to 219. Lower plot is abundance of calanoid copepods along a transect from river km 46 to 232 on September 7–8, 1993, salinity increased from 1 to 7 ppt between river km 92 and 46.

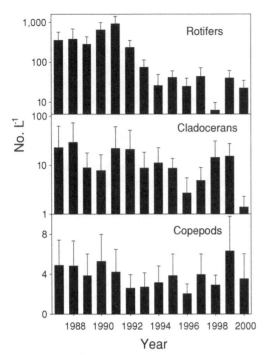

Figure 16.4. Mean annual abundance and 95% confidence intervals for rotifers, cladocerans, and post-naupliar copepods, at Kingston, New York (river km 152). Note zebra mussels invaded the Hudson in the early 1990s, establishing a large population in 1992.

would result in very different estimates and a potentially inaccurate depiction of the availability of *Bosmina* to fish.

Zooplankton and the Zebra Mussel Invasion

The invasion of the zebra mussel had important impacts on the Hudson ecosystem. Zebra mussel grazing resulted in an 80–90 percent decline in phytoplankton biomass and primary production (Caraco et al., 1997). Zebra mussels also caused a reduction in populations of native benthic bivalves and other benthic animals that feed on plankton (Strayer and Smith, 2001). Some zooplankton populations as well as zooplankton community biomass also declined (Pace et al., 1998).

The general effect of zebra mussels is evident from examining mean annual abundance from long term data. Assessments of zebra mussel effects are based on a comparison of means before and after 1992. Rotifers have clearly declined from mean densities greater than 100 l^{-1} to means less

than 50 l^{-1} since the invasion of the zebra mussel (Fig. 16.4). Other microzooplankton groups (data not shown) such as tintinnid ciliates and copepod nauplii exhibited a similar decline (Pace et al., 1998). Post-naupliar copepods have varied within a narrow range of 2–6 l^{-1} with no obvious trends, although four years of relatively low mean abundance (<3 l^{-1}) have all occurred following the invasion of the zebra mussel (Fig. 16.4). While copepod densities may have declined slightly, no substantial change has occurred, a conclusion supported by time series analysis (Pace et al., 1998).

Any change in cladocerans is difficult to assess based simply on an inspection of the annual means (Fig. 16.4). Mean abundance was low in some years following 1992 (e.g., 1996 and 2000) while other years appear quite similar to those observed prior to 1992 (e.g., 1998 and 1999). The input of fresh water to the Hudson as measured by flow over the dam at Troy, New York, has an important influence on plankton dynamics (Pace et al., 1991; Caraco et al., 1997). When mean cladoceran abundance is plotted against freshwater flow, the annual means fall cleanly into two groups representing the pre- and post-zebra mussel period (Fig. 16.5). Abundance is low in wet years and high in dry years. This pattern persists with zebra mussels but abundance has shifted to a lower level (Fig. 16.5). Thus, the mean abundance of cladocerans declined in association with the zebra mussel invasion.

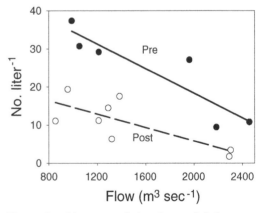

Figure 16.5. Mean annual abundance of cladocerans and mean flow for years prior to (pre) and following (post) the zebra mussel invasion. Mean flow from daily measurements of discharge made by the United States Geological Survey at the head of the estuary, Green Island, New York.

Loss of phytoplankton as food is an obvious possible mechanism that could lead to a decline in zooplankton. The most direct test of this idea, however, using available field data, is contradictory. Long-term records of egg production for *Bosmina* indicate little change in eggs per individual or clutch size following the invasion (Pace et al., 1998). Reproductive parameters are sensitive indicators of food limitation in zooplankton populations. Thus, the mechanisms whereby zebra mussels influence cladocerans are uncertain. Nevertheless, years of high freshwater flow and abundant zebra mussels are associated with reduced abundances.

Declines in various microzooplankton including tintinnid ciliates, rotifers, and copepod nauplii may be related to a loss of food, but it is equally plausible that zebra mussel predation limits these groups. Rates of zebra mussel feeding based on laboratory studies (MacIsaac et al., 1992; Wong et al., 2003) in combination with estimates of abundance in the Hudson suggest predation on microzooplankton is comparable to maximum estimated population growth rates (Pace et al., 1998).

Overall, declines in zooplankton observed in the Hudson in association with the zebra mussel invasion were size-dependent. The largest declines were observed for organisms with individual body mass less than 0.1 μg dry weight while substantial declines occurred in organisms with body mass in the range of 0.1–1 μg dry weight. For organisms with an average size greater than 1 μg (e.g., copepods) no significant change was observed. Many resident and anadromous fish exploit zooplankton especially during their earliest life history stages. Limited declines observed in larger, preferred prey items like copepods (Limburg et al., 1997) may have reduced the effects of zebra mussels on fish populations.

Zooplankton Grazing and Utilization of Autotrophic and Heterotrophic Resources

Zooplankton are typically viewed as grazers on phytoplankton, but consumption of heterotrophic organisms, especially bacteria, flagellates, and ciliates, can be significant both in terms of the mortality of heterotrophs and as a resource for zooplankton. Additionally, in many aquatic systems zooplankton constitute a significant biomass pool

and are important in the cycling of carbon, nitrogen, and phosphorus as well as other elements.

Relative zooplankton biomass, however, is not large in the Hudson ecosystem. For example, in the freshwater Hudson the biomass of benthic animals including zebra mussels averages 12 g C m^{-2} d^{-1} (Strayer and Smith, 2001) while zooplankton biomass is less than 0.1 g C m^{-2} d^{-1}. Calculations of the contribution of zooplankton to system respiration and secondary production indicate similar low relative contributions from zooplankton (Lints, Findlay, and Pace, 1992; Caraco et al., 2000). Nutrient recycling of nitrogen and phosphorus by zooplankton is also not significant as dissolved nutrients (PO$_4$, NH$_4$, and NO$_3$) are available at high concentrations (Clark et al., 1992; Lampman, Caraco, and Cole, 1999), and phytoplankton are limited primarily by light (Cole, Caraco, and Peierls, 1992).

Grazing by larger zooplankton (i.e., the micrometazoa and mesozooplankton) also has little effect on phytoplankton. For example, Lonsdale et al. (1996) found that grazing was less than 10 percent and often less than 1 percent of primary production per day during spring and summer in the lower estuary. Grazing impacts were higher (60 percent) in fall but primary production was also low at this time of the year. In the freshwater estuary, grazing by zooplankton (>73 μm) was also low, ranging from 1–13 percent d^{-1} (Pace and Findlay, unpublished data). Therefore, in both freshwater and saline sections of the estuary, direct measurements as well as extrapolations based on biomass indicate that grazing is not a major fate of phytoplankton. However, the grazing impact of smaller zooplankton, including heterotrophic flagellates and ciliates, has yet to be evaluated in the Hudson. These organisms can consume a significant fraction of phytoplankton biomass.

Flagellates and ciliates can contribute significantly to the diets of larger zooplankton such as copepods (Stoecker and Capuzzo, 1990). Ciliate concentrations in the Hudson estuary are similar to other coastal waters and preliminary research suggests that ciliates, including both nonloricate forms and tintinnids, contribute to the diets of larger zooplankton (Lonsdale, unpublished data). Copepod addition experiments, conducted in March and June using seawater collected from the Verrazano

Narrows, resulted in mean clearance rates of 2.3–5.8 ml copepod^{-1} h^{-1} for *Acartia* adults feeding on ciliates >20 μm. These clearance rates are within the range reported previously for *Acartia* (Stoecker and Capuzzo, 1990). Copepod nauplii also ingested some ciliates in both seasons. Cladocera (for example, *Bosmina*) and rotifers also prey on ciliates and heterotrophic flagellates (Sanders and Wickham, 1993).

Zooplankton also consume bacteria. Rates of consumption by heterotrophic flagellates, ciliates, and cladocerans are similar to those observed in other systems (Vaqué et al., 1992). Copepods probably do not feed directly on bacteria, at least the unattached forms that dominate numerically in the Hudson. However, detritus and the associated microbial populations do contribute to copepod diets in the estuary (Chervin, 1978; Chervin, Malone, and Neale, 1981), and observations from the Columbia River estuary suggest most consumption by copepods in the turbidity maximum is on bacteria associated with particles (Simenstad, Small, and McIntire, 1990). Copepods also are often selective for flagellates and ciliates that, in turn, are significant consumers of bacteria (Sherr and Sherr, 1987; Stoecker and Capuzzo, 1990; Merrell and Stoecker, 1998).

Zooplankton grazing does not appear to be sufficient to balance bacterial production (Vaqué et al., 1992). Nevertheless, grazing is an important fate of bacteria with an average of 10 to 20 percent; of bacteria consumed daily. Further, estimates of carbon requirements of zooplankton suggest that ingestion of bacteria can satisfy much of their demand. Bacterial production in the Hudson is largely uncoupled from primary production (Findlay et al., 1991), hence much of the carbon that ultimately fuels zooplankton production may arise from the watershed and move through into the food web via bacteria and bacterial predators. This conjecture, however, is based on limited evidence and more direct analysis using appropriate tracers (for example, stable isotopes, fatty acids) is needed to substantiate the hypothesized linkage.

Regulation of Zooplankton

Zooplankton biomass in rivers and estuaries is typically lower than in lakes even when comparing systems with comparable levels of phytoplankton (Pace et al., 1992). This comparison implies other features such as advective losses are important in limiting populations. During the cold temperature, high-flow periods of the year (November to May), zooplankton are rapidly advected downstream. After May, however, water residence time in the Hudson is several months. This allows ample time for zooplankton populations to increase, raising the question of what limits the abundance and biomass of zooplankton in the Hudson during the warmer, low-flow periods of the year (June to October). We hypothesize zooplankton are limited by a combination of food and predators with the latter being most important during summer.

Estuaries are areas with abundant and diverse food for consumers and in the Hudson some combination of bacteria, algae, detritus, and microzooplankton provide food for zooplankton. Does food limit the abundance of populations and overall biomass of the community? As noted above since the early 1990s, zebra mussels have caused a very large reduction of phytoplankton in the Hudson. The lack of a decline in freshwater copepods (Fig. 16.4) and the relatively constant egg ratios (eggs per female) in cladocerans indicate food limitation was not necessarily the reason for the changes in zooplankton that accompanied the zebra mussel invasion. There is evidence, however, of food limitation of egg production by copepods in the lower, saline portion of the estuary. Supplementing natural food levels with an edible algal species resulted in increased egg production by calanoid copepods relative to ambient conditions at most times (Lonsdale et al., 1996). Moreover, egg production rates were positively related to total depth-integrated primary production (also see Chervin et al., 1981). Food limitation also affects copepod production in other estuaries (Durbin et al., 1983).

Limitation by food quality is more difficult to evaluate. Ample dissolved nutrients in the Hudson argue against skewed stoichiometric ratios of major elements in the foods of zooplankton. Thus, the relative amounts of carbon, nitrogen, and phosphorus in resources are likely within ranges that do not cause food quality limitation, as has been observed in freshwater systems (DeMott and Gulati, 1999).

Nevertheless, if zooplankton are sustained by substantial quantities of detritus and/or bacteria, there is the possibility of food quality problems associated with essential fatty acids (Jonasdottir, 1994) and perhaps other nutritional requirements (for example, sterols; Harvey, Ederington, and McManus, 1997). Interestingly, the most extreme demonstration of food limitation of copepod egg production (*Pseudocalanus* sp.) in the Hudson estuary was found during a spring bloom of the diatom *Skeletonema costatum* ($\sim$3–7 $\times$ 10^6 cells ml^{-1}) when the concentration of chlorophyll *a* was relatively high ($>$10 μg L^{-1}) (Lonsdale et al., 1996). It is possible that this reduction in egg production rate was due to food quality, as diatoms as a dominant food source may provide a nutritionally inadequate diet (Kleppel, 1992).

Based on measurements of the abundance of planktivorous fishes and invertebrates, zooplankton may be heavily preyed on in the Hudson. For example, the combined abundance of young-of-year alosids, white perch, striped bass, and bay anchovy (size $<$100 mm) varies in the range 0.1 to 100 m^{-3} during summer (Limburg, 1994). A rough calculation of the impact of planktivores can be made by assuming a planktivore consumes 100 copepods d^{-1}, a rate well within the broad range observed in feeding studies. At planktivore densities of 10 m^{-3} and a copepod density of 1–10 L^{-1}, the estimated daily predation on copepods is 10 to 100 percent of the standing stock. Such mortality rates are significant given likely specific copepod growth rates in the range of 0.1–0.75 d^{-1} for summer water temperatures (Huntley and Lopez, 1992). Obviously, lower densities of planktivores or lower consumption rates would indicate a more modest impact, but it is very likely that the fish surveys underestimate actual abundance and under many conditions the abundance of invertebrate planktivores (*Leptodora*, *Neomysis*, ctenophores, amphipods) is at least 1 animal m^{-3} and often far greater.

The inference of significant predatory regulation of crustacean zooplankton during the warmer, low-flow period of the year is consistent with findings from other systems. Kiørboe (1998) using data on growth rates for copepods in coastal systems concluded that food was generally not the primary limiting factor. Case studies from other temperate estuaries provide evidence that planktivory may be limiting for copepodids and adult copepods, particularly in summer and fall (Mehner and Thiel, 1999; Adrian et al., 1999).

Two additional features of the Hudson zooplankton support the notion of strong predatory effects. Community structure is indicative of a system where vertebrate planktivory is important. In the freshwater section, small-bodied species less visible to predators and those with good escape abilities (cyclopoids) are dominant. The Hudson assemblage resembles that found in lakes that experience intense planktivory. In the estuarine section larger-bodied calanoids are dominant. Some of these species (for example, *Acartia*), however, have numerous morphological and life history traits thought to be adaptations to predation including body shape, rapid escape responses, and broadcast spawning of eggs (Kiørboe, 1998).

Not all planktivores are subject to regulation by predators. Ctenophores are, at times, very abundant in the lower Hudson and probably exert strong predatory effects on zooplankton, including copepods, rotifers, and ciliates (Deason and Smayda, 1982; Stoecker et al., 1987). There are a variety of predators of ctenophores (e.g., scyphozoan medusae; Feigenbaum and Kelly, 1984), but ctenophores are not apparently subject to intense predation by fish commonly found in the Hudson (Kremer, 1994). Thus, planktivory may be little affected in this case by alterations in the fish predator community.

Zooplankton – Food Web Connections to Fish

Many Hudson fish depend on zooplankton as a food resource. This is especially true for the early life history stages of resident and anadromous fishes. Striped bass, for example, consume zooplankton during their larval stage. Copepods and *Bosmina* are primary prey, but the smallest striped bass larvae also consume rotifers, copepod nauplii, and even zebra mussel veligers while larger larvae switch to larger zooplankton such as *Leptodora*. Selectivity is positive for larger copepods. Limburg et al. (1997) observed striped bass larvae with copepod eggs in their guts, suggesting consumption of ovigerous females was important. Striped bass switch to benthic and epibenthic prey such as am-phipods and shrimp as they develop from the lar-val to juvenile stage (Hurst and Conover, 2001). Juveniles still prey on animals that are partially planktonic such as *Neomysis americana*. Atlantic tomcod (*Microgadus tomcod*) also exhibit a simi-lar ontogenetic shift in prey items, switching from copepods such as *Eurytemora affinis* to mysids and amphipods (Grabe, 1978). In addition to fish that utilize zooplankton primarily during early life stages, some species are largely planktivorous including American shad, alewife, blueback her-ring, gizzard shad, bay anchovy, menhaden, and Atlantic silverside (Grabe, 1996). For these organ-isms, zooplankton are a primary resource during their residence in the Hudson.

For the smallest of some fish larvae, ciliates may be an important food resource. In the laboratory, small larval menhaden fed preferentially on tintin-nids compared to copepod nauplii while larger lar-vae preferred nauplii (Stoecker and Govoni, 1984). To date, however, little is known about the impor-tance of ciliates in larval diets of fish in the Hudson River. This may be due, in part, to the use of gut con-tent analysis of preserved specimens as the primary method of determining fish feeding preferences. Although fish have been known to consume cili-ates, rapid digestion or cell disintegration due to preservation may explain the absence of these or-ganisms in gut contents. Chemical and immuno-logical approaches could help in determining if Hudson fish utilize ciliates and other microbes as food resources.

Overall, exploitation of zooplankton as prey is a critical feature of the Hudson ecosystem. Re-ductions in zooplankton would presumably affect planktivorous fish unless these fish can compen-sate by some mechanism (e.g., increased feeding or switching to alternate resources). The zebra mus-sel invasion provides a means of testing the depen-dence of fish on zooplankton with the provision that the most selected prey of fish (that is, cope-pods) underwent little change in abundance. The long-term data on fish populations in the Hudson resulting from monitoring studies by utilities and state agencies indicate planktivorous fish exhibited changes in abundance, growth, and distribution in association with the zebra mussel invasion (Strayer, Hattala, and Kahnle, 2004).

Future Research Needs

While many of the linkages involving zooplankton in the Hudson food web are known, uncertainty remains concerning their importance to popula-tions. Are predator-prey interactions tightly cou-pled to the respective dynamics of individual pop-ulations or are these associations "loose" in the sense that specific trophic interactions have lit-tle affect on dynamics? Loose linkages could be the case if populations are highly omnivorous. In this view the estuary represents a dynamic feed-ing tableau with sufficient resources to support population growth. Exploitation is a matter of ever changing opportunities, and resources have little influence on populations. Alternatively, the highly repeatable dynamics of some populations (for ex-ample, *Bosmina freyi*) suggest there are structured interactions that determine population processes and that some of these are related to trophic effects. The Hudson probably contains both loose and tight trophic interactions and sorting the causes and consequences of these relationships remains a goal for future study.

Zooplankton by definition are animals in the water column and are often studied in isolation from interactions with benthic processes. Mero-planktonic animals, however, arise from the ben-thos and return there after a brief pelagic phase. More permanent members of the plankton have resting stages that reside in the bottom and shal-lows of the Hudson. These stages likely seed the blooms and population increases of many species. Further, planktonic animals retreat to the bottom or near-bottom environment as part of daily migra-tions probably to avoid visual predators but also to maintain position and retention within the estu-ary in association with tides. These few examples of benthic-pelagic interactions point to an area of limited knowledge. A more fully integrated under-standing of zooplankton requires a better apprecia-tion of how benthic-pelagic interactions influence populations and food web interactions.

We have argued that zooplankton are a critical trophic linkage to fish in the Hudson and much of their functional significance in the ecosystem de-rives from this role. Fish populations are, however, quite variable. Large interannual variations are ob-served. In addition, populations vary substantially in time and space within a year and hence predation from fish on zooplankton may be highly episodic. The consequences of this presumably variable interaction between fish and zooplankton remain poorly understood. Means for measuring predatory mortality and variation in these rates are critical to testing many of the ideas posed in this chapter.

REFERENCES

Adrian, R., Hansson, S., Sandin, B., De Stasio, B., and Larsson, U. 1999. Effects of food availability and predation on a marine zooplankton community – A study on copepods in the Baltic Sea. *Internationale Revue der Gesamten Hydrobiologie* **84**:609–26.

Caraco, N. F., Cole, J. J., Findlay, S. E. G., Fischer, D. T., Lampman, G. G., Pace, M. L., and Strayer, D. L. 2000. Dissolved oxygen declines in the Hudson River associated with the invasion of the zebra mussel (*Dreissena polymorpha*). *Environmental Science and Technology* **34**:1204–1210.

Caraco, N. F., Cole, J. J., Raymond, P. A., Strayer, D. L., Pace, M. L., Findlay, S. E. G., and Fischer, D. T. 1997. Zebra mussel invasion in a large, turbid, river: phytoplankton response to increased grazing. *Ecology* **78**:588–602.

Chervin, M. B. 1978. Assimilation of particulate organic carbon by estuarine and coastal copepods. *Marine Biology* **49**:265–75.

Chervin, M. B., Malone, T. C., and Neale, P. J. 1981. Interactions between suspended organic matter and copepod grazing in the plume of the Hudson River. *Estuarine and Coastal Shelf Science* **13**: 169–83.

Christy, J. H., and Morgan, S. G. 1998. Estuarine immigration by crab postlarvae: mechanisms, reliability and adaptive significance. *Marine Ecology Progress Series* **174**:51–65.

Clark, J. F., Simpson, H. J., Bopp, R. F., and Deck, B. 1992. Geochemistry and loading history of phosphate and silicate in the Hudson Estuary. *Estuarine and Coastal Shelf Science* **34**:213–233.

Cole, J. J., Caraco, N. F., and Peierls, B. L. 1992. Can phytoplankton maintain a positive carbon balance in a turbid, fresh-water, tidal estuary? *Limnology and Oceanography* **37**:1608–1617.

Cyr, H., Downing, J. A., Lalonde, S., Baines, S., and Pace, M. L. 1992. Sampling larval fish populations: choice of sample number and size. *Transactions of the American Fisheries Society* **121**:356–68.

Day, Jr., J. W., Hall, C. A. S., Kemp, W. M., and Yáñez-Arancibia, A. 1989. *Estuarine Ecology*. New York: John Wiley & Sons.

Deason, E. E., and Smayda, T. J. 1982. Ctenophore-zooplankton-phytoplankton interactions in Narragansett Bay, Rhode Island, USA, during 1972–1977. *Journal of Plankton Research* **4**: 203–217.

DeMott, W. R., and Gulati, R. D. 1999. Phosphorous limitation in *Daphnia*: Evidence from a long-term study of three hypereutrophic Dutch lakes. *Limnology and Oceanography* **44**:1557–64.

Durbin, E. G., Durbin, A. G., Smayda, T. J., and Verity, P. G. 1983. Food limitation of production by adult *Acartia tonsa* in Narragansett Bay, Rhode Island. *Limnology and Oceanography* **28**:1199–1213.

Feigenbaum, D., and Kelly, M. 1984. Changes in the lower Chesapeake Bay food chain in the presence of the sea nettle *Chrysaora quinquecirrha* (Schyphomedusa). *Marine Ecology Progress Series* **19**: 39–47.

Findlay, S., Pace, M. L., Lints, D., Cole, J. J., Caraco, N. F., and Peierls, B. 1991. Weak coupling of bacterial and algal production in a heterotrophic ecosystem: The Hudson River estuary. *Limnology and Oceanography* **36**:268–78.

Gasol, J. M., and Vaqué, D. 1993. Lack of coupling between heterotrophic nanoflagellates and bacteria: A general phenomenon across aquatic systems. *Limnology and Oceanography* **38**:657–65.

Grabe, S. A. 1978. Food and feeding habits of juvenile Atlantic tomcod, *Microgadus tomcod*, from Haverstraw bay, Hudson River. *Fisheries Bulletin* **76**:89–94.

Grabe, S. A. 1996. Feeding chronology and habits of *Alosa* spp., (Clupeidae) juveniles from the lower Hudson River estuary, New York. *Environmental Biology of Fishes* **47**:321–6.

Harvey, H. R., Ederington, M. C., and McManus, G. B. 1997. Lipid composition of the marine ciliates *Pleuronema* sp. and *Fabrea salina*: Shifts in response to changes in diet. *Journal of Eukaryotic Microbiology* **44**:189–93.

Huntley, M. E., and Lopez, M. D. G. 1992. Temperature-dependent production of marine copepods: A global synthesis. *American Naturalist* **140**:201–42.

Hurst, T. P., and Conover, D. O. 2001. Diet and consumption rates of overwintering YOY striped bass, *Morone saxatilis*, in the Hudson River. *Fisheries Bulletin* **99**:545–53.

Jonasdottir, S. H. 1994. Effects of food quality on the reproductive success of *Acartia tonsa* and *Acartia hudsonica*: laboratory observations. *Marine Biology* **121**:67–81.

Kerfoot, W. C. 1980. *Ecology and Evolution of Zooplankton Communities*. Special Symposium Volume 3, American Society of Limnology and Oceanography, University Press of New England, Durham, New Hampshire.

Kiørboe, T. 1998. Population regulation and role of mesozooplankton in shaping marine pelagic food webs. *Hydrobiologia* **363**:13–27.

Kleppel, G. S. 1992. Environmental regulation of feeding and egg production by *Acartia tonsa* off southern California. *Marine Biology* **112**:57–65.

Kremer, P. 1994. Patterns of abundance for *Mnemiopsis* in U.S. coastal water: a comparative review. *ICES Journal of Marine Science* **51**:347–54.

Kunze, H. B. 1995. "Distribution and transport of larvae within the Hudson River estuary." M. S. Thesis, State University of New York at Stony Brook, Stony Brook, New York.

Lampman, G. G., Caraco, N. F., and Cole, J. J. 1999. Spatial and temporal patterns of nutrient concentration and export in the tidal Hudson River. *Estuaries* **22**:285–96.

Limburg, K. E. 1994. "Ecological constraints on growth and migration of juvenile American shad (*Alosa sapidissima* Wilson) in the Hudson River estuary, New York." Ph.D. Dissertation, Cornell University, Ithaca, New York.

Limburg, K. E., Pace, M. L., Arend, K. K. 1999. Growth, mortality, and recruitment of larval *Morone* spp. in relation to food availability and temperature in the Hudson River. *Fisheries Bulletin* **97**:80–91.

Limburg, K. E., Pace, M. L., Fischer, D., and Arend, K. K. 1997. Consumption, selectivity, and use of zooplankton by larval striped bass and white perch in a seasonally pulsed estuary. *Transactions of the American Fisheries Society* **126**:607–21.

Lints, D., Findlay, S. E. G., and Pace, M. L. 1992. Biomass and energetics of consumers in the lower food web of the Hudson River, in C. L. Smith (ed.), *Estuarine Research in the 1980s*. Albany, NY: State University of New York Press, pp. 466–57.

Lonsdale, D. J., Cosper, E. M., and Doall, M. 1996. Effects of zooplankton grazing on phytoplankton size-structure and biomass in the lower Hudson River estuary. *Estuaries* **19**:874–89.

MacIsaac, H. J., Sprules, W. G., Johansson, O. E., and Leach, J. J. 1992. Filtering impacts of larval and sessile zebra mussels (*Dreissena polymorpha*) in western Lake Erie. *Oecologia* **92**:30–9.

Mauchline, J. 1998. The biology of calanoid copepods, in Blaxter, J. H. S., Southward, A. J., and Tyler, P. A. (eds.), *Advances in Marine Biology*, Vol. 33. San Diego, CA: Academic Press, pp. 1–710.

Mehner, T., and Thiel, R. 1999. A review of predation impact by 0+ fish on zooplankton in fresh and brackish waters of the temperate northern hemisphere. *Environmental Biology of Fishes* **56**:169–81.

Merrell, J. R., and Stoecker, D. K. 1998. Differential grazing on protozoan microplankton by developmental stages of the calanoid copepod *Eurytemora affinis* Poppe. *Journal of Plankton Research* **20**:289–304.

Omori, M., and Ikeda, T. 1984. *Methods in Marine Zooplankton Ecology*, New York: John Wiley & Sons.

Pace, M. L., Findlay, S. E. G., and Fischer, D. 1998. Effects of an invasive bivalve on the zooplankton community of the Hudson River. *Freshwater Biology* **38**:103–116.

Pace, M. L., Findlay, S. E. G., and Lints, D. 1991. Variance in zooplankton samples: evaluation of a predictive model. *Canadian Journal of Fisheries and Aquatic Science* **48**:146–51.

1992. Zooplankton in advective environments: The Hudson River community and a comparative analysis. *Canadian Journal of Fisheries and Aquatic Science.* **49**:1060–9.

Sanders, R. W., and Wickham, S. A. 1993. Planktonic protozoa and metazoa: predation, food quality and population control. *Marine Microbial Food Webs* **7**:197–223.

Sherr, E. B., and Sherr, B. F. 1987. High rates of consumption of bacteria by pelagic ciliates. *Nature* **325**:710–711.

Simenstad, C. A., Small, L. F., and McIntire, C. D. 1990. Consumption processes and food web structure in the Columbia River estuary. *Progress in Oceanography* **25**:271–97.

Stepien, J. C., Malone, T. C., and Chervin, M. B. 1981. Copepod communities in the estuary and coastal plume of the Hudson River. *Estuarine and Coastal Shelf Science* **13**:185–95.

Stoecker, D. K., and Capuzzo, J. M. 1990. Predation on protozoa: its importance to zooplankton. *Journal of Plankton Research* **12**:891–908.

Stoecker, D. K., and Govoni, J. J. 1984. Food selection by young larval gulf menhaden (*Brevoortia patronus*). *Marine Biology* **80**:299–306.

Stoecker, D. K., Verity, P. G., Michaels, A. E., and Davis, L. H. 1987. Feeding by larval and postlarval ctenophores on microzooplankton. *Journal of Plankton Research* **9**:667–83.

Strayer, D. L., Caraco, N. F., Cole, J. J., Findlay, S., and Pace, M. L. 1999. Transformation of freshwater ecosystems by bivalves: a case study in the Hudson River. *BioScience* **49**:19–27.

Strayer, D. L., and Smith, L. C. 2001. The zoobenthos of the freshwater tidal Hudson River and its response to the zebra mussel (*Dreissena polymorpha*) invasion. *Archive für Hydrobiologia Supplement* **139**:1–52.

Strayer, D. L., Hattala, K., and Kahnle, A. 2004. Effects of an invasive bivalve (*Dreissena polymorpha*) on fish in the Hudson River estuary. *Canadian Journal of Fisheries and Aquatic Sciences* **61**:924–41.

Vaqué, D., Pace, M. L., Findlay, S. E. G., and Lints, D. 1992. Fate of bacterial production in a heterotrophic ecosystem: Grazing by protists and metazoans in the Hudson Estuary. *Marine Ecology Progress Series* **89**:155–63.

Wong, W. H., Levinton, J. S., Twining, B. S., and Fisher, N. 2003. Assimilation of micro- and mesozooplankton by zebra mussels: A demonstration of the food web link between benthic predators and zooplankton. *Limnology and Oceanography* **48**:308–312.

17 Submersed Macrophyte Distribution and Function in the Tidal Freshwater Hudson River

Stuart Findlay, Cathleen Wigand, and W. Charles Nieder

ABSTRACT In the tidal freshwater Hudson River submerged aquatic vegetation (SAV) occupies on average 6 percent of the river area with much greater coverage in the mid-Hudson (Kingston – Hudson) and much lower areal coverage south of Hyde Park. The native water celery (*Vallisneria americana*) is by far the predominant species in terms of areal coverage but the invasive water chestnut (*Trapa natans*) attains a higher standing stock on a smaller area. *Vallisneria* is light-limited in all but the shallowest depths and produces sufficient oxygen to maintain super-saturated conditions in some plant beds for a large proportion of summertime daylight hours. SAV supports abundant and diverse invertebrate and fish faunas with distinct differences between *Vallisneria* and *Trapa*. Turbidity in *Vallisneria* is frequently greater than in the main channel in contrast to the baffling and enhanced sediment deposition generally expected in plant beds. Overall, SAV plays several important and unique roles in shaping the habitats and ecosystem functioning of the Hudson River.

Introduction

Submersed aquatic vegetation (SAV) plays a critical role in many aquatic systems, contributing to primary productivity, nutrient cycling and sediment dynamics, as well as providing important habitat for fishes and invertebrates (Rozas and Odum, 1987; Heck et al., 1995). Aquatic macrophyte communities are some of the most productive natural ecosystems and have been found to support numerous and diverse wildlife populations (Dennison et al., 1993; Kemp, Boynton, and Twilley, 1984). More than twenty aquatic plant species are found in the SAV beds of the Hudson River (see Table 17.1, Fig. 17.1). In almost all areas, the native *Vallisneria americana* (wild celery, water celery, tape grass) is the predominant plant, occurring in over 90 percent of the benthic grabs containing plants. In the Hudson River, SAV occupies shallows and shoals where the water depth is less than 3 m (Moran and Limburg, 1986; Muenscher, 1937), and although their distribution is limited, they can form dense conspicuous beds (Menzie, 1979; Harley and Findlay, 1994), and achieve rates of primary production as high as $5.0 \text{ g O}_2 \text{ m}^{-2} \text{ day}^{-1}$ (Garritt and Howarth, 1988).

Aside from its value as habitat and its contribution to ecosystem primary productivity, the spatial extent and temporal stability of SAV have been used as indicators of water quality. For example, the resurgence of submersed macrophytes in the tidal Potomac River has been attributed to reduced nutrient inputs from sewage and concurrent improvements in water clarity (Carter and Rybicki, 1986). On the other hand, Short and Burdick (1996) documented a replacement of SAV with macroalgae in response to increased housing density (and nutrient loads) in Waquoit Bay, Massachusetts. The mechanism behind SAV reduction appears to be the decreased light availability due to phytoplankton increase under high nutrient loads. A variety of other plants (phytoplankton, epiphytic microalgae, and benthic macroalgae) increase following nutrient additions (Short, Burdick, and Kaldy, 1995) reducing growth of submersed vascular plants. There have been extensive efforts to quantify the habitat requirements (light, nutrient concentrations) associated with successful plant growth (Dennison et al., 1993; Stevenson, Staver, and Staver, 1993) and monitoring of SAV spatial extent has become a central component in assessments of estuarine "health."

This chapter reviews what is known about the distribution, abundance, and ecological functions associated with submersed vegetation in the tidal freshwater Hudson River. There is relatively little historical information to use as a baseline for assessing change in extent of SAV or potential changes in species composition.

Table 17.1. Plant species composition of SAV beds on the Hudson River

Ceratophyllaceae	**Potamogetonaceae**
Ceratophyllum	Potamogeton
demersum	bupleuroides
Elatineceae	P. crispus
Elatine americana	P. epihydrus
Haloragaceae	P. foliosus
Myriophyllum spicatum	P. nodosus
M. exalbescens	P. pectinatus
Proserpinaca palustris	P. perfoliatus
Hydrocharitaceae	P. pusillus
Elodea canadensis	P. richardsonii
Elodea nuttallii	P. spirillus
Elodea occidentalis	P. vaseyi
Vallisneria americana	P. zosteriformis
Najadaceae	**Trapaceae**
Najas flexilis	Trapa natans
N. guadalupensis var.	
guadalupensis	
N. guadalupensis var.	
muenscheri	
N. minor	

List compiled from Svenson (1924), Svenson (1935), Muenscher (1937), Buckley and Ristich (1976), Schmidt and Kiviat (1988), and the Bard College Field Station Herbarium collection.

SAV DISTRIBUTION AND BED CHARACTERISTICS

A first attempt to map the extent of SAV in the Hudson was initiated in 1995. A Geographical Information System (GIS) coverage derived from aerial photography was used to assess several characteristics of SAV beds along the reach of the Hudson from Hyde Park to Castleton. The submersed beds, predominantly *Vallisneria americana* and the floating leafed exotic *Trapa natans* were mapped as separate patch types. The extent of SAV varies markedly along the river with as much as 17 percent of the river area occupied by plant beds in the Cementon-Saugerties reach (Fig. 17.2). For this stretch of the Hudson, the percent cover by SAV averages 13 percent. For the stretch from Troy to Piermont the percent cover is about 6.5 percent of the river surface area for *Vallisneria* and 2 percent for *Trapa*.

Biomass of *Vallisneria* in the Hudson River ranges as high as 550 g dry mass m^{-2} with signifi-

cant variability among sites. Mean standing stock based on about fifty Ponar grabs was 142 g dry mass m^{-2} with a standard deviation of 152. The median area of *Vallisneria* beds (3,072 m^2) was substantially larger than the median area of *Trapa* (1,300 m^2) and there are roughly three times as many *Vallisneria* beds as patches of *Trapa*. Consequently, the area covered by the native water celery is about three times the area covered by water chestnut.

The limit to distribution of *Vallisneria* is almost certainly light availability and given the relatively turbid nature of the Hudson River, maximum depths are generally less than 3 m. *Vallisneria* is the predominant species of submersed plant, possibly because of its ability to maintain photosynthesis at low light levels. Harley and Findlay (1994) found that *Vallisneria* produced more oxygen per gram of leaf material at light levels below about 10 percent of full sun than either *Myriophyllum* or *Potamogeton*. When comparing *Myriophyllum spicatum* (L) and *V. americana* (Michx.), Titus and Adams (1979) found that *V. americana* is a much more efficient fixer of carbon at low light intensities. In another study, *V. americana* was the most shade-adapted of five submersed macrophytes (Meyer et al., 1943). This light-harvesting ability together with significant belowground biomass of vegetative and storage structures may contribute to *Vallisneria's* ability to persist and thrive under relatively poor light conditions and in habitats subject to considerable wave and current stress. One species able to outcompete *V. americana* in the shallows of the river is *Trapa natans*. This exotic species concentrates its biomass at the surface in a dense canopy of floating rosettes, which allows for increased light availability for the leaves and dense shade beneath the canopy. It seems likely (although untested) that areas currently occupied by *T. natans* were previously occupied by *V. americana*.

Functions of SAV in the Hudson

Primary production. The ability of any plant in the turbid Hudson to fix carbon and produce oxygen will be largely related to light availability (see chapter by Cole and Caraco). Water masses traversing SAV beds are known to be significantly super-saturated with oxygen (Garritt and Howarth,

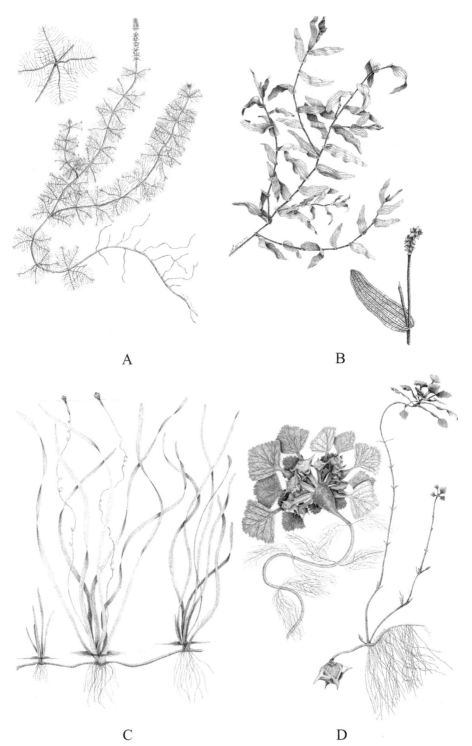

Figure 17.1. Line drawings of common plants found in shallow water habitats of the Hudson River estuary. Pictured are: A. *Myriophyllum spicatium*, B. *Potamogeton perfoliatus*, C. *Vallisneria americana*, and D. *Trapa natans*. Original artwork by L. B. McCloskey.

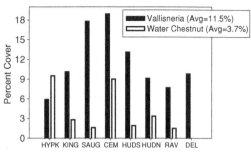

Figure 17.2. Percent cover by the native submersed *Vallisneria* and exotic *Trapa*. X-axis labels refer to USGS topographic quadrangles arranged from the south end of the study reach near Hyde Park to the north end near Castleton (Hyde Park, Kingston East, Saugerties, Cementon, Hudson South, Hudson North, Ravena, and Delmar). Water-chestnut was not present in the Delmar quadrangle.

1988; Carter, Rybicki, and Hammerschlag, 1991; Barrett and Findlay, 1993) suggesting these plants may be significant in river-scale primary productivity. For instance, continuous measurements of dissolved oxygen in several SAV beds shows that these sites are super-saturated with oxygen approximately 30 percent of the time and O_2 concentrations can be as high as 150 percent of saturation (Fig. 17.3). Recent modelling efforts based on photosynthesis-irradiance relationships for both phytoplankton and submersed plants show that oxygen production by SAV is a large component of midsummer oxygen budgets (see Cole and Caraco, chapter 9, this volume). The relative importance of submersed macrophytes as primary producers has increased dramatically since the zebra mussel invasion (1992). Prior to 1992, SAV Net Primary Production (NPP) and Gross Primary Production (GPP) were roughly 10 percent of phytoplankton NPP and GPP. Since the zebra mussels (see chapter by Strayer) have dramatically depressed phytoplankton, SAV NPP and GPP are currently about half phytoplankton values.

SAV CONTRIBUTION TO FOOD WEBS AND METABOLISM

The stable carbon signatures of several important consumers in the mid-Hudson are intermediate between carbon signatures of SAV and phytoplankton, suggesting a mixed diet (Caraco et al., 1998). Whether this has always been the case or is a recent shift due to zebra mussel depletion

of the phytoplankton food resource (Caraco et al., 1997) remains an open question. The reduction in phytoplankton primary production together with the modest increase in water clarity (Caraco et al., 1997) suggests that both the relative and absolute importance of SAV are greater now than in the recent past. Benthic invertebrates in the Hudson River appear to have been insulated from the loss of phytoplankton and benthos density in shallow vegetated habitats has increased in the past decade (see chapter 19, this volume). Perhaps the availability of organic matter from submersed plants has acted to buffer the large decline in phytoplankton allowing many shallow water benthic invertebrates to maintain or increase their population.

EFFECTS OF SAV ON SUSPENDED SEDIMENTS

As the largest sessile organisms in these communities, macrophytes can have quite an impact upon their physical environment. One of their most important effects is the reduction of water velocity through a bed (Carpenter and Lodge, 1986; Losee and Wetzel, 1988; Rybicki et al., 1997) commonly resulting in increased rates of sedimentation and decreased resuspension of fine grain sediments (Kenworthy, Zieman, and Thayer, 1982; Kemp et al., 1984; Ward, Kemp, and Boynton, 1984; Posey, Wigand, and Stevenson, 1993). Riverine beds of aquatic vegetation have been shown to act as a sieve, retaining suspended particulates and hastening the decomposition of trapped allochthonous organic matter (Kenworthy et al., 1982; Fisher and Carpenter, 1976; Fonseca and Fisher, 1986; Rybicki et al., 1997). Sediment

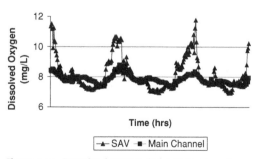

Figure 17.3. Dissolved oxygen diel patterns in a dense bed of *Vallisneria* (triangles) compared to the main channel (squares). O_2 concentrations as high as 150% of saturation have been observed when low tide corresponds to mid-day.

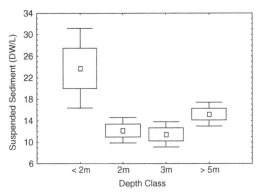

Figure 17.4. Suspended sediment concentrations collected when drifting from deep waters over vegetated shallows. (Class 1 is less than 2 m deep and occupied by dense SAV; Class 4 is >5 m and unvegetated.)

dynamics are of particular interest in a turbid system, such as the Hudson, where light limitation controls growth of phytoplankton and submersed vegetation (Malone, 1977; Moran and Limburg, 1986; Cole, Caraco, and Peierls, 1992; Harley and Findlay, 1994). Moreover, the dynamics of suspended sediment affect the distribution and trophic availability of particle-associated contaminants.

It is now obvious that suspended sediment dynamics during low-flow conditions (June–October of most years) are dictated by the likelihood of local resuspension and deposition (Findlay, Pace, and Fischer, 1997). In general, submersed vegetation is expected to act as a baffle, reducing local concentrations of suspended sediment (e.g., Posey et al., 1993). In shallow areas of the Hudson, even those with dense SAV beds, there is a marked increase in suspended sediment concentrations as water masses traverse SAV beds (Fig. 17.4) (see also Barrett and Findlay, 1993), suggesting vegetated areas do not function uniformly as sediment traps. There was also considerable variability among beds in both suspended sediment concentration and dissolved oxygen, suggesting that factors such as plant density, species composition, or actual location (east, west, or mid-channel) may influence the degree to which SAV functions as a sediment trap.

Macrophyte communities in the Hudson seem to have a variable impact on suspended matter, and do not conform to models from other systems. Differences in plant density, species composition, and shear stress may account for variation within

the Hudson, as well as among systems. We suggest that the factor affecting the impact of SAV on near-shore sediment dynamics will be the relationship between the critical depth for wave-driven resuspension and the maximum depth of SAV colonization. In turbid systems, light limitation may preclude SAV colonization of areas shallow enough to be susceptible to critical erosion stress. In these cases, macrophyte patches cannot mitigate the occurrence of resuspension until a water mass reaches vegetated depths. In less turbid systems SAV might colonize greater depths, and abundant vegetation at depths of critical erosion stress will decrease the likelihood of resuspension (c.f. Ward et al., 1984). This interplay between these two critical depths may well explain intersystem variability in the effects of SAV on suspended sediment.

SAV and Nutrient Interactions

Most research on nutrients and submersed vegetation has focused on excess nutrient supply and detrimental effects on water clarity and epiphyte growth (e.g., Short and Burdick, 1996; Dennison et al., 1993) or potential limitation of plants by sediment porewater nutrient pools (e.g., Wigand, Stevenson, and Cornwell, 1997). In the relatively high nutrient conditions prevalent in the Hudson (see Cole and Caraco, chapter 9, this volume) both phytoplankton and epiphytes are likely light-limited and so fluctuations in nutrients will have less effect on light penetration. Moreover, SAV in the Hudson are not necessarily dependent on long-term nutrient stores in the sediment nor are they nutrient-limited. Nitrogen and phosphorus concentrations of leaf tissue exceed critical threshold limits by 100 percent or more (Wigand et al., 2001). Although SAV are reported to most often rely on the sediment for nutrient acquisition (Carignan and Kalff, 1980), it appears that SAV in the Hudson may incorporate nutrients from the overlying water as well. The accumulation of allochthonous particulates in grassbeds and subsequent microbial processing in the overlying water may result in a source of nutrients for *V. americana*. In fact, recent research in the Hudson River has shown that microbial assimilation of dissolved inorganic nitrogen (DIN) is enhanced in the river because of high loads of both terrestrial organic matter and DIN (Caraco et al., 1998). Concentration of these allochthonous particulates in the grass-beds and subsequent DIN mineralization would allow for a single particle to repeatedly transport nutrients to areas of SAV. Other data in support of *V. americana* usage of newly distributed and remineralized organic material is that stable ^{15}N isotope analysis of leaves ($\delta^{15}N = 8$) collected from the field show a signal intermediate between the overlying water seston ($\delta^{15}N = 10$–12) and sediment ($\delta^{15}N = 4.5$) (Caraco et al., 1998). In contrast, lab-grown *V. americana* leaves ($\delta^{15}N = 6.5$) have a lower $\delta^{15}N$ signal, which is closer to sediment values ($\delta^{15}N = 4.5$) (Wigand et al., 2001).

Beds of *V. americana* appear to enrich rather than deplete nutrient porewater pools in the turbid mid-Hudson River with higher porewater concentrations of ammonium and phosphate inside plant beds compared to bare sediment (Wigand et al., 2001). Also, porewater N and P concentrations are maximal in summer when plant biomass is high again, suggesting that plant demand is insufficient to draw down available nutrient pools in the sediments. Porewater nitrogen pools could be enriched by the deposition of fine, organic particulates and subsequent mineralization in the sediment. In tidal rivers there may be large inputs of high-nutrient particulate material from upstream and tidal currents might redistribute these allochthonous materials across broad areas. The process whereby particulates are intercepted and trapped in some beds may be attributed to the slowing of currents in grassbeds with the rise and fall of the tide (Rybicki et al., 1997). Nutrient exchange and retention in grassbeds results from the interplay of physical forces (i.e., tides; currents), the structure of the grassbeds (i.e., canopy; understory), and biological processes (i.e., mineralization; root and leaf uptake).

Particulate mineralization could provide from 50 to 100 percent of nutrients necessary to sustain SAV in the Hudson depending upon the presence or absence of zebra mussels (Wigand et al., 2001). Particulate mineralization processes prior to the zebra mussel invasion could provide for most of the estimated plant nutrient demand. Since the invasion of zebra mussels and the subsequent reduction in phytoplankton biomass (Caraco et al., 1997), particulate mineralization could only provide about

50 percent of SAV nutrients (Wigand et al., 2001). However, in the presence of large populations of zebra mussels, the transfer of mussel feces and pseudofeces to shallow areas might provide an additional nutrient-rich and labile organic substrate which could fuel mineralization in the grassbeds (Strayer et al., 1999). In addition, soluble reactive phosphorus in the Hudson increased after the zebra mussel invasion, presumably due to lowered pressure on the dissolved phosphorus pools by the reduced phytoplankton stocks (Strayer et al., 1999). These additional nutrient sources could help support SAV growth since the zebra mussel invasion.

Although we have not measured the nutrient transfer due to the decay of the highly labile leaves of *V. americana* and other submersed macrophytes in the Hudson, we suspect that similar to other systems (Carpenter, 1980; Smith and Adams, 1986) a nutrient pulse following the decay of sloughed leaves in the fall could fuel pelagic phytoplankton, bacteria, and benthic animals (e.g., Cheng et al., 1993, see Strayer, chapter 19, this volume). Mass loss from blades of *Vallisneria* was extremely rapid in a microcosm study (~3%/day; Bianchi and Findlay, 1991) and would presumably be at least that rapid in the more turbulent river. Therefore, any nutrients remaining in the aboveground portion will be rapidly returned to the water column following plant senescence.

SAV as Habitat

INVERTEBRATE USE OF SAV

SAV beds may be an important habitat for invertebrates, typically containing higher densities and diversities of invertebrates than an equivalent area of unvegetated sediments (Cyr and Downing, 1988a, b; Chilton, 1990; Thorp, Jones, and Kelso, 1997). However, there have been relatively few studies focusing on the role shallow water vegetation beds play in supporting macroinvertebrate communities on the Hudson River (Feldman, 2001; Lutz and Strayer, 2000; Strayer and Smith, 2000; Findlay, Schoeberl, and Wagner, 1989; Menzie, 1980). Menzie (1980) found high densities of macroinvertebrates within an SAV bed (*M. spicatum*) in Bowline Pond with almost two orders of magnitude greater biomass of chironomids found within the

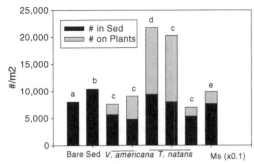

Figure 17.5. Abundance of invertebrates on plants (gray portion of bar) or in sediments under plants comparing different plant species and a river-wide mean for deeper bare sediments. Letters above bars refer to data source [a = Simpson et al., 1986, b = Strayer and Smith 2000, c = Lutz and Strayer 2000, d = Findlay et al., 1989, e = Menzie 1980 who used a smaller mesh size (0.12 mm)].

SAV bed than in unvegetated deeper waters. Findlay et al. (1989) also found high densities of invertebrates in *T. natans* in Tivoli South Bay. In the freshwater tidal portion of the estuary, Strayer and Smith (2001) found a large difference in the invertebrate community between vegetated, shallow water habitat and unvegetated deeper water sites with many taxa being strongly positively correlated with the aquatic vegetation. In the chapter on freshwater benthos, Strayer proposes that presence/absence of SAV is one of three major environmental controls (salinity, vegetation, grain size) on the composition of the macroinvertebrate community.

The invertebrate community of plant beds differs qualitatively from that of bare sediments as well. In particular, the invertebrate community of plant beds often is especially rich in the large or active animals (for example, amphipods, mayflies, caddisflies) that contribute disproportionately to fish diets. Beds of *Myriophyllum sp.* and *T. natans* are known to support dense communities of invertebrates, especially chironomids (Menzie, 1980; Findlay et al., 1989, Feldman, 2001)(Fig. 17.5). Strayer and Smith (2001) also found much greater numbers of chironomids within SAV beds than on unvegetated substrate. Thus, macrophyte beds may be important sources of fish food, because of the richness of the invertebrate community and the relative abundance of large, attractive prey. *V. americana* beds were sampled as part of a broad survey of the Hudson River zoobenthos (Strayer,

Smith, and Hunter, 1998 and unpublished) and in a smaller scale study of invertebrate distribution (Lutz and Strayer, 2000). The invertebrate fauna directly associated with the plants (epiphytic) is a large proportion of the total number of animals occurring in vegetated habitats and the numbers of individuals in sediments of vegetated areas is frequently higher than in sediments of unvegetated sites (Lutz and Strayer, 2000).

The importance of these habitats for invertebrates appears to have changed over time. Before zebra mussels arrived in the Hudson, invertebrate density was about the same in these *V. americana* beds as on open, unvegetated sediments. After the zebra mussel invasion, which drastically reduced phytoplankton biomass and increased water transparency (see Cole and Caraco, chapter 9, this volume), invertebrate density rose in *V. americana* beds and fell in unvegetated habitats, suggesting that benthic primary production may have become increasingly important to the Hudson River food web (Strayer et al., 1998).

FISH USE OF SAV

Fish may acquire plant-associated animals from macrophyte beds either by moving into these beds and feeding on the resident animals or by remaining outside macrophyte beds and feeding on animals that are carried away from the plants by currents. This latter pathway may be significant because it allows fish to remain in deepwater habitats and could distribute animals (and ultimately, macrophyte carbon) produced in macrophyte beds throughout the river. Although movement of benthic animals through the water column (drift) is very well known in small streams (e.g., Allan, 1995) where it may form a large part of the diet of stream-dwelling fish, it has scarcely been investigated in large rivers or estuaries like the Hudson. Although we often see benthic animals in our plankton samples, showing that drift does occur in the Hudson, there are no previous estimates of the size or source of this drift. The few studies that have been done in large rivers (Berner, 1951; Eckblad, Volden, and Weilgart, 1984) show that drift of benthic animals may be substantial (100–1,000 macroinvertebrates/m^3), and thus has the potential to form a large part of riverine fish diets. Menzie (1980) noted that Grabe and Schmidt found high

Table 17.2. Fish species composition in *Vallisneria americana*, *Trapa natans* and *Myriophyllum spicatum*

		V. americana	*T. natans*	*M. spicatum*
Anguillidae	**Freshwater Eels**			
Anguilla rostrata	American eel	X	X	
Atherinidae	**Silversides**			
Menidia beryllina	Inland silverside	X		
Menidia menidia	Atlantic silverside			X
Centrarchidae	**Sunfishes**			
Ambloplites rupestris	Rock bass		X	
Lepomis auritus	Redbreast sunfish		X	X
Lepomis gibbosus	Pumpkinseed	X		X
Micropterus salmoides	Largemouth bass		X	X
Clupeidae	**Herrings**			
Alosa aestivalis	Blueback herring	X		X
Alosa pseudoharengus	Alewife	X		X
Alosa sapidissima	American shad			X
Brevoortia tyrannus	Atlantic menhaden			X
Dorosoma cepedianum	Gizzard shad		X	X
Cyprinidae	**Carps and Minnows**			
Carassius auratus	Goldfish		X	
Cyprinus carpio	Common carp	X	X	
Hybognathus regius	Silvery minnow		X	
Notemigonus crysoleucas	Golden shiner		X	X
Notropis hudsonia	Spottail shiner	X	X	X
Engraulidae	**Anchovies**			
Anchoa mitchilli	Bay anchovy			X
Fundulidae	**Killifishes**			
Fundulus d. diaphanus	Banded killifish	X	X	X
Fundulus heteroclitus	Mummichog		X	X
Gasterosteidae	**Sticklebacks**			
Apeltes quadracus	Fourspine stickleback	X	X	
Ictaluridae	**Catfishes**			
Ameiurus catus	White catfish		X	
Moronidae	**Temperate River Basses**			
Morone americana	White perch	X	X	X
Percidae	**Perches**			
Etheostoma olmstedi	Tessellated darter	X	X	
Pomatomidae	**Bluefishes**			
Pomatomus saltatrix	Bluefish			X

Gilchrest and Schmidt (1998), Schmidt and Hamilton (1992), Hankin and Schmidt (1992), Schmidt and Kiviat (1988), Menzie (1980)

densities of chironomids in the gut contents of clupeids captured in and around a Hudson River SAV bed in Bowline Pond, suggesting these fish use the SAV as foraging grounds. Menzie studied this same plant bed and found high densities and production of chironomids in the bed. The high chironomid production ($2 \text{ g m}^{-2}\text{yr}^{-1}$) in Bowline Pond coupled with the fact that juvenile fish tend to congregate and feed in this area indicate that the SAV are important nursery feeding grounds for fish (Menzie, 1981).

A site-specific comparison on the Hudson River showed that fish abundances are higher in *T. natans* compared to *V. americana* beds (Schmidt and Kiviat, 1988), but again we have no way of assessing the generality of these findings. With a larger species pool and different environmental factors, use of SAV beds in the main river may be quite different from patterns described within tidal marshes and embayments. Menzie (1980) found many fish species associated with the *M. spicatum* bed he was studying. Several studies have shown that even low densities of *T. natans* supported a large and relatively diverse fish assemblage (Coote, Schmidt, and Caraco, 2001; Sanford, 2000; Gilchrest and Schmidt, 1998). Deploying three replicate pop nets in a water chestnut bed Pelczarski and Schmidt (1991) caught on average seventeen individuals distributed among five species, which is comparable to catch rates in *T. natans* in Tivoli North Bay. Pop nets are one of the enclosure methods suggested for sampling fish in shallow estuarine habitats (Rozas and Minello, 1997). Table 17.2 contains a list of fish found in association with *V. americana*, *T. natans*, and *Myriophyllum* sp. beds.

Management Issues

Despite the reasonably well-documented beneficial functions of SAV beds in the Hudson they are not presently the target of specific efforts at protection. Aerial photographs show evidence of boat scars in many beds. Also, many beds are close to shore and so modifications of shorelines (hardening of shoreline; extension of bulkheads; docks and piers) may well affect beds of SAV. Efforts to provide information to management agencies, marina operators, and boaters are underway and are expected to reduce damage to these relatively invisible habitats.

Trapa natans comprises roughly 25 percent of the areal coverage of submersed rooted plants in the tidal freshwater Hudson and is generally considered a nuisance to boaters. Water chestnut entered the Hudson within the past 100 years and was previously a target of eradication efforts by the NYS DEC. Water chestnut has both "beneficial" and "negative" effects. It clearly serves as habitat for fishes and invertebrates, supporting densities greater than non-vegetated areas and occasionally higher densities than the native *Vallisneria* (Lutz and Strayer, 2000). Water chestnut also allows dissolved oxygen levels within the bed to fall to very low levels (Caraco and Cole, 2002) although negative consequences for fishes do not appear to be strong (Coote et al., 2001). In some instances, efforts at invasive plant eradication have both positive and negative consequences (Findlay, Groffman, and Dye, in press) and the relative benefits must be weighed prior to undertaking large-scale efforts at eradication.

REFERENCES

Allan, J. D. 1995. *Stream Ecology: Structure and Function of Running Waters*. New York: Chapman and Hall.

Barko, J. W., Gunnison, D., and Carpenter, S. R. 1991. Sediment interactions with submersed macrophyte growth and community dynamics. *Aquatic Botany* **41**:41–65.

Barrett, J., and Findlay, S. 1993. Ecosystem effects of Submersed aquatic vegetation in the Tidal freshwater Hudson River, in J. Waldman and E. A. Blair (eds.), *Final Reports of the Tibor T. Polgar Fellowship Program, 1992*. Hudson River Foundation, New York, NY, Section VIII:1–48.

Berner, L. M. 1951. Limnology of the lower Missouri River. *Ecology* **32**:1–12.

Bianchi, T. S., and Findlay, S. 1991. Decomposition of Hudson estuary macrophytes: Photosynthetic pigment transformations and decay constants. *Estuaries* **14**:65–73.

Buckley, E. H., and Ristich, S. S. 1976. Distribution of rooted vegetation in the estuarine marshes of the Hudson River. In *Hudson River Ecology, Fourth Symposium on Hudson River Ecology*. Bear Mountain, New York. March 28–30, 1976.

Cafrey, J. M., and Kemp, M. 1990. Nitrogen cycling in sediments with estuarine populations of *Potamogeton perfoliatus* and *Zostera marina*. *Marine Ecology Progress Series* **66**:147–60.

Caraco, N. F., and Cole, J. J. 2002. Contrasting impacts of a native and alien macrophyte on dissolved oxygen in a large river. *Ecological Applications* **12**:1496–1509.

Caraco, N. F., Cole, J. J., Raymond, P. A., Strayer, D. L., Pace, M. L., Findlay, S. E. G. and Fischer, D. T. 1997. Zebra mussel invasion in a large, turbid river: Phytoplankton response to increased grazing. *Ecology* **78**:588–602.

Caraco, N. F., Lampman, G., Cole, J. J., Limburg, K. E., Pace, M. L., and Fischer, D. 1998. Microbial assimilation of DIN in a nitrogen rich estuary: implications for food quality and isotope studies. *Marine Ecology Progress Series* **167**:59–71.

Carignan, R., and Kalff, J. 1980. Phosphorus sources for aquatic weeds: water or sediments? *Science* **207**:987–9.

Carpenter, S. R. 1980. Enrichment of lake Wingra, Wisconsin, by submersed macrophyte decay. *Ecology* **61**:1145–55.

Carpenter, S. R., and Lodge, D. M. 1986. Effects of submersed macrophytes on ecosystem processes. *Aquatic Botany* **26**:341–70.

Carter, V., and Rybicki, N. 1986. Resurgence of submersed aquatic macrophytes in the Tidal Potomac River, Maryland, Virginia, and the District of Columbia. *Estuaries* **9**(4B):368–75.

Carter, V., Rybicki, N. B., and Hammerschlag, R. 1991. Effects of submersed macrophytes on dissolved oxygen, pH, and temperature under different conditions of wind, tide, and bed structure. *Journal of Freshwater Ecology* **6**:121–33.

Cheng, I.-J., Levinton, J. S., McCartney, M., Martinez, D., and Weissburg, M. J. 1993. A bioassay approach to seasonal variation in the nutritional value of sediment. *Marine Ecology Progress Series* **94**:275–85.

Chilton, E. W. 1990. Macroinvertebrate communities associated with three aquatic macrophytes (*Ceratophyllum demersum, Myriophyllum spicatum,* and *Vallisneria americana*) in Lake Onalaska, Wisconsin. *Journal of Freshwater Ecology* **5**:455–66.

Cole, J. J., Caraco, N. F., and Peierls, B. 1992. Phytoplankton primary production in the tidal freshwater Hudson River, New York (USA). *Verhandlungen der Internationalen Vereinigun fur Theoretische und Angewandte Limonologie* **24**:1715–1719.

Coote, T. W., Schmidt, R. E., and Caraco, N. 2001. Use of a periodically anoxic *Trapa natans* bed by fishes in the Hudson River, in J. R. Waldman and W. C. Nieder (eds.), *Final Reports of the Tibor T. Polgar Fellowship Program, 2000.* Hudson River Foundation, Section IV:1–20.

Cyr, H., and Downing, J. A. 1988a. Empirical relationships of phytomacrofaunal abundance to plant biomass and macrophyte bed characteristics. *Canadian Journal of Fisheries and Aquatic Sciences* **45**:976–84.

1988b. The abundance of phytophilous invertebrates on different species of submersed macrophytes. *Freshwater Biology* **20**:365–74.

Dennison, W. C., Orth, R. J., Moore, K. A., Stevenson, J. C., Carter, V., Kollar, S., Bergstrom, P. W., and Batiuk, R. A. 1993. Assessing water quality with submersed aquatic vegetation. *BioScience* **43**:86–94.

Eckblad, J. V., Volden, C. S., and Weilgart, L. S. 1984. Allochthonous drift from backwaters to the main channel of the Mississippi River. *American Midland Naturalist* **111**:16–22.

Feldman, R. S. 2001. Taxonomic and size structure of phytophilous macroinvertebrate communities in *Vallisneria* and *Trapa* beds of the Hudson River, New York. *Hydrobiologia* **452**:233–45.

Findlay, S., Groffman, P. M., and Dye, S. 2003. Trade-offs among ecosystem functions during restoration: *Phragmites* removal from a tidal freshwater marsh. *Wetland Ecology and Management* **11**:157–65.

Findlay, S., Pace, M. L., and Fischer, D. 1997. Spatial and temporal variability in the lower food web of the tidal freshwater Hudson River. *Estuaries* **19**:866–73.

Findlay, S., Schoeberl, K., and Wagner, B. 1989. Abundance, composition, and dynamics of the invertebrate fauna of a tidal freshwater wetland. *Journal of the North American Benthological Society* **8**:140–8.

Fisher, S. G., and Carpenter, S. R. 1976. Ecosystem and macrophyte primary production of the Fort River, Massachusetts. *Hydrobiologia* **47**:157–87.

Fonseca, M. S., and Fisher, J. S. 1986. A comparison of canopy friction and sediment movement between four species of seagrass with reference to their ecology and restoration. *Marine Ecology Progressive Series* **29**:15–22.

Garritt, R. H., and Howarth, R. W. 1988. Metabolism of submersed aquatic macrophyte beds in a freshwater portion of the Hudson River estuary, in J. Waldman and E. A. Blair (eds.), *Final reports of the Tibor T. Polgar Fellowship Program, 1997.* Hudson River Foundation, New York, NY, Section III:1–47.

Gilchrest, W. R., and Schmidt, R. E. 1998. Comparison of fish communities in open and occluded tidal freshwater tidal wetlands in the Hudson River estuary, in J. R. Waldman and W. C. Nieder (eds.), *Final Reports of the Tibor T. Polgar Fellowship Program, 1997.* Hudson River Foundation, New York, NY, Section IX:1–32.

Hankin, N., and Schmidt, R. E. 1992. Standing crop of fishes in water celery beds in the tidal Hudson River, in J. R. Waldman and W. C. Nieder (eds.), *Final Reports of the Tibor T. Polgar Fellowship Program, 1991.* Hudson River Foundation, New York, NY, Section VIII:1–23.

Harley, M. T., and Findlay, S. E. G. 1994. Photosynthesis-irradiance relationships for three species of submersed macrophytes in the tidal freshwater Hudson River. *Estuaries* **17**:200–205.

Heck, Jr., K. L., Able, K. W., Roman, C. T., and Fahay, M. P. 1995. Composition, abundance, biomass, and production of macrofauna in a New England estuary: Comparisons among eelgrass meadows and other nursery habitats. *Estuaries* **18**:379–89.

Kemp, M. W., Boynton, W. R., and Twilley, R. R. 1984. Influences of submersed vascular plants on ecological processes in upper Chesapeake Bay, in V. S. Kennedy (ed.), *The Estuary as a Filter*. Orlando, FL: Academic Press, pp. 367–94.

Kenworthy, W. J., Zieman, J. C., and Thayer, G. W. 1982. Evidence for the influence of seagrass on the benthic nitrogen cycle in a coastal plain estuary near Beaufort, North Carolina (USA). *Oecologia* **54**:152–8.

Losee, R. F., and Wetzel, R. G. 1988. Water movement within submersed littoral vegetation. *Verhandlungen Internationale Vereinigung für Theoretische und Angewandte Limnologie* **23**:62–6.

Lutz, C., and Strayer, D. 2001. Macroinvertebrates associated with *Vallisneria americana* and *Trapa natans* in Tivoli South Bay, in J. R. Waldman and W. C. Nieder (eds.), *Final Reports of the Tibor T. Polgar Fellowship Program, 2000*. Hudson River Foundation, New York, NY, Section III:1–34.

Malone, T. C. 1977. Environmental regulation of phytoplankton productivity in the lower Hudson River estuary. *Estuaries and Coastal Marine Science* **5**:157–71.

Menzie, C. A. 1979. Growth of the aquatic plant *Myriophyllum spicatum* in a littoral area of the Hudson River estuary. *Aquatic Botany* **6**:365–75.

1980. The chironomid (Insecta: Diptera) and other fauna of a *Myriophyllum spicatum* L. plant bed in the lower Hudson River. *Estuaries* **3**:38–54.

1981. Production ecology of *Cricotopus sylvestris* (Fabricius) (Diptera: Chironomidae) in a shallow estuarine cove. *Limnology and Oceanography* **26**:467–81.

Meyer, B. S., Bell, F. H., Thompson, L. C., and Clay, E. I. 1943. Effect of depth immersion on apparent photosynthesis in submersed macrophytes. *Ecology* **24**:393–9.

Moran, M. A., and Limburg, K. E. 1986. The Hudson River Ecosystem, in K. E. Limburg, M. A. Moran and W. H. McDowell (eds.), *The Hudson River Ecosystem*. New York: Springer-Verlag, pp. 6–39.

Muenscher, W. C. 1937. Aquatic vegetation of the lower Hudson area, in *A Biological Survey of the Lower Hudson Watershed. Supplement to the 26th Annual Report of the New York State Conservation Department*, Albany, NY, pp. 231–48.

Pelczarski, K., and Schmidt, R. E. 1991. Evaluation of a pop net for sampling fishes from water-chestnut beds in the tidal Hudson River, in E. A. Blair and J. R. Waldman (eds.), *Polgar Fellowship Reports of the Hudson River National Estuarine Reserve Program, 1990*. New York, NY, Section V:1–33.

Posey, M. H., Wigand, C., and Stevenson, J. C. 1993. Effects of an introduced aquatic plant, *Hydrilla verticillata*, on benthic communities in the up-

per Chesapeake Bay. *Estuarine Coastal and Shelf Science* **37**:539–55.

Rozas, L. P., and Minello, T. J. 1997. Estimating densities of small fishes and decapod crustaceans in shallow estuarine habitats: A review of sampling design with focus on gear selection. *Estuaries* **20**:199–213.

Rozas, L. P., and Odum, W. E. 1987. Fish and macrocrustacean use of submersed plant beds in tidal freshwater marsh creeks. *Marine Ecology Progress Series* **38**:101–108.

Rybicki, N. B., Jenter, H. L., Carter, V., and Baltzer, R. A. 1997. Observations of tidal flux between a submersed aquatic plant stand and the adjacent channel in the Potomac River near Washington, D.C. *Limnology and Oceanography* **42**:307–317.

Sanford, M. 2000. The effects of water chestnut (*Trapa natans*) reduction on fish communities and sedimentation, in A. R. Berkowitz, S. E. G. Findley, and S. T. A. Pickett (eds.) *Undergraduate Research Reports – Summer 1996 and 1997*. Occasional Publication of the Institute of Ecosystem Studies, Millbrook, NY, Number 14:37–42.

Schmidt, R. E., and Hamilton, A. 1992. Significance of the fishes collected by gill net in the Tivoli South Bay Ecosystem, in E. A. Blair and J. Waldman (eds.), *Final Reports of the Tibor T. Polgar Fellowship Program, 1991*. Hudson River Foundation, New York, NY, Section IX:1–16.

Schmidt, R. E., and Kiviat, E. 1988. *Communities of Larval and Juvenile Fishes Associated with Water-Chestnut, Water Milfoil and Water-Celery in the Tivoli Bays of the Hudson River*. Final Report to the Hudson River Foundation, New York, NY.

Short, F. T., Burdick, D. M., and Kaldy, III, J. E. 1995. Mesocosm experiments quantify the effects of eutrophication on eelgrass, *Zostera marina*. *Limnology and Oceanography* **40**:740–9.

Short, F. T., and Burdick, D. M. 1996. Quantifying eelgrass habitat loss in relation to housing development and nitrogen loading in Waquoit Bay, Massachusetts. *Estuaries* **19**:730–9.

Simpson, K. W., Fagnani, J. P., Denicola, D. M., and Bode, R. W. 1986. Organism-substrate relationships in the main channel of the lower Hudson River. *Journal of the North American Benthological Society* **5**:41–57.

Smith, C. S., and Adams, M. S. 1986. Phosphorus transfer from sediments by *Myriophyllum spicatum*. *Limnology and Oceanography* **31**:1312–21.

Strayer, D. L., Smith, L. C., and Hunter, D. C. 1998. Effects of the zebra mussel (*Dreissena polymorpha*) invasion on the macrobenthos of the freshwater tidal Hudson River. *Canadian Journal of Zoology* **76**:419–25.

Stevenson, J. C., Staver, L. W., and Staver, K. W. 1993. Water quality associated with survival of submersed aquatic vegetation along an estuarine gradient. *Estuaries* **16**:346–61.

Strayer, D. L., Caraco, N. F., Cole, J. J., Findlay, S., and Pace, M. L. 1999. Transformations of freshwater ecosystems by bivalves – A case study of zebra mussels in the Hudson River. *BioScience* **49**:19–27.

Strayer, D. L., and Smith, L. S. 2001. The zoobenthos of the freshwater tidal Hudson River and its response to the zebra mussel invasion. *Archiv fuer Hydrobilogie Supplement* **139**:1–152.

Svenson, H. K. 1924. Notes on some plants of eastern New York. *Rhodora* **26**:221–2.

1935. Plants of the estuary of the Hudson River. *Torreya* **35**:117–25.

Thorp, A. G., Jones, R. C., and Kelso, D. P. 1997. A comparison of water-column macroinverte-brate communities in beds of differing submersed aquatic vegetation in the tidal freshwater Potomac River. *Estuaries* **20**:86–95.

Titus, J. E., and Adams, M. S. 1979. Coexistence and the comparative light relations of the submersed macrophytes *Myriophyllum spicatum* L. and *Vallisneria americana* Michx. *Oecologia* **40**:273–86.

Ward, L. G., Kemp, W. M., and Boynton, W. R. 1984. The influence of waves and seagrass communities on suspended particulates in an estuarine embayment. *Marine Geology* **59**:85–103.

Wigand, C., Stevenson, J. C., and Cornwell, J. C. 1997. Effects of different submersed macrophytes on sediment biogeochemistry. *Aquatic Botany* **56**:233–44.

Wigand, C., Finn, M., Findlay, S., and Fischer, D. 2001. Submersed macrophyte effects on nutrient exchange in riverine sediments. *Estuaries* **24**:398–406.

18 Long-Term and Large-Scale Patterns in the Benthic Communities of New York Harbor

Robert M. Cerrato

ABSTRACT Regional benthic surveys have been conducted in the Lower Bay Complex (Lower Bay, Raritan Bay, and Sandy Hook Bay) over a four-decade period from 1957–95. The data showed that the benthos is broadly structured by the sedimentary and hydrographic regime into a north-south pattern. Species associated with muddy sediments dominated Raritan and Sandy Hook Bays and a sand fauna was prevalent in Lower Bay. Both assemblages were dominated by sessile surface depositing feeders and suspension feeders. While faunal associations have remained stable over time, community structure was characterized by high annual variability, and there was clear evidence of habitat changes over several decades. Detailed analysis of benthic community structure was hampered by a number of problems including: 1) high annual variability, 2) differences in sampling methods among regional studies, 3) goodness-of-fit problems in the multivariate analyses, and 4) weak faunal-environmental relationships.

Introduction

The Lower Bay Complex is a triangular body of water that is bounded by Brooklyn, the Atlantic Ocean and Sandy Hook on the east, New Jersey to the south, and Staten Island to the west (Fig. 18.1). It consists of three connected bays: Lower Bay, Raritan Bay, and Sandy Hook Bay. It is a generally shallow, well-mixed estuary, with only dredged ship channels, sand mining areas, and the region near the Narrows exceeding 8 m in depth. Annual

bottom water temperatures range from about 2° to greater than 24°C. Salinity along the Sandy Hook to Rockaway Beach transect reflects coastal ocean values at 32 practical salinity units (psu) but declines by as much as 10 psu both towards the Narrows and the Raritan River. A clockwise eddy off Great Kills effectively separates the Raritan River and Hudson River flows, creating different hydrographic regimes in the north (Lower Bay) and south (Raritan and Sandy Hook Bays) (Jeffries, 1962). Bottom sediments cover a full range of grain sizes from coarse gravel/shell/sand areas to fine-grained muds. Sand predominates the sediments of Lower Bay, while Raritan and Sandy Hook Bays tend to be muddy.

The Lower Bay Complex receives water from the Atlantic Ocean and mixes it with fresher water coming from many regions in the New York–New Jersey Harbor area (NYCDEP, 2000). Not only is it downstream from the Hudson and Raritan Rivers, but it also receives water from Jamaica Bay, western Long Island Sound via the East River and Upper Bay, and the Passaic and Hackensack Rivers via Newark Bay, Upper Bay and Arthur Kill (NYCDEP, 2000). This water carries a wide variety of substances, including inorganic and organic nutrients, inorganic particles, living and dead organic particles, and contaminants. These substances are altered within the Lower Bay Complex by a number of physical (e.g., dilution, sedimentation), chemical (e.g., adsorption, dissolution, oxidation, reduction), and biological (e.g., ingestion, assimilation) processes. The Lower Bay Complex is also a conduit for fish migrating into and out of the New York-New Jersey Harbor region.

Within the Lower Bay Complex, the distribution of benthic animals, i.e., those animals living on or within the bottom, varies both in space and in time. Benthic species are adapted for an association with the substrate and hydrodynamic regime in which they live (Parsons, Takahashi, and Hargrave, 1984; Barry and Dayton, 1991). Thus, barnacles are abundant only in areas with hard surfaces such as rock or shell and adequate water flow, while deposit feeding marine worms tend to be common in muddy sediments. Additional variability in the fauna is caused by physical fluctuations that are characteristic of temperate estuaries and coastal marine

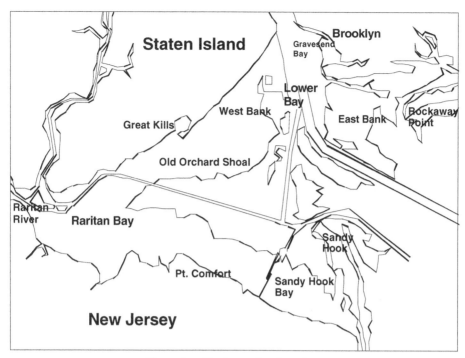

Figure 18.1. The Lower Bay Complex.

systems. Extremes in temperature, large changes in salinity, tidal scour, storm erosion, and other natural processes all represent natural disturbances that affect benthic organisms. The annual range in bottom water temperature in the Lower Bay Complex, for example, is as large as in any marine environment. Benthic communities are also patchy in space and time because of the effects of biotic factors such as competition, predation, variability in larval recruitment, and the fact that benthic organisms, especially those living in soft sediments, alter the physical and chemical properties of their associated substrate by their feeding and burrowing activities (Johnson, 1970; Rhoads, 1974; Thrush, 1991). As a result of variations in physical and biotic processes, benthic community structure in nearshore, temperate environments has been described as a spatial and temporal mosaic (e.g., Johnson, 1970; Rhoads, McCall, and Yingst, 1978).

Anthropogenic activity adds still another source of disturbance to benthic communities in New York-New Jersey Harbor. The Lower Bay Complex is surrounded by one of the largest urban and industrial regions in the world and has been subjected to considerable anthropogenic impacts

in the form of raw sewage discharges, hypoxia, oil spills, and dredging (NYCDEP, 2000). Jeffries (1962), for example, described Raritan Bay as one of the most polluted coastal areas in the United States. Most measures of sediment contaminants are higher than average in New York – New Jersey Harbor when compared to other locations in the mid-Atlantic (Adams et al., 1998).

The benthic fauna of the Lower Bay Complex has been more extensively studied than any other benthic community in the New York-New Jersey Harbor area. Several of the benthic studies (Dean, 1975; McGrath, 1974; Stainken, McCormick, and Multer, 1984; Cerrato, Bokuniewicz, and Wiggins, 1989; Adams, O'Connor, and Weisberg, 1998; NOAA-USACE, 2001) were regional in scope and attempted to cover substantial portions of the area (Table 18.1). Interestingly, these studies span a period of over four decades, from 1957 to 1995, providing the potential to examine both large-scale spatial and long-term temporal patterns in benthic community structure.

In this chapter, I will use those regional surveys that are the most compatible in terms of sampling methods to examine the large-scale spatial

Table 18.1. Characteristics of regional studies of the Lower Bay Complex

Study	Grab sampling device	Sieve size	Sampling period	Number of locations	Sampling distribution
Dean (1975)	0.1 m² Peterson or van Veen	1.5 mm	Summer 1957 Summer 1958 Summer 1959 Summer 1960	52 66 60 15	Raritan Bay (75%), Lower and Sandy Hook Bays (25%)
McGrath (1974)	0.1 m² Smith-McIntyre	1.0 mm	Jan.–Feb. 1973 April 1973 July 1973 October 1973 February 1974	65 15 18 15 8	Lower Bay Complex (1 nm spacing) Sandy Hook Bay Sandy Hook Bay Sandy Hook Bay Sandy Hook Bay
Stainken et al. (1984)	0.1 m² Smith-McIntyre	10.0 mm	June 1979– May 1980	65	Lower Bay Complex (McGrath's stations)
Cerrato (unpublished)	0.1 m² Smith-McIntyre	1.0 mm	August 1983	59	Lower Bay Complex (most of McGrath's stations)
Cerrato et al. (1989)	0.1 m² Smith-McIntyre	1.0 mm	April 1986 July 1986 October 1986 January 1987	114 114 114 114	Lower Bay Complex (most of McGrath's stations plus others)
NOAA-USACE (2001)	0.04 m² Shipek	0.5 mm	October 1994 June 1995	171 184	Lower Bay Complex
Adams et al. (1998)	0.04 m² modified van Veen	0.5 mm	Summer 1993 Summer 1994	14 14	Random within Lower Bay Complex

and long-term temporal community structure of the benthic fauna in the Lower Bay Complex. I will try to characterize community membership in general terms, attempt to relate community structure to the physical environment, and finally, describe how community structure has changed over time. In addition, I will describe the process of analyzing large faunal data sets and assess the suitability of the techniques commonly used.

Methods

Unfortunately, no two regional studies used exactly the same methods (Table 18.1). There are differences in sampling locations, season of collection, sampling device, screen sizes used to sieve the samples, and taxonomy (since different taxonomists do not always identify an organism the same way). Corrections for differences in methods do not exist, and the differences can have a substantial impact on results. Both Diaz and Boesch (1979) and Berg and Levinton (1984), in trying to compare Dean

(1975) and McGrath (1974), noted that differences in sampling locations, season of collection, and sieve sizes limited the conclusions that could be reached. Thus, any approach to comparing the regional benthic surveys must be able to overcome differences in sampling methods.

Because of large differences in methods, I will not consider Stainken et al. (1984) and Adams et al. (1998) in detail. The Stainken et al. (1984) study enumerated only very large benthic animals, and it did not provide results that can be reasonably compared to other studies. Adams et al. (1998) sampled randomly, and there was little overlap in locations between years or with other studies. To circumvent other sampling differences, I will take advantage of three factors. The survey by Cerrato et al. (1989) utilized methods that made it comparable to most of regional surveys that preceded it. It is also a good match to NOAA-USACE (2001) where both season and locations overlap, leaving only sieve size (0.5 mm vs. 1 mm) and identification differences. Secondly, species will be assigned to functional groups to reduce the effect of taxonomic differences. Finally, I will use a method called a Mantel test to compare the data sets in an indirect way that should be less sensitive to differences in methods.

Data from the regional studies consist of counts of individuals for each species present in the samples. Since there are hundreds of species and in some of the studies more than a hundred sampling locations involved, these data sets are unwieldy to examine in raw form and must be summarized in a way that allows community structure analysis. As a first step to examining large data sets, investigators often identify species that were representative of the diverse life histories present and good indicators of community structure and community change. In the present study, I assembled species lists from each regional survey using a variety of criteria and then formed a composite list. Criteria included identifying numerically abundant, cosmopolitan, and commercial species, species with interesting life history attributes, those sensitive to anthropogenic stress, important prey species, and those contributing most to community structure based on the multivariate analyses described below.

In addition to analyzing the data at the level of individual taxa, species in each data set were also assigned to functional groups on the basis of similar lifestyles. Tabulating a large taxonomically diverse benthic assemblage into functional groups loses information since the abundances of many species are added together. Functional groups do, however, reduce taxonomic discrepancies between studies and considerably reduce data sets to a smaller number of ecologically meaningful descriptors. Criteria for assigning species vary but it seems reasonable to consider the animal's primary feeding mode combined with whether the organism was infaunal or epifaunal, whether it constructed a tube or was free living, and whether it was mobile or sessile. These criteria merge two prior attempts (Woodin and Jackson, 1979; Fauchild and Jumars, 1979) at classifying the marine benthos in terms of similar lifestyles.

Most ecologists summarize large data sets for further analysis by calculating an index of ecological resemblance or association between the sampling sites or species present (Legendre and Legendre, 1998). In this study, the Bray-Curtis index was used:

$$D = \frac{\sum_{j=1}^{n} |x_{1j} - x_{2j}|}{\sum_{j=1}^{n} (x_{1j} + x_{2j})}$$

If the benthic communities at two sampling locations are being compared, the x_{ij} are the abundances (usually root or log transformed to decrease the influence of dominants) of each species present at each location, and the approach is called normal analysis. If associations between two species are being compared, the x_{ij} are abundances (again usually transformed) of the species at each sampling location in the study, and the approach is called inverse analysis. The Bray-Curtis index varies between 0 and 1, with 0 representing perfect ecological resemblance, and 1 being no similarity. When calculated for all pairs of sampling stations or species, the values can be assembled together to form a matrix of index values, called an ecological resemblance matrix.

Ordination and cluster analysis are two common, multivariate methods used to visualize relationships contained in an ecological resemblance matrix (Field, Clarke, and Warwick, 1982; Legendre and Legendre, 1998). Ordination attempts to plot the sampling stations or species in two- or three-dimensions such that the distances between points are related to the values in the ecological resemblance matrix. Cluster analysis combines stations or species into groups based on the similarity of their ecological resemblance values. Goodness-of-fit criteria exist for both methods to evaluate how well they represent the original resemblance matrix (Rohlf, 1993).

Much like the sampling methods, no two investigators studying the Lower Bay Complex used the same data analysis methods. In the present study, I attempted to examine the regional studies using a common set of multivariate methods. Abundance data were $\log_e (x + 1)$ transformed and relationships were determined using the Bray-Curtis index. Data sets for inverse analysis were reduced to eliminate rare species (<5% of a sample at all stations in entire data set) as suggested by Field et al. (1982). Numerical analysis consisted of both UPGMA (Unweighted Pair-Group Method using Arithmetic averages) clustering and ordination by nonmetric multidimensional scaling (MDS) (Legendre and Legendre, 1998). Environmental data were standardized and matrices of Euclidean distances were calculated.

In the present study, one additional technique called a Mantel test was used to examine relationships among data sets (Mantel, 1967). In the Mantel test, two resemblance matrices (e.g., sets of Bray-Curtis indices for January 1973 and January 1984 data sets) are tested for correspondence. The statistic calculated is a correlation coefficient that ranges in value from −1 to +1. Values close to +1 or −1 indicate strong positive or negative relationships, respectively. A value near zero indicates no relationship. If the resemblance matrices were calculated for normal analysis, the Mantel test determines how well the spatial community distribution, i.e., the habitat structure, matches between the two data sets. For inverse analysis, the test measures the strength of faunal associations by examining whether species or functional groups in the two data sets tend to co-occur in the same way. The Mantel test compares the relationships among sites or species and not the raw data directly. It is, therefore, somewhat less sensitive to differences in sampling methods and taxonomy than a direct comparison.

Results

BENTHIC COMMUNITY STRUCTURE

Combining all regional studies, a total of 328 benthic species have been identified in the Lower Bay Complex. The dominant taxonomic groups are polychaetes (43 percent), mollusks (17 percent), and crustaceans (31 percent). Of the taxa identified, ninety-five species emerged as being representative of the diverse life histories present and/or good indicators of community structure and community change (Tables 18.2 and 18.3). Several taxa (*Polydora cornuta* and *P. ligni*; *Ampelisca* sp. and *A. abdita*) were assigned different names but were probably the same organism. Because of the different methods used in the surveys, it is best to restrict comparisons to surveys with similar season and sieve size. For that purpose, both the 1.0 and 1.5 mm sieve results for July 1986 are included from Cerrato et al. (1989). Comparisons matching season and sieve size are always possible between the 1986–87 data and earlier surveys. Comparing the 1994–95

data to earlier studies is more problematic. Many striking differences occur for small organisms (for example, oligochaetes, the polychaetes *Mediomastus* spp. and *Streblospio benedicti*, the bivalve *Gemma gemma*, and the amphipod *Ampelisca abdita*), suggesting a large sieve size effect.

The composition of species in Tables 18.2 and 18.3 held few surprises and generally included species common to estuarine and coastal regions of the Northeast and Mid-Atlantic. The most abundant organism in the Lower Bay Complex was the amphipod *Ampelisca abdita*. This is a small (4–8 mm), tube building, surface deposit feeder that was often found at average densities exceeding 1,000 per m^2. It often represented >50% of the fauna collected and was commonly present at 70 to 90 percent of the sampling stations. Its tube building activities substantially modify the physical characteristics of the bottom, increasing the deposition of fine-grained sediments by trapping and incorporating particles into densely-packed tube mats (Rhoads, 1974). *A. abdita* is sensitive to pollutants and is extensively used in sediment toxicity tests (Redmond et al., 1994). It is an extremely important food source for winter flounder (*Pseudopleuronectes americanus*), windowpane flounder (*Scophthalmus aquosus*), scup (*Stenotomus chrysops*), weakfish (*Cynoscion regalis*), and silver hake (*Merluccius bilinearis*) (Franz and Tancredi, 1992; Steimle et al., 2000).

The polychaete *Streblospio benedicti* was another dominant. *S. benedicti* was widespread throughout the region and was found to occur on average at 37 percent of stations sampled during the regional studies. In June 1995, it was present at 97 percent of the sampling stations. Like *A. abdita*, it is a small (20 × 1 mm), tube building, surface deposit feeder (McCall, 1977). It is found in a variety of sediments and is highly opportunistic, i.e., an early colonizer on disturbed habitats with the ability to grow, mature, and reproduce quickly (McCall, 1977). *S. benedicti* is also tolerant of high levels of organic enrichment, organic contaminants, and low concentrations of dissolved oxygen (Llanso, 1991; Chandler, Shipp, and Donelan, 1997). Other widespread or cosmopolitan species, along with the average percent of stations at which they were found, included *Mulinia lateralis* (53 percent), *Ilyanassa trivittata* (50 percent), *Glycera*

Table 18.2. Species representative of the diverse life histories present in the Lower Bay Complex and good indicators of community structure and community change

Species	Functional group	Numerical dominant	Cosmopolitan species	Important as prey	MDS indicator	Other criteria
Ceriantheopsis americanus	ITSS				x	A
Metridium senile	ENSS	x				
Unidentified nematode	INMO	x			x	
Unidentified oligochaete	INMDi	x	x		x	
Peloscolex intermedius	INMDi	x				A
Peloscolex gabriellae	INMDi	x			x	A
Asabellides oculata	ITSDs	x	x	x	x	A
Capitella capitata	ITMDi	x				A,O
Capitellid A	ITMDi	x			x	A
Heteromastus filiformis	INMDi	x	x		x	A
Mediomastus ambiseta	ITMDi	x				A
Mediomastus sp.	ITMDi	x	x			A
Unidentified cirratulid	INMDs	x	x			
Cirratulus grandis	INMDs	x			x	
Tharyx acutus	INMDs	x	x			A
Pherusa affinis	INMDs		⟩	x	x	A
Glycera americana	INMC	x	x	x	x	
Glycera dibranchiata	INMO		x	x	x	
Goniadella gracilis	INMC				x	
Microphthalmus aberrans	INMDi	x			x	
Lumbrineris tenuis	INMO				x	
Magelona rosea	INMDs				x	
Nephtys bucera	INMC				x	
Nephtys incisa	INMC	x	x		x	E
Nephtys picta	INMC	x			x	
Nereis succinea	ITMDs	x	x		x	
Haploscloplos fragilis	INMDi		x		x	A
Haploscloplos robustus	INMDi					A
Asychis elongata	INMDi	x			x	
Pectinaria gouldii	ITMDi	x	x		x	
Eteone heteropoda	ENMC	x	x		x	A
Eteone lactea	ENMC		x		x	
Eumida sanguinea	ENMC	x	x		x	A
Phyllodoce groenlandica	ENMC					A
Harmothoe extenuata	ENMC				x	
Lepidonotus squamatus	ENMC				x	
Sabellaria vulgaris	ETSS	x				
Hydroides dianthus	ETSS				x	
Polydora ligni	ITMDs	x	x		x	A
Polydora cornuta	ITMDs	x	x		x	A
Spio filicornis	ITMDs	x			x	
Spio setosa	ITMDs		x			
Streblospio benedicti	ITMDs	x	x		x	A,O
Prionospio cirriferra	ITMDs					A
Autolytus cornutus	ENMC				x	
Ritaxis punctostriatus	ENMC	x	x		x	
Crepidula fornicata	ENSS	x	x		x	

(continued)

Table 18.2 (*continued*)

Species	Functional group	Numerical dominant	Cosmopolitan species	Important as prey	MDS indicator	Other criteria
Crepidula convexa	ENSS	x			x	
Crepidula plana	ENSS	x			x	
Ilyanassa obsoleta	ENMO	x	x		x	
Ilyanassa trivittata	ENMO	x	x			
Turbonilla sp.	ENMC	x			x	
Mulinia lateralis	INSS	x	x		x	A
Spisula solidissima	INMS	x		x	x	D,C
Mya arenaria	INSS	x	x		x	A,C
Modiolus modiolus	INSS	x				
Mytilis edulus	ENSS	x	x	x		A,C
Yoldia limatula	INSDi				x	E
Nucula proxima	INMDi	x	x			I
Crassostrea virginica	ENSS					C
Ensis directus	INMS	x	x	x	x	E
Macoma balthica	INSDs		x		x	A
Tellina agilis	INSDs	x	x		x	D,I
Gemma gemma	INSS	x				
Mercenaria mercenaria	INSS	x	x	x	x	C
Ampelisca abdita	ITSDs	x	x	x		D,O
Ampelisca vadorum	ITSDs					D
Ampelisca sp.	ITSDs	x	x	x	x	D,O
Unciola irrorata	ETMDs					D
Unciola serrata	ETMDs	x	x	x	x	
Corophium tuberculatum	ETMS	x	x	x		A
Erichthonius brasiliensis	ETMS					D
Gammarus lawrencianus	ENMO			x	x	
Acanthohaustorius millsi	INMDi				x	
Acanthohaustorius similis	INMDi				x	
Bathyporeia parkeri	INMDi				x	
Parahaustorius longimerus	INMDi				x	
Protohaustorius deichmannae	INMDi	x			x	
Protohaustorius wigleyi	INMDi				x	
Elasmopus levis	ENMDs	x	x		x	
Paraphoxus spinosa	INMDi	x				
Harpinia propinqua	INMDi				x	
Rheopoxynius epistomus	INMDi				x	
Stenothoe minuta	ENMDs				x	
Balanus improvisus	ENSS	x			x	
Heteromysis formosa	ENMO				x	
Neomysis americana	ENMO		x	x	x	
Cancer irroratus	ENMO			x	x	
Crangon septemspinosa	ENMO		x	x	x	
Pagurus longicarpus	ENMO			x		
Palaemonetes pugio	ENMO			x		
Callinectes sapidus	ENMO			x		C
Ovalipes ocellatus	ENMO			x		
Neopanope texana	ENMO	x			x	

Species	Functional group	Numerical dominant	Cosmopolitan species	Important as prey	MDS indicator	Other criteria
Neopanope sayi	ENMO			x		
Cyathura polita	ENMO				x	

Numerical dominants are species that represent >1% of the total fauna collected in any regional study. Cosmopolitan species are those present at 50% or more of the stations in any regional study. Important prey species were identified from an analysis of fish and lobster diets by Steimle et al. (2000). MDS indicators are species that are correlated ($r \geq 0.4$) with one or more multidimensional scaling axes during any one regional study. Other criteria: A = advantaged and D = disadvantaged by stress as determined by Pearson and Rosenberg (1978), Diaz and Boesch (1984), Diaz and Rosenberg (1995), and Adams et al. (1998). C = commercially important. O = opportunist, I = intermediate, and E = equilibrium species as identified by McCall (1977). Functional group codes are interpreted as follows. First character: I = infaunal and E = epifaunal. Second character: T = tube building and N = nontubiculous. Third character: M = motile and S = sessile. Last character: C = carnivore. Di = infaunal deposit feeder, Ds = surface deposit feeder, O = omnivore, S = suspension feeder.

americana (42 percent), *Tellina agilis* (41 percent), *Heteromastus filiformis* (39 percent), *Mya arenaria* (37 percent), *Pectinaria gouldii* (36 percent), *Nereis succinea* (34 percent), and *Mercenaria mercenaria* (31 percent). The hard clam, *Mercenaria mercenaria*, represents an important fishery species in the Lower Bay Complex. Because Lower Bay waters do not meet coliform standards, hard clams have been transplanted to other areas in New York and depurated in New Jersey prior to marketing.

The benthic fauna of the Lower Bay Complex represent twenty-three functional groups, based upon life habit and feeding traits (Table 18.4). These groups consist of from two (ITSC and ENMS) to sixty-three (ENMO) species. Nineteen of the groups are represented by species in Table 18.2. The groups that are sometimes missing (ENSC, ITSC, ITSDi, and ITSS) were absent during many of the regional studies, and when present were low in abundance. The two infaunal, tubiculous, surface deposit feeding groups ITSDs and ITMDs were particularly abundant. Often more than half of the individuals collected during a survey were from one of these two groups. The next most abundant functional groups were two sessile suspension feeding groups INSS and ENSS; they represented about 30 percent of the total fauna collected during the regional surveys. Omnivore and carnivore groups generally had low abundances.

Benthic community structure in the Lower Bay Complex follows, in a broad way, a north-south pattern that corresponds to the large-scale sedimentary and hydrodynamic regime (McGrath, 1974). The southern half of the Bay is dominated by muddy sediments running in a southeast to north-

west direction from Sandy Hook Bay to Raritan Bay (Fig. 18.2). In the northern half of the Bay, the sediments are predominantly sandy, except for muddy pit areas associated with dredging activity and a region in Gravesend Bay. The hydrographic regimes in the northern and southern parts of the Lower Bay Complex created by the eddy off Great Kills (Jeffries, 1962) closely parallel the sediment pattern (Dean, 1975).

The influence of the north-south physical regime in the Lower Bay Complex is clearly evident in the distribution of the amphipods *Ampelisca abdita* and *Corophium tuberculatum* and the blue mussel *Mytilus edulis* (Fig. 18.2). The two amphipods are associated with muddy sediments, while the blue mussel is restricted to sandy areas. Other species consistently more abundant either in the northern or southern region are given in Figure 18.3. With the exception of several dominants (i.e., the amphipods *Ampelisca abdita*, *Unciola* spp., and *Corophium tuberculatum*, and the mud crab *Neopanope texana*), most amphipod and decapod species have a higher frequency of occurrence and higher abundance in the northern region. In particular, haustorid and phoxocephalid amphipods, both of which are motile, infaunal, deposit feeders, are considerably less abundant in the south. All the decapods are omnivores and are associated with sandy areas. McGrath (1974) and Steimle and Caracciolo-Ward (1989) have discussed whether the distribution of these crustacean groups is natural or due to anthropogenic factors. The persistence of the distribution throughout all of the regional studies suggests that the differences are related to sediment preferences.

Table 18.3. Species representative of the diverse life histories present in the Lower Bay Complex and good indicators of community structure and community change

Sieve Size (mm) = Species	1957 Sum. 1.5	1958 Sum. 1.5	1959 Sum. 1.5	1960 Sum. 1.5	1973 Jan. 1.0	1973 April 1.0	1973 July 1.0	1973 Oct. 1.0	1974 Feb. 1.0	1983 Aug. 1.0	1986 April 1.0	1986 July 1.0	1986 July 1.5	1986 July 1.0	1986 Oct. 1.0	1987 Jan. 1.0	1994 Oct. 0.5	1995 June 0.5
Anthozoa:																		
Cerianthteopsis americanus																		
Metridium senile					17.6						0.4	0.4	0.5	0.4	0.1	0.2		
Aschelminthes:																		
Unidentified nematode							2.2	4.0	13.5	3.2	1.1	2.0	1.6	2.0	1.0	0.7		
Oligochaeta:																		
Unidentified oligochaete		0.0	0.1		2.9	8.3	66.3	72.0	17.3		0.0						479.2	776.8
Peloscolex intermedius					19.2	1.8	13.1	8.3	12.8									
Peloscolex gabriellae					2.5	5.1	7.2	42.3	1.3									
Polychaeta:																		
Asabellides oculata		4.3	0.2		0.2		0.2			40.7	516.1	127.9	126.4	127.9	65.7	49.7		
Capitella capitata					0.2	0.3	0.6			66.9	53.0	1.5	1.1		0.4	3.2	0.4	
Capitellid A	0.1	4.3	0.9	0.3													1.5	
Heteromastus filiformis	0.7	2.6	8.0	18.3	2.2	1.1	1.9	2.7	6.8		112.3	89.8	84.8		58.9	127.7		12.2
Mediomastus ambiseta							0.2	4.3									305.1	172.0
Mediomastus sp.																	369.3	136.3
Unidentified cirratulid					0.1												1,463.5	3,161.1
Cirratulus grandis											30.3	51.8	51.5	65.7			153.4	509.8
Tharyx acutus	0.1				47.6	1.6		7.3	4.4	202.0	22.9	5.9	3.9				0.1	117.0
Pherusa affinis		0.1			0.1		1.1			0.8	2.8	18.7	18.3	18.7	2.3	2.8	0.7	21.5
Glycera americana	1.6	3.3	4.0	8.0	3.8	2.5	7.0	7.7	6.6	6.4	37.6	24.0	23.6	24.0	20.7	21.9	96.2	26.4
Glycera dibranchiata	1.3	1.1	2.3	4.7	2.9	0.8	0.6	0.7	2.0	21.5	17.5	28.9	28.2	28.2	32.0	27.7	1.2	8.6
Goniadella gracilis					0.1		0.6	8.0										
Microphthalmus aberrans						1.3	20.6	2.7				0.0	0.4	0.0		0.0	0.8	
Lumbrineris tenuis	1.8	3.2	17.7		0.1	0.2				5.4	0.1						0.8	0.8
Magelona rosea					0.6		10.6			3.1	1.9	1.5	1.5		0.8	0.9		
Nephtys bucera		0.8	0.4	1.0	0.3	1.0		1.3		0.2	0.6	0.0	0.0	0.0	0.0	0.0		0.1
Nephtys incisa	0.8	0.5	0.4	1.0	4.8	8.9	9.0	8.7	2.8	1.4	0.6	0.3	0.3	0.4	0.4	0.3	1.6	9.5
Nephtys picta		2.5	1.2	8.0	4.2	0.3	0.2			24.4	27.6	24.5	24.0	24.0	11.6	18.2	4.2	18.2
Nereis succinea	10.2	1.1	1.0	25.0	12.5	0.7	3.1	49.7		29.0	11.6	9.4	8.9	8.9	10.9	17.4	12.4	10.1
Haploscloplos fragilis	0.8				0.8						0.3	0.5	0.5		2.0	2.3	9.8	0.4
Haploscloplos robustus															0.4	1.9		0.8
Asychis elongata						2.5			0.6		4.5	4.6	4.5			2.7	1.3	1.6

Pectinaria gouldii	7.9	1.8	6.7	2.7	5.2	2.2	31.0	12.3	18.8	2.8	14.3	13.7	28.9	11.8	18.3	3.0
Eteone heteropoda	0.1			0.4	0.1	29.5	5.3	0.5	2.2	0.0	10.0	7.9	0.0		65.2	94.8
Eteone lactea	0.4	0.8	2.6						63.7		1.1			7.7		
Eumida sanguinea	2.1	0.5	0.4	24.7	6.9		0.3		4.6	7.4	10.2	8.1	3.3	2.0		131.3
Phyllodoce groenlandica		0.1														
Harmothoe extenuata	1.9	0.3			0.3	0.2			2.9	29.6	43.2	40.8	28.8	6.0		8.8
Lepidonotus squamatus	0.3				0.1				17.1	3.2	11.8	10.8	26.2	9.3		
Sabellaria vulgaris	0.5	0.7	1.9	10.7	60.8	0.6		0.7	123.1	6.9	26.6	26.4	25.4	43.1	1.0	61.8
Hydroides dianthus	0.1								1.0	2.7	3.1	3.1	20.0	15.6	273.5	
Polydora ligni	3.9	0.7					0.7		7.3	0.5	5.6	4.3	0.7	0.8	7.5	4.2
Polydora cornuta		11.0	25.1	45.0	3.2	4.5	28.3	3.1							33.6	541.7
Spio filicornis					565.9	358.7	2.3	9.9								
Streblospio benedicti	0.4	5.5	0.7	0.7	7.5	8.9	250.0	58.3	59.3	52.0	20.7	13.7	13.6	18.0	4,958.9	2,445.0
Prionospio cirrifera		3.8	0.7	29.7	217.9	250.0	0.7									
Autolytus cornutus	0.9	0.1							1.8		0.9	0.7	1.2	0.2	1.5	20.1
Gastropoda:																
Ritaxis punctostriatus	1.1	2.4	8.0	363.7		249.0	424.3	15.3	0.5	0.1	0.1	5.5	3.7		0.1	
Crepidula fornicata		0.5		0.5	5.1	27.3	26.3	2.4	19.0	42.5	42.2	100.6	83.1	346.1	59.1	
Crepidula convexa			1.0	14.8	0.5	0.7	0.3	13.9								
Crepidula plana	0.3				0.2		0.3	0.7	9.3	27.1	27.0	56.6	30.0	60.4	11.1	
Ilyanassa obsoleta	2.1	13.8	18.3	5.2	8.7	10.7	8.5	3.2	4.7	8.2	8.2	11.4	11.1	12.1	10.7	
Ilyanassa trivittata	0.6	2.4	17.3	9.2	2.6	1.3	1.4	17.0	25.7	25.6	28.6	35.2	205.3	120.0		
Turbonilla sp.															0.1	
Bivalvia:																
Mulinia lateralis	13.6	20.4	1.3	26.1	66.7	347.3	76.7	61.4	40.4	8.2	8.1	83.9	63.2	911.0	534.4	
Spisula solidissima	35.9			79.4	3.6	4.0	22.2	8.6	43.6	27.1	50.1	10.1	33.9	14.9		
Mya arenaria	54.3	160.6	1,448.6	914.3	1.5	22.0	1,373.2	22.9	125.0	115.6	88.0	58.0	11.7	20.4		
Modiolus modiolus				0.5	12.2											
Mytilis edulus	0.1	0.5	363.7	0.4	8.7	3.3	11.1	13.4	2,310.1	1,142.2	1,141.8	692.2	95.3	7.0	364.9	
Yoldia limatula	0.1	0.3		25.4				0.3	0.0	0.0	0.1	0.1	0.0	0.1	6.8	
Nucula proxima						0.3		0.2	3.4	5.3	4.1	1.6	6.5	1.6	652.0	
Crassostrea virginica	0.6	0.1		0.1					0.1	0.2	0.2	1.6		202.2		
Ensis directus	0.6	12.0	5.3	0.1			2.8	11.2	2.6	6.7	6.7	2.9	6.5	41.1	6.8	
Macoma balthica	1.9	1.0	20.3	0.3						0.1	0.1		1.6	0.1	7.7	
Tellina agilis		12.6	1.5	15.8	1.7	51.2	25.7	50.3	39.2	42.6	37.3	27.8	37.3	79.5	116.3	
Gemma gemma		25.2	2,094.3			23.0			9.4	61.7	30.8	5.3	15.0	688.0	523.5	
Mercenaria mercenaria	1.1	1.1	1.5	2.7	2.8	19.4	6.7	9.3	4.2	5.1	4.6	4.6	5.4	5.3	17.1	14.8

(continued)

Table 18.3 (continued)

Sieve Size (mm) = Species	1957 Sum.	1958 Sum.	1959 Sum.	1960 Sum.	1973 Jan.	1973 April	1973 July	1973 Oct.	1974 Feb.	1983 Aug.	1986 April	1986 July	1986 July	1986 Oct.	1987 Jan.	1994 Oct.	1995 June
	1.5	1.5	1.5	1.5	1.0	1.0	1.0	1.0	1.0	1.0	1.0	1.0	1.5	1.0	1.0	0.5	0.5
Amphipoda:																	
Ampelisca abdita	538.2									309.8	3,516.0	2,319.9	1,601.0	3,799.6	3,116.7	14,012.1	4,629.1
Ampelisca sp.		8.8	32.1	1,694.7		0.2											
Ampelisca vadorum								0.7	0.3	0.3							
Unciola irrorata										2.5	0.9	2.6	0.0	0.1	0.6		
Unciola serrata	19.3	3.9	2.3	128.3	2.5	0.1					23.8	21.5	16.6	25.5	23.2	62.3	51.0
Corophium tuberculatum					1.3					104.4	47.8	838.3	617.5	83.2	55.8	876.3	676.6
Erichthonius brasiliensis										2.4	0.4	1.4	0.8	2.6	1.0	29.2	3.0
Gammarus lawrencianus					1.1	2.2	0.6	0.7		3.1	0.0	0.0					
Acanthohaustorius millsi					0.8					2.9	2.5	0.8	0.6	1.3	2.1	2.1	1.2
Acanthohaustorius similis											0.9	0.4	0.4	1.0	0.9	0.9	
Bathyporeia parkeri											0.4	0.1	0.1	0.4	0.2		
Parahaustorius longimerus											1.7	1.4	1.4	1.8	2.5	1.2	
Protohaustorius deichmannae					14.8						0.4	0.4		2.1	2.1	2.5	0.1
Protohaustorius wigleyi					0.8						2.9		1.1			2.1	0.7
Elasmopus levis		0.1			3.9						11.0	19.0	15.6	138.1	60.6	41.8	2.3
Paraphoxus spinosa			1.1		0.2		0.8			0.2							
Harpinia propinqua							5.6			19.5	43.8	21.7	15.3	40.7	57.9	24.6	
Rheopoxynius epistomus					3.5	2.0	6.7			2.4	3.8	1.5	1.4	11.4	4.6	1.2	1.5
Stenothoe minuta	0.0									25.3				0.0		10.1	
Cirripedia:																	
Balanus improvisus	28.3	20.9	30.0	1.0	44.8	2.7	37.0	114.7	7.5		5.5	57.3	57.3	1.8	4.3		
Mysidacea:																	
Heteromysis formosa								3.3		4.4	0.4	2.1	2.1	21.5	0.6	19.4	1.4
Neomysis americana					0.4	0.2	10.8	5.3		17.6	0.5	2.0	2.0	1.3	0.5	0.1	0.1
Decapoda:																	
Cancer irroratus	0.3				0.2		1.7		0.3	5.4	0.3	16.3	16.3	5.0	1.8	0.7	8.8
Crangon septemspinosa	0.3	0.8	0.3	6.3	1.3	0.3	5.4	4.3	0.7	0.8	0.5	5.2	4.9	0.5	1.0	0.1	2.9
Pagurus longicarpus			0.3		1.5	2.3	0.1	2.0			1.8	1.5	1.5	2.9	4.3		0.4
Palaemonetes pugio														0.1			
Callinectes sapidus		0.3													0.0		
Ovalipes ocellatus								0.7		2.5	0.5	4.3	4.3	0.2	0.2	0.4	
Neopanope texana					4.7	0.1		2.0		1.2	3.9	7.5	7.5	21.4	12.8	1.0	8.2
Neopanope sayi																	
Isopoda:																	
Cyathura polita	3.4	2.7	11.7								6.2	5.0	4.9	12.1	16.4	20.3	13.6

Values are abundance expressed as number of individuals per square meter. Data compiled from regional studies cited in text.

Table 18.4. Functional group abundances expressed as the number of individuals per square meter

	1957 Sum.	1958 Sum.	1959 Sum.	1960 Sum.	1973 Jan.	1973 April	1973 July	1973 Oct.	1974 Feb.	1983 Aug.	1986 April	1986 July	1986 July (1.5 mm)	1986 Oct.	1987 Jan.	1994 Oct.	1995 June
ITSS	0.1		0.1	0.3	0.1						0.9	1.1	1.1	1.3	1.1	13.0	5.6
ITSDi											1.0	0.7	0.7	0.5	0.4	0.1	1.4
ITSDs	539.5		32.5	1,711.7			0.2			350.8	4,032.4	2,448.0	1,727.6	3,801.8	3,020.3	14,049.3	4,652.2
ITSC			0.1		0.2	0.3					0.3	0.1	0.1	0.2	0.1	1.2	0.5
ITMDi	8.1	7.2	3.5	8.7	3.2	5.5	2.9	35.3	13.5	85.8	55.7	15.7	14.8	29.4	15.8	1,853.8	3,313.3
ITMDs	15.3	21.6	31.4	75.0	55.2	22.5	1,156.9	331.7	74.5	143.7	89.8	71.5	57.4	31.0	42.7	5,028.5	3,092.8
INSS	69.0	200.5	3,564.8	918.3	41.6	98.8	95.3	354.0	86.3	1,439.3	81.1	204.2	163.7	191.4	143.8	1,642.4	1,099.0
INSDi			0.3								0.4	0.0	0.0	0.1	0.1	0.1	7.2
INSDs	1.9	13.6	1.8	20.3	15.8	1.8	51.2	23.0	25.7	50.3	45.7	44.9	39.4	29.6	40.1	80.0	116.3
INMS	0.6	41.9	12.0	5.3	1.5	3.9	6.4	4.0	4.0	33.4	11.3	50.3	33.8	53.0	11.8	75.1	25.5
INMDi	2.0	3.9	10.3	43.3	49.1	14.2	59.1	58.0	22.7	63.7	180.5	130.8	116.4	128.4	212.9	1,134.5	1,762.2
INMDs	0.5	2.3	0.4		48.4	1.9	1.7	7.3	4.4	206.4	57.8	78.1	75.8	87.9	82.7	263.3	663.0
INMO	2.3	6.0	7.7	23.7	4.1	10.0	68.4	77.3	19.3	33.7	22.1	34.7	33.2	37.6	29.7	52.9	18.5
INMC	4.5	18.7	19.0	29.0	15.8	13.7	30.9	28.7	9.3	36.1	70.5	52.0	50.9	36.4	44.0	139.5	84.0
ETSS	0.6	0.8	1.9	10.7	60.8	0.6	0.1	0.7	3.8	124.1	9.8	29.7	29.5	45.5	58.7	286.5	102.6
ETMS				15.7	1.5					109.5	48.2	839.7	618.4	85.8	56.8	938.9	692.0
ETMDs	19.3	4.1	2.3	131.0	2.5	0.6	0.2	0.7	0.3	3.4	29.5	31.7	25.9	29.4	26.3	75.1	73.2
ENSS	35.8	72.8	32.1	374.0	83.3	28.9	48.5	150.0	58.6	45.9	2,350.8	1,278.2	1,277.4	855.3	213.6	418.6	511.4
ENSC														0.0		66.7	0.1
ENMS																	0.8
ENMDs		0.1			4.9	0.5	0.1	11.3	0.5	20.5	19.1	26.2	22.3	148.2	67.8	113.6	16.2
ENMO	3.7	8.5	5.7	52.0	15.5	14.5	26.4	28.0	12.5	67.6	44.6	83.2	80.7	112.9	104.4	547.8	354.1
ENMC	3.0	9.2	9.1	30.3	9.5	10.5	32.3	261.0	426.9	31.2	113.2	81.1	72.5	72.3	38.5	377.6	415.1
Overall Abundance	705.8	425.0	3,734.8	3,449.3	413.0	228.5	1,580.7	1,367.0	762.2	2,893.9	7,264.6	5,502.0	4,441.6	5,778.0	4,211.5	27,158.5	17,007.1
Number of stations	52	61	59	15	63	15	18	15	8	59	114	114	114	114	114	171	184

Functional group codes are as follows. First character: I = infaunal and E = epifaunal. Second character: T = tube building and N = nontubiculous. Third character: M = motile and S = sessile. Last character: C = carnivore, Di = infaunal deposit feeder, Ds = surface deposit feeder, O = omnivore, S = suspension feeder.

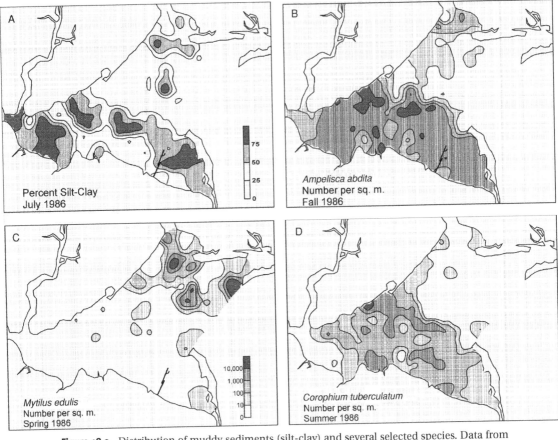

Figure 18.2. Distribution of muddy sediments (silt-clay) and several selected species. Data from Cerrato et al. (1989).

Characterizing the distribution of benthic fauna of the Lower Bay Complex into two broad geographic regimes is, of course, an oversimplification and community structure is more complex. Detailed analyses by Diaz and Boesch (1979), Steimle et al. (1989), and NOAA-USACE (2001) describe between five and ten geographic subdivisions and up to six species groups. My own attempt to examine community structure in the regional studies using a common set of multivariate methods failed. Spatial or habitat relationships were not well represented by MDS ordinations or UPGMA clustering. In most cases, goodness-of-fit measures for the 1959–60, January 1973, and August 1983 data sets were unsatisfactory. These measures were only slightly better, in the fair to good categories, for 1986–87 and 1994–95 data sets. Using functional groups instead of species as descriptors did not improve the goodness-of-fit measures.

Relationships assessed by correlating the faunal and environmental data by Mantel test while significant were also weak (Table 18.5). Thus, interpreting spatial and faunal-environmental associations based on these multivariate techniques was determined to be problematic.

Inverse analyses to examine faunal associations also resulted in a large number of goodness-of-fit problems. Goodness-of-fit measures for analyses with species were either poor or fair. Repeating the inverse analysis using functional groups as descriptors improved the goodness-of-fit only slightly, but it was enough to merit detailed analyses. Several distinct functional group associations were present (Table 18.6). Assemblage A consisted of two epifaunal, nontubiculous functional groups (ENMC and ENSS), a surface deposit feeding group (INMDs), and a suspension feeding group (ETSS). This assemblage was predominantly found in sandy

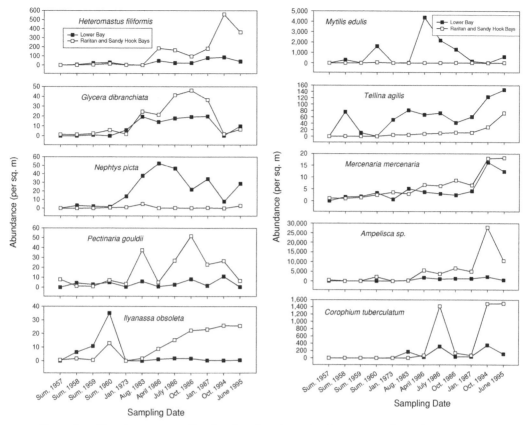

Figure 18.3. Abundance vs. sampling date for selected species. Stations were divided into northern (Lower Bay) and southern (Raritan and Sandy Hook Bay) regions using the mud-sand boundary that runs from southwest of Great Kills to the northern tip of Sandy Hook (Fig. 18.2). No correction was made for differences in sampling methods. Consequently, abundances for *Ampelisca* sp. and *Corophium tuberculatum* were probably 25–30% higher during 1957–60 than indicated. Other species shown were probably not affected by sieve size. Data from regional studies identified in the text.

sediments, and ENSS was the dominant group. Assemblage B (ITSDs, ITMDi, ITMDs, INSS, INSDs, INMS, INMDi, INMO, INMC, ENMO) was found during 1957–60 and consisted of infaunal functional groups of mixed feeding types. This assemblage with a few added groups split into two distinct assemblages (C and D) during the remaining studies. Assemblage C was associated with muddy areas in Raritan and Sandy Hook Bays and assemblage D tended to be more abundant in Lower Bay.

TEMPORAL CHANGE

The benthic fauna in the Lower Bay Complex is characterized by moderate to large seasonal fluctu-

ations. Seasonal changes in abundance can be as much as several orders of magnitude in some locations (Fig. 18.4). The more variable station plotted in Figure 18.4 was located within a pit that had been created by sand mining, and it is likely that annual declines at this location were associated with low dissolved oxygen conditions created by poor flushing and high accumulation of organic matter at the bottom of the pit. The other station in this figure was located in a nearby, shallow sandy area that had never been disturbed by sand mining. Over the entire Lower Bay Complex, the benthic fauna in finer grained sediments tends to be more abundant and to fluctuate more on a seasonal basis than in sandy areas (Figs. 18.1a and 18.5).

Table 18.5. Mantel tests of biotic-environmental relationships. Faunal and environmental data from the regional studies cited in the text. Environmental data included grain-size (% gravel, sand, silt, clay, and median), depth, temperature and salinity when available

	Species as descriptors	Functional groups as descriptors		Species as descriptors	Functional groups as descriptors
Summer 1957	–	–	July 1986	0.430 **	0.344 **
Summer 1958	0.380 **	0.253 **	October 1986	0.336 **	0.301 **
Summer 1959	0.332 **	0.204 **	January 1987	0.369 **	0.303 **
Summer 1960	–	–	October 1994	0.199 **	0.168 **
January 1973	0.354 **	0.301 **	June 1995	0.052 ns	0.008 ns
April 1986	0.359 **	0.250 **			

Asterisks indicate $p < 0.01$.

Strong seasonal associations were present in the benthic community. Statistical comparison of surveys conducted three to nine months apart (Tables 18.7 and 18.8) resulted in correlation coefficients that ranged from 0.47 to 0.75 for normal analyses and from 0.68 to 0.85 for inverse analyses. These are fairly high, but not exceptional, values for large independent data sets. In a pattern that will be repeated in other analyses, the correlation coefficients are slightly lower when functional groups instead of species were used as descriptors for normal analyses. This reflects some loss of information about spatial relationships when combining species into a group. Conversely, functional groups produced slightly higher correlation coefficients than species for inverse analyses, indicating that the variability of groups of species was less than that of individual species. Despite some differences, the results when using species or functional groups always tended

Table 18.6. Associated functional groups based on UPGMA cluster analysis and MDS ordination

Year Funct. group	1957 Sum.	1958 Sum.	1959 Sum.	1960 Sum.	1973 Jan.	1983 Aug.	1986 April	1986 July	1986 Oct.	1987 Jan.	1994 Oct.	1995 June
ITSS												
ITSDi												
ITSDs		B	B	B		C		C	C	C	C	C
ITSC												
ITMDi	B	B	B	B	C	C	C	C			C	C
ITMDs	A	B	B	A	A	C	D	D	D	D	C	C
INSS	B	B		B	C			C	C			
INSDi												
INSDs		B		B	D	D	D	D	D	D		D
INMS		B	B	B		D						
INMDi	B	B	B	B	D			C	C	C	C	C
INMDs					A			A	A	A	A	
INMO	B	B	B	B	D	D		D	D	D		
INMC	B	B	B	B	D	D	D	D	D	D		D
ETSS					A	A	A					A
ETMS		A					A	C	C	C	C	C
ETMDs	A				A		C	C	C	C		A
ENSS	A	A		A	A	A		A	A	A	A	D
ENMDs		A			A	A	C	C	C	C	A	
ENMO	B	B	B	B	A	C	C	A	C	C	C	C
ENMC	A	A		A	A	A	D	A	A	C	C	C

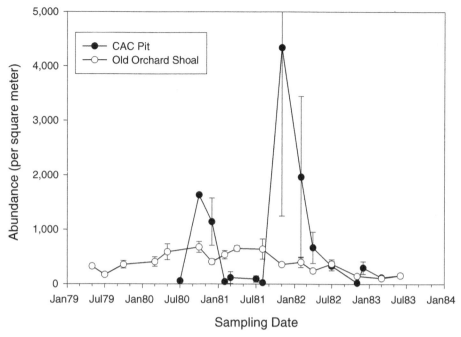

Figure 18.4. Seasonal variations in abundance at two locations in Lower Bay. Data from Cerrato and Scheier (1984).

to be comparable, suggesting that the differences in taxonomy between surveys did not have a major influence on the outcome of the Mantel tests.

Analysis of spatial and faunal associations in data sets collected during the same season, but one to three years apart, indicated considerable annual variability in the benthic community. Correlations from Mantel tests were significant but weaker than seasonal correlations (Tables 18.7 and 18.8), even if the extremely low correlations for the spatial comparison between 1957 and 1960 are excluded as possible artifacts of their small sample size (n = 10). Diaz and Boesch (1979) did not feel that changes in the benthic community during 1957–60 were associated with initiation of sewage treatment in early 1958. So the low annual correlations involving the 1957 and 1960 data cannot be explained by faunal succession.

Comparing the benthos on a decadal time scale, the abundances of many species increased substantially between the early regional studies (1957–60 and 1973–74) and the later studies (1986–87 and 1994–95) (Table 18.3 and Fig. 18.3). No species that was consistently abundant in 1957–60 or 1973–74 was rare in 1986–87 or 1994–95. Species both

from Lower Bay and those in Raritan and Sandy Hook Bays increased, indicating that the pattern was bay wide. It is also evident from Table 18.3 that fewer species were present during 1957–60 and 1973–74 compared to later surveys. This is especially obvious for amphipod and other crustacean groups. These observations cannot be explained by seasonal or sieve size differences, since methods can be matched for any comparison involving these earlier studies and the 1986–87 study. High abundances of some species such as *Streblospio benedicti* and *Ampelisca abdita* in October 1994 or June 1995 could, however, reflect sieve size differences.

Abundances of a number of species were especially different in 1973–74 compared to other sampling periods. Numerical dominants such as the amphipods *Ampelisca spp.* and *Unciola serrata*, the gastropod *Ilyanassa obsoleta*, and the bivalve *Mya arenaria* were conspicuously low during January 1973 (Table 18.3). The almost complete absence of these species persisted throughout the more limited 1973–74 sampling in Sandy Hook Bay (see Table 18.3). Although less obvious, several species, including the polychaetes *Nephtys incisa*, *Polydora ligni*, *Spio filicornis*, *Streblospio benedicti*,

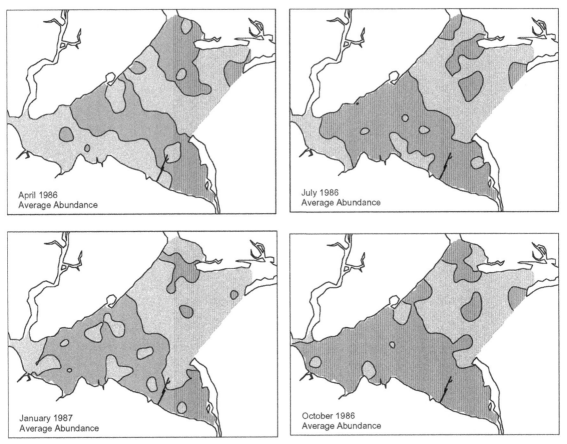

Figure 18.5. Seasonal changes, indicated clockwise, in the distribution of high and low abundance areas in the Lower Bay Complex. The contour line delineates geometric mean abundance for all four sampling periods (1,778 individuals per m^2). The darker area is above and the lighter area is below the mean. Data from Cerrato et al. (1989).

the gastropod *Ritaxis punctostriatus*, and the bivalve *Mulinia lateralis*, actually increased during this same period. Very often these species had high abundances during only one or two seasons (e.g., *Polydora ligni* in July 1973 and *Streblospio benedicti* in July and October 1973).

Most investigators have concluded that the benthic community present during the January 1973 regional study was different than other periods (McGrath, 1974; Berg and Levinton, 1984; Diaz and Boesch, 1979). McGrath (1974), based on a preliminary analysis of only forty samples, characterized the benthic community in 1973–74 as "impoverished" when compared to other regions, although reanalysis by Steimle and Caracciolo-Ward, (1989) using the entire data set showed that

the fauna in 1973–74 was somewhat more abundant and diverse than McGrath initially suggested. Diaz and Boesch (1979) in comparing Dean's 1957–60 data with McGrath's 1973–74 survey thought that the differences for dominants such as *Ampelisca abdita*, *Mya arenaria*, and *Ilyanassa obsoleta* could not be due to differences in sieve size (1.5 mm for Dean and 1.0 mm for McGrath) since the finer mesh sieve in McGrath's study would tend to retain more, not fewer, individuals. Despite other methodological differences, they believed the 1973–74 fauna densities were "extraordinarily low." Comparison of the July 1986 1.0 and 1.5 mm sieved samples in Cerrato et al. (1989) suggests that except for several small species, most differences in retention between 1.0 and 1.5 mm screens were

Table 18.7. Mantel tests of faunal associations (inverse analysis)

			Species as descriptors			Functional groups as descriptors		
			n	r		n	r	
Seasonal:								
	April 1986 vs.	July 1986	50	0.699	**	17	0.712	**
		Oct. 1986	53	0.673	**	17	0.583	**
		Jan. 1987	59	0.683	**	17	0.673	**
	July 1986 vs.	Oct. 1986	50	0.696	**	17	0.850	**
		Jan. 1987	50	0.651	**	17	0.809	**
	Oct. 1986 vs.	Jan. 1987	53	0.778	**	17	0.802	**
	Oct. 1994 vs.	June 1995	36	0.675	**	17	0.781	**
Annual:								
	Sum. 1957 vs.	Sum. 1958	19	0.222	*	14	0.458	**
	Sum. 1958 vs.	Sum. 1959	27	0.706	**	14	0.748	**
	Sum. 1959 vs.	Sum. 1960	7	–		12	0.451	**
	Sum. 1957 vs.	Sum. 1959	19	0.340	**	14	0.565	**
	Sum. 1958 vs.	Sum. 1960	7	–		12	0.349	*
	Sum. 1957 vs.	Sum. 1960	4	–		12	0.247	*
	Aug. 1983 vs.	July 1986	45	0.223	**	18	0.284	*
Long Term:								
	July 1986 vs.	Sum. 1957	9	–		10	0.275	ns
	July 1986 vs.	Sum. 1958	18	0.287	**	13	0.276	*
	July 1986 vs.	Sum. 1959	14	0.271	*	13	0.240	ns
	July 1986 vs.	Sum. 1960	3	–		6	–	
	Jan. 1987 vs.	Jan. 1973	19	0.565	**	15	0.600	**
	July 1986 vs.	June 1995	29	0.348	**	17	0.485	*
	Oct. 1986 vs.	Oct. 1994	28	0.473	**	17	0.380	*

Significance levels: * $p < 0.05$ and ** $p < 0.01$. Low sample size comparisons ($n < 10$) were not run.

less than 10 percent. This observation reinforces the conclusion by most investigators that the very low abundance throughout the Lower Bay Complex in January 1973 was real.

Are the differences in community structure between the earlier (1957–60 and 1973) and later benthic surveys (1986–87 and 1994–95) because of habitat changes or because of changes in faunal associations over time? To examine this question, I compared the regional studies using Mantel tests, with the comparison centering on the 1986–87 survey because of its compatibility in methods to prior studies. Almost all comparisons of faunal associations were significant, providing evidence of stability over decadal time scales (Table 18.7). Correlations ranged from 0.24 to 0.60, values that are comparable in magnitude to those obtained for annual faunal associations. It is especially interesting

to note that the strongest correlation in faunal associations was found between the two winter surveys, January 1973 and January 1987.

In contrast to faunal associations, spatial or habitat associations have changed over decadal time scales within the Lower Bay Complex (Table 18.8). Mantel tests indicated that spatial associations between the early surveys and the 1986–87 study were often nonsignificant, indicating little or no similarity in habitat structure between surveys. In particular, the correlations between 1959–86 and 1973–87 were close to 0 and well below the range indicated for annual variations (0.19–0.43). Even with sieve size differences, strong spatial associations in community structure were indicated in the comparisons between 1986–87 and 1994–95. All four spatial comparisons were significant, and three of the four correlations exceeded the range for

Table 18.8. Mantel tests of spatial associations (normal analysis)

			Species as descriptors			Functional groups as descriptors		
			n	r		n	r	
Seasonal:								
	April 1986 vs.	July 1986	114	0.651	**	114	0.470	**
		Oct. 1986	114	0.662	**	114	0.468	**
		Jan. 1987	114	0.615	**	114	0.502	**
	July 1986 vs.	Oct. 1986	114	0.745	**	114	0.677	**
		Jan. 1987	114	0.660	**	114	0.522	**
	Oct. 1986 vs.	Jan. 1987	114	0.667	**	114	0.537	**
	Oct. 1994 vs.	June 1995	131	0.749	**	131	0.708	**
Annual:								
	Sum. 1957 vs.	Sum. 1958	40	0.190	**	40	0.133	ns
	Sum. 1958 vs.	Sum. 1959	50	0.332	**	50	0.167	*
	Sum. 1959 vs.	Sum. 1960	14	0.396	**	14	0.431	**
	Sum. 1957 vs.	Sum. 1959	42	0.215	*	42	0.122	ns
	Sum. 1958 vs.	Sum. 1960	13	0.406	**	13	0.353	*
	Sum. 1957 vs.	Sum. 1960	10	0.010	ns	10	0.064	ns
	Aug. 1983 vs.	July 1986	25	0.293	**	25	0.207	*
Long Term:								
	July 1986 vs.	Sum. 1957	14	0.210	ns	14	0.352	*
	July 1986 vs.	Sum. 1958	29	0.302	**	29	0.235	ns
	July 1986 vs.	Sum. 1959	26	0.002	ns	26	−0.074	ns
	July 1986 vs.	Sum. 1960	11	0.230	ns	11	0.177	ns
	Jan. 1987 vs.	Jan. 1973	56	0.027	ns	56	−0.058	ns
	July 1986 vs.	June 1995	38	0.458	**	38	0.323	*
	Oct. 1986 vs.	Oct. 1994	36	0.605	**	36	0.460	**

Significance levels for the correlation coefficient (r) are * $p < 0.05$ and ** $p < 0.01$.

annual variations. This outcome strongly suggests that habitat associations have been stable between 1986–87 and 1994–95.

Discussion

The benthic fauna present in the Lower Bay Complex are typical of estuarine and coastal regions of the Northeast and Mid-Atlantic. They live in a highly fluctuating physical environment and as a result, tend to show dynamic temporal patterns. There was, however, stability or coherence in the faunal associations apparent over the four decades spanned by the regional data sets. The best example is the comparison between 1973 and 1987. A strong faunal association was found in winter between 1973 and 1987, even though the fauna in 1973 declined to low abundance and there was marked evidence for habitat differences.

Benthic community structure in the Lower Bay Complex tends to follow in a broad way the sediment and hydrographic regime that divides the area into distinct southern (Raritan and Sandy Hook Bays) and northern regions (Lower Bay). Within this broadscale pattern, habitats have changed over time. Mantel tests indicated that the habitat structure was uncorrelated when comparing the surveys of 1959–60 and 1986 and when comparing 1973 and 1987. From 1983 onward, spatial associations remained stable. It was apparent, from an examination of Tables 18.3 and 18.4 and the plots in Figure 18.3, that many members of the benthic community were more abundant during the 1980s and 1990s than in 1957–60 and 1973. This trend could not be explained by differences in survey methods.

Further detailed analysis of benthic community structure was hampered by a number of problems: 1) high annual variability, 2) differences in sampling methods among regional studies, 3) goodness-of-fit problems in the multivariate analyses, and 4) weak faunal-environmental relationships. High annual variability is a characteristic of temperate, coastal benthic communities, but little quantitative information exists on the degree of annual change, mainly because few regional studies are carried out at annual or greater time scales (Constable, 1999). In the present study, correlations declined abruptly between seasonal and annual time scales. For example, in examining spatial associations and using species as descriptors, seasonal correlations ranged from 0.65–0.75 while annual correlations were only 0.19–0.41 (Table 18.8). In contrast, McArdle and Blackwell (1989) found a gradual decline in correlation from 0.6 to 0 for *Chione stutchburyi* as sampling intervals increased from three to eighteen months. McArdle and Blackwell were, however, examining a single, long-lived species over a small spatial scale (100 m), so it would be expected to behave more predictably than a multispecies assemblage. The cause of high annual variability in the present study was probably episodic recruitment and mortality of several of the dominant species. During 1957–60 (Table 18.3), there were large annual changes in abundance of *Polydora ligni, Mya arenaria, Mytilis edulus, Gemma gemma, Ampelisca* sp., *Unciola serrata*, and other dominants. High annual variability obscures relationships with stable environmental factors such as sediment grain-size and hampers attempts to identify structure or pattern across data sets. A practical concern that must be considered in the future is the relevance of single surveys in characterizing community structure or establishing baseline levels.

The different sampling methods used in the regional studies (Table 18.1) limited the types of comparisons that could be made. Simple comparisons of abundance, relative abundance of each species, species richness, or even species presence/absence among the regional studies would have been very valuable but were avoided for the most part because no reliable corrections for methodological differences exist. To assess long term changes, future regional studies will need to seriously consider matching sampling locations, season of collection, sampling device, and sieve size to prior studies. Establishing type collections and a specimen repository would also be worthwhile, since they would reduce variability in taxonomy among studies.

The ordination and cluster analysis techniques used in this study did not perform well. Goodness-of-fit problems arose in all attempts, indicating that a simple two- or three-dimensional display for ordination or a tree-diagram for cluster analysis would not accurately represent relationships. It was not possible, therefore, to confidently use these methods to identify spatial and faunal associations for the regional studies, let alone use them to assess change in associations between studies. The goodness-of-fit criteria used in this study are an essential part of the process of validation of a multivariate method, that is, determining whether the structure or relationships being displayed are real or an artifact created by the analytical method (Legendre and Legendre, 1998). Although validation is important, validation methods are generally not available in statistical packages (Legendre and Legendre, 1998) and are not commonly examined as a regular step in an analysis.

It is possible that an index other than the Bray-Curtis measure, or a different choice of ordination and clustering algorithm, would have performed better than those selected for the present study. More likely, a different approach is required to handle these large, complex data sets. A rapidly expanding class of multivariate methods, generally called "direct comparison" by Legendre and Legendre (1998) and "direct analysis" by ter Braak (1996), may provide a partial solution. A direct analysis examines faunal data and environmental data together within a single multivariate technique. Canonical correspondence analysis (CCA) is one example (ter Braak 1996). CCA would produce an ordination of stations and/or species arranged along gradients in grain-size, temperature, salinity, and other environmental data. This approach has not been applied to data from the Lower Bay Complex.

Simply applying direct analyses to existing data, however, would not totally resolve the analytical problem, since community structure was only weakly related to sediment grain-size, depth, salinity, and temperature data (Table 18.5), only about 10 to 15 percent of the spatial variation was explained by these variables. This highlights a need for additional environmental data useful in characterizing habitats. Interestingly, collection and use of new environmental data for habitat analyses has already begun in the Lower Bay Complex. Side-scan sonar imagery is available for some areas (Schwab et al., 1997), and NOAA-USACE (2001) has generated very high resolution habitat maps for the Lower Bay Complex based on extensive use of sediment-profile and sediment-surface imagery. By combining these data with water quality, sediment contaminant, and sediment toxicity data, it should be possible to substantially increase the amount of explained variation and make direct analyses meaningful.

What caused the observed habitat change and especially the decline in 1973–74? Diaz and Boesch (1979) and Berg and Levinton (1984) in comparing 1957–60 to 1973–74 data felt that the environmental data available to them, particularly data on pollutants in sediments, were not adequate to assign specific causes. Diaz and Boesch (1979) thought that the cause was anthropogenic, particularly because the numerical dominants (*Ampelisca abdita*, *Cyathura polita*, *Mya arenaria*, and *Ilyanassa obsoleta*) all declined. They indicated that low abundance was not a typical organic enrichment response; low dissolved oxygen and high sulfides, conditions that are associated with enrichment, generally allow dense populations of a few stress tolerant species to occur. Instead, they suggested that the response was more consistent with toxicants. *Ampelisca abdita* in particular is sensitive to contaminants and is often used in sediment toxicity tests (e.g., Wolfe, Long, and Thursby, 1996). Other possibilities suggested by investigators included sewage and industrial pollution (Franz, 1982), dredging (Franz, 1982; MacKenzie, 1983), siltation (MacKenzie, 1983), increased salinity (MacKenzie, 1983), heavy metals (Diaz and Boesch, 1979; Steimle and Caracciolo-Ward, 1989), chlorinated pesticides and PCBs (Diaz and Boesch, 1979), and extractable hydrocarbons (Steimle and Caracciolo-Ward, 1989).

Stainken (1984), sampling along two transects in Raritan Bay in June and September–October 1977, reported little relationship between biotic indices of diversity and specific sediment contaminants. He did, however, find a trend of increased abundance and diversity with distance from inner Raritan Bay that correlated with both decreasing silt-clay content and decreasing levels of PAHs, PCBs, and extractable hydrocarbons. Faunal abundances were depressed in general, and perhaps even more significantly, *Ampelisca abdita* was not reported in any of his samples. Even with the 1.5 mm mesh used in his study, Stainken should have retained some individuals of this species had it been present. Combining McGrath's 1973–74 data (Table 18.3) with Stainken's 1977 study suggests that a dominant mud species, *Ampelisca abdita*, may have been absent for several years. By 1983, this species had clearly returned as a dominant (Table 18.3).

A specific cause for the observed habitat change will probably never be identified. In fact, Franz (1982) suggested that major habitat change actually began to occur in the Lower Bay Complex by the late 1800s, that is, well before any recent studies. By comparing the number of molluscan species from studies conducted in the late 1800s and 1920s, he concluded that many species were eliminated when eelgrass and oyster beds declined. Extensive oyster beds were present in western Raritan Bay during the late 1800s and once supported an active oyster industry (MacKenzie, 1983).

Adams et al. (1998) reported that the benthos in 1993–94 in the Lower Bay Complex was the least impacted in New York-New Jersey Harbor. The most extensive sediment contaminants in the Harbor were mercury, chlordane, and PCBs, and high concentrations were restricted to muddy areas. Similar results were also obtained for toxicity tests both in 1991 (Wolfe et al., 1996) and 1993–94 (Adams et al., 1998). Overall, contaminant concentrations and sediment toxicity were lower compared to Newark Bay and Upper Bay, but New York-New Jersey Harbor was generally more contaminated than other sites in the mid-Atlantic region from Cape Cod to Chesapeake Bay.

Even without identifying a specific cause for the poor health of the benthic community from the

1950s to the 1970s, improvement in the benthic fauna by the 1980s is almost certainly due to a significant improvement in water quality in the 1970s. This occurred primarily as a result of the Clean Water Act, when existing plants in the region were upgraded to secondary treatment and additional plants were constructed (Brosnan and O'Shea, 1996). Secondary treatment resulted in decreased loadings of organic carbon, phosphorus, metals such as cadmium, copper, and lead, and PCBs. Untreated water discharges into the Lower Hudson River, for example, decreased from 19.7 m^3/s in 1970 to 0.2 m^3/s in 1988 (Brosnan and O'Shea, 1996). Indicators of water quality, such as fecal coliform and dissolved oxygen, in the Lower Bay Complex showed noticeable improvement from the 1970s to the 1990s (NYCDEP, 1995), and with the exception of some results in western Raritan Bay, the Lower Bay Complex met water quality standards for the fifteen-year period from 1985–2000 (NYCDEP, 2000).

Despite impressive gains in controlling inputs, it is likely that contaminant concentrations and sediment toxicity such as that observed by Adams et al. (1998) will continue to persist in muddy areas for at least several more decades due to the high binding capacity of fine-grained sediments. Improvements in the benthic fauna should continue in the Lower Bay Complex but at a slower rate than seen during the past 20 years. A reasonable goal would be the restoration of eelgrass and oyster beds to the Bay as was typical of a century ago. That goal is certainly obtainable but probably decades off.

Acknowledgments

Special thanks to Frank Steimle, Pace Wilber, and Robert Will for sharing regional survey data with me, to Mark Wiggins for his meticulous work on the 1986–87 study, to Shawn MacCafferty for early help with data analysis, and to the Hudson River Foundation for providing partial support.

REFERENCES

Adams, D. A., O'Connor, J. S., and Weisberg, S. B. 1998. Sediment Quality of the NY/NJ Harbor System. Environmental Protection Agency Final Report EPA/902-R-98-001.

Barry, J. P., and Dayton, P. K. 1991. Physical heterogeneity and the organization of marine communities, in J. Kolska and S. T. A. Pickett (eds.) *Ecological Heterogeneity.* New York: Springer, pp. 207–320.

Berg, D. L., and Levinton, J. S. 1984. *The Biology of the Hudson-Raritan Estuary with Special Emphasis on Fishes.* NOAA Technical Memorandum. NOS OMA 16.

Brosnan, T. M., and O'Shea., M. L. 1996. Long-term improvements in water quality due to sewage abatement in the Lower Hudson River. *Estuaries* 19:890–900.

Cerrato, R. M., Bokuniewicz, H. J., and Wiggins, M. H. 1989. *A Spatial and Seasonal Study of the Benthic Fauna of the Lower Bay of New York Harbor.* Marine Sciences Research Center Special Report No. 84. State University of New York, Stony Brook, NY.

Cerrato, R. M., and Scheier, F. T. 1984. *The Effect of Borrow Pits on the Distribution and Abundance of Benthic Fauna in the Lower Bay of New York Harbor.* Marine Sciences Research Center Special Report No. 59. State University of New York, Stony Brook, NY.

Chandler, G. T., Shipp, M. R., and Donelan, T. L. 1997. Bioaccumulation, growth and larval settlement effects of sediment-associated polynuclear aromatic hydrocarbons on the estuarine polychaete *Streblospio benedicti. Journal of Experimental Marine Biology and Ecology* 213:95–110.

Constable, A. J. 1999. Ecology of benthic macroinvertebrates in soft-sediment environments: A review of progress towards quantitative models and predictions. *Australian Journal of Ecology* 24:452–76.

Dean, D. 1975. *Raritan Bay Macrobenthos Survey, 1957–60.* NOAA National Marine Fisheries Service Data Report 99, Washington, DC.

Diaz, R. J., and Boesch, D. F. 1979. The macrobenthos of the Hudson-Raritan Estuary, in D. F. Boesch (ed.) *The Ecology of Macrobenthos of the New York Bight Region.* Technical Report to the National Oceanic and Atmospheric Administration, Marine Ecosystems Analysis Program, Washington, DC.

Fauchild, K., and Jumars, P. A. 1979. The diet of worms: a study of polychaete feeding guilds. *Oceanography and Marine Biology Annual Review* 17:193–284.

Field, J. G., Clarke, K. R., and Warwick, R. M. 1982. A practical strategy for analyzing multispecies distribution patterns. *Marine Ecology Progress Series* 8:37–52.

Franz, D. R. 1982. An historical perspective on mollusks in Lower New York Harbor, with emphasis on oysters, in G. F. Mayer (ed.) *Ecological Stress and the New York Bight: Science and Management.* Estuarine Research Federation, Columbia, SC, pp. 181–97.

Franz, D. R., and Tancredi, J. T. 1992. Secondary production of the amphipod *Ampelisca abdita* (mills) and its importance in the diet of juvenile winter flounder in Jamaica Bay. *Estuaries* **15**: 193–203.

Jeffries, H. P. 1962. Environmental characteristics of Raritan Bay, a polluted estuary. *Limnology and Oceanography* **7**:21–31.

Johnson, R. G. 1970. Variations in diversity within benthic communities. *American Naturalist* **104**:285–300.

Legendre, P., and Legendre, L. 1998. *Numerical Ecology,* Amsterdam: Elsevier.

Llanso, R. J. 1991. Tolerance of low dissolved-oxygen and hydrogen-sulfide by the polychaete *Streblospio benedicti. Journal of Experimental Marine Biology and Ecology* **153**:165–78.

MacKenzie, C. L. 1983. A History of oystering in Raritan Bay, with environmental observations, in A. L. Pacheco (ed.) *Raritan Bay: Its Multiple Uses and Abuses. Proceedings of the Walford Memorial Convocation, Sandy Hook Lab Technical Series Report No. 30.* Sandy Hook, NJ, pp. 37–66.

Mantel, N. 1967. The detection of disease clustering and a generalized regression approach. *Cancer Research* **27**:209–20.

McArdle, B. H., and Blackwell, R. G. 1989. Measurement of density variability in the bivalve *Chione stutchburyi* using spatial autocorrelation. *Marine Ecology Progress Series* **52**:245–52.

McCall, P. L. 1977. Community patterns and adaptive strategies of the infaunal benthos of Long Island Sound. *Journal of Marine Research* **35**:221–66.

McGrath, R. A. 1974. Benthic macrofaunal census of Raritan Bay – Preliminary results, in *Proceedings of the 3rd Symposium of Hudson River Ecology.* Hudson River Environmental Society, Altamont, NY.

NOAA-USACE. 2001. *Benthic Habitats of the New York/New Jersey Harbor.* National Oceanic and Atmospheric Administration and U. S. Army Corps of Engineers, NOAA Coastal Services Center, Charleston, SC.

NYCDEP 1995. *New York Harbor Water Quality Survey Appendices.* New York City Department of Environmental Protection, New York, NY.

NYCDEP 2000. *Regional Harbor Survey.* New York City Department of Environmental Protection, New York, NY.

Parsons, T. R., Takahashi, M., and Hargrave, B. 1984. *Biological Oceanographic Processes.* Oxford, UK: Pergamon Press.

Redmond, M. S., Scott, K. J., Swartz, R. C., and Jones, J. K. P. 1994. Preliminary culture and life-cycle experiments with the benthic amphipod *Ampelisca abdita. Environmental Toxicology and Chemistry* **13**:1355–65.

Rhoads, D. C. 1974. Organism-sediment relations on the muddy seafloor. *Oceanography and Marine Biology Annual Review* **12**:263–300.

Rhoads, D. C., McCall, P. L., and Yingst, J. Y. 1978. Disturbance and production on the muddy seafloor. *American Scientist* **66**:577–86.

Rohlf, F. J. 1993. *NTSYS-pc: Numerical Taxonomy and Multivariate Analysis System.* Setauket, NY: Exeter Software.

Schlacher, T. A., and Wooldridge, T. H. 1996. How sieve mesh size affects sample estimates of estuarine benthic macrofauna. *Journal of Experimental Marine Biology and Ecology* **201**:159–71.

Schwab, W.C., Allison, M. A., Corso, W., Lotto, L. L., Buttman, B., Buchholtz ten Brink, M., Denny, J., Danforth, W. W., and Foster, D. S. 1997. Initial results of high-resolution sea-floor mapping offshore of the New York – New Jersey metropolitan area using sidescan sonar. *Northeastern Geology and Environmental Sciences* **19**:243–62.

Stainken, D. M. 1984. Organic pollution and the macrobenthos of Raritan Bay. *Environmental Toxicology and Chemistry* **3**:95–111.

Stainken, D. M., McCormick, J. M., and Multer, H. G. 1984. Seasonal survey of the macrobenthos of Raritan Bay. *Bulletin of the NJ Academy of Science* **29**:121–32.

Steimle, F. W., and Caracciolo-Ward, J. 1989. A reassessment of the status of the benthic macrofauna of the Raritan Estuary. *Estuaries* **12**:145–56.

Steimle, F. W., Caracciolo-Ward, J., Fromm, S., and McGrath, R. 1989. *The 1973–74 Benthic Macrofaunal and Sediment Survey of Raritan Bay: Data Report.* Northeast Fisheries Center Reference Document 89–07. National Marine Fisheries Service, Northeast Fisheries Center, Highlands, NJ.

Steimle, F. W., Pikanowski, R. A., McMillan, D. G., Zetlin, C. A., and Wilk, S. J. 2000. *Demersal Fish and American Lobster Diets in the Lower Hudson-Raritan Estuary.* NOAA Technical Memorandum NMFS-NE-161.

ter Braak, C. J. F. 1996. Canonical correspondence analysis: a new eigenvalue technique for multivariate direct gradient analysis. *Ecology* **67**:1167–79.

Thrush, S. A. 1991. Spatial patterns in soft-bottom communities. *Trends in Ecology and Evolution* **6**:75–9.

Wolfe, D. A., Long, E. R., and Thursby, G. B. 1996. Sediment toxicity in the Hudson-Raritan Estuary: Distribution and correlations with chemical contamination. *Estuaries* **19**:901–912.

Woodin, S. A., and Jackson, J. B. C. 1979. Interphyletic competition among marine benthos. *American Zoologist* **19**:1029–43.

19 The Benthic Animal Communities of the Tidal-Freshwater Hudson River Estuary

David L. Strayer

ABSTRACT Benthic animals (those that live in or on sediments or vegetation) are of key importance in the Hudson River ecosystem. They are the major source of food to the Hudson's fish and regulate the abundance and composition of phytoplankton in the river. Benthic animals probably are important in mixing sediments, an activity that may affect the movement and ultimate fate of toxins in the river, although this process is not well studied in the Hudson. The benthic animal community of the Hudson is diverse, containing several hundred species of worms, mollusks, crustaceans, insects, and other invertebrates. These animals represent a wide array of life histories, feeding types, distributions, and adaptations. Community structure and population density vary greatly from place to place in the Hudson, and are determined chiefly by salinity, the presence of rooted plants, and the nature of the sediment (hard vs. soft). Nevertheless, a great deal of site-to-site variation in benthic community structure in the Hudson and other large rivers is unexplained. Human activities (especially water pollution and alteration of the channel for navigation) probably had large effects on the benthic communities of the Hudson, but these effects have not been well documented. The recent invasion of the Hudson by the zebra mussel (*Dreissena polymorpha*) profoundly changed the benthic communities of the river, altering their composition and function in the ecosystem.

Introduction

Benthic animals (collectively called the zoobenthos) are a diverse community of animals living in or on sediments, aquatic plants, or other solid surfaces under the waters. The zoobenthos of the Hudson is one of the most diverse communities in the river, containing several hundred species of varied habits. Benthic animals play key roles in the river's ecosystem. They are the predominant food for many of the river's fish, regulate populations of phytoplankton and zooplankton, and probably are important in determining the movement and fate of nutrients and toxins in the river. Despite this importance, much remains unknown about the Hudson's benthic animals and their roles in the river's ecosystem. My goal in this chapter is to describe the animals that make up the Hudson's zoobenthos, discuss how different habitats within the river support different kinds of benthic animals, review how benthic animal communities in the river have changed over time, especially in response to the zebra mussel invasion, and evaluate the importance of benthic animals in the Hudson's ecosystem.

Sources of Information

Studies of the Hudson's zoobenthos have been spotty, limiting our insight into this part of the ecosystem. The earliest naturalists collected specimens from the Hudson and made incidental observations on benthic animals (e.g., Say, 1821; Lea, 1829; Dekay, 1844; Gordon, 1986), but the first systematic survey of the Hudson's zoobenthos was done by Townes (1937), who made a few collections from the middle estuary as part of the Conservation Department's survey of New York's fisheries resources. In the 1970s, the Boyce Thompson Institute (Ristich, Crandall, and Fortier, 1977; Weinstein, 1977) surveyed the benthos of the lower estuary (Manhattan to Poughkeepsie), and in 1983–84 researchers from the New York State Department of Health (Simpson et al., 1984, 1985, 1986; Bode et al., 1986) made a detailed study of the zoobenthos of the main channel of the freshwater Hudson from Troy to New Hamburg. Two vegetated areas (Bowline Pond – Menzie, 1980, and Tivoli South Bay – Findlay, Schoeberl, and Wagner, 1989) were studied during the same time period. Finally, my colleagues and I have studied the zoobenthos of the freshwater tidal section of the river (Troy to Newburgh) since 1990, a period that included the zebra mussel invasion (Strayer et al., 1994, 1996, 1998; Strayer and Smith, 1996, 2000, 2001).

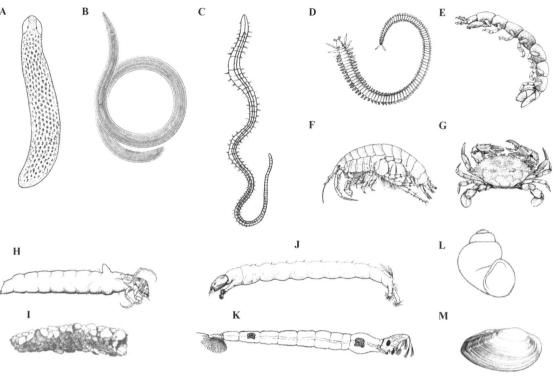

Figure 19.1. Some benthic animals that are common in the Hudson River. A. the flatworm *Hydrolimax grisea*, B. the nematode *Dorylaimus stagnalis*, C. a tubificid oligochaete, D. the polychaete *Eteone heteropoda*, E. the isopod *Cyathura polita*, F. the amphipod *Leptocheirus plumulosus*, G. the blue crab *Callinectes sapidus*, H. the caddisfly *Oecetis inconspicua*, and I. its case, J. the chironomid *Ablabesmyia*, K. the phantom midge *Chaoborus*, L. the snail *Amnicola limosa*, M. the mussel *Anodonta implicata*. From Thorne and Swanger (1936), Hyman and Jones (1959), Burch (1975), Weinstein (1977), Oliver and Roussel (1983), Fryer (1991), Jokinen (1992), and Wiggins (1996).

In addition to these large studies, a number of studies more limited in scope (e.g., Hirschfield, Rachlin, and Leff, 1966; Howells, Musnick, and Hirschfield, 1969; Williams, Hogan, and Zo, 1975; Crandall, 1977; Yozzo and Steineck, 1994) have contributed information on the Hudson's zoobenthos. Together, these studies offer a moderately clear picture of benthic animal communities of the freshwater tidal river in 1983–2000, a glimpse into communities of the lower river in the mid-1970s, and only hints of the benthic communities that lived anywhere in the river before 1970.

Further, most of the studies in the Hudson have been focused on the macrofauna (animals large enough to be caught on a 0.5–1 mm mesh screen), and have excluded the numerous smaller animals as well as larger mobile forms such as crabs and shrimp. Typically, these excluded forms constitute 5–75 percent of benthic biomass, production, and diversity (e.g., Strayer, 1985; Hakenkamp, Morin, and Strayer, 2002). Consequently, benthic animals in the Hudson are more numerous and more diverse than existing studies on the Hudson suggest.

Biology of the Zoobenthos

Approximately three hundred species of macrobenthic animals have been recorded from the Hudson River (Ristich et al., 1977; Simpson et al., 1986; Strayer and Smith, 2001). This fauna includes animals with a wide array of body sizes and shapes (Fig. 19.1), life histories, and ecological habits. In terms of numbers, biomass, and species richness, the most important groups in the Hudson's zoobenthos are annelids, mollusks, crustaceans, and insects.

Three major groups of annelids are common in the Hudson: leeches, oligochaetes, and polychaetes. Although leeches are well known (and reviled!) as bloodsuckers, only a few species of leeches are parasites of humans and other vertebrates. Most leech species are scavengers or predators of invertebrates. About ten species of leeches have been reported from the freshwater parts of the Hudson. Leech densities usually are low in the Hudson, but these animals may be locally important as predators in plant beds, where their densities are highest. Most oligochaetes and polychaetes burrow in soft sediments or crawl on vegetation or rocks and are deposit-feeders, feeding on sediment bacteria and organic matter. Many species are macroscopic, and reach lengths of 3–30 mm as adults. Polychaetes are predominately marine, and are dominant in the polyhaline and mesohaline parts of the Hudson (river kilometer (RKM) 0–75). Only one species (the microscopic *Manayunkia speciosa*) lives in the freshwater part of the estuary. Oligochaetes live throughout the river, but are especially common in the freshwater estuary (RKM 100–248), where they often constitute >75 percent of macrobenthic animals. Scientists have thus far found twenty to thirty species each of oligochaetes and polychaetes in the Hudson.

Mollusks (clams, mussels, and snails) are among the most familiar of the benthic animals in the Hudson. About fifty species have been reported from the river. Bivalve mollusks (clams and mussels) feed either on phytoplankton and other suspended material (suspension-feed) or on organic matter deposited on the sediments (deposit-feed). While some bivalves are among the largest invertebrates in the river, reaching >10 cm long, others never reach 5 mm long, even as adults. The life cycles of our bivalves are highly varied. Most of the brackish-water species have free-living larvae, but most freshwater species either have larvae that are parasitic on fish (pearly mussels) or no larvae at all (pea clams). The pearly mussels may live for decades. Some of the bivalves in the Hudson are edible (for example, oysters, mussels), and have been fished in prehistoric (e.g., Schaper, 1989) and recent times (because of widespread contamination, it is probably not a good idea to eat mollusks from the river today). Most of the Hudson's snails graze on attached algae or deposit feed on

organic sediments; a few are able to suspension feed. Several alien mollusk species have been introduced to the Hudson (e.g., the zebra mussel *Dreissena polymorpha*, the dark false mussel *Mytilopsis leucophaeta*, the Atlantic rangia *Rangia cuneata*, the faucet snail, *Bithynia tentaculata*) and are now common in the river.

Although only about thirty species of benthic crustaceans (isopods, amphipods, barnacles, and decapods) have been reported from the Hudson, the crustaceans are among the most important benthic animals in the river. They often are abundant, and many are especially choice food for fish (Table 19.1). Isopods (relatives of the familiar terrestrial pill bug) are common on unvegetated sediments throughout the river. Amphipods (scuds, sideswimmers) are small shrimp-like crustaceans common throughout the river that are one of the most important fish foods in the river (Table 19.1). Barnacles live on rocky shorelines as far north as Beacon (RKM 99). The decapods (crabs, crayfish, and shrimp) are another important fish food, but have received little study in the Hudson. Crayfish live in freshwater habitats, grass shrimp (*Paleomonetes*) live in brackish habitats, and blue crabs (*Callinectes sapidus*) migrate from the lower estuary as far north as Troy in some summers. Blue crabs (color plate 7) are widely fished for food in the Hudson and elsewhere; in recent years, the commercial catch in the river was ~40,000 kg/yr (NYSDEC, 1993). Many marine crustaceans have free-swimming larvae, and larval crabs and barnacles are common in the plankton on the lower Hudson. In contrast, most freshwater crustaceans have no larval stage, and develop directly from egg to juvenile to adult.

Benthic insects are common in the Hudson, especially in freshwater habitats. The chironomid midges (larvae of non-biting flies) are by far the most abundant and species-rich of the insects (color plate 8). Chironomid densities in the freshwater Hudson typically are ~1,000/m^2. More than 70 species of chironomids have been identified from the Hudson, and true diversity probably exceeds 100 species. The chironomids are a diverse group that includes predators, suspension-feeders, and grazers. Other insects that may be locally abundant in the freshwater Hudson include Ephemeroptera (mayflies), Odonata (damselflies),

Table 19.1. Importance of benthic invertebrates in the diets of some Hudson River fishes.

Fish species	% of diet	Dominant items in diet	Source
Shortnose sturgeon (YOY)	100 (V)	Chironomids	Carlson and Simpson, 1987
Shortnose sturgeon	100 (V)	Chironomids, mollusks, oligochaetes	Curran and Ries, 1937
Atlantic sturgeon	100 (V)	Chironomids, oligochaetes	Curran and Ries, 1937
Blueback herring (YOY)	49 (V)	Copepods	Limburg, 1988
American shad (YOY)	~65 (N,V)	Chironomids, *Chaoborus*	Townes, 1937; Limburg, 1988
Spottail shiner	>50 (N)	Microcrustaceans, chironomids	Smith and Schmidt, 1988
Tomcod	99 (N)	Amphipods	McLaren et al., 1988
Banded killifish	>50 (N)	Microcrustaceans, chironomids	Richard and Schmidt, 1986
White perch	91–99 (N)	Amphipods	Curran and Ries, 1937; Bath and O'Connor, 1985
Striped bass (YOY)	85 (N)	Amphipods	Townes, 1937; Gardinier and Hoff, 1983
Striped bass (yearlings)	76 (N)	Amphipods	Gardinier and Hoff, 1983
Striped bass (2-yr old)	14 (N)	Fish	Gardinier and Hoff, 1983
Tessellated darter	>50 (N)	Chironomids, microcrustaceans	Duryea and Schmidt, 1986

Importance is expressed as % of number (N) or volume (V) of items in the gut contents that were benthic invertebrates.
YOY = young-of-year fish
Modified from Strayer and Smith (2001).

Trichoptera (caddisflies), Coleoptera (beetles), Ceratopogonidae (no-see-ums), and Chaoboridae (phantom midges).

While annelids, mollusks, crustaceans, and insects dominate the Hudson's zoobenthos, many other animals are present. Porifera (sponges), Cnidaria (hydras, jellyfish), Turbellaria (flatworms), Nematoda (roundworms), and Acari (mites) may be locally abundant in the Hudson and add to its biological richness.

The Hudson's fauna resembles that of other tidal rivers in northeastern North America, from the James to the St. Lawrence. The macrozoobenthos of the freshwater parts of these rivers is usually strongly dominated by *Limnodrilus hoffmeisteri* and other tubificid oligochaetes, and often contains dense populations of predatory chironomids (for example, *Coelotanypus scapularis*, *Procladius* spp., *Cryptochironomus* spp.) and sphaeriid clams (Massengill, 1976; Crumb, 1977; Vincent, 1979; Ettinger, 1982; Diaz, 1989). Most of the freshwater species in these tidal rivers also occur widely in lakes and warm water rivers, but the fauna is distinctive in two ways. Several species common in the Hudson and other northeastern estuaries (for example, the cumacean crustacean *Almyracuma proximoculi*, the amphipod *Monoculodes edwardsi*, the isopods *Chiridotea almyra*

and *Cyathura polita*, and the snail *Littoridinops tenuipes*) usually live in oligohaline estuaries and coastal waters, and introduce a distinctively estuarine element to the "freshwater" fauna. Also, net-spinning caddisflies and burrowing mayflies, two groups of suspension-feeding insects that are important in many large rivers worldwide, are very rare in the freshwater tidal rivers of the Northeast, perhaps because rapidly changing tidal currents interfere with the construction and operation of the fixed burrows and nets used in feeding.

Spatial Variation in the Hudson Zoobenthos

Benthic communities vary enormously from place to place along the Hudson, in terms of both the number and kinds of animals that are present. Four factors are correlated with this variation: position along the course of the river, salinity, the presence or absence of rooted plants, and the nature of the bottom (hard vs. soft).

It appears that the density of benthic macroinvertebrates in the Hudson follows a W-shaped pattern, with peaks near Manhattan, Kingston, and Albany, and deep, broad troughs between these peaks (Fig. 19.2). This pattern is very strong, with densities in the peaks about 100-fold higher than

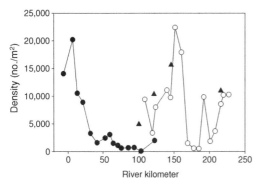

Figure 19.2. Long-river variation in density of benthic macroinvertebrates in the Hudson River. Data from mid-channel samples from Ristich et al. (1977) (black circles) and Simpson et al. (1984) (white circles), and from cross-channel transects in 1990–92 by Strayer et al. (unpublished). Because the three studies were done at different times and used different methods, the data are not exactly comparable across studies.

verse communities that are rich in insects and snails. Dozens of species of benthic animals in the Hudson are essentially confined to plant beds (Strayer and Smith, 2001). Likewise, rocky bottoms support more diverse communities than unvegetated soft sediments, including animals like mayflies and beetles that are rare elsewhere in the river. In contrast, the communities of various kinds of soft sediments (that is, sand vs. mud) differ little from one another, at least in the freshwater part of the Hudson (Strayer and Smith, 2001).

Nevertheless, most of the site-to-site variation in benthic communities in the Hudson and other large rivers is unexplained by factors like salinity, rooted plants, the grain size and organic content of the sediments. For example, the amphipod

in the troughs. The W-shaped pattern may arise through a combination of stress and food subsidies. Unstable salinities in RKM 20–100 and unstable, sandy sediments in RKM 170–210 may suppress benthic communities (cf. Simpson et al., 1986). Inputs of sewage from New York City, and of phytoplankton from the Bight and near RKM 150 (Cole, Caraco, and Peierls, 1992) may further contribute to the development of the peaks.

The composition of benthic communities in the Hudson is a strong function of salinity (Fig. 19.3). Near Manhattan, the fauna is dominated by characteristically marine animals (polychaetes, bivalves such as *Mya* and *Macoma*), while above Newburgh, the benthos is dominated by freshwater species of oligochaetes, insects, and bivalves. In the intermediate zone of moderate and fluctuating salinity, the fauna contains a few species (for example, the polychaete *Marenzelleria viridis*, the amphipod *Leptocheirus plumulosus*) that thrive in brackish water. Nevertheless, there is a good deal of blurring of the fauna along the salinity gradient, and it is common to find supposedly marine or brackish-water animals (e.g., the crab *Callinectes sapidus*, the cumacean *Almyracuma proximoculi*) well into the freshwater Hudson (Simpson et al., 1985).

The nature of the substratum also has a strong influence on the character of the zoobenthos (Table 19.2). Compared to nearby unvegetated habitats, beds of rooted vegetation support di-

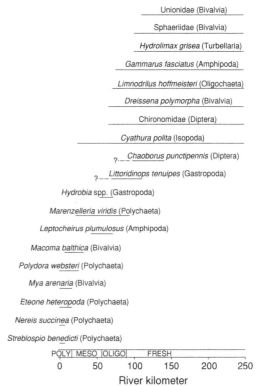

Figure 19.3. Approximate longitudinal distribution of dominant benthic animals in the Hudson River estuary, showing succession along the salinity gradient. The typical late-summer salinity zonation is shown just above the X-axis. FRESH = freshwater (< 0.5 ppt), MESO = mesohaline (5–18 ppt), OLIGO = oligohaline (0.5–5 ppt), POLY = polyhaline (18–30 ppt). Based on Ristich et al. (1977), Weinstein (1977), Simpson et al. (1986), and Strayer and Smith (2001). Uncertainties indicated by dashes and question marks.

Table 19.2. Composition of macrobenthic communities in three habitats of the freshwater tidal Hudson near Kingston, based on % numerical abundance

Taxon	Soft bottom	Beds of submersed vegetation	Rocky shoreline
Oligochaeta	70%	41%	9.2%
Amphipoda	13%	0.4%	3.7%
Bivalvia	6.8%	16%	0.5%
Diptera	5.6%	21%	45%
Turbellaria	2.9%	1.7%	5.5%
Others	1.3%	0.4%	3.1%
Nematoda	0.6%	18%	20%
Non-dipteran insects	0.1%	0.3%	6.3%
Gastropoda	0.02%	2.3%	7.1%

From Strayer and Smith (2000, 2001).

Gammarus tigrinus is common throughout the freshwater tidal Hudson River. Like other benthic animals, its local density varies from place to place by more than 1,000-fold. Of this variation, 11 percent can be attributed to sampling error, 14 percent can be explained by environmental variables like bottom type, and 75 percent remains unexplained (Strayer and Smith, 2001). This unexplained variation could be due to biological factors (e.g., sediment bacteria, amphipod behavior, fish predation), disturbance history, unmeasured characteristics of the environment (e.g., local current regime, sediment stability), and so on. Understanding the causes and consequences of spatial variation in large-river benthic communities represents a major research challenge.

Temporal Variation in the Hudson Zoobenthos

Benthic communities vary over time in response to season, disturbances, species invasions, human alteration of riverine habitats, long-term climate change, and so on. Unfortunately, very little is known about how the Hudson's benthos varies over time. Based on work done in other rivers and estuaries, we can assume that there are significant seasonal changes in the community (for example, Wolff, 1983; Beckett, 1992). The Hudson's zoobenthos must have changed greatly over the

past one hundred to two hundred years in response to pollution and habitat alteration by humans. Further, it seems likely that there has been natural long-term variation in the benthic community. However, we know almost nothing about the nature of these changes. The only temporal change in the zoobenthos that has been well studied in the Hudson is its response to the zebra mussel invasion.

Zebra mussels first appeared in the river in May 1991 and by the end of 1992 constituted over half of heterotrophic biomass in the freshwater tidal Hudson (Strayer, Chapter 21, this volume). They reduced the biomass of phytoplankton and small zooplankton by 80–90 percent (Caraco et al., 1997; Pace, Findlay, and Fischer, 1998; Chapter 9, this volume; Chapter 16, this volume), changed the species composition of the remaining phytoplankton (Smith et al., 1998), increased water clarity by 45 percent (Caraco et al., 1997), changed concentrations of dissolved oxygen and plant nutrients (Caraco et al., 2000), and increased numbers of bacterioplankton (Findlay, Pace, and Fischer, 1998).

The zoobenthos showed three kinds of response to the zebra mussel invasion. First, there was an overall depletion of the zoobenthos other than zebra mussels (Fig. 19.4, upper). Riverwide, we estimated a loss of about 4,000 animals/m^2 (Strayer and Smith, 2001), or roughly three benthic animals lost for every zebra mussel that appeared. Taken together with losses in the zooplankton (Pace et al., 1998), we estimated that about half of the biomass of invertebrates useful for fish forage was lost from the Hudson with the zebra mussel invasion (Strayer and Smith, 2001).

Second, the response of benthic species to the zebra mussel invasion depended on their trophic group. Species that feed on plankton (that is, suspension-feeders plus the phantom midge *Chaoborus punctipennis*, which eats small zooplankton) declined much more severely than species that feed on benthic food (that is, predators and deposit-feeders) (Fig. 19.4, middle). Since the zebra mussel invasion, benthic planktivores have declined by 46–100 percent, and several formerly common species appear to be on the verge of disappearing from the Hudson. Because these benthic planktivores constituted more than half of heterotrophic biomass in the freshwater tidal Hudson River before the zebra mussel invasion,

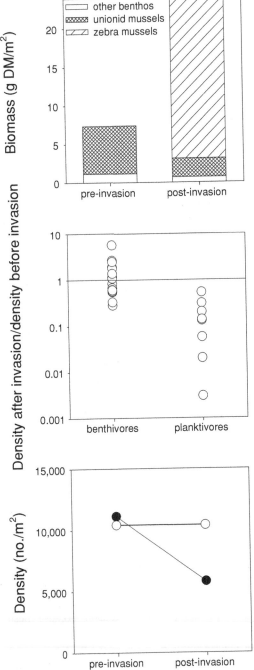

these large losses may have important ecological ramifications.

Third, the habitat occupied by benthic animals determined their response to the zebra mussel invasion. The zoobenthos of deep-water (>3 m deep), unvegetated, soft-bottom habitats declined sharply, while the zoobenthos of shallow-water, vegetated, soft-bottom habitats did not change (Fig. 19.4, bottom). Together, trophic group and habitat accounted for 51 percent of the variation in the response of benthic species to the zebra mussel invasion (Strayer and Smith, 2001).

It appears that loss of planktonic food, especially phytoplankton, was responsible for the large effects of the zebra mussel invasion on the Hudson's zoobenthos. Several pieces of evidence point to this conclusion: (a) benthic animals that feed on plankton declined, while those that feed on benthos did not (Fig. 19.4); (b) the body condition (body mass for a given body length) of unionid mussels declined, suggesting that they were receiving insufficient food (Strayer and Smith, 1996); and (c) population declines and body conditions of unionid mussels (which eat plankton) were uncorrelated with fouling rates by zebra mussels, suggesting that exploitative competition (rather than interference competition) was involved (Strayer and Smith, 1996). Thus, even though phytoplankton production forms only a small part of organic matter inputs to the Hudson, it appears to be of key importance in supporting higher trophic levels.

Figure 19.4 Effects of the zebra mussel invasion on the macrobenthos of the freshwater tidal Hudson River. Upper. Biomass of various parts of the community before and after the invasion. Middle. Effect of the zebra mussel invasion on populations of benthic animals in the freshwater tidal Hudson River according to trophic group. Each point represents the change in density of a taxon (usually a species) between 1990–92 and 1993–97 (animals other than unionids) or 1993–99 (unionids). The mean change for planktivores was significantly different than that for benthivores (t-test, $p < 0.0001$). Lower. Mean densities of all macrobenthos at deep water (black circles) and shallow water (white circles) stations before and after the zebra mussel invasion in the Hudson River. The interaction between habitat and the zebra mussel invasion is significant ($p < 0.02$). Based on Strayer and Smith (2001).

Table 19.3. Outputs of organic carbon from the freshwater tidal Hudson River. Because the different terms in the budget were estimated at different times and using different methods and assumptions, the overall budget is very approximate.

	Output (g C/m²-yr)
Phytoplanktonic respiration	230
Submerged macrophyte respiration	10
Bacterial respiration	220
Zooplanktonic respiration	10
Macrozoobenthic respiration (before zebra mussel)	**8**
Macrozoobenthic respiration (after zebra mussel)	**110**
Export to downriver at RKM 100	360
Burial in sediments	40

Modified from Howarth, Schneider, and Swaney (1996), Caraco et al. (2000), and Strayer and Smith (2001).

Importance of Benthic Animals in the Hudson River Ecosystem

We know enough to assess the roles of benthic animals in the Hudson ecosystem only for the freshwater parts of the estuary, although there is no reason to doubt that they are important further downriver. Furthermore, because we have essentially no information about the meiofauna and mobile epifauna in the river, all of our assessments underestimate the importance of benthic animals in the Hudson.

Most often, when ecologists speak of the "importance" of a group of organisms, they are referring vaguely to their abundance, biomass, or contribution to metabolic processes in the ecosystem. There are approximately 10,000 benthic animals/m² of river bottom, and these animals constitute more than half of heterotrophic biomass in the ecosystem (e.g., Strayer et al., 1996). With the arrival of the zebra mussel, zoobenthic respiration changed from a minor term to a major term in the organic carbon budget of the Hudson (Table 19.3), which was large enough to significantly reduce dissolved oxygen concentrations in the freshwater tidal Hudson (Caraco et al., 2000). However, these conventional assessments give limited insight into the roles that benthic animals play in the Hudson River ecosystem. It may be more useful to consider three specific roles that benthic animals play in the Hudson ecosystem: as suspension feeders, as forage for fish, and as sediment mixers.

Suspension-feeders feed on particles that are suspended in the water column, and thus have the potential to affect the number and kind of phytoplankton and other suspended particles. Prior to the arrival of the zebra mussel, benthic animals (chiefly unionid mussels) were responsible for a little more than half of suspension-feeding activity in the freshwater tidal Hudson (Fig. 19.5), and may have exercised modest control over plankton in the upper river (RKM 213–248) (Caraco et al., 1997, Strayer et al., 1994). After the zebra mussel invasion, the activity of benthic suspension-feeders became enormous, and was a primary control on the amount and kind of phytoplankton in the freshwater estuary (Caraco et al., 1997; Cole and Caraco, Chapter 9, this volume), with effects that ramified into many other parts of the ecosystem (Findlay et al., 1998; Pace et al., 1998; Strayer et al., 1999; 2001; Caraco et al., 2000).

Benthic animals also serve as an important source of food to higher trophic levels, particularly fish. Except for very early life stages, every fish that has been the subject of a detailed dietary study in the Hudson has been found to feed

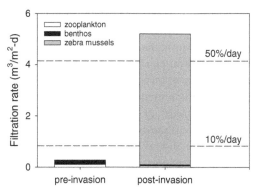

Figure 19.5. Estimated filtration rates of all suspension-feeders, averaged over the entire freshwater tidal Hudson River, before and after the zebra mussel invasion. The dashed lines show the percentage of the water in the freshwater tidal estuary that would theoretically be cleared of particles by suspension-feeders feeding at such rates, if particle retention were perfectly efficient. Based on Strayer and Smith (2001).

primarily on benthic animals, or on benthivorous fish (Table 19.1). Thus, benthic animals form the main link between phytoplankton, macrophytes, and allochthonous inputs at the base of the Hudson's food chain, and fish at its top. Because the zebra mussel invasion radically reduced the biomass of invertebrates that serve as fish food in the Hudson (Pace et al., 1998; Strayer and Smith, 2001), we might expect to see consequent changes in the Hudson's fish communities.

Finally, the feeding, burrowing, and movement of benthic animals mix sediments. Such mixing activities may alter exchanges of materials between sediment and overlying water (e.g., McCall and Tevesz, 1982; Robbins, 1982; Van de Bund et al., 1994). Although sediment mixing by benthic animals has not been investigated in the Hudson, its benthos is dominated by animals that are known to be effective sediment mixers (i.e., tubificid oligochaetes, chironomids, amphipods, and unionid mussels – Robbins, 1982; Van de Bund, Goedkoop, and Johnson, 1994; McCall et al., 1995), and many important substances in the river (notably PCBs) are associated with the sediments. Thus, it seems likely that benthic animals play important roles as sediment mixers in the Hudson.

The role of benthic animals in the Hudson ecosystem is thus larger and more complex than would be suggested from a conventional assessment of biomass or metabolism. The overall importance of the zoobenthos in the ecosystem differs across specific roles, as does the importance of different members of the zoobenthos. Thus, bivalves are important suspension-feeders, amphipods are especially important as fish food, and oligochaetes probably are important in mixing sediments. Even this brief consideration of a few specific roles of benthic animals shows that they form a vital part of the Hudson River ecosystem.

The relative importance of the two major groups of invertebrates – zooplankton and zoobenthos – differs across types of aquatic ecosystems. Pace et al. (1992) pointed out that zooplankton densities are lower in advective habitats such as estuaries and rivers than in still-water habitats such as lakes. In contrast, because benthic animals are not carried en masse downriver by water flow, we would expect that benthic animal densities could be just as high in rivers and estuaries as in lakes. Available data support this idea, and further show

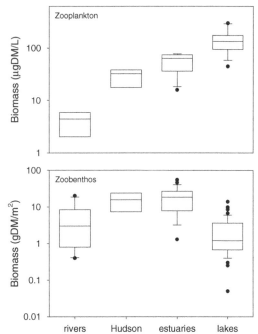

Figure 19.6. Biomass of zooplankton and zoobenthos in large rivers, the freshwater tidal Hudson River, estuaries, and lakes. Boxes show 25th and 75th percentiles (horizontal line is the median), whiskers show 5th and 95th percentiles, and dots show outliers. For zoobenthos, sample sizes are as follows: large rivers (10), Hudson River (2; i.e., pre- and post zebra mussel invasion), estuaries (23), and lakes (41). Zooplankton data from Pace, Findlay, and Lints (1992); zoobenthos data compiled from various sources.

that benthic biomass is especially high in estuaries (Fig. 19.6). Perhaps estuaries support higher benthic biomass than lakes because estuaries have greater inputs of physical energy (especially tidal currents), which leads to better vertical mixing and higher rates of food supply to the sediments (Nixon, 1988). The beneficial effects of physical energy may be reduced in rivers because of high temporal variance in energy supply rates, leading to scour, fill, and disturbance of the benthos. Further, food quality may be lower in rivers than in estuaries because of greater relative inputs of detrital allochthonous material of low nutritional quality. Thus, although site-to-site variation will be high, zoobenthos/zooplankton ratios might be highest in rivers, intermediate in estuaries, and lowest in lakes.

Traditionally, the ecological communities of the sediments and open water are considered separately, probably because the different habitats

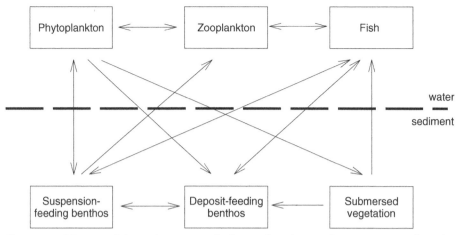

Figure 19.7. Diagram of the major community interactions in aquatic ecosystems such as the Hudson River. Arrows show the hypothesized direction of control. Note that many interaction arrows cross the sediment-water interface.

are studied by different groups of scientists using different methods. Nevertheless, connections between the benthos and the overlying water of the Hudson are numerous and strong (Fig. 19.7). Benthic suspension-feeders, especially bivalves, can regulate the amount and kind of plankton (Dame, 1996; Strayer et al., 1999), as was shown most clearly by the zebra mussel invasion of the Hudson (Cole and Caraco, Chapter 9, this volume; Pace and Lonsdale, Chapter 16, this volume). The benthic animal community in turn depends on the amount and kind of plankton as a key food source. Seasonal, interannual (Johnson, Bostrom, and van de Bund, 1989), or long-term changes in the plankton can cause large changes in the zoobenthos. In the Hudson, the removal of edible suspended particles by zebra mussels led to large changes in the zoobenthos (Fig. 19.4). Benthic plant communities likewise depend on the amount of suspended particles, which regulate the amount of light that penetrates to the sediments. A concrete example of this link was the possible increase in rooted plants (Caraco et al., 2000; Findlay et al., Chapter 17, this volume) and associated animals (Fig. 19.4) after zebra mussels reduced plankton biomass in the Hudson. Further, rooted plants may negatively influence phytoplankton, through a complex series of interactions (Scheffer, 1998). Finally, as shown in Table 19.1, benthic prey dominates fish diets in the Hudson, so that there may be strong reciprocal links between fish and zoobenthos in aquatic ecosystems (e.g., Strayer, 1991).

Thus, many aquatic ecosystems, especially shallow, well mixed habitats like the Hudson, function more as unified systems than as the isolated boxes suggested by compartmentalized research studies and textbook diagrams.

Acknowledgments

I appreciate the dedicated assistance of Chris Anderson, Chris Borg, Karyl Brewster-Geisz, David Cohen, Chris Edelstein, David Fischer, Dean Hunter, Jeff Janota, Carolyn Klocker, Craig Jankowski, Greg Lampman, Colleen Lutz, Heather Malcom, Erik Molinaro, Alex Nixon, Elizabeth Pangia, Sarah Poppenhouse, Bill Shaw, Lane Smith, Martha Young, and Brian Zielinski, and the continued intellectual support of my colleagues Nina Caraco, Jon Cole, Stuart Findlay, and Mike Pace. Stuart Findlay offered helpful comments on the manuscript. I am grateful to the Hudson River Foundation and the National Science Foundation for their support of my work on the Hudson's zoobenthos. This is a contribution to the program of the Institute of Ecosystem Studies.

REFERENCES

Bath, D. W., and O'Connor, J. M. 1985. Food preferences of white perch in the Hudson River estuary. *New York Fish and Game Journal* **32**: 63–70.

Beckett, D. C. 1992. Phenology of the larval Chironomidae of a large temperate Nearctic river. *Journal of Freshwater Ecology* **7**: 303–316.

Bode, R. W., Novak, M. A., Fagnani, J. P., and Denicola, D. M. 1986. *The Benthic Macroinvertebrates of the Hudson River from Troy to Albany, New York.* Final Report to the Hudson River Foundation, New York.

Burch, J. B. 1975. *Freshwater unionacean clams (Mollusca, Pelecypoda) of North America.* Revised edition. Hamburg, MI: Malacological Publications.

Caraco, N. F., Cole, J. J., Findlay, S. E. G., Fischer, D. T., Lampman, G. G., Pace, M. L., and Strayer, D. L. 2000. Dissolved oxygen declines associated with the invasion of the zebra mussel (*Dreissena polymorpha*). *Environmental Science and Technology* **34**: 1204–1210.

Caraco, N. F., Cole, J. J., Raymond, P. A., Strayer, D. L., Pace, M. L., Findlay, S. E. G., and Fischer, D. T. 1997. Zebra mussel invasion in a large, turbid river: phytoplankton response to increased grazing. *Ecology* **78**: 588–602.

Carlson, D. M., and Simpson, K. W. 1987. Gut contents of juvenile shortnose sturgeon in the Upper Hudson River estuary. *Copeia* 1987: 196–202.

Cole, J. J., Caraco, N. F., and Peierls, B. 1992. Can phytoplankton maintain a positive carbon balance in a turbid, freshwater, tidal estuary? *Limnology and Oceanography* **37**: 1608–1617.

Crandall, M. E. 1977. Epibenthic invertebrates of Croton Bay in the Hudson River. *New York Fish and Game Journal* **24**: 178–86.

Crumb, S. E. 1977. Macrobenthos of the tidal Delaware River between Trenton and Burlington. *Chesapeake Science* **18**: 253–65.

Curran, H. W., and Ries, D. T. 1937. Fisheries investigations in the lower Hudson River, in E. Moore (ed.). *A Biological Survey of the Lower Hudson watershed.* Supplement to the 26th Annual Report of the New York State Conservation Department, Albany, NY, pp. 124–45.

Dame, R. F. 1996. *Ecology of Marine Bivalves: An Ecosystem Approach.* Boca Raton, FL: CRC Press.

Dekay, J. E. 1844. *Zoology of New York. Part 5. Mollusca.* Albany, NY: Carroll and Cook.

Diaz, R. J. 1989. Pollution and tidal benthic communities of the James River estuary, Virginia. *Hydrobiologia* **180**: 195–211.

Duryea, M. and Schmidt, R. E. 1987. Feeding biology of tesselated darter (*Etheostoma olmstedi atromaculatus*) at Tivoli North Bay, Hudson River, New York, in E. A. Blair and J. C. Cooper (ed.). *Polgar Fellowship reports of the Hudson River National Estuarine Research Reserve Program, 1986.* Hudson River Foundation, New York, NY, pp. III-1–III-19.

Ettinger, W. S. 1982. Macrobenthos of the freshwater tidal Schuylkill River at Philadelphia, Pennsylvania. *Journal of Freshwater Ecology* **1**: 599–606.

Findlay, S., Pace, M. L., and Fischer, D. T. 1998. Response of heterotrophic planktonic bacteria to the zebra mussel invasion of the tidal freshwater Hudson River. *Microbial Ecology* **36**: 131–40.

Findlay, S., Schoeberl, K., and Wagner, B. 1989. Abundance, composition, and dynamics of the invertebrate fauna of a tidal freshwater wetland. *Journal of the North American Benthological Society* **8**: 140–8.

Fryer, G. 1991. *A Natural History of the Lakes, Tarns and Streams of the English Lake District.* Ambleside, UK: Freshwater Biological Association.

Gardinier, M. N., and Hoff, T. B. 1983. Diet of striped bass in the Hudson River estuary. *New York Fish and Game Journal* **29**: 152–65.

Gordon, M. E. 1986. Rafinesque's Hudson River mussels: a re-evaluation. *Malacology Data Net* **1**: 141–4.

Hakenkamp, C. C., Morin, A., and Strayer, D. L. 2002. The functional importance of freshwater meiofauna, in S. D. Rundle, A. L. Robertson, and J. M. Schmid-Araya (eds.). *Freshwater Meiofauna: Biology and Ecology.* Leiden, The Netherlands: Backhuys Publication, pp. 321–35.

Hirschfield, H. I., Rachlin, J. W., and Leff, E. 1966. A survey of the invertebrates from selected sites of the lower Hudson River, in M. Eisenbud and D. B. Stevens (eds.). *Hudson River Ecology.* Hudson River Valley Commission, Poughkeepsie, NY, pp. 220–57.

Howarth, R. W., Schneider, R., and Swaney, D. 1996. Metabolism and organic carbon fluxes in the tidal freshwater Hudson River. *Estuaries* **19**: 848–65.

Howells, G. P., Musnick, E., and Hirschfield, H. I. 1969. Invertebrates of the Hudson River, in G. P. Howells and G. J. Lauer (eds.). *Hudson River ecology: proceedings of a symposium.* New York State Department of Environmental Conservation, Albany, NY, pp. 262–80.

Hyman, L. H., and Jones, E. R. 1959. Turbellaria, in W. T. Edmondson (ed.). *Fresh-water Biology.* Second edition. New York: Wiley, 323–65.

Johnson, R. K., Bostrom, B., and van de Bund, W. 1989. Interactions between *Chironomus plumosus* and the microbial community in surficial sediments of a shallow, eutrophic lake. *Limnology and Oceanography* **34**: 992–1003.

Jokinen, E. H. 1992. *The Freshwater Snails (Mollusca: Gastropoda) of New York State. Bulletin of the New York State Museum* 482: Albany, New York, pp. 1–112.

Lea, I. 1829. Description of a new genus of the family of naiades, including eight new species, four of which are new; also the description of eleven new species of the genus *Unio* from the rivers of the United States: with observations on some of the characters of the naiads. *Transactions of the American Philosophical Society* **3**(N.S.): 403–457 + plates vii–xiv.

Limburg, K. E. 1988. Studies of young-of-the-year river herring and American shad in the Tivoli Bays, Hudson River, New York, in J. R. Waldman and E. A. Blair (ed.). *Polgar Fellowship reports of the Hudson River Research Reserve Program, 1987*, Hudson River Foundation, New York, NY, pp. VII-1–VII-62.

Massengill, R. R. 1976. Benthic fauna: 1965–1967 versus 1968–1972, in D. Merriam and L. M. Thorpe (eds.). *The Connecticut River ecological study: the impact of a nuclear power plant. American Fisheries Society Monograph* **1**: 39–59.

McCall, P. L., and Tevesz, M. J. S. 1982. The effects of benthos on physical properties of freshwater sediments, in P. L. McCall and M. J. S. Tevesz (eds.). *Animal-Sediment Relations: The Biogenic Alteration of Sediments*. New York: Plenum Press, pp. 105–76.

McCall, P. L., Tevesz, M. J. S., Wang, X., and Jackson, J. R. 1995. Particle mixing rates of freshwater bivalves: *Anodonta grandis* (Unionidae) and *Sphaerium striatinum* (Pisidiidae). *Journal of Great Lakes Research* **21**: 333–9.

McLaren, J. B., Peck, T. H., Dey, W. P., and Gardinier, M. 1988. Biology of Atlantic tomcod in the Hudson River estuary. *American Fisheries Society Monograph* **4**: 102–112.

Menzie, C. A. 1980. The chironomid (Insecta: Diptera) and other fauna of a *Myriophyllum spicatum* L. Plant bed in the lower Hudson River. *Estuaries* **3**: 38–54.

New York State Department of Environmental Conservation. 1993. *Hudson River Estuary Quarterly Issues Update and State of the Hudson Report*. Hudson River Estuary Management Program, New York State Department of Environmental Conservation.

Nixon, S. W. 1988. Physical energy inputs and the comparative ecology of lake and marine ecosystems. *Limnology and Oceanography* **33**: 1005–25.

Oliver, D. R., and Roussel, M. E. 1983. *The insects and arachnids of Canada. Part 11. The genera of larval midges of Canada: Diptera: Chironomidae*. Agriculture Canada Publication 1746.

Pace, M. L., Findlay, S. E. G., and Fischer, D. T. 1998. Effects of an invasive bivalve on the zooplankton community of the Hudson River. *Freshwater Biology* **39**: 103–116.

Pace, M. L., Findlay, S. E. G., and Lints, D. 1992. Zooplankton in advective environments: the Hudson River community and a comparative analysis. *Canadian Journal of Fisheries and Aquatic Sciences* **49**: 1060–9.

Richard, E., and Schmidt, R. E. 1987. Feeding biology of the banded killifish (*Fundulus diaphanus*) at Tivoli North Bay, Hudson River, New York, in E. A. Blair and J. C. Cooper (eds.). *Polgar Fellowship reports of the Hudson River National Estuarine Research Reserve Program, 1986*. Hudson River Foundation, New York, NY, pp. II-1–II-20.

Ristich, S. S., Crandall, M. E., and Fortier, J. 1977. Benthic and epibenthic macroinvertebrates of the Hudson River. I. Distribution, natural history and community structure. *Estuarine and Coastal Marine Science* **5**: 255–66.

Robbins, J. A. 1982. Stratigraphic and dynamic effects of sediment reworking by Great Lakes zoobenthos. *Hydrobiologia* **92**: 611–22.

Say, T. 1821. Descriptions of univalve shells of the United States. *Journal of the Philadelphia Academy of Sciences* **2**: 150–78.

Schaper, H. F. 1989. Shell middens in the lower Hudson valley. *Journal of the New York Archaeological Association* **98**: 13–24.

Scheffer, M. 1998. *Ecology of Shallow Lakes*. New York: Chapman and Hall.

Simpson, K. W., Bode, R. W., Fagnani, J. P., and Denicola, D. M. 1984. *The freshwater macrobenthos of the main channel, Hudson River, part B: biology, taxonomy and distribution of resident macrobenthic species. Final report to the Hudson River Foundation*, New York, NY, 203 pp.

Simpson, K. W., Fagnani, J. P., Bode, R. W., Denicola, D. M., and Abele, L. E. 1986. Organism-substrate relationships in the main channel of the lower Hudson River. *Journal of the North American Benthological Society* **5**: 41–57.

Simpson, K. W., Fagnani, J. P., Denicola, D. M., and Bode, R. W. 1985. Widespread distribution of some estuarine crustaceans (*Cyathura polita, Chiridotea almyra, Almyracuma proximoculi*) in the limnetic zone of the lower Hudson River, New York. *Estuaries* **8**: 373–80.

Smith, S., and Schmidt, R. E. 1988. Trophic status of the spottail shiner (*Notropis hudsonius*) in Tivoli North Bay, a Hudson River freshwater tidal marsh, in J. R. Waldman and E. A. Blair (eds.). *Polgar Fellowship reports of the Hudson River Research Reserve Program, 1987*, Hudson River Foundation, New York, NY, pp. VI-1–VI-25.

Smith, T. E., Stevenson, R. J., Caraco, N. F., and Cole, J. J. 1998. Changes in phytoplankton community structure during the zebra mussel (*Dreissena polymorpha*) invasion of the Hudson River, New York. *Journal of Plankton Research* **20**: 1567–79.

Strayer, D. 1985. The benthic micrometazoans of Mirror Lake, New Hampshire. *Archiv für Hydrobiologie Supplementband* **72**: 287–426.

1991. Perspectives on the size structure of the lacustrine zoobenthos, its causes, and its consequences. *Journal of the North American Benthological Society* **10**: 210–221.

Strayer, D. L., Caraco, N. F., Cole, J. J., Findlay, S., and Pace, M. L. 1999. Transformation of freshwater ecosystems by bivalves: a case study of zebra mussels in the Hudson River. *BioScience* **49**: 19–27.

Strayer, D. L., Hunter, D. C., Smith, L. C., and Borg, C. K. 1994. Distribution, abundance, and roles of freshwater clams (Bivalvia, Unionidae) in the freshwater tidal Hudson River. *Freshwater Biology* **31**: 239–48.

Strayer, D. L., Powell, J., Ambrose, P., Smith, L. C., Pace, M. L., and Fischer, D. T. 1996. Arrival, spread, and early dynamics of a zebra mussel (*Dreissena polymorpha*) population in the Hudson River estuary. *Canadian Journal of Fisheries and Aquatic Sciences* **53**: 1143–9.

Strayer, D. L., and Smith, L. C. 1996. Relationships between zebra mussels (*Dreissena polymorpha*) and unionid clams during the early stages of the zebra mussel invasion of the Hudson River. *Freshwater Biology* **36**: 771–9.

2000. Macroinvertebrates of a rocky shore in the freshwater tidal Hudson River. *Estuaries* **23**: 359–66.

2001. The zoobenthos of the freshwater tidal Hudson River and its response to the zebra mussel (*Dreissena polymorpha*) invasion. *Archiv für Hydrobiologie Supplementband* **139**: 1–52.

Strayer, D. L., Smith, L. C., and Hunter, D. C. 1998. Effects of the zebra mussel (*Dreissena polymorpha*) invasion on the macrobenthos of the freshwater tidal Hudson River. *Canadian Journal of Zoology* **76**: 419–25.

Thorne, G., and Swanger, H. H. 1936. A monograph of the nematode genera *Dorylaimus* Dujardin, *Aporcelaimus* n.g., *Dorylaimoides* n.g. and *Pungentus* n.g. *Capita Zoologica* **6**(4): 9–223.

Townes, H. K. 1937. Studies on the food organisms of fish, in. E. Moore (ed.). *A Biological Survey of the Lower Hudson Watershed.* Supplement to the 26th Annual Report of the New York State Conservation Department, Albany, NY, pp. 217–30.

Van de Bund, W., Goedkoop, W., and Johnson, R. K. 1994. Effects of deposit-feeder activity on bacterial production and abundance in profundal lake sediment. *Journal of the North American Benthological Society* **13**: 532–9.

Vincent, B. 1979. Étude du benthos d'eau douce dans le haut-estuaire du Saint-Laurent (Québec). *Canadian Journal of Zoology* **57**: 2171–82.

Weinstein, L. H. (ed.). 1977. *An Atlas of the Biologic Resources of the Hudson Estuary.* Yonkers, NY: Boyce Thompson Institute for Plant Research.

Wiggins, G. B. 1996. *Larvae of the North American caddisfly genera (Trichoptera).* Second edition. Toronto: University of Toronto Press.

Williams, B. S., Hogan, T., and Zo, Z. 1975. The benthic environment of the Hudson River in the vicinity of Ossining, New York, during 1972 and 1973. *New York Fish and Game Journal* **22**: 25–31.

Wolff, W. J. 1983. Estuarine benthos, in B. H. Ketchum (ed.). *Estuaries and Enclosed Seas.* New York: Elsevier Scientific, pp. 151–82.

Yozzo, D., and Steineck, P. L. 1994. Ostracoda from tidal freshwater wetlands at Stockport, Hudson River estuary: abundance, distribution, and composition. *Estuaries* **17**: 680–4.

20 Tidal Wetlands of the Hudson River Estuary

Erik Kiviat, Stuart E. G. Findlay,
and W. Charles Nieder

ABSTRACT There are about 2,900 ha of tidal wetlands in the Hudson River. Tidal flow between wetlands and the "main river" moves sediment, nutrients, organic matter, and organisms in and out of the wetlands. Sediment deposition rates in the tidal wetlands are about 0.05–2.9 cm yr^{-1}. In wetlands separated from the main river by a railroad, scoured pools remain just inside the openings and large tidal creeks radiate into the gradually-filling landward part of the wetland. Although large areas of the estuary have been filled, there has been a net gain of wetland area. Sediments, vegetation, animal communities, and ecosystem functions may be different in the railroad-sheltered wetlands and the wetlands on sandy dredged material than they were in unaltered wetlands. In Hudson River tidal wetlands, the elevation gradient, from near Mean Low Water through the intertidal zone to near Mean High Water, is correlated with increases in sediment organic matter (SOM), plant litter cover and litter mass, and aboveground peak biomass, height, and species richness of vascular plants. Among different marshes, SOM is correlated with abundance and diversity of benthic macroinvertebrates and fish species richness. Tidal waters are the main source of nitrogen for the marshes, whereas phosphorus appears to come from upland tributaries or decay of organic matter in sediments. The lower intertidal zone is nearly bare of vascular vegetation in the more brackish and the more sandy wetlands; in silty freshwater tidal wetlands this zone is occupied by spatterdock and pickerelweed. The middle intertidal zone is occupied by saltmarsh cordgrass in the most brackish marsh, but by a mixture of many broadleaf and grasslike plants in lower salinity wetlands. The upper intertidal zone is most often dominated by cattail or common reed. Areas near

Mean High Water may be dominated by common reed or saltmeadow cordgrass in the most brackish marsh, and in lower salinity wetlands are typically dominated by common reed, shrubs, or trees. Components of the tidal marsh fauna have low to moderate diversity and include a number of rare or habitat-dependent species. Many animals move in and out of the marshes on seasonal, daily, or tidal cycles.

Introduction

Scientists, managers, and educators are interested in estuarine wetlands because they are "hotspots" of ecological processes, biological diversity, and human activity and impact within the estuary. Tidal wetlands occur at the land edges of the Hudson River from the Troy Dam to Manhattan, especially from just south of Albany to the New Jersey state line. There are about 2,895 hectares (7,151 acres) of tidal wetland in the estuary, including 443 hectares (ha) of mudflats, 601 ha of broadleaf marsh, 1,236 ha of graminoid marsh (dominated by grasslike plants), and 617 ha of tree or shrub swamp (Picard, 2002). These wetlands are freshwater tidal north of about Constitution Marsh (Cold Spring), and brackish tidal from about Constitution south to Piermont Marsh (Piermont); Piermont is the southernmost major wetland (Fig. 20.1). Except for Piermont Marsh, the cordgrass (*Spartina* spp.) dominated "salt" marshes are outside the nominal Hudson River in New York Bay, the Arthur Kill, Jamaica Bay, the Hackensack Meadowlands, and other estuarine areas associated with the mouth of the Hudson.

Low salinity tidal wetlands such as those of the Hudson River have been studied less than salt marshes. Nonetheless, since about 1970, there has been considerable research on fresh-tidal and brackish-tidal wetlands in the Hudson River and elsewhere on the U.S. Atlantic Coast (see Kiviat, 1981 and Yozzo, Smith, and Lewis, 1994 for bibliographies). These studies have discovered that low salinity tidal marshes have different ecological structure and function than salt marshes (Odum, 1988), but are as important to the estuarine landscape, and in many cases are more threatened because low salinity wetlands occur mostly in the upper reaches of tidal rivers and bays where urban, industrial, and transportation uses tend to be concentrated. Many examples in this chapter refer

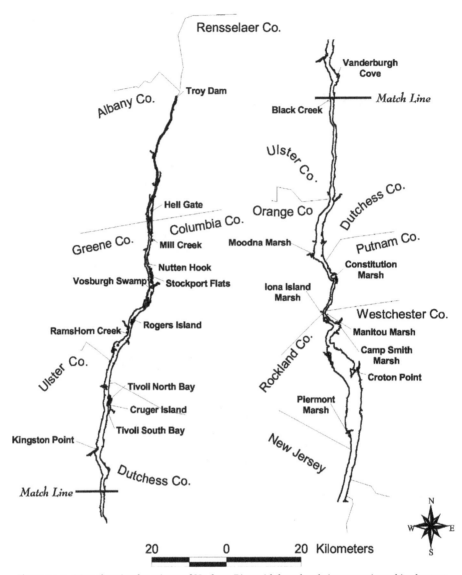

Figure 20.1. Map showing locations of Hudson River tidal wetland sites mentioned in the text.

to the tidal wetlands at Tivoli Bays on the Hudson River; ecological structure and function at Tivoli are similar to other Hudson River tidal marshes, acknowledging variation due to salinity and exposure to tidal energy in different parts of the river (see Mihocko et al., 2003).

Development and Types of Wetlands

Water control (by restricted openings in the railroads, sandbars, or other barriers) affects hydrology, sedimentation, vegetation, animal use, and biogeochemistry. Most organisms move between wetlands and estuary, or wetlands and uplands, actively or passively. Dissolved and suspended matter, plant propagules, drifting and swimming organisms, mobile higher animals, and pollutants move in and out of wetlands on tidal, daily, seasonal, or irregular schedules. After death, some of the plant production of the wetlands is exported to the estuary in the form of particulate and dissolved organic matter (collectively "detritus"). This makes the wetlands very "open" systems, and means that the biota and function of the wetlands are shaped to a significant degree by external influences, both natural and anthropogenic.

Table 20.1. Sediment deposition rates (cm · yr⁻¹) within Hudson River tidal wetlands as determined using radionuclide techniques (^{210}Pb and ^{137}Cs)

	Piermont Marsh	Iona Island	Tivoli Bays	Stockport Flats
Benoit et al., 1999			0.59–2.92	
Robideau, 1997	0.053–0.51	0.31–0.62	0.72–1.16	0.16–1.05
Peller & Bopp, 1986	0.7–0.8	0.2–0.7	0.1	0.3–0.9
Stevenson et al., 1986			0.29	0.32

Tidal exchange between the estuary and a wetland drives not only the sedimentation process but also many other processes within the wetland. Vertical tidal range varies from about 0.75 to 1.8 m along the river. The intercreek marsh ("high marsh") of most marshes is inundated by all but neap tides and at spring tides there may be 20–30 cm or more of standing water on the marsh surface. The position of the tidal wetland in the landscape (that is, in relation to both open water and uplands), and the presence of anthropogenic features (for example, railroad, road causeways, other areas of fill), affect the "hydrodynamic energy" level of the marsh which shapes its ecological structure and function.

Sediments must build up to the low tide level (Mean Low Water or MLW) to support wetland development. Wetlands occur in several types of sites in the Hudson River estuary: separated from the main river by a railroad, road, or sandbar ("enclosed" wetlands); not separated by such an obstruction but partly sheltered by an island, headland, fill, or other natural or artificial feature ("sheltered" wetlands); in the mouth of a tributary; narrow wetlands along exposed shorelines often of dredge spoil ("fringe" wetlands); broad wetlands exposed to the main river on one side; or occasionally in mid-river and exposed to deeper water on all sides (Green Flats and Upper Flats, Fig. 20.1). Physical shelter allows continued deposition of suspended sediment from estuarine waters and upland tributaries, and the surface elevation of a wetland continues to increase apparently until it reaches a steady state of deposition versus erosion (and decomposition) of sediment. Different wetland types support different ecological structure, biota, and function.

Spatial Patterns and Rates of Deposition

Sedimentation rates within the tidal marshes of the Hudson River National Estuarine Research Reserve (HRNERR) have been measured using radionuclide (^{210}Pb and ^{137}Cs) dating techniques (Peller and Bopp, 1986; Stevenson, Armstrong, and Schell, 1986; Robideau, 1997; Benoit et al., 1999). Most of the cores that were dated were collected from shallow subtidal areas (both tidal creeks and pools) with smaller numbers from intertidal marshes and tidal swamps. Deposition rates ranged from 0.053 to 2.92 cm yr⁻¹ with the highest rates in the shallow subtidal and intertidal mudflats of Tivoli South Bay. Tables 20.1 and 20.2 summarize the rates in both the marshes and marsh habitat types.

Goldhammer and Findlay (1988) measured tidal fluxes of suspended inorganic materials in Tivoli South Bay over several tidal cycles and estimated a mean deposition rate of 1.2 cm · yr⁻¹. Benoit et al. (1999), combining their data with the Goldhammer and Findlay (1988) data, concluded that the

Table 20.2. Sediment deposition rates (cm · yr⁻¹) within vegetated tidal marsh habitats of the Hudson River as determined using radionuclide techniques (^{210}Pb and ^{137}Cs). IT = intertidal zone. Sample sizes are in parentheses

	Shallow subtidal	Lower IT	Upper IT	Tidal swamp
Benoit et al., 1999	0.59–2.92 (6)			
Robideau, 1997	0.12–1.16 (13)	0.31 (1)	0.21–0.53 (2)	
Stevenson et al., 1986				0.29–0.32 (2)

measured tidal flux was not high enough to account for an average sediment accumulation rate of 1.18 cm · yr^{-1}. However, Benoit et al. (1999) noted that these flux studies were performed from May to November, which is typically a period of low freshwater discharge. Storms and higher flow periods in the spring could account for a greater import of sediment into Tivoli South Bay.

The Tivoli Bays contain areas of shrub or tree-dominated tidal swamp in the mouths of tributaries and in a 15 hectare neck between Cruger Island and the mainland. These areas of woody vegetation evidently represent pre-European (or at least pre-railroad) wetlands. The tributary mouth deposits are deltas where sediment suspended by swift currents in the tributary is deposited upon reaching the quiet waters of the bays. The shape of the Cruger Island neck and the sand underlying the organic sediments suggest the neck was a tombolo (a double sand spit swept out to the island by bidirectional currents along the mainland shore). In Tivoli North Bay, which was separated from the estuary by the railroad circa, 1850, the present form of the marsh was already recognisable by circa 1900 (ground photos) and 1936 (aerial photo; Roberts and Reynolds, 1938). Since then, the two large interior pools have progressively filled in whereas the two large pools just inside the railroad trestles have remained the same size. Apparently, the tidal currents rushing under the railroad trestles deposited sediments in the quiet waters of the bay, forming flood tidal deltas comparable to those at inlets through barrier beaches (Reinson, 1979). These deltas comprised shoals within the pool and a natural levee around the pool at a certain distance inside the trestle, with three to five primary tidal creeks radiating into the bay from the pool. Pools and primary creeks are relatively deep and hold water at low tide. Gradually the areas of the bay more distant from the trestles filled with sediment, forming progressively shrinking intertidal pools that do not hold water at low tide. Woody vegetation (especially tree and shrub willows, *Salix* spp., and false-indigo, *Amorpha fruticosa*) is established on the relatively stable levees of the trestle pools, and shrubs are scattered along the banks of the primary tidal creeks. Following the primary creeks into the bays, there is less vegetational evidence of a natural levee, and a shift from woody vegetation or purple loosestrife to narrowleaf cattail on the creek banks. This spatial pattern of one or more trestle pools with natural levees and radiating tidal creeks is characteristic of many of the marshes. Because the Hudson River has such diverse topography and historic alteration, however, individual marshes vary greatly in landscape position, size, stage of development, and other features.

Although deposition is dominant in most Hudson River tidal wetlands, some areas are actively eroding where the main river or large tidal creeks scour wetland edges. Fringe marshes on dredge spoil are subject to relatively high levels of hydrodynamic energy, and are expected to be stable or eroding rather than depositing. In addition to currents, wind and boat waves, and ice, certain animals cause resuspension of fine sediments in tidal marshes. Snapping turtle (Kiviat, 1980b), muskrat (*Ondatra zibethicus*) (Kiviat, 1994; Connors et al., 2000), beaver (*Castor canadensis*), European carp, killifishes, and American eel treading, burrowing, and rooting, and human boating and treading all contribute to resuspension of sediments.

During pre-European time, the Hudson River had some large wetlands. For example, Piermont Marsh (now 114 ha) and Iona Island Marsh (64 ha) are several thousand years old (Newman et al., 1969). The distribution of pre-European wetlands was altered because railroads on both sides of the river, roads, disposal of dredged material (dredge spoil), historic industries such as brick works and ice houses, and other development along the Hudson destroyed many wetlands but also created or enlarged certain wetlands. The railroads alone border 54 percent of the eastern shore and 63 percent of the western shore between the Troy Dam and Piermont (Squires, 1992). Based on old maps, Squires estimated that 121 ha (300 acres) of emergent marsh were lost to filling in the past 500 years but that there has been a net gain of 769 ha of wetlands. Squires also estimated that 2,713 ha of estuary overall were filled for spoil disposal, 810 ha for railroad construction, 729 ha for industrial development, and 445 ha for other purposes. We think that 121 ha of filled marsh is an underestimate because many maps do not show wetlands accurately; for example, old maps of Tivoli Bays variously show wetland or not in the Cruger Island neck between North Bay and South Bay

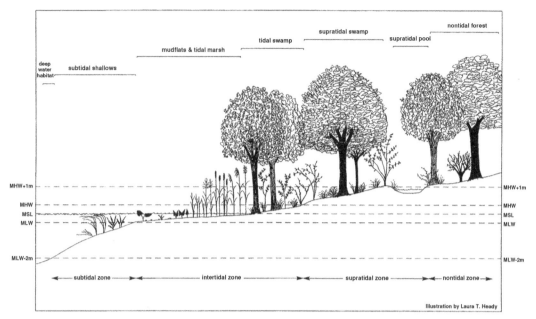

Figure 20.2. Diagram of tidal zones and plant communities of the Hudson River tidal wetlands. (Drawn by Laura T. Heady for Biodiversity Assessment Manual for the Hudson River Estuary Corridor, E. Kiviat and G. Stevens, New York State Department of Environmental Conservation, copyright © Hudsonia Ltd., 2001.)

(Kiviat, personal observation). Squires (1992) also estimated that 850 ha of marsh were created by the railroads and other changes.

The wetlands of Tivoli Bays were probably restricted to small areas in the mouths of tributaries and in the Cruger Island neck (Kiviat, 1974) amounting to <30 ha; construction of the east shore railroad circa 1850 caused more rapid deposition of sediments and expanded the wetlands to the approximately 240 hectares (600 acres) present today. Farther upriver, many wetlands and subtidal shallows were filled with dredge spoil and new wetlands formed on portions of the spoil. Most of the dredge spoil is sandy and many recently created wetlands on dredge spoil have large areas of soil lacking vascular vegetation, and low densities of benthic macroinvertebrates and fish (Mihocko et al., 2003). A few marshes such as Stockport Flats and the marsh at Hell Gate (Fig. 20.1) appear to have silty deposits over sand and are functionally intermediate between sandy fringe marshes and silty or mucky sheltered and enclosed marshes; Stockport and Hell Gate may represent the development of more "natural" marsh conditions on older, lower elevation spoil deposits (see Mihocko et al.,

2003). Because most currently existing wetlands are apparently different than pre-European wetlands in sediment type, vegetation, and other characteristics, the management and restoration of Hudson River wetlands are a challenge to science and policy.

Vegetation

Table 20.3 shows the dominant plants of typical tidal wetlands. Figure 20.2 shows idealized plant communities along the marsh elevation gradient. Tidal wetland plant species distributions are delimited by substrate (sediment) elevation because different species tolerate different lengths of inundation and exposure. The intertidal zone is the vertical stratum between low tide level (MLW) and high tide level (Mean High Water or MHW). In the Hudson River, the tidal amplitude or height of the intertidal zone varies from about 0.75 to 1.8 m, lowest in the Hudson Highlands and highest in the southern and northern ends of the estuary. Tidal wetlands have substrate levels within the intertidal zone, and supratidal wetlands have substrates <1 m above MHW (Kiviat and Stevens, 2001).

Table 20.3. Predominant plant species of Hudson River tidal wetlands. IT = intertidal zone

Elevation – community	Brackish water	Freshwater – fine sediment	Freshwater – sandy dredge spoil
Tidal swamp	Lower diversity than freshwater; very restricted in the more brackish sites	Red maple (*Acer rubrum*), red ash (*Fraxinus pennsylvanica* s.l.), black ash (*Fraxinus nigra*), swamp white oak (*Quercus bicolor*), smooth alder (*Alnus serrulata*), silky dogwood (*Cornus amomum*), Bell's honeysuckle (*Lonicera X bella*), spicebush (*Lindera benzoin*), willows (*Salix* spp.), purple loosestrife (*Lythrum salicaria*), etc.	Similar to fine sediment
Marsh – supratidal	Common reed (*Phragmites australis*), saltmeadow cordgrass (*Spartina patens*), saltgrass (*Distichlis spicata*), bulrushes (*Scirpus* spp.), marsh straw sedge (*Carex hormathodes*)	Lake sedge (*Carex lacustris*), purple loosestrife, common reed	Common reed
Marsh – upper IT	Common reed, narrowleaf cattail (*Typha angustifolia*), swamp rose mallow (*Hibiscus moscheutos*)	Narrowleaf cattail, hybrid cattail (*Typha X glauca*),[a] purple loosestrife, common reed, arrow arum (*Peltandra virginica*)	Purple loosestrife, common reed
Marsh – middle IT	Saltmarsh cordgrass (*Spartina alterniflora*)	Arrow arum, river bulrush (*Scirpus fluviatilis*) sweetflag (*Acorus*), wild-rice (*Zizania aquatica*), pickerelweed (*Pontederia cordata*), broadleaf arrowhead (*Sagittaria latifolia*), dotted smartweed (*Polygonum punctatum*), rice cutgrass (*Leersia oryzoides*), tidewater-hemp (*Amaranthus cannabinus*), nodding bur-marigold (*Bidens cernua*), narrowleaf cattail, hybrid cattail,[a] purple loosestrife, others	American threesquare (*Scirpus pungens*)
Marsh – lower IT	Little or no vascular vegetation	Spatterdock (*Nuphar advena*), pickerelweed, awl-leaf arrowhead (*Sagittaria subulata*), stunted submergent species	Spatterdock, American threesquare
Shallow subtidal zone[b] and "mudflats" just above mean low water (MLW)	Sago pondweed (*Potamogeton pectinatus*), Eurasian watermilfoil (*Myriophyllum spicatum*)	Wild-celery (*Vallisneria americana*), Eur. watermilfoil, clasping pondweed (*Potamogeton perfoliatus*), water-chestnut (*Trapa natans*), coontail (*Ceratophyllum demersum*), waterweeds (*Elodea canadensis, E. nuttallii*), water star-grass (*Zosterella dubia*)	Wild-celery, etc. (sparse)

[a] The hybrid of narrowleaf cattail and broadleaf cattail (*Typha latifolia*) is variable and has probably often been misidentified as one of the parent species. Hybrid cattail seems to dominate where there is more anthropogenic alteration or less muskrat activity (Kiviat, unpublished data).

[b] Not wetland in the strict sense.

The lower third of the intertidal zone in the fresh wetlands supports 1 m tall plants with very large heart-shaped leaf blades. Some areas of the lower intertidal zone are nearly bare "mudflats" (texture varies from sandy to sandy silt, silty, or organic), which may have sparse cover of submergent species or small emergent species. In the brackish wetlands, vascular plants are scarce or absent in the lower intertidal zone because no vascular plant species thrives in this combination of salinity and prolonged tidal flooding alternating with exposure to the air. The middle third of the intertidal zone supports a diverse mixture of plants in the fresh marshes; this community often forms a narrow (one to a few meters wide) belt along pool and creek banks, and may colonize intercreek areas, where ice, muskrats, or other agents disturb soil and vegetation (Connors et al., 2000).

Cattail, purple loosestrife, or common reed (color plate 4) typically dominate the upper intertidal zone in fresh or brackish marshes. Areas at or just above MHW in fresh-tidal wetlands support vegetation dominated by herbs, shrubs, or trees; in the most brackish wetland (Piermont Marsh) there are common reed (*Phragmites australis*) stands as well as salt meadows with a mixture of several dense low grass-like plants. Where MHW is situated at the upland edge of fresh-tidal marshes there is a diverse assemblage of wetland and upland plants influenced by irregular brief tidal flooding; rare plants or habitat-limited species may occur (for example, winged monkeyflower [*Mimulus alatus*] Sharma and Kiviat, 1994, cardinalflower [*Lobelia cardinalis*], and closed gentian [*Gentiana andrewsii*]). Vascular plants were discussed by Kiviat (1974, 1978a), Ristich, Fredrick, and Buckley (1976), Buckley and Ristich (1976), Kiviat et al. (1982), DeVries and DeWitt (1987), Senerchia-Nardone, Reilly, and Holland (1986), Reschke (1990), Kiviat and Beecher (1991), Stevens (2001), and Kiviat and Stevens (2001).

Swamps. "Marshes" are dominated by herbaceous plants although the marshes of the Hudson often contain scattered shrubs or trees; "swamps" are dominated by woody plants (shrubs or trees). Tidal swamps may be dominated by trees, shrubs, or both; each vegetation layer (tree, shrub, herb, moss) may be species rich or poor. At lower elevations, trees tend to be small (less than 30 cm diameter-at-breast-height [dbh]) and often have damaged crowns or multiple stems, whereas larger, healthier-looking trees grow at higher elevations on creek bank levees or in other supratidal habitats. The shrub layer is about 2–3 m tall and may be quite dense. Purple loosestrife (*Lythrum salicaria*), arrow arum (*Peltandra virginica*), and more than 50 other species of herbs occur in tidal swamps (Westad and Kiviat, 1986; Westad, 1987). The herbs grow mostly on top of the "hummocks" or woody root crowns formed by red maple and certain shrubs; a few herbs (for example, purple loosestrife, arrow arum) occur in the "hollows" on the swamp floor, on soil between the hummocks. As the substrate elevation increases from intertidal swamp to supratidal swamp, hummocks are smaller and fewer, and herbs occur more in the hollows. Bryophyte communities (mosses and liverworts) are well developed in fresh-tidal swamps (Leonardi and Kiviat, 1990; Leonardi, 1991) and these nonvascular plants often cover the hummocks, bases of tree and shrub stems, and logs.

Species diversity. Species richness (number of species) of vascular plants on 0.25 m^2 sampling plots tends to increase with elevation in Hudson River tidal marshes, although this is not consistent across all elevation levels or marsh types. In 1996 data on the vegetation of fifteen reference marshes, richness was zero to six species in the subtidal shallows and lower intertidal zone, and zero to ten species in the middle and upper intertidal zones (Kiviat et al., unpublished data). Subtidal vegetation may comprise a single, dominant species such as wild celery or, in more sheltered areas such as quiet secondary tidal creeks, a mixture of several species. Even in dense water-chestnut beds there may be three kinds of duckweeds (*Lemna minor*, *Spirodela polyrrhiza*, *Wolffia*) among the water-chestnut leaves. In the lower intertidal zone, spatterdock is often highly dominant; however, there can be mixtures of several species. Middle and upper intertidal zones tend to be species-rich, especially in the sheltered, high-organic matter marshes where muskrat or human activities, or the creek-associated disturbances, have reduced dominance by cattail (*Typha*). It is these seemingly haphazard assemblages of arrow arum, purple loosestrife, broadleaf arrowhead, dotted smartweed, water-hemp, cattails, and other plants, and the birds and butterflies attracted to them, that characterize the creek banks that many human visitors see from a boat.

Biomass. Peak aboveground standing crop (biomass) of vascular vegetation increases with elevation in the Hudson River marshes. Biomass is about 140 g dry mass $\cdot$ m^{-2} in submergent vegetation, 360 in water-chestnut, 150 in spatter-dock, 210 in pickerelweed, and 1,100 in cattail in fresh marshes (Kiviat and Beecher, 1991; also see Mihocko et al., 2003). In brackish marshes, biomass is roughly 1,000 g dry mass $\cdot$ m^{-2} in cattail, big cordgrass, saltmarsh cordgrass, purple loosestrife, and common reed, and 400 in spike grass, salt-meadow cordgrass, arrow arum, and pickerelweed (common reed attains the highest values) (Buckley and Ristich, 1977). These data are from dominant stands, optimum salinities, and seasonal peaks of biomass; biomass varies considerably. Peak biomass is attained about mid-July to mid-August, although some species (e.g., arrow-arum, river bulrush) may reach peak biomass early and begin to senesce and lose aboveground biomass in August.

Basal area (the aggregate, cross-sectional area of tree stems per unit area of ground at 1.4 m above the soil) is a good indicator of the dominance of trees. Three Hudson River tidal swamps (Mill Creek, Cruger Island Neck, and Mudder Kill) supported 8–34 m$^2 \cdot$ ha^{-1} basal area, low to moderately high values (Kiviat, unpublished data). Like herbaceous plant biomass, tree basal area also increases with elevation from the upper intertidal zone to the supratidal zone. Species richness of trees, shrubs, and herbs often increases with elevation in swamps as well. The swamps studied had five to ten tree species (with stems equal to or greater than 2.5 cm dbh) and 70–467 tree stems $\cdot$ ha^{-1}. Many trees (8–28 percent) had multiple stems, indicating ice damage or other stress.

Lower "plants." The algae are important organisms of the mud and plant surfaces in the intertidal zone, as well as of the plankton. Sixty-three genera of phytoplankton were sampled in a small, recently restored marsh at Camp Smith near Peekskill (Ristich et al., 1976). The generic composition of the phytoplankton in the marsh was considered similar to that in the main river. Bryophytes (mosses and liverworts) are prominent, even lush, on woody stem bases and exposed roots, purple loosestrife bases, logs, duckblinds, pilings, and lumber in the upper intertidal zone and (especially) the suprati-dal zone of the swamps and to a lesser extent marshes. A single floristic study has been conducted on tidal swamp bryophytes (Leonardi and Kiviat, 1989, 1990; Leonardi, 1991). Lichens occur on live and dead woody materials in the tidal wetlands (especially on bases, stems, and branches of swamp trees and shrubs), as well as on rocks in the upper intertidal zone and supratidal zone (Feeley-Connor, 1978; Royte, 1985). Lichens appear neither diverse nor abundant in the tidal wetlands, probably due to air (and water?) pollution.

Vegetation patterns in space and time. Vegetation displays spatial patterns and also changes over time. Temporal change in low salinity tidal wetlands, absent major disturbance, generally includes increase in stature, biomass, persistence aboveground in winter, resistance to decay, and abundance of woody species. Vegetation change is driven mainly by increase in substrate elevation from tidal deposition of sediment and in situ production of organic matter. In Tivoli North Bay, the sequence of change generally passes from SAV to spatterdock (and pickerelweed) to mixed middle intertidal species to narrowleaf cattail to woody species (or common reed). This pattern is not necessarily representative of other Hudson River wetlands, due to effects of sea level rise, variable rates of sediment deposition, different dominant plant species, and a variety of disturbances such as scouring by floods and ice. Common reed presumably speeds the buildup of the marsh surface (Rooth, Stevenson, and Cornwell, 2003) but how long Hudson River reed stands are stable, and whether they are invaded by woody plants, is unknown.

In 1991 and 1997, plant communities at the time of peak aboveground biomass (late July – early September) were mapped with true color stereo aerial photography. Simplified cover types of four emergent marshes are shown in Figure 20.3. With the partial exception of Stockport Flats, the

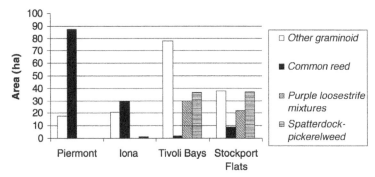

Figure 20.3. Emergent vegetation of four major tidal marshes at the Hudson River National Estuarine Research Reserve sites in summer 1997. The "other graminoid" class includes: narrowleaf cattail and sweetflag in Tivoli Bays; narrowleaf cattail, sweetflag, and bulrushes (*Scirpus* spp.) at Stockport Flats; narrowleaf cattail and bulrushes at Iona; and narrowleaf cattail, saltmarsh cordgrass, saltmeadow cordgrass, saltgrass, and bulrushes at Piermont (Hudson River National Estuarine Research Reserve, unpublished data).

marshes are dominated by graminoid vegetation. The vegetated lower intertidal zone, dominated by emergent broadleaf plants (spatterdock and pickerelweed), makes up a significant portion of Tivoli Bays and Stockport Flats. Wild rice is also abundant in the lower to middle intertidal zone at Stockport Flats.

Common reed occurs at all four marshes and is the dominant cover type at Piermont and Iona. Reed has been spreading at the Reserve sites for many years (Winogrond and Kiviat, 1997). At Iona and Tivoli the spread was nearly exponential in 1991 and continued at a high rate to at least 1997 (Fig. 20.4). Although purple loosestrife is prominent in Tivoli North Bay, it occurs mainly in mixed stands with narrowleaf cattail. Purple loosestrife

has declined in some marshes during the past three decades (Kiviat, personal observation).

Qualitative comparisons of the descriptions of sites in the 1930s and 1940s (Muenscher, 1935, 1937; Foley and Taber, 1951) with today's vegetation suggests a large increase in common reed and water-chestnut, and decreases in river bulrush, wild rice, and "muskgrass" or "stonewort" (Charophyta). Wild rice was rare in the early 1970s and has increased since, perhaps due to the mid-1970s cessation of herbicide use for water-chestnut control (Kiviat, personal observation). Wild celery has become much more abundant relative to the "invasive" Eurasian watermilfoil in the Tivoli Bays area during the same period (Kiviat, personal observation).

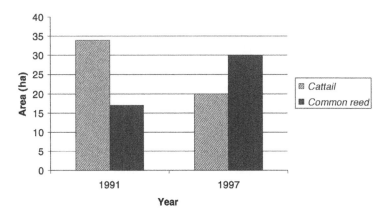

Figure 20.4. Decrease in cattail and and increase in common reed cover at Iona Island Marsh, 1991 to 1997 (Hudson River National Estuarine Research Reserve, unpublished data).

Table 20.4. Fauna of Hudson River tidal wetlands

Group	References	Findings
Mammals	Kiviat, 1978b, 1980a, 1994, personal observations; Connors et al., 2000; McGlynn and Ostfeld, 2000	Low diversity, few resident species; muskrat and beaver shape ecosystem via influences on sediments, vegetation, fauna
Birds	Kiviat, 1978a, 1996, personal observations; Kiviat and Tulmage, submitted; Kiviat et al., 1982, 1996; Stapleton and Kiviat, 1989; Swift, 1989	Low diversity but high density of certain species; wetlands important to certain rare and habitat-dependent species; breeding, migrant, and wintering faunas different; large numbers roost in marshes especially in common reed; high density of breeding birds on railroad causeways
Reptiles and amphibians	Kiviat, 1980b, 1997–1998; Stone, Kiviat, and Butkas, 1980; Rozycki and Kiviat, 1996; Rubbo and Kiviat, 1999; Simoes and Chambers, 1999; Stevens, 2001	Low diversity, diversity increases at higher elevations; snapping turtle abundant in lower salinity wetlands
Fishes	Kiviat et al., 1982; Schmidt, 1986; Duryea and Schmidt, 1987; Richard and Schmidt, 1987; Schmidt, 1993; Mihocko et al., 2003	Moderate diversity; higher diversity with greater physiographic diversity in marsh and higher SOM; resident, spawning-nursery, foraging, and transient faunas different; mummichog numerically dominant, important food for other organisms
Benthic macroinvertebrates near MLW	Mihocko et al., 2003	Dominated by chironomid midge larvae and oligochaetes; number of higher taxa and density correlated with SOM
Litter invertebrates beneath common reed and narrowleaf cattail	Kiviat unpublished data	Dominated by mites and springtails; at higher taxonomic levels, fauna of reed and cattail similar
Insects on and inside emergent plants	Krause, Rietsma, and Kiviat, 1997; Kiviat, unpublished data	Biomass higher on common reed than purple loosestrife or narrowleaf cattail in spring, all about the same in summer
Water-lily leaf beetle on water-chestnut	Schmidt, 1986	Eggs, larvae and adults abundant but little leaf biomass removed
Butterflies	Barbour and Kiviat, 1986; Kiviat personal observations	25 species found in tidal swamp and upland and railroad edges of a tidal marsh; few species in tidal marsh interior

Fauna

Many animals move actively or passively among wetland habitats and along the elevation gradient; movements between the tidal wetlands and either the main river or the uplands are also common and may follow seasonal, daily, or tidal cycles (see Kiviat, 1989). The tidal wetland fauna is summarized by taxonomic groups in Table 20.4.

Organic Matter and Nutrients

Organic matter on the marsh surface is derived from plant litter, settles out of tidal water, and to a lesser extent is delivered from upland tributaries. Sediments in North Bay range from about 8 percent to 45 percent organic matter (dry mass) in the upper 5 cm (Kiviat and Beecher, 1991). SOM in the upper 15 cm in fifteen reference marshes averaged 11.6 percent with an observed range of 1–80 percent and half the observations in the range 4–16 percent (Kiviat et al., unpublished data). SOM (on a small plot basis) is correlated with marsh surface elevation, aboveground biomass and stature of vascular vegetation, and plant species richness, benthic macroinvertebrate and taxon richness, and (on a whole-marsh basis) fish species richness and mummichog density (Findlay et al., 2002a; Mihocko et al., 2003).

Plant Litter: Abundance, Decay, and Microbial Growth

In most wetlands the majority of plant production is not consumed during the lifetime of the plant parts but enters a detritus-based food web (Odum et al., 1984) and serves as a growth substrate for various microbes and food for many benthic invertebrates (Vos et al., 2002). In the tidal freshwater wetlands of the Hudson, quantities of plant litter vary among marsh types, along elevational gradients within a marsh and among plant communities (Kiviat and Beecher, 1991; Mihocko et al., 2003). Litter cover was highest in the high marsh zone with values approaching 100 percent; in the marshes overall, median litter cover was 1 percent with half the observations in the range 0–25 percent. As suggested by the coarser-scale sampling, maximal litter abundance occurs in communities of intertidal emergent plants with standing stocks of litter on the order of 500–1000+ g dry mass $\cdot$ m^{-2}. These high standing stocks are probably due to a combination of high rates of litter production, relatively slow decay, and limited opportunity for export. Lower intertidal areas occupied by broadleaf (e.g., spatterdock, arrow arum) or floating-leaf plants (e.g., water-chestnut) have much less recognizable litter and what is shed from the plants is rapidly decomposed or exported with tidal waters (Findlay, Howe, and Austin, 1990).

Decay of litter by microbes is typically a major fate of detritus and rates of decomposition are known to vary significantly among plant species (Odum and Heywood, 1978; Brinson, Lugo, and Brown, 1981). Loss of mass from recognizable fragments of plant litter occurs via a number of separate processes including mechanical fragmentation into smaller, unrecognizable particles, leaching of dissolved organic components, and mineralization to carbon dioxide (CO_2) by bacteria and fungi. Decay rates for cattail, reed, and loosestrife are such that less than half the litter decays within a year from plant senescence (exponential mass loss coefficients 0.3–0.4 $\cdot$ year^{-1}). As a general rule, the "softer" broadleaf plants have the highest rates of mass loss such that litter decomposes completely within a year (or less). In contrast the predominant grasslike plants of intertidal marshes generate litter with much slower decay and, for instance, roughly 50 percent of the litter from reed is still retained in coarse-mesh litter bags three years after the death of aerial stems (Findlay, Dye, and Kuehn, 2002b). For many emergent species, plants will spend as much as a year as standing dead material where the culms may serve as habitat for invertebrates (Krause, Rietsma, and Kiviat, 1997) and provide physical structure on the marsh. In contrast to previous work in other wetland systems (e.g., Newell and Porter, 2000), there appears to be no mass loss from the standing dead phase of common reed although there is an abundant fungal community. Also, litter mass loss over the winter months appears to be minimal.

There is a clear transition from fungal-dominated communities on relatively large litter as is common through the first few years of decay to a bacteria-dominated community in the sediments and associated with finer particles of organic matter (Sinsabaugh and Findlay, 1995; Findlay et al., 2002b). In relatively intact litter over the first two to three years of decay, fungal biomass can be hundreds of times greater than bacterial biomass and fungal production is much greater than bacterial production. Bacterial production in surface sediments of the Hudson wetlands is well within the range for bacterial growth reported from other wetland and shallow aquatic habitats (Austin and Findlay, 1989).

Nutrient Cycling

NUTRIENTS: SOURCES AND TRANSFORMATIONS

The largest mass of nutrients is delivered by incoming tidal waters and, for example, a square meter of marsh inundated twice a day by 25 cm of tidal water carrying 0.5 mg dissolved inorganic $N \cdot L^{-1}$ has a potential supply of 250 mg $N \cdot m^{-2} \cdot d^{-1}$. At least a portion of this potential N supply is retained within some marshes since ebb-tide concentrations of nitrate were roughly 1 mg $NO_3 \cdot L^{-1}$, lower than mean nitrate concentrations in the mainstem, where NO_3 is 2.5 mg $NO_3 \cdot L^{-1}$ (Lampman, Caraco, and Cole, 1999). Phosphorus (P) concentrations in ebb-tide waters range from 40 to 80 μg $PO_4 \cdot L^{-1}$ and are not demonstrably lower than in the mainstem ($PO_4 \sim 60 \, \mu$g $\cdot L^{-1}$; Lampman et al., 1999). Given the significant plant demand for PO_4, it suggests there must be reasonably large sources of PO_4 to balance plant removal and maintain rough equality in flood versus ebb tide concentrations. This P source may be from tributary inputs since many tributaries (for example, Stony Creek and Saw Kill in the Tivoli Bays) receive treated sewage leading to greatly elevated P concentrations. Sediment P release is another likely candidate for this source of P since porewater concentrations are quite high (see below). If porewaters can bypass the surface oxidized layer where P is effectively scavenged (Vernon, 2002), the large reservoir of inorganic P in deeper sediment layers (ultimately derived from decay of organic materials) may contribute to the net efflux of P from Hudson marshes. There is essentially no information on sources or exchanges of organic nutrients (dissolved organic N, dissolved organic P, etc.) although some Hudson marshes act as minor sources of dissolved organic C to the mainstem (Findlay et al., 1998).

Tributary inputs of nutrients to Hudson River marshes vary greatly among sites due to both variation in size of tributary relative to area of marsh and variation in nutrient concentration, the latter of which seems related to agricultural lands and human population (Parsons and Lovett, 1992; Nieder, unpublished). Tributaries are only occasionally a large source compared to tidal waters; for instance, at Tivoli North Bay, Stony Creek has a relatively high dissolved inorganic N concentration (1998 mean ≥ 2 mg $NO_3 \cdot L^{-1}$; Hudson River National Estuarine Research Reserve, unpublished data) and a modest discharge ($\sim 100 \cdot L \, s^{-1}$ summer) resulting in a potential contribution of about 40 mg $N \cdot m^{-2} \, d^{-1}$ (assuming an intertidal marsh area of 1,000,000 m^2 based on area of cattail plus purple loosestrife), much less than the potential tidal water contribution (250 mg $N \cdot m^2 \cdot d$).

Porewater nutrients represent a large potential pool and more importantly are the proximate source of nutrients for the emergent vascular plants. Typical growing season porewater concentrations are 0.25–1 mg ammonium $\cdot L^{-1}$ with frequently low nitrate concentrations of 0.1 mg $N \cdot L^{-1}$ or less. Porewater phosphate is typically high with concentrations >1–2 mg PO_4-P $\cdot L^{-1}$ and significant variability among plant species (Templer et al., 1998). Porewater nutrient concentrations vary among marsh types, with two to three times higher concentrations in enclosed marshes (NH_4-N = 0.5 mg $\cdot L^{-1}$; $PO_4 = 9$ mg $\cdot L^{-1}$) versus sheltered or fringe (0.22 and 1.64 mg $\cdot L^{-1}$, respectively). Phosphate was significantly, positively ($r = 0.68$) related to sediment organic content, which varies among marsh types. Plant demand for porewater nutrients is large relative to porewater nutrient standing stocks and plant uptake is sufficient to turn over porewater pools several times during the growing season.

NUTRIENT BUDGETS

For Tivoli North Bay there are sufficient data to construct a rough annual N budget. The site is a net sink for N as indicated by the lower ebb-tide (0.23 mg NO_3-N $\cdot L^{-1}$) than flood-tide (0.56 mg NO_3-N $\cdot L^{-1}$) concentrations. Net tidal input is estimated as the mean concentration difference X tidal volume/marsh area = 0.33 mg $N \cdot L^{-1}$ X 250 $L \cdot m^{-2}$ = net loss of 3.3 mg $N \cdot m^{-2}$ per tidal cycle during the summer. Assuming 100 days of N removal per year (non-summer ebb nitrate concentrations are not significantly below mainstem values) this yields a net removal from tidal waters of 14 g $N \cdot m^{-2} \cdot yr$. Atmospheric deposition directly to the marsh surface is about 1 g $N \cdot m^{-2} \cdot yr$ using a regional estimate of deposition (10 kg N ha yr). The tributary input from Stony Creek is about 24 g $N \cdot m^{-2} \cdot yr$ (1994 means: annual mean flow 1,450 $L \cdot s^{-1}$ X mean concentration 3.34 mg $NO_3 \cdot L^{-1}$, total area = 1.4 × 10^6 m^2; Nieder, unpublished). The removal of NO_3 from tidal waters is probably due to a combination of plant and microbial uptake and denitrification. Plant demand for N is fairly large with, for example, 5 g $\cdot$ N m^{-2} in aboveground biomass of narrowleaf cattail (Templer, Findlay, and Wigand, 1998) and over 10 g $N \cdot m^{-2}$ in common reed (Findlay et al.,

Table 20.5. Topics for future study of Hudson River tidal wetlands

Component	Question	Implications
Water control structures (trestles, culverts)	Would enlargement reverse sedimentation?	Vegetation and habitat management; restoration design
Sewage effluent from local treatment plants	Effects on marshes?	May stimulate undesirable vegetation and habitat change
Dumps in or adjoining wetlands	Effects on wetlands?	Possible toxicity
Sediment organic matter	Functional relationships to other ecosystem components?	Restoration design
Temporal vegetation change ("succession")	Patterns and causes?	Management to maintain certain habitats; restoration design
Invasive plants (e.g., Eurasian watermilfoil, purple loosestrife, common reed, false-indigo)	Negative, neutral, and positive effects on biodiversity, ecological structure and function?	Management to maintain biodiversity and ecological services including fishery support; restoration design
Muskrat populations	Why have muskrat populations remained low since mid-1970s?	Muskrat management; changes in biota due to reduced muskrat activity
Beaver ecology	How do dams, lodges, food caches, and cutting of trees and shrubs affect tidal wetland biota and ecosystems?	Beaver management; restoration design; biodiversity conservation
Landscape ecology of mobile consumers	How and why do mobile insects, spiders, fishes, amphibians, reptiles, birds, and mammals move between wetlands and other habitats? What critical resources do wetlands provide?	Function of wetlands in landscape; management of economic and pest species; restoration design; biodiversity conservation
Winter ecology	Where and how do organisms overwinter?	Function of wetlands in winter landscape; limiting factor for, e.g., amphibians and reptiles, terrestrial invertebrates
Toxic contaminants	What effects on animal populations?	Understanding scarcity or absence of many species; biodiversity conservation
Recreation, e.g., motorized and non-motorized boating	Effects on sediments, vegetation, fauna?	Recreation management; biodiversity conservation
Little-studied taxa	Species abundance, reliance on wetlands, role in ecosystem?	Biodiversity conservation; wetland management

2002b). Some of this demand is met by translocation from belowground reserves but half the aboveground N remains in the standing dead litter, suggesting only half the N has been recovered prior to plant senescence. Therefore, plant demand in the predominant cattail community is about $2.5 \, g \, N \cdot m^{-2} \cdot yr$. Burial of organic matter is a major fate of N in this and other marshes and has been estimated at roughly $5 \, g \, N \cdot m^{-2} \cdot yr^{-1}$ (Merrill, 1998). Actual estimates of denitrification are rare

but estimates for Tivoli North Bay are about $2 \, g \, N \cdot m^{-2} \cdot yr^{-1}$ (Merrill, 1998). Clearly the budget is dominated by the tidal input, atmospheric deposition and losses to burial and denitrification. Estimated losses exceed inputs in accordance with the net removal of nitrate from tidal waters. We cannot estimate all the terms in a PO_4 budget but again the tidal concentrations imply a net source within the marsh and the high porewater concentrations suggest a sediment source.

Research Needs

Most research has been conducted in geomorphically well-developed marshes protected from tidal erosion by artificial structures and dominated by robust colonial emergent plants such as cattail or reed. Research is needed to determine how marsh function varies in different geomorphic types, salinity regimes, soil types, and plant communities. Table 20.5 lists additional specific research questions that would improve the ability to manage Hudson River tidal wetlands for their ecosystem services and biodiversity resources.

Acknowledgments

We acknowledge assistance from our colleagues and students at Hudsonia Ltd., Bard College, Institute of Ecosystem Studies, and Hudson River National Estuarine Research Reserve. Key studies and syntheses were supported by New York State Department of Environmental Conservation – Hudson River Estuary Program, Hudson River Foundation including Hudson River Improvement Fund, National Oceanic and Atmospheric Administration, U.S. Environmental Protection Agency, and Geoffrey C. Hughes Foundation. Bard College Field Station – Hudsonia Contribution 84 and Contribution to the Program of the Institute of Ecosystem Studies.

REFERENCES

Austin, K., and Findlay, S. 1989. Benthic bacterial biomass and production in the Hudson River Estuary. *Microbial Ecology* **18**:105–16.

Barbour, S., and Kiviat, E. 1986. A survey of Lepidoptera in Tivoli North Bay (Hudson River estuary), in J. C. Cooper (ed.), *Polgar Fellowship Reports of the Hudson River National Estuarine Sanctuary Program, 1985*. New York State Department of Environmental Conservation, [Albany, NY], pp. IV-1 to IV-20.

Beecher, E. C. 1984. "The accumulation of cadmium and lead in the rhizomes of *Typha angustifolia* and *Typha glauca* from fresh-water tidal marshes." Senior Project, Bard College, Annandale, New York.

Benoit, G., Wang, E. X., Nieder, W. C., Levandowsky, M., and Breslin, V. 1999. Sources and history of heavy metal contamination and sediment deposition in Tivoli South Bay, Hudson River, New York. *Estuaries* **22**:167–78.

Brinson, M. M., Lugo, A., and Brown, S. 1981. Primary productivity, decomposition and consumer activity in freshwater wetlands. *Annual Review of Ecology and Systematics* **12**:123–61.

Buckley, E. H., and Ristich, S. S. 1976. Distribution of rooted vegetation in the brackish marshes and shallows of the Hudson River estuary, Paper 20, in *Hudson River Ecology*, Fourth Symposium on Hudson River Ecology, Bear Mountain, New York, 28–30 March 1976. Hudson River Environmental Society, [Poughkeepsie, NY].

1977. Rooted vegetation, in L. H. Weinstein (ed.), *An Atlas of the Biologic Resources of the Hudson Estuary*. Boyce Thompson Institute for Plant Research, Yonkers, New York, pp. 12–33, 95–96.

Connors, L. M., Kiviat, E., Groffman, P. M., and Ostfeld, R. S. 2000. Muskrat (*Ondatra zibethicus*) disturbance to vegetation and potential net nitrogen mineralization and nitrification rates in a fresh-tidal marsh. *American Midland Naturalist* **143**:53–63.

DeVries, C., and DeWitt, C. B. 1986. Freshwater tidal wetlands community descriptions and relation of plant distribution to elevation and substrate, in J. C. Cooper (ed.), *Polgar Fellowship Reports of the Hudson River National Estuarine Sanctuary Program, 1985*. Hudson River Foundation, New York, NY, pp. IX-1 to IX-43.

Duryea, M., and Schmidt, R. E. 1987. Feeding biology of the tessellated darter (*Etheostoma olmstedi atromaculatum*) at Tivoli North Bay, Hudson River, New York, in E. A. Blair and J. C. Cooper (eds.), *Polgar Fellowship Reports of the Hudson River National Estuarine Research Reserve Program, 1986*. New York State Department of Environmental Conservation, [Albany, NY], pp. III-1 to III-19.

Feeley-Connor, B. 1978. "The ecology of corticolous lichens in northern Dutchess County, New York." Senior Project, Bard College, Annandale, New York.

Fernberg, L. S. 1997. "Causes and consequences of purple loosestrife (*Lythrum salicaria*) invasions on native wetlands." Doctoral Dissertation. Fordham University, Bronx, New York.

Findlay, S., Dye, S., and Kuehn, K. A. 2002b. Microbial growth and nitrogen retention in litter of *Phragmites australis* and *Typha angustifolia*. *Wetlands* **22**:616–25.

Findlay, S., Howe, K., and Austin, K. 1990. Comparison of detritus dynamics in two tidal freshwater wetlands. *Ecology* **71**:288–95.

Findlay, S. E. G., Kiviat, E., Nieder, W. C., and Blair, E. A. 2002a. Functional assessment of a reference wetland set as a tool for science, management and restoration. *Aquatic Sciences* **64**:107–17.

Findlay, S. E. G., Sinsabaugh, R. L., Fischer, D. T., and Franchini, P. 1998. Sources of dissolved organic carbon supporting planktonic bacterial production in the tidal freshwater Hudson River. *Ecosystems* 1:227–39.

Foley, D. D., and Taber, R. W. 1951. *Lower Hudson Waterfowl Investigation*. Pittman-Robertson Project 47-R. New York State Conservation Department, Albany, New York.

Goldhammer, A., and Findlay, S. 1988. Estimation of suspended material flux between a *Trapa natans* stand and the Hudson River estuary, in J. R. Waldman and Blair, E. A. (eds.), *Polgar Fellowship Reports of the Hudson River National Estuarine Research Reserve Program, 1987*. Hudson River Foundation, New York, NY, pp. VIII-1 to VIII-43.

Howard, T. G., Jaycox, J. W., and Weldy, T. W. 2002. *Rare Species and Significant Natural Communities of the Significant Biodiversity Areas in the Hudson River Valley*. Report to Cornell University and New York State Department of Environmental Conservation – Hudson River Estuary Program. New York Natural Heritage Program, Albany, New York.

Kiviat, E. 1974. *A Fresh-water Tidal Marsh on the Hudson, Tivoli North Bay*, in Third Symposium on Hudson River Ecology. Hudson River Environmental Society, Bronx, NY, Paper 14, 36 unnumbered pages.

1978a. *Hudson River East Bank Natural Areas, Clermont to Norrie*. The Nature Conservancy, Arlington, Virginia.

1978b. Vertebrate use of muskrat lodges and burrows. *Estuaries* 1:196–200.

1980a. *Are Muskrats Declining in New York? Why? A Preliminary Study*. Report to Wildlife Pathology Unit, New York State Department of Environmental Conservation, Delmar, New York.

1980b. A Hudson River tidemarsh snapping turtle population. *Transactions of the Northeast Section*, The Wildlife Society, **37**:158–68.

1981. *Hudson River estuary shore zone annotated natural history bibliography with index*. Scenic Hudson, Poughkeepsie, New York.

1989. The role of wildlife in estuarine ecosystems, in J. W. Day, et al. (eds.). *Estuarine Ecology*. New York: John Wiley & Sons, pp. 437–75.

1994. Muskrat: Manager of the marsh. *News from Hudsonia* **10**(3):1–3.

1996. American goldfinch nests in purple loosestrife. *Wilson Bulletin* **108**(1):182–6.

1997. Where are the reptiles and amphibians of the Hudson River? Part 1. *News from Hudsonia* **12**(2–3):1, 3–5.

1998. Where are the reptiles and amphibians of the Hudson River? Part 2. *News from Hudsonia* **13**(3):1–7.

Kiviat, E., and Beecher, E. 1991. *Vegetation in Fresh-Tidal Habitats of Tivoli Bays, Hudson River National Estuarine Research Reserve*. Report to National Oceanic and Atmospheric Administration. Hudsonia Ltd., Annandale, New York.

Kiviat, E., Stapleton, J. J., Schmidt, R. E., and Zeising, N. 1982. *Final Environmental Impact Statement; Proposed Estuarine Sanctuary grant award to the State of New York for a Hudson River Estuarine Sanctuary*. U.S. Department of Commerce, Washington, D.C.

Kiviat, E., and Stevens, G. 2001. B*iodiversity Assessment Manual for the Hudson River Estuary Corridor*. New York State Department of Environmental Conservation, New Paltz, New York.

Kiviat, E., and Talmage, E. Submitted. Bird use of common reed and cattail in a Hudson River freshwater tidal marsh. *Journal of Field Ornithology*.

Krause, L. H., Rietsma, C., and Kiviat, E. 1997. Terrestrial insects associated with *Phragmites australis*, *Typha angustifolia*, and *Lythrum salicaria* in a Hudson River tidal marsh, in W. C. Nieder and J. R. Waldman (eds.), *Final Reports of the Tibor T. Polgar Fellowship Program 1996*. Hudson River Foundation, New York, NY, pp. V-1 to V-35.

Lampman, G., Caraco, N. F., and Cole, J. J. 1999. Spatial and temporal patterns of nutrient concentration and export in the tidal Hudson River. *Estuaries* 22:285–96.

Leonardi, L. 1991. Bryophytes of two New York State freshwater tidal swamps. *Evansia* **8**(1):22–5.

Leonardi, L., and Kiviat, E. 1989. *A Moss and Liverwort Survey of Freshwater Tidal Swamps along the Hudson River*. Report to the Alan DeVoe Bird Club.

1990. Bryophytes of the Tivoli Bays tidal swamps, in J. R. Waldman and E. A. Blair (eds.), *Final Reports of the Tibor T. Polgar Fellowship Program 1989*. Hudson River Foundation, New York, NY, pp. III-1 to III-23.

McGlynn, C. A., and Ostfeld, R. S. 2000. A study of the effects of invasive plant species on small mammals in Hudson River freshwater marshes, in J. R. Waldman and W. C. Nieder (eds.), *Final Reports of the Tibor T. Polgar Fellowship Program, 1999*. Hudson River Foundation, New York, NY, pp. VIII-1 to VIII-21.

Merrill, J. Z. 1998. *Tidal Freshwater Marshes of the Hudson River as Nutrient Sinks: Long-term Retention and Denitrification*. Final Report to the Hudson River Foundation, Fellowship GF/03/96.

Mihocko, G., Kiviat, E., Schmidt, R. E., Findlay, S. E. G., Nieder, W. C., and Blair, E. A. 2003. *Assessing Ecological Functions of Hudson River Fresh-Tidal Marshes; Reference Data and a Modified Hydrogeomorphic (HGM) Approach*. Report to New York State Department of Environmental

Conservation, Hudson River Estuary Program. Hudsonia Ltd., Annandale, New York.

Muenscher, W. C. 1935. *Aquatic Vegetation of the Mohawk Watershed*. Biological Survey 9 (Mohawk-Hudson Watershed), Supplement to the Annual Report, New York State Conservation Department **24**:228–49.

——— 1937. *Aquatic Vegetation of the Lower Hudson Area*. Biological Survey 11 (Lower Hudson Watershed), Supplement to the Annual Report, New York State Conservation Department **26**:231–48.

Newell, S. Y., and Porter, D. 2000. Microbial secondary production from saltmarsh-grass shoots, and its known and potential fates, in M. P. Weinstein and D. A. Kreeger (eds.), *Concepts and Controversies in Tidal Marsh Ecology*. Dordrecht, The Netherlands: Kluwer Academic Publishers, pp. 159–85.

Newman, W. W., Thurber, D. H., Zeiss, H. S., Rokach, A., and Musich, L. 1969. Late Quaternary geology of the Hudson River estuary; A preliminary report. *Transactions of the New York Academy of Sciences Series 2*, **31**:548–70.

Odum, W. E. 1988. Comparative ecology of tidal freshwater and salt marshes. *Annual Review of Ecology and Systematics* **19**:147–76.

Odum, W. E., and Heywood, M. A. 1978. Decomposition of intertidal freshwater marsh plants, in R. E. Good, D. Whigham, R. L. Simpson and C. G. Jackson (eds.), *Freshwater Wetlands*. New York: Academic Press, pp. 89–97.

Odum, W. E., Smith III, T. J., Hoover, J. K., and McIvor, C. C. 1984. *The Ecology of Tidal Freshwater Marshes of the United States East Coast: A Community Profile*. U.S. Fish and Wildlife Service, Washington, D.C. FWS/OBS-83-17.

Parsons, T. L., and Lovett, G. M. 1992. Land use effects on Hudson River tributaries, in J. R. Waldman and E. A. Blair (eds.), *Final Reports of the Tibor T. Polgar Fellowship Program 1991*. Hudson River Foundation, New York, NY, pp. IX-1 to IX-34.

Peller, P., and Bopp., R. 1986. Recent sediment and pollutant accumulation in the Hudson River National Estuarine Sanctuary, in J. C. Cooper (ed.), *Polgar Fellowship Reports of the Hudson River National Estuarine Sanctuary Program, 1985*. Hudson River Foundation, New York. NY, Section VII, pp. VII-1 to VII-29.

Picard, E. 2002. 1998. *Tidal Wetland Inventory Draft, Tappan Zee Bridge to Troy Dam*. New York State Department of Environmental Conservation and New England Interstate Water Pollution Control Commission.

Reinson, G. E. 1979. Barrier island systems, in R. G. Walker (ed.), *Facies Models*. Geoscience

Canada Reprint Series 1, Geological Association of Canada, Toronto, Ontario, pp. 57–74.

Reschke, C. 1990. *Ecological Communities of New York State*. New York Natural Heritage Program, Latham, New York.

Richard, E., and Schmidt, R. E. 1987. Feeding ecology of the banded killifish (*Fundulus diaphanus*) at Tivoli North Bay, Hudson River, New York, in E. A. Blair and J. C. Cooper (eds.), *Polgar Fellowship Reports of the Hudson River National Estuarine Research Reserve Program, 1986*. New York State Department of Environmental Conservation, [Albany, NY], pp. II-1 to II-20.

Ristich, S. S., Fredrick, S. W., and Buckley, E. H. 1976. Transplantation of *Typha* and the distribution of vegetation and algae in a reclaimed estuarine marsh. *Bulletin of the Torrey Botanical Club* **103**(4):157–64.

Roberts, E. A., and Reynolds, H. W. 1938. *The Role of Plant Life in the History of Dutchess County*. Privately published, Vassar College, Poughkeepsie, New York.

Robideau, R. M. 1997. "Sedimentation rates in Hudson River marshes as determined by radionuclide dating techniques." Master's thesis, Rensselaer Polytechnic Institute, Troy, New York.

Rooth, J. E., Stevenson, J. C., and Cornwell, J. C. 2003. Increased sediment accretion rates following invasion by *Phragmites australis*: The role of litter. *Estuaries* **26**:476–84.

Royte, J. L. 1985. "The lichen community of Skillpot Island." Senior Project, Bard College, Annandale, New York.

Rozycki, C., and Kiviat, E. 1996. A low density, tidal marsh, painted turtle population, in E. A. Blair and J. R. Waldman (eds.), *Final Reports of the Tibor T. Polgar Fellowship Program 1995*. Hudson River Foundation, New York, NY, pp. V-1 to V-35.

Rubbo, M. J., and Kiviat, E. 1999. A herpetological survey of Tivoli Bays and Stockport Flats, in W. C. Nieder and J. R. Waldman (eds.), *Final Reports of the Tibor T. Polgar Fellowship Program 1998*. Hudson River Foundation, New York, NY, pp. VIII-1 to VIII-22.

Schmidt, K. A. 1986. The life history of the chrysomelid beetle *Pyrrhalta nymphaeae* (Galerucinae) on water chestnut, *Trapa natans* (Hydrocariaceae [sic]) in Tivoli South Bay, Hudson River, NY, in J. C. Cooper (ed.), *Polgar Fellowship Reports of the Hudson River National Estuarine Sanctuary Program, 1985*. New York State Department of Environmental Conservation, [Albany, NY], pp. V-1–V-38.

Schmidt, R. E. 1986. *Fish Community Structure in Tivoli North Bay, a Hudson River Freshwater Tidal*

Marsh. NOAA Technical Report Series OCRM/ SPD, U.S. Department of Commerce.

Schmidt, R. E. 1993. *Fishes of Manitou Marsh with Comments on other Aquatic Organisms.* Report to Museum of the Hudson Highlands. Hudsonia Ltd., Annandale, NY.

Schmidt, R. E., and Kiviat, E. 1988. *Communities of Larval and Juvenile Fish Associated with Waterchestnut, Watermilfoil and Water-celery in the Tivoli Bays of the Hudson River.* Report to Hudson River Foundation, New York, NY.

Senerchia-Nardone, P., Reilly, A., and Holland, M. M. 1986. Comparison of vascular plant zonation at Iona Island Marsh (Hudson River estuary) and Lord's Cove (Connecticut River estuary), in J. C. Cooper (ed.), *Polgar Fellowship Reports of the Hudson River National Estuarine Sanctuary Program, 1985.* New York State Department of Environmental Conservation, [Albany, NY], pp. III-1 to III-35.

Sharma, V., and Kiviat, E. 1992. Habitats of the monkeyflowers *Mimulus alatus* and *Mimulus ringens* on the Hudson River, in E. A. Blair and J. R. Waldman (eds.), *Final Reports of the Tibor T. Polgar Fellowship Program, 1991.* Hudson River Foundation, New York, NY, pp. V-1 to V-36.

Simoes, J. C., and Chambers, R. M. 1999. The diamondback terrapins of Piermont Marsh, Hudson River, New York. *Northeastern Naturalist* **6**:241–8.

Sinsabaugh, R. L., and Findlay, S. 1995. Microbial production, enzyme activity and carbon turnover in surface sediments of the Hudson River Estuary. *Microbial Ecology* **30**:127–41.

Squires, D. F. 1992. Quantifying anthropogenic shoreline modification of the Hudson River and estuary from European contact to modern time. *Coastal Management* **20**:343–54.

Stapleton, J., and Kiviat, E. 1979. Rights of birds and rights of way: Vegetation management on a railroad causeway and its effect on breeding birds. *American Birds* **33**(1):7–10.

Stevens, G. (ed.). 2001. *Natural Resource / Human Use Inventory of Six State-Owned Properties on the Hudson River in Columbia and Greene Counties.* Report to New York State Department of Environmental Conservation. Hudsonia Ltd., Annandale, New York.

Stevenson, K. A., Armstrong, R. and Schell, W. R. 1986. Chronological determination of mercury, lead, and cadmium in two Hudson River freshwater tidal marshes, in J. C. Cooper (ed.), *Polgar Fellowship Reports of the Hudson River National Estuar-*

ine Sanctuary Program, 1985. Hudson River Foundation, New York, NY, pp. VIII-1 to VIII-27.

Stone, W. B., Kiviat, E., and Butkas, S. A. 1980. Toxicants in snapping turtles. *New York Fish and Game Journal* **27**(1):39–50.

Swift, B. L. 1989. *Avian Breeding Habitats in Hudson River Tidal Marshes.* Report to the Hudson River Foundation. New York State Department of Environmental Conservation, Delmar, New York.

Templer, P., Findlay, S., and Wigand, C. 1998. Sediment chemistry associated with native and non-native emergent macrophytes of a Hudson River marsh ecosystem. *Wetlands* **18**:70–8.

Vernon, M. 2002. Phosphorous saturation in wetland soils: The relationship between loading history and removal rates in freshwater tidal wetlands, in A. R. Berkowitz, S. E. G. Findlay, F. Keesing and R. S. Ostfeld (eds.), *Occasional Publication of the Institute of Ecosystem Studies No. 16,* pp. 83–8.

Vos, J. H., van den Ende, P. J., Ooijevaar, M. A. G., Oosthoek, A. J. P., Postma, J. F., and Admiraal, W. 2002. Growth response of a benthic detritivore to organic matter composition in sediments. *Journal of the North American Benthological Society* **21**:443–56.

Weinstein, L. H. (ed.) 1977. *An Atlas of the Biologic Resources of the Hudson Estuary.* Boyce Thompson Institute for Plant Research, Inc. Yonkers, NY.

Westad, K. E. 1987. Addendum to flora of freshwater tidal swamps at Tivoli Bays, in E. A. Blair and J. C. Cooper (eds.), *Polgar Fellowship Reports of the Hudson River National Estuarine Research Reserve Program, 1986.* New York State Department of Environmental Conservation, [Albany, NY], p. X-1.

Westad, K. E., and Kiviat, E. 1986. Flora of freshwater tidal swamps at Tivoli Bays Hudson River National Estuarine Sanctuary, in J. C. Cooper (ed.), *Polgar Fellowship Reports of the Hudson River National Estuarine Sanctuary Program, 1985.* New York State Department of Environmental Conservation, Hudson River Foundation, and U.S. Department of Commerce, pp. III-1–III-20.

Winogrond, H. G., and Kiviat, E. 1997. Invasion of *Phragmites australis* in the tidal marshes of the Hudson River, in W. C. Nieder and J. R. Waldman (eds.), *Final Reports of the Tibor T. Polgar Fellowship Program 1996.* Hudson River Foundation, New York, NY, pp. VI-1–VI-29.

Yozzo, D. J., Smith, D. E., and Lewis, M. L. 1994. *Tidal Freshwater Ecosystems: Bibliography.* Virginia Sea Grant College Program VSG-94-12, Charlottesville, Virginia.

21 Alien Species in the Hudson River

David L. Strayer

ABSTRACT Like most estuaries, the Hudson has been heavily invaded by alien species (those moved out of their native ranges by human activities). The Hudson and its tributaries now contain more than 100 alien species, which are abundant in every habitat in the basin. Invasions of the freshwater part of the basin (aliens in brackish waters of the basin have not been systematically studied) were underway by the early nineteenth century, and continue at a rate of ~7 new species per decade. Most of these species came from Europe or the Great Lakes through shipping activities, the Erie Canal, or deliberate introductions. Case studies of selected aliens (the zebra mussel, black bass, water-chestnut, Atlantic rangia, and Asian shore crab) show that alien species have had large and varied ecological impacts on all parts of the Hudson estuary. The impacts of alien species on the Hudson are likely to increase in the future as new aliens become established. We may be able to reduce future undesirable impacts of aliens on the Hudson by controlling or eradicating undesirable species, in the few cases where this is feasible; aggressively reducing the numbers of alien species that are inadvertently transported by human activities; and adopting more stringent criteria for allowing the intentional introduction of species.

Introduction

Most people know that humans have deeply affected the Earth's ecosystems by pollution, changes in land use, and overharvesting of wild plants and animals. It is much less well known that humans have caused large, widespread, and irreversible changes to ecosystems around the globe by introducing alien species (e.g., Office of Technology Assessment, 1993; Vitousek et al., 1996; Cox, 1999). (**Alien species** are those moved outside of their native ranges by human activities which subsequently establish self-sustaining populations. They are also known as exotic, introduced, or nonindigenous species). Humans have introduced many alien species to the Hudson River that have profoundly changed the nature of the river's ecosystems. This chapter briefly discusses the numbers and origins of alien species in the Hudson, reviews the biology and impacts of selected alien species in the Hudson, shows that species introductions are one of the most important ways that humans have affected the Hudson ecosystem, and makes recommendations for improving the management of alien species.

Numbers, Origins, and Characteristics of Aliens in the Hudson

How many alien species live in the Hudson River? Where did they come from, how did they get here, and when did they arrive? We do not yet have complete answers to these questions, but a study of alien species in the freshwater parts of the Hudson basin (Mills et al., 1996, 1997) provides partial answers. Mills et al. concluded that at least 113 alien plant and animal species have become established in the fresh waters of the Hudson basin (Table 21.1). This estimate is probably far too low, because we do not have good distributional or historical information on microscopic organisms, and so have no way to distinguish native species from aliens. Thus, a large part of the freshwater flora and fauna of the Hudson basin is not native, but was brought here by humans.

Records of species introductions are incomplete, so the time-course of invasions shown in Figure 21.1 is only approximate. Nonetheless, alien species had already arrived in the Hudson basin by the beginning of the nineteenth century, and invasions continue to this day. It appears that the invasion rate has been relatively constant (about 7 species per decade) since the mid-nineteenth century. The kinds of invaders have changed markedly over that period, though, from mostly plants to mostly animals (Fig. 21.1).

Table 21.1. Numbers of native and alien species in fresh waters of the Hudson River basin, modified from Mills et al. (1996)

Group	Native	Alien	% alien
Aquatic mammals	6	0	0
Aquatic birds[a]	23	1	4
Aquatic reptiles	8	0	0
Amphibians	24	0	0
Fish	70	33	32
Crayfish	4	5	56
Mollusks	75	20	21
Aquatic vascular plants[b]	164	33	17

[a] regular breeders only
[b] because of the difficulty in estimating the number of "aquatic" plants throughout the basin, these figures refer to a single representative community: plants found below the high tide mark in the middle part of the freshwater tidal Hudson River (Kiviat, 1978)

The alien species in the freshwater parts of the Hudson basin came from two major sources: Europe and the American Interior Basin (i.e., the Great Lakes and Mississippi drainages) (Fig. 21.2). Alien plants in the Hudson basin are chiefly from Europe, while animals originated largely from the Interior Basin (Fig. 21.2). Alien species were brought into the basin by several methods (Table 21.2). European species came into the basin in the solid ballast and ballast water of ships, as agricultural escapes and weeds, and as deliberate introductions. In contrast, Interior Basin species moved into the Hudson mainly through the Erie Canal, and secondarily through deliberate introductions.

Patterns of species invasions reflect the extent to which human activities break natural barriers to dispersal. Plant invasions were most frequent in the nineteenth century because solid ballast and agriculture brought many alien plants over the previously insurmountable barrier of the Atlantic Ocean. Plant invasions slowed in the twentieth century, in part because solid ballast was replaced by ballast water. At the same time, the switch to ballast water opened a gate for freshwater animals that could not cross the ocean in solid ballast but could survive the oceanic voyage in ballast tanks, and invasion rates of aquatic

animals rose. Likewise, the opening of the Erie Canal in 1825 breached a major barrier to eastward dispersal of aquatic animals, many of which then invaded the Hudson Basin. The Hudson Basin does not have many alien plants from the Interior Basin because the Alleghenian Divide between the Interior Basin and the Hudson Basin was never a significant barrier to natural dispersal of plants.

Although we know that alien species live in the brackish waters of the lower Hudson estuary, we do not have a comprehensive analysis of invasions like that done by Mills et al. (1996, 1997). Nonetheless, we can guess about aliens in the lower Hudson based on the probable vectors that brought aliens into this area. Shipping activities probably brought many aliens into the lower Hudson, either as ballast or as fouling organisms on ships' hulls. Because of the long history of ship traffic between Europe and New York harbor, shipping probably brought aliens into the lower Hudson beginning in the sixteenth century, and continues to bring in new aliens today. Invaders from early in this period may be so widely naturalized along the East Coast that they appear to be native [Carlton (1996) called these "cryptogenic species" because their foreign origin is so obscured]. In contrast to the situation in fresh water, canals probably were insignificant as a vector. Thus, the lower Hudson probably contains many (>100) alien species; most of them arrived in or on ships, especially from Europe; the lower Hudson was already well invaded before 1800 by aliens that are so well established that they may appear to be natives; and plants and invertebrates, rather than fish, constitute the bulk of invaders.

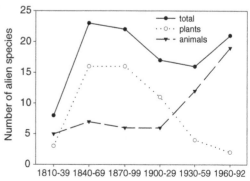

Figure 21.1. Time-course of the establishment (i.e., first detection in the wild) of alien species in the fresh waters of the Hudson River basin. Modified from Mills et al. (1996, 1997).

Table 21.2. Major vectors that have brought alien aquatic species into the Hudson basin, modified from Mills et al. (1997).

Vector	Description
Deliberate	Release of an organism with the intent of establishing a population in the wild
Unintentional	Release of organisms without the intent of establishing populations in the wild
Aquarium	Release of aquarium pets or plants
Cultivation	Escape of cultivated plants into the wild
Fishing	Release of organisms from bait buckets or with intentionally stocked fish
Accidental	Accidental release of organisms by any other means
Shipping	
Fouling	Transport of organisms on the hulls of ships
Solid ballast	Transport of organisms with the solid ballast of ships
Ballast water	Transport of organisms with the ballast water of ships
Canals	Movement of organisms through canals (but not on or in ships)

The high invasion rates in the Hudson are not unusual; estuaries and other aquatic habitats near centers of human activity typically contain large and increasing numbers of aliens (Table 21.3). However, the invasion history of the Hudson differs from that of the Great Lakes and San Francisco Bay (Fig. 21.3). Invasion rates in the Hudson were relatively high in the nineteenth century, but rose less sharply in the late twentieth century than rates in the Great Lakes and San Francisco Bay. These differences presumably reflect differences in human commerce in the three areas, with the Hudson subject to high inputs of solid ballast and immigrants from the Erie Canal in the nineteenth century, while

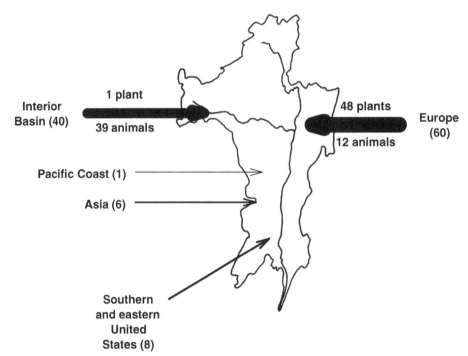

Figure 21.2. Sources of alien species now established in the fresh waters of the Hudson River basin, based on data of Mills et al. (1996, 1997). Arrow widths are proportional to the number of aliens arriving from each source region, which is also given in parentheses after the name of the source region.

Table 21.3. Numbers of alien species known from some American waters. Because data on microscopic organisms are inadequate, all of the values in this table are underestimated to an unknown degree

Body of water	Number of known aliens	Current rate at which new aliens are established (species/yr)	Notes
Hudson River basin	113	0.7	Freshwater, macroscopic organisms only; Mills et al. (1996, 1997)
Great Lakes basin	139	1.4	Mills et al. (1993)
San Francisco Bay and Delta	234	3.7	Fresh and brackish waters; Cohen and Carlton (1998)
Chesapeake Bay	196	–	Fresh and brackish waters; Ruiz (1999)

the other two systems have received increasing inputs of ballast water (in the case of the Great Lakes due in part to the opening of the St. Lawrence Seaway in 1959).

Case Studies of Selected Aliens in the Hudson

The following section contains case histories of five alien species that have invaded the Hudson River, including the chronology of the invasions, the current distribution and abundance in the river, probable ecological and economic impacts, and feasible control methods. I chose the five species because they are ecologically or economically important in the Hudson, and because they show the diversity

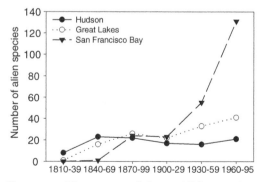

Figure 21.3. Time-course of the establishment (i.e., first detection in the wild) of alien species in the fresh waters of the Hudson River basin, the Great Lakes basin, and fresh and brackish waters of the San Francisco Bay and Delta. From data of Mills et al. (1993, 1996, 1997) and Cohen and Carlton (1998).

of invasion histories, habitats, biological traits, effects, and costs or benefits of alien species.

I. ZEBRA MUSSEL (*Dreissena polymorpha*)
Zebra mussels are small bivalves with black-and-white striped shells (Fig. 21.4, color plate 5). The life cycle of zebra mussels is unusual for a freshwater invertebrate, and includes a free-swimming larva called a *veliger*. During warm periods (usually late May to the end of summer in the Hudson), adults shed eggs and sperm into the water, where fertilization occurs. Fertilized eggs develop into veligers, which spend one to several weeks feeding in the plankton. When larval development is complete, these animals settle onto hard objects such as stones, plants, wood, concrete, fiberglass, steel, etc. They are sexually mature after one year, and may live for from four to six years, reproducing each summer. Both adult and larval zebra mussels are suspension feeders, subsisting on phytoplankton, small zooplankton, large bacteria, and organic detritus. In turn, zebra mussels are eaten by some fish (for example, sturgeons, freshwater drum, some sunfishes and suckers), waterfowl (for example, coots, scaup, goldeneyes), and decapods (for example, blue crabs, crayfish).

Zebra mussels are native to fresh and brackish waters in southeastern Europe and western Asia, and spread throughout Europe since ~1800 as a result of canal-building and other human activities. In about 1985, a ship from a European port released ballast water containing live zebra mussel veligers into Lake St. Clair near Detroit (Hebert,

Figure 21.4. Selected alien species now established in the Hudson estuary: (a) the zebra mussel, *Dreissena polymorpha*; (b) the largemouth bass, *Micropterus salmoides*; (c) a bed of water-chestnut, *Trapa natans*, in Tivoli South Bay; (d) the spiny nut of the water-chestnut; (e) *Rangia cuneata*; (f) the Japanese shore crab *Hemigrapsus sanguineus*. Photographs from David Strayer (a, d, e), F. Eugene Hester and the United States Geological Survey (b), Stuart Findlay (c), and Diane Brousseau (f).

Muncaster, and Mackie, 1989). Zebra mussels have since spread rapidly into lakes and rivers in eastern North America, especially in waters that are used heavily for navigation or recreation, activities that readily spread zebra mussels. Zebra mussels were first seen in the Hudson near Catskill in May, 1991. By the end of 1992, they were found everywhere in freshwater and oligohaline parts of the Hudson estuary, and had a biomass greater than the combined biomass of all other consumers in the river (Strayer et al., 1996). Zebra mussels have remained abundant on hard substrata throughout the freshwater and oligohaline Hudson estuary since 1992.

The theoretical *daily* filtration activity of the zebra mussel population during the summer has been 25–100 percent of the volume of the freshwater estuary.

Zebra mussels caused vast changes to the freshwater tidal Hudson (Strayer and Smith, 1996, 2001; Caraco et al., 1997, 2000; Strayer et al., 1999, 2004; Smith et al., 1998; Pace et al., 1998; Findlay et al., 1998). Populations of phytoplankton and small zooplankton fell sharply because of direct consumption by zebra mussels (Table 21.4). In contrast, populations of copepod zooplankton did not change, and populations of planktonic

Table 21.4. Changes in the Hudson River ecosystem caused by the zebra mussel invasion. Data are summertime (June–August) means; all biomasses given as g dry mass/m²

Variable	Pre-invasion	Post-invasion	Change
Light extinction[a] (m⁻¹)	1.9	1.3	−29%
Soluble reactive P[a] (μg/L)	12	28	+125%
Dissolved oxygen[a] (mg/L)	8	7	−12%
Phytoplankton biomass[a]	20	4	−80%
Bacterioplankton biomass[a]	3.3	4.7	+42%
Microzooplankton biomass[a]	0.5	0.1	−76%
Macrozooplankton biomass[a]	0.2	0.1	−52%
Native bivalve biomass[b]	6	2	−72%
Zoobenthos biomass (shallow water)[b]	0.9	1.1	+20%
Zoobenthos biomass (deep water)[b]	1.2	0.7	−40%

[a] mean for long-term monitoring station near Kingston.
[b] mean for the freshwater estuary.
From Strayer and Smith (1996, 2001), Caraco et al. (1997, 2000), Strayer et al. (1999), Pace, Findlay, and Fischer (1998), and Findlay, Pace, and Fischer (1998).

bacteria increased substantially. Native plankton-feeders declined sharply, probably because their phytoplankton food was so depleted. Growth, abundance, and distribution of young-of-year fish changed substantially after the zebra mussel invasion. Physical and chemical characteristics of the Hudson changed as well. Water clarity and dissolved nutrients rose in response to the loss of phytoplankton. The increase in water clarity probably led to an increase in the size and thickness of submersed vegetation, although good pre-invasion data are lacking. Even dissolved oxygen concentrations in the Hudson fell because of respiration by the enormous zebra mussel population. Thus, the zebra mussel invasion led to a series of large, ecologically important changes in the Hudson ecosystem that probably are long-lasting (decades) to permanent.

In addition to these ecological changes, zebra mussels cause economic damage in the Hudson. They attach to water intakes, boat hulls, and other submerged objects, increasing costs for inspecting and maintaining submerged equipment. Power plants and drinking water intakes have increased the frequency of intake inspections, and most now add anti-fouling chemicals such as chlorine, potassium permanganate, or polyquaternary ammonium compounds to prevent fouling by zebra mussels. Annual costs probably are in the range of $100,000 to 1,000,000/per year.

II. BLACK BASS (*Micropterus spp.*)

Most of the freshwater sport fish in eastern New York (including rainbow and brown trout, northern pike, largemouth and smallmouth bass, rock bass, black and white crappie, bluegill, and walleye) are not native to this region, but were deliberately introduced in the late nineteenth and early twentieth century (Mills et al., 1996, 1997). Of these, the black bass (the largemouth bass, *Micropterus salmoides*, and the smallmouth bass, *M. dolomieu*) are the most important in the Hudson River.

Until the late nineteenth century, black bass were widespread in the Great Lakes and Mississippi River drainages, but absent from the Northeast (Robbins and MacCrimmon, 1974). They moved eastward into the Hudson basin along the Erie Canal when it was opened in 1825, and were stocked into hundreds of lakes and rivers in the Northeast in the late nineteenth century (Cheney, 1895). Both species of black bass are now among the most common freshwater fish in the region. Largemouth bass typically occur in quiet, weedy waters such as ponds, lakes, and slow-moving rivers, while smallmouth bass prefer running waters or rocky lakeshores (e.g., Robbins and MacCrimmon, 1974; Smith, 1985).

Both species occur throughout the freshwater and oligohaline Hudson River. The largemouth is the more common species (10,000–30,000 fish >280 mm long; Carlson, 1992; Green et al., 1993); the smallmouth is less common (5,000–10,000 fish >280 mm long) and found chiefly in the upper and middle parts of the estuary.

Black bass are important in the Hudson because of their value to the sport fishery and their impacts on prey populations. Black bass are among the most popular sport fish in the freshwater estuary. Between 1986 and 1991, 50–60 bass tournaments were held annually in the Hudson estuary, averaging 1,500 angler-days of effort per year (Green et al., 1993). The economic benefit of these tournaments was considerable. Of course, people fish for black bass in the Hudson outside of the organized tournaments, resulting in many hours of recreation and many dollars spent in the local economy. The ecological impacts of black bass in the Hudson have not been studied, but can be roughly assessed. Black bass are large, omnivorous predators which have important effects that cascade through food webs (e.g., Carpenter and Kitchell, 1993; Fuller, Nico, and Williams, 1999). Based on their biomass and typical physiological efficiencies, the black bass populations in the Hudson estuary probably consume very roughly 10^7 g dry mass of prey each year. While this is less than 1 percent of the annual production of forage fish and invertebrates in the freshwater estuary (Lints, Findlay, and Pace, 1992), black bass are highly localized (Carlson, 1992; Nack et al., 1993) and have strong preferences for specific prey, so it is likely that the black bass invasion has affected at least the abundance of preferred prey in local areas in the Hudson.

III. WATER CHESTNUT (*Trapa natans*)

Water chestnut is a striking aquatic plant (Fig. 21.4, color plate 5) native to Eurasia. Its biology was well summarized by Kiviat (1993), from whom much of the present account was drawn. The plant consists of a rosette of floating leaves, buoyed by air bladders in the petioles, which is attached to the sediments by a long, tough stem. This annual plant produces hard, spiny nuts (Fig. 21.4) that are viable for a decade or more. Although the seed encased in this nut is edible, *Trapa* is not the familiar water chestnut of Chinese cuisine, which is a sedge

(*Eleocharis*). Water chestnut lives in quiet waters up to 5 m deep, and may form dense, nearly inpenetrable stands of >1 kg dry matter/m^2.

Water chestnut was introduced into North America in the late nineteenth century by well-meaning botanists, one of whom wrote: "but that so fine a plant as this, with its handsome leafy rosettes, and edible nuts, which would, if common, be as attractive to boys as hickory nuts now are, can ever become a nuisance, I can scarcely believe" (Kiviat, 1993). It arrived in the Hudson basin when it was deliberately introduced into Collins Lake near Schenectady in 1884. It escaped into the Mohawk River by the 1920s, and then into the Hudson estuary in the 1930s. By the 1950s, water chestnut was a nuisance in the Hudson. It is now widespread in quiet bays and backwaters of the Hudson estuary from Troy to Iona Island, with larger beds reaching 10–100 hectares in extent.

Water chestnut is a nuisance because its thick beds impede boating and other recreational activities, and because its spiny nuts can injure swimmers. In addition, water chestnut has been accused of having undesirable ecological impacts, including outcompeting native plants, increasing sedimentation rates, and lowering dissolved oxygen, thereby reducing the value of shallow-water habitats to fish and waterfowl. Because water chestnut has floating leaves that release photosynthetic oxygen into the air while shading out and preventing photosynthesis in the underlying water, dissolved oxygen concentrations can fall to zero in large, dense beds (Fig. 21.5; Caraco and Cole, 2002). Nevertheless, water chestnut supports dense communities of invertebrates and fish, although not necessarily the same species that live in native vegetation (Findlay, Schoeberl, and Wagner, 1989; Pelczarski and Schmidt, 1991; Hankin and Schmidt, 1992; Gilcrest and Schmidt, 1998; Strayer et al., 2003).

Because of its negative impacts, people have tried to eradicate water chestnut from the Hudson. In the 1960s and early 1970s, the Department of Environmental Conservation used 2,4-D as a control. Since high doses of 2,4-D have been banned, hand-pulling or cutting in local areas (for example, around marinas and beaches) is the only control that has been practiced. There has been considerable interest in using herbivorous insects as a

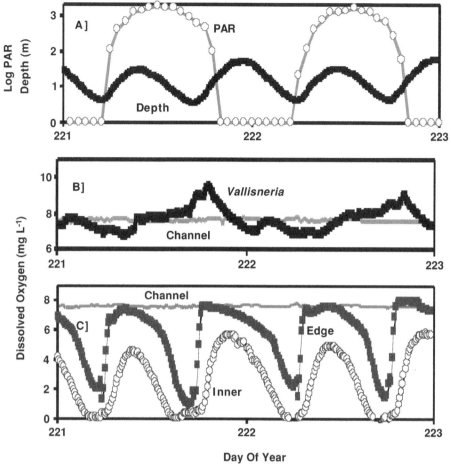

Figure 21.5. Dissolved oxygen dynamics over two summer days in a large bed of *Vallisneria americana* near Catskill, a nearby large bed of *Trapa natans*, and the adjoining open channel. The upper panel shows photosynthetically active radiation (PAR) and water depth (i.e., tidal activity). From Caraco and Cole (2002).

biological control, but this approach has not yet been perfected.

IV. ATLANTIC RANGIA (*Rangia cuneata*)

The Atlantic rangia is a characteristically estuarine clam native to the Gulf Coast. Adults are 2–6 cm long (Fig. 21.4, color plate 8). In the summer, adults release eggs and sperm into the water, where fertilization occurs. In the James River (Virginia), juveniles settled chiefly in the fall and winter (Cain, 1975). Adults are burrowing suspension-feeders, and may live for ten to fifteen years. Atlantic rangia live in estuaries where the salinity is usually less than 20 ppt. Adults can survive in fresh water, but larvae cannot develop, so the landward border of rangia populations is in areas with some sea salt.

Populations of Atlantic rangia often reach densities >100 adults/m² and may dominate benthic biomass in low-salinity estuaries. Further information on the Atlantic rangia was summarized by LaSalle and de la Cruz (1985), on which much of this account was based.

Atlantic rangia are widespread and abundant along the Gulf Coast. Fossil shells are common from New Jersey to Florida, but living animals weren't reported along the East Coast until 1955. Since 1955, the species has become widespread and common in estuaries from Florida to the Hudson River. It is unclear whether this spread represents an entirely new introduction of populations from the Gulf Coast or a resurgence of the population from a post-glacial refuge along the East Coast. In either case, the spread of rangia from estuary to estuary almost certainly was aided by human movement of animals in ballast water, for bait or food, and with oyster shells used in oyster re-establishment programs (Carlton, 1992). Atlantic rangia were first seen in the Hudson River in 1988. Although the population has not been systematically studied, Atlantic rangia is abundant in Haverstraw Bay and the Tappan Zee (Llanso et al., 2001), and is found as far north as Newburgh (Strayer and Smith, 2001). It is not known how rangia reached the Hudson, but humans probably carried the species into the river in some way.

Atlantic rangia is important both ecologically and economically. Like the zebra mussel, Atlantic rangia may have large, far-reaching effects on aquatic ecosystems. The ecological impacts of rangia in the Hudson have not been studied, but the shallow, well-mixed waters of Haverstraw Bay would be susceptible to impacts from a benthic suspension feeder. Atlantic rangia is an important food for waterfowl and some fish and crabs. Atlantic rangia also is edible and is sometimes harvested commercially (taking and eating rangia from the Hudson is illegal and possibly hazardous). Finally, Atlantic rangia is so abundant along the Gulf Coast that it is harvested for use in road building, where its shells are used as a substitute for gravel (another common name for the species is the "Louisiana road clam"). In 1967, 21.2 million tons of rangia (living and dead) were taken along the Gulf Coast (LaSalle and de la Cruz, 1985).

V. ASIAN SHORE CRAB (*Hemigrapsus sanguineus*)

This small crab (Fig. 21.4) is native to east Asia, where it lives on rocky shores from Hong Kong to Sakhalin Island (McDermott, 1998a). It lives in the upper intertidal zone to the upper subtidal zone, and often hides under rocks. It feeds on a mixed diet of algae and small crustaceans and mollusks (Lohrer and Whitlatch, 1997; McDermott, 1998a; Ledesma and O'Connor, 2001). *H. sanguineus* produces two to five broods during the summer (McDermott, 1998b). It takes about two months for an egg to develop into a small crab, during which time the planktonic larvae may disperse widely.

H. sanguineus was first seen in the United States in New Jersey in 1988. It is spreading rapidly, and by 1996 was common on rocky shores from North Carolina to Cape Cod Bay (McDermott, 1998a). Based on its Asian range, the species may spread along the East Coast from Florida to the Gulf of St. Lawrence, and probably will occupy mesohaline estuaries as well as the open coast (Ledesma and O'Connor, 2001). *H. sanguineus* was first seen in the Hudson in 1995, and is now common along the piers on the Lower West Side of Manhattan (Cathy Drew, personal communication).

H. sanguineus may have strong impacts on populations of competitors and prey (Jensen, McDonald, and Armstrong, 2002; Lohrer and Whitlatch, 2002a,b). It lives in many of the same habitats as the European green crab (*Carcinus maenus* – another abundant alien species that was introduced to the East Coast in the early nineteenth century, and which is itself presumed to have strong ecological impacts; Grosholz and Ruiz, 1996) and mud crabs, and feeds on broadly similar foods. *H. sanguineus* is dominant over co-occurring *C. maenus* and displaced this species from intertidal habitats in the Northeast (Jensen et al., 2002; Lohrer and Whitlatch, 2002a). It further appears that *H. sanguineus* may cause populations of the blue mussel (*Mytilus edulis*) to decline (Lohrer and Whitlatch, 2002a). In the Hudson, Cathy Drew has noticed that green crabs and mud crabs have become scarce on the upper parts of piers, perhaps as a result of the shore crab invasion (personal communication).

Ecological and Economic Impacts of Aliens in the Hudson

We cannot make a rigorous accounting of the effects of alien species in the Hudson because (1) we don't have a full list of aliens in the river; (2) fewer than 10 percent of known aliens in the Hudson have received serious study; and (3) there has been no attempt to investigate the interactions among alien species, or between species introductions and other human impacts on the ecosystem. Nevertheless, the effects of alien species in the Hudson ecosystem surely are large and pervasive. Alien species have altered water chemistry, flow, and clarity, and biogeochemical cycling. They have become important predators, prey, and competitors of the native biota, thereby changing the complexion of biological communities throughout the estuary. Alien species have become valuable parts of the fishery, but interfered with boating and swimming and intake of drinking and cooling water. They have affected the ecology of the main channel, the shallows, rocky shorelines, and wetlands, and have presumably affected the brackish and marine sections of the estuary as well as the freshwater estuary. There probably is no habitat, general ecological process, or important human use of the river that has not been significantly changed by alien species. Introduction of alien species is one of the most important ways that humans have affected the Hudson River ecosystem.

The impacts of alien species on the Hudson seem certain to increase in the future as new invaders establish themselves in the river. Mills et al. (1996) estimated that about 15 percent of the aliens in the freshwater part of the Hudson basin have strong ecological effects, and current invasion rate is about seven species per decade. This suggests that we might see a new, ecologically important alien about once a decade in the freshwater part of the basin, in addition to new arrivals in the lower estuary. Alien species with strong ecological effects that probably will appear in the Hudson in the next five to fifty years include *Corophium curvispinum*, a filter-feeding amphipod that is spreading through Europe fouling pipes and crowding out other benthic animals, including the zebra mussel (!) (van den Brink, van der Velde, and bij de Vaate, 1993; Paffen et al., 1994); *Echinogammarus ischnus*, another Caspian amphipod that already is widespread in the Great Lakes, where it is displacing native amphipods (Dermott et al., 1998); the New Zealand mudsnail *Potamopyrgus antipodarum*, established in the Great Lakes and elsewhere in North America, Australia, and Europe, where it has strong ecological effects (Hall, Tank, and Dybdahl, 2003); the Chinese mitten crab *Eriocheir sinensis*, now established on the West Coast (Cohen and Carlton, 1997) as well as in Europe, a species that migrates hundreds of kilometer into fresh waters and destroys dikes and river banks with its extensive burrows; and the round goby *Neogobius melanostomus*, a benthic fish that is now extremely abundant along Great Lakes shorelines (Charlebois et al., 1997). As these and other species appear in the Hudson,

the cumulative impacts of alien species will increase.

As is apparent from the case studies, eradication or comprehensive control of alien species is rarely attempted and usually unsuccessful. Aside from local control programs (for example, cutting water chestnut near marinas, poisoning zebra mussels in water intakes), only the water chestnut and purple loosestrife (Malecki et al., 1993) have been the objects of serious eradication programs in the Hudson. Whether the impacts of aliens are desirable or undesirable, they usually are irreversible.

Alien Species as an Environmental Issue

Why are alien species regarded as an environmental problem? As the case studies show, while some alien species have negative impacts, others have mixed or even highly positive impacts. One problem with alien species is that their impacts are difficult to predict, so that species thought of as useful have turned out to be pests (for example, water chestnut, carp). Even worse, the impacts of alien species have scarcely been considered when conducting activities that bring in alien species (for example, shipping, canal-building, the pet trade). Thus, we have been flooded with a largely indiscriminant (from the point of view of impacts) group of alien species. Alien species have high risks of undesirable impacts; the Office of Technology Assessment (1993) estimated that one-third of alien species in North America have been harmful. The problem with alien species is not so much that some species have undesirable impacts as that the human activities that bring in species do not adequately separate the desirable from the undesirable species. Because many alien species have large, probably irreversible impacts, the absence of sound controls and screening of species introductions has serious long-term ecological consequences.

What routes are open to reduce the undesirable effects of alien species? Three lines of action should be pursued: (1) selective control or eradication of aliens with clearly undesirable impacts, in cases where such programs are economically sensible and environmentally acceptable; (2) aggressively reducing the numbers of aliens that are unintentionally carried around the globe by humans; and

(3) adopting more stringent criteria for allowing the intentional introduction of species.

Once alien species become firmly established, they usually are difficult to control or eradicate. Biological control of alien species has been successful in some cases. In biological control, enemies (predators, parasites, competitors) of the pest are introduced or encouraged. Biological control is attractive because it can suppress a pest over large areas and long periods of time without harmful chemicals, but requires careful matching of the enemy to the target pest species. Biological control is being attempted or considered for pest species like purple loosestrife (Malecki et al., 1993), water chestnut, and the zebra mussel (Molloy et al., 1997). Nevertheless, biological control has been successful in only 10–20 percent of the cases in which it has been attempted, and is never attempted in many cases, especially for aquatic animals. Further, the longstanding image of biological control as environmentally benign has recently been challenged by critics who suggest that effects of biological control agents on non-target species has been vastly understated (e.g., Strong and Pemberton, 2000; Henneman and Memmott, 2001).

It usually is simpler and far more effective to prevent the arrival of an alien species than to control it after it is established. The major vectors that bring aquatic aliens into the Northeast today are ballast water and unintended releases of species used for pets, bait, and aquaculture, both of which could be brought under better control. Ballast water management is currently an active area of policy change and research (Carlton and Holohan, 1998). Ballast water is water that is taken on by ships to improve their stability and performance. Because ships carry large volumes of ballast water, which is not usually treated to exclude or kill organisms, ballast water is a major vector for species introductions worldwide (e.g., Carlton and Geller, 1993; National Research Council, 1996). Currently, under the National Invasive Species Act of 1996, ballast water of ships entering the Great Lakes or Hudson River (above the George Washington Bridge) must be treated to kill organisms, retained within the ship, or exchanged in the open ocean, which prevents spread of freshwater organisms. Ships entering other parts of the United States are asked to participate in a voluntary ballast-water exchange program. Further, research is proceeding on better ways to prevent moving organisms around in ballast water (Carlton and Holohan, 1998). Wider application of existing methods of ballast management and development of better methods of ballast management could substantially reduce the number of new invasions of aquatic aliens.

The second major group of vectors includes releases leading to unintended establishment of alien species, including the release of unwanted pets, the release of unused bait, and the escape of organisms from aquaculture. Plants and animals sold as pets may be released into the wild when the owner tires of them or they outgrow the aquarium. Many species have been established in North America as a result of such releases (Crossman and Cudmore, 1999a; Mackie, 1999). Anglers sometimes release unused bait at the end of a day of fishing. These organisms (which may include contaminant species other than those purchased) may establish a self-sustaining population (Litvak and Mandrak, 1999; Goodchild, 1999). For example, the European rudd is now appearing widely through eastern and central North America as a result of bait-bucket releases (Fuller et al., 1999). Releases from aquaculture may occur when the animal that is being raised escapes from captivity (Crossman and Cudmore, 1999b). For example, three species of carp (grass, silver, and bighead carp) have established breeding populations in North America, probably from animals that escaped from cultivation (Fuller et al., 1999). Alternatively, aquaculturists may inadvertently bring in undesirable aliens with the species that are intended to be cultured. Throughout the world, many species have been transported with living oysters or with oyster shells used to reestablish oyster beds (Carlton, 1992). Thus, attempts to reinvigorate oyster populations in the lower Hudson by bringing large volumes of old shell into New York Harbor (Revkin, 1999) may accidentally bring more alien species into the river. It may be possible to reduce rates of these unintentional introductions with better laws and improved enforcement of existing laws about the pet, bait, and aquaculture trades. Ultimately, though, reducing inadvertent introduction of aliens through releases will require better education of the public as to the risks of introducing alien species. People need to realize that releasing foreign plants and animals into the wild is an act of environmental recklessness comparable to tossing a lighted match into a forest.

Next, we need better controls over the deliberate establishment of alien species. Many species that were deliberately established in North America have had undesirable effects. In fact, the Office of Technology Assessment (1993) estimated that negative effects resulted as frequently from species that were intentionally introduced as from those that were unintentionally brought to North America! This suggests that past screening procedures have been nearly useless. The problem lies partly with the weakness of existing laws and screening procedures (Ruesink et al., 1995), which tend to allow importation of alien species if they are not known to have deleterious properties (i.e., the species are considered to be innocent until proven guilty). The case of the black carp (*Mylopharyngodon piceus*) is a particularly appalling example of the shortcomings of existing legal controls on species importation into the United States (Ferber, 2001; Williams, 2001). This species, which probably will escape from cultivation and establish wild populations throughout North America, was allowed into the United States on the authority of the Mississippi Department of Agriculture, despite strong opposition from twenty-eight states in the Mississippi River basin and several groups of professional biologists and a negative risk assessment by the United States Fish and Wildlife Service (Nico and Williams, 1996). More effective control over undesirable alien species can be achieved if species are imported only after being shown that the risk of deleterious effects is minimal (e.g., Townsend and Winterbourne, 1992).

Finally, attempts to deal with alien species nationally or internationally have been hampered by the patchwork of state and Federal programs, usually not coordinated with one another, that claim authority over various aspects of alien species management (Ruesink et al., 1995). A recent executive order (number 13112, signed 3 February 1999) establishing the Invasive Species Council to expand and coordinate programs of Federal agencies to combat alien species could be a step in the right direction.

Acknowledgments

I thank Jim Carlton, Cathy Drew, Tom Lake, John Waldman, and my colleagues at IES for helpful discussions. My own work on alien species has been supported by the Hudson River Foundation, the National Science Foundation, and the New York State Department of Environmental Conservation. This is a contribution to the program of the Institute of Ecosystem Studies.

REFERENCES

Cain, T. D. 1975. Reproduction and recruitment of the brackish water clam *Rangia cuneata* in the James River, Virginia. *United States National Marine Fisheries Service Fishery Bulletin* **73**: 412–30.

Caraco, N. F., and Cole, J. J. 2002. Contrasting impacts of a native and alien macrophyte on dissolved oxygen in a large river. *Ecological Applications* **12**: 1496–1509.

Caraco, N. F., Cole, J. J., Findlay, S. E. G., Fischer, D. T., Lampman, G. G., Pace, M. L., and Strayer, D. L. 2000. Dissolved oxygen declines in the Hudson River associated with the invasion of the zebra mussel (*Dreissena polymorpha*). *Environmental Science and Technology* **34**: 1204–1210.

Caraco, N. F., Cole, J. J., Raymond, P. A., Strayer, D. L., Pace, M. L., Findlay, S. E. G., and Fischer, D. T. 1997. Zebra mussel invasion in a large, turbid river: phytoplankton response to increased grazing. *Ecology* **78**: 588–602.

Carlson, D. M. 1992. Importance of winter refugia to the largemouth bass fishery in the Hudson River estuary. *Journal of Freshwater Ecology* **7**: 173–80.

Carlton, J. T. 1992. Introduced marine and estuarine mollusks of North America: an end-of-the-20th-century perspective. *Journal of Shellfish Research* **11**: 489–505.

1996. Biological invasions and cryptogenic species. *Ecology* **77**: 1653–5.

Carlton, J. T., and Geller, J. B. 1993. Ecological roulette: the global transport of nonindigenous marine organisms. *Science* **261**: 78–82.

Carlton, J. T., and Holohan, B. A. (compilers). 1998. *USA Ballast Book: Ballast Research in the United States of America*. Maritime Studies Program, Williams College – Mystic Seaport. 204 pp.

Carpenter, S. R., and Kitchell, J. F. (eds.). 1993. *The Trophic Cascade in Lakes*. Cambridge, UK: Cambridge University Press.

Charlebois, P. M., Marsden, J. E., Goettel, R. G., Wolfe, R. K., Jude, D. J., and Rudnika, S. 1997. The round goby, *Neogobius melanostomus* (Pallas), a review of European and North American literature. *Illinois-Indiana Sea Grant Program and Illinois Natural History Survey Special Publication* **20**: 1–76.

Cheney, A. N. 1895. Black bass and their distribution in the waters of the state of New York. *Annual*

Report of the Commissioners of Fisheries, Game, and Forests of the State of New York, pp. 176–84.

Cohen, A. N., and Carlton, J. T. 1997. Transoceanic transport mechanisms: introduction of the Chinese mitten crab, *Eriocheir sinensis*, to California. *Pacific Science* **51**: 1–11.

1998. Accelerating invasion rate in a highly invaded estuary. *Science* **279**: 555–8.

Cox, G. W. 1999. *Alien Species in North America and Hawaii*. Washington, DC: Island Press.

Crossman, E. J., and Cudmore, B. C. 1999a. Summary of North American fish introductions through the aquarium/horticulture trade, in R. Claudi and J. H. Leach (eds.). *Nonindigenous Freshwater Organisms: Vectors, Biology, and Impacts*. Boca Raton, FL: Lewis Publishers, pp. 129–33.

1999b. Summary of North American fish introductions through the aquaculture vector and related human activities, in R. Claudi, and J. H. Leach (eds.). *Nonindigenous Freshwater Organisms: Vectors, Biology, and Impacts*, Boca Raton. FL: Lewis Publishers, pp. 297–303.

Dermott, R., Witt, J., Um, Y. M., and Gonzalez, M. 1998. Distribution of the Ponto-Caspian amphipod *Echinogammarus ischnus* in the Great Lakes and replacement of native *Gammarus fasciatus*. *Journal of Great Lakes Research* **24**: 442–52.

Ferber, D. 2001. Will black carp be the next zebra mussel? *Science* **292**: 203.

Findlay, S., Pace, M. L., and Fischer, D. T. 1998. Response of heterotrophic planktonic bacteria to the zebra mussel invasion of the tidal freshwater Hudson River. *Microbial Ecology* **36**: 131–40.

Findlay, S., Schoeberl, K., and Wagner, B. 1989. Abundance, composition, and dynamics of the invertebrate fauna of a tidal freshwater wetland. *Journal of the North American Benthological Society* **8**: 140–8.

Fuller, P. L., Nico, L. G., and Williams, J. D. 1999. *Nonindigenous Fishes Introduced into Inland Waters of the United States*. American Fisheries Society Special Publication 27.

Gilcrest, W. R., and Schmidt, R. E. 1998. Comparison of fish communities in open and occluded freshwater tidal wetlands in the Hudson River estuary, in J. R. Waldman and W. C. Nieder (eds.). Final Reports of the Tibor T. Polgar Fellowship Program for 1997. New York: Hudson River Foundation, pp. IX-1 to IX-32.

Goodchild, C. D. 1999. Ecological impacts of introductions associated with the use of live baitfish, in R. Claudi and J. H. Leach (eds.). *Nonindigenous Freshwater Organisms: Vectors, Biology, and Impacts*. Boca Raton, FL: Lewis Publishers, pp. 181–200.

Green, D. M., Landsberger, S. E., Nack, S. B., Bunnell, D., and Forney, J. L. 1993. *Abundance and Winter Distribution of Hudson River Black Bass*. Final report to the Hudson River Foundation on grants 001/88B and 009/91A. 49 pp.

Grosholz, E. D., and Ruiz, G. M. 1996. Predicting the impact of introduced marine species: lessons from the multiple invasions of the European green crab *Carcinus maenus*. *Biological Conservation* **78**: 59–66.

Hall, R. O., Tank, J. L., and Dybdahl, M. F. 2003. Exotic snails dominate nitrogen and carbon cycling in a highly productive stream. *Frontiers in Ecology and the Environment* **1**: 407–411.

Hankin, N., and Schmidt, R. E. 1992. Standing crop of fishes in water celery beds in the tidal Hudson River, in J. R. Waldman and E. A. Blair (eds.). *Final Reports of the Tibor T. Polgar Fellowship Program for 1991*. New York: Hudson River Foundation, pp. VIII-1 to VIII-23.

Hebert, P. D. N., Muncaster, B. W, and Mackie, G. L. 1989. Ecological and genetic studies on *Dreissena polymorpha* (Pallas): a new mollusc in the Great Lakes. *Canadian Journal of Fisheries and Aquatic Sciences* **46**: 1587–91.

Henneman, M. L., and Memmott, J. 2001. Infiltration of a Hawaiian community by introduced biological control agents. *Science* **293**: 1314–1316.

Hopkins, S. H., and Andrews, J. D. 1970. *Rangia cuneata* on the East Coast: thousand mile range extension, or resurgence. *Science* **167**: 868–9.

Jensen, G. C., McDonald, P. S., and Armstrong, D. A. 2002. East meets west: competitive interactions between green crab *Carcinus maenus* and native and introduced shore crab *Hemigrapsus* spp. *Marine Ecology Progress Series* **225**: 251–62.

Kiviat, E. 1978. *Hudson River East Bank Natural Areas, Clermont to Norrie*. Arlington, VA: The Nature Conservancy.

1993. Under the spreading water-chestnut. *News from Hudsonia* **9**(1): 1–6.

LaSalle, M. W., and de la Cruz., A. A. 1985. Species profiles: life histories and environmental requirements of coastal fishes and invertebrates (Gulf of Mexico) – common rangia. *U.S. Fish and Wildlife Service Biological Report*. 82 (11.31). U.S. Army Corps of Engineers, TR EL-82-4. 16 pp.

Ledesma, M. E., and O'Connor, N. J. 2001. Habitat and diet of the non-native crab *Hemigrapsus sanguineus* in southeastern New England. *Northeastern Naturalist* **8**: 63–78.

Lints, D., Findlay, S., and Pace, M. 1992. Biomass and energetics of consumers in the lower food web of the Hudson River, in C. L. Smith (ed.). *Estuarine*

Research in the 1980's. Albany, NY: SUNY Press, pp. 446–57.

Litvak, M. K., and Mandrak, N. E. 1999. Baitfish trade as a vector of aquatic introductions, in R. Claudi and J. H. Leach (eds.). Nonindigenous freshwater organisms: vectors, biology, and impacts. Boca Raton, FL: Lewis Publishers, pp. 163–80.

Llanso, R., Southerland, M., Vølstad, J., Strebel, D., Mercurio, G., Barbour, M., and Gerritsen, J. 2001. Hudson River Estuary Biocriteria: Results Report for Year 2000. Report to the New York State Department of Environmental Conservation, Albany, NY.

Lohrer, A. M., and Whitlatch, R. B. 1997. Ecological studies on the recently introduced Japanese shore crab (Hemigrapsus sanguineus), in eastern Long Island Sound, in N. C. Balcom (ed.). Proceedings of the Second Northeast Conference on Nonindigenous Aquatic Nuisance Species. Connecticut Sea Grant Publication CTSG 97-02, pp. 49–60.

2002a. Interactions among aliens: apparent replacement of one exotic species by another. Ecology 83: 719–32.

2002b. Relative impacts of two exotic brachyuran species on blue mussel populations in Long Island Sound. Marine Ecology Progress Series 227: 135–44.

Mackie, G. L. 1999. Mollusc introductions through aquarium trade, in R. Claudi and J. H. Leach (eds.). Nonindigenous Freshwater Organisms: Vectors, Biology, and Impacts. Boca Raton, FL: Lewis Publishers, pp. 135–49.

Malecki, R. A., Blossey, B., Hight, S. D., Schroeder, D., Kok, L. T., and Coulson, J. R. 1993. Biological control of purple loosestrife. BioScience 43: 680–6.

McDermott, J. J. 1998a. The western Pacific brachyuran (Hemigrapsus sanguineus: Grapsidae), in its new habitat along the Atlantic coast of the United States: geographic distribution and ecology. ICES Journal of Marine Science 55: 289–98.

1998b. The western Pacific brachyuran Hemigrapsus sanguineus (Grapsidae) in its new habitat along the Atlantic coast of the United States: reproduction. Journal of Crustacean Biology 18: 308–316.

Mills, E. L., Leach, J. H., Carlton, J. T., and Secor, C. L. 1993. Exotic species in the Great Lakes: a history of biotic crises and anthropogenic introductions. Journal of Great Lakes Research 19: 1–54.

Mills, E. L., Scheuerell, M. D., Carlton, J. T., and Strayer, D. L. 1997. Biological invasions in the Hudson River basin: an inventory and historical analysis. Circular of the New York State Museum 57: 1–51.

Mills, E. L., Strayer, D. L., Scheuerell, M. D., and Carlton, J. T. 1996. Exotic species in the Hudson River basin:

a history of invasions and introductions. Estuaries 19: 814–23.

Molloy, D. P., Karatayev, A. Y., Burlakova, L. E., Kurandina, D. P., and Laruelle, F. 1997. Natural enemies of zebra mussels: predators, parasites, and ecological competitors. Reviews in Fishery Science 5: 27–97.

Nack, S. B., Bunnell, D., Green, D. M., and Forney, J. L. 1993. Spawning and nursery habitats of large-mouth bass in the tidal Hudson River. Transactions of the American Fisheries Society 122: 208–216.

National Research Council. 1996. Stemming the Tide: Controlling Introductions of Nonindigenous Species by Ships' Ballast Water. Washington, DC: National Academy of Sciences Press, 141 pp.

Nico, L. G., and Williams, J. D., 1996. Risk Assessment on Black Carp (Pisces: Cyprinidae). Report to the Risk Assessment and Management Committee of the Aquatic Nuisance Species Task Force, Gainesville, Florida.

Office of Technology Assessment. 1993. Harmful Nonindigenous Species in the United States. Office of Technology Assessment, U.S. Congress, Washington, DC.

Pace, M. L., Findlay, S. E. G., and Fischer, D. 1998. Effects of an invasive bivalve on the zooplankton community of the Hudson River. Freshwater Biology 39: 103–116.

Paffen, B. G. P., van den Brink, F. W. B., van der Velde, G., and bij de Vaate, A. 1994. The population explosion of the amphipod Corophium curvispinosum in the Dutch lower Rhine. Water Science and Technology 29: 53–5.

Pelczarski, K., and Schmidt, R. E. 1991. Evaluation of a pop net for sampling fishes from water-chestnut beds in the tidal Hudson River, in E. A. Blair and J. R. Waldman (eds.). Final Reports of the Tibor T. Polgar Fellowship Program for 1990. New York: Hudson River Foundation, pp. V-1 to V-33.

Revkin, A. C. 1999. Making up their beds and hoping the oysters will move in. The New York Times, 24 June 1999, pp. B1, B5.

Robbins, W. H., and MacCrimmon, H. R. 1974. The Black Bass in America and Overseas. Ontario Canada Biomanagement and Research Enterprises. 196 pp.

Ruesink, J. L., Parker, I. M., Groom, M. J., and Kareiva, P. M. 1995. Reducing the risks of nonindigenous species introductions: guilty until proven innocent. BioScience 45: 465–77.

Ruiz, G. M., Fofonoff, P., Hines, A. H., and Grosholz, E. D. 1999. Non-indigenous species as stressors in estuarine and marine communities: assessing invasion impacts and interactions. *Limnology and Oceanography* **44**: 950–72.

Schmidt, R. E., Anderson, A. B., and Limburg, K. 1992. Dynamics of larval fish populations in a Hudson River tidal marsh, in C. L. Smith (ed.). *Estuarine Research in the 1980s*. Albany, NY: State University of New York Press, pp. 458–75.

Smith, C. L. 1985. *The Inland Fishes of New York State*. New York State Department of Environmental Conservation, Albany, NY.

Smith, T. E., Stevenson, R. J., Caraco, N. F., and Cole, J. J. 1998. Changes in phytoplankton community structure during the zebra mussel (*Dreissena polymorpha*) invasion of the Hudson River. *Journal of Plankton Research* **20**: 1567–79.

Strayer, D. L., Caraco, N. F., Cole, J. J., Findlay, S., and Pace, M. L. 1999. Transformation of freshwater ecosystems by bivalves: a case study of zebra mussels in the Hudson River. *BioScience* **49**: 19–27.

Strayer, D. L., Hattala, K., and Kahnle, A. 2004. Effects of an invasive bivalve (*Dreissena polymorpha*) on fish populations in the Hudson River estuary. *Canadian Journal of Fisheries and Aquatic Sciences* **61**:924–41.

Strayer, D. L., Lutz, C., Malcom, H. M., Munger, K., and Shaw, W. H. 2003. Invertebrate communities associated with a native (*Vallisneria americana*) and an alien (*Trapa natans*) macrophyte in a large river. *Freshwater Biology* **48**: 1938–49.

Strayer, D. L., Powell, J., Ambrose, P., Smith, L. C., Pace, M. L., and Fischer, D. T. 1996. Arrival, spread, and early dynamics of a zebra mussel (*Dreissena polymorpha*) population in the Hudson River estuary. *Canadian Journal of Fisheries and Aquatic Sciences* **53**: 1143–9.

Strayer, D. L., and Smith, L. C. 1996. Relationships between zebra mussels (*Dreissena polymorpha*) and unionid clams during the early stages of the zebra mussel invasion of the Hudson River. *Freshwater Biology* **36**: 771–9.

2001. The zoobenthos of the freshwater tidal Hudson River and its response to the zebra mussel (*Dreissena polymorpha*) invasion. *Archiv für Hydrobiologie Supplementband* **139**: 1–52.

Strong, D. R., and Pemberton, R. W. 2000. Biological control of invading species – risk and reform. *Science* **288**: 1969–70.

Townsend, C. R., and Winterbourne, M. J. 1992. Assessment of the risk posed by an exotic fish: the proposed introduction of channel catfish (*Ictalurus punctatus*) to New Zealand. *Conservation Biology* **6**: 273–82.

van den Brink, F. W. B., van der Velde, G., and bij de Vaate, A. 1993. Ecological aspects, explosive range extension and impact of a mass invader, *Corophium curvispinosum*, in the lower Rhine (The Netherlands). *Oecologia* **93**: 224–32.

Vitousek, P. M., D'Antonio, C. M., Loope, L. L., and Westbrooks, R. 1996. Biological invasions as global environmental change. *American Scientist* **84**: 469–78.

Williams, T. 2001. Want another carp? *Fly Rod and Reel*, June 2001. http://www.flyrodreel.com/archive/consvarch/conservation0601.html.

**Contaminants and Management Issues
of the Hudson River Estuary**

22 The History and Science of Managing the Hudson River

Dennis J. Suszkowski and
Christopher F. D'Elia

ABSTRACT For nearly four centuries humans have been affecting Hudson River resources, with the most profound human influences occurring during the last 150 years. Economic issues have been at the root of most environmental management decisions. Problems and controversies, like dealing with New York City's sewerage, Westway and the Hudson River Power Case, have shaped both regional and national environmental policies. The current intricate matrix of governmental institutions, nongovernmental organizations, and multiple and multidisciplinary issues involved greatly complicates environmental management in the United States. New management structures have emerged to deal with problems that cross political and institutional boundaries, and for which no single entity has full responsibility to resolve. Successes in conquering regional problems have shared the same characteristics: the development of sound technical information to understand the problem and its potential solution; the formation of appropriate partnerships that include all appropriate decision makers; pressure from stakeholders and concerned individuals outside the management agencies for specific outcomes; the acquisition of funds appropriate to the task; and an institutional structure to implement the solution. There is a disconnect between the institutions that fund research and the management agencies that use the information that the funded research generates. With growing demands for watershed planning, habitat restoration, contaminant reduction, and biodiversity protection, agencies will require better understandings of ecosystem processes in order to formulate credible and predictive management strategies.

Introduction

Each year, many decisions are made that involve the utilization and conservation of Hudson River natural resources, or involve projects that impact those resources. Collectively, these decisions constitute the management of the Hudson River. Regardless of the magnitude and scope of the project or action, each decision exhibits the same common characteristics: it is made by a governmental body in the face of some degree of uncertainty, contention, and public expense. Decisions are made at various governmental levels, from municipal to federal, and the consequences of these actions can affect river resources at local or regional geographic scales.

For nearly four centuries, humans other than native Americans have been affecting river resources, with the most profound human influences occurring during the last 150 years. Responding to economic and social needs of a growing population, commercial navigation channels were dredged, dams were constructed, industries blossomed, forests were cleared for agriculture and wetlands were filled to create new land. By the end of the nineteenth century, the Erie Canal was completed, navigation channels throughout the Hudson River were dredged, dikes were built along the banks of the Hudson to increase the "rise of the tide at Albany and Troy" (Klawonn, 1977), the population within the watershed had risen to over 3 million (Hetling et al., 2003), and vast amounts of raw sewage from that growing population were discharged to the river. Changes to the biological, chemical, and physical makeup of the Hudson caused by human intervention escalated during the twentieth century leading to pioneering programs in New York State, such as Governor Nelson Rockefeller's Pure Waters Bond Act of 1965, and of important pieces of Federal environmental legislation from 1969 through 1972.

Today more than ever, there is a tremendous awareness of all the Hudson River has to offer. Besides the ongoing use of resources for human use, there is a growing appreciation that the river is part of the fabric and culture of the region. As its mysteries are unlocked through scientific observation and personal contact, the river's ecosystem is increasingly being celebrated and embraced as a friendly and valued neighbor. Fortunately, great strides have been made over the past thirty years to clean up and restore the river, but much remains to be done. Goals have been established through several government initiatives to preserve that relationship. But are these goals realistic and will they be achieved? Have we learned important lessons from the past? Are there mechanisms in place or contemplated for the future to effectively manage the river? How do we enhance our understanding of the river and use that knowledge to make the best decisions possible?

History of Environmental Management

MAJOR ENVIRONMENTAL CONCERNS
AND JURISDICTIONS

The intricate matrix of governmental institutions, nongovernmental organizations and multiple and multidisciplinary issues involved greatly complicates environmental management in the United States. The U.S. Constitution vests considerable authority and responsibility at the state level, and only in cases where what happens in one state affects another or has national implications does the Federal government readily exercise major authority. Of course, since many environmental policy issues clearly transcend state borders, such as air and water pollution, they do appropriately fall under Federal jurisdiction. However, inasmuch as land use is now regarded to be an important determinant of environmental quality at a larger scale, many have advocated stronger land-use planning legislation. Others view this as inconsistent with state sovereignty, New York State's strong tradition of home rule and traditional American values of individual property ownership. Some threatened private interests have strongly opposed any authority seeking to regulate their lands, such as for example, by invoking the "takings clause" of the fifth Amendment in the courts.

In the early days of the Union, scant attention was paid to environmental legislation or regulation. Promoting economic and political well-being were the principal concerns. With time, states started to take an interest in stewardship of resources and began to evince concern for pollution and land-use issues. As it became more obvious to Congress that environmental issues often transit state boundaries, an increasing federal role developed, but even today, the Federal government has shown reluctance to involve itself in issues of land-use planning and management, which many believe lie at the core of environmental stewardship. Thus, until recently, the Federal role in non-point source pollution management and regulation of non-tidal wetlands has very much remained within the purview of an individual state, and the different states, in turn, vest differing levels of authority with state and municipal agencies.

As will be discussed below, one of the earliest environmental concerns in New York State related to land use, and even there, the matter required the State to establish its own authority over local entities by legislation creating the Adirondack Park. The history of home rule is well established in New York, and accordingly, land use is very much relegated to local authority (Kleppel, 2002; Nolon, 1999) leading to a patchwork approach to management of the landscape.

One might conveniently divide the major environmental concerns into the following groupings:

1. *Point and non-point source pollution.* Nutrients, sewage solids, and toxic wastes from publicly-owned sewerage facilities and industries now come under state and Federal controls. Runoff from the land, atmospheric deposition, both of nutrients and toxic compounds have largely been local and state concerns until the most recent reauthorization of the Clean Water Act.

2. *Disposal of solid wastes and dredged material.* Solid wastes from households and industry, sludge from sewage treatment plants, and sediments dredged from harbors and rivers must all be disposed of. A variety of Federal and state laws pertain.

3. *Land use.* To the extent that land use affects non-point pollution, land use falls under the previous grouping and the pertinent Federal and state legislation. To the extent that land use affects the ecological communities on them and their biological integrity, it has

generally been left up to the local planning and zoning boards in New York to exercise primary authority.

4. *Recovery of polluted areas.* The Comprehensive Environmental Response, Compensation, and Liability Act (CERCLA, PL 96–510, enacted in 1980), commonly known as "Superfund," was enacted by Congress in 1980 to eliminate the health and environmental threats posed by hazardous waste sites. This law is highly pertinent to contaminated areas in the Hudson River Valley.

5. *Resource use.* The planning, implementation, and regulation of projects and activities, including navigation, fisheries, biodiversity, water supply, power generation and a wide variety of commercial and recreational uses. Both state and Federal authority pertain.

HUDSON RIVER ENVIRONMENTAL HISTORY

Although a complete environmental history of the Hudson River and surrounding areas is well beyond consideration in this paper, we provide here an overview of key issues and events that have had particular bearing on either the management of the river or in a larger sense, on environmental policy in the United States. We divide this history into two major periods, the first being prior to the 1960s when issues for the Hudson and its watershed focused legislative and managerial action primarily at the state level, and the second being from the late 1960s to the present, when the Hudson figured heavily in changing the course of environmental management at the national level. Table 22.1 summarizes environmental concerns and issues, institutional drivers, and economic drivers of management and policy.

EARLY HISTORY: BEFORE THE 1960S

While the most vexing environmental problems we now face, such as the cleanup of toxic materials, are clearly rooted in post-Industrial Age technological developments, early colonial activities nonetheless began to have profound effects on the landscape and these, in turn, affected the Hudson River itself. In 1609, as he navigated up the river that is now his namesake, Captain Henry Hudson was impressed

with the extensive, dense forest he saw along the entire route, and he noted in his log that it "abounds in trees of every description" (Boyle, 1979). Farming settlements were established on both sides of the river after 1630 (Howe, 2002). Within 100 years, much of the land from the river's eastern bank to the Atlantic Ocean would be substantially cleared (e.g., Foster, Motzkin, and Slater, 1998) to provide fuel for winter heat, lumber for the construction of dwellings, farm buildings, and ships, and open land suitable for cultivation. Within the next 100 years, an expansion westward would extend similar effects through the Mohawk Valley, and by 1825 the completion of the Erie Canal would further accelerate westward development. Shortly thereafter, deforestation occurred even in remote mountainous areas of the Hudson's watershed (Stanne, Panetta, and Forist, 1996).

One of the earliest New World developments of commerce and industry focused squarely on technical improvements in transportation, which has historically been one of the most important uses of the Hudson River proper and the land along its banks. Under the able leadership of Governor DeWitt Clinton, the construction of the Erie Canal (1817–25) was among the most ambitious public works programs ever undertaken and completed. The canal opened the primary trade route to the Great Lakes and Midwest and led to the rapid development of New York City as the nation's center of commerce and finance. Along with the Delaware and Hudson Canal, constructed from 1825–29 to the south, the Erie Canal provided coastal access to the coal fields in Pennsylvania and Ohio; to the fur trade of Canada and Upstate New York; to vast lumber resources for building and fuel; for tannins used to cure leather; to sand, gravel, and stone used in the construction industry; and to the rich agricultural resources in the Midwest. The period from 1825–60 saw substantial regional expansion as the Troy and Albany region contributed to the rapid increase in northeastern manufacturing and transportation (Howe, 2002). In the westward direction, the finest European manufactured products would now make frontier life more bearable for early settlers. Accordingly, it is not surprising that in the earliest days, the governmental role that related to the environment was aimed squarely

Table 22.1. Environmental concerns and issues, institutional and economic drivers, and key enabling legislation related to management of the Hudson River

Time period	Environmental concerns and issues	Major institutional drivers	Major economic drivers	Enabling legislation
17th and 18th centuries	• Colonial clearing forest	• Colonial rule	• Agricultural production	
1st half of 19th century	• Forest clearing • Pre-industrial era and transportation	• New York State and City commercial interests	• Agricultural production • Lumbering • Commerce and trade	• Federal navigation projects • 1855 Harbor Commission – NYS
2nd half of 19th century	• Forest clearing • Industrialization and development of transportation	• New York State and City business interests • State government	• Commerce and trade • Lumbering Industrial development	• Federal navigation projects • 1885 Adirondacks Forest Preserve – NYS • Federal 1888 Supervisor of the Harbor Act • Federal 1899 River and Harbor Act
1st half of 20th century	• Industrialization and urban development • Public health • Declining water quality in river, estuary and harbor	• New York State and City business interests • State government • Major corporate interests	• Commerce and trade • Industrial development	• Federal navigation projects • 1903 NY Bay Pollution Commission – NYS • 1906 Metropolitan Sewerage Commission – NYS • 1936 Tri-State Compact – NY, NJ & CT • 1948 Federal Water Pollution Control Act
1960s–1970s	• Environmental impact assessment of projects affecting river • Storm King proposal • Sewage disposal • Industrial wastes • Fisheries management • Endangered species • Dredged material disposal	• New York State and City business interests • State government • Major corporate interests • Federal government • NGOs	• Commerce and trade • Industrial development • Power generation	• Federal navigation projects • 1965 Pure Waters Bond Act – NYS • Federal 1965 Anadromous Fish Conservation Act • Federal 1973 Endangered Species Act • 1969 National Environmental Policy Act • 1972 Clean Water Act • Federal 1972 Marine Protection, Research and Sanctuaries Act (*Ocean Dumping Act*) • Federal 1972 Coastal Zone Management Act
1980s – present	• PCBs and other contaminants • Exxon dumping of oil-polluted waters • Power plant impacts • Wetlands and nearshore filling • Dredged material disposal • Public access	• State government • NGOs • Federal government	• Commerce and trade • Industrial and residential development • Power generation	• Federal 1980 Comprehensive Environmental Response, Compensation, and Liability Act (CERCLA or *Superfund*) • 1987 Hudson River Estuary Management Act – NYS • Federal 1987 Clean Water Act – National Estuary Program • Federal 1996 Magnuson-Stevens Conservation and Management Act • Hudson River Greenway Act

at enhancing commerce, such as by ensuring that the waterways were passable and navigable.

The visionary inventor-entrepreneur Robert Fulton recognized that steam could be harnessed to propel commercial traffic in reliable, scheduled service, and his steamer, the *North River*, later called the *Clermont*, took its maiden voyage from New York City to Albany in 1807. The importance of Fulton's steam-powered service cannot be underestimated: not only did it accelerate trade and commerce, but it also created a new demand for fuel to power steam engines, which proliferated rapidly throughout the ensuing Industrial Revolution. In the early days, the source of fuel was invariably wood, and the need for wood fuel along with a demand for tannins obtained from hemlock trees led, in turn, to increased logging pressures throughout the Hudson's watershed (McMartin, 1992). This demand continued to intensify with the development of the railroad, and by the 1860s, the combination of logging for fuel and construction had taken a noticeable toll on the forest resources of the Adirondack and Catskill mountains (Terrie, 1994).

Deforestation in the late nineteenth century continued until a public outcry from a variety of strange bedfellows led to one of the first major environmental protections in the United States. In Terrie's (1994, p. 83) words, "The key authors of the Adirondack conservation story were journalists, wealthy businessmen, cut-and-run loggers, government officials, aristocratic hunters and anglers trying to protect their sport, and transportation interests worried about water levels in the Hudson River." The culminating event was the adoption of state constitutional protection of the Adirondack Park in 1894 as "forever wild," which has made it nearly invulnerable to the whimsy of a governor and legislature.

While science was not the determining factor in the development of environmental legislation to protect the Hudson River watershed, scientific information and advice played an essential role in framing the issues and raising awareness of them. George Perkins Marsh's historic book, *Man and Nature; or, Physical Geography as Modified by Human Action* (1864), led to a more widespread understanding that mountain forests control runoff, erosion, sediment input and regional microclimate. Verplanck Colvin, who for three decades surveyed the length and breadth of the Adirondacks, reported back trenchantly to the legislature about the steady demise of forested areas. His persistence raised awareness of the immensity of the problem in the halls of power in Albany. Great men of learning of the time, Harvard Professor C.S. Sargent and Dr. F. B. Hough, through their testimony and own publications, gave further credence to the concerns raised by Marsh, Colvin, and others.

Irrespective of the voices calling for environmental protection per se, natural resource management efforts during this period were dominated by economic interests (Johnson, 2000), and the Hudson River and watershed continued to experience significant change as a result of economic development and population growth. Public works projects (for example, navigation channels, hydroelectric power plants, flood control projects, etc.) were designed and constructed to meet economic needs, with little or no consideration of the impacts of these activities on river resources, other than navigation. At the turn of the century, the principal objectives for government regulations associated with the lower Hudson River and New York Harbor included: the prevention of the dumping of solid materials into navigation channels by the federal government; the management of a quarantine by New York State to limit the spread of infectious diseases from vessel passengers; and New York City's prevention of "local nuisances along the shore." (Metropolitan Sewerage Commission, 1910)

By the turn of the nineteenth century, the Port of New York was the busiest and most important in the country (Klawonn, 1977). A vast network of navigation channels and berthing facilities was created in the lower Hudson River and New York Harbor. Disposal of sediments dredged from the construction and maintenance of these channels was problematic. Much of the dredged material was dumped in sites in the entrance channels to the harbor, creating new navigation hazards. In addition, the lower river and harbor were convenient dumping grounds for street sweepings and construction debris. Because these practices were seriously affecting navigation by clogging shipping channels, the Federal 1888 Supervisor of the Harbor Act was enacted to prevent the discharge of solid materials into the harbor and its tributaries. The Act established dumping grounds for dredged material and other materials in areas offshore of the entrance to the estuary. To further prevent hazards, Section 13 (the Refuse Act) of the River and Harbor Act of 1899 was enacted by the U.S. Congress to prevent the discharge of any refuse matter that might impede or obstruct navigation.

By the 1870s, landfilling along the banks of the lower Hudson River was a widespread concern. As the Manhattan and New Jersey shorelines grew closer together, changes in sediment deposition patterns followed. While natural depositional patterns caused sediments to accumulate on the New Jersey side of the river, it was believed by some that shoaling had increased by the "artificial" scour produced by the narrowing of the river (Klawonn, 1977). The first Federal water legislation was enacted by Congress in 1886 as the River and Harbor Act. Eventually harbor lines were established to guide the placement of bulkheads and piers, and a permit program was established under the amended River and Harbor Act of 1899 to review the placement of materials into navigable waterways which extended beyond the harbor lines, with the U.S. Army Corps of Engineers as the responsible Federal agency. These new authorities brought a halt to significant incursions of new land into the lower Hudson River; however, they had little effect on the massive filling of wetlands and mudflats in other areas of the lower estuary (Squires, 1992).

While Federal government interest was primarily vested in protecting navigation with good reason, the states and New York City focused attention on public health issues affecting the harbor. *The New York Times* (1890) called the New York City's sewerage system an "abomination" and warned that deposits of sewage sludge accumulating in New York Harbor are "far from being innocuous to the health of the people." The early pollution of the harbor is graphically summarized by Waldman (1999), who terms it "ecological strangulation." In 1903, the New York Bay Commission, created by a special act of the New York State Legislature, found the harbor to be seriously polluted and recommended that a metropolitan sewerage district be established to deal with the sewage problem. Following up on the Bay Pollution Commission's recommendations, the New York State Legislature passed the New York Bay Pollution Act of 1906, directing the City of New York

to create the Metropolitan Sewerage Commission to devise ways of correcting the sewage problem.

The Commission did a remarkable and comprehensive job of investigating conditions in New York Harbor, which they found to be "more polluted than public health and welfare should allow" (Metropolitan Sewerage Commission, 1910). The results of the Commission's work are contained in several large volumes, published between 1906 and 1914, and include: detailed scientific and engineering investigations, including data from an extensive monitoring program started in 1909 and continuing today as the New York Harbor Survey; opinions of prominent scientists, engineers, and public health officials; and a plan for a new sewerage system for New York City. The technical information was unambiguous about the need for improvements to the sewerage system, and the Commission's findings paved the way for vast improvements to the water quality of the lower Hudson River.

When a problem transcends state boundaries, it falls under Federal jurisdiction. However, if there are no Federal programs designed to address the issue, states form alliances or compacts with one another to seek solutions. Because interstate alliances and compacts could unduly encroach upon Federal authority and violate Federal laws, the U.S. Constitution (Article 1, Section 10, Clause 3) requires that states gain Congressional approval before entering into such agreements. Of the thirty-six interstate compacts authorized by Congress prior to 1921, virtually all were established to resolve rudimentary issues, such as the settlement of boundary disputes (Mountjoy, 2003).

Compacts can, however, provide states the freedom to find creative solutions to complex problems of mutual concern, and put the development of those solutions in the hands of the people who are most familiar with the issues (Sundeen and Runyon, 1998). In fact, important and powerful interstate agencies have been created through compacts. The first, and probably the most famous, is the Port Authority of New York and New Jersey, which was established in 1921 to improve port management in the country's largest port. The shoreline and bottom of New York Harbor have been reshaped by port interests, much of which by the Port Authority, as the need for deeper channels and greater wharf space grew throughout the twentieth century. After the Port Authority was established, more than 150 other compacts were formed throughout the country over the next seventy-five years. Their purposes ranged from conservation and resource management to civil defense (Mountjoy, 2003).

In the 1930s, the New York metropolitan region had moved ahead with plans for the abatement of sewage-related problems, with partnerships forming not only between the states of New York and New Jersey, but with the state of Connecticut as well. Because the Federal government had little to offer, and because the expertise and funding for developing engineering solutions were at the regional level, a Tri-State Compact was formed. In 1936, the Interstate Sanitation Commission, authorized by the compact, held its first meeting (Interstate Sanitation Commission, 1937). It was given many responsibilities, including developing water quality classifications for the Sanitation District (which generally includes the lower Hudson River, New York Harbor and Long Island Sound), inspection of sewage treatment facilities, enforcement of non-compliance with the compact, and technical planning and monitoring. The Commission's work over the years focused attention on the problems created by inadequate sewage disposal systems on New York Harbor and is given large credit for keeping capital improvement projects on track.

From the 1930s through 1968, modest changes were made to the overall management structure affecting the Hudson River Estuary to include the consideration of factors other than public health and navigation. The Federal government was gradually assuming more responsibilities in environmental management through new legislation and regulation revision. The Anadromous Fish Conservation Act (PL 89–304) was enacted in 1965 (Limburg et al., Chapter 14, this volume), the Corps of Engineers' regulatory program was revised to include a "public interest review" of proposed actions instead of just a review of the project's effects on navigation, the Federal Water Pollution Control Act and Amendments (1948, 1956, 1965) were enacted, which stressed the need for water quality standards and sewage treatment upgrades, and the Pure Waters Program was established in New York State (Chapter 23, this volume). During this period the

Federal role in water pollution control was purely advisory, and administered through the Public Health Service (O'Connor, 1990).

A Case Study in Early Management: The New York City Sewerage System

In 1906, the Metropolitan Sewerage Commission was given three objectives (Metropolitan Sewerage Commission, 1910):

"First. To establish the facts attending the discharge of sewage;

Second. To determine the extent to which these conditions were injurious to the public health; and,

Third. To ascertain the way in which it would be necessary to improve the conditions of disposal in order to meet the reasonable requirements of the present and future."

Under the terms of the Bay Pollution Act of 1906, five persons were appointed by the Mayor of New York to serve as members of the Metropolitan Sewerage Commission. One of its original members, George A. Soper, became president in 1908. Soper, a sanitary engineer working for the New York City Health Department, gained considerable recognition in 1906 by tracking down the source of a typhoid epidemic to one Mary Mallon, a cook who became commonly known as "Typhoid Mary." Soper made medical history by being the first person ever to document that typhoid could be spread by a healthy carrier (Bourdain, 2001).

In 1910, the Commission made its first set of findings public, which included a detailed description of the horrific water quality conditions in the harbor, a general design for a new sewerage system, and recommendations for public policy changes to deal with the growing sewage problems. It strongly endorsed a joint and permanent sewerage commission to be created by the states of New York and New Jersey. Clearly both New York and New Jersey contributed to the problem and both would need to part of the solution. However, tension between the states existed over the proposed construction of an outfall pipe by the Passaic Valley Sewerage Commission in Upper New York Bay. The new pipeline would divert vast amounts of sewage from being discharged into the Passaic River in northern New

Jersey to a point on the New York/New Jersey border within the Harbor. The State of New York vigorously opposed the plan and battled New Jersey in court for nearly twenty years. This battle not only inhibited the creation of an interstate commission but also caused New Jersey to boycott participation in proceedings of the Metropolitan Sewerage Commission.

One influential business group, the Merchant's Association, became a strong advocate for sewerage improvements. The Association, like *The New York Times*, supported the technical conclusions of the Commission, but had other ideas concerning the most expedient approach to getting some action. It advocated enlisting the services of the Federal government to require a "standard of purity" and let "all abutters and defilers" conform to that standard (*The New York Times*, 1910). If water quality standards were set, New York City and other municipalities surrounding the harbor would be forced to make improvements.

The Association pressured New York City officials for many years to take action, advocating that nothing was more important than the City's health and that a healthy harbor was in the best interest of the business community. Its frustration culminated in 1923 with the release to *The New York Times* of correspondence with Mayor Hylan that demonstrated his refusal to devote attention to the sewage disposal problem (*The New York Times*, 1923). The Mayor's position regarding the "alleged germ-laden water around the harbor," was that, "When the immediate and necessary problems are overcome, one of which is transit, it will then be time enough to take up the question to which you refer." Before leaving office in 1926, Mayor Hylan did devote considerable attention to transit issues, creating the city-owned, Independent Subway line (the IND), which opened after he left office, but did little to further the cause of sewage abatement.

From the time of the Commission's release of its final report in 1914, until actual construction of a new sewerage system began in New York City, nearly thirty years had expired. The delays in implementation can be linked to poor regional cooperation, a lack of protection standards, the aftermath of the First World War, changing social issues, funding limitations, and political indifference. None of the policy strategies recommended by the Com-

mission and others to speed up the process took hold during this period. But with continued pressure from the business and engineering communities, and the fallout from a typhoid epidemic linked to contaminated shellfish, a joint legislative committee of the States of New York, New Jersey, and Connecticut was formed in 1924 to form a new Sanitary Committee to revisit the sewage problem and recommend solutions. After exhaustive study, the Committee issued its final report in 1927 that recommended immediate adoption of a comprehensive plan of sewage disposal in greater New York. In 1931, New York City announced that it had finally developed a financing plan for the sewerage improvements (*The New York Times*, 1931) and construction of a new system, patterned on many of the recommendations of the Metropolitan Sewerage Commission, commenced.

The New York City sewerage story highlights several important challenges to developing regional management strategies for the Hudson River. They include: the development of sound and credible technical information to characterize the problem and to reduce the uncertainties in forecasting the benefits (or consequences) of taking action; the formation of partnerships that include all appropriate decision makers for the geographic scope of the problem and its causes; the inclusion of specific goals to be met; the active participation of user groups and stakeholders; the development of political support; and the creation of funding strategies for both planning and implementation.

A New Era: 1960s–1990s

A growing public concern over the environment prompted dramatic new Federal action in the late 1960s and early 1970s, much of it motivated by events affecting the Hudson River. The National Environmental Policy Act (NEPA, PL 91-190) enacted in 1969 forced Federal agencies to write environmental impact statements before proceeding with management decisions deemed to be "significant." The Federal Water Pollution Control Act of 1972 (PL 92–500, in subsequent authorizations referred to as the "Clean Water Act"), proclaiming "it is the national goal that the discharge of all pollutants waters into navigable waters be eliminated by 1985," was the most comprehensive water pollution control legislation ever enacted. It was a major transition point from its timid predecessors to the much more comprehensive legislation embodied by the various authorizations of the Clean Water Act that followed. The Act authorized huge Federal expenditures for sewage treatment construction grants, institutionalized a permit program for industrial dischargers (including power plants), required states to make regular evaluations of water quality, required secondary treatment for all municipal wastes, established environmental criteria for dredged material disposal, regulated the filling of wetlands, and provided new direction for water quality standards and criteria with the goal of creating "fishable, swimmable waters."

An avalanche of new programs and organizations cascaded into the environmental management structure at the state and municipal levels (see Table 22.2). The U.S. Environmental Protection Agency, the New York Department of Environmental Conservation, the New Jersey Department of Environmental Protection, and the New York City Department of Environmental Protection were created, and other Federal and state agencies were revamped, all designed to address the new and growing environmental mandates that the public was demanding. In addition, states developed legislation to complement the recently enacted Federal legislation. For example, to provide for the Environmental Impact Statements at the state level – in essence, the New York State counterpart to NEPA's similar provisions – the State Environmental Quality Review Act (SEQRA) took effect in November, 1978. The overall management structure that emerged was one of strong Federal controls initially, with gradual delegation of responsibilities to the states over time as the state programs matured.

Legions of environmental managers were now hard at work correcting environmental problems. Some of their successes are chronicled in Chapter 23 of this volume and Steinberg et al. (2004). While much of the day-to-day activities of these managers went unnoticed by the public, some key regulatory actions proved to be lightning rods for environmental activism and public debate. Westway and the Hudson River Power Case, discussed below, are two examples of controversial regulatory proceedings that focused regional and national attention on Hudson River environmental issues.

Prompted by the growing awareness of environmental issues in the Hudson River brought about by the Power Case, Congressman Richard Ottinger, along with several other prominent Democrats in the U.S. Congress, supported legislation in 1966 to create an interstate compact for a Hudson River Scenic Riverway. Not to be outdone by the Democrats and seeking to keep issues under State control, Rockefeller established his own state run entity, the Hudson River Valley Commission (HRVC), and pushed through the Pure Waters Bond Act aimed at cleaning up sewage throughout the state, with an emphasis on the Hudson River. In addition, Rockefeller stalled efforts to negotiate an interstate agreement with New Jersey for many years and the Congressional deadline for ratifying a compact expired in 1974 (Dunwell, 1991).

Rockefeller's HRVC was composed of influential New Yorkers, but had limited powers and was described by Robert Boyle (1979) as a "bad joke." It compiled information about the Hudson's resources and conducted site plan reviews of large projects. Though it did not have the power to stop projects, it could delay them by holding extensive hearings. It was successful in redesigning projects to reduce their scenic impacts and facilitating the creation of new parks like Hudson Highlands State Park (Dunwell, 1991). After a period of time it lost its momentum and local support, and eventually was dissolved.

With vanishing of hope for an interstate compact and the limited authority of the HRVC, the Rockefeller Foundation stepped forward in 1973 and funded a three-year study of environmental problems and institutional issues called the Hudson River Basin Project. This impressive effort, which produced over 4,000 pages of memoranda, working documents, and reports after consulting with approximately 125 people, is synthesized in a two-volume report published in 1979. The need to strengthen environmental management institutions was identified as the most important problem to be tackled in the Hudson River Basin (Richardson and Tauber, 1979). The overall project unfortunately turned out to be a purely academic exercise. It had no official connection to any individual or agency of the executive or legislative branch

Table 22.2. Agencies with management responsibilities

Level	Agency	Responsibilities
Federal	National Oceanic and Atmospheric Administration (National Marine Fisheries Service and National Ocean Survey)	– Review and comment on permits – Endangered species – Nautical charts – Natural Resource Damage Assessment (NRDA)
	U.S. Coast Guard	– Pollution response – Homeland Security – Boater safety
	U.S. Environmental Protection Agency	– Clean Water Act oversight and enforcement – National Estuary Program (HEP) – Superfund – Review and comment on permits
	U.S. Geological Survey	– Collect data tributary flow and sediment data
	U.S. Department of the Interior (National Park Service and Fish and Wildlife Service)	– Manage park facilities – Review and comment on permits – Habitat inventories
	U.S. Army Corps of Engineers	– Navigation projects – Regulation of activities in waterways – Flood and beach erosion control – Dredged material management – Floating drift collection
	U.S. Food and Drug Administration	– Seafood quality standards
State	New Jersey Department of Environmental Protection	– Clean Water Act delegated programs – Coastal and waterfront permitting – Navigation and coastal protection – Monitoring and research – Enforcement – Seafood consumption advisories – Fisheries management – NRDA
	New Jersey Department of Health	– Assists in beach water quality monitoring – Certifies shellfish handling
	New York State Department of Environmental Conservation	– Hudson River Estuary Management Program – Clean Water Act delegated programs – Fisheries management – Enforcement – State Environmental Quality Review Act – NRDA – Monitoring
	New York State Department of Health	– Seafood consumption advisories – Beach water quality
	New York State Department of State	– Coastal zone management
Municipal	New York City Department of Environmental Protection	– Construction and operation of treatment plants – NY Harbor Survey – Floating drift collection
	New York City Department of Health	– Beach water quality monitoring
	New York City Department of Parks – Natural Resources Group	– Park and natural area management – Habitat restoration
Regional	Port Authority of NY and NJ	– Operate port facilities
	Interstate Environmental Commission	– Water quality monitoring – Enforcement
	Hackensack Meadowlands Commission	– Manage wetlands and open space – Monitoring and education

within New York State government, nor did it enlist the support of outside organizations to lobby for changes of the present system. Consequently, the project had little effect on changing policy related to the Hudson River.

A few years later in 1976, another planning effort was initiated to comprehensively analyze the resources of the Hudson River Basin, this time by New York State with Federal funding. The Hudson River Level B Study assessed the basin's existing conditions and projected water and related land needs and problems to the year 2000. It provided a series of recommendations, including the creation of "new management structure with a unified approach to conservation and development of land and water" (New York State Department of Environmental Conservation, 1979). The recommendations from the Level B Study suffered the same fate, however, as the Hudson River Basin Project. Though sponsored by government, the project was purely a planning exercise and had no effect on changing existing policies.

During the 1980s, significant changes were made to the management structure guiding decisions about the Hudson River. The Hudson River Estuary Management Program and the New York/New Jersey Harbor Estuary Program both came into effect in the late 1980s and resulted in the first sustainable and comprehensive programs to deal with estuary and river issues. They will be discussed in greater detail in a subsequent section of this paper.

The Federal Superfund program was authorized by the U.S. Congress in 1980 and had particular significance to the Hudson River. Unacceptably high concentrations of PCBs and cadmium in sediments within two distinct portions of the Hudson could now be dealt with through a Federal initiative.

Also, in recent years citizens have been demanding greater access to the river and better protection of the aesthetic resources of adjacent land areas. New programs, like New York State's Hudson River Greenway established in 1991, are now successfully preserving and enhancing the scenic, historic, cultural, and recreational resources of the Hudson River Valley.

WESTWAY

Westway was a project developed in the early 1970s to rebuild the crumbling West Side Highway and create over 200 acres of developable land and parks in Manhattan. A new highway was to be sunk in a landfill created in the Hudson River that extended over four miles, and at a cost of approximately $2 billion. As the project was designed to be part of the Federal interstate highway system, the Federal government would pay 90 percent of the bill. The project sponsors were required to obtain a permit from the U.S. Army Corps of Engineers (Corps) because fill would be placed into the Hudson to create the landfill. The Corps' permit review process provided a forum for individuals, groups, and agencies to voice support or opposition to the plan. While there were many issues debated in the Westway case, the one that resulted in the project's demise was the potential impact of the proposed landfill on the population of striped bass in the Hudson River.

The aquatic environment that the landfill would displace was originally characterized by the project sponsors as being biologically impoverished. This assessment was based upon very little field information. Federal actions, like the Westway permit review by the Corps of Engineers, trigger impact assessments in accordance with the National Environmental Policy Act of 1969 (NEPA), and require scientific counsel (Limburg, Moran, and McDowell, 1986). As more information was collected so the Corps could complete its environmental assessment, and as that information was reviewed by other agencies and groups, the project area was found to be inhabited by far more organisms than previously thought. Juvenile striped bass were observed in the inter-pier areas of the project site during winter months, prompting scientists to hypothesize that the Westway area was an important wintering area for these young fish. The Corps rejected that hypothesis and issued a permit 1981. The decision was challenged in court and the permit was vacated.

The Court allowed the project sponsors, the New York State Department of Transportation, to reapply for a landfill permit, but the Corps was required to prepare a supplemental environmental impact statement (SEIS) addressing specifically the impact of Westway on Hudson River fishery resources. The Corps' final SEIS estimated, according to a most probable worst case analysis, that Westway could displace one-quarter of the juvenile striped bass population (New York District, U.S. Corps of Engineers, 1985). But what would become of displaced fish if the project were built? And if these fish perished, would the overall population of striped bass be adversely affected? All of the experts consulted agreed that it was impossible to design a study to determine the answer to those questions. The population dynamics of striped bass would have to be better understood through longer term research before accurate impact predictions could be made.

For Westway's permit decision, the answers would have to come from expert opinion and qualitative judgments. That decision rested on whether the Corps believed that the construction of Westway would harm Hudson River striped bass and result in a finding of "unacceptable adverse impact," and whether there were any practicable alternatives to the project that would lessen impacts to the aquatic environment, the criteria used in determining whether projects are in compliance with Section 404 of the Clean Water Act. The Corps concluded that displaced fish would likely survive and that Westway would not cause a "significant adverse impact" to the Hudson and Coastal striped bass stocks. Consequently the Corps approved a permit in January 1985.

The permit was immediately challenged in court, and Corps representatives had great difficulty explaining to Judge Thomas Griesa how they reached their decision. The final SEIS used language in describing aquatic impacts that was dramatically different from language in the draft SEIS. The term "significant," which has both a regulatory and statistical meaning, was freely and loosely used in the draft SEIS to describe impacts. The Court eventually found that the Corps' decision to grant the permit was arbitrary and violated NEPA and the Clean Water Act (Sierra Club vs. United States Army Corps of Engineers, 81 Civ. 3000 Opinion, August 7, 1985).

The Westway saga had a chilling effect on any future plans for large-scale filling of the Hudson River. An unwritten new regulatory commandment of "Thou shalt not fill" propagated throughout the region. In addition, the Westway case not only highlighted the need to obtain appropriate scientific information and expertise prior to decisionmaking, but also demonstrated the limitations in our understandings of fundamental ecosystem processes, making impact assessment very difficult, especially in cases where there are potential population-level effects.

HUDSON RIVER POWER CASE AND HUDSON RIVER FOUNDATION

The Hudson River Power Case, involving the permitting of several power plants in the mid-Hudson River, has focused considerable attention to human impacts on fisheries resources and led ultimately to the formation of a foundation to conduct environmental research. The conflicts between the power-generating industry – which uses Hudson River water to run steam turbines and cool them – and those concerned with the conservation of natural resources proved to be an enormously important milestone in environmental policy development for the Hudson, and indeed the nation itself.

In 1962, the electric power generating company, Consolidated Edison (Con Ed), proposed construction of a "pumped storage generating plant" drawing water from the River at historic and beautiful Storm King Mountain in the Hudson Highlands. An enormous outcry ensued and soon thereafter the Scenic Hudson Preservation Conference[1] was formed and later, the Hudson River Fishermen's Association[2]. The Second Circuit Court's decision in the case, *Scenic Hudson Preservation Conference v. Federal Power Commission* (1965) set an important precedent for environmental law in the United States by affording citizens' groups legal standing to sue over environmental and aesthetic issues[3]. From the perspective of the present paper, though, the nearly protracted legal battle that preceded the final settlement in 1980 with Con Ed led to the widespread recognition that "the fundamental environmental information needed to make many management decisions was simply not available," nor was any public agency adequately prepared to fund necessary studies.

Under the terms of the "Hudson River Settlement Agreement," which also pertains to thermal pollution problems associated with the Indian Point Nuclear Power Plant and two other plants, the Storm King project was abandoned and steps were taken to reduce fish mortality, particularly

---

[1] Now known as Scenic Hudson.
[2] Now known as Riverkeeper.
[3] Before, only those with a direct economic interest could be construed to be an "injured party" in cases before the courts.

during spawning times. Of particular significance is the recognition of the need for better scientific information that was articulated and promoted very passionately and cogently by environmental activist Robert Boyle (1979). Accordingly, the utilities also agreed to conduct biological monitoring that still continues today and to provide a $12 million endowment for a new foundation for independent environmental research on the Hudson River. Thus, the Hudson now has an institutional resource that no other river or estuary we are aware of anywhere has, the Hudson River Foundation (HRF). HRF, a private not-for-profit organization, sponsors research in the natural sciences and public policy, and promotes efforts to improve management policies through the integration of science. Since 1983, the Foundation has funded approximately 460 individual projects totaling approximately $30 million, contributing to more than 60 percent of the research conducted about the Hudson River since that time.

In addition to its contributions to the broader understanding of the ecological function of the river, the HRF is generally regarded to have made important research contributions regarding the operation of power plants and the potential effects they have on the populations of several species of Hudson River fish. The continuing need for regulatory action argues for the need to incorporate cutting-edge, unbiased, and credible scientific information into environmental decision making. As in the Westway matter, current science may not be able to make significant reductions in uncertainties with respect to important impacts, particularly in cases where population-level effects are possible. Clearly, more focused and sustained research on fundamental ecosystem processes will be needed, as will be better ways to enable managers to incorporate the results of basic research into their policies and decisions.

PCBs IN THE UPPER HUDSON RIVER

Among the most vexing and persistent challenges to the Hudson River science and management are the PCBs[4] that have accumulated in the river north

---

[4] PCBs – polychlorinated biphenyls – are very stable organic compounds with chlorine atoms in a variety of configurations that are used as insulators in transformers and other industrial applications.

of the Troy Dam. From 1947 to 1977 General Electric (GE) plants at Fort Edwards and Hudson Falls, New York, released an estimated 590,000 kg (1.3 million pounds) of PCBs into the river, and although GE stopped using PCBs after 1977, some PCBs have since leached from its plant sites.

In the ensuing years – almost three decades have passed since the legal actions first began – this problem has motivated one of the most high profile and vitriolic environmental debates in the United States, pitting environmentalists, who have sought to have PCB-contaminated sediments removed from the river, against GE and its supporters.

As growing awareness of toxic organics developed in the decade after the publication of Rachel Carson's *Silent Spring* (1962), attention began to be focused on the health risks of PCBs. Studies soon linked PCBs to developmental and neurological disorders, as well as cancer, reduced diseased resistance and reproductive problems not only in humans, but also in animal populations in the vicinity of the Hudson.

Monitoring and science have played critical roles in dealing with the Upper Hudson PCB problem, and several numerical models exist to predict the distribution and mobility of PCBs in the freshwater and estuarine parts of the river. Chapter 24 in this volume summarizes the science behind several of the key factors involved in the decision to dredge PCBs from the Upper Hudson River. Finally, in February 2002, the U.S. Environmental Protection Agency issued a record of decision calling for targeted environmental dredging and removal of approximately two million cubic meters of PCB-contaminated sediment from a 65-km (40-mile) stretch of the Upper Hudson.

The Present Management Structure

The Hudson River management structure, once only afforded protections related to navigation and public health, now has a broad range of programs that seek to conserve and protect the aquatic ecosystem and a wide variety of human uses. These initiatives are administered by no fewer than nine Federal agencies, five state agencies, three regional authorities, and countless municipalities. While there is much to celebrate about these programs, Adler (1995) points out that it is difficult to imagine a political system as complicated and as fragmented as that used for protecting and managing water resources in the United States.

Harbor Estuary Program and Hudson River Estuary Program. In the late 1980s new Federal and state legislation significantly changed the management structure for the Hudson River Estuary. At the Federal level, the Clean Water Act was amended in 1987 to include the establishment of a National Estuary Program (NEP), patterned after the successful operations of the Chesapeake Bay Program. The governors of New York and New Jersey successfully petitioned the U.S. Environmental Protection Agency to include the Hudson River Estuary (also known as the "New York/New Jersey Harbor Estuary") as "an estuary of national significance." Inclusion of the New York/New Jersey Harbor Estuary Program (HEP) into the NEP in 1988 provided an excellent opportunity to take stock of the current environmental conditions and to develop plans to correct unacceptable conditions found in the lower estuary. Though the Harbor Estuary encompasses all of the tidal waters of New York Harbor and its tributaries, including the Hudson River to the Federal lock and dam in Troy, the HEP has focused its attention on a "core area" that includes the harbor, its direct tributaries, and the Hudson River north to the vicinity of Piermont Marsh (km 40 – Milepoint 25).

The overall goal of HEP is "to establish and maintain a healthy and productive ecosystem with full beneficial uses" by first characterizing the environmental conditions in the estuary, developing a comprehensive plan that recommends actions to improve conditions, implementing those actions, and monitoring the health of the estuary to determine the effectiveness of the actions taken. A "Comprehensive Conservation and Management Plan" (CCMP) was adopted in 1996 and the program is now in its implementation phase.

In 1987, the New York legislature enacted the Hudson River Estuary Management Act, which declared that it is the policy of the State of New York to "preserve, protect and, where possible, restore and enhance the natural resources, the species, the habitat and the commercial and recreational values of the Hudson River Estuary." The Act established

an "estuarine district" from the Troy lock and dam to the Verrazano-Narrows in New York Harbor, and required the development of a Hudson River Estuary Management Program (HREMP) by the New York State Department of Environmental Conservation (DEC) for the district in consultation with an advisory committee, which included representatives of commercial fishing, sportsmen, research, conservation, and recreation.

Both management programs have similar challenges that relate to institutional, financial and technical constraints. These challenges must be overcome if there is any hope of achieving the lofty goals established by both programs. Management responsibilities are fragmented and spread among several layers of government and among different political jurisdictions. Overlapping responsibilities of agencies can lead to conflicts in protection objectives and inefficiencies in resource allocations. The management of complex, important issues is often artificially fragmented within an agency's structure. Some issues may require that two or more different divisions or bureaus within agencies be involved. Lack of coordination and confusion of responsibilities can lead to a dilution of effort. Probably the most important problem, however, is the existence of gaps in authority to deal with complex problems over geographically broad areas, leading to serious problems in program implementation and funding.

An important function that HEP and HREMP provides is coordination. Both programs provide a structured way for agencies, organizations, and individuals to communicate with one another on an ongoing basis. While coordination alone does not ensure that individual organizations will agree to take on expanded responsibilities or that collaborations will be formed, the role that HEP and HREMP play cannot be underestimated in facilitating the creation of new partnerships to achieve the goals that all have agreed upon. Both programs have a sustainable, long term component missing from previous efforts to provide direction toward comprehensive management. They each had a planning phase, and now have an implementation and action phase that is supported by annual funding for essential program functions.

HEP has characterized problems of the estuary and recommended actions to solve those problems in a comprehensive planning document endorsed by the governors of New York and New Jersey and the administrator of EPA. An implementation phase is now in place where resources are being sought to fund the recommended actions. Lindblom (1995) has cautioned that some comprehensive planning models, that is, ones that seek clear objectives and require explicit evaluations of all potential decisions before proceeding, are attractive for use in solving complex problems, but rarely can be used by policy and decision makers and when used, prove to be unproductive. He states that an intense comprehensive analysis "assumes intellectual capacities and sources that men simply do not possess." Successful solutions and policies to complex problems have generally evolved through step-by-step, incremental planning and execution.

Both estuary programs have no choice but to approach the countless goals and objectives in their respective management plans in incremental ways. Moreover, the development and application of technically sound tools, like mathematical models, have been given high priority by both programs to help forecast future conditions in the estuary in light of management actions that may be taken.

Though both programs have made important progress, the Chesapeake Bay Program is still generally considered the premier estuarine management program in the United States. Much of that success can be linked to the establishment of incremental goals and targets that prescribe for the bay what people concerned about it bay want, and by when they want it. The acceptance and endorsement of these targets by elected officials has led to the allocation of resources to implement the solutions needed to reach those targets. An important aspect of the target setting is that it forces the management structure to assess scientifically how the targets can best be reached and whether they can be reached in the time frames contemplated. Both HEP and HREMP have embarked on similar approaches to the one adopted for the Chesapeake, and at the writing of this chapter, have target-oriented plans awaiting final endorsement by state and Federal officials.

The new estuary management structure that has emerged in recent years through the work of HEP

and HREMP has had to deal with the gaps and constraints of existing authorities. Smith (2002) in an analysis of estuary management in Australia found that traditional management responsibilities emanating from legislation and regulation, which he terms de jure, often evolves into de facto responsibilities because of external pressures exerted on management authorities. Pressures for change from environmental organizations and champions of certain issues, a lack of response to these pressures from agencies, and new knowledge from scientific researchers have forced officials and agencies to assume expanded management roles. New attention to emerging issues has created de facto management structures which are more responsive to estuarine problems; however, they are inherently unstable. The de facto structure requires continued pressures from external sources to keep its priority at a high level and to generate a continued supply of resources.

Within the HEP structure, two major initiatives have emerged which follow the de facto management scenario described above. Concern for greater habitat protection and restoration has been strongly expressed at public meetings convened by HEP, and through members of the Habitat Work Group of HEP. Many organizations, including national and local environmental groups, watershed associations, civic organizations, and resource management agencies serve on the Work Group. In 2001, the Work Group identified eighty-eight sites for restoration and sixty sites for acquisition surrounding the lower estuary (Habitat Work Group, 2001). Since thousands of acres of wetland and aquatic areas have been filled or altered over the years to create new land for an expanding metropolis, HEP is now devoted to saving the remaining important habitat areas and working to restore those sites that have been physically or chemically altered. Since there were no agencies with de jure responsibilities to conduct restoration or purchase sites, creative ways had to be found to move the habitat initiative forward. Groups and individuals, working with the "blueprint" created by the Habitat Work Group, have administratively and legislatively committed approximately $100 million to support the habitat efforts.

Another major de facto effort is the Contamination Assessment and Reduction Project (CARP).

In the early 1990s, dredging activities in New York Harbor came to a halt because of environmental concerns over the disposal of dredged sediments at an ocean dump site. Without dredging, ships that carry international cargo and oil products could not safely navigate the waters of the harbor. Their exclusion would be devastating to the regional economy.

Several workshops sponsored by EPA, called the "Dredged Material Forum," were convened to discuss the dredging dilemma among a variety of port stakeholders, including Federal, state and local government agencies, labor unions, regional port officials, environmental organizations, engineering consultants and scientists. While workshop participants were deeply divided on many issues, all agreed that the region needed to address dredging and disposal issues in a more comprehensive way. In particular, new disposal strategies for contaminated sediments needed to be researched and implemented as soon as possible. Also, since contaminants were at the heart of the crisis, a plan should be developed to reduce or eliminate the sources of contaminants that were causing the sediments to be deemed too contaminated for ocean disposal. A work group was established to develop a plan and present its recommendations to the Policy Committee of HEP for inclusion into HEP's comprehensive plan.

The primary management objectives were: (1) to identify sources of contaminants that needed to be reduced or eliminated in order to render future dredged material "clean" (as defined in applicable guidelines and criteria); (2) to define what actions will be the most effective in abating the sources; and (3) to determine how long it will take for freshly deposited sediments to achieve "clean" status.

The work group made several findings. First, addressing the management questions required that a comprehensive technical analysis be made to understand the linkages between inputs of contaminants to the estuary and their ultimate fate in water, sediment, and biota. Second, since it was important to forecast future conditions in light of potential contaminant reductions, a mathematical modeling framework would have to be developed. Third, new data would have to be collected to quantify ambient contaminant concentrations and develop credible loading estimates for specific contaminant sources. Even though contaminants like PCBs, dioxins, and PAHs were routinely tested in connection with dredged material management, there was very little complementary testing of these chemicals in other media by government agencies or regulated parties. Lastly, the Work Group found that specific government authority (that is, de jure management responsibility) for taking action to reduce contaminants that were violating dredged material criteria was nonexistent. A new de facto management framework, the Contamination Assessment and Reduction Project (CARP) was devised to deal with the issue. A management committee now guides the progress of CARP and is composed of representatives from the Hudson River Foundation, the Port Authority of New York and New Jersey, New Jersey Department of Environmental Protection, New Jersey Maritime Resources, New York Department of Environmental Conservation, the Empire State Development Corporation, Environmental Defense, the U.S. Environmental Protection Agency, and the U.S. Army Corps of Engineers. To the present, funding for CARP totals approximately $27 million. The majority of that amount emanates from the Port Authority through a bistate dredging agreement endorsed by the governors of New York and New Jersey.

CARP is perhaps the largest and most ambitious contaminant assessment effort ever undertaken. Nearly one million individual contaminant analyses have been performed. The utilization of these data in an ad hoc management framework is truly remarkable and demonstrates the benefits of having cooperative arrangements, like HEP, in place to bring different parties together to tackle new management challenges.

Collecting Scientific Information

Scientific information about environmental conditions and understanding of ecosystem processes are essential for management of the river's resources. The utilization of this information generally proceeds through a two-step process: a "characterization phase" that involves the collection of new information describing the problem or particular portion of the system that requires protection, and an "interpretation phase" that places the information in the context of the present

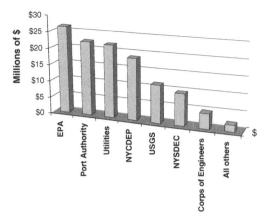

Figure 22.1. Annual support for monitoring, impact assessment, and resource inventories by funding sources: 1990–2000. (The data contained in this figure and Figure 22.2 were obtained from 39 individuals representing 25 different organizations. In addition, data from the National Science Foundation were obtained from its website.)

understanding of natural processes. Moreover, for impact assessment, managers must evaluate how the proposed human action will affect those processes.

Government agencies and regulated parties routinely spend considerable funds in the characterization phase, collecting and managing technical data about the river and estuary. Between 1990 and 2000, approximately $117 million was directed to data collection in connection with monitoring programs, impact assessments, and resource inventories (Fig. 22.1). State and Federal agencies funded about 64 percent of that amount. New York City spent nearly $19 million, half of which was devoted to its Annual Harbor Survey that started in 1909 with the Metropolitan Sewerage Commission.

Managers generally rely on existing scientific literature and experience of their technical staffs for current understandings of ecosystem processes. They sometimes discover that there are serious deficiencies in the understanding of these processes, however, rarely do managers sponsor research to fill needed gaps in that understanding. Many are constrained within their institutional authority to even consider research as a management tool. Regulatory programs typically limit most assessments to narrowly defined short-term objectives. After digesting years of scientific and legal debate in connection with the Hudson River Power

Case, Barnthouse, Klauda, and Vaughn (1988) concluded that long-term monitoring and research were clearly needed to improve future assessments, but these efforts require funding and management independent of the regulatory process. Since settlement of the power case in the early 1980s, more than $41 million has been invested in research about the river and estuary (Fig. 22.2). Only very modest funding was provided by management agencies. More than half of the research funding emanated from the Hudson River Foundation.

Broader planning programs like HEP and HREMP have recognized the importance of new research being incorporated into their planning and implementation efforts. In fact, one of the first initiatives of HREMP was to outline a science program that would support better and more effective management of the Hudson River Estuary. After several meetings with both managers and the research community, a Science/Management Paradigm was developed (Schubel, 1992). The elements of the paradigm include research, modeling, monitoring, synthesis, education, outreach, and partnerships between scientists and resource managers. It recognizes that managers need information, not simply data, to make decisions. Data may be derived from monitoring programs, research projects, or both, depending on the nature of the problem being addressed. Data collected through research and monitoring efforts can then be interpreted and synthesized into information that can be used in decision making. To sustain the paradigm, scientists, managers, and the public should form ongoing

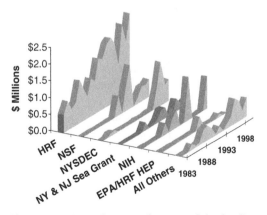

Figure 22.2. Annual support for research by funding sources: 1983 through 2000.

partnerships, and an education program should be established to enhance public understanding. The paradigm was envisioned to be funded through a large endowment of approximately $100 million.

Inasmuch as securing an endowment of $100 million was highly unlikely, it soon became apparent that the "paradigm" was unrealistic as originally contemplated. Developing a single comprehensive research and monitoring program to address the many problems plaguing the Hudson was far too ambitious (Suszkowski and Schubel, 1994). However, the paradigm did provide a model whose components deserved further examination and application on a smaller scale, and the Hudson River Foundation subsequently used these concepts to develop a special research initiative concerning Atlantic sturgeon.

In the late 1980s, commercial fishermen in the river observed that they were capturing fewer small sturgeon as incidental catches in their gill nets, which was corroborated by other fish surveys conducted in the river. Although the reasons for this remained unknown, it was starkly evident that there would be fewer sturgeon available to commercial fishermen in future years. At the same time, commercial fishing for the Atlantic sturgeon stock had increased dramatically, particularly in ocean waters offshore of New Jersey (Waldman, Hart, and Wirgin, 1996).

In response to a growing recognition that the Atlantic sturgeon population of the Hudson River might be in trouble, the Hudson River Foundation convened a workshop, inviting noted sturgeon research scientists and fishery managers to discuss potential courses of action. The workshop concluded that key scientific information was lacking about the reproductive condition of the fish, the size of the Hudson River population, and movement patterns of the sturgeon. This information was deemed critical to the management of the stock.

After establishing sturgeon as a "special interest area" in the Foundation's 1993 call for proposals, several research projects were funded to ascertain the health of the stock at an initial investment of approximately $700,000. The research soon confirmed the hypotheses that there were dwindling numbers of Atlantic sturgeon and that the overall Hudson River population was very small.

The reproductive condition of the sturgeon was found to be healthy, and was not a cause of the stock's decline. Modeling analyses performed by New York State biologists, working in concert with the Foundation-sponsored investigators and using their research findings, demonstrated that the sturgeon stock could not withstand a fishing pressure sufficient for an economically viable fishery.

A moratorium on the harvesting of Hudson River Atlantic sturgeon was enacted in New York based upon the research and modeling. A subsequent moratorium was also enacted in New Jersey following legislative hearings in which the results of the Foundation's sponsored research were presented. Commercial fishing will be unlikely to resume for several decades while sturgeon stock rebuilds itself to a sustainable population. In the meantime, New York State is supporting a monitoring program to complement the Foundation's research by watching the progress in sturgeon recruitment. This monitoring will be the important ingredient to successful management of this species in the future.

Managing Scientific Research

During the two decades of its existence, there has quite naturally been considerable discussion of how to direct the Hudson River Foundation's funding to the most meritorious and important projects headed by the best qualified principal investigators. Regardless of the context, management of research funding is a challenge: for corporate research and development managers, for Federal and state management offices, for Federal basic science agencies and for foundations and nongovernmental organizations the desire is to direct funding for the most efficacious purpose. No perfect formula exists for the best mix of research topics, and irrespective of this, philosophical differences abound as to what the highest purpose is. Environmental activists might argue that research must be directly relevant to the problems of the day and thus provide immediate feedback for management actions. In contrast, many scientists might argue that fundamental research should have the largest role, and that only by understanding the environment in depth will we be able to manage it.

HRF has migrated to several principles in managing scientific research over the years. In 1999, it clarified its mission as making science integral to decision making with regard to the Hudson River and its watershed and to support competent stewardship. This purpose is being pursued in large part through support of quality scientific research relevant to public policy. The most important aspect of selecting projects of the highest quality is the reliance on a peer review process with the following important characteristics: use of outside mail reviews and inside panel discussions; avoidance of conflict of interest, real or perceived; use of interdisciplinary evaluation; evaluation of prior results; involvement of scientists from many institutions, including outside of the region; evaluation of proposal significance; and availability of multiyear funding, when feasible.

HRF further believes that investments in environmental research should be distributed in ways to best address short and long term issues. This "portfolio approach" is akin to what financial managers might recommend to investors, that is, instead of making all investments in a single category, one should diversify one's holdings. Thus, HRF seeks to have a flexible blend of research projects, addressing scientific and public policy questions that may or may not have time constraints associated with them, but nonetheless relate to important areas in need of scientific inquiry. The categories considered are as follows:

- Long-term or fundamental importance, that is, what is believed to be necessary in order to understand basic ecological function and thus of potential long-range bearing on management approaches. This is often referred to as "basic" research that is intended to advance the state of knowledge where the possible applications of the results of the research are many years away. Example: studies of lower food web processes in the tidal freshwater portion of the river.
- Near-term importance, that is, what is anticipated will have important bearing on an environmental issue in the next five to ten years. This may have both "basic" and "applied" components. Example: studies of the fate, transport, and potential effects of toxic chemicals.
- Immediate importance of high priority, that is, what needs to be known now for a compelling environmental problem of present interest. This

typically is what is often referred to as "applied" research. This research is intended to provide needed information for issues facing the Hudson over the near term, say in the next several years. In addition, HRF recognizes the need to direct resources at emerging issues that need clarity before management actions can even be contemplated. Example: studies in connection with the decline of Atlantic sturgeon.

Managing its grants program as a "portfolio" and making its programs as responsive to public policy issues as possible makes it incumbent upon HRF to understand the pressing management problems and issues facing the Hudson River and the role that science can play in developing solutions to them. This requires active participation by HRF staff in management deliberations, particularly those of HEP and HREMP. We note that a major disconnect exists between organizations that need scientific information for management, and organizations, like HRF, that fund research. As pointed out in the discussion of the Science/Management Paradigm, most complex environmental problems require some combination of research, monitoring, and modeling to formulate solutions. Determining which combination of technical tools is appropriate to solve the problem is crucial, and this process can greatly benefit from the participation of research organizations and scientists who are currently engaged in research or have recently completed studies of the river. Establishment of collaborations and partnerships is perhaps the greatest challenge to resolving complex environmental issues in the future that cross political and administrative boundaries, and where the need for scientific information to reduce the uncertainty in decision making is critical.

Conclusions

For almost four centuries, human activities have profoundly affected the Hudson River, its estuary, and its watershed. Our brief review of the history of human activities and their relationship to the Hudson system, its science, and its management leads us to the following major conclusions:

- The Hudson River cannot simply be viewed as a river isolated from the rest of the environment.

Indeed, the crucial role of the watershed that feeds fresh water to the river and the Atlantic Ocean that provides salt water to the estuary and powers its tides are important considerations in the Hudson system's ecological functioning and health.

- Economic issues have been at the root of most environmental management decisions. Indeed, it was not until a landmark decision in 1965 regarding power generation on the river that issues related to natural resources and aesthetics had any legal standing in environmental litigation.

- While the overall management structure for the river and estuary has dramatically changed over the last 100 years, successes in conquering regional problems have shared the same characteristics: the development of sound technical information to understand the problem and its potential solution; the formation of appropriate partnerships that include all appropriate decision makers; pressure from stakeholders and concerned individuals outside the management agencies for specific outcomes; the acquisition of funds appropriate to the task; and an institutional structure to implement the solution.

- Science per se rarely motivates managerial actions. However, science that is appropriately available to managers when needed is often essential to making the most effective managerial decisions. Science and environmental management may at times seem incompatible, but without proper incorporation of scientific information into decision making, serious errors will result.

- For solving complex environmental problems, it is not enough to collect environmental data by means of monitoring or other survey programs alone. Process-oriented information must also be obtained from research and modeling, either mathematical or conceptual. For there to be real hope for such scientific results to be useful to managers, synthetic and interpretive value must be added.

- Land use is a key issue affecting all parts of the Hudson ecosystem's components. Regulating land use is an aspect of environmental management that is challenging to implement due to a patchwork of regulations in different jurisdictions, the strong tradition of home rule in New York State and U.S. Constitutional protections of the rights of individual land owners.

- The role of the Federal government has gradually increased particularly in the latter part of the last century due to recognition of the interconnectedness of different factors affecting the environment. This has had beneficial results regarding environmental management, but has also complicated the role of government in this activity.

- Although prior to the 1960s primary responsibilities for management of the Hudson, its estuary, and its watershed fell to just a few agencies, there is now a complex maze of government agencies at the Federal, state, and local levels whose jurisdictions and purview often overlap. To effect successful environmental management of the Hudson system, substantial interagency interaction and coordination is necessary. Mechanisms that foster interagency and cooperation are important. Of greatest importance is collaboration on issues where gaps in authority and responsibility are preventing regional solutions from being developed and implemented.

- New management structures (that is, de facto management responsibilities) have emerged to deal with problems that cross political and institutional boundaries, and for which no single entity has full responsibility to resolve. Programs like CARP and habitat restoration efforts demonstrate that external pressures on existing management agencies can generate new collaborations and new funding strategies, and bridge gaps in existing authorities.

- Both HEP and HREMP provide excellent fora to set goals for the future of the river and estuary, and provide a starting place and "umbrella" for new management structures to develop and take on the tasks necessary to achieve the goals.

- There is a "disconnect" between the institutions that fund research and the management agencies that use the information that the funded research generates. With growing demands for watershed planning, habitat restoration, contaminant reduction, and biodiversity protection, agencies will require better understandings of ecosystem processes in order to formulate credible and predictive management strategies. Consequently more research, modeling, and synthesis will be required than ever before. If the present model of sponsoring research continues, new sources of funding will be required and stronger ties between management agencies and research organizations will have to be forged.

- The Hudson River Foundation has been an important source of funding for scientific research. Much of this research has had bearing, directly and indirectly, on issues related to the management of the Hudson's resources, and accordingly has been sought and used by management agencies. Nonetheless, one of the great challenges of managers of research is to find ways to "translate" the results of research to practical application and to keep managers and policymakers informed of the latest scientific information that bears on their responsibilities.

REFERENCES

Adler, R. W. 1995. Addressing Barriers to Watershed Protection. *Environmental Law* 25:973–1106.

Barnthouse, L. W., Klauda, R. J., and Vaughn, D. S. 1988. *What We Didn't Learn about the Hudson River, Why, and What it Means for Environmental Assessment.* American Fisheries Society Monograph 4:329–35.

Boyle, R. H. 1979. *The Hudson River: A Natural and Unnatural History.* New York: Norton.

Bourdain, A. 2001. *Typhoid Mary: An Urban Historical.* New York: Bloomsbury, USA.

Carson, R. 1962. *Silent Spring.* Greenwich, CT: Fawcett.

Dunwell, F. F. 1991. *The Hudson Highlands.* New York: Columbia University Press.

Foster, D. R., Motzkin, G., and Slater, B. 1998. Land-use history as long-term broad-scale disturbance: regional forest dynamics in central New England. *Ecosystems* 1:96–119.

Habitat Work Group. 2001. *New York/New Jersey Harbor Estuary Program Habitat Workgroup 2001 Status Report: A Regional Model for Estuary and Multiple Watershed Management.* New York, NY.

Hetling, L. J., Stoddard, A., Brosnan, T. M., Hammerman, D. A., and Norris, T. M. 2003. Effects of Water Quality Management Efforts on Wastewater Loadings over the Past Century, *Water Environment Federation,* 75:30–8.

Howe, E. T. 2002. The Hudson-Mohawk Region Industrializes: 1609–1860. *Hudson River Valley Review* 19:40–57.

Interstate Sanitation Commission. 1937. *Annual Report of Interstate Sanitation Commission for the Year 1937.* Trenton, NJ.

Johnson, M. D. 2000. A Sociocultural Perspective on the Development of U.S. Natural Resource Partnerships in the 20th Century. March 13–16 2000; Tucson, AZ. Proceedings RMRS-P-13. Fort Collins, CO: U.S. Dept. of Agriculture, Forest Service, Rocky Mountain Research Station, pp. 205–12.

Klawonn, M. J. 1977. *Cradle of the Corps: A History of the New York District, U.S. Army Corps of Engineers – 1775–1975.* U.S. Army Corps of Engineers, New York District publication.

Kleppel, Gary S. 2002. Urbanization and Environmental Quality: Implications of Alternative Development Scenarios. *Albany Law Environmental Outlook* 8:38–64.

Limburg, K. E., Levin, S. A., and Harwell, C. C. 1986. Ecology and Estuarine Impact Assessment: Lessons Learned from the Hudson River (U.S.A.) and Other Estuarine Experiences. *Journal of Environmental Management* 22:255–80.

Limburg, K. E., Moran, M. A., and McDowell, W. H. 1986. *Hudson River Ecosystem.* New York: Springer-Verlag.

Lindblom, C. E. 1995. The Science of Muddling Through. *Public Policy: The Essential Readings.* S. Theodoulou and M. Cahn (eds.). Englewood Cliffs, NJ: Prentice Hall, pp. 113–27.

Marsh, G. P. 1864. Man and Nature; or, Physical Geography as Modified by Human Action. New York: C. Scribner.

McMartin, B. 1992. *Hides, Hemlocks, and Adirondack History: How the Tanning Industry Influenced the Region's Growth.* Utica, NY: North Country Books.

Metropolitan Sewerage Commission. 1910. *Report of the Metropolitan Sewerage Commission,* New York, NY.

Mountjoy, J. J. 2003. *Interstate Compacts: An Alternative for Solving Common Problems Among States.* The 2003 Edition of the Report on Trends in the State Courts. The National Center for State Courts, Williamsburg, VA.

New York/New Jersey Harbor Estuary Program. 1996. *Final Comprehensive Conservation and Management Plan.* New York/New Jersey Harbor Estuary Program, New York, NY.

New York District, U.S. Army Corps of Engineers. 1985. Record of Decision with attached Section 404(b)(1) Evaluation for Westway. New York, NY.

New York State Department of Environmental Conservation. 1979. *Hudson River Basin: Water and Related Land Resources.* Level B Study Report and Environmental Impact Statement. Albany, NY.

New York Times, The. 1890. "A Poor Sewage System," July 28, 1890. p. 8.

1910. "Cleansing the Harbor," March 8, 1910, p. 8.

1923. "Sewage Disposal Deferred by Mayor," April 9, 1923, p. 18.

1931. "City Will Act Today on Sewage Disposal." May 8, 1931, p. 27.

Nolon, J. 1999. Grassroots regionalism through inter-municipal land use compacts. *St. John's Law Review* 73:1011–39.

O'Connor, D. J. 1990. A Historical Perspective: Engineering and Scientific. *Cleaning Up Our Coastal Waters: An Unfinished Agenda.* Proceedings of a conference co-sponsored by Manhattan College and the Management Conferences for the Long Island Sound Study, the New York-New Jersey Harbor Estuary Program and the New York Bight Restoration Plan. March 12–14, 1990. pp. 49–67.

Richardson, R. W., and Tauber, G. (eds). 1979. The Hudson River Basin: Environmental Problems and Institutional Response, Volume 1. Academic Press, New York, NY. 354 p.

Scenic Hudson Preservation Conference v. Federal Power Commission. 1965. 453 F. 2d 463 (2d Cir 1971).

Schubel, J. R. 1992. *A Research Program for the Hudson River Estuary: Report on the Development of an Estuarine Science-Management Paradigm.* Hudson River Estuary Management Program, September 1992. New York State Department of Environmental Conservation, Albany, NY. 72 pp.

Smith, T. F. 2002. *Institutional Analysis for Estuary Management.* Proceedings of Coast to Coast 2002: Australia's National Coastal Conference, Queensland Environmental Protection Agency and Coastal Council of New South Wales.

Squires, D. F. 1992. Quantifying Anthropogenic Shoreline Modification of the Hudson River and Estuary from European Contact to Modern Time. *Coastal Management* 20:343–54.

Stanne, S. P., Panetta, R. G., Forist, B. E., and Hudson River Sloop Clearwater, Inc. 1996. *The Hudson: An Illustrated Guide to the Living River.* New Brunswick, NJ: Rutgers University Press.

Steinberg, N., Suszkowski, D. J., Clark, L., and Way, J. 2004. *Health of the Harbor: The First Comprehensive Look at the State of the NY/NJ Harbor Estuary.* New York: Hudson River Foundation.

Sundeen, M., and Runyon, L. C. 1998. *Interstate Compacts and Administrative Agreements: State Legislative Report.* Washington, DC: National Conference of State Legislatures, March 1998, Vol. 23, No. 8.

Suszkowski, D. J., and Schubel, J. R. 1994. Hope for the Hudson: New Opportunities for Managing an Estuary. *Changes in Fluxes in Estuaries,* ECSA22/ERF Symposium. Olssen & Olsen, Fredensborg, Denmark, pp. 395–400.

Terrie, P. 1994. *Forever Wild: A Cultural History of Wilderness in the Adirondacks.* Syracuse, NY: Syracuse University Press.

U.S. Environmental Protection Agency. 1972. *The Challenge of the Environment: A Primer on EPA's Statutory Authority.* EPA publication, Washington, D.C. (Available online at http://www.epa.gov/history/topics/fwpca/05.htm.)

Waldman, J. 1999. *Heartbeats in the Muck: The History, Sea Life, and Environment of New York Harbor.* Guilford, CT: The Lyons Press.

Waldman, J., Hart, J. T., and Wirgin, I. I. 1996. Stock composition of the New York Bight Atlantic Sturgeon fishery based on analysis of mitochondrial DNA. *Transactions of the American Fisheries Society,* 125:364–71.

23 Hudson River Sewage Inputs and Impacts: Past and Present

Thomas M. Brosnan, Andrew Stoddard, and Leo J. Hetling

ABSTRACT The quality of the Hudson River estuary has been negatively impacted for many years by the discharge of untreated sewage. The abatement of these discharges due to construction and upgrading of wastewater treatment plants (WTP) in the Hudson valley from the 1930s to the 1990s has significantly reduced loadings of suspended solids, oxygen demanding organics, floatables, and pathogens, with lesser reductions observed for nitrogen and phosphorus. In response, water quality conditions have improved significantly. Dissolved oxygen has increased from critically low levels to summer averages that exceed 5 mg l^{-1} and pollution sensitive insects and marine borers have returned to the estuary. Sanitary quality has also improved with most of the Hudson today considered to meet swimmable water quality standards. Consequently, shellfish beds and bathing beaches have been reopened in New York/New Jersey Harbor and additional beaches are being considered throughout the river. Priorities for the future include: increased capital and operations and maintenance investments for WTPs, improved capture and treatment of combined sewer overflows (CSO), and investigation of the need for nutrient removal.

Introduction

The Hudson River south of the Federal dam at Troy comprises an approximately 240 km long estuarine system that has been subjected to an enormous loading of pollutants from a variety of sources for over three hundred years. Until relatively recently, this loading included the discharge of millions of liters of untreated sewage per day. Water quality impacts in this and other estuaries from untreated or partially treated sewage have included: closed shellfish beds and beaches from pathogenic microorganisms; depressed oxygen concentrations from the bacterial breakdown of organic compounds; turbidity from suspended solids; and beach closings, wildlife entanglement, and interference with navigation from a variety of "floatables," including sewage-related paper and plastics (Suszkowski, 1990; Brosnan and O'Shea, 1996a). In response, sewage treatment has focused on reducing the discharge of pathogens, organic total suspended solids, and floatables. More recently, concerns over the contribution of nutrients such as nitrogen and phosphorus to algae blooms and depressed dissolved oxygen (eutrophication) have focused investigations into removal of these nutrients from sewage effluents (USEPA, 1996; O'Shea and Brosnan, 2000).

The purpose of this chapter is to document the history of municipal sewage pollution in the Hudson River, highlight impacts of sewage abatement, and discuss remaining challenges related to management and treatment of municipal sewage in the Hudson valley.

Study Area, Scope, Data Sources, and Methods

Study Area. The Hudson River basin can be divided geographically into four subbasins: (1) upper Hudson River basin, extending from its source at Lake Tear of the Clouds to the Federal dam at Troy, New York; (2) Mohawk River basin; (3) middle Hudson River basin, from the Federal dam at Troy, New York to the Bronx-Westchester County boundary; and (4) lower Hudson in the New York-New Jersey metropolitan region from the Bronx-Westchester County line to the Verrazano-Narrows Bridge. This chapter focuses on the middle Hudson and lower Hudson River basins (Fig. 23.1). The watersheds of the middle Hudson basin include most of the area of Albany, Columbia, Dutchess, Greene, Orange, Putnam, Rensselaer, Rockland, Ulster, and Westchester counties. The lower Hudson (metropolitan New York-New Jersey region) basin includes portions of the five boroughs of New York City (Queens, Bronx, Brooklyn, Staten Island, and Manhattan) and Bergen, Passaic, Essex, Morris,

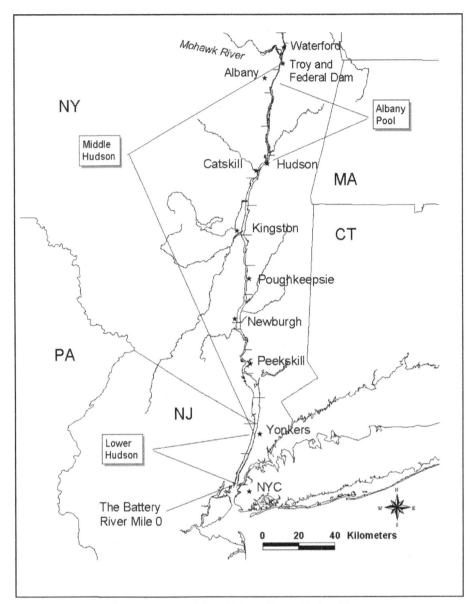

Figure 23.1. Map of the middle and lower Hudson River.

Hudson and Union counties in New Jersey. For this study, the lower Hudson estuary includes the Hudson River from the Bronx-Westchester County line to the Verrazano-Narrows Bridge, and includes the Harlem River, the East River to Throgs Neck, and the Kill van Kull.

Scope of study. Pollutants are discharged to the Hudson River from municipal and industrial wastewater treatment plants (WTP), combined sewer overflows (CSO), urban storm water,

tributaries, and nonpoint sources including dry and wet atmospheric deposition and land runoff. In this chapter, we present trends in municipal wastewater pollutant loads discharged directly or indirectly to the middle Hudson and lower Hudson basins. Historical data have been compiled from 1900–2000 to show trends in population served by different categories of treatment plants, wastewater flow and effluent loading rates of 5-day biochemical oxygen demand (BOD_5), total suspended solids (TSS), total nitrogen (TN) and total phosphorus (TP). Historical pollutant-loading and water quality data are presented to document the problem caused by ignoring the waste disposal side of the urban water cycle during the first half of the twentieth century and the effectiveness of state and federal regulations and WTP construction subsidies enacted in the 1970s to improve waste disposal practices. Finally, contemporary WTP loads are put in the context of a total point and nonpoint source budget for the 1990s.

Data sources. The data sources, methodology, and assumptions used to estimate wastewater flow and pollutant loads for the middle and lower Hudson basins are documented in Johnson (1994), Johnson and Hetling (1995) and Hetling et al. (2003).

History of Sewage Abatement in the Hudson River Estuary

Management of sewage pollution in the Hudson River estuary has been a problem since the earliest days of settlement. In the seventeenth century, the practice of collecting sewage in pails and dumping it into local waterways created such unsanitary conditions that the Governor ordered a common sewer to be built in southern Manhattan in 1680 (Tetra Tech and Stoddard, 2000; Stoddard et al., 2002). Construction of a sewer and wastewater collection system in NYC began in 1696, with many sewers in lower and central Manhattan built from 1830–1870. When not clogged, street sewers constructed primarily to relieve flooding discharged a foul mixture from overflowing privies and manure heaps into nearby boat slips, such that in 1868, the water was described as poisoned and the air contaminated (Suszkowski, 1990). Gross sewage pollution including seas of floating garbage were reported in the early 1900's within 15 miles of Manhattan (Metropolitan Sewerage Commission, 1912). Outbreaks of typhoid linked to oysters from Raritan Bay in 1904 and Jamaica Bay in 1918 closed the oyster fishery by 1925 (Franz, 1982).

Sanitary conditions in the Albany Pool (Fig. 23.1) were similarly degraded and possibly worse since at least the early 1900s (Boyle, 1969). Early in the twentieth century, the City of Albany used the Hudson River as a water supply and typhoid epidemics were common (City of Albany, 1997). As recently as the 1960s, this 35–50 km section below the Troy Dam

was described as coated in sewage fungus, permeated with floating oil and animal parts, essentially devoid of oxygen and fish in summer months, and reeking of sulfur dioxide (Boyle, 1969).

The abatement of sewage discharges into the estuary can largely be attributed to the Metropolitan Sewerage Commission in the early 1900s, the New York State Environmental Bond Act of the mid-1960's, and the Federal Water Pollution Control Act or Clean Water Act of 1972 (see Stoddard et al., 2002, Hetling et al., 2003, and others). The Metropolitan Sewerage Commission was established in 1906 to study sewage problems in New York Harbor. It established a water quality monitoring program that still exists today (see below) and recommended significant improvements to regional sewerage systems, including the construction of up to thirty-five WTPs (Metropolitan Sewerage Commission, 1912; Suszkowski, 1990). Implementation of the commission's report did not begin until 1929 and modifications to the Commission's Master Plan guided construction of WTPs in the region for several decades. Recognizing the regional nature of water pollution, the Interstate Sanitation Commission was established in 1936 by New York, New Jersey, and Connecticut to develop common water quality standards and document regional progress in pollution abatement.

New York State initiated a water pollution control program in 1949 that initially consisted largely of inventorying pollution sources and assigning usage classifications for streams (for example, for drinking water supply). The most significant progress in pollution abatement occurred after 1965 when a State environmental bond issue provided $1.7 billion under the Pure Waters Program for construction of municipal WTPs (Hetling et al., 2003).

Stimulated by environmental activism and increasing public awareness of the national scope of water pollution problems, a new national policy was embodied in the 1972 Clean Water Act (CWA) that firmly rejected the historically accepted use of rivers, lakes, and harbors as receptacles for inadequately regulated waste disposal practices. The U.S. Congress' objective was clear: "restore and maintain the chemical, physical and biological integrity of the nation's waters" and attain "fishable and swimmable" waters throughout the nation. To comply with the CWA, the U.S. Environmental

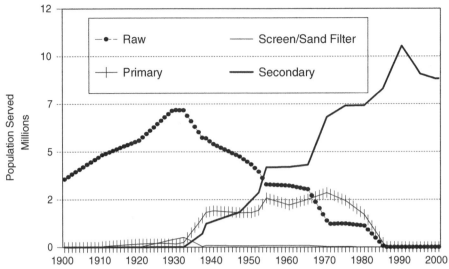

Figure 23.2. Trends of wastewater flow to the middle and lower Hudson River (combined) from ca. 1900–2000, including untreated flows, primary and secondary treatment flows, and total flows.

Protection Agency (EPA) invested $61.1 billion ($96.5 billion in 1995 dollars) during the period from 1970–95 under EPA's Construction Grants Program to build and upgrade the nation's municipal WTPs. Approximately $3.26 billion ($5.52 billion in 1995 dollars) has been allocated to municipalities of the middle and lower Hudson River (Tetra Tech and Stoddard, 2000; Stoddard et al., 2002). The next section quantifies the changes in loadings associated with these efforts.

Trends in Municipal Wastewater Loads: 1900–2000

Population Served. Figure 23.2 displays the type of sewage treatment received over time by the population in the middle and lower Hudson basins. During the course of the twentieth century, the total population served by municipal wastewater facilities has more than doubled from 3.4 million in 1900 to 8.5 million by 2000. This increase reflects the growth of the population of the New York and New Jersey metropolitan region and, beginning in about 1880, the increasing proportion of the population in the metropolitan drainage basin that was connected to urban sewerage collection systems (see Suszkowski, 1990). Reflecting the movement of people to the suburbs following WWII, the

sewered population served by wastewater facilities in the middle Hudson basin rose from 10 percent of the total in the mid-1950s to 18 percent by 2000 (Fig. 23.3a).

The population served by facilities discharging untreated sewage steadily increased during the period from 1900 to the 1930s (Fig. 23.2). In the middle Hudson, raw sewage was discharged by 0.4 million people in 1900 with a peak of 0.5 million in 1930. In the lower Hudson, no treatment was provided to 3 million people in 1900, increasing to over 6 million by 1938. From the mid-1930s to the late-1980s, the population discharging untreated sewage steadily declined as raw discharges received primary treatment, which typically removes 30 percent of the biochemical oxygen demand (BOD) and total suspended solids (TSS) load. Following master plans from the Metropolitan Sewerage Commission (1912), primary WTPs were constructed in 1924 at Passaic Valley, New Jersey and in Yonkers, New York in 1933. By 1938, three plants were discharging to the East River (Tetra Tech and Stoddard, 2000; Stoddard et al., 2002). By 1952, a total of seven primary WTPs were operational in New York City in the study area. The population served by primary facilities increased from 1.05 million in the late 1930s to a peak of 2 million in the 1960s. Completion of Manhattan's North River WTP in

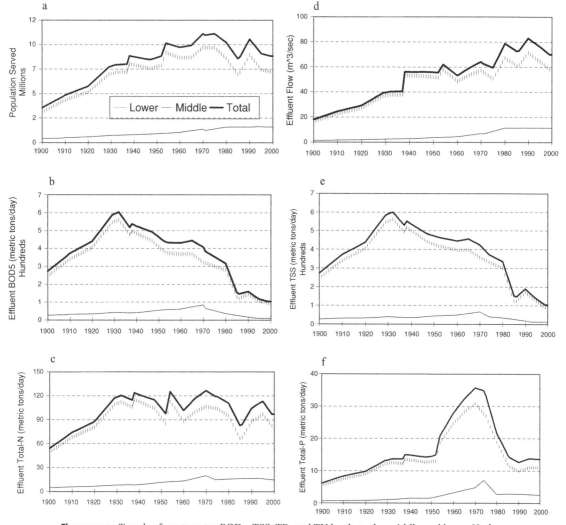

Figure 23.3. Trends of wastewater BOD$_5$, TSS, TP, and TN loads to the middle and lower Hudson River ca. 1900–2000.

1986 and Brooklyn's Red Hook WTP in 1987 as advanced primary facilities eliminated the discharge of 5.3 m^3 s^{-1} of raw sewage into the lower Hudson River and lower East River (Brosnan and O'Shea, 1996a).

Driven by the regulatory controls of the 1972 CWA and an aggressive New York State program, public works officials throughout the region embarked upon programs to upgrade all WTPs to full secondary levels of treatment (that is, 85 percent removal of BOD$_5$ and TSS) during the 1970s and 1980s. From 1979 to 1994, eight of the nine WTPs in New York City in our study area were upgraded to full secondary treatment, with the Red Hook and

North River plants upgraded to full secondary in 1989 and 1991, respectively. WTPs in the rest of New York and New Jersey were also upgraded to secondary treatment at this time. Planning for upgrading of the Newton Creek plant on the lower East River to full secondary treatment is ongoing. As a result of the regulatory requirements of the 1972 CWA and the availability of significant Federal and state construction grants, the population served by secondary treatment plants has increased from 1.8 million in the late 1930s to 8.6 million by 1990 in the lower Hudson basin. A similar change is seen in the middle Hudson basin where the population served by secondary increased slowly during the 1960s to

0.25 million by 1970. After the 1972 CWA and an establishment of a significant state construction grant program, the population served by secondary plants in the middle Hudson increased to 1.5 million by 1999.

Wastewater effluent flow. Following the long-term trend in population served by sewers, effluent flow from municipal facilities in the middle and lower Hudson basins increased steadily over the course of the twentieth century (Fig. 23.3d). At the turn of the century, a total of $18\,m^3\,s^{-1}$ of untreated sewage was discharged to the Hudson River. Increases in population and increasing per capita consumption of water resulted in a steady increase in effluent flow to $83\,m^3\,s^{-1}$ by 1990. Declines in population served from 1990–2000 and a New York City water conservation program then resulted in a decline of total effluent flow to $70\,m^3\,s^{-1}$ by 2000. Effluent flow from municipal wastewater facilities in the middle Hudson basin accounted for about 8 percent of the total effluent flow in 1900, 5 percent in the 1940s and 1950s, and 15 percent by 1990–2000.

BOD₅ and TSS loads. With the same per capita loading rate (81.6 grams/capita per day) used to estimate effluent loads for BOD_5 and TSS, the trends for BOD_5 (Fig. 23.3b) and TSS (Fig. 23.3e) are quite similar. The small differences in the estimated effluent loads are dependent on the BOD_5 and TSS removal efficiency assigned to primary and secondary treatment plants (Hetling et al., 2003). Following a steadily increasing trend similar to that shown for effluent flow and population served, total BOD_5 and TSS loads from raw sewage discharges to the middle and lower Hudson basins increased from 273 mt d^{-1} in 1900 to a peak loading rate of 600 mt d^{-1} by the early 1930s. With the construction of primary treatment plants in the late 1920s and 1930s and subsequent upgrades to secondary treatment during the 1940s, 1950s, and 1960s, effluent BOD_5 and TSS loads gradually declined by more than 50 percent from that to approximately 400 mt d^{-1} in 1970. After enactment of the CWA in 1972, and the upgrades of WTPs in the middle and the lower Hudson to full secondary treatment, effluent loads of BOD_5 and TSS continued to decline to approximately 1 mt d^{-1} by 1999. Effluent loads

of BOD_5 and TSS from municipal wastewater facilities in the middle Hudson basin accounted for about 10 percent of the total BOD_5 and TSS effluent load in 1900, 10–25 percent in the 1950s-1960s, 15 percent during the 1980s and 10–14 percent by 1990–2000.

Total Nitrogen (TN) loads. Total Nitrogen (TN) loads from raw sewage discharges to the middle and lower Hudson basins increased from 60 mt/d in 1900 to a peak loading rate of almost 125 mt/d by 1938 (Fig. 23.3c). With the construction of primary WTPs in the late 1920s and 1930s and subsequent upgrades to secondary treatment during the 1940s, 1950s, and 1960s, effluent TN loads by 1970 were virtually unchanged from 1938. After upgrades to full secondary treatment, effluent loads to the estuary declined by 32 percent to approximately 85 mt/d by the mid-1980s. Full secondary plants, although not specifically designed for the removal of nitrogen, typically can achieve about 40 percent removal of TN (Hetling et al., 2003). Note however, that New York City WTP removals are approximately 20 percent or less, primarily due to weak (that is, diluted) influent (O'Shea and Brosnan, 2000). TN loads in the lower Hudson increased in the early 1990s due to the Ocean Dumping Ban Act of 1988. This act required several municipalities in New York and New Jersey to cease ocean disposal of sewage biosolids. To facilitate land-based management of biosolids, the biosolids were dewatered and the nitrogen-rich centrate was discharged to several WTPs, and ultimately to area waterways. Implementation of nitrogen removal technologies at some WTPs have reduced nitrogen loads back to pre-biosolids centrate levels (O'Shea and Brosnan, 2000). Effluent loads of TN from municipal wastewater facilities discharging to the middle Hudson accounted for about 9 percent of the combined TN effluent load in 1900, 7–14 percent from the 1940s–1950s, 18–22 percent from the 1970s–1980s, and 18 percent by the 1990s.

Total Phosphorus (TP) loads. Total Phosphorus (TP) loads from raw sewage discharges to the middle and lower Hudson basins increased by 117 percent from 6 mt/d to 13 mt/d by the late 1930s (Fig. 23.3f). Even with the construction of primary treatment plants in the late 1920s and 1930s and subsequent upgrades to secondary treatment from the 1940s through the 1960s, effluent TP loads continued to increase to a peak of 36 mt d^{-1} by 1970. Effluent loads of TP increased from 1938 to 1970 even as raw sewage discharges were eliminated and WTPs were upgraded to primary and secondary treatment for three key reasons: (1) population served and influent wastewater flow increased; (2) removal efficiency of TP for both primary and secondary plants is only 30 percent; and (3) influent concentration of TP steadily increased after the introduction of phosphorus-based detergents in 1945 (Hetling et al., 2003). After state legislative bans of phosphorus-based detergents in 1973 and the required upgrades of WTPs to full secondary treatment, effluent loads of TP declined sharply by 61 percent to approximately 14 mt/d by 2000. Since the removal efficiency of 30 percent for phosphorus is similar for both primary and secondary treatment, the decline in effluent loading of TP has resulted primarily from the ban on phosphorus-based detergents (Clark et al., 1992; Hetling et al., 2003). The slight increase in TP loads to the lower river reflects in part the addition by New York City in late 1992 of a phosphate-based buffer to inhibit corrosion of copper distribution pipes (O'Shea and Brosnan, 2000).

Point versus Nonpoint Source Pollutant Loads in the 1990s

Municipal wastewater discharges account for only one source of pollutants to the Hudson River. In order to properly place the magnitude of municipal wastewater loads in the context of the total pollutant loads discharged to the Hudson River, estimates of the contributions from the Upper Hudson and Mohawk river basins discharging over the dam at Troy, New York and nonpoint sources from the middle and lower Hudson basins have been compiled as a budget based on conditions during the 1990s. Loadings were based on estimates from Johnson (1994), Johnson and Hetling (1995), and HydroQual (1991) as described in Hetling et al. 2003. Point sources include municipal and industrial WTPs and CSOs. Nonpoint sources include land-use-dependent surface runoff of water and pollutant loads. Land uses of the Hudson basin are broadly categorized as urban, forest, crops,

and pasture lands to estimate nonpoint source loading rates (Johnson and Hetling, 1995). Annual averaged flow and nonpoint pollutant loading rates for the Upper Hudson and Mohawk basin at the Troy Dam and the middle Hudson basin are taken from Johnson (1994) and Johnson and Hetling (1995). Estimates of annual average flow and nonpoint and CSO flow and pollutant loads to the lower Hudson New York-New Jersey metropolitan region are taken from HydroQual (1991).

Over 79 percent of the population served by WTPs in the Hudson River watershed is from the lower Hudson metropolitan area (Fig. 23.4). The less densely populated middle and upper Hudson watersheds contain only 19 percent of the basin's total population. However, the predominant source of flow (67 percent) in the watershed is from its major subbasin, the upper Hudson above the Troy Dam.

In part reflecting this geographic disparity in distribution of population and sources of flow, the principal components of loading to the Hudson River watershed vary considerably by the type of contaminant. For example, the Upper Hudson contributes 71 percent of the TSS to the system (Fig. 23.4). With solids loads greatly reduced by upgrading to full secondary treatment, the solids contribution from WTPs (ca. 90 mt d^{-1}) represents only 6 percent of the total solids budget.

While flows and TSS are dominated by contributions from above the Federal dam at Troy, sources of BOD$_5$ are more evenly distributed between lower Hudson point sources (38 percent), middle and lower Hudson nonpoint sources (33 and 34 percent), and contributions from above the dam (25 percent). Lower Hudson point sources dominate loadings of nitrogen and phosphorus at 57 percent and 65 percent, respectively. The other nutrient sources in order of significance include the upper Hudson, and middle Hudson point and nonpoint sources (Fig. 23.4).

Note that CSOs contribute 1–3 percent of the total input of TSS, BOD$_5$, and nutrients. However, as noted below, they are the dominant source of fecal coliform bacteria and floatables. Thus the principal reason for controlling CSOs is not to reduce TSS and BOD$_5$ or nutrients, but rather to alleviate impacts from floatables and pathogens.

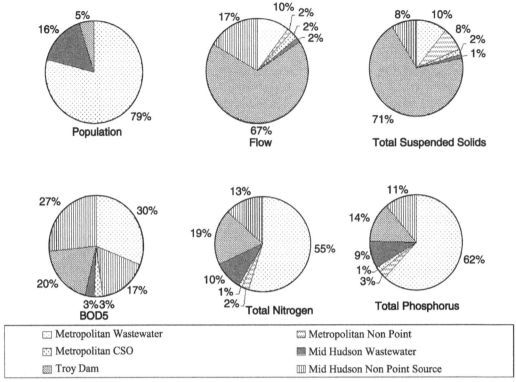

Figure 23.4. Percentage distribution of population served (8.41 million), flow (4.78e7 m³ d⁻¹), and effluent loads of BOD_5 (238 mt d⁻¹), TSS (1,469 mt d⁻¹), TN (145 mt d⁻¹) and TP (17.1 mt d⁻¹) for point and nonpoint sources of the middle Hudson and lower Hudson basins ca. 1990s.

Trends in Ambient Water Quality and Aquatic Resources

Declines in the quality of aquatic resources in the Hudson drainage are clearly linked to increases in population and associated destruction of habitat, changes in land use, over-harvesting of fisheries, and the discharge of municipal and industrial effluents (Suszkowski, 1990). As noted at the beginning of this chapter, impacts associated with the discharge of untreated sewage into the Hudson River Estuary have been recorded since the seventeenth century.

Estimating water quality improvements due to sewage treatment is primarily achieved by tracking two key indicators of sewage-related pollution: dissolved oxygen (DO) as an indicator of the quality of the habitat to sustain life, and fecal coliform bacteria as an indicator of sanitary quality. For this analysis, long-term water quality data for the Albany Pool were retrieved from the U.S. Environmental Protection Agency's STORET system in October 2000.

Data for the lower Hudson were provided by the New York City Department of Environmental Protection's Harbor Survey Program. Methods used by the NYCDEP are documented in Brosnan and O'Shea (1996a).

Trends in aquatic health. Oxygen dissolved in the water column is necessary for respiration by all aerobic forms of aquatic life, including fish, crabs, clams, and insects. Dissolved Oxygen (DO) levels between 4.8 mg l⁻¹ and 3.5 mg l⁻¹ are generally protective of all but the most sensitive aquatic species, while levels below 2.3 mg l⁻¹ may cause severe lethal and sub-lethal effects (USEPA 2000). DO varies seasonally, typically being lowest in summer and highest in early winter and spring. Year to year variability can be affected by a variety of natural and anthropogenic factors including weather, runoff, temperature and salinity stratification, tidal and gravitational circulation, algae blooms, the quality of water entering an area, and especially flushing

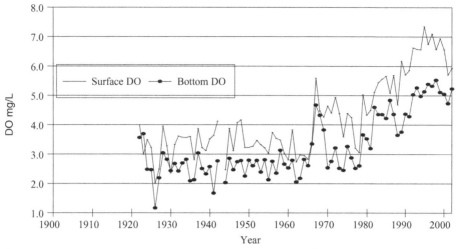

Figure 23.5. Dissolved oxygen trends in the Hudson River off of 42nd St., Manhattan, NY, ca. 1910–2002. Data represent surface and bottom summer average concentrations of 8–14 samples per summer.

rate and river flow (Clark et al., 1995). The bacterial decomposition of high organic carbon loads from untreated sewage can deplete DO, especially in the warm summer months, rendering the water unfit for most aquatic life. DO is therefore used as one of the most universal indicators of overall water quality and a means of determining sewage impacts on habitat and ecosystem conditions.

DO has been depressed in the Hudson River for most of the twentieth century. For example, summer average DO was typically between 2 and 4 mg l^{-1} in surface and bottom waters off of Manhattan from circa 1910–70 (Fig. 23.5). Minimum values were often less than 1 mg l^{-1} and average summer percent saturation varied between 25 and 50 percent (Brosnan and O'Shea, 1996b). Despite the construction of several WTPs throughout the estuary since the 1930s, no clear impact on DO in the lower Hudson was observed during this period. This is in contrast to other regional waterways (for example, the East River and the Arthur Kill) where DO increases have been observed since the 1940s (O'Shea and Brosnan, 2000). The most significant abatement of sewage loadings into the lower Hudson River did not occur until after the late 1970s when most of the existing WTPs were upgraded to secondary treatment and additional plants were constructed (Figs. 23.2 and 23.3). Up until the mid-1980s, over 5 m^3 s^{-1} of raw sewage was still being discharged into the lower Hudson from the western shore of Manhattan and the northwestern shore of Brooklyn. Completion of the 3.6 m^3 s^{-1} North River WTP at 125th Street in Manhattan in 1986 and the 1.7 m^3 s^{-1} Red Hook plant in the lower East River in 1987, coupled with upgrades of the Yonkers, New York and Passaic Valley, New Jersey and other regional WTPs, resulted in significant water quality improvements (Brosnan and O'Shea, 1996b). By the late 1990s, summer average DO off of Manhattan was typically between 5 and 7 mg l^{-1} (Fig. 23.5) and bottom minima typically exceeded 3.5 mg l^{-1}. Average percent saturation values in the late 1990s approached 70–90 percent. Surveys conducted by Clark et al. (1995) from Haverstraw Bay to New York Harbor also document DO improvements from 1978–93.

Limited data from the Albany Pool from the 1940s through the mid-1980s indicate average summer concentrations of less than 1 mg l^{-1} to less than 5 mg l^{-1} were common prior to 1970 and the minimum recorded value often approached 1 mg l^{-1} or less (Fig. 23.6). Average saturation values ranged from 10–40 percent. However, with the additional abatement of sewage loadings that accompanied the passage of the Clean Water Act in 1972, DO improved significantly with summer average concentrations typically between 6 and 8 mg l^{-1} in the 1980s (Fig. 23.6). Summer minima during the 1980s typically exceeded 6–7 mg l^{-1} and average percent saturation was typically 70–85 percent.

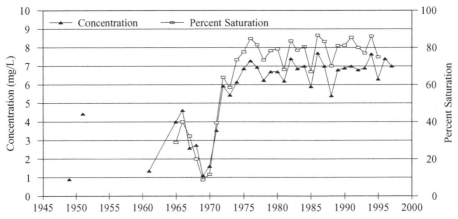

Figure 23.6. Dissolved oxygen trends in the Hudson River in the Albany Pool near Glenmont, NY, ca. 1949–1997. Data represent summer average concentrations and percent saturation of 6–14 samples per summer, except for 1949, 1951, 1961, 1965, 1975, and 1987–97, which represent 1–4 samples per summer, and 1966 which represents 38 samples.

These increases in DO have improved the ability of the Hudson River to sustain life. Biological monitoring using resident benthic macroinvertebrate communities (for example, aquatic insects, worms, clams) as indicators of water quality has documented significant improvements in many sites in watersheds throughout New York State. Of 216 sites monitored periodically statewide from 1972–92, eighty-three sites improved. Improvements at 53 percent of these eighty-three sites was attributed to improved sewage treatment, 9 percent was due to industry, and 25 percent was due to a combination of improvements in municipal and industrial discharges (Bode, Novak, and Abele, 1993). The Albany Pool was cited as one of the ten greatest success stories, with all biological indices improved since 1972. The replacement of pollution tolerant tubifex worms and midges with pollution sensitive mayflies, stoneflies, and caddisflies is attributed to the completion of secondary WTPs in the Albany and Rensselaer county sewer districts (Bode et al., 1993).

Improvements in New York Harbor, as well as other east and west coast harbors, have resulted in a resurgence of marine borers such as shipworms (*Teredo* spp.) and gribbles (*Limnoria* spp.) that devour natural driftwood and manmade wooden structures such as boats and pilings. Previously abundant populations of pollution intolerant borers were decimated as water quality declined well into the twentieth century. Improved water quality conditions in the mid-1980s has coincided with

a severe re-infestation of borers and rapid deterioration of wood pilings and other submerged wooden structures in New York Harbor (Abood, Ganas, and Matlin, 1995). Improved benthic communities in Lower New York Bay have also been documented (Steimle and Caracciolo-Ward, 1989; Cerrato, Bokuniewicz, and Wiggins, 1989; Chapter 18, this volume).

Trends in sanitary quality. Fecal coliform bacteria are used by various water quality monitoring programs as indicators of sewage-related pollution. Elevated concentrations in the aquatic environment indicate the presence of fecal contamination and the potential presence of pathogenic bacteria, fungi, and viruses often associated with untreated wastewater pollution. New York State water quality standards use fecal coliform bacteria as indicators of the sanitary quality of area waterways for uses such as shell fishing, swimming, and secondary contact recreation.

Declining concentrations of fecal coliform bacteria indicate that the sanitary quality of both the middle and lower Hudson River has also improved significantly in response to improved capture and treatment of sewage over the last three decades (Fig. 23.7). Undisinfected wastewater contains 10^7 cells/100 mL of coliform bacteria (Thomann and Mueller, 1987). Seasonal chlorination (May–September) using either sodium hypochlorite or chlorine gas started in the 1940s for the WTPs in Staten Island, and included all fourteen of New

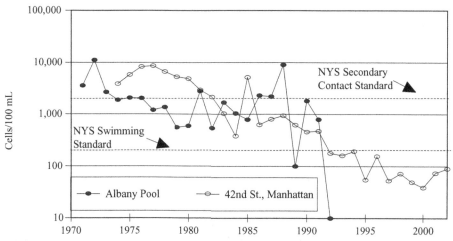

Figure 23.7. Fecal coliform bacteria trends (as summer geometric means) in the Hudson River in the Albany Pool near Glenmont, NY and off of 42nd St., Manhattan, NY. Albany Pool data represent 6–8 samples per summer, except for 1975, 1976, and 1987–92 which represent 4 or less samples per summer. Data collected off of Manhattan represent 8–14 samples per summer. The NYS Primary Contact or "Swimming" Standard of 200 cells per 100 ml and Secondary Contact Standard (e.g., for wading, boating, fishing) of 2,000 cells per 100 ml are also depicted.

York City's WTPs by 1985 (personal communication, Diane Hammerman, NYCDEP). Disinfection reduces wastewater concentrations dramatically, for example, the average discharge from New York City WTPs in 1998 was less than 150 cells/100 mL (NYCDEP, 1999). In response, fecal coliform levels off of Manhattan have declined by two orders of magnitude from almost 10,000 cells/100 mL in the mid-1970s to less than 100 cells/100 mL in the 1990s (Fig. 23.7). The most significant decline occurred after the North River and Red Hook WTPs achieved primary treatment in 1986 and 1987, respectively. Further declines in coliform bacteria levels in the lower Hudson have been achieved by additional improvements in the operation of NYC's sewage collection system that has reduced bypassing by 96 percent, abated over 9,500 m^3 d^{-1} of illegal discharges harborwide, and reduced the incidence and volume of combined sewer overflow (CSO) discharges (Brosnan and Heckler, 1996). The result is that by the mid-1990s, average summer fecal coliform levels off of Manhattan were estimated to meet the New York State swimming standard (Fig. 23.7).

Note, however, that data collected shortly after rain events show that coliform concentrations increase significantly due to CSOs (Brosnan and Heckler, 1996). Many older cities in the country, including many cities along the Hudson in New York and New Jersey, have combined sewer systems, that is, sewers that convey household and industrial waste to WTPs during dry weather, as well as surface water runoff during rain events. When runoff flows exceed the hydraulic capacity of the WTPs, a mixture of untreated sewage and urban runoff is discharged to the local waterways. CSO discharges have been estimated to contain 3.5 million fecal coliform cells/100 mL and are responsible for over 95 percent of the current coliform load to New York Harbor (NYCDEP, 1999). In the lower Hudson, CSOs can cause fecal coliform concentrations to increase from less than 100 cells/100 mL to over 2,000 cells/100 mL (NYCDEP, 1999). CSOs are also responsible for 85 percent of the floatables load, with an average of 1.5 million floatable items (primarily plastic street litter and less than 1 percent sanitary or medical waste) discharged each month into New York Harbor from surrounding communities in New York and New Jersey (Leo, St. John, and McMillan, 1992).

Improvements in the sanitary quality of the Hudson River have led to increased human use of the resource. In lower New York Harbor, over 67,800 acres of shellfish beds have been upgraded since 1985, including removal of restrictions on 30,000 acres off the Rockaways for direct harvest and in

Raritan Bay for a site relay program in the late 1980s (USEPA, 1996). Seagate Beach on Coney Island re-opened in 1988 for the first time in forty years and South Beach and Midland Beach on Staten Island reopened in 1992 for the first time in twenty years (Brosnan and Heckler, 1996). Wet weather advisories were also lifted at seven of ten New York City public beaches and the wet advisory was reduced at the other three. Closures of beaches in New York City and New Jersey due to floatables have been virtually eliminated since the early 1990s.

Examples of recovered human uses in the middle Hudson include the town of Bethlehem tapping an aquifer fed by the Albany Pool for drinking water in 1996 and the reopening of Croton Point Beach in Westchester County for the first time in a decade (Stevens, 1996). The NYSDEC classifies the "Best Usage" of the river as swimmable from northern Columbia County to Manhattan and a series of public meetings were held to discuss the feasibility of developing additional public swimming sites in the Hudson River Estuary (NYSDEC, 2000).

Priorities and Outlook for the Future

Priorities for the future of wastewater management in the Hudson River Estuary include the need for continued investment in WTP maintenance and upgrades, the need to further abate remaining sources of untreated sewage, and the need to investigate if nutrient removal should be required to reduce eutrophication. These are discussed briefly below.

WTP maintenance and upgrades. A continued Federal, state, and local commitment to provide the necessary capital and operations and maintenance investments for municipal wastewater facilities is critical to maintain the dramatic improvements in water quality that have been achieved since the 1972 CWA. At a minimum, aging sewer mains and pumping stations will need to be maintained and replaced to reduce leaks and bypasses. Projected population increases are another significant concern. New York metropolitan area population is projected to increase by 12 percent by 2020 (New York Metropolitan Transportation Council, 1999).

Abatement of remaining sources of untreated sewage. Although CSOs are not a significant contributor to TSS, BOD_5 and nutrients, they are the dominant source of coliform bacteria and floatables. Control of CSO discharges is expensive and difficult. However, some improvements can be achieved for a relatively modest investment. New York City's implementation of EPA's common sense "Nine Minimum Controls" for minimizing CSO discharges has reduced unintentional bypasses by 96 percent, abated 9,500 m^3 d^{-1} of illegal discharges, improved capture of CSOs from 18 percent in 1989 to 44 percent in 1998, increased the capture of floatables from 18–68 percent, and reduced coliform concentrations in the harbor by 50 percent (NYCDEP, 1999). Aggressive implementation of the Nine Minimum Controls by all communities in the estuary would likely achieve further improvements. Untreated discharges from boats can also be locally significant sources of coliforms. New York State's recent efforts to have the U.S. EPA declare the Hudson River a "No Discharge Area," which would prohibit all sewage discharge from vessels from Troy to the Battery, could provide further local improvements (Pataki, 2000).

Nutrients. Wastewater treatment plants (WTPs) are a significant source of nitrogen and phosphorus to the estuary. Recent National Academy reports have listed eutrophication as perhaps the biggest problem in the coastal zone of the United States (NAS, 1993), as one of the greatest research needs for coastal ecology (NAS, 1994), and as one of the two biggest threats to biodiversity in marine ecosystems (NAS, 1996). In order to evaluate the need for nutrient removal, the impact of WTP nutrient loading to the Hudson-Raritan estuary on eutrophication and depressed bottom water dissolved oxygen levels in outer areas of New York Harbor, including western Long Island Sound, Raritan Bay, Jamaica Bay, and the nearshore New Jersey coast is currently being investigated using state-of-the-art hydrodynamic and water quality models (O'Shea and Brosnan, 2000).

Acknowledgments

The authors would like to thank the following for their assistance: Dan Parker of EPA for providing STORET water quality data for the Hudson River near Albany and Troy, New York; Naji Yao, Yin Ren, and Beau Ranheim for providing NYC water quality data and statistics; Diane Hammerman and Theresa Norris for New York City wastewater data; Robert Bode for New York State Department of Environmental Conservation macroinvertebrate data; and Peter Sattler of the Interstate Sanitation Commission for assistance in obtaining historic reports of the Commission.

DISCLAIMER

The information in this chapter reflects the views of the authors and does not necessarily reflect the official positions or policies of NOAA or the Department of Commerce.

REFERENCES

Abood, K. A., Ganas, M. J., and Matlin, A. 1995. The *Teredos* are coming! The *Teredos* are coming!, in M. A. Knott (ed.), *Ports '95*, Volume 1. Conference Proceedings, March 13–15, 1995. Tampa, Florida. American Society of Civil Engineers, New York, pp. 677–90.

Blumberg, A. F., Kahn, L. A., and St. John, J. 1998. Three dimensional hydrodynamic simulations of the New York Harbor, Long Island Sound, and the New York Bight. *Journal of Hydraulic Engineering* **125**:799–816.

Bode, R. W., Novak, M. A., and Abele, L. E. 1993. *Twenty Year Trends in Water Quality of Rivers and Streams in New York State*. New York State Department of Environmental Conservation, Albany, New York.

Boyle, R. 1969. *The Hudson River*. New York: W. W. Norton and Company, Inc.

Brosnan, T. M., and Heckler, P. C. 1996. The benefits of CSO control: New York City implements nine minimum controls in the harbor. *Water Environment & Technology* **8**:75–9.

Brosnan, T. M., and O'Shea, M. L. 1996a. Long-term improvements in water quality due to sewage abatement in the lower Hudson River. *Estuaries* **19**:890–900.

1996b. Sewage abatement and coliform bacteria trends in the lower Hudson-Raritan Estuary since passage of the Clean Water Act. *Water Environment Research* **68**:25–35.

Cerrato, R. M., Bokuniewicz, H. J., and Wiggins, M. H. 1989. *A Spatial and Seasonal Study of the Benthic Fauna of the Lower Bay of New York Harbor*. Special Report 84, Reference 89–1. Marine Sciences Research Center, State University of New York, Stony Brook, New York.

City of Albany, 1997. *Water for a City* Department of Water and Water Supply, Volume 2, Number 3, Albany, New York.

Clark, J. F., Simpson, H. J., Bopp, R. F., and Deck, B. L. 1992. Geochemistry and loading history of phosphate and silicate in the Hudson Estuary. *Estuarine, Coastal, and Shelf Science* **34**:213–33.

1995. Dissolved oxygen in the lower Hudson Estuary: 1978–93. *Journal of Environmental Engineering* **121**:760–3.

Franz, D. R. 1982. An historical perspective on molluscs in lower New York Harbor, with emphasis on oysters, in G. F. Mayer (ed.), *Ecological Stress and the New York Bight: Science and Management*. Columbia, SC: Estuarine Research Foundation, pp. 181–98.

Hetling, L. J., Stoddard, A., Brosnan, T. M., Hammerman, D. A., and Norris, T. M. 2003. Effect of water quality management efforts on wastewater loadings over the past century. *Water Environment Research* **75**:30–8.

HydroQual, Inc. 1991. *Assessment of Pollutant Loadings to New York–New Jersey Harbor*. Draft final report to U.S. Environmental Protection Agency, Region 2, for Task 7.1, New York/New Jersey Harbor Estuary Program. Hydroqual, Inc., Mahwah, New Jersey.

Johnson, C. 1994. "Evaluation of BOD, SS, N and P Loadings into the Lower Hudson River Basin from Point and Nonpoint Sources." M.S. thesis, Rensselaer Polytechnic Institute, Troy, NY.

Johnson, C., and Hetling, L. 1995. *A Historical Review of Pollution Loadings to the Lower Hudson River*. Paper presented at New York Water Environment Association Meeting, New York City, NY, January 31.

Leo, W. M., St. John, J. P., and McMillan, W. E. 1992. Floatable materials in New York Harbor: Sources and solutions. *Clearwaters* **22**:28–32.

Metropolitan Sewerage Commission. 1912. *Present Sanitary Conditions of New York Harbor and the Degree of Cleanness Which is Necessary and Sufficient for the Water*. Report of the Metropolitan Sewerage Commission of New York, August 1, 1912. Wyncoop Hallenbeck Crawford Co., New York.

National Academy of Sciences. 1993. *Managing Wastewater in Coastal Urban Areas*. Washington, DC: National Academy of Sciences Press.

1994. *High Priority Science to Meet National Coastal Needs*. Washington, DC: National Academy of Sciences Press.

1996. *Understanding Marine Diversity*. Washington, DC: National Academy of Sciences Press.

NYCDEP (New York City Department of Environmental Protection). 1999. *New York Harbor Water Quality Survey 1998*. Marine Sciences Section, Wards Island, New York.

New York Metropolitan Transportation Council. 1999. *Transportation Models, Technical Memorandum No. 8.9.* Parsons Brinckerhoff Quade and Douglas, New York, New York.

NYSDEC (New York State Department of Environmental Conservation). 2000. *Public Meetings to Discuss Feasibility of Hudson River Swimming.* Press Release, 7/17/2000. www.dec.state.ny.us/website/press/pressrel/2000-94.html.

O'Shea, M. L., and Brosnan, T. M. 2000. Trends in indicators of eutrophication in Western Long Island Sound and the Hudson-Raritan Estuary. *Estuaries* **23**:877–901.

Pataki, G. 2000. *Declare Hudson River a No Discharge Area.* Press release from the Governor of the State of New York, Albany, New York. 10/27/2000.

Steimle, F., and Caracciolo-Ward, J. W. 1989. A reassessment of the benthic macrofauna of the Raritan Estuary. *Estuaries* **12**:145–56.

Stevens, W. 1996. "Shaking Off Mankind's Taint, The Hudson Pulses With Life," *The New York Times* June 9, pp. 1, 46–7.

Stoddard, A., Harcum, J. B., Simpson, J., Pagenkopf, J. R., and Bastian, R. K. 2002. *Municipal Wastewater Treatment: Evaluating Improvements in National Water Quality.* New York: John Wiley & Sons, Inc.

Suszkowski, D. J. 1990. Conditions in the New York/New Jersey Harbor Estuary, in K. Bricke and R. V. Thomann (eds.), *Cleaning Up Our Coastal Waters: An Unfinished Agenda.* March 12–14, 1990. Dynamac Corporation, Rockville, Maryland, pp. 105–31.

Tetra Tech, Inc. and Andrew Stoddard & Associates. 2000. *Progress in Water Quality: An Evaluation of the National Investment in Municipal Wastewater Treatment.* EPA-832-R-00-008. U.S. Environmental Protection Agency, Office of Water, Washington, DC.

Thomann, R. V., and Mueller, J. A. 1987. *Principles of Surface Water Quality Modeling and Control.* New York: Harper and Row Publishers.

USEPA (United States Environmental Protection Agency). 1996. *Comprehensive Conservation and Management Plan.* NY/NJ Harbor Estuary Program, U.S. Environmental Protection Agency, Region 2, New York, New York.

USEPA. 2000. Ambient aquatic life water quality criteria for dissolved oxygen (saltwater): Cape Cod to Cape Hatteras. Office of Water, EPA-822-R-00-012, Nov. 2000. 49 pp.

24 PCBs in the Upper and Tidal Freshwater Hudson River Estuary: The Science behind the Dredging Controversy

Joel E. Baker, W. Frank Bohlen,
Richard F. Bopp, Bruce Brownawell,
Tracy K. Collier, Kevin J. Farley,
W. Rockwell Geyer, Rob Nairn,
and Lisa Rosman

Introduction

From the latter 1940s until 1977, the General Electric Corporation (GE) discharged an estimated 200,000 to 1.3 million pounds (U.S. Environmental Protection Agency, 2000a) of polychlorinated biphenyls (PCBs) into the Hudson River from two electrical capacitor manufacturing plants at Hudson Falls and Fort Edward, New York (Fig. 24.1). In 1977, under a settlement agreement with the New York State Department of Environmental Conservation, GE stopped direct discharges of PCBs to the river, although leakage of PCBs from the factory sites to the river continues to this day. PCBs used at the GE plants were oily liquids containing dozens of distinct PCB compounds. Most of these components are persistent in the environment, attach strongly to soils and river sediments, and readily accumulate in fish, wildlife, and humans (National Research Council, 2001a). These properties, combined with the large discharges of PCBs from the GE plants over 50+ years, have led to elevated levels of PCBs in the water, sediments, and biota of the Upper Hudson River (defined here as the stretch upstream of the Troy lock and dam). Levels of PCBs in the Hudson River ecosystem are among the highest in the United States.

PCB contamination in the Hudson River is a management problem for the public because it has likely increased human health risks (primarily from consumption of fish), increased ecological risks to fish and fish-eating birds and mammals,

and caused losses of river use and the resulting economic impacts (catch and release only fishery; advisories on fish consumption; restrictions on navigational dredging limiting access to the Champlain Canal; restrictions on and the increased costs of dredging; and commercial fishery closure). PCB levels found in the Upper Hudson between Hudson Falls and the Federal Dam at Troy exceed numerous risk-based guidelines (U.S. Environmental Protection Agency, 2000a), and PCB transport over the Federal Dam is a major source of contamination affecting the lower tidal river and estuary (Bopp et al., 1985; Schroeder and Barnes, 1983; Thomann et al., 1989; U.S. Environmental Protection Agency, 1991; QEA, 1999; U.S. Environmental Protection Agency, 2000b). Consequently, the U.S. Federal government is compelled to address the problem of PCBs in the Upper Hudson River.

Public awareness of PCBs in the Upper Hudson River dates back to the early 1970s. In 1976, the New York State Department of Environmental Conservation banned all fishing from Hudson Falls to the Federal Dam and commercial fishing for striped bass in the lower Hudson (New York State Department of Health, 1998). Investigations of the sources and impacts of PCB contamination were conducted, and in 1984, the U.S. Environmental Protection Agency (EPA) designated the lower 200 miles of the Hudson River a "Superfund" site (U.S. Environmental Protection Agency, 2000a). It is among the largest Superfund sites in the country. Under Federal law, listing a Superfund site sets in motion a series of policy and management steps to evaluate the extent of the problem, identify the parties responsible for the contamination, design and implement cleanup and restoration, and assess economic damages. In 1984, EPA selected an interim 'No Action' remedy for the contaminated sediments because the agency believed that the feasibility and effectiveness of sediment remediation technologies was too uncertain (U.S. Environmental Protection Agency, 2000a). In 1995, the NYS Department of Environmental Conservation replaced the ban on all fishing in the Upper Hudson River with a "catch-and-release" program, but the ban on commercial fishing for striped bass in the Lower Hudson River remains in effect (New York State Department of Health, 1998).

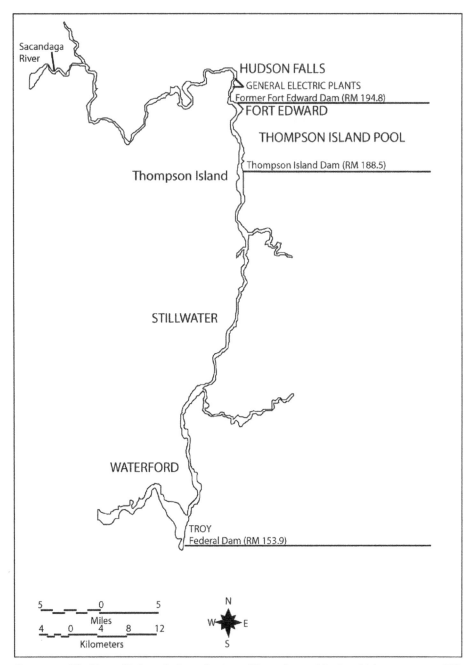

Figure 24.1. The Upper Hudson drainage basin and Sacandaga subbasin which represents ~38% of the total area. Models of the 100-year flood event assume that the dam for the Sacandaga will provide significant flow control and limit water discharge to 8,000 cfs. Under the more conservative and reasonable assumption that the reservoir will fill up during such an event, flows from the Sacandaga subbasin could exceed 12,000 cfs. [Figure prepared by Edward Shuster of RPI. Discussion based on his analysis of a 100-year flood event (RPI, 2001).]

In December 2000, EPA published its 'Superfund Proposed Plan' for the Upper Hudson River (U.S. Environmental Protection Agency, 2000a), in which it recommended that 2.65 million cubic yards of contaminated sediments, containing over 100,000 pounds of PCBs, be dredged from the Upper Hudson River. In August 2001, EPA Administrator Whitman announced that EPA would continue to pursue that cleanup plan (U.S. Environmental Protection Agency press release, 2001).

During the twenty-five years since PCB contamination in the Hudson River was first brought to the public's attention, a large number of studies have been conducted to determine the sources, movements, ultimate fates, and effects of PCBs in the system. Studies of PCB contamination have generally resulted in high quality data, with excellent measurements of PCB concentrations in Hudson River water, sediments, and fish (see http://www.epa.gov/hudson/dbr_exsum.htm). These data, along with complementary analyses and modeling studies, have provided us with a detailed description of PCB distributions in the Hudson River and a good understanding of many key aspects of PCB fate and transport under present conditions. Although these studies have been extensive, one could still argue that our understanding of the science behind the PCB problem is not complete and that further studies are necessary to add to our knowledge and to help reduce the uncertainty surrounding the issue. However, after two decades of study, there is likely to be a point of diminishing returns and there are costs in further delaying the decision. In the case of the Hudson River, as with any policy debate centering on a technically-complex issue, decisions must be made based upon the preponderance of the data, knowing full well that our ability to predict the consequences of our actions is not perfect.

The fact that our scientific understanding of PCBs in the Hudson River is not perfect has led to a vigorous debate as to the nature of the PCB problem and to the most effective course of remediation. Such a debate, which is critical to resolving complex technical issues, has allowed all sides of the PCB problem to be explored in detail and has played a critical role in advancing the state of the science. Controversy, however, still surrounds the interpretation of technical information on PCB fate and effects, and on the effectiveness of dredging technologies. Nevertheless, we believe that PCBs in the Upper Hudson River have been extensively studied and debated, and informed decisions can be made now.

This report has been written by a panel of independent experts convened by the Hudson River Foundation. Our charge was to critically examine the science underlying the controversy, deduce the relevant principles, and draw conclusions based on the available science. Volumes have been written about PCBs in the Hudson River, ranging from exhaustive scientific and technical reports to numerous articles in the popular press. While we have reviewed much of this information, our objective here is not to comprehensively summarize all of this material. Rather, we wish to convey those aspects of the problem for which we believe the science and engineering are clear. We take a "weight-of-evidence" approach to reach our findings based on our considerable collective expertise and experience. We believe these findings are supported by the available scientific information and are consistent with underlying scientific principles.

Key Questions

The role of science in public policy is not to make decisions per se, but to provide clear interpretations of existing information relevant to key issues, and to project possible consequences of societal actions. After reviewing the science of the issue, we conclude that the decision of whether and how to clean up the PCBs in the Upper Hudson River hinges on four key questions:

1. Are the current levels of PCBs in the Upper Hudson River causing harm to the residents and environment of the Upper and Lower Hudson River?

2. Are the PCBs in the Upper Hudson River sediments an important continuing source of contamination to the Lower Hudson under average flow conditions?

3. What are the chances that a large quantity of the PCBs currently buried in the sediments of the Upper Hudson River will be released sometime in the future under extreme weather conditions?

4. Can active remediation be implemented in such a way that it provides a net long-term benefit to the Hudson River?

Discussion of Key Questions

KEY QUESTION 1. Are the current levels of PCBs in the upper Hudson River causing harm to the residents and environment of the upper and lower Hudson River?
Findings:

1. PCB levels in Hudson River fish far exceed those believed to impact the health of people who consume fish, based upon risk-based levels established by credible toxicological methods.
2. Concentrations of PCBs in fish and wildlife exceed levels believed to cause harm, based upon risk-based levels established by credible toxicological methods.

Effects of PCBs on people. The effects of PCBs on individual humans and on human populations have been studied extensively over the past thirty years (Agency for Toxic Substances and Disease Registry, 1999; Robertson and Hansen, 2001).

As a result of this research, PCBs have been labeled "probable human carcinogens" by the EPA, and are also suspected of inducing developmental and learning disorders, impairing human immune systems, and causing low birth weights. Production of these chemicals has been banned internationally under terms of the United Nations' recent treaty on Persistent Organic Pollutants (see http://www. chem.unep.ch/pops/POPs_Inc/dipcon/meeting-docs/conf_2/en/conf_2e.pdf).

It is very difficult to prove that exposure to an environmental contaminant harms people, as evidenced by debates over tobacco smoke and asbestos. Risks usually have to be judged in terms of probabilities. The science of risk assessment has matured considerably since the National Academy of Sciences endorsed it (National Research Council, 1983). Risk assessment has been widely adopted within the public health profession. The risk to people exposed to PCBs in the fish they eat depends upon the amount of fish they consume, the PCB

concentrations in those fish, and their vulnerability to PCB-induced diseases. Only the first two of these factors can be controlled.

To determine the "safe" level of PCB exposure for a human population, environmental epidemiologists first decide what level of risk is "acceptable." The U.S. Food and Drug Administration (FDA) has set the acceptable PCB level in fish sold for human consumption in interstate commerce at 2 parts per million (ppm, or milligram PCB per kilogram of edible fish tissue on a wet weight basis). This guidance, now seventeen years old, was based on the average amount of fish consumed by the American public and the known PCB effects on humans at the time. Since the FDA guidance level was set, the average U.S. diet has changed to include more fish (Reinert et al., 1991). Also, our understanding of the subtle impacts of PCBs on humans, including non-cancer effects such as developmental impairment has greatly improved (Agency for Toxic Substances and Disease Registry, 1999, Robertson and Hansen, 2001). More recent human health risk assessments of PCBs suggest that the FDA guidance level does not protect recreational fishers, certain ethnic groups, and coastal dwellers who consume more fish than the average U.S. resident. Non-cancer threats of PCBs, especially to children and women of child-bearing age, have led some coastal states to set more stringent PCB guidelines (see http://www.epa.gov/watescience/fish/ for most recent fish consumption advisories). Although the EPA provides some advice on how the states should evaluate PCB risks and set guidelines (see http://www.epa.gov/ost/sish/guidance.html for EPA's guidance to the states to set advisories), each individual state currently sets its own PCB advisory level. Many coastal states are following the Great Lakes Protocol, a risk-based approach (Table 24.1) for setting PCB advisory levels developed by a consortium of eight Great Lakes states (Great Lakes Sport Fish Advisory Task Force, 1993). While the public health advisories produced by individual states vary somewhat, in general they are very close to the Great Lakes Protocol.

In the Upper Hudson River, mean PCB levels in edible fillets of fish commonly caught in recreational fisheries range (Table 24.2) from 2 to 41 ppm (U.S. Environmental Protection Agency, 2000c). These levels exceed by more then ten-fold the

Table 24.1. The Great Lakes Protocol Risk-Based PCB Advisory

PCB concentration in edible fish tissue	Advisory
Less than 0.05 ppm	Unlimited consumption, no advisory
0.06–0.2 ppm	Restrict intake to one fish serving per week
0.21–1.0 ppm	Restrict intake to one fish serving per month
1.1–1.9 ppm	Restrict intake to one fish serving every 2 months
Greater than 2 ppm	Do not eat

Source: Great Lakes Sport Fish Advisory Task Force, 1993.

most recent risk-based levels developed to protect human health by coastal and Great Lakes states.

Even below the Federal Dam at Troy, PCB levels in fish are up to five times the Great Lakes criterion for no consumption. The closure of the striped bass fishery in the Lower Hudson River due to PCB contamination has resulted in a significant economic impact. Since the consumption advisory program in New York State is linked to the licensing program for recreational fishing, advisories are only provided in non-tidal waters above the Federal Dam where licenses are required. Some local residents have probably consumed enough Hudson River fish to affect their health. Possible effects, however, have not yet been quantified in any comprehensive epidemiological studies.

Effects on fish and wildlife. PCBs are persistent bioaccumulating compounds that cause a wide range of biological dysfunction in exposed biota. A substantial body of literature describes the results of laboratory and field investigations on the consequences of PCB exposure to a variety of animals (invertebrates, fish, reptiles, birds, and mammals – Eisler, 2000; Giesy et al., 1994a,b; Safe, 1994; Elliot, Norstrom, and Smith, 1996; Monosson, 2000). Some of the more common effects seen after animals have been exposed to PCBs include reproductive dysfunction (including feminization

of males), impaired development, reduced growth, immunotoxicity, induction of histological changes, and alterations in biochemical processes, including induction of enzyme synthesis as well as inhibition of enzyme activities.

A substantial issue to be considered in the Hudson River decision-making process is whether current exposures of animals to PCBs pose ecological risks. The most recent data show that many species sampled in and adjacent to the Upper Hudson River continue to have substantial body burdens of PCBs (NOAA, 2001). The most comprehensive Hudson River PCB data set, compiled by the New York State Department of Environmental Conservation (New York State Department of Environmental Conservation, 2001b), is for fish, with the majority of the analyses conducted on fish fillets. Concentrations in fillets are relevant to human fish consumption, but they may underestimate those in whole fish bodies, which tend to be consumed almost entirely by fish and wildlife predators.

For several species in the Upper Hudson (Table 24.2), average fillet PCB concentrations range

Table 24.2. Comparing PCB levels in Upper Hudson River fish to those from other coastal waters

	Mean PCB concentration, ppm
Hudson River (U.S. Environmental Protection Agency, 2000c)	
Thompson Island Pool	7–29
Stillwater Reach	1.6–41
Waterford Reach	3–19
Below Federal Dam	1.1–11
Great Lakes (see U.S. Environmental Protection Agency Great Lakes Office http://www. epa.gov/grtlakes/glindicators/ fish/topfish/topfishb.html)	0.4–1.9
Delaware Bay (Ashley et al., 2003)	0.4–0.7
Chesapeake Bay (Liebert et al., 2001)	0.05–1.0

Source: From U.S. Environmental Protection Agency 2000c.

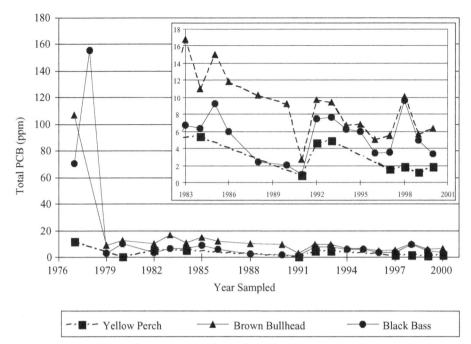

Figure 24.2. PCB levels in fish (wet weight basis) from the Upper Hudson long-term trends site (Stillwater/Coveville). Recent year-to-year variation is most clearly seen in the inset. [Figure supplied by Ron Sloan of the New York State Department of Environmental Conservation (NYSDEC), based on data from New York State Department of Environmental Conservation 2001.]

from 1.6 ppm to 41 ppm PCBs (U.S. Environmental Protection Agency, 2000c; New York State Department of Environmental Conservation, 2001a). For the same species in the Lower Hudson within eleven miles of the Federal Dam, concentrations range from 1.1 ppm to 11 ppm. PCB concentrations vary greatly within each species, and PCB levels in individual fish have exceeded these mean values by several fold. In recent years, maximum PCB concentrations in fillets from individual Hudson River fish have been found to be as high as 480 ppm in common carp, 290 ppm in white sucker, 160 ppm in American eel, 150 ppm in largemouth bass, 50 ppm in red-breast sunfish, 42 ppm in walleye, 39 ppm in smallmouth bass, 37 ppm in brown bullhead, 30 ppm in yellow perch, and 27 ppm in black crappie (NOAA letter, 2000). In the lower Hudson River, recent maximum concentrations of 77 ppm in shortnose sturgeon liver, 42 ppm in Atlantic sturgeon gonad, and 31 ppm in striped bass fillet have been documented (NOAA letter, 2000) Fewer data are available for wildlife species other than fish, but several bird and mammal species sampled near the Hudson River also exhibit increased levels of PCBs

in their tissues (McCarty and Secord, 1999; Secord and McCarty, 1997; Secord et al., 1999; New York State Department of Environmental Conservation, 2001b).

For Upper Hudson River fish, PCB concentrations declined substantially between the 1970s and 1980s and experienced an increase in the early 1990s due to the Allen Mill event (the collapse of a wooden gate structure adjacent to the riverbank at the GE Hudson Falls plant site that resulted in a release of PCBs). The most recent data (Fig. 24.2) show considerable year-to-year variability and less obvious declining trends (New York State Department of Environmental Conservation, 2001a,b). Comparing these tissue burdens of PCBs with published guidelines demonstrates that the current levels of exposure of fish and wildlife in the upper Hudson River drainage basin are high enough to cause concern for environmental effects. To protect piscivorous wildlife in the Great Lakes, a guideline for total PCB loads in fish of approximately 0.1 ppm was recommended by the International Joint Commission (Newell, Johnson, and Allen, 1987; International Joint Commission, 1989;

Canadian Council of Ministers of the Environment, 2001).

Some of the strongest evidence of adverse PCB consequences to fish-eating animals has been documented for mink and otter, two mammals that are especially sensitive to PCBs (Golub, Donald, and Reyes, 1991; Heaton et al., 1995; Halbrook et al., 1999; Moore et al., 1999). When mink eat fish containing PCB levels comparable to those recently and historically reported in the Upper Hudson fish, they experience impaired reproduction, reduced offspring (kit) survival, and reduced kit body weight. Results of three long-term studies in which PCB-contaminated fish were fed to mink allowed development of a dose-response curve relating the rate of PCB ingestion (milligram of PCB ingested per kg body weight per day, mg/kg-day) to a decline in fecundity (Golub et al., 1991; Heaton et al., 1995; Moore et al., 1999; Halbrook et al., 1999). That analysis suggests that a daily dose of 0.69 mg PCB/kg-day (corresponding to approximately 5 ppm PCBs wet weight in their food) will result in a greater than 99 percent decline in mink reproductive fecundity, while approximately 0.1 and 0.025 mg/kg-day (equivalent to approximately 0.7 and 0.2 ppm) will result in 50 percent and 10 percent declines in mink reproduction and fecundity, respectively (Golub et al., 1991; Heaton et al., 1995; Moore et al., 1999; Halbrook et al., 1999). PCB levels in Hudson River fish exceed levels demonstrated to cause reproductive impairment in mink. Moreover, recent analyses of PCBs in the livers of mink and otter collected from the Upper Hudson River valley showed levels in some individuals that exceed values reported to cause negative impacts (New York State Department of Environmental Conservation, 2001 b,c).

Thus, our current knowledge strongly suggests that the health of some sensitive mammalian species, such as mink and otter, may be seriously impaired along the Upper Hudson River. EPA considers otter to be at slightly greater risk than mink, because otter diets have higher proportions of fish, and the agency has designated whole-body fish concentrations of 0.03–0.3 ppm (mg/kg) total PCBs (approximately corresponding to 0.012–0.12 mg/kg total PCBs in fish fillets) as the upper limit for protection of otter (U.S. Environmental Protection Agency, 2000c). Fish concentration goals designed

to protect mink and otter should afford protection to the other less sensitive species that inhabit the Hudson River ecosystem. A corollary to this is that the less sensitive species should recover sooner in response to decreasing PCB levels in the Hudson River than the more sensitive species.

Besides being a source of PCB contamination to consumers, fish themselves are vulnerable to these chemicals. Recommended levels for protecting fish from exposure to PCBs range from a median threshold value of 1.1 ppm total PCBs in whole body (Meador, Collier, and Stein, 2002) to 25–70 ppm in adult fish liver (Monosson, 2000), and 5–125 ppm in the body of fish larvae. Current levels of PCB contamination in Upper Hudson River fish often exceed those associated with health effects on fish and wildlife. Because PCBs have such wide-ranging effects on the health of biota, and are so persistent once exposure occurs, it is very likely that current levels of contamination are causing injury to species that depend on the Upper Hudson River ecosystem.

KEY QUESTION 2. Are the PCBs in the upper Hudson River sediments an important continuing source of contamination to the lower Hudson under average flow conditions?
Findings:

1. PCBs leaking from the GE plant sites and remobilized from the sediments continue to add PCBs to the Hudson River and to the food chain.

2. In recent years, contaminated sediments have become the dominant source of PCBs to the river. As a result of source controls being implemented at the plant site, contaminated sediments are expected to serve as the dominant source of PCBs to the river for years to come.

3. Analyses conducted to date by both GE and EPA using relatively coarse-scale numerical models (QEA, 1999; U.S. Environmental Protection Agency, 2000d) lack the required fine-scale spatial resolution in the sediment transport model and use of an overly simplistic PCB distribution and bioaccumulation model. These deficiencies limit the ability of either model to accurately project future

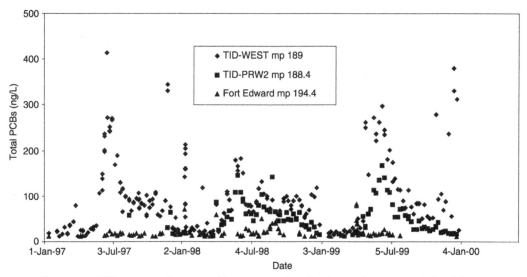

Figure 24.3. PCB concentrations in weekly water sample collections at the upstream (▲) and downstream (■, ◆) ends of the Thompson Island Pool in 1997 through 1999. Increased levels at the downstream end indicate that the contaminated sediments in the Thompson Island Pool are the major current source of PCBs to the Upper Hudson River water column, contributing on the order of 180 kg/y. (Plot prepared by Jennifer Tatten as part of RPI (2001) based on data from General Electric Company as reported in the database supplied by GE to NYSDEC).

PCB levels in the Upper Hudson River, with or without active remediation. More sophisticated field evaluations and models would greatly improve efforts to define and monitor the remediation of the Hudson River.

The current releases of PCBs from the GE facilities are substantially less than those during active operation of the plants. GE has spent and will continue to spend considerable amounts of money to stem the flow of PCBs from their properties. Nonetheless, given the large amount of PCB contamination on these sites, and their immediate proximity to the Hudson, a small but significant amount of PCBs is expected to continue to enter the river from the GE sites for many years. Based on the amount of PCB in the river near the GE facilities, this small amount of leakage is presently estimated to be no more than 3 ounces per day (or 30 kilograms per year, see next paragraph), whereas the average PCB releases from the facilities were 2,700 to 16,000 kilograms per year between the 1940s and 1977 (United States Environmental Protection Agency, 2000a). In addition to this recognized leakage of PCBs from the plant sites, PCBs that were previously discharged from the plants and now reside in river sediments

downstream from the plants are being released into the river's waters. PCBs may be released from the sediments during resuspension by currents and by diffusion and mixing of PCBs.

To estimate the relative importance of these two sources of PCBs to the Upper Hudson River, we examined monitoring data collected by GE (O'Brien and Gere Engineers, 1998; QEA, 2000, 2001; RPI, 2001) at two locations downstream of their facilities (Fig. 24.3). The first site is at Rogers Island downstream of GE's Fort Edward Plant (Fig. 24.1). Here PCB concentrations are (relatively) low and quite constant. By multiplying the PCB concentration in the river by the river's flow rate at Fort Edward, we estimate that about 30 kilograms of PCBs per year were moving down the river at this point in the late 1990s.[1] In contrast, PCB concentrations in the waters passing over the Thompson Island Dam six miles downstream were much higher and more variable than at the upstream site (Fig. 24.3).

[1] Weekly PCB mass loadings were calculated as the product of measured PCB concentrations (nanograms/liter $\times 10^{12}$ nanograms/ kilogram = kg PCB/liter) and the corresponding total flow for the period (usually weekly; cubic feet/second converted to liters/week). The annual mass loading of PCBs was calculated as the sum of weekly loadings.

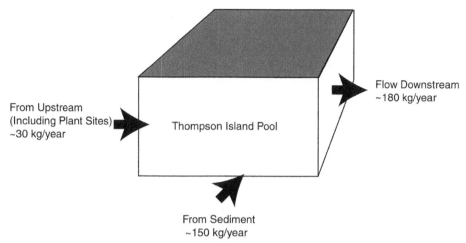

From Upstream (Including Plant Sites) ~30 kg/year

Thompson Island Pool

Flow Downstream ~180 kg/year

From Sediment ~150 kg/year

Figure 24.4. Approximate mass balance for PCB fluxes in the Thompson Island Pool for 1998, based on data shown in Figure 24.3.

These higher PCB concentrations, multiplied by the river flow, yield an estimate of 180 kilograms of PCBs per year passing over the Thompson Island Dam. We conclude, therefore, that about 150 kilograms of PCBs per year enter the river as it moves through the Thompson Island Pool (Fig. 24.4). The only plausible source of these PCBs is release from the Thompson Island Pool sediments. These sediments are highly contaminated with PCBs that can be released into the water column under a variety of flow conditions and there are no other likely significant PCB sources to this stretch of the river. It is important to note that these releases have occurred during relatively typical flow conditions.

These observations are consistent with our understanding of PCB behavior in rivers. Measurements of PCBs in the river indicate that the release of PCBs from sediments in the Upper Hudson River, including those below the Thompson Island Pool, is currently occurring and that this release is the dominant source of PCBs to the Hudson River downstream from the GE facilities at Hudson Falls and Fort Edward. GE has asserted that this current ongoing PCB supply is transient, resulting from the contamination of near surface sediments in the Thompson Island Pool (and, presumably, a number of other spots downstream) by the Allen Mill gate failure (1991) and more recent releases from the plant sites. Both the GE and EPA models indicate that the Thompson Island Pool is a region of net deposition and GE maintains that its ongoing

program to control releases from the plant sites will lead to burial by relatively clean materials in short order, isolating these sediments and associated PCBs from the overlying water column (see QEA, 1999; also GE interpretation of model projections – http://www.hudsonvoice.com). As a result, the company says, dredging of contaminated sediments would be counterproductive, invasive, and expensive because it could expose deeply buried, highly PCB-contaminated sediment layers and increase downstream transport of contaminated sediments. If this were the case, monitored natural attenuation of PCB impacts by allowing new sediments to bury the contaminated sediments within the Thompson Island Pool and elsewhere would clearly be the preferred course.

If the Thompson Island Pool were a quiescent area of net deposition, one would expect that the sediments would accumulate in a rather orderly fashion, layer by layer, forming a stable, stratified deposit in which the deeper, older sediments and their associated contaminant burden would be efficiently isolated from the surface layers and the overlying waters. Transport and material exchange would be confined to the immediate surface layers even during the extreme flow events. This idealized description of sediment accumulation, however, is not consistent with the bulk of the available data. While there are a few sediment cores that show orderly and progressive deposition as evidenced by radionuclide dating, there are many more showing a disturbed and irregular sediment column in which the record of sediment accumulation cannot be readily deciphered (Bopp et al., 1985; United States Environmental Protection Agency, 1997; O'Brien & Gere Engineers, 1999). In contrast to the well-ordered cores, these irregular distributions of properties provide clear indication that significant areas of the sediment deposit resident within the Thompson Island Pool are subject to time-variant disturbance involving vertical distances similar in magnitude to the observed depths of contaminant burial. When viewed collectively (rather than selectively), these disparate field data indicate that the Thompson Island Pool sediment deposit is not an ordered, stratified mass with near horizontal uniformity in sediment properties, but rather is more accurately described as a spatially heterogeneous "patchwork quilt." In this deposit, sediment characteristics and the associated PCB concentrations display significant spatial variability. These variations affect the ability of the sediment to be moved by bottom currents under average ambient flows as well as the aperiodic high energy storm event. As a result, a given flow condition might find some areas of the pool experiencing net deposition while other areas erode. A change in flow state could significantly alter the locations of deposition and erosion and might change the pool from net depositional to net erosional or vice versa.

We believe that the heterogeneous nature of the Thompson Island Pool sediment deposit in space and time makes it impossible to specify the "age" of the PCBs being added to the water passing by. Whether the PCBs being added to the water at present are simply remnants of those introduced by the Allen Mill gate failure or contaminants introduced much earlier and subsequently remobilized by physical and biological processes, or some combination of these two sources, cannot be accurately determined from the field data alone. Nonetheless, we conclude that under the prevailing average flow conditions the sediments of the Thompson Island Pool are a continuing source of PCBs to the overlying waters.

Having concluded that PCB release from the sediments of the Upper Hudson River is the dominant *current* source of these contaminants to the water column and food web, the next question is how

long this condition will persist in the river. Will PCBs continue to bleed from the sediments indefinitely, or will natural processes gradually sequester the PCBs within the river's sediments? If all of the PCBs in the Thompson Island Pool sediments (approximately 15,000 kg – U.S. Environmental Protection Agency, 2000a) were available to be reintroduced back into the river and the rate of release continued at the present level (150 kg/year), there would be sufficient PCB in the sediment to support release for 100 years. This approximation is not realistic, however, as some of the 15,000 kg are undoubtedly trapped within the sediments, and one would not expect the release rate to remain constant in the face of declining PCB inventories in the sediments. To refine this estimate requires a coherent understanding of the movements of water, sediments and PCBs in the river, as well as addressing the difficult problem of quantifying remobilization of sediment. Predicting the future consequences of environmental actions is quite difficult, especially in a dynamic river system that has already been altered through the construction of locks and dams, reservoirs, canals, and dredged channels. Numerical models are tools used to estimate how PCB levels in the Hudson River sediments, water, and biota will change in the future, with and without active remediation. If the main motivation for active remediation is to reduce PCB levels in the future, our ability to design and evaluate the effectiveness of proposed remediation depends almost entirely on the accuracy of such models.

Both GE and EPA have developed numerical models that describe PCB transport in the Upper Hudson River (QEA, 1999; U.S. Environmental Protection Agency, 2000d). While these two models share many similarities, there are also some key differences related to the extent of PCB release from the sediments. The two models predict similar levels of PCBs in the Upper Hudson River during the next several decades.[2] Both models predict slowly declining PCB levels in the Upper Hudson River over the next several decades as the system continues to respond to the gradual depletion of PCBs in the 'active' layer of sediment. In other words, the results of the models are driven by the underlying

---

[2] For a side-by-side comparison of the USEPA and GE models, see pages 143–5 in National Research Council (1983).

assumption that the sediments are a source of PCBs to the river water, but that the magnitude of this source will gradually decrease over the next several decades. This decrease results from the continued burial of PCBs by ongoing deposition of clean "new" sediment and from the release into the overlying water. Neither model predicts that the PCB levels will approach zero within the next 65+ years, reflecting both the likely continual chronic release of PCBs from upstream and the inherently slow response time of the system. As discussed above, it is not clear to us that the Thompson Island Pool is net depositional. Therefore, we question whether ongoing burial will significantly deplete PCBs in the surface sediment as fast as predicted by these models.

Because the long-term recovery of the river from PCBs depends explicitly on the amount of PCBs in the river sediments and the rate at which these PCBs are removed from the active surface sediment, our ability to assess the future course of PCB levels in the Hudson River, with or without active remediation, depends upon our ability to model sediment transport processes. This is a challenging exercise because the sediment transport regime with the upper river is highly dynamic and is significantly variable in space and time. River sediments are constantly being reworked and those which settle in one location are often later resuspended and displaced. A fraction of these materials may accumulate within the Thompson Island Pool, while others move downstream. The extent of this "trapping" of sediments within any stretch of river is difficult to estimate. The retention efficiency of the Thompson Island Pool (that is, the fraction of the solids entering the pool that remain in the pool for long times) is believed to be low, and the associated sedimentation rates are low (on the average of a few tenths of a centimeter per year, averaged over the entire pool) (QEA, 1999). Temporal variations in sediment transport and accumulation result in a heterogeneous sediment deposit whose characteristics vary significantly over small vertical and horizontal distances. As a result, the bottom throughout the upper river is a complex mosaic of fine sands, silts, clays, wood chips, and other organics formed by the combination of constantly changing currents and sediment supplies. Predicting sediment and PCB transport within such

a system requires the use of a numerical model with sufficient spatial resolution to accurately represent this heterogeneity. Unfortunately, the models used by both the EPA and GE employ relatively coarse spatial segmentation that effectively masks the heterogeneity of the river bottom. Only the GE model attempts to address the complexities associated with the transport of sediments of mixed composition. This approach, although commendable, is essentially untested, leaving its accuracy open to question.

In addition, we feel that the numerical models used by both EPA and GE to describe PCB transport and accumulation in biota are too simplistic in their chemical descriptions. Although a large amount of high quality measurements of PCB components were made in the Hudson River, the models treat the complex and variable mixture of PCB components as a single 'chemical' (called Tri+ PCB, equal in concentration to the sum of all PCB components in the Hudson with three or more chlorines). The behavior of the PCB mixture varies markedly depending on the properties of the individual PCB components, especially as a function of the number of chlorines. The PCB composition changes with space and time in the Hudson. We are concerned that extrapolating a PCB model into the future that has been calibrated primarily on data collected over a relatively short period in which the PCB composition has not varied markedly introduces important uncertainties into the projections of long-term recovery. Based on our knowledge of PCB behavior, we believe that the recovery time of the more highly chlorinated PCB congeners (those that accumulate most in the food web) could be longer than that projected by the models.

Both the EPA and GE models appear to reasonably match previous field measurements. One should not conclude from this general agreement, however, that the underlying processes are correctly modeled. As noted above, we are concerned that the lack of fine-scale spatial resolution in the sediment transport model and the use of an overly simplistic PCB distribution and bioaccumulation model limits the ability of either model to accurately project future PCB levels in the Upper Hudson River, with or without active remediation. More sophisticated field evaluations and models would greatly improve the efforts to define and monitor the remediation of the Hudson River.

KEY QUESTION 3. What are the chances that the PCBs currently buried in the upper Hudson River will be released sometime in the future under extreme weather conditions?

Findings:

1. The extent of remobilization of "buried" PCB-contaminated sediments during episodic high flow events (for example, 100-year or 200-year floods) may have been underestimated and remains a concern.
2. Based on current releases of PCBs from sediments and potential remobilization of "buried" PCBs during episodic events, we do not see monitored natural attenuation as a sufficient remedy.

As if modeling sediment and PCB movements in the dynamic Upper Hudson River was not difficult enough, the modeling of extreme weather events, such as a 100- or 200-year flood, is particularly challenging. Models are calibrated with available data, which typically do not include extreme events and often do not include flood periods. The spatial patterns of sediment erosion and deposition vary as functions of river flow. It is quite likely that an extreme event such as a 100-year storm will occur in the Upper Hudson River during the recovery period. Whereas a 100-year storm is an event that occurs, on average, every 100 years, there is a 10 percent probability of a 100-year storm occurring in the next 10 years, a 25 percent probability in the next 30 years, and a 40 percent probability within the next 50 years. A question central to the PCB issue in the Upper Hudson is the depth of remobilization of sediments under different flow conditions. More energy in the river in the form of water currents can cause a deeper disturbance of the sediments and a greater release of the associated PCBs to the water column. To assess the potential impact of high flow events, both GE and EPA modeled the bottom current velocities under a high flow of 47,000 cubic feet per second (QEA, 1999; U.S. Environmental Protection Agency, 2000d). The two models predict substantially different amounts of non-cohesive sediment remobilization in the Thompson Island Pool, with the

EPA model predicting as much as 13 cm eroded (averaged over the pool – see U.S. Environmental Protection Agency 2000d) versus 0.14 cm from the GE model (QEA, 1999). This important discrepancy underscores the difficulty in using hydrodynamic and sediment transport models to estimate sediment remobilization during extreme events in the Upper Hudson River.

We are also concerned that the flows used to model the impact of extreme events do not adequately account for high flows from the Sacandaga Reservoir, which drains to the Hudson upstream from the GE plants. Since the Sacandaga River was dammed in 1930, one storm (May 1983) was large enough to cause water to spill over the dam and raised flows in the Sacandaga River above 12,000 cubic feet per second[3] which is 50 percent higher than the worst-case Sacandaga River flows used in the sediment transport modeling. In addition, the operation of the Sacandaga dam has recently changed. Relicensing agreements between Orion Power and surrounding communities on the Sacandaga Reservoir and along the downstream Hudson River dictate that Orion Power will keep the reservoir at higher levels both during summer and winter months (Bucciferro, 2000). The new agreement signals a shift in management practices away from one favoring flood control, toward one favoring recreational uses of the reservoir and river. This loss in reservoir capacity decreases the dam's ability to hold back precipitation during extreme events, and increases the likelihood of flows through the Upper Hudson River that have not been experienced since the dam was constructed seventy years ago.

Neither the GE nor the EPA model adequately explains the observed current PCB releases from the Thompson Island Pool. We believe this is partly due to the coarse spatial and temporal resolution of those models and their corresponding inability to properly represent small-scale and ongoing redistribution of sediments within the pool. As we mentioned previously, both GE and EPA maintain that the Thompson Island Pool is net depositional, without any supporting geophysical evidence. The

---

[3] River flow data have been recorded daily since 1907 at the Sacandaga River at Stewarts Bridge near Hadley, NY (USGS Station 01325000).

overall result of their modeling is that less than 20 percent of the total reservoir of PCBs in the Thompson Island Pool will be released over the next thirty years without dredging, with the remainder buried indefinitely (QEA, 1999; U.S. Environmental Protection Agency, 2000b). Due to shortcomings of the modeling with respect to the ongoing redistribution of sediments under low to moderate flows and large-scale changes under extreme flood events, we believe the eventual release of PCBs from the Thompson Island Pool could be much greater than the 20 percent of the current PCB reservoir predicted by the models. We believe that both GE and EPA have likely underestimated the magnitude and probability of PCB release from the sediments and subsequent transport downstream.

KEY QUESTION 4. Can active remediation be implemented in such a way that it provides a net long-term benefit to the Hudson River?
Findings:

1. In other locations, active remediation of contaminated sediments resulted in lower contaminant levels and risk in wildlife. While the most sensitive species will continue to be impacted for decades, other less sensitive species will benefit sooner from declining PCB levels resulting from active remediation.

2. With the best dredging techniques, only a very small fraction of PCBs are released to the water, likely less than 2 percent of the total PCBs dredged. In the Thompson Island Pool, this short-term release is comparable to the rate at which PCBs are currently being released from the sediments. Thus, with properly designed and executed techniques, dredging may result in no more than a doubling of the present day PCB flux during the project period.

3. Effectively managing the dredged materials stream is critical to the success of the active remediation.

4. Dredging with appropriate techniques is technically feasible, but requires rigorous oversight to minimize contaminant dispersion and community disruption.

5. There will be short-term impact of the dredging operations on local communities and

habitats but, properly managed, these impacts need be no greater than those of other large construction activities (road/bridge construction, navigation dredging, lock and dam repair and maintenance).

The estimated average concentration of PCBs in surface sediment in Thompson Island Pool is approximately 40 ppm, with maximum concentrations reaching 2,000 ppm (U.S. Environmental Protection Agency, 2000a). Elsewhere, concentrations of this magnitude and less required or led to remedial actions under state and Federal laws. For example, sediment remediation in Commencement Bay near Tacoma, Washington is proposed to reduce the PCB level to 0.45 ppm, although the National Oceanic and Atmospheric Administration and the Department of the Interior, the Federal stewards of natural resources, have requested a lower target of 0.2 ppm in the interests of chinook salmon and fish-eating birds (Weiner, 1991; United States Fish and Wildlife Service and National Oceanic and Atmospheric Administration, 1999). Target PCB concentrations have been set at 1 ppm for cleanup of the Housatonic River (Connecticut – Massachusetts), the St. Lawrence and Raquette rivers (New York), the Kalamazoo River (Michigan), and the Delaware River (New Jersey – Pennsylvania); at 0.5 ppm for the Sheboygan River and harbor (Wisconsin); and at 0.25 ppm for the Fox River (Wisconsin).[4]

Although active PCB remediations have not always been successful due to design and operational problems (General Electric, 2000), there are other examples where biological benefits have followed active remediation. We note that whether a specific remediation is deemed 'successful' depends upon the criteria established for that project. Short-term degradation resulting from the dredging activity can mask eventual benefits, and one must recognize that judging the 'success' or 'failure' of a remediation will likely require a long-term view. Examples where biological benefits followed active remediation include Sweden's Lake

---

[4] See the Major Contaminated Sediments Sites (MCSS) Database, a joint effort of the General Electric Co., Applied Environmental Management, Inc., and Blasland, Bouck & Lee, Inc. at http://www.hudsonvoice.com/mcss/index.html for details on specific contaminated sediment sites in North America.

Järnsjön, where after two years PCB concentrations in one-year-old Eurasian perch in the lake and fifty miles downstream were half those before dredging (Bremle and Larsson, 1998a,b; Bremle, Okla, and Larsson, 1998). Removal of PCB-contaminated soils and near shore sediments along the Upper Hudson River at Queensbury, New York (upstream from the two GE plants) led to significant declines of PCBs in yellow perch except near a remnant hot spot.[5]

Active remediation has relieved stress from other contaminants as well. Marsh and open-water sediments along the Lower Hudson River at Cold Spring were badly polluted with heavy metals (mainly cadmium but also cobalt and nickel). These sediments were excavated or dredged. The marsh area was covered with an absorptive clay fabric liner and clean fill and then replanted. Subsequently, five years of monitoring showed notable decreases of cadmium in the bodies of local plants, birds, invertebrates, and test fish.[6]

Similar findings have been reported for sediments contaminated with polycyclic aromatic hydrocarbons (PAHs), a class of synthetic organic compounds that are toxic to animals. Brown bullheads living over PAH-contaminated sediments in the Black River, Ohio, had high prevalences of liver tumors. Dredging of the sediments brought a temporary increase in tumors among resident bullheads, but bullheads spawned after the dredging had no tumors four years later (Baumann and Harshbarger, 1995, 1998). The age class structure of the bullhead population improved, and the benefit of dredging was greater than that observed after onshore source control of the PAHs (Baumann, Blazer, and Harshbarger, 2001). Similarly, liver tumors in English sole at a PAH Superfund site in Eagle Harbor of Puget Sound, Washington, decreased fifteenfold over the six years after the site was capped with cleaner sediments (Myers et al., 2001). Eleven years of monitoring before this remediation had shown

no evidence of natural PAH attenuation in either the sediments or the fish (Baumann and Harshbarger, 1995, 1998).

These case studies indicate that active remediation of contaminated sediments can more effectively reduce toxic pollution in most aquatic systems than natural dissipation of the pollutants. In addition to reducing surface contaminant concentrations, dredging will greatly reduce the reservoir of buried contaminants that could be remobilized during an extreme event. Lessening the risk of event-driven release of PCBs is one of the most valuable long-term benefits of dredging. Our professional opinion is that removal of contaminated sediments from the Upper Hudson River will accelerate recovery of the river.

Dredging will bring problems, of course. Some contaminants inevitably will be released when dredging disturbs the sediments. Previously buried muds with high PCB concentrations might be encountered and disturbed. Aquatic habitats will be disrupted in and downstream of dredging areas. Management of waste sediments will be a large and challenging operation. Nearby human communities will be bothered by noise, lights, odors, and temporary closures of roads and navigation channels. We believe these problems are less serious than commonly perceived and can be minimized.

Dredging technology has greatly improved in the past decade (National Research Council, 2001a). An ability to "surgically" dredge has developed in response to demand for such technology around the world, and firms specializing in remediation dredging (as distinct from navigation dredging) now exist. As with any engineering project, success or failure of Hudson River dredging will depend equally on the quality of the project design and the rigor and responsiveness of the project's oversight. Both factors can be encouraged and facilitated by performance-based contracting, but it will be very important to carefully specify the expected outcomes of dredging in terms of contaminant removal. Detailed site assessments will be needed before dredging begins to refine our knowledge of the current spatial distributions of sediments and contaminants in PCB hot spots. The collection and analysis of high spatial resolution data detailing sediment and PCB distributions through the project area will allow managers to select the

---

[5] Ronald Sloan, New York Department of Environmental Conservation, personal communication. New York State Department of Environmental Conservation (2001b) Hudson River PCB Biota Database. Bureau of Habitat, Division of Fish, Wildlife and Marine Resources, Albany, NY, Updated 13 March 2001.

[6] See http://life.bio.sunysb.edu/marinebio/foundryframe. html for a history of the Foundry Cove site at Cold Spring, NY.

best removal technology (for example, hydraulic versus mechanical dredging), access points, and waste management procedures. Such information also is needed for accurately estimating overall project costs.

Any disturbance of contaminated sediments can release both particle-associated and dissolved PCBs. Operations must be designed to minimize these releases. In a well-documented study in the Fox River, Wisconsin (Steuer, 2000), the release of particulate and dissolved contaminants was 2 percent of the total weight of PCBs removed. No particular attempt was made to optimize PCB confinement in this project. We believe that substantial improvements can be realized and that ultimate losses will be less than 2 percent. However, even at the 2 percent loss level, the additional release and downstream transport of PCBs would amount to 180 kilograms per year under the proposed EPA alternative,[7] an amount comparable to the current annual release from the Thompson Island Pool sediments. In this "worst case," the total amount of PCBs released into the Upper Hudson with dredging could be doubled, relative to not dredging, over the duration of the project period.

Dredging will temporarily destroy habitat in several ways besides changing the substrate: local flows will be altered and submerged aquatic vegetation and marginal wetlands will be lost. However, aquatic vegetation will readily recolonize disturbed areas from upriver sources once dredging is finished. Wetlands can be restored by established techniques with full consideration of the concerns raised recently by the National Research Council (2001b) regarding implementation, monitoring, and selection of success criteria. Fish undoubtedly will be driven from areas of dredging because of bottom disruptions, turbidity, and noise. The stress of displacement and of crowding on established populations elsewhere may increase fish mortality for a period of time. However, fish and aquatic invertebrates typically recolonize abandoned areas rapidly after disturbances have ended. Scheduling

of operations to avoid known periods of spawning and migration will be important nonetheless.

Management of waste sediments can greatly disturb adjacent human communities if it is not carefully designed and implemented (National Research Council, 2001a). The plan as presented calls for the wastes to be ultimately transported to an out-of-state Hazardous Waste Landfill (U.S. Environmental Protection Agency 2000a), but operational aspects must be considered. These include the dewatering facility, waste transfer stations, and transport of waste from the dredging site to the processing site by pipeline, barge, or rail. The dewatering facility consists of a settling basin and a filter press to remove interstitial water from dredged sediments. Residual waters will be treated to remove PCBs and returned to the river. Dried sediments may be moved directly or barged to a transfer station for out-of-state rail transport and disposal. If these operations are sited and managed to minimize the number of times sediment is handled, community impacts will be lower than otherwise. Efforts to reduce these impacts will benefit from early and continuing consultation with community representatives.

No data indicate that dredging operations themselves will directly affect public health. Despite claims to the contrary,[8] construction projects similar in magnitude to and larger than the proposed Hudson River dredging occur regularly in densely populated areas and are accommodated by the affected communities. Although the entire proposed dredging operation along the upper Hudson will take several years, particular communities will be affected for much shorter times. Economic impacts can be offset by care in planning and scheduling and, when unavoidable, financial compensation. Lighting and noise intrusions often can be reduced to below expectations. Continuous operations (night and day, seven days per week) are most efficient and therefore preferred from an

---

[7] This estimate of 180 kilograms of PCBs per year potentially released from the dredging operation was calculated as follows. Approximately 100,000 pounds of PCBs are to be dredged from the Upper Hudson River over a five-year period (equal to about 9,100 kg/year). If 2 percent of this is released, 180 kg/year (9,100 kg/year dredged times 2 percent released) could be released.

[8] For two contrasting views on the efficacy and impact of environmental dredging, see General Electric (2000) *Environmental Dredging: An Evaluation of its Effectiveness in Controlling Risk*, General Electric Company Corporate Environmental Program, Albany, New York (http://207.141.150.134/downloads/whitepaper/DREDGE.PDF), and Scenic Hudson (2000) Results of Environmental Cleanups Relevant to the Hudson River (http://www.scenichudson.org/pcb_dredge.pdf).

operational standpoint, but more accommodating schedules might be adopted in areas of high population density. Innovation and a willingness to compromise will be needed by all.

Conclusions

Based on our evaluation of the current levels of PCBs in the Upper Hudson River relative to a wide variety of benchmarks, we conclude that PCBs are very likely causing harm to the environment and are sufficiently high to pose risks to human health. PCB levels in the upper river have declined since the discharges from the GE facilities were curtailed, and will continue to decrease over the next century even without active remediation. However, the large quantity of PCBs residing in the sediments of the Upper Hudson River are not permanently sequestered, but rather are currently leaking back into the water, comprising the largest single source of PCBs to the river. Based on our review of field data and models, we believe that both EPA and GE have likely underestimated both the potential magnitude of PCB release from these sediments under typical conditions and the probability of large releases during extreme weather conditions. For these reasons, we believe active remediation such as the planned dredging is beneficial, as it takes advantage of the present opportunity to permanently remove this large quantity of PCBs from the environment. We recognize that cleaning up the PCBs that had been discharged into the Hudson over the past 50+ years will be expensive and will take many years. The technology exists to dredge, treat, and dispose of the contaminated sediments. Successful dredging, which will require careful planning and diligent execution, will accelerate the recovery of the Upper Hudson River and substantially reduce the risks to the Lower Hudson. The issue of PCBs in the Hudson River has been studied and debated for a generation. We conclude that the risks are real, the problem will not solve itself, and that the proposed remediation (with monitoring) is feasible, appropriate, and prudent.

Acknowledgments

We thank Edward Shuster (RPI) for his insights on the hydrology of the Upper Hudson River, Ross Norstrom (National Wildlife Research Centre, Environment Canada) for his insights into environmental toxicology and his review of this paper, and Robert Kendall for editorial assistance. This paper is slightly modified from a "white paper" first prepared for the Hudson River Foundation.

REFERENCES

Agency for Toxic Substances and Disease Registry. 1999. *Public Health Implications of Exposure to Polychlorinated Biphenyls (PCBs)*, U.S. Public Health Service, http://www.epa.gov/ost/fish/pcb99.html

Ashley, J. T. F., Horwitz, R., Ruppel, B., and Steinbacher, J. 2003. A comparison of accumulated PCB patterns in American eels and striped bass from the Hudson and Delaware River estuaries. *Marine Pollution Bulletin* **486**: 1294–1308.

Baumann, P., Blazer, V., and Harshbarger, J. C. 2001. Bullhead tumor prevalence as affected by point source closure and remedial dredging in the Black River, OH, in *Coastal Zone 01. Proceedings of the 12 Biennial Coastal Zone Conference, Cleveland, OH, July 15–19, 2001.* published by U.S. National Oceanic and Atmospheric Administration. NOAA/CSC/20120-CD. CD-ROM. Charleston, SC: NOAA Coastal Services Center.

Baumann, P. C., and Harshbarger, J. C. 1995. Decline in liver neoplasms in wild brown bullhead catfish after coking plant closes and environmental PAHs plummet. *Environmental Health Perspectives* **103**: 168–70.

1998. Long term trends in liver neoplasm epizootics of brown bullhead in the Black River, Ohio. *Environmental Monitoring Assessment* **53**: 213–23.

Bopp, R. F., Simpson, H. J., and Deck, B. L. 1985. *Release of Polychlorinated Biphenyls from Contaminated Hudson River Sediments.* Final report prepared for NYS Department of Environmental Conservation, contract NYS C00708, June, 1985.

Bopp, R. F., Simpson H. J., Olsen, C. R., and Kostyk, N. 1981. PCB's in sediments of the tidal Hudson River, New York, *Environmental Science and Technology* **15**: 210–16.

Bremle, G., and Larsson, P. 1998a. PCBs in Eman river ecosystem. *Ambio* **27** (5): 384–92.

1998b. PCB concentration in fish in a river system after remediation of contaminated sediment. *Environmental Science and Technology* **32** (22): 3491–5.

Bremle, G., Okla, L., and Larsson, P. 1998. PCB in water and sediment of a lake after remediation of contaminated sediment. *Ambio* **27** (5): 398–403.

Bucciferro, M. M. 2000. "Floods in Glens Falls Led to Push for Dam." *The Post-Star*, Glens Falls, NY, May 29, 2000, p. A3.

Canadian Council of Ministers of the Environment. 2001. *Canadian Environmental Quality Guidelines.* Canadian tissue residue guidelines for the protection of wildlife consumers of aquatic biota: Summary table. Winnipeg, MB (http://www.ec.gc.ca/ceqg_rcqe/tissue.htm).

Eisler, R. 2000. *Handbook of Chemical Risk Assessment: Health Hazards to Humans, Plants, and Animals.* Vol. 1–3. Boca Raton, FL: Lewis Publishers, 1903 pp.

Elliot, J. E., Norstrom, R. J., and Smith, G. E. J. 1996. Patterns, trends, and toxicological significance of chlorinated hydrocarbon and mercury contaminants in bald eagle eggs from the Pacific Coast of Canada, 1990–1994. *Archives of Environmental Contamination and Toxicology* **31**: 354–67.

General Electric. 2000. *Environmental Dredging: An Evaluation of its Effectiveness in Controlling Risk*, General Electric Company Corporate Environmental Program, Albany, New York.

Giesy, J. P., Verbrugge, D. A., Othout, R. A., Bowerman, W. W., Mora, M. A., Jones, P. D., Newsted, J. L., Vandervoort, C., Heaton, S. N., Aulerich, R. J., Bursian, S. J., Ludwig, J. P., Ludwig, M., Dawson, G. A., Kubiak, T. J., Best, D. A., and Tillitt, D. E. 1994a. Contaminants in fishes from Great Lakes-influenced section and above dams of three Michigan rivers. I: Concentrations of organochlorine insecticides, polychlorinated biphenyls, dioxin equivalents, and mercury. *Archives of Environmental Contamination and Toxicology* **27**: 202–12.

1994b. Contaminants in fishes from Great Lakes-influenced section and above dams of three Michigan rivers. II: Implications for health of mink. *Archives of Environmental Contamination and Toxicology* **27**: 213–23.

Golub, M. S., Donald, J. M., and Reyes, J. A. 1991. Reproductive toxicity of commercial PCB mixtures: LOAELs and NOAELs from animal studies. *Environmental Health Perspectives* **94**: 245–53.

Great Lakes Sport Fish Advisory Task Force. 1993. *Protocol for a Uniform Great Lakes Sport Fish Consumption Advisory.*

Halbrook, R. S., Aulerich, R. J., Bursian, S. J., and Lewis, L. 1999. Ecological Risk Assessment in a large river-reservoir: 8. Experimental study of the effects of polychlorinated biphenyls on reproductive success in mink. *Environmental Toxicology and Chemistry* **18**: 649–54.

Heaton, S. N., Bursian, S. J., Giesy, J. P., Tillitt, D. E., Render, J. A., Jones, P. D., Verbrugge, D. A., Kubiak, T. J., and Aulerich, R. J. 1995. Dietary exposure of mink to carp from Saginaw Bay, Michigan. 1. Effects on reproduction and survival, and the potential risks to wild mink populations. *Archives of Environmental Contamination and Toxicology* **28**: 334–43.

International Joint Commission. 1989. *Revised Great Lakes Water Quality Agreement of 1978.* Office Consolidation, International Joint Commission, United States and Canada, September, 1989.

Liebert, D., Baker, J. E., Ko, F. C., Connell, D., Burrell, T., Poukish, C., Luckett, C., Foprest, Q., Beaty, W., Burch, V., Fairall, B., McKay, J., Evans, W., and Johnson, D. 2001. *Bioaccumulative Toxic Chemicals in Fish from Maryland Waters, Fall 2000.* Final report to the Maryland Department of the Environment, University of Maryland Report [UMCES]CBL01-0133.

McCarty, J. P., and Secord, A. L. 1999. Nest-building behavior in PCB-contaminated tree swallows. *The Auk* **116**: 55–63.

Meador, J. P., Collier, T. K., and Stein, J. E. 2002. Determination of a tissue and sediment threshold for tributyltin to protect prey species of juvenile salmonids listed under the US Endangered Species Act. *Aquatic Conservation* **12**: 539–51.

Monosson, E. 2000. Reproductive and developmental effects of PCBs in fish: a synthesis of laboratory and field studies. *Reviews in Toxicology* **3**: 25–75.

Moore, D. R. J., Sample, B. E., Suter, G. W., Parkhurst, B. R., and Teed, R. S. 1999. A probabilistic risk assessment of the effects of methylmercury and PCBs on mink and kingfishers along East Fork Poplar Creek, Oak Ridge Tennessee, USA. *Environmental Toxicology and Chemistry* **18**: 2941–53.

Myers, M. S., Anulacion, B. F., French, B. L., Hom, T., Reichert, W. L., Buzitis, J., and Collier, T. K. 2001. *Biomarker and Histopathologic Responses in Flatfish after Site Remediation in Eagle Harbor, Washington, USA*, in T. Droscher (ed.). Proceedings of the 2001 Puget Sound Research Conference, Puget Sound Action Team, Olympia, WA.

National Research Council. 1983. *Risk Assessment in the Federal Government: Managing the Process*, Washington, DC: National Academy of Sciences Press.

2001a. *A Risk-Management Strategy for PCB-Contaminated Sediments*, Washington, DC: National Academy of Sciences Press.

2001b. *Compensating for Wetlands Losses Under the Clean Water Act*. Washington, DC: National Academy of Sciences Press.

New York State Department of Environmental Conservation, 2001a. *Injuries to Hudson River Fishery*

Resources: Fisheries Closures and Consumption Restrictions. Hudson River Natural Resource Damage Assessment Final Report, Albany, New York. http://www.dec.state.ny.us/website/dfwmr/habitat/nrd/index.htm.

2001b. *Hudson River PCB Biota Database.* Bureau of Habitat, Division of Fish, Wildlife and Marine Resources, Albany, NY, Updated 13 March 2001.

2001c. *DEC: Mammals, Soil Near Hudson River Have Elevated PCB Levels.* Press Release, April 2, 2001. www.dec.state.ny.us/websites/press/pressrel/2001-52.html.

New York State Department of Health, 1998. *Health Consultation: Survey of Hudson River Anglers And an Estimate of Their Exposure to PCBs.* Albany, New York.

Newell, A. J., Johnson, W., and Allen, L. K. 1987. *Niagara River Biota Contamination Project: Fish Flesh Criteria for Piscivorous Wildlife.* New York State Department of Environmental Conservation, Technical Report 87-3, Albany, NY.

NOAA letter, 2000. Comments on December 2000 Hudson River PCBs Reassessment RI/FS Phase 3 Report: *Feasibility Study and the December 2000 Superfund Proposed Plan for the Hudson River PCBs Superfund Site.* Letter from NOAA Coastal Resource Coordinator to U.S. EPA Region , 17 April 2001. Numbers cited are rounded to two significant figures here.

O'Brien & Gere Engineers, Inc. 1998. *Fort Edward Dam PCB Remnant Containment, 1997 Post-Construction Remnant Deposit Monitoring Program, Summary Report.* Monitoring performed pursuant to Consent Decree 1990; 90-CV-575 between the United States and General Electric Company. Report prepared for General Electric Company, Albany, NY, November, 1998.

1999. *1998 Upper Hudson Sediment Coring Program.* Final report prepared for General Electric Company Corporate Environmental Programs, Albany, NY.

QEA, 1999. *PCBs in the Upper Hudson River.* Report prepared for General Electric, Albany, NY, May, 1999. http://hudsonvoice.com/PDF/Executive_Summary.pdf.

2000. *Hudson River Monitoring Program, Final 1998 Summary Report.* Monitoring performed pursuant to Consent Decree 1990; 90-CV-575 between the United States and General Electric Company. Report prepared for General Electric Company, Albany, NY.

2001. *Hudson River Monitoring Program, Final 1998 Summary Report.* Monitoring performed pursuant to Consent Decree 1990; 90-CV-575 between the United States and General Electric

Company. Report prepared for General Electric Company, Albany, NY.

Reinert, R. E., Knuth, B. A., Kamrin, M. A., and Stober, Q. J. 1991. Risk assessment, risk management, and fish consumption advisories in the United States. *Fisheries* 6: 5–12.

Robertson, L. W., and Hansen, L. G. (eds.). 2001. *PCBs: Recent Advances in the Environmental Toxicology and Health Effects.* Lexington, KY: The University Press of Kentucky.

RPI, 2001. *Analysis of Hudson River Water Column PCB Data and 100-Year Flood Estimate.* Task 3 Final Report to NYSDEC, Contract C003844, Hudson River Sediment Consultation, Richard Bopp, Project Director.

Safe, S. 1994. Polychlorinated biphenyls (PCBs): environmental impact, biochemical and toxic responses, and implications for risk assessment. *Critical Reviews in Toxicology,* 24: 87–194.

Schroeder, R. A., and Barnes, C. R. 1983. *Trends in Polychlorinated Biphenyl Concentrations in Hudson River Water Five Years After Elimination of Point Sources.* U.S. Geological Survey, Water Resources Investigations, Report 83–4206.

Secord, A. L., and McCarty, J. P. 1997. Polychlorinated biphenyl contamination of tree swallows in the Upper Hudson River Valley, New York. *Effects on Breeding Biology and Implications for Other Bird Species,* New York Field Office, USFWS, Cortland, New York.

Secord, A. L., McCarty, J. P., Echols, K. R., Meadows, J. C., Gale, R. W., and Tillitt, D. E. 1999. Polychlorinated biphenyls and 2,3,7,8-tetrachlordibenzo-p-dioxin equivalents in tree swallows from the Upper Hudson River, New York State, USA. *Environmental Toxicology and Chemistry* 18: 2519–25.

Steuer, J. J. 2000. *A mass-balance approach for assessing PCB movement during remediation of a PCB-contaminated deposit on the Fox River, Wisconsin.* USGS Water-Resources Investigations Report 00-4245.

Thomann, R. V., Mueller, J. A., Winfield, R. P., and Huang, C. R. 1989. *Mathematical Model of the Long-Term Behavior of PCBs in the Hudson River Estuary.* Report prepared for the Hudson River Foundation. Grant Nos. 007/87A/030 and 011/88A/030.

United States Environmental Protection Agency, 1991. *Phase 1 Report – Review Copy – Interim Characterization and Evaluation, Hudson River PCB Reassessment RI/FS.* USEPA Work Assignment No. 013–2N84. Prepared for USEPA by TAMS Consultants, Inc. and Gradient Corporation.

1997. *Phase 2 Report, Further Site Characterization and Analysis,* Volume 2C – Data Evaluation and

Interpretation Report (DEIR), Hudson River PCBs RI/FS. Prepared for USEPA Region 2 and USACE by TAMS Consultants, Inc., the Cadmus Group, Inc., and Gradient Corporation.

2000a. Hudson River PCB Superfund Site (New York) Superfund Proposed Plan, December.

2000b. *Further Site Characterization and Analysis, Revised Baseline Modeling Report (RBMR), Hudson River PCB Reassessment RI/FS*. Prepared for USEPA Region 2 and USACE Kansas City District by TAMS Consultants, Inc., Limno-Tech, Inc., Menzie-Cura & Associates, Inc., and Tetra-Tech, Inc.

2000c. *Revised Baseline Ecological Risk Assessment, Hudson River PCB Reassessment*, Volume 2E, http://www.epa.gov/hudson/revisedbera_tables.pdf.

2000d. *Revised Baseline Modeling Report, Hudson River PCB Reassessment*, Volume 2D, http://www.epa.gov/Hudson/rbmr_bk1&2_chpt1_5.pdf.

2001. *Whitman Decides to Dredge Hudson River*, Press Release, 1 August 2001. (www.epa.gov/hudson/augpressrelease.pdf).

United States Fish and Wildlife Service and National Oceanic and Atmospheric Administration. 1999. Letter to the U.S. EPA from the Commencement Bay Trustees.

Weiner, K. S. 1991. *Commencement Bay Near shore/Tidal flats Superfund Completion Report*. Report for St. Paul Waterway Sediment Remedial Action. Submitted to the U.S. Environmental Protection Agency for Simpson Tacoma Kraft Company and Champion International Corporation.

25 Transport, Fate, and Bioaccumulation of PCBs in the Lower Hudson River

Kevin J. Farley, James R. Wands,
Darin R. Damiani, and
Thomas F. Cooney, III

ABSTRACT A mass balance model was developed to examine the transport, fate, and bioaccumulation of Polychlorinated Biphenyls (PCBs) in the Lower Hudson River. The model was applied to five (di- through hexa-) PCB homologues over a fifteen-year simulation period (1987–2002) and results compared well to observed PCB homologue concentrations in river sediments and fish. From model evaluations, we found that partitioning of PCBs to suspended solids appears to be largely controlled by phytoplankton. Phytoplankton production and subsequent decomposition of phytoplankton-derived material in sediments plays a particularly important role in scavenging PCBs from the water column and accumulating them in sediments. In addition, there is a continuous exchange of PCBs between the overlying water and surface sediments associated with settling of phytoplankton and other suspended organic matter, resuspension of sedimentary organic matter, and pore water diffusion of dissolved and dissolved organic carbon (DOC)-bound contaminant. These processes, along with the large capacity of sediments to store contaminants, work to sequester PCBs in sediments during periods of high contaminant loads and subsequently release them to the overlying water. This results in highly dampened responses of PCBs in water, sediments and fish in the mid estuary, and in "smearing" the effects of increased PCB loads from the Upper Hudson in the early 1990s. Model results clearly demonstrate that both the magnitude and distribution of PCBs in sediments and fish are strongly dependent on homologue-specific partitioning behavior (as expressed in terms of hydrophobicity and K_{ow} values). Finally, the migration of striped bass also plays a critical role in limiting their exposure to PCBs in the mid estuary.

Introduction

Public awareness of polychlorinated biphenyl (PCB) contamination in the Hudson River dates back to the early 1970s when elevated levels of the contaminant were discovered in river sediments and fish. This contamination was largely attributed to two General Electric (GE) capacitor manufacturing plants that were operated along the Upper Hudson River approximately 65 km (40 mi) north of Albany, New York. Although highest concentrations of PCBs were reported just downstream of the GE facilities, contamination extended well beyond this section of the river, into the tidal fresh and estuarine waters of the Lower Hudson, and down into New York Harbor.

Although production of PCBs in the United States was banned in 1977, contamination of the Lower Hudson remains a serious concern to this day. This is due to the slow breakdown of PCBs in the environment and the long residence times of PCBs in river and fish. In addition, PCBs continue to enter the Lower Hudson from the Upper Hudson as well as from downstream sources (including wastewater treatment plants and combined sewer overflows in the New York metropolitan area, and the atmosphere). Understanding how levels of PCB contamination in the Lower Hudson will change in time centers on the following questions:

1. How are PCBs transported through the Lower Hudson River?
2. What processes control the fate of PCBs in the Lower Hudson River?
3. How are PCBs transferred through the Lower Hudson food chain and accumulated in higher predatory fish such as striped bass?

We explored these questions using a mass balance model for PCBs in the Lower Hudson. A description of our modeling approach is first presented. Model results are then compared to observed PCB concentrations in sediments and fish, and are used to examine the critical processes affecting the transport, fate, and bioaccumulation of PCBs in the Lower Hudson.

Model Development

The purpose of our studies was to construct a model to examine the transport, fate, and subsequent

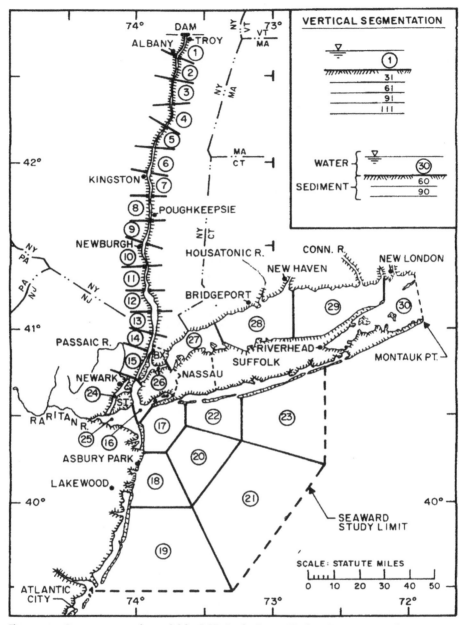

Figure 25.1. Large-space scale model for PCBs in the Lower Hudson River, New York-New Jersey Harbor, New York Bight, and Long Island Sound.

food-chain bioaccumulation of PCBs in the Lower Hudson. In this approach, PCB loadings from the Upper Hudson and from downstream sources were used in conjunction with model calculations for chemical transport and fate processes, and bioaccumulation to evaluate PCB responses in river water, sediment, and fish. A fifteen-year simulation period (from 1987 to 2002) was used for model calculations.

Long-term time scales (seasons and decades) were chosen for model application based on the decades-long extent of PCB inputs, the long-term "memory" of the sediment, the life span of striped bass, and the long-term projection period. The geographic extent of the model was specified from the Federal Dam at Troy out into the New York Bight and Long Island Sound (Fig. 25.1). A large spatial segmentation of the water column was employed

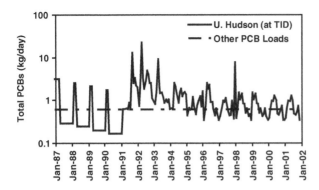

Figure 25.2. Estimates of monthly-averaged loads for total (di- through hexa-) PCBs from the Upper Hudson and from other PCB sources (including the Mohawk River, New Jersey tributaries, wastewater treatment plants, combined sewer overflows and the atmosphere). TID = Thompson Island Dam.

based on estuarine mixing behavior and the migration patterns of striped bass. Underlying each water column segment was placed two to fourteen sediment segments for a total of 30 water column segments and 120 sediment segments (see Farley et al., 1999 for details).

Although total PCB was used as a state variable in many previous model investigations (for example, the Great Lakes: Thomann and DiToro, 1983; New Bedford Harbor: Connolly, 1991), this approach was not considered adequate for this study. This is because PCBs represent a family of 209 possible compounds, with each compound containing one to ten chlorines on the biphenyl structure and exhibiting different physical-chemical and biochemical behavior. Modeling the transport, fate, and bioaccumulation of a large number of individual PCB compounds over decadal time periods in a 150 segment model, however, was not considered readily tractable. As a compromise solution, model calculations were performed for the five PCB homologue groups representing di- through hexachlorobiphenyl (CB) that contain the largest mass of PCBs. Description of PCB loads during the 1987–2002 simulation period is presented below and is followed by discussions of PCB transport and fate, and PCB bioaccumulation models.

PCB LOADS

PCB concentrations in the Lower Hudson are strongly linked to external loads from the Upper Hudson and downstream sources. For model applications, PCB loads from the Upper Hudson were specified on a monthly basis over the fifteen-year simulation period as follows. For January 1987–April 1991, PCB homologue loads were determined

by adjusting the exponentially decreasing average annual load function given in Thomann et al. (1989) to monthly PCB homologue loads. This was accomplished by assigning 68 percent of the annual load to the March–April high flow period and 32 percent of the annual load to the remaining ten months. For May 1991–December 1998, monthly PCB homologue loads were calculated from measured concentrations (O'Brien and Gere, 1997) and estimated flows at Thompson Island Dam (Kilometer Point (km) 304; River Mile (RM) 189). Monthly PCB loadings for all years after 1998 were assumed to follow 1998 monthly loads (without the January 1998 high flow event). The resulting distribution of monthly-averaged loads from the Upper Hudson is given in Figure 25.2. Elevated loads for the early 1990s, which were estimated to be as high as 10–15 kilograms per day, were largely attributed to scouring of PCB contaminated sediments from an old water intake structure and PCB oil seeps through the fractured bedrock underlying the Hudson Falls facility (Rhea, Connolly, and Haggard, 1997). Controls subsequently implemented at the Hudson Falls facility have been effective in reducing PCB loads to the river, and by the late 1990s, estimated loads to the Lower Hudson decreased to approximately 0.5 kilograms per day. These later loads are believed to be dominated by leaching of PCBs from contaminated sediments in the Upper Hudson (for example, Thompson Island Pool) (Garvey and Hunt, 1997).

All other PCB homologue loads were considered constant throughout the model simulation period. These included the Mohawk River (0.16 kg d^{-1}), the New Jersey tributaries (0.12 kg d^{-1}), New York City and New Jersey wastewater treatment plants

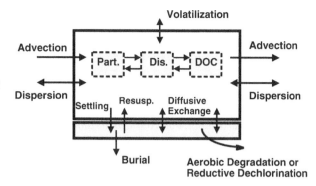

Figure 25.3. Schematic diagram of processes affecting the transport and fate of PCB homologues in water column and surface sediment segments.

(0.26 kg d^{-1}), combined sewer overflows to New York Harbor (0.14 kg d^{-1}), and direct atmospheric loads to the Lower Hudson and New York Harbor (0.03 kg d^{-1}). Details of the calculations are given in Farley et al. (1999). The total PCB load from all these sources is denoted by the horizontal line in Figure 25.2 and is shown to be a significant portion of the load, particularly for the late 1990s.

PCB TRANSPORT AND FATE MODELING

The chemical transport and fate of PCBs in the Lower Hudson and New York Harbor is affected by hydrodynamic and sediment transport of dissolved and particulate PCBs, water column-pore water exchange, volatilization, and chemical transformations. To evaluate the overall effect of these processes on PCBs, we constructed mass conservation equations for each water column and sediment segment based on the schematic diagram shown in Figure 25.3. For water column segments, the mass conservation equation for total (that is, freely-dissolved, DOC-bound plus particulate) concentration for each PCB homologue is given as:

$$V_i \frac{dC_i}{dt} = \sum Q_{ji} C_j - \sum Q_{ij} C_i$$
$$+ \sum E_{ij}(C_j - C_i) + W_{C_i} - w_s A_{s_i} m_i \Gamma_i$$
$$+ w_{u_i} A_{s_i} m_{sed_i} \Gamma_{sed_i}$$
$$+ k'_f A_{s_i} \left(C_{dis+DOC_{sed_i}} - C_{dis+DOC_i} \right)$$
$$- k'_v A_{s_i} C_{dis} - k_i V_i C_{dis_i}$$

where the first term represents the change of the total PCB homologue mass in water column segment 'i' with time; the second and third terms represent the mass rate of PCB homologue flowing into and out of segment 'i', respectively; the fourth term represents PCB homologue entering or leaving

segment 'i' by tidal dispersion; the fifth term represents PCB homologue input into segment 'i' from external sources (e.g., tributary input or wastewater discharge); the sixth term represents PCB homologue loss from the water column by settling; the seventh term represents PCB homologue gain from resuspension; the eighth term represents diffusive exchange between freely-dissolved and DOC-bound PCB homologue concentrations in the water column and pore waters; the ninth term represents the transfer of PCB homologue across the air-water interface (that is, volatilization); and the last term represents transformation losses from the water column (for example, by aerobic degradation). A complete listing of terms used in the equation is given in the appendix of this chapter.

A similar equation can be written for total (that is, freely-dissolved, DOC-bound plus particulate) concentrations for each PCB homologue in the surface sediment layer:

$$V_{sed_i} \frac{dC_{sed_i}}{dt} = w_s A_{s_i} m_i \Gamma_i - w_{u_i} A_{s_i} m_{sed_i} \Gamma_{sed_i}$$
$$- w_{b_i} A_{s_i} m_{sed_i} \Gamma_{sed_i} - k'_f A_{s_i} \left(C_{dis+DOC_{sed_i}} \right.$$
$$\left. - C_{dis+DOC_i} \right) - k_{sed_i} V_{sed_i} C_{dis_{sed_i}}$$
$$+ k'_f A_{s_i} \left(C_{dis+DOC_{deepsed_i}} - C_{dis+DOC_{sed_i}} \right)$$

where the first term represents the change in the total PCB homologue mass in sediment segment 'i' with time; the second term represents the gain of PCB homologue by settling from the overlying water; the third and fourth terms represent the loss of PCB homologue by resuspension and burial into deeper sediments, respectively; the fifth term represent diffusive exchange of freely-dissolved and DOC-bound PCB homologue with the overlying water; and the sixth term represents transformation losses from the sediments (for example, by anaerobic dechlorination); and the last term represents diffusive exchange of freely-dissolved and DOC-bound PCB homologue with the deeper sediment pore water. Chemical gain, for example, by dechlorination of higher chlorinated homologues, is also possible.

For model calculations, flows through the model domain were specified on a seasonal basis based on aggregated results from the Blumberg-Mellor three-dimensional, intratidal hydrodynamic model for the 1989 water year (see Miller and St. John, Chapter 11). Tidal dispersion coefficients were taken from Thomann et al. (1989). Seasonal estimates of suspended solids concentrations, re-suspension rates, burial rates and downstream transport of suspended solids were determined from seasonal solids balances using estimates of sediment loads, measured deposition rates from dated sediment cores, aerial estimates of deposition zones, dredging records, and a specified settling velocity of 3.2 m d^{-1} (Farley et al., 1999). Particulate (POC) and dissolved organic carbon (DOC) concentrations were specified on a seasonal basis based upon aggregated results from the System-Wide-Eutrophication-Model (SWEM) for the 1989 water year (see Chapter 11, this volume).

In addition, hydrodynamics, sediment transport, and organic carbon distributions, model descriptions for PCB partitioning between the freely-dissolved, DOC-bound, and particulate phases are essential in describing the various flux terms in the mass conservation equations. In our modeling studies, PCB partitioning is assumed to be fast compared to other environmental processes and is modeled as instantaneous (or equilibrium) reactions. PCB concentrations in the various phases can then be expressed in terms of the total PCB concentrations using the equilibrium partitioning relationships to solids and DOC ($K_d = \Gamma./C_{dis}$) and $K_{DOC} = (C_{DOC}/DOC)/C_{dis}$) and the total mass conservation equation ($C = \phi C_{dis} + \phi C_{DOC} + .m\Gamma$).

For our current model applications, partitioning between freely-dissolved and DOC-bound phases is described as a direct function of K_{ow} ($K_{DOC} = a_{DOC} K_{ow}$) where the factor a_{DOC} is used to account for differences in PCB partitioning to lower molecular weight DOC compounds and octanol. Partitioning between freely-dissolved and sediment

phases is also expressed as a direct function of K_{ow} and the organic carbon fraction (f_{oc}) of the sediment ($K_d = f_{oc} K_{ow}$) (Karickhoff, 1981; DiToro et al., 1991). This simple "$f_{oc} K_{ow}$" relationship, however, may not provide an adequate description of PCB partitioning to suspended solids for cases like the Lower Hudson where phytoplankton comprise a large portion of the suspended organic material. PCB partitioning between the freely-dissolved and suspended solid phases is therefore expressed by a more general relationship that accounts for enhanced partitioning for lower chlorinated homologues (possibly due to the stronger binding of PCBs to cell membranes) and reduced partitioning of higher chlorinated homologues (due to occurrence of cell growth during the longer periods of PCB uptake for higher chlorinated homologues) (Skoglund and Swackhamer, 1994). This relationship is given as:

$$K_d = \frac{a_{phyto}\, f_{oc} K_{ow}}{1 + \left(\frac{k_g}{k_u}\right) a_{phyto}\, f_{oc} K_{ow}}$$

where a_{phyto} is the sorption enhancement factor for PCBs to phytoplankton cells and k_g/k_u is the ratio of phytoplankton growth to the PCB uptake rate. (Setting $a_{phyto} = 1$ and $k_g/k_u = 0$ reduces this expression to our previous formulation, $K_d = f_{oc} K_{ow}$.)

Homologue-specific K_{ow} values for the model were determined from weighted averages of observed congener distributions in 1992 high-resolution surface sediments and 1993 perch data (TAMS/Gradient, 1995) and K_{ow} values for individual PCB congeners (as reported in Hawker and Connell, 1988). Resulting log K_{ow} values are given as 5.0 (di-CB), 5.6 (tri-CB), 6.0 (tetra-CB), 6.45 (penta-CB), and 6.85 (hexa-CB). The value of a_{DOC} is taken as 0.1. This represents an order of magnitude decrease in the PCB partitioning to DOC and is consistent with results of Burkhard (2000). The remaining two sorption coefficients, a_{phyto} and k_g/k_u, were not specified a priori but were considered as adjustable parameters in calibrating the fate model results to observed PCB homologue concentrations in surface sediments.

In addition to PCB partitioning behavior, specification of kinetic rate coefficients for volatilization, pore water exchange, and chemical transformations are also required. The volatilization rate coefficient was calculated using the two-layer model of the air-water interface (Schwarzenbach, Gschwend, and Imboden, 1993), and assuming that PCB transfer through the water side of the interface is controlling the overall volatilization rate. A volatilization rate coefficient of 0.5 m d^{-1} was estimated using the O'Connor-Dobbins formula (O'Connor and Dobbins, 1958) with an average tidal velocity of 0.5 m s^{-1}, an average depth of 6 m, and an average PCB molecular diffusivity coefficient of 0.4×10^{-5} cm^2 s^{-1}. This value is consistent with results of Clark et al. (1996) for gas exchange rates as determined from a sulfur hexafluoride and helium-3 tracer study in the tidal freshwater Hudson.

Dissolved chemical exchange between pore water and the overlying water column has been shown in recent studies of the Upper Hudson to occur at fairly high rates ($k_f' = 1$–15 cm d^{-1}) (Connolly et al., 2000). These high rates of pore water exchange have been attributed to mixing of sediment particles by bioturbation coupled with diffusion of dissolved contaminant through the water side of the benthic boundary layer (Thibodeaux, Valsaraj, and Reible, 2001). For our current model application, k_f' was specified as 5 cm d^{-1}. Even with this higher rate of exchange, settling and resuspension of particle-bound PCBs still appeared to dominate the PCB transfer rates across the water-sediment interface in the tidal freshwater and mid-estuary regions.

Finally, a number of studies have shown that certain PCB congeners may be transformed in aquatic environments by degradation under aerobic conditions or microbial dechlorination under anaerobic conditions (Abramowicz, 1990). Although these processes were found to be active in altering PCB distributions in the Upper Hudson, aerobic degradation and anaerobic dechlorination do not appear to be significant in the Lower Hudson River. PCB transformation rates for the Lower Hudson and New York Harbor were therefore considered to be negligible in our model calculations.

PCB BIOACCUMULATION MODELING

Accumulation of PCBs in Hudson River white perch and striped bass is calculated using the food chain model of Thomann et al. (1992a,b). In this approach, PCB accumulation within a given organism is viewed as a dynamic process that depends on direct uptake from the water, ingestion

of contaminated prey, depuration (from urine excretion and egestion of fecal matter), and metabolic transformation of PCBs within the organism.

Model equations for the uptake and release of PCBs into a given organism are typically written in terms of μg PCB g^{-1} (wet weight) of organism (v_k) (Thomann et al., 1992a,b). The general form of this equation is given as:

$$\frac{dv_k}{dt} = k_{u_k} C_{dis} - k_{b_{kl}} v_k + \sum \alpha_{kl} I_{kl} v_l - [k_e + k_m + k_g] v_k$$

where the first term represents the change in PCB homologue concentration in organism 'k' with time; the second term represents the direct uptake of PCB homologues from the water phase by diffusion across an external cell or gill membrane; the third term represents back diffusion of PCB homologues across the membrane; the fourth term represents PCB homologue uptake through the ingestion of contaminated food or prey and is dependent on the chemical assimilation efficiency (α_{kl}) and the food consumption rate (I_{kl}) for organism 'k' feeding on organism 'l'; and the last term represents decreases in PCB homologue concentration in organism 'k' due to excretion (k_e), metabolic transformation (k_m), and growth dilution (k_g). In this equation, growth dilution is included as a loss term to account for the reduction in PCB homologue concentration due to the increase in size of the organism. A complete listing of terms in the equation is given in the appendix to this chapter.

A time-variable, age-dependent striped bass food chain model was previously developed for the Hudson River Estuary by Thomann et al. (1989; 1991). The model includes a five component, water-column food chain that consists of phytoplankton, zooplankton, small fish, seven age classes of perch, and seventeen age classes of striped bass. In applying the model to the Lower Hudson, PCB homologue concentrations in water and phytoplankton are taken directly from the transport and fate model calculations. Phytoplankton are preyed upon by a zooplankton compartment, the characteristics of which is considered to be represented by *Gammarus*. The small fish compartment, which feeds on zooplankton, is meant to reflect a mixed diet of fish of about 10 g in weight and includes age 0–1 tomcod and herring.

White perch is considered as a representative size-dependent prey of the striped bass and is assumed to feed exclusively on zooplankton. Based on feeding studies where stomach contents of striped bass were examined (Gardinier and Hoff, 1982; O'Connor, 1984; Setzler et al., 1980), the 0–2-year-old striped bass are assumed to feed on zooplankton; 2–5-year-old striped bass are assumed to feed on a mixture of small fish and 0–2-year-old perch; and 6–17-year-old striped bass are assumed to feed on 2–5-year-old perch.

Growth rates were determined from results of Poje, Riordan, and O'Connor (1988) for zooplankton; from a generalized growth-weight relationship for small fish (Thomann et al., 1989); from the age-weight data of Bath and O'Connor (1982) for white perch; and from the age-weight data of Setzler et al. (1980) and Young (1988) for striped bass. Details of age-dependent weights and growth rates are given in Thomann et al. (1989) and are summarized in Farley et al. (1999).

Respiration rates for zooplankton, small fish, white perch, and striped bass were estimated using formulations given in Thomann and Connolly (1984) and Connolly and Tonelli (1985). Details of respiration rates, along with lipid content, dry weight fractions, and food assimilation efficiency are given in Farley et al. (1999). These values are used with the gill transfer efficiency (β.), chemical assimilation efficiency from food (.α) and PCB homologue-specific parameters for K_{ow}, to calculate gill uptake rates ($k_u = \beta R_{oxygen}/C_{oxygen}$), back-diffusion rates ($k_b = k_u/(f_{lipid}\,K_{ow})$), and food ingestion rates ($I = (R+k_g)/a$). Log K_{ow} values were previously given as 5.0, 5.6, 6.0, 6.45, and 6.85 for di- through hexa-CB. The chemical assimilation efficiency (α.) was set equal to the food assimilation efficiency (a) of 0.3 for zooplankton and 0.8 for fish. Gill transfer efficiency (β.) was the only remaining parameter and was adjusted in calibrating model results to observed PCB homologue concentrations in white perch. This value was then used for all fish species throughout the Lower Hudson, New York Harbor, Long Island Sound, and New York Bight.

In bioaccumulation calculations, migration of striped bass adds a further complication in specifying time-dependent exposure concentrations. Migration patterns used in the calculations were assigned based on Waldman (1988); Waldman et al.,

(1990) and are described in Thomann et al. (1989; 1991). These are summarized as follows: Striped bass are born on May 15 of each year and the yearlings are assumed to remain in the mid estuary (as defined by Km 30 to 126; RM 18.5 to 78.5). The 2–5-year-old striped bass are considered to migrate from the mid estuary into New York Harbor in June and spend the summer months (July through September) in Long Island Sound and the New York Bight. Lastly, 6–17-year-old striped bass are assumed to spend most of their year in the open ocean, but migrate into Long Island Sound and the New York Bight around March 15 and return to the mid estuary around April 15 to spawn. They remain in the mid estuary until the middle of July.

Model Results and Discussion

PCB TRANSPORT AND FATE

Transport and fate model calculations for five PCB homologues (di- through hexa-CB) were performed for a simulation period beginning in January 1987. The model was tested by comparing computed results to observed 1992 PCB homologue concentrations in surface sediments. For this evaluation, partitioning of PCBs to suspended solids was initially specified as a direct function of octanol-water partition coefficients ($K_d = f_{oc}\,K_{ow}$). Although these results provided a reasonable description for tetra-, penta-, and hexa-CB, the model underestimated observed concentrations of di- and tri-CB in surface sediments. A more generalized partitioning relationship (previously discussed) was then used to describe PCB partitioning to suspended solids. The coefficients a_{phyto} and k_g/k_u were adjusted to values of 6.3 (dimensionless) and 6×10^{-7} (kg C L^{-1}), respectively, to obtain the final model calibration.

Comparisons of model results to observed 1992 surface sediment concentration are shown in Figure 25.4 for the tri- and penta-CB. In this figure, homologue concentrations in surface sediments are shown as a function of distance down the Hudson River from Troy (Km 246; RM 153) past Kingston (Km 143; RM 89) to the Battery in New York City (Km 0; RM 0) and out into New York Harbor and the New York Bight. Data points shown by the open symbols in Figure 25.4 were not considered in these

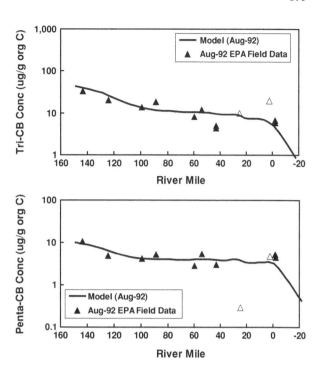

Figure 25.4. Model-field data comparisons for tri- and penta-CB concentrations in surface sediments (presented as organic carbon normalized concentrations) for 1992. (Data are from 1992 EPA Region 2 high resolution sediment cores (TAMS/Gradient 1995).)

comparisons for the following reasons: First, the sediment core at Km 41.5 (RM 25.8) was collected in Piermont Marsh – an area that has limited exchange with suspended solids in the main portion of the river. Second, the tri-CB concentrations at Km 3.9 (RM 2.4) are exceptionally high compared to other homologues in the sample, strongly suggesting that there was an analytical error in quantification (for example, matrix interference) or a very localized source of tri-CB near this sampling location. The resulting longitudinal distributions for di-CB (not shown) and tri-CB (Fig. 25.4) exhibit a more pronounced decline in concentrations with distance downstream. This is due to the lower partitioning of di- and tri-CB to suspended solids and DOC which results in more of these homologues remaining in the freely-dissolved phase and available for loss by volatilization.

The above model evaluations clearly demonstrate that both the magnitude and longitudinal distributions of PCBs in sediments are strongly dependent on homologue-specific partitioning behavior. Enhanced partitioning of the lower chlorinated homologues through the adjustment of "a_{phyto}" was critical in increasing surface sediment concentrations of di- and tri-CB, and reduced

partitioning of the high chlorinated homologues through the specification of "k_g/k_u" had an important (albeit smaller) effect on sediment concentrations of penta- and hexa-CB. These results are consistent with PCB partitioning to phytoplankton (as observed by Skoglund and Swackhamer, 1994), and strongly suggest that phytoplankton are important in controlling PCB partitioning to suspended solids. In addition, phytoplankton production in the water column and subsequent decomposition of phytoplankton-derived material in sediments play a key role in scavenging PCBs from the water column and accumulating them in sediment. Without this trapping mechanism, PCB accumulation in sediments would be greatly reduced.

Time history/projections of dissolved PCBs in the water column and particulate PCBs in sediments are given in Figure 25.5 for the model simulation period of January 1987 to December 2001. Dissolved PCB concentrations at Km 207 (RM 128.5), which is 40 km (25 mi) downstream from Troy, clearly show the effect of changing loads from the Upper Hudson (Fig. 25.2). As shown, dissolved PCB concentrations at Km 207 (RM 128.5) decreased during the period of exponentially decreasing loads in the late 1980s. A large peak in dissolved PCB

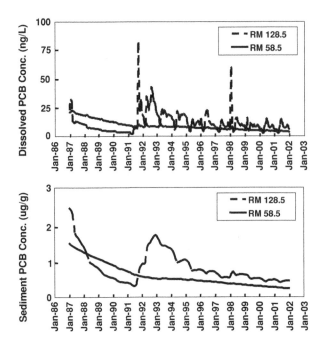

Figure 25.5. Time history/projections for dissolved PCBs in the water column and particulate PCBs in surface sediments for River Mile 128.5 (in the tidal freshwater region) and River Mile 58.5 (in the mid estuary).

concentrations occurred in September/October 1991, corresponding to the flooding and scouring of highly contaminated PCB sediments from an old water intake structure just downstream from the GE facility at Hudson Falls (Rhea et al., 1997). Subsequent peaks in dissolved PCB concentrations occurred in the following years and are consistent with elevated PCB loads that are believed to be associated with seepage of PCB oil from the GE Hudson Falls plant site and the remobilization of deposited PCBs from Upper Hudson sediments, particularly during high flow events. For example, the large peak in dissolved PCB concentrations in January 1998 is associated with a large flow event that occurred in the Hudson River.

In contrast to Km 207 (RM 128.5), dissolved PCB concentrations 113 km (70 mi) downstream at Km 94 (RM 58.5) show a relatively smooth and slow decline of PCBs with time and no apparent variation corresponding to changing loads from the Upper Hudson. Although this could be interpreted as a large loss of PCBs (for example, by volatilization) during downstream transport, PCB responses at Km 94 (RM 58.5) are largely the result of the buffering capacity of sediments. In this case, the continuous interaction of the overlying water with sediments (through settling, resuspension, and pore water exchange) and the large capacity

of the sediments to sorb PCBs work together to dampen the PCB responses downstream. This is demonstrated in the bottom panel of Figure 25.5 which shows PCB surface sediment concentrations at Km 207 (RM 128.5) increasing in the early 1990s in response to increased loads from the Upper Hudson. Later in the mid-to-late 1990s (as PCB loads from the Upper Hudson were reduced), PCBs stored in these sediments were slowly released to the overlying water and transported downstream. Although difficult to discern from Fig. 25.5, this downstream transport of PCBs was typically higher during spring high flow due the larger volume of water and suspended solids being transported downstream. The overall effect of trapping and subsequently releasing PCBs from sediments is to slow PCB transport down the river, and to smear downstream responses of PCBs to changes in Upper Hudson loads.

BIOACCUMULATION

Dissolved and phytoplankton-bound PCB homologue concentrations from the transport and fate model calculations were used as exposure concentrations in subsequent bioaccumulation model calculations for zooplankton, small fish, white perch, and striped bass. Since little or no data were available for PCB accumulation in zooplankton

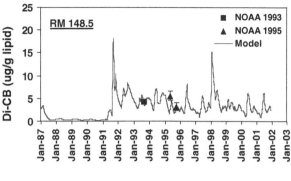

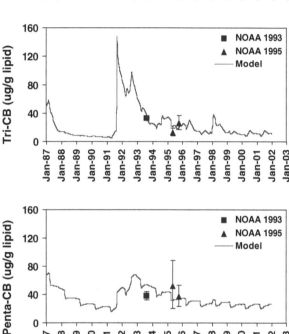

Figure 25.6. Model-field data comparisons for di-, tri- and penta-CB concentrations in white perch at River Mile 148.5 (in the tidal freshwater region). (Data are for 1993 EPA/NOAA samples from (TAMS/Gradient, 1995) and for 1995 EPA/NOAA samples from (McGroddy et al., 1997).)

and small fish, testing of the model was performed by comparing model results to observed PCB homologue concentrations in white perch. All parameters for this evaluation were previously specified except for the gill transfer efficiency coefficient (β). which was adjusted to 0.25 for simulation results presented below.

A good comparison of model results to observations was obtained for di- through hexa-CB concentrations in white perch at Km 239 (RM 148.5) (see Fig. 25.6 for di-, tri- and penta-CB comparisons) and Km 191 (RM 118.5) (not shown). Di-CB accumulations in perch are quite low (approx. 5 μg g^{-1}(lipid)) and appear to rapidly adjust to variations in PCB exposure concentration in this portion of the river (for example, see dissolved PCB concentrations in Fig. 25.5). In contrast, accumulations of higher chlorinated homologues in perch are greater (ranging from 10 to 60 μg g^{-1} (lipid)). This is largely due to increased hydrophobicity (as represented by the increased K_{ow} value) of the higher chlorinated homologues which favor their accumulation in the lipid of fish. Accumulation of the more-chlorinated homologues by perch show a clear increase in the early 1990s (corresponding to increased PCB loads from the Upper Hudson). Higher frequency variations that are apparent for dissolved PCB concentrations (see Fig. 25.5) and for di-CB in perch (Fig. 25.6), however, are largely attenuated. This is due to the relatively

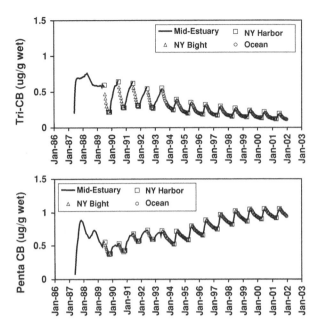

Figure 25.7. Calculated concentrations of tri- and penta-CB for a 1987 striped bass cohort.

slow rates (of several months or more) for the accumulation and loss of more chlorinated homologues by perch.

Calculated PCB homologue concentrations in white perch further downstream in the mid estuary at Km 94 (RM 58.5) (not shown) also compared well to observed data. At this location, PCB responses in perch exhibit a slow decline, largely in response to the slow decline in exposure concentrations (as previously shown in Fig. 25.5 for dissolved PCBs). The resulting concentrations of PCBs in perch at Km 94 (RM 58.5) decreased from a high of 5 $\mu g\,g^{-1}$ (wet weight) in 1987 to approximately 1 $\mu g\,g^{-1}$ (wet weight) at the end of our simulation period in 2002. Perch in this portion of the river are particularly important as a food source for striped bass.

PCB accumulation in striped bass, however, is further complicated by fish migration behavior. This is best illustrated by examining the accumulation of tri- and penta-CB in a striped bass cohort born in 1987. As shown in Figure 25.7, the 1987 cohort quickly accumulates PCBs during the first two years of life in the mid estuary (solid lines in Fig. 25.7). As the cohort ages, fish begin to migrate from the mid estuary into the New York Bight (open triangles), and for older fish, the Atlantic Ocean (open circles). During their time out of the estuary, striped bass feed on less contaminated prey

and their stored PCB concentrations are reduced by depuration and growth dilution. Each year, as striped bass migrate back into the estuary, their PCB concentrations increase as fish again feed on more contaminated prey.

Differences in homologue behavior are shown in Figure 25.7. As shown, there is a significant loss of tri-CB from striped bass during their migration to less contaminated waters. This is accompanied by a slow decline in tri-CB concentrations over many years. In contrast, penta-CB shows only moderate reductions in concentration during migration. Since the reduction in penta-CB is less than the accumulation of penta-CB by striped bass during their return to the mid estuary, a long-term buildup in penta-CB concentrations occurs over the years. Differences in homologue responses are related to their hydrophobicity (as measured by the log K_{ow}). In this case, penta-CB has a greater affinity to remain in fish lipids and its loss by depuration occurs at very slow rates. Reduction in penta-CB concentrations in striped bass is therefore slow and is largely controlled by growth dilution. This results in a slow decline of penta-CB during migration and ultimately leads to a long-term buildup of penta-CB over time. A shift in PCB homologue distributions to high chlorinated homologues is therefore expected for older striped bass.

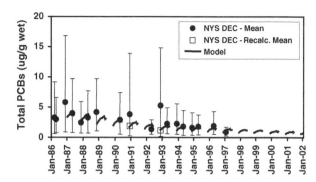

Figure 25.8. Model-field data comparison for PCB concentrations in 2–5 year old striped bass in the mid estuary. Data are from NYS DEC fish monitoring data (TAMS/Gradient 1995) and are reported as means with 5 and 95 percentiles.

Lastly, comparison of PCB striped bass model simulation results and 1987–97 field data (TAMS/Gradient, 1995) are shown for 2–5-year-old striped bass in the mid estuary (Fig. 25.8). Simulated results are denoted by disconnected lines to represent only the portion of the year that striped bass are in the mid estuary. Field data are presented as seasonal (three-month) average concentrations with 5 and 95 percentiles. For fall 1990 and fall 1992, average concentrations were recalculated after eliminating a few high outliers from the sample distributions (Farley et al., 1999). As shown in Figure 25.8, model results are consistent with average observed concentrations in striped bass, and show a slight increase from fall to spring as the young fish overwinter in the mid estuary. A slow decline in PCB concentrations in 2–5-year-old striped bass is also determined with average concentrations of approximately $1\ \mu g\ g^{-1}$(wet weight) at the end of the simulation period in 2002. Similar responses are obtained for PCB accumulations in older striped bass (not shown) with average concentrations of approximately $2\ \mu g\ g^{-1}$(wet weight).

Conclusions and Future Work

A mass balance model was developed to examine the transport, fate, and bioaccumulation of PCB homologues in the Lower Hudson River. A 15-year simulation period (1987–2002) was considered for model application and included the period of increased PCB loads from the Upper Hudson during the early 1990s. Results of the model provide a good description of observed PCB homologue concentrations in surface sediments and in fish.

A closer examination of model results indicated the following:

1. Sorption of PCBs to phytoplankton appears to control the partitioning of PCB homologues to suspended solids in the Lower Hudson River.

2. Organic carbon cycles, which are largely described by phytoplankton production and subsequent deposition and decomposition in sediments, act to scavenge PCBs from the water column and accumulate them in sediments.

3. During downstream transport, exchange of PCBs between the water column and sediments and the large capacity of sediments to store PCBs work together to dampen downstream responses to changes in Upper Hudson loads.

4. Differences in the hydrophobicity of di- through hexa-CBs (as expressed by a two order of magnitude variation in K_{ow} values) largely explain differences in PCB homologue accumulations in sediments and fish, in volatilization losses, and in temporal variations in white perch and striped bass.

5. Migration of striped bass plays a critical role in limiting their exposure to PCBs.

Although the current model provides a reasonable description for PCB transport, fate and bioaccumulation in the Lower Hudson, gaps remain in our understanding of several key processes. In particular, further studies are needed to address the partitioning of PCBs to different types of POC (for example, phytoplankton, fresh detritus, refractory organic material). In addition, our present understanding of sediment transport and how it affects the movement of POC (and POC-bound contaminants) in the Lower Hudson is limited and needs further evaluation. Finally, current model descriptions for PCB bioaccumulation, provide useful information on the transfer of PCBs through the Lower Hudson food web. Continued investigations of bioaccumulation, however, are needed to provide us with a better understanding of PCB transfer pathways (including interactions with the benthic food web). Specific attention should also be given to differences in migration behavior, feeding patterns, and other processes that may explain intraspecies variability of PCB accumulations in fish.

Acknowledgments

Support for this work was provided by the Hudson River Foundation with contributing funds from the Port Authority of New York and New Jersey, and the U.S. Environmental Protection Agency, Region 2. The guiding advice of Bob Thomann is gratefully acknowledged. Views expressed in this chapter do not necessarily reflect the beliefs or opinions of our sponsoring agencies.

Appendix. Notation

The following symbols are used in this chapter:

a = food assimilation efficiency (dimensionless);

a_{DOC} = factor relating K_{DOC} to K_{ow} (dimensionless);

a_{phyto} = enhancement factor for PCB sorption to phytoplankton (dimensionless);

A_s = surface area (m^2);

C = total (freely-dissolved plus DOC-bound plus particulate) PCB concentration ($\mu g\,L^{-1}$);

C_{dis} = freely-dissolved PCB concentration ($\mu g\,L^{-1}$);

C_{DOC} = DOC-bound PCB concentration ($\mu g\,L^{-1}$);

C_{oxygen} = dissolved oxygen concentration in water ($mg\,L^{-1}$);

E_{ij} = bulk dispersion coefficient for mixing between segments 'i' and 'j' ($m^3\,s^{-1}$);

f_{lipid} = fraction of organism mass that is comprised of lipids (g(lipid) g^{-1} (wet weight));

f_{oc} = fraction organic carbon (gC g^{-1} (dry weight));

K_d = equilibrium partition coefficient between particulate and freely-dissolved phases ($L\,kg^{-1}$);

K_{DOC} = equilibrium partition coefficient between DOC and freely-dissolved phases ($L\,kg^{-1}$);

K_{ow} = octanol-water partition coefficient ($L\,kg^{-1}$);

k = PCB transformation rate coefficient (d^{-1});

k_b = PCB back-diffusion rate coefficient across organism membrane or gill (d^{-1});

k_e = PCB excretion rate coefficient (d^{-1});

k_f' = porewater-water column exchange rate coefficient ($m\,d^{-1}$);

k_g = growth dilution rate coefficient (d^{-1});

k_m = PCB metabolic rate coefficient (d^{-1});

k_u = PCB uptake rate coefficient across organism membrane or gill ($L\,g^{-1}$ (wet weight) d^{-1});

k_v' = volatilization rate coefficient ($m\,d^{-1}$);

I_{kl} = consumption rate of organism 'k' feeding on organism 'l' (g(wet prey) g^{-1} (wet pred.) d^{-1});

m = solids concentration ($mg\,L^{-1}$);

Q_{ij} = flow rate from segment 'i' to segment 'j' ($m^3\,s^{-1}$);

R = respiration rate in wet weight equivalents (g(wet weight respired) g^{-1} (wet weight) d^{-1});

R_{oxygen} = respiration rate in oxygen equivalents (g(O_2 respired) g^{-1} (wet weight) d^{-1});

t = time (d);

V = volume (m^3);

W_C = PCB input rate from external sources, e.g., tributaries, effluent discharges ($kg\,d^{-1}$);

w_b = burial rate for solids (cm yr^{-1});

w_s = solids settling velocity ($m\,d^{-1}$);

w_u = solids resuspension velocity ($m\,d^{-1}$);

α_{kl} = PCB assimilation efficiency for organism 'k' feeding on organism 'l' (dimensionless);

β = gill transfer efficiency (dimensionless);

Γ = solid phase PCB concentration ($\mu g\,g^{-1}$ (dry weight));

v = biota PCB concentration (ug g^{-1} (wet weight));

ϕ = porosity (dimensionless);

The following subscripts are used in this chapter:

sed = surface (active) sediment layer;
phyto = phytoplankton.

REFERENCES

Abramowicz, D. A. 1990. Aerobic and anaerobic biodegradation of PCBs: A review. *Critical Reviews in Biotechnology* **10**:241–51.

Bath, D. W., and O'Connor, J. M. 1982. The biology of the white perch, *Morone americana*, in the Hudson River Estuary. *Fisheries Bulletin* **80**:599–610.

Burkhard, L. P. 2000. Estimating dissolved organic carbon partition coefficients for nonionic organic chemicals. *Environmental Science and Technology* **34**(22):4663–8.

Clark, J. F., Schlosser, P., Stute, M., and Simpson, H. J. 1996. SF6–3He tracer release experiment: A new method of determining longitudinal dispersion coefficients in large rivers. *Environmental Science and Technology* **30**:1527–32.

Connolly, J. P. 1991. Application of a food chain model to polychlorinated biphenyl contamination of the lobster and winter flounder food chains in New Bedford Harbor. *Environmental Science and Technology* **25**:760–70.

Connolly, J. P., and Tonelli, R. 1985. Modeling Kepone in the striped bass food chain of the James River Estuary. *Estuarine, Coastal and Shelf Sciences* **20**:349–66.

Connolly, J. P., Zahakos, H. A., Benaman, J., Ziegler, C. K., Rhea, J. R., and Russell, K. 2000. A model of PCB fate in the Upper Hudson River. *Environmental Science and Technology* **34**:4076–87.

DiToro, D. M., Zarba, C. S., Hansen, D. J., Berry, W. J., Swartz, R. C., Cowan, C. E., Pavlou, S. P., Allen, H. E., Thomas, N. A., and Paquin, P. R. 1991. Technical basis for establishing sediment quality criteria for nonionic organic chemicals using equilibrium partitioning. *Environmental Toxicology and Chemistry* **10**:1541–83.

Farley, K. J., Thomann, R. V., Cooney, III, T. F., Damiani, D. R., and Wands, J. R. 1999. *An Integrated Model of Organic Chemical Fate and Bioaccumulation in the Hudson River Estuary*. Final Report to the Hudson River Foundation. Manhattan College, Riverdale, NY.

Gardinier, M. N., and Hoff, T. B. 1982. Diet of striped bass in Hudson River Estuary. *New York Fish and Game Journal* **29**:152–65.

Garvey, E. A., and Hunt, C. 1997. Long term fate of PCBs in the Hudson River sediments. *Clearwaters*, **27**(2):17–22.

Hawker, D. W., and Connell, D. W. 1988. Octanol-water partition coefficients of polychlorinated biphenyl congeners. *Environmental Science and Technology* **22**:383–7.

Karickhoff, S. W. 1981. Semi-empirical estimation of sorption of hydrophobic pollutants on natural sediments and soils. *Chemosphere* **10**:833–46.

McGroddy, S. E., Read, L. B., Field, L. J., Severn, C. G., and Dexter, R. N. 1997. *Hudson River Congener-Specific Analysis: Data Summary and Analysis Report*. National Oceanographic and Atmospheric Administration, Seattle, WA.

O'Brien and Gere Engineers, Inc. 1997. *Correction of Analytical Biases in the 1991–1997 GE Hudson River PCB Database*. Prepared for General Electric Company, East Syracuse, NY.

O'Connor, D. J., and Dobbins, W. E. 1958. Mechanisms of reaeration in natural streams. *Transactions of the American Society of Civil Engineers* **641**: 123.

O'Connor, J. M. 1984. PCBs: Dietary dose and burdens in Striped Bass from the Hudson River. *Northeastern Environmental Science* **3**(3/4):152–8.

Poje, G. V., Riordan, S. A., and O'Connor, J. M. 1988. Food habits of the amphipod *Gammarus tigrinus* in the Hudson River and the effects of diet upon its growth and reproduction, in C. L. Smith (ed.), *Fisheries Research in the Hudson River*. Albany, NY: State University of New York Press, pp. 255–70.

Rhea, J., Connolly, J., and Haggard, J. 1997. Hudson River PCBs: A 1990s perspective. *Clearwaters* **27**(2):24–8.

Schwarzenbach, R. P., Gschwend, P. M., and Imboden, D. M. 1993. *Environmental Organic Chemistry*, New York: John Wiley & Sons, Inc.

Setzler, E. M., Boynton, W. R., Wood, K. V., Zion, H. H., Lubbers, L., Mountford, N. K., Fere, P., Tucker, L., and Mihursky, J. A. 1980. *Synopsis of Biological Data on Striped Bass*, Morone saxatilis (Waldbaum). NMFS Cir. 433, FAO Synopsis No. 121, U.S. Department of Commerce, Rockville, MD.

Skoglund, R. S., and Swackhamer, D. L. 1994. Fate of hydrophobic organic contaminants: Processes affecting uptake by phytoplankton, in L. A. Baker (ed.), *Environmental Chemistry of Lakes and Reservoirs*. Washington, D.C.: American Chemical Society, pp. 559–73.

TAMS/Gradient. 1995. *Further Site Characterization and Analysis Database Report*. Phase 2 Report. EPA Contract No. 68-S9-2001, U.S. Environmental Protection Agency, Region 2.

Thibodeaux, L. J., Valsaraj, K. T., and Reible, D. D. 2001. Bioturbation-driven transport of hydrophobic organic contaminants from bed sediment. *Environmental Engineering Science* **18**:215–23.

Thomann, R. V., and Connolly, J. P. 1984. Model of PCB in the Lake Michigan Trout food chain. *Environmental Science and Technology* **18**:65–71.

Thomann, R. V., Connolly, J. P., and Parkerton, T. F. 1992a. An equilibrium model of organic chemical accumulation in aquatic food webs with sediment interaction. *Environmental Toxicology and Chemistry* **11**:615–29.

1992b. Modeling accumulation of organic chemicals in aquatic food webs, in F. A. P. C. Gobas and J. A. McCorquodale (eds.), *Chemical Dynamics in Fresh Water Ecosystems*. Chelsea, MI: Lewis Publishers, pp. 153–86.

Thomann, R. V., and DiToro, D. M. 1983. Physicochemical model of toxic substances in the Great Lakes. *Journal of Great Lakes Research* **9**: 474–96.

Thomann, R. V., Mueller, J. A., Winfield, R. P., and Huang, C.-R. 1989. *Mathematical Model of the Long-Term Behavior of PCBs in the Hudson River Estuary*. Final Report to the Hudson River Foundation, Grant Numbers 007/87A/030, 011/88A/030, Manhattan College, Riverdale, NY.

1991. Model of fate and accumulation of PCB homologues in Hudson Estuary. *Journal of Environmental Engineering* **117**:161–78.

Waldman, J. R. 1988. *1986 Hudson River Striped Bass Tag Recovery Program*. Hudson River Foundation, New York, NY.

Waldman, J. R., Dunning, D. J., Ross, Q. E., and Mattson, M. T. 1990. Range dynamics of Hudson River striped bass along the Atlantic coast. *Transactions of the American Fisheries Society* **119**: 910–919.

Young, B. H. 1988. A study of the striped bass in the marine district of New York V., New York State Department of Environmental Conservation (DEC), Division of Marine Resources, Stony Brook, NY.

26 Contaminant Chronologies from Hudson River Sedimentary Records

Richard F. Bopp, Steven N. Chillrud,
Edward L. Shuster, and H. James Simpson

ABSTRACT Analyses of sections from dated sediment cores have been used to construct contaminant chronologies in the Hudson River Basin and the New York/New Jersey Harbor complex. Dating information was derived primarily from radionuclide analyses. The known input history of ^{137}Cs, a radionuclide derived from global fallout and nuclear reactor discharges, places important constraints on estimates of net sediment accumulation rates. ^{7}Be, a natural radionuclide with a 53 day half-life is detectable in surficial samples with a significant component of particles deposited within a year of core collection. Persistent contaminants analyzed in dated Hudson sediments include PCBs, dioxins, chlorinated hydrocarbon pesticides, and trace metals such as copper, lead, zinc, cadmium, chromium, and mercury. The combination of temporal and geographic information from these analyses is most valuable and provides a general basinwide perspective on the significant improvement in contaminant levels in the Hudson over the past several decades. It has also allowed us to trace the influence of several major contamination incidents in the basin, including PCB and trace metal inputs to the Upper Hudson River and dioxin and DDT discharges to the Lower Passaic River.

Introduction

Over the past several decades, many thousands of sediment samples have been collected from the Hudson River, its tributaries and the New York/New Jersey (NY/NJ) Harbor complex (Fig. 26.1). This chapter will focus on insights gained from analyses on a very select subset of those samples – sections of dated sediment cores. While it may be fairly obvious that information about the period of deposition represented by any given sediment sample is useful, we would argue that for many important applications involving contaminant sources, transport, and behavior, it is essential. The importance of dating information is derived from two inescapable characteristics of the system, the short-distance-scale heterogeneity of depositional environments (geographic variability) and the large range in contaminant levels in the system over time (temporal variability).

Estimating the Time of Sediment Deposition

The depth distribution of ^{137}Cs in sediment cores provides information on the timing of sediment deposition. The sources of ^{137}Cs to the Hudson River Basin include fallout from atmospheric testing of nuclear weapons, liquid releases from Indian Point Nuclear Power Generating Facility (IPNPGF) on the lower Hudson River, and liquid releases from Knolls Atomic Power Laboratory (KAPL) on the Mohawk River. For dating purpose, the utility of ^{137}Cs comes from the fact that it is relatively easy to measure and that all of these sources have been monitored over the last several decades.

The annual delivery rates for these sources are reported in Chillrud (1996). ^{137}Cs, derived from atmospheric weapons testing, first entered drainage basins on a global scale in significant amounts in the early 1950s. In cores with semicontinuous and relatively rapid sediment accumulation (on the order of 0.5 cm yr^{-1} or greater), maximum activities of fallout ^{137}Cs can be associated with maximum fallout delivery (Olsen et al., 1981; Ritchie and McHenry, 1990; Fig. 26.2). The largest recorded annual liquid release from KAPL occurred in 1963 while the largest annual liquid release from IPNPGF was in 1971. In a very small number of cores from the lower Hudson estuary that showed rapid particle accumulation rates, two peaks in a Cs-137 depth profile were observed. The first can be associated with the 1971 release from IPNPGF and the deeper peak with the mid-1960s global fallout maximum (Bopp and Simpson, 1989; Fig. 26.2B).

Monitoring of all three sources showed insignificant levels of inputs since the 1980s. Most of

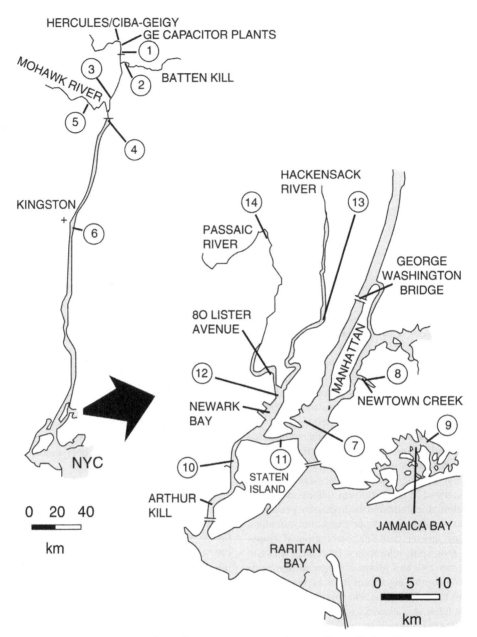

Figure 26.1. Sampling sites in the Hudson River Basin. 1) Main stem, Upper Hudson River upstream of the Thompson Island Dam; 2) Batten Kill; 3) main stem, Upper Hudson River upstream of lock 2; 4) main stem, Hudson River downstream of the Federal Dam at Troy, NY; 5) Mohawk River; 6) main stem, Hudson River near Kingston, NY; 7) main stem, Hudson River, NY/NJ Harbor; 8) Newtown Creek; 9) Jamaica Bay; 10) Arthur Kill; 11) Kill Van Kull; 12) Newark Bay; 13) Hackensack River; 14) Passaic River upstream of the Dundee Dam.

the integrated fallout ^{137}Cs that deposits onto a drainage basin is stored in watershed soils. Erosion of these soils is now the largest source of ^{137}Cs to the Hudson River. This decrease in source strength is reflected in depth profiles of undisturbed cores, where the activity of ^{137}Cs decreases exponentially toward the sediment-water interface (Bopp et al., 1982, Fig. 26.2). With no significant atmospheric inputs of ^{137}Cs for many years, the current exponential rate of decrease in sediment cores

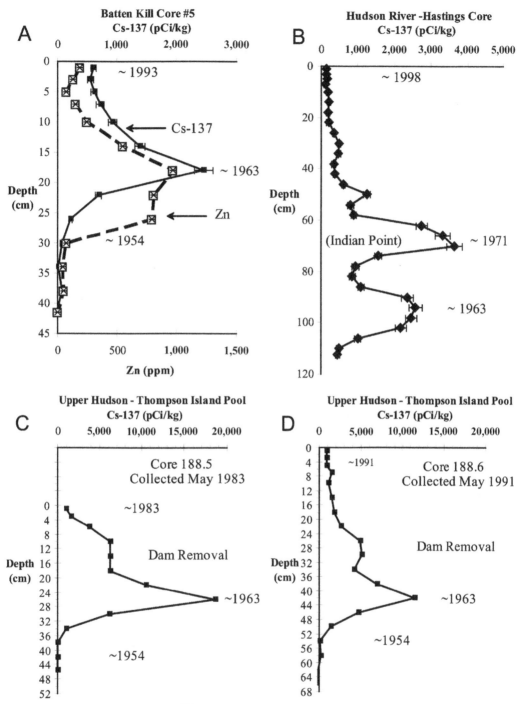

Figure 26.2. The distribution of ^{137}Cs activity with depth in four Hudson Basin sediment cores. Core A was collected from the Batten Kill (site 2; Fig. 26.1). Also shown is the history of Zn contamination at this site. Core B was collected by NYSDEC personnel from the main stem Hudson at mile point 21.6 (21.6 statute miles upstream of the southern tip of Manhattan). The Cs-137 profile appears to reflect the influence of both global fallout (1963 peak) and inputs from the IPNPGF (1971 peak) at mile point 43. Figures C and D are depth profiles from two cores at site 1 (Fig. 26.1) collected eight years apart. In addition to providing contaminant chronologies, paired samples from these cores were used to study in situ reductive dechlorination of PCBs (McNulty, 1997).

is approaching the decay rate of Cs-137 ($t_{1/2} = 30$ y) (Chillrud, 1996).

Confirmation that the uppermost section of a core contains recently accumulated sediment comes from analysis of [7]Be, a cosmic-ray produced radionuclide with a half-life of 53 days. Depth sections with measurable activity of [7]Be have a significant component of particles deposited within about a year prior to sampling. At sites with very rapid sediment accumulation rates (on the order of several cm yr^{-1}), depth profiles of [7]Be can be used to estimate sedimentation rates (Bopp and Simpson, 1989; Feng et al., 1998).

[7]Be analysis has been useful at several sites in the New York/New Jersey Harbor where extremely rapid deposition (sometimes exceeding 10 cm yr^{-1}) and disturbances of the sediment column caused by human activities such as dredging are commonly encountered. These factors make collection of cores with continuous decades-long records of sediment accumulation most difficult. Under such circumstances, surface sediments from areas of rapid deposition, if they contain detectable [7]Be, define a time horizon within about a year prior to sample collection (Bopp and Walsh, 1994; Chillrud, 1996).

Dating information can also be obtained from depth profiles of the natural radionuclides ^{210}Pb and [234]Th. [210]Pb ($t_{1/2} = 22$ y) provides information on a time-scale of decades; [234]Th ($t_{1/2} = 24$ days) on a time-scale of weeks (see Chapter 6, Cochran et al., this volume).

[210]Pb dating has been used extensively in lakes where low net accumulation rates (on the order of 0.1 cm yr^{-1}) result in high specific activities on recently deposited particles (Alderton, 1985). In depositional areas of the Hudson, however, the surface sediment activity of excess ^{210}Pb is relatively low. While this limits the utility of ^{210}Pb as a primary dating tool, depth profiles have been used to confirm ^{137}Cs based dating assignments in Hudson River sediment cores (Bush et al., 1987; Robideau, 1997; Benoit et al., 1999). A combination of ^{210}Pb and ^{137}Cs data was used to date a core from Central Park Lake, Manhattan and chronologies of atmospheric fluxes of lead and several other trace metals to the New York/New Jersey Harbor area were developed. The historical use of municipal solid waste incinerators was found to be a dominant source (Chillrud et al., 1999).

[234]Th has been used to study particle reworking in sediments of the New York Bight (Cochran and Aller, 1979) and for dating surface sediments of the Hudson Estuary (Feng et al., 1998). The temporal constraints on deposition are similar to those obtained from [7]Be analyses. It has been suggested that for Hudson Estuary sediments, [234]Th analysis does not provide sufficient additional dating information to warrant the higher level of effort involved in its analysis (Feng et al., 1998).

In the Upper Hudson River (upstream of the Federal Dam at Troy, NY; Fig. 26.1), stable lead isotopes provide additional stratigraphic control (Chillrud et al., 2003; Chillrud et al., 2004). The Upper Hudson River is heavily contaminated with several metals, including lead, that appear to be derived from discharges from a pigment manufacturing facility in Glens Falls, New York. The total range in lead isotope ratios observed in Upper Hudson sediments through the last several decades is large, for example, for [206]Pb/[207]Pb from 1.1364 to 1.2496, on the order of 10 percent. This large range provides an extremely sensitive tracer since mass spectrometers can measure this ratio to a precision of better than 0.05 percent. For purposes of stratigraphy, the key observation is that there have been four large shifts in isotope composition (each one being about half of the total range) occurring in the 1950s, 1960s, 1970s, and 1980s. The temporal trend in [206]Pb/[207]Pb is essentially identical in sediment cores collected from over a twenty-mile stretch of the upper river, and even 100 miles downstream the lead isotope composition at critical time periods is consistent with a predominant lead source derived from the Upper Hudson (Chillrud et al., 2004).

Heterogeneity of Depositional Environments

The short-distance-scale heterogeneity of net particle deposition rates in the Hudson has been recognized for decades. Examples based on the distribution of ^{137}Cs activity with depth in sediment cores were reported by Olsen et al. (1978). Bopp and Simpson (1989) found ^{137}Cs penetration depths ranging from 0 (no detectable ^{137}Cs in the surficial sediment) to 200 cm in sixteen cores from a six-mile reach of the river near Kingston, New York (Fig. 26.1). A range of 0 to >64 cm of sediment with ^{137}Cs activity had previously been found at three coring sites separated by a total distance of less than half a mile (Bopp, 1979). In the Arthur Kill (site 10; Fig. 26.1) cores Kill 20 and Kill 21, collected less than 20 meters apart, had detectable levels of ^{137}Cs to depths of 4 cm and 160 cm, respectively. Analyses of samples from Kill 21 are being used to develop detailed contaminant chronologies for this area of the New York/New Jersey Harbor complex.

Spatial heterogeneity of depositional environments greatly complicates any attempt to interpret spatial distributions of particle-associated contaminants in the Hudson (Gibbs, 1994; Feng et al., 1998). The approach that we have employed consistently over the past twenty-five years is to focus our contaminant analyses on cores from specific sites. The ideal site is one of continuous, fairly rapid deposition of fine-grained sediments. Such sites are often found in coves, marshes, and other sheltered areas of the river and can be thought of as "sampling" the fine-grained suspended matter transported with the main flow. Our best cores are composed of homogeneous mud that is dominated by silt and clay-sized particles with little down-core variation in organic matter content. The ^{137}Cs approach significantly constrains the estimate of timing of particle deposition over the past fifty years (Fig. 26.2). Sites like these are neither easy to locate nor so rare as to exclude detailed interpretation of spatial distributions of contaminant levels. Data from eighteen such sites in the Hudson River, its major tributaries, and the New York/New Jersey Harbor complex have been used to summarize the spatial and temporal distributions of PCBs, dioxins, and chlorinated hydrocarbon pesticides (Bopp et al., 1998). Similar data for several trace metals are presented below.

PCBs, Dioxins, DDT, and Chlordane

PCBs. The particle-associated contaminant most closely associated with the Hudson River is PCBs. In December 2000, the USEPA proposed the dredging of 2.65 million cubic yards of sediment from the Upper Hudson River containing an estimated 150,000 pounds of PCBs from the discharges of two General Electric capacitor plants (USEPA, 2000; Baker et al., 2001; Fig. 26.1). The analysis of dated sediment samples and the development of contaminant

chronologies played a critical role in the evolution of our understanding of the importance of this and other PCB sources to the Hudson.

The development of PCB chronologies provided direct evidence that the removal of the first dam downstream of the General Electric inputs to the Upper Hudson resulted in an unprecedented PCB downstream transport event (Bopp et al., 1982; Bopp and Simpson, 1989). PCB component analysis has been used to determine the influence of the Upper Hudson source on sediments depositing in the New York/New Jersey Harbor along the main stem of the Hudson (Bopp et al., 1981; Bopp and Simpson, 1989; Chillrud, 1996). Analyses of dated sediments from other parts of the harbor complex have provided information on significant PCB sources to the western side of New York/New Jersey related to discharges of municipal wastewater (Bopp et al., 1991; Bopp et al., 1998). Recent work has focused on the characterization of atmospheric PCB sources through the analysis of dated sediment core samples from Central Park Lake and reservoirs of the New York City municipal water supply (Chaky et al., 1998; Chaky, 2003).

Dioxin. The best known case of dioxin contamination in the area involves the synthesis of compounds used in the formulation of Agent Orange at what is now commonly referred to as the 80 Lister Avenue Superfund site on the lower Passaic River in the western part of New York/New Jersey Harbor (Fig. 26.1). This dioxin source is characterized by a high relative proportion of 2,3,7,8-TCDD (Hay, 1982; Bopp et al., 1991), the congener with the highest toxic equivalency factor (TEF) (NATO, 1988; van den Berg et al., 1998). Its influence has been traced to Newark Bay and possibly up the Hackensack River as a result of tidal flow (Bopp et al., 1991). More recent analysis, based on the ratio of 2,3,7,8-TCDD to total TCDDs, suggests that as much as half of the 2,3,7,8-TCDD in main stem Hudson sediments as far upstream as the George Washington Bridge (Fig. 26.1) could be related to this source (Chaky, 2003). Significant dioxin contamination has also been found in sediments of the Upper Hudson and at a site just downstream of the Federal Dam at Troy, New York (Bopp et al., 1998). The total toxic equivalents are comparable to those found in Newark Bay sediments, but are derived dominantly from hexa-through octachlorinated congeners.

DDT and chlordane. The 80 Lister Avenue site also plays a significant role in the DDT contamination in sediments of the New York/New Jersey Harbor. DDT was manufactured at the facility from the mid-1940s to 1958–59 when production was moved to Texas (Diamond Shamrock Corporation, 1983). This production history imparts a unique temporal signal on sediment chronologies influenced by this source – a peak in DDT-related compounds in samples deposited in the 1940s through the early 1950s. In other natural water systems (Alderton, 1985), including the mid-tidal Hudson (site 6; Fig. 26.1; Bopp et al., 1982) and Jamaica Bay (site 9; Fig. 26.1; Bopp et al., 1991), peak levels of DDT-derived compounds occur in samples deposited in the 1960s to early 1970s, reflecting overall U.S. production and use history. A 1940s to early 1950s peak in DDT-related compound levels was clearly seen in Newark Bay sediments (site 12; Fig. 26.1; Bopp et al., 1991) and has been reported in sediments from the Arthur Kill (site 10; Fig. 26.1; Robinson, 2002). In a core from southern Raritan Bay (Fig. 26.1) peak levels of DDT-derived compounds were found near the bottom of the core in sediments that dated from the 1950s (Robinson, 2002). In recently deposited sediments (1980s to 1990s), cores from the Arthur Kill and Kill Van Kull (site 11; Fig. 26.1) have the highest levels of DDT-derived compounds of any of our Hudson Basin sites (Bopp et al., 1998; Robinson, 2002). The data suggest a local source.

Based on analyses of dated sediment samples, the Passaic and Hackensack Rivers have been identified as major sources of chlordane to the western harbor (Bopp et al., 1998). Although relatively few samples have been analyzed, levels of chlordane in Hudson sediments upstream of New York/New Jersey Harbor appear to be quite low relative to those observed in the western part of the harbor complex (Robinson, 2002).

PAH and Saturated Hydrocarbons

Polycyclic aromatic hydrocarbon and saturated hydrocarbon chronologies in sediments deposited from the 1940s to the 1980s have been developed at several sites throughout the Hudson Basin and the New York/New Jersey Harbor complex, including sites 1, 6, 7, 9, and 12 shown on Figure 26.1 (Keane, 1998). The highest levels of PAH were found in Newark Bay (site 12; Fig. 26.1) in samples deposited in the 1940s and 1950s. Upstream of the harbor along the main stem of the Hudson, peak levels of PAH and saturated hydrocarbons were found in samples from the late 1960s and early 1970s. In the more recent samples, the levels were significantly lower. In several cases, saturated hydrocarbon concentrations dropped to less than 10 percent of peak levels. Several Jamaica Bay samples (site 9; Fig. 26.1) had relatively high proportions of lower molecular weight saturated hydrocarbons consistent with inputs of jet fuel from nearby Kennedy International Airport.

Individual PAH compounds in many of the harbor samples have been analyzed for stable carbon isotope ratios. This technique, known as compound specific gas chromatography isotope ratio mass spectrometry (GC/IRMS) provides a powerful tool for PAH source partitioning (O'Malley, Abrajano, and Hellou, 1996). The historical record in Newark Bay cores shows several shifts in the ^{13}C to ^{12}C ratio that correspond to changes in individual PAH level ratios. Both of these tracers indicate that there have been significant changes in the relative importance of combustion-related and petroleum-derived sources of PAH to Newark Bay sediments over the past sixty years (Perry et al., 2002). Recent work on dated sediment samples has utilized both isotopic and molecular PAH tracers to study temporal and geographic changes in PAH sources to the Lower Hudson Basin (Yan, 2004; Yan et al., 2004).

Trace Metals

While the Hudson and New York/New Jersey Harbor complex are best known for incidents of PCB and dioxin contamination, the sediments are also among the nation's most contaminated with trace metals (Table 26.1).

The use of ^{137}Cs analyses to guide interpretation of trace metal data in Hudson sediment samples dates back to the 1970s (Williams et al., 1978). Copper, lead, and zinc levels were interpreted in terms of three-endmember mixing. The "recent harbor" endmember had detectable levels of ^{137}Cs and the highest trace metal levels. Recent Hudson samples

Table 26.1. Trace metal levels in Hudson sediments – nationwide perspective

| | **NOAA National Status and Trends Program[1]** | | | | **Highest level reported in Figs. 26.3–26.5 (μg/g)** | |
	Highest reported level (μg/g)	Tenth highest reported level (μg/g)	Number of the top ten located in the Hudson Basin and New York Harbor Complex	Background concentration[2] (μg/g)	1960s	Recent
Cd	11	2.5	3	0.5	115	5.08
Cr	3,400	320	0	60	1,440	166
Cu	320	180	6	25	1,395	317
Pb	280	200	6	20	1,560	307
Hg	4.3	1.7	6	0.18	20	4.94
Zn	570	380	4	95	1,100	559

[1] National Oceanic and Atmospheric Administration 1988. (A summary of selected data on chemical contaminants in sediments collected during 1984–1987 at about 200 coastal and estuarine sites)

[2] Based on data compiled by Bowen (1979).

(upstream of the harbor) had detectable ^{137}Cs and trace metal levels that were lower, but still significantly elevated above background. Old (preindustrial) Hudson sediments had near-background levels of the metals, comparable to those reported for average shale. Detailed chronologies of these metals in sediments from the mainstem harbor (site 7; Fig. 26.1) and mid-tidal Hudson (site 6; Fig. 26.1) were reported in the late 1980s (Bopp and Simpson, 1989). A few years later, dated sediment cores from Jamaica Bay, a sewage-impacted coastal embayment, were used to derive chronologies for an expanded list of metals, including cadmium, chromium, and mercury, and for persistent chlorinated hydrocarbon contaminants (Bopp et al., 1993).

Recent efforts to extend and expand trace metal chronologies in Hudson sediments have been productive. The history of atmospheric trace metal inputs to the New York metropolitan area has been elucidated through analyses of sediment core samples from Central Park Lake, Manhattan (Chillrud et al., 1999). The development of sediment chronologies has allowed characterization of major trace metal sources to the Arthur Kill associated with smelting at a National Lead site (Chillrud, 1996) and to the Hackensack River from the Berry's Creek Superfund site (Goeller, 1989). In the Upper Hudson Basin, significant sources of zinc

could be related to pulp and paper plant operations and other metals, including lead, chromium, and cadmium come from discharges associated with pigment manufacturing at a Hercules/Ciba-Geigy Plant (Fig. 26.1; Chillrud et al., 2004; also Zamek, 2002).

Consideration of a limited amount of data from the sampling sites in Figure 26.1 provides a useful basinwide perspective on trace metal contamination in Hudson sediments. The figures that follow list the background concentrations of the metal expected for uncontaminated sediments (based on data compiled by Bowen, 1979) and the probable effects level (PEL; Smith et al., 1996), a common regulatory benchmark developed for freshwater ecosystems. While the PEL is not directly applicable to the brackish and saline environment of the NY/NJ Harbor sites, it does provide a point of reference. No similar benchmark is currently available for marine systems. Concentrations in mid-1960s deposits (identified by the fallout ^{137}Cs peak) and in the most recent sediments that we have analyzed (^{7}Be bearing surficial samples) are reported at each site. A similar approach has been applied to chlorinated hydrocarbon contamination in Hudson Basin sediments (Bopp et al., 1998).

The copper data (Fig. 26.3A) illustrate a pattern common to all the metals. At every site, there is a significant decrease in levels between the mid-1960s

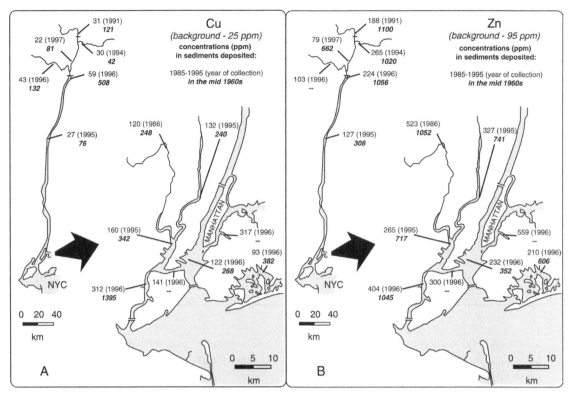

Figure 26.3. Levels of Cu and Zn in Hudson Basin sediment samples reported in parts per million on a dry weight basis. Upper numbers represent the concentrations in samples deposited between the mid 1980s and mid 1990s. The numbers in bold type are concentrations in mid 1960s samples. The probable effects level (PEL) is 197 ppm for Cu and 315 ppm for Zn (Smith et al., 1996).

and the most recent samples, reflecting the success of regulatory efforts at controlling point-source inputs and improving wastewater treatment. At only two sites do the most recent levels exceed the PEL for Cu – the Arthur Kill (site 10; Fig. 26.1), one of the most contaminated waterways in the New York/New Jersey Harbor (Chillrud, 1996; Bopp et al. 1998), and Newtown Creek (site 8; Fig. 26.1), a tidal embayment that receives the discharge from one of the largest New York City wastewater treatment plants. From the mid-tidal Hudson (site 6; Fig. 26.1) upstream levels in the most recent samples are at or near background. The highest Cu levels in mid-1960s samples are found in the Arthur Kill and near Troy (site 4; Fig. 26.1). Much lower levels upstream of the Troy site suggest a significant local source.

Zinc levels in recent samples (Fig. 26.3B) exceed the PEL in the Upper Passaic (site 14; Fig. 26.1) and

mid Hackensack (site 13; Fig. 26.1) Rivers as well as in the Arthur Kill and Newtown Creek. Mid-1960s levels exceeding 1,000 ppm are seen in the Arthur Kill and Upper Passaic River as well as at three sites in the Upper Hudson Basin. While zinc oxide was used at the Hercules/Ciba-Geigy pigment plant upstream of site 1 (Fig. 26.1), the high levels in the Batten Kill (site 2; Fig. 26.1) are upstream of a dam and cannot be related to this source. We suspect a pulp and paper plant source of zinc to the Batten Kill. Comparison of ^{137}Cs and Zn profiles with depth in a Batten Kill core (Fig. 26.2A) clearly indicates that the major Zn inputs occurred in the 1950s and 1960s. Recent analysis of mid-1960s samples from the main stem of the Hudson upstream of Hercules/Ciba-Geigy pigment plant also gave zinc levels of over 1,000 ppm (Zamek, 2002) suggesting a pulp and paper plant source further upstream on the Hudson.

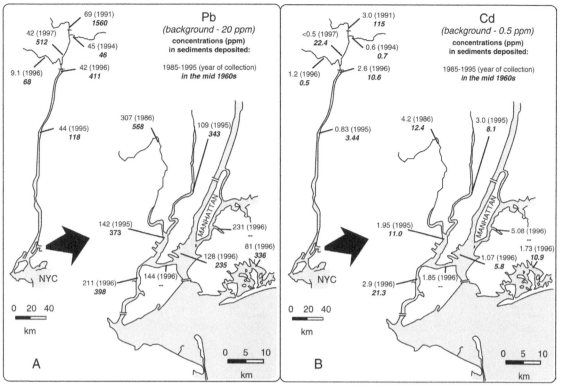

Figure 26.4. Levels of Pb and Cd in Hudson Basin sediment samples. The PEL is 91 ppm for Pb and 3.5 ppm for Cd (Smith et al., 1996). See Figure 26.3 caption for additional details.

The major Pb (Fig. 26.4A), Cd (Fig. 26.4B), and Cr (Fig. 26.5A) source to the main stem Upper Hudson sites appears to be the Hercules/Ciba-Geigy pigment plant (Rohmann, 1985; Eckenfelder Inc., 1991; Bopp et al., 1996; Chillrud, 1996; Chillrud et al., 2003; Chillrud et al., 2004). The mid-1960s Pb concentration at site 1 (1,560 ppm) was the highest at any Hudson site sampled. It is noteworthy that in 1991 deposition, the Pb level (69 ppm) was less than one-twentieth of the mid-1960s value, less than four times background, and below the PEL. Except for Jamaica Bay (site 9; Fig. 26.1), the recent samples from the New York/New Jersey Harbor area exceed the PEL. As expected, levels in mid-1960s samples were all significantly higher. The mid-1960s concentration at the Arthur Kill site, 398 ppm, is somewhat misleading. Samples at this site dating from the early twentieth century had lead levels up to 2,000 ppm, reflecting the smelting history at the nearby National Lead plant (Chillrud, 1996). The Cd data indicate the importance of the

Hercules/Ciba-Geigy source to the Upper Hudson sites. The lack of other significant Cd sources is indicated by the near-background levels at Upper Hudson tributary sites. More detailed data analysis suggests that Hercules/Ciba-Geigy discharges were the main source of Cd to sediments as far downstream as Kingston (site 6; Fig. 26.1; Chillrud, 1996; Chillrud et al., 2004). Thirty-five miles farther downstream, discharges from a battery manufacturing facility on Foundry Cove were an additional significant source of Cd to the lower Hudson (Bower et al., 1978; Knutson, Klerks, and Levinton, 1987). The data for Cr are much more limited. They are consistent with a Hercules/Ciba-Geigy source and significant inputs to the Hackensack River (site 13; Fig. 26.1) from the Berry's Creek Superfund site (Goeller, 1989).

Hg is a toxic metal of particular concern because of its propensity to bioaccumulate in the methylated form. Of all the contaminants monitored in fish of the Upper Hudson, Hg ranks second in

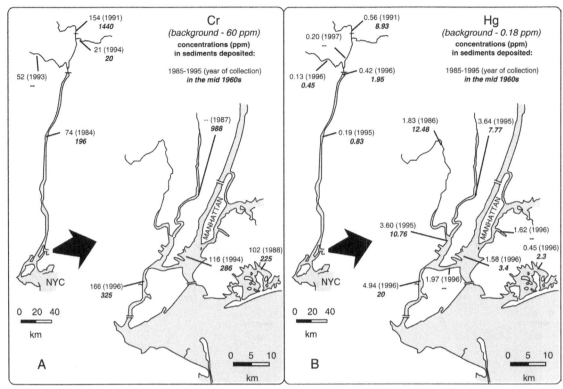

Figure 26.5. Levels of Cr and Hg in Hudson Basin sediment samples. The PEL is 90 ppm for Cr and 0.49 ppm for Hg (Smith et al., 1996). See Figure 26.3 caption for additional details.

significance, behind only PCBs (Sloan, 1999). At site 1 in the Upper Hudson, the high level of Hg in the mid-1960s sample (Fig. 26.5B) is consistent with the production of mercury-based pigments at the Hercules/Ciba-Geigy plant and reports of Hg contamination in soils at the plant site (Eckenfelder Inc., 1991). With the exception of the 1996 sample from Jamaica Bay all the New York/New Jersey Harbor samples exceeded the PEL. The mid-1960s samples provide evidence of major, but poorly characterized, historical sources of Hg, especially to the western harbor complex (Kroenke et al., 1998).

Multiple Co-Located Sediment Cores

Sites in the Hudson Basin that have yielded well-dated sediment cores in the past are typically re-visited every few to several years to extend contaminant chronologies. This procedure, collecting multiple sediment cores spaced several years apart at the same site, was first applied to the

Hudson at our site just downstream of the Statue of Liberty (site 7; Fig. 26.1; Bopp and Simpson, 1989). The initial core, collected in 1979, provided samples dating back to the mid-1950s. A second core collected in 1984 contained several samples that overlapped and confirmed the contaminant chronologies from the first core. Since 1984, we have extended the chronologies at this site through analyses of surficial samples that contained detectable levels of ^{7}Be collected in 1989, 1994, 1998, and 2001. We also conducted similar monitoring at four other mainstem sites in the harbor and in the Kill Van Kull (site 11; Fig. 26.1) and Newtown Creek (Bopp and Walsh, 1994; Chillrud, 1996; Robinson, 2002).

Jamaica Bay cores collected in 1982 and 1988 were used to develop trace metal and chlorinated hydrocarbon chronologies (Bopp et al., 1993). Pb, Zn, Cd, Cr and Hg were each strongly correlated with Cu suggesting that the primary source of these metals to Jamaica Bay was from waste water treatment plants. Cu, Pb, and Zn were analyzed

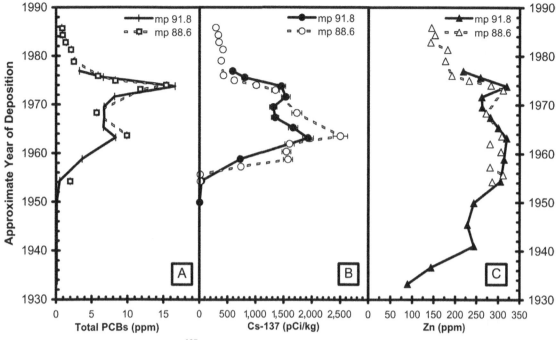

Figure 26.6. Total PCBs (A), [137]Cs (B), and Zn (C) plotted against approximate year of deposition for two sediment cores from the Kingston area (site 6; Fig. 26.1). Model II assigns sedimentation rates of 0.9 to 1.9 cm yr[−1] to the core at mile point 91.8 and 0.85 to 4.0 cm yr[−1] to the core at mile point 88.6. Application of this model produces excellent agreement of the total PCB, ^{137}Cs and Zn chronologies, although some minor discrepancies still exist for other tracers. (Source: Chillrud, 1996)

in several samples from the period of overlap and showed that data from the two cores could be combined in a single extended chronology. This approach was confirmed by trace metal analyses on sections of a third core from this site collected in 1996. Chronologies of Cu, Pb, Zn, Ag, and Cd showed almost perfect agreement with those developed from the 1988 core. The results also indicate that chronologies of metal loadings to Jamaica Bay derived from dated sediment core depth profiles are not significantly affected by pore water mobility of these elements in the anoxic sediments found at the site (Chillrud, unpublished data).

In the mid-tidal Hudson (site 6; Fig. 26.1) cores collected in 1979 and 1986 provided contaminant chronologies extending back several decades (Bopp and Simpson, 1989). With dating based on ^{137}Cs and PCB level time horizons, chronologies developed from the two cores showed excellent agreement (Fig. 26.6; Chillrud, 1996). Analysis of surficial sediment with detectable levels of [7]Be collected in

1995 provided the recent trace metal data reported for this site (Figs. 26.3–26.5).

Cores collected from a cove on the Upper Hudson (site 1; Fig. 26.1) in 1983 (Fig. 26.2C) and 1991 (Fig. 26.2D) had near ideal profiles of ^{137}Cs activity with depth. Trace metal chronologies showed excellent agreement and reflected the importance of Hercules/Ciba-Geigy inputs (Chillrud et al., 2003). These and several other cores from the same cove provided detailed information on the history of PCB inputs to the Upper Hudson from the GE capacitor plants several miles upstream (Brown et al., 1984; Bush et al., 1987; Bopp and Simpson, 1989; TAMS, 1996; McNulty, 1997).

Paired, well-dated cores collected years apart at the same site also provide an excellent means of studying in situ processes such as transformations of organic contaminants. Samples from two co-located cores can be paired on the basis of time of deposition. The paired samples would have similar initial contaminant compositions and concentrations and would have experienced similar depositional and microbial environments. Differences in contaminant composition between paired samples can be interpreted as the result of transformations that occurred during the period between the dates of core collection – an in situ incubation period. This approach was first applied to the microbial reductive dechlorination of PCBs in the mid-tidal Hudson cores from site 6 (Fig. 26.6; Chillrud, 1996) collected seven years apart, in 1979 and 1986. Only minor changes in composition consistent with reductive dechlorination were reported. This study was expanded to include congener-specific PCB analysis and the Upper Hudson cores from site 1 (Figs. 26.2C & D; McNulty, 1997) where PCB concentrations were much higher and in situ PCB dechlorination had been discovered (Brown et al., 1984). For the paired cores from site 1, the in situ incubation period was eight years (1983 to 1991). The observed dechlorination pathways were consistent with those widely reported in laboratory studies (Bedard and Quensen, 1995), but the overall rate and extent of in situ dechlorination at site 1 were significantly less than had been reported in a number of much shorter laboratory incubation experiments. At site 3, the congener-specific PCB analyses revealed minor compositional changes consistent with initial stages of microbial dechlorination (McNulty, 1997) and earlier observations.

The co-located core technique has been recently applied to another class of contaminants, alkylphenol ethoxylate (APEO) metabolites. APEOs are surfactants found in many detergents. The metabolites are of concern because they are persistent in the environment and are endocrine disruptors (Servos, 1999). Jamaica Bay has received significant inputs of APEOs associated with discharges of municipal wastewater. Analyses of sections from the cores collected there in 1988 and 1996 have been used to determine the input history of APEOs and to study the pathways and rates of APEO metabolism (Ferguson et al., 2003).

Conclusions

The natural waters of the Hudson Basin provide some of the best examples of the use of dated sediment cores to derive contaminant chronologies. The chronologies provide a basinwide, multicontaminant perspective that has significantly added

to our understanding of the sources, fate, and transport of particles and associated contaminants in the Hudson. The success of regulatory efforts is evidenced in the significant declines in concentration of many contaminants over the past few decades. Analyses of dated sediments also play a central role in areas of continuing concern and research interest, including the transport of PCBs and metals from the Upper Hudson, the spread of contaminants from other Superfund sites, biologically mediated transformations of contaminants, and atmospheric fluxes of contaminants.

The archiving of well-dated sediment samples is a critical component of our research approach. Samples initially collected and analyzed for PCBs, chlorinated hydrocarbon pesticides, and a few metals (Cu, Pb, and Zn) have formed the basis of our studies of dioxins, PAH, APEO, and a number of additional trace metals (Hg, Cr, As, Sn, Cd, Sb, Ag and others). We are currently using archived harbor sediment samples to provide historical perspective on levels of polybrominated diphenyl ethers, contaminants associated with the World Trade Center disaster. We look forward to more detailed studies of several contaminants (Hg, APEOs, chlordane) and to continued application of state of the art analytical techniques (for example, compound specific GC/IRMS) to extract the maximum amount of information from a unique set of sediment samples.

Acknowledgments

The study of contaminant chronologies in sediments of the Hudson River and the New York/New Jersey Harbor complex is a long term, multicontaminant effort that combines data and insights gained from many specific studies carried out over several decades. Grants from the Hudson River Foundation (HRF), U.S. Environmental Protection Agency, U.S. Department of Energy, National Oceanic and Atmospheric Administration, NYS Department of Environmental Conservation (NYSDEC), NJ Department of Environmental Protection, and the National Institute of Environmental Health Science (NIEHS) have funded numerous scientists and graduate students at the Lamont-Doherty Earth Observatory and RPI where much of the work summarized above was carried out and continues. We specifically thank the HRF for support spanning more than two decades, the NIEHS for support of the Superfund Basic Research Program grant to Mt. Sinai Medical Center (P42 ES07384), and an Environmental Health Center grant to the Columbia University Mailman School of Public Health (P30 ES09089), and NYSDEC for current funding supporting collaboration with scientists of the Contaminated Sediments Section, true partners in the search for well-dated cores. This is LDEO contribution number 6447.

REFERENCES

Alderton, D. H. M. 1985. Sediments, in *Historical Monitoring*, Monitoring and Assessment Research Center, MARC Report No. 31, London. pp. 1–95.

Baker, J. E., Bohlen, W. F., Bopp, R., Brownawell, B., Collier, T. K., Farley, K. J., Geyer, W. R., and Nairn, R. 2001. *PCBs in the Hudson River: The Science Behind the Controversy*. White Paper prepared for the Hudson River Foundation, released October 29, 2001.

Bedard, D. L., and Quensen, III, J. F. 1995. Microbial reductive dechlorination of polychlorinated biphenyls, in L. Y. Young and C. E. Cerniglia (eds.), *Microbial Transformation and Degradation of Toxic Organic Chemicals*. New York: Wiley-Liss, Inc. pp. 127–216.

Benoit, G., Wang, E. X., Nieder, W. C., Levandowsky, M., and Breslin, V. T. 1999. Sources and history of heavy metal contamination and sediment deposition in Tivoli South Bay, Hudson River, New York. *Estuaries* 22:167–78.

Bopp, R. F. 1979. "The geochemistry of polychlorinated biphenyls in the Hudson River," Ph.D. dissertation, Columbia University, New York.

Bopp, R. F., Butler, J. A., Chaky, D. A., Shuster, E. L., Chillrud, S. N., and Estabrooks, F. D. 1996. Geographic and temporal distribution of particle-associated contaminants in sediments of the Hudson River Basin. Abstract, Society of Environmental Toxicology and Chemistry – 17th Annual Meeting, Washington, D.C.

Bopp, R. F., Chillrud, S. N., Shuster, E. L., Simpson, H. J., and Estabrooks, F. D. 1998. Trends in chlorinated hydrocarbon levels in Hudson River Basin sediments. *Environmental Health Perspectives* 106(supplement 4):1075–81.

Bopp, R. F., Gross, M. L., Tong, H. Y., Simpson, H. J., Monson, S. J., Deck, B. L., and Moser, F. C. 1991. A major incident of dioxin contamination: Sediments of New Jersey estuaries. *Environmental Science and Technology* 25:951–56.

Bopp, R. F., and Simpson, H. J. 1989. Contamination of the Hudson River: The sediment record, in *Contaminated Marine Sediments Assessment and Remediation*. Washington, D.C., National Research Council, NAS, pp. 401–416.

Bopp, R. F., Simpson, H. J., Chillrud, S. N., and Robinson, D. W. 1993. Sediment-derived chronologies of persistent contaminants in Jamaica Bay, New York. *Estuaries* 16:608–616.

Bopp, R. F., Simpson, H. J., Olsen, C. R., and Kostyk, N. 1981. Polychlorinated biphenyls in sediments of the tidal Hudson River, New York. *Environmental Science and Technology* 15:210–216.

Bopp, R. F., Simpson, H. J., Olsen, C. R., Trier, R. M., and Kostyk, N. 1982. Chlorinated hydrocarbons and radionuclide chronologies in sediments of the Hudson River and Estuary, New York. *Environmental Science and Technology* 16:666–76.

Bopp, R. F., and Walsh, D. C. 1994. Rivers and estuaries: A Hudson perspective, in *Environmental Science in the Coastal Zone: Issues for Further Research*. Washington, D.C. National Research Council, NAS, pp. 49–66.

Bowen, H. J. M. 1979. *Environmental Chemistry of the Elements*. London: Academic Press.

Bower, P. M., Simpson, H. J., Williams, S. C., and Li, Y. H. 1978. Heavy metals in the sediments of Foundry Cove, Cold Spring, New York. *Environmental Science and Technology* 12:683–7.

Brown, J. F. Jr., Wagner, R. E., Bedard, D. L., Brennan, M. J., Carnahan, J. C., May, R. J., and Tofflemire, T. J. 1984. PCB transformations in upper Hudson sediments. *Northeastern Environmental Science* 3:167–79.

Bush, B., Shane, L. A., Wahlen, M., and Brown, M. P. 1987. Sedimentation of 74 PCB congeners in the Upper Hudson River. *Chemosphere* 16:733–44.

Chaky, D. A. 2003. "The geochemistry of polychlorinated biphenyls, dibenzo-p-dioxins and dibenzofurans in recent sediments of the New York Metropolitan Area," Ph.D. dissertation, Rensselaer Polytechnic Institute, Troy, NY.

Chaky, D. A., Chillrud, S. N., Bopp, R. F., Shuster, E. L., Estabrooks, F. D., and Swart, J. 1998. Chlorinated hydrocarbon contamination of the New York/New Jersey Metropolitan Area: The urban atmospheric influence. *EOS, Transactions of the American Geophysical Union* 79:S86.

Chillrud, S. N. 1996. "Transport and fate of particle associated contaminants in the Hudson River basin," Ph.D. dissertation, Columbia University, NY, 277 pp.

Chillrud, S. N., Bopp, R. F., Ross, J. M., Chaky, D. A., Hemming, S., Shuster, E. L., Simpson, H. J., and Estabrooks, F. 2004. Radiogenic lead isotopes and time stratigraphy in the Hudson River, New York. *Water, Air and Soil Pollution: Focus* **4**:469–82.

Chillrud, S. N., Bopp, R. F., Simpson, H. J., Ross, J., Shuster, E. L., Chaky, D. A., Walsh, D. C., Chin Choy, C., Tolley, L. R., and Yarme, A. 1999. Twentieth century atmospheric metal fluxes into Central Park Lake, New York City. *Environmental Science and Technology* **33**(5):657–62.

Chillrud, S. N., Hemming, S., Shuster, E. L., Simpson, H. J., Bopp, R. F., Ross, J., Pederson, D. C., Chaky, D. A., Tolley, L.-R., and Estabrooks, F. D. 2003. Stable lead isotopes, contaminant metals and radionuclides in upper Hudson River sediment cores: Implications for improved stratigraphy and transport processes. *Chemical Geology* **199**:53–70.

Cochran, J. K., and Aller, R. C. 1979. Particle reworking in sediments from the New York Bight apex: Evidence from ^{234}Th/^{238}U disequilibrium. *Estuarine and Coastal Marine Science* **9**:739–47.

Diamond Shamrock Corporation. 1983. *Report on Lister Avenue Facility*. Prepared for the New Jersey Department of Environmental Protection, Trenton, NJ.

Eckenfelder, Inc. 1991. State-Wide Soil Sampling Report, Ciba-Geigy Main Plant Site, Glens Falls, NY. Prepared for Hercules Inc., Wilmington, DE.

Feng, H., Cochran, J. K., Hirschberg, D. J., and Wilson, R. E. 1998. Small-scale spatial variations of natural radionuclide and trace metal distributions in sediments from the Hudson River Estuary. *Estuaries* **21**:263–80.

Ferguson, P. L., Bopp, R. F., Chillrud, S. N., Aller, R. C., and Brownawell, B. J. 2003. Biogeochemistry of nonlyphenol ethoxylates in urban estuarine sediments. *Environmental Science and Technology* **37**:3499–3506.

Gibbs, R. J. 1994. Metals in the sediments along the Hudson River Estuary. *Environment International* **20**:507–516.

Goeller, A. F. III. 1989. "Heavy metals and radionuclides in sediments of the Hackensack River, New Jersey," Master's thesis, Rutgers University, Newark, NJ.

Hay, A. 1982. *The Chemical Scythe: Lessons of 2,4,5-T and Dioxin*. New York: Plenum Press.

Keane, D. P. 1998. "Temporal trends of saturated and polycyclic aromatic hydrocarbons in the sediments of the Hudson and Passaic River systems," Master's thesis, Rensselaer Polytechnic Institute, Troy, NY.

Knutson, A. B., Klerks, P. L., and Levinton, J. S. 1987. The fate of metal contaminated sediments in Foundry Cove, New York. *Environmental Pollution* **45**:291–304.

Kroenke, A. E., Bopp, R. F., Chaky, D. A., Chillrud, S. N., Shuster, E. L., Estabrooks, F. D., and Swart, J. 1998. Atmospheric Deposition and Fluxes of Mercury in Remote and Urban Areas of the Hudson River Basin, Abstract, *EOS, Transactions of the American Geophysical Union* **79**:S86.

McNulty, A. K. 1997. "In situ anaerobic dechlorination of PCBs in Hudson River sediments," Master's thesis, Rensselaer Polytechnic Institute.

National Oceanic and Atmospheric Administration. 1988. *National Status and Trends Program – A summary of selected data on chemical contaminants in sediments collected during 1984, 1985, 1986, and 1987*. NOAA Technical Memo. NOS OMA 44, Rockville, MD.

NATO. 1988. *International toxicity equivalency factor (I-tef) method of risk assessment for complex mixtures of dioxins and related compounds*, North Atlantic Treaty Organization, Report Number 176.

Olsen, C. R., Simpson, H. J., Bopp, R. F., Williams, S. C., Peng, T.-H., and Deck, B. L. 1978. A geochemical analysis of sediments and sedimentation in the Hudson Estuary. *Journal of Sedimentary Petrology* **48**:401–418.

Olsen, C. R., Simpson, H. J., Peng, T.-H., Bopp, R. F., and Trier, R. M. 1981. Sediment mixing and accumulation rate effects on radionuclide depth profiles in Hudson Estuary sediments. *Journal of Geophysical Research* **86**:11020–28.

O'Malley, V. P., Abrajano Jr., T. A., and Hellou, J. 1996. Stable carbon isotopic apportionment of individual polycyclic aromatic hydrocarbons in St. John's Harbour, Newfoundland. *Environmental Science and Technology* **30**:634–9.

Perry, E. A., Bopp, R., Keane, D., and Abrajano, T. A. 2002. *History of polycyclic aromatic hydrocarbon (PAH) deposition in the New York Harbor*. Abstract, Geological Society of America Northeastern Section – 37th Annual Meeting, Springfield, MA.

Ritchie, J. C., and McHenry, J. R. 1990. Application of radioactive fallout 137Cs for measuring soil erosion and sediment accumulation rates and patterns: A review. *Journal of Environmental Quality* **19**:215–33.

Robideau, R. M. 1997. "Sedimentation rates in Hudson River marshes as determined by radionuclide dating techniques," Master's thesis, Rensselaer Polytechnic Institute, Troy, NY.

Robinson, K. A. 2002. "Chlordane and DDT in the Hudson River Basin, Master's thesis," Rensselaer Polytechnic Institute, Troy, NY.

Rohmann, S. O. 1985. *Tracing a River's Toxic Pollution: A Case Study of the Hudson*. New York: Inform, Inc.

Servos, M. R. 1999. Review of the aquatic toxicity, estrogenic responses and bioaccumulation of alkylphenols and alkylphenol polyethoxylates. *Water Quality Research Journal of Canada* 34: 123–77.

Sloan, R. J. 1999. *Hudson River Fish and the PCB Perspective.* Presentation to the NRC Committee on Remediation of PCB Contaminated Sediments, November 8, 1999, Albany, NY.

Smith, S. L., MacDonald, D. D., Keenleyside, K. A., Ingersoll, C. G., and Field, L. J. 1996. A preliminary evaluation of sediment quality assessment values for freshwater ecosystems. *Journal of Great Lakes Research* 22:624–38.

TAMS Consultants, Inc. and Gradient Corporation. 1996. Database for the Hudson River PCBs Reassessment, Phase 2 Report, *Further Site Characterization and Analysis Database Report, Volume 2A,* U.S. Environmental Protection Agency, Washington, D.C.

USEPA. 2000. *Hudson River PCBs Superfund Site, New York.* Superfund proposed plan, EPA Region 2.

Van den Berg, M., Birnbaum, L., Bosveld, A. T. C., Brunström, B., Cook, P., Feeley, M., Giesy, J. P., Hanberg, A., Hasegawa, R., Kennedy, S. W., Kubiak, T., Larsen, J. C., Van Leeuwen, F. X. R., Liem, A. K. D., Nolt, C., Peterson, R. E., Poellinger, L., Safe, S., Schrenk, D., Tillitt, D., Tysklind, M., Younes, M., Wærn, F., and Zacharewski, T. 1998. Toxic equivalency factors (TEFs) for PCBs, PCDDs, and PCDFs for humans and wildlife. *Environmental Health Perspectives* 106:775–92.

Williams, S. C., Simpson, H. J., Olsen, C. R., and Bopp, R. F. 1978. Sources of heavy metals in sediments of the Hudson River Estuary. *Marine Chemistry* 6:195–213.

Yan, B. 2004. "PAH sources and depositional history in sediments from the lower Hudson River basin," Ph.D. dissertation, Rensselaer Polytechnic Institute, Troy, NY.

Yan, B., Benedict, L. A., Chaky, D. A., Bopp, R. F., and Abrajano, T. A. 2004. Levels and patterns of PAH distribution in sediments of the New York/New Jersey Harbor complex. *Northeastern Geology and Environmental Science* 26(1&2):113–22.

Zamek, E. 2002. "Trace metal chronologies in sediments of the upper Hudson and Mohawk Rivers," Master's thesis, Rensselaer Polytechnic Institute, Troy, NY.

27 Atmospheric Deposition of PCBs and PAHs to the New York/New Jersey Harbor Estuary

Lisa A. Totten, Steven J. Eisenreich,
Cari L. Gigliotti, Jordi Dachs,
Daryl A. VanRy, Shu Yan, and
Michael Aucott

ABSTRACT The objective of this work is to quantify the atmospheric inputs of polychlorinated biphenyls (PCBs) and polycyclic aromatic hydrocarbons (PAHs) to the New York/New Jersey Harbor Estuary. Atmospheric deposition was quantified by measuring eighty-six PCBs and thirty-four PAHs in air (gas and aerosol) and precipitation at three sites: Jersey City (Liberty Science Center), Sandy Hook, and New Brunswick. These sites are part of the New Jersey Atmospheric Deposition Network (NJADN), a research and monitoring network operated on a twelve-day sampling frequency since 1997. The measured concentrations in the three media were used to calculate atmospheric deposition fluxes to the estuary via three processes: (1) gas absorption, (2) dry particle deposition, and (3) wet deposition. Concentrations of PCBs and PAHs were generally highest at Liberty Science Center and lowest at Sandy Hook. For the sum of all PCBs measured (ΣPCBs), these three modes combined deposit between 21 and 56 $\mu g\,m^{-2}\,yr^{-1}$ to the estuary, or about 13 to 41 kg yr^{-1}. Gas absorption is the dominant mode of deposition for most PCBs, due to their relatively high vapor pressures, which cause them to exist primarily in the gas phase in the atmosphere. This input is small compared to the inputs to the estuary from wastewater treatment plants and the upper Hudson River, and also in comparison to the volatilization of PCBs from the water column to the atmosphere. It is two to ten times larger, however, than atmospheric deposition fluxes of PCBs to similar ecosystems, such as the Great Lakes and Chesapeake Bay. For PAHs, the three deposition modes result in loadings of 414–1,890 $\mu g\,m^{-2}\,yr^{-1}$ of phenanthrene, 79–356 $\mu g\,m^{-2}\,yr^{-1}$ for pyrene, and 8–42 $\mu g\,m^{-2}\,yr^{-1}$ for benzo[a]pyrene (BaP). Gas absorption

is the dominant mode of atmospheric deposition for phenanthrene and pyrene. Gas absorption is negligible for BaP due to its higher molecular weight and lower vapor pressure. As with PCBs, these values are two to ten times higher than fluxes of the same PAHs to the Great Lakes and Chesapeake Bay. This difference suggests that the intense urbanization and industrial activity surrounding the New York/New Jersey Harbor Estuary has a large impact on atmospheric loadings of both PCBs and PAHs to the estuary.

Introduction

Atmospheric deposition is the major atmospheric pathway for persistent organic pollutant (POP) input to the large water bodies such as the Great Lakes and Chesapeake Bay (Baker et al., 1997; Eisenreich, Hornbuckle, and Achman, 1997) (Fig. 27.1). For semivolatile organic compounds, such as polychlorinated biphenyls (PCBs) and polycyclic aromatic hydrocarbons (PAHs), atmospheric deposition occurs via three processes: (1) wet deposition via rain and snow, (2) dry deposition of fine and coarse particles, and (3) gaseous air-water exchange. Because atmospheric particles are scavenged efficiently by precipitation, the magnitudes of both wet and dry deposition are usually controlled by the concentration of a pollutant on atmospheric particles. In contrast, gaseous air-water exchange consists of the volatilization of dissolved contaminants into the gas phase, and the opposite effect of absorption of gas-phase pollutants into the water column. Thus, the magnitude of gaseous deposition (absorption) is controlled by the concentration of the pollutant in the gas phase.

PCBs and PAHs are of particular concern in aquatic ecosystems due to their persistence, their tendency to bioaccumulate, and their toxicity. Although other major sources of these contaminants exist within the estuary (for example, wastewater treatment discharges), atmospheric deposition may still be important, especially as management strategies are implemented to reduce point discharges, leaving atmospheric deposition as an uncontrolled source. PCBs are of particular interest in the Hudson River ecosystem due to the well-documented contamination introduced into the Upper Hudson River by plants operated by General Electric (USEPA, 2001). The Upper Hudson has therefore long been recognized as a source of PCBs

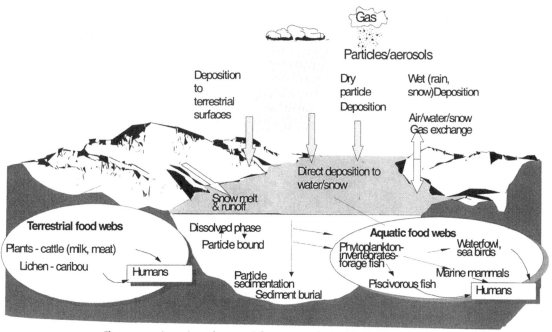

Figure 27.1. Aquatic and terrestrial ecosystem linkages to pollutant cycles.

to the New York/New Jersey Harbor Estuary. Until recently, however, little information was available about sources of PCBs to the New York/New Jersey Harbor other than the Upper Hudson. In particular, almost nothing was known about atmospheric deposition of PCBs to the estuary. In order to quantify these inputs, the New Jersey Atmospheric Deposition Network (NJADN) was established. This network was designed based on the findings of two earlier atmospheric deposition networks, the Integrated Atmospheric Deposition Network (IADN) operating in the Great Lakes (Hoff et al., 1996; Hillery et al., 1998) and the Chesapeake Bay Atmospheric Deposition Study (CBADS) (Baker et al., 1997). Both of these earlier networks were designed to capture the *regional* atmospheric signal, and thus monitoring sites were located in background areas away from local sources. However, many urban/industrial centers are located on or near coastal estuaries (for example, NY/NJ Harbor Estuary and NY Bight) and the Great Lakes (for example, Chicago, IL and southern Lake Michigan). Emissions of pollutants into the urban atmosphere are reflected in elevated local and regional pollutant concentrations and localized intense atmospheric deposition that are *not* observed in the regional signal (Hoff et al., 1996). Higher at-

mospheric concentrations are ultimately reflected in increased precipitation (Offenberg and Baker, 1997) and dry particle fluxes of PCBs and PAHs (Franz, Eisenreich, and Holsen, 1998) and trace metals (Paode et al., 1998; Caffrey et al., 1998) to the coastal waters as well as enhanced air-water exchange fluxes of PCBs (Zhang et al., 1999; Nelson, McConnell, and Baker, 1998; Totten et al., 2001) and PAHs (Bamford et al., 1999; Gigliotti et al., 2001).

Processes of wet and dry deposition and air-water exchange of atmospheric pollutants reflect loading to the water surface directly. This is especially important for aquatic systems that have large surface areas relative to watershed areas (for example, Great Lakes; coastal seas). Water bodies may also be sources of contaminants to the local and regional atmosphere representing losses to the water column. This has been demonstrated in the New York/New Jersey Harbor Estuary for PCBs, PAHs, PCDDs/Fs and nonylphenols (Dachs, Van Ry, and Eisenreich, 1999; Van Ry et al., 2000; Lohmann et al., 2000; Brunciak et al., 2001b; Totten et al., 2001; Gigliotti et al., 2001). However, many aquatic systems have large watershed to lake/estuary areas emphasizing the importance of atmospheric deposition to the watershed (forest, grasslands, crops, paved areas, and wetlands) and the subsequent

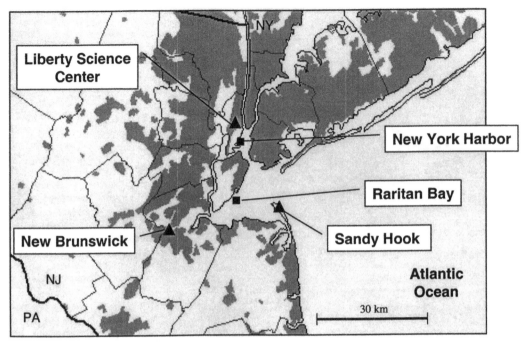

Figure 27.2. Map showing monitoring site locations (triangles) at Liberty Science Center, New Brunswick, and Sandy Hook, and over-water sampling sites (squares) in Raritan Bay and New York Harbor.

leakage of deposited contaminants to the downstream water body (Fig. 27.1). Most lakes and estuaries in the Mid-Atlantic states have large watershed/water area ratios (for example, New York/New Jersey Harbor Estuary, Chesapeake Bay, Delaware River Estuary) emphasizing the potential importance of atmospheric pollutant loading to the watershed and subsequent release to rivers, lakes, and estuaries.

The NJADN was established a) to support the atmospheric deposition component of the New York/New Jersey Harbor Estuary Program; b) to support the Statewide Watershed Management Framework and the National Environmental Performance Partnership System (NEPPS) for New Jersey; c) to assess the magnitude of toxic chemical deposition throughout the State; and d) to assess in-state versus out-of-state sources of air toxic deposition. The NJADN is a collaborative effort of Rutgers University, the New Jersey Department of Environmental Protection (NJDEP), and the Hudson River Foundation. The NJADN is a *research and monitoring* network designed to provide scientific input to the management of the various affected aquatic and terrestrial resources. This

chapter will present results of NJADN through January 2001, including atmospheric concentrations and deposition of PCBs and PAHs relevant to the New York/New Jersey Harbor Estuary.

Description of the Atmospheric Deposition Sites in the New York/ New Jersey Harbor Estuary

The NJADN was initiated in October 1997 with the establishment of a suburban master monitoring and research site at the New Brunswick meteorological station/Rutgers Gardens near Rutgers University (Fig. 27.2). In February 1998, an identical site was established at Sandy Hook to reflect the marine influence on the atmospheric signals and deposition at a coastal site on the New York/New Jersey Harbor Estuary and Raritan Bay. In July 1998, a site was established at the Liberty Science Center in Jersey City to reflect the urban/industrial influence on atmospheric concentrations and deposition in the area of the estuary.

At each land site, a suite of PCB congeners (n = 86) and PAH compounds (n = 34) were measured in atmospheric samples in gaseous and particulate phases, and precipitation; total suspended particulate matter (TSP), PM2.5, and particulate organic carbon and elemental (black or soot) carbon (POC/EC) in PM2.5 aerosol in the majority of samples. Atmospheric samples of gas and particulate phases (organics) were collected one day (24 hours) every twelfth day, and wet-only integrated precipitation was collected over twenty-four days or two air-sampling cycles. Meteorological data were obtained from nearby established meteorological stations.

Framework for Estimating Atmospheric Deposition

Atmospheric deposition may occur by dry particle deposition, wet deposition via rain and snow, and gaseous chemical partitioning into the water from the atmosphere. In this study, deposition to the water surface of the New York/New Jersey Harbor Estuary was calculated as the sum of dry particle deposition, wet deposition, and gaseous chemical absorption into the water column. Deposition was estimated at each of the sites surrounding the estuary (as shown in Fig. 27.1). The framework for converting the PCB and PAH concentrations in the atmosphere and rain to deposition is described in the next sections.

DRY PARTICLE DEPOSITION

Dry deposition describes the process of aerodynamic transport of a particle to the near-surface viscous sublayer where diffusion, turbulent diffusion and gravitational settling deliver the particle to the surface. Zufall et al. (1998) provide convincing evidence that particle deposition is dominated by large particles even though atmospheric particle size distributions are dominated by particles less than 1 μm mass median diameter (mmd). Therefore, the dry deposition flux is calculated as:

$$\text{Flux}_{\text{dry part}} \ (\text{ng m}^{-2}\text{d}^{-1})$$
$$= V_d \ (0.5 \text{ cm s}^{-1}) \times [\text{SOC}_{\text{part}}] \ (\text{pg m}^{-3})$$
$$\times \ 864 \ (\text{unit adjustment}) \tag{1}$$

We selected a value for the V_d of 0.5 cm s^{-1} reflecting the disproportionate influence that large particles have on atmospheric deposition, especially in urbanized and industrialized regions (see Franz et al., 1998; Zufall et al., 1998; Caffrey et al., 1998). We

believe that this may be an underestimate and studies are underway to better estimate particle size – dependent deposition velocities.

WET DEPOSITION

Wet deposition describes the process by which gases and particles are scavenged from the atmosphere (in cloud or below cloud) by raindrops and delivered to the ground. The best way to estimate wet deposition is to collect all rainfall in suitable samplers, measure the contaminant concentrations, and calculate seasonal wet fluxes of chemicals. Thus wet fluxes are estimated as seasonal deposition at each site equipped with a wet-only integrating collector. The collector has a stainless steel surface with a surface area of 0.21 m^2.

$$\text{Flux}_{\text{wet,total}} \ (\text{ng m}^{-2} \text{ yr}^{-1})$$
$$= \text{VWM} \ (\text{ng m}^{-3}) \times \ P \ (\text{m yr}^{-1}) \tag{2}$$

where VMW is the volume weighted concentration (ng m^{-3}), and P is the Precipitation Intensity (m yr^{-1}). Precipitation intensity typically is 1.05 to 1.15 m yr^{-1} in New Jersey.

GASEOUS ABSORPTIVE DEPOSITION

The concepts of air-water exchange and mass transfer of organic chemicals across water surfaces have been described in detail elsewhere (Eisenreich et al., 1997; Liss and Duce, 1997). Diffusive air-water exchange refers to the transfer of chemical across an air-water interface and may be visualized as diffusive transfer of a chemical across near-stagnant layers of 0.1 to 1.0 mm thickness. At low wind speeds, insufficient wind energy exists to mix the air and water films or boundary layers, and a stagnant boundary layer is established (Stagnant Two-Film Model). Higher wind speeds generate more turbulence in the boundary layers, parcels of air and water are forced to the surface, and exchange is dependent on the renewal rate of air and water parcels. In highly turbulent seas, gas exchange is enhanced by breaking waves and bubble ejection. Under turbulence and wind conditions normally occurring in estuaries and lakes, the first two models are most applicable although wind extremes may be very important. The gas-phase concentration in the atmosphere (C_g) attempts to reach equilibrium with the concentration of dissolved gas in water (C_w).

When equilibrium is achieved, the ratio of the gas activities in air and water are constant at a given temperature and are represented by Henry's Law constant (H): $(H = C_g \, C_w^{-1}; \text{Pa m}^3 \text{ mol}^{-1})$. The direction of chemical transfer is from the water to the air when the fugacity in the water exceeds the fugacity (gas phase concentration) in air and is referred to as volatilization. Chemical transfer from the air to the water occurs when the fugacity (that is, activity) in the air $(C_a \, (RT)^{-1})$ exceeds the chemical fugacity in water $(C_w H^{-1})$ and is referred to as gas absorption. The processes of gas absorption and volatilization occur simultaneously, and their difference contributes to the net flux. The magnitude of mass transfer is determined by a mass transfer coefficient (K, m d^{-1}) and the concentration difference:

$$F_{gas,net} = K_{OL} \left(C_d - \frac{C_a}{H'} \right) \qquad (3)$$

where $F_{gas,net}$ is the net flux (ng m^{-2} d^{-1}), K_{OL} (m d^{-1}) is the overall mass transfer coefficient, and $(C_d - C_a/H')$ describes the fugacity gradient (ng m^{-3}); C_d (ng m^{-3}) is the dissolved phase concentration of the compound in water; C_a (ng m^{-3}) is the gas phase concentration of the compound in air which is divided by the dimensionless Henry's Law Constant, H', $H' = H/RT$; R is the universal gas constant (8.315 Pa m^3 K^{-1} mol^{-1}); H is the temperature-specific Henry's Law Constant (Pa m^3 mol^{-1}); and T is the temperature at the air-water interface (K). For the New York/New Jersey Harbor Estuary, we estimated only the gaseous chemical absorption (F$_{abs}$) across the water surface; volatilization was not estimated because it is a loss rather than depositional term, and spatially- and temporally-distributed dissolved water concentrations were not available. The relevant equation then becomes:

$$F_{abs} \text{ (ng m}^{-2} \text{ d}^{-1})$$
$$= K_{OL} \text{ (m d}^{-1})(-C_g RT/H)(\text{ng m}^{-3}) \qquad (4)$$

The negative sign on the flux simply means that the direction of transfer is from the air to the water. The mass transfer coefficient is dependent on turbulent mixing in the boundary layers on either side of the air-waxster interface, which is highly correlated with wind speed (Wanninkhof, 1992; Wanninkhof and McGillis, 1999). In addition, the K$_{OL}$ is dependent on the Henry's Law Constant, which is a func-

tion of temperature and the diffusivity of the compound in air and water. Examples of the application of the calculation can be found in Zhang et al. (1998), Nelson et al. (1998), Bamford et al. (1999), Totten et al. (2001), and Gigliotti et al. (2001).

It is important that the corresponding volatilization term also be estimated for mass budget calculations but this requires dissolved water concentrations of the target chemical. Later in this chapter, results of intensive field measurements of air and water concentrations measured simultaneously in the estuary in July 1998 will be reported, and the resulting absorption, volatilization, and net air-water exchange fluxes for PCBs and PAHs. Technically, only gas absorption contributes to atmospheric deposition. In the future, we will estimate the seasonal and annual cycle of air-water exchange fluxes (absorption, volatilization, and net air-water exchange) for PCBs and PAHs utilizing water concentrations measured in all seasons.

NJADN in the New York/New Jersey Harbor Estuary

The time-dependent concentrations of many organic compounds at the three sites that are used to estimate deposition to the estuary exhibit significant variability. Therefore, we will present first summaries of the meteorological and hydrological data, followed by examples of the variability in concentrations for some compounds. This will be followed by a series of tables describing annual atmospheric loading resulting from dry particle deposition, wet deposition/and gas absorption across the water surface of the estuary based on measurements at New Brunswick, Sandy Hook, and the Liberty Science Center through January 2001.

AIR AND WATER TEMPERATURES, WIND SPEED, AND PRECIPITATION

Calculation of dry particle deposition, wet deposition, and gas absorptive fluxes of target organic chemicals to the New York/New Jersey Harbor Estuary requires knowledge of the air temperatures and wind speeds at the three sites surrounding the estuary (New Brunswick, Sandy Hook, Liberty Science Center), and the mean surface skin temperature of the water body. Figure 27.3 (upper panel) portrays the mean daily air temperatures for the

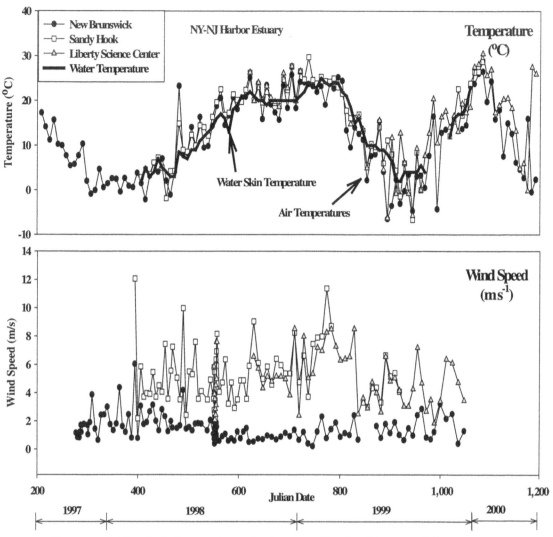

Figure 27.3. Meteorological parameters at the three sampling sites. Upper panel shows temperatures at Liberty Science Center, New Brunswick, and Sandy Hook as well as water surface skin temperatures in Raritan Bay measured by remote sensing. Lower panel shows wind speeds at Liberty Science Center, New Brunswick, and Sandy Hook.

New Brunswick, Sandy Hook, and Liberty Science Center sites from October 1997 through June 2000. The winter mean daily temperatures ranged from approximately 0°C in the winter to 22–25°C in the summer. The mean daily surface skin temperature in the open estuary, determined by remote sensing in the IR band, followed the air temperature very closely as expected due to coupling of the air and water. The mean daily wind speeds at the Sandy Hook and Liberty Science Center sites on the estuary were significantly higher than at the land-locked New Brunswick site yielding

conservative estimates of exchange at the latter. Typical daily mean wind speeds at New Brunswick varied from $\sim$2–4 m s^{-1} whereas wind speeds at the other sites ranged from 2 to as much as 12 m s^{-1} depending on storm activity, season, and sea breezes.

Precipitation intensity or volumes were summed over the four seasons of winter (Dec–Feb), spring (Mar–May), summer (Jun–Aug), and fall (Sep–Nov). The mean annual precipitation (thirty-year average) for the estuary is $\sim$1.1 m yr^{-1}. Precipitation intensity over the study period ranged from

Figure 27.4. Gas-phase ΣPCB concentrations (pg m^{-3}) measured at Liberty Science Center (triangles), New Brunswick (diamonds) and Sandy Hook (squares).

0.9 m yr^{-1} at New Brunswick to 1.68 m yr^{-1} at the Liberty Science Center, the latter being mostly due to high summer rains locally at the Liberty Science Center. Although precipitation volumes used in deposition calculations derive from measurements at each site, they are similar to the data collected at the major regional airports of Newark International and JFK International.

POLYCHLORINATED BIPHENYLS (PCBs)

As is typical for atmospheric samples, about 90 percent of the total PCBs in the atmosphere at the three sampling sites was in the gas phase, with the other ∼10 percent sorbed to airborne particles (aerosols). This percentage sorbed to particles is higher during colder sampling periods due to the decrease in vapor pressure of PCB congeners at lower temperatures, increasing sorption onto airborne particles. The percentage is also higher for the higher MW PCBs. For the octa- and nonachloro congeners, for example, perhaps 50 percent of their total atmospheric concentration is in the particle phase during the warmer months, while essentially 100 percent is sorbed to particles in the winter. Thus the gas-phase PCB concentrations are best used to illustrate spatial differences between

the three sampling sites. ΣPCB gaseous concentrations varied from 96 to 3,800 pg m^{-3} at Liberty Science Center, from 40 to 2,300 pg m^{-3} at New Brunswick, and from 77 to 1,800 pg m^{-3} at Sandy Hook. Although the temporal trends of total concentrations were significantly different at the three sites ($p < 0.01$), PCB congener profiles were similar ($r^2 > 0.90, p < 0.001$), implicating a dominant emission type and/or process. The concentrations were typically highest at the Liberty Science Center and lowest at Sandy Hook. Temporal changes in congener distribution at the suburban site are consistent with the preferential atmospheric removal of 3 to 5 Cl-substituted biphenyls by hydroxyl radical attack with estimated half-lives of 0.7 to 1.8 years (Brunciak et al., 2001b).

The gaseous ΣPCB concentrations are driven primarily by temperature and take the same shape as the annual variation in temperature (Fig. 27.4). One way to investigate the effect of temperature on gas-phase chemical concentrations is to plot the natural log of the gas-phase concentration versus the inverse of the temperature (in degrees K), similar to a Clausius-Clapeyron plot. When this is done for the data from the three sites, the R^2 values are greater than 0.5, suggesting that temperature

Table 27.1. Annual PCB deposition fluxes ($\mu g\ m^{-2}\ yr^{-1}$)

Site	Liberty Science Center			New Brunswick			Sandy Hook		
Deposition mode	Wet	Dry	Gas	Wet	Dry	Gas	Wet	Dry	Gas
Homolog group									
2	0.12	0.032	7.4	0.032	0.0050	0.72	0.028	0.0019	2.6
3	0.47	1.3	22	0.22	0.61	1.9	0.090	0.43	7.9
4	0.74	1.8	11	0.21	0.89	1.1	0.26	0.45	6.0
5	0.86	1.5	3.5	0.25	0.66	0.43	0.15	0.40	1.8
6	0.86	2.0	1.6	0.21	0.57	0.18	0.11	0.35	0.72
7	0.43	1.3	0.66	0.091	0.29	0.089	0.066	0.19	0.25
8	0.38	0.74	0.28	0.081	0.16	0.044	0.047	0.11	0.098
9	0.043	0.092	0.011	0.011	0.021	0.0016	0.0065	0.014	0.0044
ΣPCBs	3.9	8.4	46	1.1	3.4	4.4	0.75	1.9	19

explains more than 50 percent of the variability in gas-phase ΣPCB concentrations at these sites. In addition, the PCB congener profiles are very similar amongst sampling sites and also with the dissolved phase PCB profile from the water of the New York/New Jersey Harbor Estuary (Brunciak et al., 2001b; Totten et al., 2001). This suggests that PCBs are volatilized into the atmosphere from the water and land surfaces in and near the urban area during periods of higher temperature and deposited during periods of low temperatures.

Table 27.1 presents a summary of the dry particle deposition, wet deposition (VanRy et al., 2002) and gas absorption of ΣPCBs, selected PCB congeners and PCB homologues on an annual basis at the Liberty Science Center, Sandy Hook, and New Brunswick ($\mu g\ m^{-2}\ yr^{-1}$). The gaseous PCB concentrations at New Brunswick were included in the calculation of gas absorption into the New York/New Jersey Harbor Estuary even though the site is physically removed from the estuary. The PCB gas absorptive fluxes at New Brunswick will be an underestimate based on lower observed wind speeds.

These are the first comprehensive estimates of PCB deposition to the New York/New Jersey Harbor Estuary and the Lower Hudson River Estuary. Table 27.2 compares the atmospheric ΣPCB fluxes on an annual basis for wet and dry particle deposition, and gas absorption to values published for the Great Lakes from IADN (Hoff et al., 1996; Hillery et al., 1998) and Chesapeake Bay from CBADS (Baker et al., 1997). Atmospheric fluxes to the estuary due to precipitation and dry particle deposition are perhaps two to ten times fluxes reported for the other systems. If gas absorptive inputs are included,

Table 27.2. Comparison of Atmospheric Fluxes of ΣPCBs ($\mu g\ m^{-2}\ yr^{-1}$) to various aquatic ecosystems

	Wet	Dry	Gas	Total
NY/NJ Harbor Estuary				
Liberty Science Center	1.4	8.4	46	56
New Brunswick	0.47	3.4	4.4	8.3
Sandy Hook	0.29	1.9	19	21
Chesapeake Bay (Elms, CBADS)	0.4–1.9	1.4	—	1.8–3.3
(Baker et al., 1997)				
Great Lakes (Michigan, IADN)	0.57	0.4–1.9	—	1.0–2.5
(Hoff et al., 1996; Hillery et al., 1998)				
Coastal Wetlands, Long Island Sound				5–150
(Personal communication, B. Brownawell, SUNY/SB)				

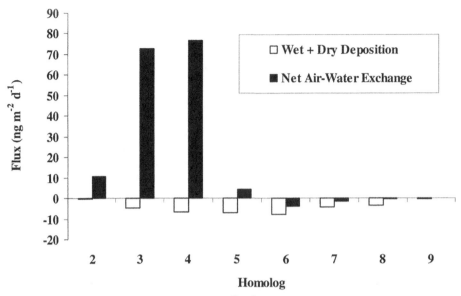

Figure 27.5. Net air-water exchange fluxes (ng m^{-2} d^{-1}) of PCB homologs measured in Raritan Bay during 1999–2001 (black bars) and wet plus dry atmospheric deposition fluxes measured at Jersey City during 1998–2001. The total interaction of the estuary with the atmosphere, encompassing gas exchange, dry and wet deposition, results in a net loss of low MW PCBs (congeners containing 3–4 chlorines) from the water column, but a net input of PCBs containing 6–9 chlorines.

total atmospheric fluxes increase by five to ten times. These fluxes are lower than the PCB accumulation rates in wetland sediments at the lower end of Long Island Sound, which may represent an atmospheric input signal (personal communication; B. Brownawell, State University of New York at Stony Brook).

The absorptive input of gaseous PCBs dominates the atmospheric deposition signal. However the high concentrations of PCBs in the water column of the estuary coming from upstream flow in the Hudson River, other tributary inputs, and discharges from the approximately twenty wastewater treatment facilities contribute to a large volatilization flux (for example, see Totten et al., 2001, and Yan, 2003). Totten et al. (2001) and Yan (2003) report the absorptive, volatilization, and net fluxes of PCBs from the estuary for July 1998 through April 2001 based on simultaneously measured air and water concentrations of PCBs in Raritan Bay and New York Bay and estimated air-water fluxes based on fugacity gradients and mass transfer driven by wind-induced turbulence. Not surprisingly, volatilization greatly exceeds absorption, even though absorption dominates total atmospheric deposition.

Figure 27.5 demonstrates that air-water exchange (the balance between gas absorption and volatilization) is dominated by low molecular weight PCBs (those with three or four chlorines). For these congeners, the dry and wet deposition fluxes are comparatively small, and the overall interaction of the estuary with the atmosphere results in a net loss of these congeners. In contrast, for the high molecular weight PCBs (those having six or more chlorines), air-water exchange is near equilibrium, such that wet and dry deposition result in a net loading of PCBs from the atmosphere to the estuary. Thus the total interaction of the estuary with the atmosphere, encompassing gas exchange, dry and wet deposition, probably results in a net loss of low MW PCBs (congeners containing 3–4 chlorines) from the water column, but a net input of PCBs containing 6–9 chlorines.

Compared with other inputs of PCBs to the New York/New Jersey Harbor Estuary, atmospheric deposition is small. Durell and Lizotte (1998) estimate that the twenty-six water pollution control plants on the estuary discharge about 88 kg of PCBs per year into the estuary. In addition, Farley et al. (1999) estimate that the annual input of PCBs from the upper Hudson River at the Federal Dam in Troy,

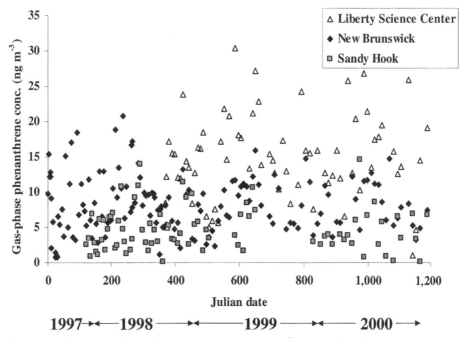

Figure 27.6. Gas-phase phenanthrene concentrations (ng m^{-3}) measured at Liberty Science Center (triangles), New Brunswick (diamonds) and Sandy Hook (squares).

New York is about 250 kg (1997 numbers). Assuming that the plume of atmospheric contamination extends throughout the New York/New Jersey Harbor Estuary (surface area ~ 811 km^2 from Klinkhammer and Bender, 1981), the current estimates of atmospheric deposition result in about 13–41 kg yr^{-1} of ΣPCBs being deposited into the estuary.

POLYCYCLIC AROMATIC HYDROCARBONS (PAHs)

Polycyclic aromatic hydrocarbons (PAHs) are ubiquitous compounds containing two to eight rings that arise from the incomplete combustion of fossil fuels and wood. Forest fires and volcanoes contribute to the PAH burden, but by far, anthropogenic sources are responsible for the majority of the PAH input to the atmosphere, which in turn contributes to depositional loadings to aquatic and terrestrial systems. The largest anthropogenic sources of PAHs are vehicular emissions from both gasoline and diesel powered vehicles, coal and oil combustion, petroleum refining, natural gas consumption, and municipal and industrial/municipal incinerators. Once they enter the atmosphere, PAHs redistribute between the gas and particle phases and are subject to removal

mechanisms such as oxidative and photolytic reactions, and wet and dry deposition.

Gigliotti et al. (2000) and Gigliotti (2003) report PAH data from Liberty Science Center, New Brunswick, and Sandy Hook. Thirty-six PAHs were analyzed at both sites including phenanthrene and benzo[a]pyrene (BaP) whose concentrations ranged from 0.18 to 31.5 ng m^{-3} and from below detection limit to 1.4 ng m^{-3}, respectively. PAH concentrations at the suburban site were about two times higher than concentrations measured at the coastal site, consistent with the closer proximity of New Brunswick to urban/industrial regions than Sandy Hook. The seasonal trends of particulate PAH concentrations indicate that PAH sources such as fuel consumption for domestic heating and vehicular traffic drive their seasonal occurrence. Gas-phase concentrations of methylated phenanthrenes and pyrene and particle-phase concentrations of most high molecular weight PAHs were higher during the winter. In contrast, phenanthrene and fluoranthrene show the opposite seasonal trend with concentrations peaking in the summer months. Because temperature accounted for less than 25 percent of the variability in atmospheric concentrations of these two PAHs in

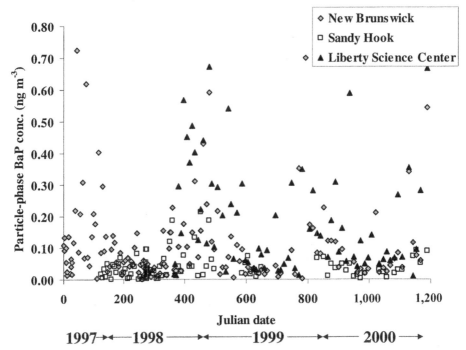

Figure 27.7. Particle-phase benzo[a]pyrene concentrations (ng m^{-3}) measured at Liberty Science Center (triangles), New Brunswick (diamonds) and Sandy Hook (squares).

the Clausius-Clapeyron plots, seasonal variability could not be attributed to temperature-controlled air-surface exchange. PAH concentrations in the New Jersey coastal atmosphere indicate the importance of local and regional sources originating from urban/industrial areas to the north, northeast, and southwest. As expected, PAH concentrations at the Liberty Science Center in the heart of the urban-industrial region of the estuary were nearly always greater than those measured at New Brunswick and Sandy Hook.

Gas-phase phenanthrene concentrations are highest at the Liberty Science Center and typically lowest at the coastal Sandy Hook site (Fig. 27.6). On average, the concentrations of phenanthrene are about 2.5 times lower at Sandy Hook than at New Brunswick. Phenanthrene concentrations at Sandy Hook vary between $\sim$2–5 ng m^{-3} in the summer but may increase to perhaps 5–10 ng m^{-3} in the colder months.

In contrast to phenanthrene, which is found almost exclusively in the gas phase, Figure 27.7 shows the measured particulate concentrations of BaP, which is found almost exclusively in the particle phase. BaP is a well-known product of fossil fuel combustion. The concentrations of particulate BaP (typically ten times lower than phenanthrene concentrations) are perhaps five to ten times higher in the winter atmosphere than in summer, and are considerably higher at the urban-industrial and suburban sites than at the coastal Sandy Hook site.

Table 27.3 is a summary of the dry particle deposition, wet deposition, and gas absorption of PAHs on an annual basis (μg m^{-2} yr^{-1}) to the estuary as represented by the Liberty Science Center, New Brunswick, and Sandy Hook sites. The gaseous PAH concentrations at New Brunswick were included in the calculation of gas absorption into the estuary even though the site is physically removed from the estuary.

As with PCBs, these are the first comprehensive estimates of PAH deposition to the New York/New Jersey Harbor Estuary and the Lower Hudson River Estuary. Comparing only wet and dry particle deposition amongst the systems (Table 27.4), the New York/New Jersey Harbor Estuary is loaded at a rate of approximately two to ten times the rates reported for the Great Lakes from IADN (Hoff et al., 1996; Hillery et al., 1998) and Chesapeake Bay from CBADS (Baker et al., 1997) from the 1990s. The

Table 27.3. PAH deposition fluxes µg m^{-2} yr^{-1}

PAH	Liberty Science Center			New Brunswick			Sandy Hook		
	wet	dry	gas	wet	dry	gas	wet	dry	gas
Fluorene	8.9	7.8	579	1.6	6.6	78	2.1	3.5	212
Phenanthrene	45	48	1,797	10	33	371	9.4	16	644
Anthracene	5.1	14	88	0.80	4.2	11	1.0	2.6	17
1 Methylfluorene	6.6	8.6	250	3.4	6.9	44	3.4	1.9	121
Dibenzothiophene	5.1	14	189	0.93	6.3	24	2.7	3.0	62
4,5-Methylenephenanthrene	6.9	11	174	0.96	4.9	24	1.1	2.4	49
Methylphenanthrenes	50	91	1,839	7.4	52	443	9.5	28	788
Methyldibenzothiophenes	3.8	12	157	0.49	5.6	21	0.94	3.2	68
Fluoranthrene	42	71	419	10	41	75	6.4	18	136
Pyrene	31	67	258	6.5	31	41	4.2	14	72
3,6-Dimethylphenanthrene	3.5	10	100	0.48	4.5	11	0.93	1.8	31
Benzo[a]fluorene	6.2	29	39	1.4	10	3.3	1.5	4.1	7.0
Benzo[b]fluorene	2.7	13	9.6	0.47	4.8	1.2	0.46	1.7	1.8
Retene	1.5	12	11	0.37	5.6	3.2	0.40	2.9	6.0
Benzo[b]naphtho[2,1-d]thiophene	3.0	15	2.8	0.59	6.0	0.21	0.66	2.3	1.7
Cyclopenta[cd]pyrene	0.93	12	1.3	0.70	6.2	0.51	0.45	1.7	0.086
Benz[a]anthracene	11	39	1.7	1.6	15	0.22	1.3	5.1	0.25
Chrysene/Triphenylene	18	70	7.5	4.6	34	1.6	2.9	14	2.0
Naphthacene	26	8.7	0.55	0.46	1.8	0.17	0.40	0.50	0.032
Benzo[b+k]fluoranthrene	17	110	1.6	7.5	65	0.42	5.4	26	0.30
Benzo[e]pyrene	13	65	0.70	4.1	27	0.21	2.6	12	0.23
Benzo[a]pyrene	11	30	0.65	2.5	16	0.14	1.6	6.6	0.16
Perylene	3.8	9.1	0.15	2.2	3.7	0.033	0.89	1.6	0.035
Indeno[1,2,3-cd]pyrene	22	86	0.49	6.3	37	0.12	3.5	18	0.13
Benzo[g,h,i]perylene	10	68	0.36	3.1	35	0.18	2.0	14	0.10
Dibenzo[a,h+a,c] anthracene	2.8	8.3	0.064	0.46	5.2	0.014	0.31	2.1	0.020
Coronene	6.7	84	0.28	2.0	34	0.11	1.4	14	0.14

Table 27.4. Fluxes (µg m^{-2} yr^{-1}) of Phenanthrene, Pyrene and Benzo[a]pyrene to the NY/NJ Harbor Estuary: Comparison to Lake Michigan and the Chesapeake Bay

		Liberty Science Center	New Brunswick	Sandy Hook	Lake Michigan[a]	Chesapeake Bay[b]
Phenanthrene	wet	45	10	9	4.4	5.7
	dry	48	33	16	1.7	9.1
	gas	1,797	371	644	133	300
	total	1,890	414	669	139	315[c]
Pyrene	wet	31	6.5	4.2	2.7	10
	dry	67	31	14	2	9.6
	gas	258	41	72	34	50
	total	356	79	90	39	70[c]
Benzo[a]pyrene	wet	11	2.5	1.6	2.4	2
	dry	30	16	6.6	1	3.3
	gas	0.65	0.14	0.16	1.7	–
	total	42	19	8	5.1	5.3

Sources: [a] Hoff et al., 1996; [b] Baker et al., 1997; [c] Nelson et al., 1998.

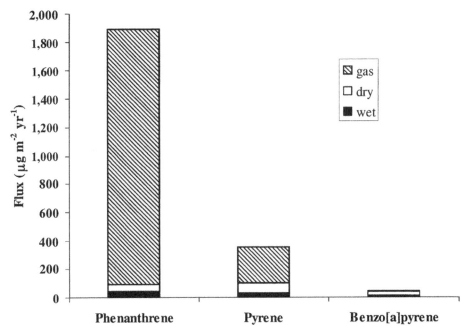

Figure 27.8. Atmospheric deposition fluxes (μg m^{-2} yr^{-1}) of three PAHs measured at Liberty Science Center via gas absorption (striped), wet deposition (black), and dry particle deposition (white).

absorptive input of gaseous PAHs dominates the atmospheric signal for the more volatile phenanthrene but plays no significant role for the mostly particle-bound BaP. The elevated atmospheric deposition of PAHs to the New York/New Jersey Harbor Estuary is consistent with the proximity of higher local and regional emissions in the estuary and near the monitoring stations.

Figure 27.8 depicts the atmospheric deposition of phenanthrene, pyrene, and BaP at Liberty Science Center. Whereas the deposition of phenanthrene (which exists largely in the gas phase) is overwhelmingly dominated by gas absorption, dry particle deposition and precipitation inputs dominate for BaP, which exists primarily in the particle phase in the atmosphere. Phenanthrene deposition is more or less uniform over the seasons, whereas BaP is dominated by higher deposition in the winter months due to higher particulate emissions.

Summary

The New York/New Jersey Harbor Estuary receives substantial inputs of organic contaminants from upstream Hudson River flow, other tribu-

tary flow, discharge of wastewater treatment plants and CSOs, resuspension of historically contaminated sediments, and atmospheric deposition. Farley et al. (1999) has described the PCB and other organic chemical inputs to the New York/New Jersey Harbor Estuary and has concluded that PCB volatilization from the river and estuarine waters may be an important loss term for the water column. We have estimated the contributions of wet and dry particle deposition and atmospheric gas phase absorption across the water surface of PCBs and PAHs to the estuary to total atmospheric deposition. Although gas absorption of PCBs dominates inputs, loss by volatilization exceeds atmospheric deposition by approximately five times. Total PCB loading from the atmosphere is about 30–90 ng m^{-2} d^{-1} depending on which land-based data are used. Atmospheric fluxes to the estuary due to precipitation and dry particle deposition are perhaps two to ten times fluxes reported for the other systems. If gas absorptive inputs are included, total atmospheric fluxes increase by five to ten times. These fluxes are lower than the PCB accumulation rates in wetland sediments at the lower end of Long Island Sound, which may represent an atmospheric input signal. Comparing only wet and dry particle deposition for PAHs amongst the New York/New Jersey Harbor Estuary, Great Lakes, and Chesapeake Bay, the New York/New Jersey Harbor Estuary is loaded at a rate of approximately two to ten times the rates reported for the Great Lakes from IADN (Hoff et al., 1996; Hillery et al., 1998) and Chesapeake Bay from CBADS (Baker et al., 1997) from the 1990s. The absorptive input of gaseous PAHs dominates the atmospheric signal for the more volatile phenanthrene but plays no significant role for the mostly particle-bound BaP. The elevated atmospheric deposition of PAHs to the estuary is consistent with the proximity of higher local and regional emissions in the estuary and near its monitoring stations.

REFERENCES

Baker, J. E., Poster, D. L., Clark, C. L., Church, T. M., Scudlark, T. L., Ondov, J. M., Dickhut, R. M., and Cutter, G. 1997. Loadings of atmospheric trace elements and organic contaminants to the Chesapeake Bay, in J. E. Baker(ed.), *Atmospheric Deposition of Contaminants in the Great Lakes and Coastal Waters*. Pensacola, FL: SETAC Press, pp. 171–94.

Bamford, H. A., Offenberg, J. H., Larsen, R. K., Ko, F.-C., and Baker, J. E. 1999. Diffusive exchange of polycyclic aromatic hydrocarbons across the air-water interface of the Patapsco River, an urbanized subestuary of the Chesapeake Bay. *Environmental Science and Technology* 33:2138–44.

Bidleman, T. F., Alegria, H., Ngabe, B., and Green, C. 1998. Trends of chlordane and toxaphene in ambient air of Columbia, South Carolina. *Atmospheric Environment* 32:1849–56.

Brunciak, P. A., Dachs, J., Franz, T. P., Gigliotti, C. L., Nelson, E. D., Turpin, B. J., and Eisenreich, S. J. 2001a. Polychlorinated biphenyls and particulate organic/elemental carbon in the atmospheres of Chesapeake Bay, USA. *Atmospheric Environment* 35:5663–77.

Brunciak, P. A., Dachs, J., Gigliotti, C. L., Nelson, E. D., and Eisenreich, S. J. 2001b. Atmospheric polychlorinated biphenyl concentrations and apparent degradation in coastal New Jersey. *Atmospheric Environment* 35:3325–39.

Caffrey, P. F., Ondov, J. M., Zufall, M. J., and Davidson, C. I. 1998. Determination of size-dependent dry particle deposition velocities with multiple intrinsic elemental tracers. *Environmental Science and Technology* 32:1615–22.

Cotham, W. E., and Bidleman, T. F. 1995. Polycyclic aromatic hydrocarbons and polychlori-nated biphenyls in air at an urban and a rural site near Lake Michigan. *Environmental Science and Technology* 29:2782–9.

Dachs, J., Van Ry, D. A., and Eisenreich, S. J. 1999. Occurrence of estrogenic nonylphenols in the urban and coastal atmosphere of the lower Hudson River Estuary. *Environmental Science and Technology* 33:2676–9.

Durell, G. S., and Lizotte, R. D. 1998. PCB levels at 26 New York City and New Jersey WPCPs that discharge to the New York/New Jersey Harbor Estuary. *Environmental Science and Technology*. 32:1022–31.

Eisenreich, S. J., Gigliotti, C. L., Brunciak, P. A., Dachs, J., Glenn, IV, T. R., Nelson, E. D., Totten, L. A., and Van Ry, D. A. 2000. Persistent organic pollutants in the coastal atmosphere of the Mid-Atlantic States of the United States of America, in Lipnick, R., J. L. M. Hermens, K. C. Jones, and D. C. G. Muir (eds.), *Persistent Bioaccumulative and Toxic Chemicals*. American Chemical Society Symposium Series, Washington DC, pp. 28–57.

Eisenreich, S. J., Hornbuckle, K. C., and Achman, D. R. 1997. Air-water exchange of semivolatile organic chemicals in the Great Lakes, in Baker, J. E. (ed.), *Atmospheric Deposition of Contaminants to the Great Lakes and Coastal Waters*. Boca Raton, FL: SETAC Press, pp. 109–36.

Eisenreich, S. J., Reinfelder, J. R., Gigliotti, C. L., Totten, L. A., VanRy, D. A., Glenn, IV, T. R., Brunciak, P. A., Nelson, E. D., Dachs, J., Yan, S., and Zhuang, Y. 2001. *The New Jersey Atmospheric Deposition Network (NJADN)*. Report to the New Jersey Department of Environmental Protection.

Farley, K. J., Thomann, R. V., Cooney, III, T. F., Damiani, D. R., and Wands, J. R. March 1999. *Report: An Integrated Model of Organic Chemical Fate and Bioaccumulation in the Hudson River Estuary*. The Hudson River Foundation, New York.

Franz, T. P., Eisenreich, S. J., and Holsen, T. M. 1998. Dry deposition of particulate polychlorinated biphenyls and polycyclic aromatic hydrocarbons to Lake Michigan. *Environmental Science and Technology* 32:3681–8.

Gigliotti, C. L. 2003. "Environmental origin, chemical transport, and fate of hazardous pollutants in atmospheric and aquatic systems in the Mid-Atlantic region." Ph.D. thesis. Department of Environmental Sciences, Rutgers University, New Brunswick, NJ.

Gigliotti, C. L., Brunciak, P. A., Dachs, J., Glenn, IV, T. R., Nelson, E. D., Totten, L. A., and Eisenreich, S. J. 2001. Air-water exchange of polycyclic aromatic hydrocarbons in the NY–NJ Harbor Estuary. *Environmental Toxicology and Chemistry* 21:235–44.

Gigliotti, C. L., Dachs, J., Nelson, E. D., Brunciak, P. A., and Eisenreich, S. J. 2000. Polycyclic aromatic hydrocarbons in the New Jersey coastal atmosphere. *Environmental Science and Technology* **34**:3547–54.

Harner, T., and Bidleman, T. F. 1998. Octanol-air partition coefficient for describing particle/gas partitioning of aromatic compounds in urban air. *Environmental Science and Technology* **32**:1494–1502.

Hillery, B. R., Simcik, M. F., Basu, I., Hoff, R. M., Strachan, W. M. J., Burniston, D., Chan, C. H., Brice, K. A., Sweet, C. W., and Hites, R. A. 1998. Atmospheric deposition of toxic pollutants to the Great Lakes as measured by the integrated atmospheric deposition network. *Environmental Science and Technology* **32**:2216–21.

Hoff, R. M., Strachan, W. M. J., Sweet, C. W., Chan, C. H., Shackleton, M., Bidleman, T. F., Brice, K. A., Burniston, D. A., Cussion, S., Gatz, D. F., Harlin, K., and Schroeder, W. H. 1996. Atmospheric deposition of toxic chemicals to the Great Lakes: A review of data through 1994. *Atmospheric Environment* **30**:3505–27.

Klinkhammer, G. P., and Bender, M. L. 1981. Trace metal distributions in the Hudson River estuary. *Estuarine, Coastal and Shelf Science* **12**:629–43.

Liss, P. S., and Duce, R. A. (eds). 1997. *The Sea Surface and Global Change*. Cambridge, UK: Cambridge University Press.

Lohmann, R., Nelson, E. D., Eisenreich, S. J., Jones, K. C. 2000. Evidence for Dynamic Air-Water Exchange of PCDD/Fs: A Study in the Raritan Bay/Hudson River Estuary. *Environmental Science and Technology* **34**:3086–93.

Miller, S. M., Green, M. L., DePinto, J. V., and Hornbuckle, K. C. 2001. Results from the Lake Michigan Mass Balance Study: Concentrations and fluxes of atmospheric polychlorinated biphenyls and trans-nonachlor. *Environmental Science and Technology* **35**:278–85.

Nelson, E. D., McConnell, L. L., and Baker, J. E. 1998. Diffusive exchange of gaseous polycyclic aromatic hydrocarbons and polychlorinated biphenyls across the air-water interface of the Chesapeake Bay. *Environmental Science and Technology* **32**:912–19.

Offenberg, J. H., and Baker, J. E. 1997. Polychlorinated biphenyls in Chicago precipitation: Enhanced wet deposition to near-shore Lake Michigan. *Environmental Science and Technology* **31**:1534–8.

———. 1999. Influence of Baltimore's urban atmosphere on organic contaminants over the northern Chesa-peake Bay. *Journal of the Air and Waste Management Association* **49**:959–65.

Paode, R. D., Sofuoglu, S. C., Sivadechathep, J., Noll, K. E., Holsen, T. M., and Keeler, G. J. 1998. Dry deposition fluxes and mass size distributions of Pb, Cu, and Zn measured in southern Lake Michigan during AEOLOS. *Environmental Science and Technology* **32**:1629–35.

Simcik, M. F., Zhang, H., Eisenreich, S. J., and Franz, T. 1997. Urban contamination of the Chicago/coastal Lake Michigan atmosphere by PCBs and PAHs during AEOLOS. *Environmental Science and Technology* **31**:2141–7.

Totten, L. A., Brunciak, P. A., Gigliotti, C. L., Dachs, J., Glenn, IV, T. R., Nelson, E. D., and Eisenreich, S. J. 2001. Dynamic air-water exchange of polychlorinated biphenyls in the NY/NJ Harbor Estuary. *Environmental Science and Technology* **35**:3834–40.

USEPA. 2001. "Hudson River PCBs Site New York." Record of Decision. New York, NY.

VanRy, D. A., Dachs, J., Gigliotti, C. L., Brunciak, P. A., Nelson, E. D., and Eisenreich, S. J. 2000. Atmospheric seasonal trends and environmental fate of alkylphenols in the Lower Hudson River Estuary. *Environmental Science and Technology* **34**:2410–2417.

VanRy, D. A., Gigliotti, C. L., Glenn, IV, T. R., Nelson, E. D., Totten, L. A., and Eisenreich, S. J. 2002. Wet deposition of polychlorinated biphenyls in urban and background areas of the Mid-Atlantic states. *Environmental Science and Technology* **36**:3201–3209.

Wanninkhof, R. 1992. Relationship between gas exchange and wind speed over the ocean. *Journal of Geophysical Research* **97**:7373–81.

Wanninkhof, R., and McGillis, W. R. 1999. A cubic relationship between air-sea CO2 exchange and wind speed. *Geophysical Research Letters* **26**:1889–92.

Yan, S. 2003. "Air-water exchange controls phytoplankton concentrations of polychlorinated biphenyls in the Hudson River Estuary." Master of Science Thesis. Department of Environmental Sciences, Rutgers University, New Brunswick, NJ.

Zhang, H., Eisenreich, S. J., Franz, T. P., Baker, J. E., and Offenberg, J. H. 1999. Evidence for increased gaseous PCB fluxes to Lake Michigan from Chicago. *Environmental Science and Technology* **33**:2129–37.

Zufall, M. J., Davidson, C. I., Caffrey, P. F., and Ondov, J. M. 1998. Airborne concentrations and dry deposition fluxes of particulate species to surrogate surfaces deployed in southern Lake Michigan. *Environmental Science and Technology* **32**:1623–8.

28 Toxic Substances and Their Impacts on Human Health in the Hudson River Watershed

Philip J. Landrigan, Anne L. Golden, and H. James Simpson

ABSTRACT In this chapter, we examine the impacts on human health of persistent environmental pollutants found in the watershed of the Hudson River, with particular focus on the potential of these contaminants to cause injury to the developing human brain. Polychlorinated biphenyls (PCBs), organochlorine pesticides, and mercury have been shown to be widespread in bottom sediments as well as in edible species of fish, shellfish, and crustaceans in the lower Hudson River and the New York Harbor complex. Interview surveys of anglers have documented that local residents consume fish, shellfish, and crustaceans from the lower Hudson, despite longstanding advisories by health officials. Poor people and people of color are the most likely to consume locally caught fish. In a recent pilot survey of levels of PCBs, organochlorine pesticides, and mercury in the blood and hair of local anglers, we documented that anglers who consume fish from the lower Hudson River and New York Harbor have higher levels than anglers who consume no locally caught fish. A positive exposure-response relationship was seen in these findings, with the highest levels of PCBs, pesticides, and mercury observed in those anglers who ate the most fish. Within the local fish-eating population, pregnant women and women of childbearing age are the groups at greatest risk. Intrauterine and early postnatal exposures to PCBs and mercury, at levels similar to the levels found in Hudson River aquatic species, have been shown in carefully conducted prospective epidemiological studies of human infants and children to cause loss of intelligence and alteration of behavior. Decisions about reopening the commercial striped bass fishery on the Hudson or dredging to remove PCB-contaminated sediments from the upper Hudson

River need to take into account the developmental toxicity of PCBs and other persistent pollutants. The 2 parts per million (ppm) exposure tolerance limit established by the United States Food and Drug Administration for PCBs in commercial fish was set at a level intended to protect adult health and is almost certainly not protective of the fetal or neonatal brain. Additional research must be undertaken to further document patterns of human exposure to persistent pollutants in the Hudson River watershed. A new risk assessment paradigm, which specifically considers the neurodevelopmental toxicity of these exposures, must be developed to guide upcoming decisions on management of the Hudson River Estuary.

Introduction

The persistent environmental pollutants found in the Hudson River watershed include chemicals with potential to disrupt development of the human nervous system and to interfere with human reproduction. Pollutants of greatest concern in this region are the polychlorinated biphenyls (PCBs), organochlorine pesticides, dioxins, and methylmercury. The potential risks from exposures to these chemicals are greatest for sensitive subgroups within the population, in particular, infants, young children, and pregnant and nursing women, and more generally for people who are chronically and heavily exposed (Rice, 1995; Longnecker, Rogan, and Lucier, 1997). Exposure of the developing brain to PCBs or mercury during critical early periods of vulnerability can produce serious and possibly irreversible decrements in cognitive and behavioral function (Kurland, Faro, and Siedler, 1960; Bakir, Damlogi, and Amin-Zaki, 1973; Chen, Guo, and Hsu, 1992; Schantz, Moshtaghian, and Ness, 1995; Jacobson and Jacobson, 1996b). Prospective epidemiologic data from environmentally exposed populations in the United States and Europe suggest that even relatively low levels of exposure may have detectable adverse effects on the developing nervous system (Gladen and Rogan, 1991; Patandin et al., 1999).

The Hudson River watershed and New York Harbor complex are home to about 17 million people, approximately 6 percent of the population of the United States. The watershed has been densely populated for more than 350 years and industrialized for over 200 years and encompasses hundreds of hazardous waste disposal sites. Twenty-one of these sites in New York as well as seventy in New Jersey have been placed by the United States Environmental Protection Agency (USEPA) on the National Priorities List (NPL) and thus are designated as Superfund sites (USEPA, 1992). Most important among the hazardous waste sites in the Hudson River watershed are:

1. The Hudson River itself, the nation's longest Superfund site, is contaminated for over 300 kilometers of its length by PCBs principally derived from the General Electric transformer manufacturing plants in upstate New York (USEPA, 2002a).
2. The 80 Lister Avenue site in Newark, New Jersey, is located on the western edge of New York Harbor. The herbicide Agent Orange, a 50:50 mix of 2,4-dichlorophenoxyacetic acid (2,4-D) and 2,4,5-trichlorophenoxyacetic acid (2,4,5-T), was manufactured there for use in the Vietnam War. Dioxin (2,3,7,8-tetrachlorodibenzo-p-dioxin), formed as a byproduct of 2,4,5-T synthesis, has leached into soil and into adjacent sediments of the western Harbor and has moved north up the tidal Hudson as far as the George Washington Bridge. The organochlorine insecticide 2,2-bis(p-chlorophenyl)-1,1,1-trichloroethane (DDT) was also produced at 80 Lister Avenue, and DDT-derived residues are found in adjacent soils and harbor sediments (USEPA, 2002b).
3. The Hudson River below Glens Falls, New York, contains a complex mixture of lead, chromium, and cadmium downstream of a pigment plant (USEPA, 2001).
4. The Hackensack Meadowlands estuary in northern New Jersey has been rated by the National Oceanic and Atmospheric Administration as among the worst areas of mercury contamination in the United States (USEPA, 2002c).

Non-point sources of environmental pollutants, for example, pesticide applications, are also prevalent in this region. In 1997, 16.7 million pounds of pesticides were used by commercial applicators and farmers in New York state, and additional, unquantified amounts of pesticides were applied privately. Continued leaching, runoff, or illegal disposal of commercial and residential organochlorine insecticides that were banned from use in the United States since the 1970s – including chlordane, dieldrin, and DDT – have prolonged the contamination of the sediments and the food chain of this aquatic ecosystem (Bopp et al., 1998). Organochlorine pesticides are extant in both the aquatic and the terrestrial chains. As was discussed elegantly by Clarkson (1995), some control exists over the quality of crop production and animal husbandry in terrestrial food chains (plants, meat, poultry, and dairy products) because these foods are monitored through a series of governmental inspections and regulatory checks. In contrast, in aquatic food chains, there exists little if any control over the environments in which fish develop and grow or on the contaminant burdens that are ultimately consumed by those who eat the fish.

Despite numerous advisories and fishing bans by public health officials, several questionnaire surveys of anglers indicate that residents of the lower Hudson watershed, including women and children, continue to eat fish from the Hudson River, its tributaries, and New York Harbor (Barclay, 1993; Burger, Staine, and Gochfeld, 1993; May and Burger, 1996; Burger et al., 1999; NYSDOH, 1999; Pflugh et al., 1999). These studies found that poor people and people of color are most likely to consume locally caught fish and shellfish. White, middle-class anglers typically release many of the fish that they catch, while poorer anglers of color are more likely to keep their catch and share it with family and friends (Burger et al., 1999).

In this chapter, we will review the current evidence regarding the toxicity and human health impacts of the major persistent environmental pollutants found in the Hudson River watershed.

Polychlorinated Biphenyls (PCBs)

Chemistry. Polychlorinated biphenyls (PCBs) are a family of 209 chemicals (congeners), each with a common two-ring structure and one to ten substituted chlorine atoms (ATSDR, 1998). PCBs were used commercially as insulating material in electrical equipment because of their unusual chemical properties: they resist oxidation and

Table 28.1. PCB residue levels in edible fish, bivalves, and crustaceans from the New York-New Jersey Harbor Estuary, Fall, 1993

Species	No. of samples	Total PCB concentration (ppm) Arithmetic mean	Range
Finfish			
American Eel	24	3.79	0.02–18.25
Atlantic Herring	8	0.29	0.12–0.53
Atlantic Tommy Cod	9	0.34	0.17–0.49
Bluefish: <559 mm	34	0.99	0.16–3.06
>559 mm	24	2.27	0.20–8.80
Striped Bass: <610 mm	48	1.21	0.22–3.97
>610 mm	38	2.06	0.25–13.40
White Perch	22	2.83	0.21–10.92
Bivalves			
Blue Mussel	11	0.32	<0.03–1.06
Eastern Oyster	11	0.30	0.22–0.46
Crustaceans			
Lobster: Muscle	11	0.07	<0.03–0.18
Hepatopancreas	11	13.16	0.40–78.00
Blue Crab: Muscle	25	0.03	<0.03–0.07
Hepatopancreas	25	6.55	0.26–23.80

Source: Adapted from Skinner et al., 1996. Samples were taken from six areas in the New York-New Jersey Harbor estuary: the New York Bight apex; lower bay; upper bay; Arthur Kill, Kill van Kull, and Newark Bay; Jamaica Bay; and East and Harlem Rivers.

reduction, they are thermally stable, and they are nonflammable. Because of their stability, PCB mixtures of thirty to seventy congeners ranging from clear oils to viscous waxy compounds were used extensively in the United States from the 1930s until the 1970s. Their widest application was in the manufacture of dielectric fluids used for insulation in electrical generators and transformers. PCBs were also used in carbonless copy papers, lubricants, printing inks, and as "inert" ingredients in pesticides. Heating or incomplete combustion of PCBs can give rise to dioxins and furans.

Environmental distribution. The chemical stability that made PCBs so useful in industrial applications makes them extremely persistent in the environment. Although manufacture of PCBs was halted in the United States in 1978 because of concern for their potential to cause adverse health effects, PCBs continue to be found widely. Across the United States, PCBs have been detected in 432 Superfund hazardous waste disposal sites (ATSDR, 1998).

PCBs are present in high concentrations in upper Hudson River sediments and in fish from Hudson Falls, New York (the site of a former General Electric transformer manufacturing facility) to at least the southern tip of Manhattan (Bopp et al., 1981; Bopp et al., 1982; Kennish et al., 1992; Kennish and Ruppel, 1996a; Skinner et al., 1996).

PCBs are lipid-soluble and bioaccumulative, and they can reach very high concentrations in fish. As seen in Table 28.1, samples taken from throughout the New York Harbor estuary by the New York State Department of Environmental Conservation show especially high levels occur in predator species high on the aquatic food chain, such as striped bass and bluefish, as well as in predatory, bottom-feeding species, such as eels, crabs, and lobsters (Skinner et al., 1996). In recent years, levels of PCBs in Hudson River fish have declined appreciably. With this decline, there has been a change in the mix of PCB congeners, with a relative decline in abundance of the less highly chlorinated species and persistence of the more heavily chlorinated moieties (Bopp et al., 1998).

Human exposure. Virtually the entire United States population has been exposed to at least low levels of PCBs through their diet (Robinson et al., 1990). The United States Food and Drug Administration (USFDA) regards PCBs as "unavoidable environmental contaminants" of foods; nevertheless, they have set tolerance limits for PCBs of 3 ppm in poultry, 2 ppm in fish and shellfish, 1.5 ppm in cow's milk and manufactured dairy products, and 0.2 ppm in infant and junior foods (USFDA, 2000). Consumption of contaminated fish and shellfish is considered the most significant route of human exposure to PCBs outside of the workplace (ATSDR, 1998; Laden et al., 1999).

While pregnant women and women of childbearing age comprise only a small fraction of the fish-eating population, they are the groups at greatest risk within that population. PCBs and other persistent pollutants that enter the bodies of childbearing women can result in transplacental and lactational exposures of human fetuses and nursing infants (Longnecker et al., 1997). These contaminants have been shown to cross the placenta without hindrance, and because they are lipid-soluble, they tend to concentrate in human breast milk (Craan and Haines, 1998). In a study of pregnant African American and Hispanic women in New York City, the levels of PCBs were similar for the two groups, but the two highest levels (10 parts per billion (ppb) and 18 ppb) were in African American women (Berkowitz, Lapinski, and Wolff, 1996). Other recent studies of older women by the same authors revealed higher serum PCB levels in African Americans as compared to Hispanics (median 5–6 ppb versus 3 ppb) in New York City. Comparable body burdens of PCBs were measured in women residing in the Northeast and Midwest regions of the United States (mean 5.6 ppb), which were significantly higher than levels in women from the South or West (mean 4.5 ppb) (Laden et al., 1999).

Toxicity. Neurodevelopmental toxicity in infants and children is the health effect of greatest current concern from PCB exposure (Longnecker et al., 1997). A growing body of evidence indicates that PCBs have negative neurodevelopmental effects even at the relatively low levels found in the general population of the United States (Gladen

and Rogan, 1991; Patandin et al., 1999). Primarily because of the potential for PCBs in fish to cause developmental neurotoxicity, the state health departments of New York and New Jersey currently advise women of childbearing age to consume no fish from the Hudson River and associated waters (NYSDOH, 2000; NJDEP, 1995).

Public health concern about the neurodevelopmental effects of PCBs was triggered initially by reports of toxicity in the children of women who were exposed to high levels of PCBs and dioxin analogues in two incidents in Asia. In the Yusho and Yu-Cheng oil disease episodes in Japan and Taiwan respectively, cooking oil was contaminated by PCBs and other related compounds, especially furans (Chen et al., 1992; Guo, Lai, and Chen, 1995). Children exposed prenatally exhibited a variety of toxic effects including low birth weight, abnormal skin pigmentation, delayed developmental milestones, and lower intelligence quotients (IQs) as compared to unexposed siblings.

Of most relevance in the United States today are data suggesting that even low levels of exposure to PCBs may have effects on the developing nervous system (Gladen and Rogan, 1991; Jacobson and Jacobson, 1996b; Patandin et al., 1999). Gladen and Rogan examined a general population cohort of children in North Carolina to study the effects of PCB exposure in the top fifth percentile of exposure (PCB levels above 3.5 ppm in fat of maternal breast milk). They found lower scores in these children at eighteen and twenty-four months than in peers on several scales of psychomotor development (Gladen and Rogan, 1991). Antenatal exposures appeared more hazardous than postnatal breast milk exposures. Furthermore, preliminary analyses show associations between antenatal exposure to PCBs in these children and early onset of puberty (Gladen, Ragan, and Rogan, 2000).

Jacobson has followed a cohort of Michigan children with above-average intrauterine exposure to PCBs via maternal consumption of contaminated Lake Michigan fish (Jacobson and Jacobson, 1996b and 1997). They observed adverse effects on McCarthy Verbal and Memory Scale scores at age four years that appeared to be dose-dependent across a range of cord serum PCB levels (Jacobson and Jacobson, 1996a). When PCB exposures were expressed in terms of maternal breast milk PCB levels, effects were limited to children in the highest exposure category, defined as a breast milk fat PCB level >1.25 ppm (Jacobson and Jacobson, 1996a). In a subsequent follow-up of the Michigan cohort at age eleven (Jacobson and Jacobson, 1996b), full scale IQ was inversely associated with prenatal exposure to PCBs rather than postnatal exposure via breast milk. Experimental animal studies of the neurodevelopmental toxicity of PCBs are generally consistent with the human data in terms of the relative importance of pre- versus postnatal exposure and in the general functional domains affected (Lilienthal and Winneke, 1991; Schantz et al., 1995; Herr, Goldey, and Crofton, 1996; Mundy et al., 1998).

The carcinogenicity of PCBs has been established in animal species as well as in humans. PCBs have been declared probable human carcinogens by EPA, the Occupational Safety and Health Administration (OSHA), the National Institute for Occupational Safety and Health (NIOSH), and the World Health Organization (WHO). In animal studies, chronic dietary exposure to PCBs results in the development of liver toxicity and liver cancers (Kimbrough, 1995, Mayes et al., 1998). In epidemiologic studies of PCB-exposed workers, the most notable finding has been an increased death rate from cancer of the liver, cancer of the kidney, and melanoma (Brown, 1987; Brown and Jones, 1981; Longnecker et al., 1997; Sinks et al., 1992). A recent epidemiologic study of the mortality experience of General Electric workers in upstate New York reported no excess cancer mortality (Kimbrough, Doemland, and LeVois, 1999). Several serious flaws and limitations were noted, however, in the methodology of that study; of most importance, the majority of workers had no opportunity for occupational exposure to PCBs, resulting in probable dilution of any excess risk of cancer mortality (Bove, Slade, and Canady, 1999; Frumkin and Orris, 1999).

Concern about a possible role of PCBs in the etiology of hormonally-related diseases such as breast cancer has prompted several investigations of the effects of environmental (that is, dietary) PCB exposure in women. Overall, these epidemiologic data on PCB exposure and breast cancer suggest no substantial increase in risk (Krieger et al., 1994; Longnecker et al., 1997; Helzlsouer et al., 1999; Wolff et al., 2000b; Zheng et al., 2000), although the importance of prenatal exposures to hormonally active chemicals in cancer development is a new and intriguing area of research that has only begun to be explored (Wolff and Toniolo, 1995).

Organochlorine Pesticides

Chemistry. Organochlorine pesticides were introduced in the 1940s to replace the acutely toxic arsenical pesticides that had been their principal predecessors. They were used extensively in agriculture, in forestry, in the control of insect-borne diseases such as malaria and typhus, and for pest control in homes and neighborhoods. Among the most commonly used organochlorines were 2,2-bis(p-chlorophenyl)-1,1,1-trichloroethane (DDT) and the termiticide chlordane (a mixture of at least fifty different compounds with the majority constituents being cis and trans chlordane; heptachlor; cis and trans nonachlor; alpha, beta, and gamma chlordane). The general mechanism of the organochlorine pesticides' toxicity in insects is central nervous system stimulation and/or depression, depending on the compound and dose. Because the compounds showed little or no acute toxicity in humans, they were initially believed to be safe.

In 1962, with publication of Rachel Carson's *Silent Spring*, the potential of the organochlorine pesticides for long-term persistence in the environment, for bioaccumulation, and most importantly, for neuroendocrine and reproductive toxicity became evident. Carson showed that through its ability to disrupt endocrine function, DDT had caused extensive reproductive failure in eagles and ospreys, species high on the food chain that had accumulated large body burdens. In 1972, DDT production and use were banned in the United States by the newly created EPA.

Environmental distribution. A large number of chlorinated hydrocarbon pesticides and their breakdown products contaminate sediments in the Hudson River basin. The most significant of these contaminants are DDT derivatives, chlordane and its metabolites, and dioxins (Bopp and Simpson, 1989; Bopp et al., 1998). Dieldrin and hexachlorocyclohexane (HCH, sometimes misnamed benzene hexachloride or BHC), also prototypical organochlorines, are also detectable but less common.

In the lower Hudson River and New York Harbor, residues of organochlorine pesticides are found in various aquatic species (Hauge et al., 1994; Skinner et al., 1996; Kennish and Ruppel, 1996b; Kennish and Ruppel, 1997). For example, DDT levels were found to exceed the regulatory criterion of 5,000 ng/g for human health protection in some samples of American eel. DDT compounds were dominated by their longer half-life degradation products, DDE and DDD. Greatest total DDT concentrations were found in the Newark Bay complex and appear to be associated with the former Diamond Alkali production facility at 80 Lister Avenue (Bopp et al., 1991).

Chlordane, banned since 1988, was used in 24 million United States homes, usually as a termiticide, and it has been detected in the home environment as long as thirty-five years after use (Wright, Leidy, and Dupree, 1994). Chlordane concentrations in the Hudson River estuary have been found to exceed regulatory criteria for human health protection for several specimens of American eel, white perch, and the hepatopancreas of blue crab (Skinner et al., 1996). However, only blue crab hepatopancreas showed average concentrations that exceeded the regulatory criterion of 300 ng/g. Greatest concentrations were found in samples taken from the East River and the Newark Bay complex and are possibly due to residential applications for termite control.

Dieldrin concentrations exceeded 50 ng/g only in the hepatopancreas of blue crabs, but even those samples did not exceed the regulatory criterion of 300 ng/g. Hexachlorobenzene, mirex, endrin, and toxaphene were seldom or never detected (Skinner et al., 1996).

Human exposure. Organochlorine pesticides are persistent lipophilic compounds that are highly resistant to biodegradation in the environment (ATSDR, 1994). With the decrease in use of these compounds, body burden levels in United States residents have fallen in recent decades; for example, levels of DDT in the 1960s were about five times higher than current levels (Kutz, Wood, and Bottimore, 1991; Craan and Haines, 1998; Wolff, 1999). Nevertheless, they are ubiquitous in air, soil, water, and sediments, and the primary source of exposure to the general population is through the

food chain. Children have an additional route of exposure to organochlorines through breast milk. Meat, dairy products, and fish are the main sources of exposure for adults, and residues have also been measured in fruits, vegetables, and grains (particularly foodstuffs imported from developing countries where DDT is still used). Several studies have examined ethnic differences in environmental exposures to organochlorine pesticides and PCBs. They found that African Americans have higher DDT levels than Caucasians, and the data suggest that this disparity has existed since 1960 (Krieger et al., 1994). In recent studies among 278 women approximately fifty-five years old from New York City who were tested during 1994–96, both African American and Hispanic women had serum levels of DDE almost twice as high as Caucasian women (Wolff et al., 2000a).

The synergistic health effects exerted by complex mixtures of organochlorine pesticides and PCBs are inadequately explored, but are potentially important, since these compounds generally occur together in the environment (Bopp et al., 1998). Recent analyses of body burdens of these pollutants in anglers who eat fish and crabs from the lower Hudson River watershed corroborate that there exists a strong congruence among levels of highly chlorinated PCB congeners and organochlorine pesticides in anglers' blood (A. L. Golden, unpublished data).

Toxicity. Organochlorine pesticides are carcinogenic, they upregulate cytochrome P450 enzymes, and they cause reproductive failure in wildlife (Longnecker et al., 1997). These pollutants are known to modulate hormonal activity, as displayed in various in vitro and in vivo test systems, in wildlife and human populations (ATSDR, 1994). They have both estrogenic and antiestrogenic potential. Workers who are highly exposed to DDT exhibit acute neurological symptoms (Longnecker et al., 1997) and low-dose in utero exposure to DDT during critical periods of development can lead in animal models to irreversible aberrations in adult brain function, including motor, sensory, and cognitive changes (Eriksson and Talts, 2000). However, ambient exposure levels in children, assessed in one study from North Carolina, have not been associated with neurologic or developmental abnormalities in humans (Gladen and Rogan, 1991; Gladen et al., 2000).

Mercury

Chemistry. Mercury (Hg) is a metal that exists in three basic forms: (a) elemental mercury (part of the earth's natural geochemistry), (b) inorganic mercury (as mercuric salts), and (c) organic mercury (methylmercury compounds). Inorganic mercury comprises the vast majority of the total mercury found in Hudson River sediments, but it is the small fraction of mercury that is methylated by microorganisms in the aquatic environment, enters the food chain, and bioaccumulates in fish that is of greatest toxicologic concern (ATSDR, 1999).

Environmental distribution. Mercury is found widely in the environment across the United States. It is encountered at 46 percent of Superfund sites on the NPL (ATSDR, 1999). High concentrations of mercury are found in the Hackensack Meadowlands, a tidal estuary at the western margin of New York Harbor. The highest levels of methylmercury in fish from the lower Hudson are found in large striped bass (mean: 517 ng/g), and two of thirty-eight large striped bass tested in 1993 exceeded the regulatory criterion of 1,000 ng/g (Skinner et al., 1996).

Human exposure. Chronic poisoning by mercury occurs in two distinct clinical forms, depending upon whether exposure has been to inorganic or to organic compounds of mercury (Hunter, 1969; Clarkson, 1997; ATSDR, 1999). Only organic mercury toxicity is relevant to this discussion of exposure from the aquatic environment. Poisoning by the organic compounds of mercury, including methylmercury, produces an almost purely neurologic illness (Clarkson, 1997; ATSDR, 1999). Early symptoms include paresthesias, perioral numbness and other manifestations of sensory neuropathy. With continued exposure, the syndrome progresses to a triad of dysarthria, ataxia, and visual field constriction (Hunter, 1969).

Acute devastating outbreaks of organic mercury poisoning have been reported. Infants and children have been most seriously affected. Diet has been the usual route of exposure. The first of these epidemics occurred in Minimata Bay, Japan,

where exposure resulted from ingestion of contaminated shellfish (Kurland et al., 1960). Later epidemics occurred in Iraq (Bakir et al., 1973), Pakistan (Hag, 1976), and Guatemala (Ordonez, Carillo, and Miranda, 1966), where exposure was caused by consumption of seed grain that had been treated with mercurial fungicides. An episode of poisoning by organic mercury occurred in the United States among members of a New Mexico family who ate pork from hogs that had been fed mercury-treated seed grain (Pierce, Thompson, and Likosky, 1972).

Toxicity. A major focus of current research surrounds the question of whether low-level exposure to organic mercury is capable of causing subclinical developmental neurotoxicity. To answer this question, three major prospective epidemiologic studies have been initiated and are ongoing: one among children in the Seychelles Islands in the Indian Ocean (Marsh et al., 1995), the second among children in the Faroe Islands in the North Atlantic (Grandjean et al., 1998), and the third among children in New Zealand (Kjellström et al., 1989; Crump et al., 1998). Maternal exposure to methylmercury during pregnancy has been assessed in each study through determination of mercury levels in scalp hair, and neurological development in their children has been tested postnatally. To date, the Seychelles study has found no association between low levels of exposure and any sign of neurodevelopmental toxicity. By contrast, the Faroe study, which employed more sensitive assessment instruments, has found evidence of subclinical impairment. There was concomitant exposure to PCBs in the Faroe Islands, but this does not seem to account for the findings. The New Zealand study also has found that prenatal exposure to low levels of methylmercury is associated with neurobehavioral impairment in six- and seven-year-old children. After a careful weighing of the data from these three studies, the United States National Academy of Sciences has declared methylmercury a fetal neurotoxin (NRC, 2000). The USFDA recently announced an advisory and comprehensive educational program to warn pregnant women, women of childbearing age, and their health care providers about the hazard posed to the unborn child from consuming fish that may contain high levels of methylmercury (USFDA, 2001).

Human Exposure to Persistent Pollutants in the Hudson River Watershed

THE HUDSON RIVER ANGLERS HEALTH STUDY

In the fall of 1998, in collaboration with two local fishing clubs and the New Jersey Department of Environmental Protection (NJDEP), researchers at Mount Sinai School of Medicine began a pilot study of anglers who frequent fishing and crabbing sites in the lower Hudson River and New York Harbor. The purpose of this preliminary "Hudson River Anglers Health Study" was to characterize the fish and shellfish consumption patterns and the body burdens of persistent environment chemicals among these anglers, as well as to better understand the links between fishing behavior, fish consumption, and health risk

The forty-six volunteer study participants were mostly white males, with a mean age of fifty (A. L. Golden, unpublished data). As members of organized fishing clubs, they were presumably better informed than the general population about New York or New Jersey state fishing advisories, with 83 percent reporting some knowledge of the advisories' contents. Nevertheless, their fish consumption practices put them at substantial health risk. Most reported eating local fish or shellfish at least once a month during the previous fishing season, with 48 percent eating at least one locally-caught fish or shellfish meal each week. The data show clear associations between self-reported frequency of consuming locally caught fish and markers of exposure for several environmental contaminants known to have serious health effects. For example, as seen in Table 28.2, eating at least one meal a week of any fish or shellfish was related to higher concentrations of highly chlorinated PCBs, DDT, and mercury. Those who frequently consumed blue crabs showed elevated levels of DDE and highly chlorinated PCB congeners.

The findings of the Hudson River Anglers Study suggest that, despite health advisories, a significant proportion of recreational anglers in the Hudson River Estuary do consume contaminated fish and shellfish from these waters. Those with the highest consumption of fish and shellfish have significantly increased body burdens of environmental toxins. Since the anglers reported often sharing their catch with others, some of their friends and family members also share the health risk along with the food.

The average body burdens of mercury, PCBs, DDT, and DDE measured in the Hudson River Anglers Study are similar to those found for male fish eaters in other recent reports from the Great Lakes region (Anderson et al., 1998.; Falk et al., 1999; Hanrahan et al., 1999) and northern New York State (Fitzgerald et al., 1999). The long-term and subclinical impact of exposures at these levels are just beginning to be addressed in longitudinal studies designed to address the health effects that have been found with higher occupational exposures.

THE HUDSON RIVER COMMUNITIES PROJECT

In 1999, the New York State Department of Health initiated a research project, "PCBs and Health: The Hudson River Communities Project," with funding from the Federal Agency for Toxic Substances and Disease Registry (ATSDR). This study is designed to compare neurologic test results in adults who have lived for at least twenty-five years in Fort Edward or Hudson Falls (the site of PCBs release from GE manufacturing plants) to a similar group from Glens Falls (a control community upriver from the contamination sources). The project aims to determine whether current and past exposures from consumption of contaminated fish or inhalation of airborne PCBs are associated with neurotoxicity in adults. One shortcoming will be the inability of this study to address neurodevelopmental toxicity in children.

ANGLER SURVEYS IN THE HUDSON RIVER WATERSHED

A growing body of research has assessed the knowledge, attitudes, and consumption practices of United States anglers who fish in contaminated waters. Among these studies, several focus specifically on anglers in the lower Hudson River (Belton, Roundy, and Weinstein, 1986; Barclay, 1993; Burger et al., 1993; May and Burger, 1996; Burger et al., 1999; NYSDOH, 1999; Pflugh et al., 1999). Studies

Table 28.2. Comparison of age-adjusted least-squares geometric mean levels of persistent pollutants (ng/mL), by frequency of fish or crab consumption, in blood samples from the Hudson River Anglers Health Study

	N	Total low PCBs[a]	Total high PCBs[b]	PCB congener 118	PCB congener 153	Chlordane residues[c]	p, p' – DDT	p, p' – DDE	Total mercury
Overall:	37								
Mean		1.11	4.70	0.31	1.27	0.91	0.60	4.82	2.82
Standard Deviation		1.67	1.79	2.21	2.03	1.93	1.37	2.82	4.79
Range		0.48–6.63	1.83–16.88	0.06–1.57	0.30–9.47	0.33–4.72	0.37–2.54	0.83–57.80	0–22
Any fish or shellfish:									
<1 meal/week	18	1.03	4.22	0.25	1.05	0.87	0.54	4.78	1.87
≥1 meal/week	19	1.20	5.23	0.40*	1.51	0.95	0.66*	4.85	4.17
Striped Bass:									
<1 meal/week	27	1.10	4.75	0.32	1.23	0.88	0.58	5.10	2.55
≥1 meal/week	10	1.15	4.56	0.29	1.39	0.98	0.64	4.13	3.93
Blue Crab:									
<1 meal/week	29	1.15	4.42	0.29	1.20	0.90	0.60	4.46	2.94
≥1 meal/week	8	1.00	5.98	0.42	1.55	0.96	0.57	6.41	2.46

* p-value < 0.05 for Student's t-test comparing age-adjusted least-squares geometric means according to consumption frequency.

[a] Total Low PCB congeners = (IUPAC # 56 + 66 + 74 + 99 + 101)

[b] Total High PCB congeners = (IUPAC #105 + 118 + 138 + 146 + 153 + 156 + 167 + 170 + 172 + 174 + 177 + 178 + 180 + 183 + 187 + 199 + 203).

[c] Chlordane residues = (trans-nonachlor + oxychlordane).

in the New York-New Jersey area document that, relative to white anglers, minority anglers are more likely to consume unsafe fish and less likely to be informed about health advisories and health hazards related to local fish (Burger et al., 1999). Middle-class anglers predominantly fish for sport rather than subsistence. Among low-income minority anglers, both for income reasons and as a matter of cultural tradition, fishing is likely to represent not only recreation but also an important source of food (Burger, 1998). Therefore, the health risk may be even higher in low-income minority communities in the Hudson River watershed, particularly for women of childbearing age who eat fish that are caught in local waters. An informal survey of twenty New York City anglers conducted along shores of the East and Harlem Rivers found that almost all of them ate their catch; all gave fish to others at least sometimes; and they reported that locally caught fish are commonly sold, with some anglers believing this is not illegal (P. J. Landrigan, unpublished data).

Major inconsistencies exist between the anglers' knowledge of the hazards of pollutants in fish and their behavior. In surveys conducted in the highly contaminated Arthur Kill estuary and New Jersey shore area, 60 percent of the fishermen and crabbers interviewed reported having heard warnings about consuming fish from these waters (Burger et al., 1999; Pflugh et al., 1999). Nevertheless, 70–76 percent reported that they eat their catch. These anglers rationalized the inconsistency with a number of inaccurate but strongly-held beliefs – for example, locally caught fish are good for you because they are "fresher;" you can make fish completely safe by cooking it; certain fishing locations have escaped pollution; crabs can "filter out" hazardous chemicals; if you eat the fish and don't get sick immediately, the fish was safe. Many distrusted the advisories, doubting the motives behind government warnings. A 1993 angler survey by Hudson River Sloop Clearwater, Inc., found similar beliefs, noting that "the idea of soaking the fish (in beer, water, lemon juice, vinegar, etc.) to detoxify it was reported with disturbing frequency," and is indicative of fundamental misunderstanding about the nature of chemical contaminants found in fish (Barclay, 1993).

HEALTH AND POLICY IMPLICATIONS OF HUMAN EXPOSURES TO PERSISTENT POLLUTANTS

Health advisories. The federal government sets standards that are enforced through the Food and Drug Administration for chemicals in food that is sold commercially, including fish (USFDA, 2000), but such rules do not apply to the private consumption of sportfish. States, tribal organizations, and the USEPA issue fish consumption advisories in the United States and territories. (The USEPA fish consumption advisory can be downloaded in several languages from http://www.epa.gov/ost/fish). These advisories include recommendations to limit or avoid eating non-commercial fish and wildlife from certain bodies of water. In New York State, the Department of Environmental Conservation (DEC) routinely monitors contaminant levels in fish and game, and the Department of Health (DOH) issues advisories when sportfish have contaminant levels greater than federal standards. Fish from more than seventy bodies of water in New York State have contaminant levels that are greater than federal standards. For these waters, DOH recommends either limiting or not eating specific species of fish (NYSDOH, 2000). Similar advisories are issued for relevant waterways in New Jersey (NJDEP and NJDOH, 1995).

The New York State DOH advisory for sportfish states that no more than one meal (one-half pound) per week of fish should be taken from the state's fresh waters and some marine waters at the mouth of the Hudson River. These include the waters of the Hudson River, Upper Bay of New York Harbor (north of Verrazano Narrows Bridge), Arthur Kill, Kill Van Kull, Harlem River and the East River to the Throgs Neck Bridge. This general advisory is designed to protect against eating large amounts of fish that have not been tested or that may contain unidentified contaminants. Specific advice is also given for infants, children under the age of fifteen, and women of childbearing age. DOH recommends that these groups not eat any fish from the specific bodies of water listed in the advisory.

Management of the watershed. Data on human exposures to persistent pollutants and on the health impacts of these exposures are extremely important for decision making about management of the Hudson River estuary.

Whether to reopen the Hudson River commercial striped bass fishery is one major question that is receiving urgent consideration from federal and state agencies now that levels of PCBs in these prized and beautiful game fish have declined appreciably. However, a major health-based impediment to reopening the fishery is that the current standard for PCBs of 2 ppm in fish is based on a risk assessment that centers on the prevention of cancer in adults. The standard was established before the developmental neurotoxicity of PCBs was recognized. Consequently, it pays no consideration to the fact that PCBs are now known to be capable of causing adverse effects on fetal development at levels of exposure well below 2 ppm. It may therefore be unwise to reopen the Hudson River striped bass fishery for many years.

Another major policy issue confronting EPA and state agencies in New York is the dredging of sediments in the upper Hudson River to remove PCBs and other toxins. Recent geochemical data suggest that PCBs are much more persistent in the environment than some had predicted and that natural degradation is occurring at a very slow rate (Bopp et al., 1998) These data, in combination with body burden data from the Hudson River Anglers Study and information on the developmental toxicity of PCBs supplied, should inform decisions related to dredging.

Another difficult policy issue currently confronting EPA and the New York State DEC is the question of how best to manage heavy metal contamination in the upper Hudson River below Glens Falls, New York. Lead, cadmium, and copper from a pigment factory in Glens Falls have contaminated the Hudson for more than 80 kilometers downstream. All of these metals are potent human toxins.

Future Work

Continuing research on the developmental toxicity of exposures to PCB and methylmercury during pregnancy and early childhood will help to formulate a new paradigm for assessing the risks of human exposures to these persistent pollutants. The impacts of exposure to environmental toxins on the health of children are particularly critical in forming public policy. Children are the most susceptible subset within a population, and their developmental processes are extremely vulnerable and easily disrupted. During fetal development, when complex development and differentiation of the nervous system, the immune system, the reproductive organs, and other organ systems is proceeding at a rapid rate, exposures to even minute concentrations of compounds such as PCBs, methylmercury, and DDT can cause devastating damage with lifelong consequences. It is imperative that policy decisions regarding the management of persistent pollutants in the Hudson River watershed emphasize the risks these chemicals pose to human health, with particular consideration of their impact on the development and health of children.

REFERENCES

Anderson, H. A., Falk, C., Hanrahan, L., Olson, J., Burse, V. W., Needham, L., Paschal, D., Patterson Jr., D., and Hill, Jr., R. H. 1998. Profiles of Great Lakes critical pollutants: a sentinel analysis of human blood and urine. *Environmental Health Perspectives* **106**:279–89.

ATSDR (Agency for Toxic Substances and Disease Registry). 1994. *Toxicological Profile for 4,4'-DDT, 4,4'-DDE, 4,4'-DDD (Update)*. U.S. Department of Health and Human Services, Public Health Service, Atlanta, Georgia.

——— 1998. *Draft Toxicological Profile for Polychlorinated Biphenyls (PCBs)*. U.S. Department of Health and Human Services, Public Health Service, Atlanta, Georgia.

——— 1999. *Toxicological Profile for Mercury*. U.S. Department of Health and Human Services, Public Health Service, Atlanta, Georgia.

Bakir, F., Damlogi, S., and Amin-Zaki, L. 1973. Methylmercury poisoning in Iraq. *Science* **181**: 230–41.

Barclay, B. 1993. *A report on the adherence to fish consumption health advisories among Hudson River anglers*. Hudson River Sloop Clearwater, Inc. Poughkeepsie, New York.

Belton, T., Roundy, R., and Weinstein, N. 1986. Urban fishermen: Managing the risks of toxic exposure. *Environment* **28**:19–37.

Berkowitz, G. S., Lapinski, R. H., and Wolff, M. S. 1996. The role of DDE and polychlorinated biphenyl levels in preterm birth. *Archives of Environmental Contamination and Toxicology* **30**:139–41.

Bopp, R. F., Chillrud, S. N., Shuster, E. L., Simpson, H. J., and Estabrooks, F. D. 1998. Trends in chlorinated hydrocarbon levels in Hudson River basin sediments. *Environmental Health Perspectives* **106**(suppl. 4):1075–81.

Bopp, R. F., Gross, M. L., Tong, H. Y., Simpson, H. J., Monson, S. J., Deck, B. L., and Moser, F. C. 1991. A major incident of dioxin contamination: sediments of New Jersey estuaries. *Environmental Science and Technology* **25**:951–6.

Bopp, R., and Simpson, H. 1989. Contamination of the Hudson River – the sediment record, in A. Correll (ed.). *Contaminated Marine Sediments: Assessment and Remediation*. Washington, DC: National Academy of Sciences Press.

Bopp, R. F., Simpson, H. J., Olsen, C. R., and Kostyk, N. 1981. Polychlorinated biphenyls in sediments of the tidal Hudson River, New York. *Environmental Science and Technology* **15**:210–216.

Bopp, R. F., Simpson, H. J., Olsen, C. R., Trier, R. M., and Kostyk, N. 1982. Chlorinated hydrocarbons and radionuclide chronologies in sediments of the Hudson River and estuary, New York. *Environmental Science and Technology* **16**:666–76.

Bove, F. J., Slade, B. A., and Canady, R. A. 1999. Evidence of excess cancer mortality in a cohort of workers exposed to polychlorinated biphenyls. *Journal of Occupational and Environmental Medicine* **41**:739–41.

Brown, D. P. 1987. Mortality of workers exposed to polychlorinated biphenyls – an update. *Archives of Environmental Health* **42**:333–9.

Brown, D. P., and Jones, M. 1981. Mortality and industrial hygiene study of workers exposed to polychlorinated biphenyls. *Archives of Environmental Health* **36**:120–9.

Burger, J. 1998. Fishing and risk along the Savannah River: possible intervention. *Journal of Toxicology and Environmental Health* **55**:405–419.

Burger, J., Pflugh, K. K., Lurig, L., Von Hagen L. A., and Von Hagen S. 1999. Fishing in urban New Jersey: ethnicity affects information sources, perception, and compliance. *Risk Analysis* **19**:217–29.

Burger, J., Staine, K., and Gochfeld, M. 1993. Fishing in contaminated waters: knowledge and risk perception of hazards by fishermen in New York City. *Journal of Toxicology and Environmental Health* **39**:95–105.

Carson, R. 1994. *Silent Spring*. New York: Houghton Mifflin Co.

Chen, Y., Guo, C., and Hsu, C. 1992. Cognitive development of children prenatally exposed to polychlorinated biphenyls (Yu-Cheng children) and their siblings. *Journal of the Formosa Medical Association* **91**:704–707.

Clarkson, T. W. 1995. Environmental chemicals in the food chain. *American Journal of Clinical Nutrition* **61** (suppl.):682S–6S.

Clarkson, T. 1997. The toxicology of mercury. *Critical Reviews in Clinical Laboratory Science* **34**:369–403.

Craan, A. G., and Haines, D. A. 1998. Twenty-five years of surveillance for contaminants in human breast milk. *Archives of Environmental Contamination and Toxicology* **35**:702–710.

Crump, K. S., Kjellstrom, T., Shipp, A. M., Silvers, A., and Stewart, A. 1998. Influence of prenatal mercury exposure upon scholastic and psychological test performance: benchmark analysis of a New Zealand cohort. *Risk Analysis* **18**:701–713.

Eriksson, P., and Talts, U. 2000. Neonatal exposure to neurotoxic pesticides increases adult susceptibility: a review of current finding. *Neurotoxicology* **21**:37–47.

Falk, C., Hanrahan, L., Anderson, H. A., Kanarek, M. S., Draheim, L., Needham, L., Patterson, D., and the Great Lakes Consortium. 1999. Body burden levels of dioxin, furans, and PCBs among frequent consumers of Great Lakes sport fish. *Environmental Research* **80**:S19–S25.

Fitzgerald, E. F., Deres, D. A., Hwang, S., Bush, B., Yang, B., Tarbell, A., and Jacobs, A. 1999. Local fish consumption and serum PCB concentrations among Mohawk men at Akwesasne. *Environmental Research* **80**:S97–S103.

Frumkin, H., and Orris, P. 1999. Evidence of excess cancer mortality in a cohort of workers exposed to polychlorinated biphenyls. *Journal of Occupational and Environmental Medicine* **41**:741–2.

Gladen, B., and Rogan, W. 1991. Effects of perinatal polychlorinated biphenyls and dichloroethene dichlorodiphenyl on later development. *Journal of Pediatrics* **119**:58–63.

Gladen, B. C., Ragan, N. B., and Rogan, W. J. 2000. Pubertal growth and development and prenatal and lactational exposure to polychlorinated biphenyls and dichlorodiphenyl dichloroethene. *Journal of Pediatrics* **136**:490–6.

Grandjean, P., Weihe, P., White, R., and Debes, F. 1998. Cognitive performance of children prenatally exposed to "safe" levels of methylmercury. *Environmental Research* **77**:165–72.

Guo, Y., Lai, T., and Chen, S. 1995. Gender-related decrease in Raven's progressive matrices scores in children prenatally exposed to polychlorinated biphenyls and related contaminants. *Bulletin of Environmental Contamination and Toxicology* **55**:8–13.

Hag, I. 1976. Agrosan poisoning in Nau. *British Medical Journal* 1579–82.

Hanrahan, L. P., Falk, C., Anderson, H. A., Draheim, L., Kanarek, M. S., and Olson, J. 1999. Serum PCB and DDE levels of frequent Great Lakes sport fish consumers – a first look. The Great Lakes Consortium. *Environmental Research* 80:S26–S37.

Hauge, P. M., Belton, T. J., Ruppel, B. E., Lockwood, K., and Mueller, R. T. 1994. 2,3,7,8-TCDD and 2,3,7,8-TCDF in blue crabs and American lobsters from the Hudson-Raritan estuary and the New York Bight. *Bulletin of Environmental Contamination and Toxicology* 52:734–41.

Helzlsouer, K. J., Alberg, A. J., Huang, H. Y., Hoffman, S. C., Strickland, P. T., Brock, J. W., Burse, V. W., Needham, L. L., Bell, D. A., Lavigne, J. A., Yager, J. D., and Comstock, G. W. 1999. Serum concentrations of organochlorine compounds and the subsequent development of breast cancer. *Cancer Epidemiology, Biomarkers and Prevention* 8:525–32.

Herr, D., Goldey, E., and Crofton, K. M. 1996. Developmental exposure to Arochlor 1254 produces low-frequency alterations in adult rat brainstem auditory evoked responses. *Fundamental and Applied Toxicology* 33:120–8.

Hunter, D. 1969. *The Diseases of Occupations*, 4th ed. Boston, MA: Little, Brown and Co.

Jacobson, J., and Jacobson, S. 1996a. Dose response in perinatal exposure to polychlorinated biphenyls (PCBs): the Michigan and North Carolina cohort studies. *Toxicology and Industrial Health* 12:435–45.

1996b. Intellectual impairment in children exposed to polychlorinated biphenyls in utero. *New England Journal of Medicine* 335:783–9.

Jacobson, J. L., and Jacobson, S. W. 1997. Evidence for PCBs as neurodevelopmental toxicants in humans. *Neurotoxicology* 18:415–24.

Kennish, M. J., Belton, T. J., Hauge, P., Lockwood, K., and Ruppel, B. E. 1992. Polychlorinated biphenyls in estuarine and coastal marine waters of New Jersey: a review of contamination problems. *Reviews in Aquatic Science* 6:275–93.

Kennish, M. J., and Ruppel, B. E. 1996a. Polychlorinated biphenyl contamination in selected estuarine and coastal marine finfish and shellfish of New Jersey. *Estuaries* 19:288–95.

Kennish, M. J., and Ruppel, B. E. 1996b. DDT contamination in selected estuarine and coastal marine finfish and shellfish of New Jersey. *Archives of Environmental Contamination and Toxicology* 31:256–62.

Kennish, M. J., and Ruppel, B. E. 1997. Chlordane contamination in selected freshwater finfish of New Jersey. *Bulletin of Environmental Contamination and Toxicology* 58:142–9.

Kimbrough, R. D. 1995. Polychlorinated biphenyls (PCBs) and human health: an update. *Critical Reviews in Toxicology* 25:133–63.

Kimbrough, R. D., Doemland, M. L., and LeVois, M. E. 1999. Mortality in male and female capacitor workers exposed to polychlorinated biphenyls. *Journal of Occupational and Environmental Medicine* 41:161–71.

Kjellström, T., Kennedy, P., Wallis, S., Stewart, A., Friberg, L., Lind, B., Wutherspoon, T., and Mantell, C. 1989. *Physical and Mental Development of Children with Prenatal Exposure to Mercury from Fish*. National Swedish Environmental Protection Board Report No. 3642. Solna, Sweden.

Krieger, N., Wolff, M., Hiatt, R., Rivera, M., Vogelman, J., and Orentreich, N. 1994. Breast cancer and serum organochlorines: a prospective study among white, black and Asian women. *Journal of the National Cancer Institute* 86:589–99.

Kurland, L., Faro, S. N., and Siedler, H. 1960. Minimata disease. *World Neurology* 1:370–90.

Kutz, F. W., Wood, P. H., and Bottimore, D. P. 1991. Organochlorine pesticides and polychlorinated biphenyls in human adipose tissue. *Reviews in Environmental Contaminants and Toxicology.* 120:1–82.

Laden, F., Neas, L. M., Spiegelman, D., Hankinson, S. E., Willett, W. C., Ireland, K., Wolff, M. S., and Hunter, D. J. 1999. Predictors of plasma concentrations of DDE and PCBs in a group of U.S. women. *Environmental Health Perspectives* 107:75–81.

Lilienthal, H., and Winneke, G. 1991. Sensitive periods for behavioral toxicity of polychlorinated biphenyls: determination by cross-fostering in rats. *Fundamental and Applied Toxicology* 17:368–75.

Longnecker, M., Rogan, W., and Lucier, G. 1997. The human health effects of DDT (Dichlorodiphenyltrichloroethane) and PCBs (polychlorinated biphenyls): an overview of organochlorines in public health. *Annual Review of Public Health* 18:211–44.

Marsh, D., Clarkson, T., Myers, G., Davidson, P., Cox, C., Cernichiari, E., Tanner, M., Lednar, W., Shamlaye, C., Choisy, O., Hoareau, C., and Berlin, M. 1995. The Seychelles study of fetal methylmercury exposure and child development: Introduction. *Neurotoxicology* 16:583–96.

May, H., and Burger, J. 1996. Fishing in a polluted estuary: fishing behavior, fish consumption, and potential risk. *Risk Analysis* 16:459–71.

Mayes, B. A., McConnell, E. E., Neal, B. H., Brunner, M. J., Hamilton, S. B., Sullivan, T. M., Peters, A. C., Ryan, M. J., Toft, J. D., Singer, A. W., Brown Jr., J. F. Menton, R. G., and Moore, J. A. 1998. Comparative carcinogenicity in Sprague-Dawley rats of the polychlorinated biphenyl mixtures Aroclors 1016, 1242, 1254, and 1260. *Toxicological Sciences* **41**:62–76.

Mundy, W. R., Bushnell, P. J., Crofton, K. M., Herr, D. W., Moser, V. C., and Kodavanti, P. R. 1998. Neurobehavioral effects of developmental Aroclor 1254 exposure. *Toxicologist* **42**:34–5.

NRC (National Research Council). 2000. Committee on the Toxicological Effects of Methylmercury. *Toxicological Effects of Methylmercury*. Washington, DC: National Academy of Sciences Press.

NJDEP and NJDOH (New Jersey Department of Environmental Protection and New Jersey Department of Health). 1995. *A Guide to Health Advisories for Eating Fish and Crabs Caught in New Jersey Waters: What You Need to Know About Recreational Fishing and Crabbing*. Trenton, NJ.

NYSDOH (New York State Department of Health). 1999. *Health Consultation: 1996 Survey of Hudson River Anglers*. Center for Environmental Health. Albany, New York.

——— 2000. *2000–2001 Health Advisories: Chemicals in Sportfish and Game*. Division of Environmental Health Assessment. Albany, New York.

Ordonez, J., Carillo, J., and Miranda, M. 1966. Epidemiological study of an illness in the Guatemala highlands believed to be encephalitis. *Boletín de la Oficina Sanitaria Panamericana* **60**: 18–24.

Patandin, S., Lanting, C. I., Mulder, P. G., Boersma, E. R., Sauer, P. J., and Weisglas-Kuperus, N. 1999. Effects of environmental exposure to polychlorinated biphenyls and dioxins on cognitive abilities in Dutch children at 42 months of age. *Journal of Pediatrics* **134**:33–41.

Pflugh, K. K., Lurig, L., VonHagen, L. A., VonHagen, S., and Burger, J. 1999. Urban anglers' perception of risk from contaminated fish. *Science of the Total Environment* **228**:203–218.

Pierce, P., Thompson, J., Likosky, W., Nickey, L. N., Barthel, W. F., and Hinman, A. R. 1972. Alkyl mercury poisoning in humans: a report of an outbreak. *Journal of the American Medical Association* **200**:1439–42.

Rice, D. C. 1995. Neurotoxicity of lead, methylmercury, and PCBs in relation to the Great Lakes. *Environmental Health Perspectives* **103** (suppl. 9):71–87.

Robinson, P. E., Mack, G. A., Remmers, J., Levy, R., and Mohadjer, L. 1990. Trends in PCB, hexachlorobenzene, and beta-benzene hexachloride levels in the adipose tissue of U.S. populations. *Environmental Research* **53**:175–92.

Schantz, S., Moshtaghian, J., and Ness, D. 1995. Spatial learning deficits in adult rats exposed to ortho-substituted PCB congeners during gestation and lactation. *Fundamental and Applied Toxicology* **26**:117–26.

Sinks, T., Steele, G., Smith, A. B., Watkins, K., and Shults, R. A. 1992. Mortality among workers exposed to polychlorinated biphenyls. *American Journal of Epidemiology* **136**:389–98.

Skinner, L., Jackling, S., Kimber, G., Waldman, J., Shastay, Jr., J., and Newell, A. 1996. *Chemical Residues in Fish, Bivalves, Crustaceans and Cephalopods from the New York-New Jersey Harbor Estuary: PCB, Organochlorine Pesticides and Mercury*. New York State Department of Environmental Conservation, Division of Fish and Wildlife, Albany, New York.

USEPA (U.S. Environmental Protection Agency). 1992. *Superfund: Progress at National Priority List Sites, New York, 1992 Update*. EPA/540/R-93/030. Publication #9200.5-732B. USEPA Office of Program Management, Washington, D.C. (http://www.epa.gov/region02/superfund/npl).

——— 2001. *Glens Falls, NY*, EPA ID#: NYD002069748, (http://www.epa.gov/Region2/waste/ciba_h725.pdf).

——— 2002a. *Hudson River, NY*, EPA ID#: NYD980763841, (http://www.epa.gov/region02/superfund/npl/0202229c.pdf).

——— 2002b. *80 and 120 Lister Avenue/Diamond Alkali*, EPA ID#: NJD980528996, (http://www.epa.gov/region02/superfund/npl/0200613c.pdf).

——— 2002c. *Hackensack, NJ, Meadowlands*, EPA ID# NJD980529879, (http://www.epa.gov/region02/superfund/npl/0200674c.pdf).

USFDA (United States Food and Drug Administration). 2000. *Unavoidable Contaminants in Food for Human Consumption and Food-packaging Tolerances for PCBs*. Code of Federal Regulations. Title 21, Volume 2, Part 109, Section 109.30. Washington, D.C.: U.S. Government Printing Office.

——— 2001. Center for Food Safety and Applied Nutrition. *Consumer Advisory: An Important Message for Pregnant Women and Women of Childbearing Age Who May Become Pregnant About the Risks of Mercury in Fish*. (http://vm.cfsan.fda.gov/~dms/admehg.html).

Whitmore, R., Immerman, F. W., Camann, D. E., Bond, A. E., Lewis, R., and Schaum, J. 1994.

Non-occupational exposures to pesticides for residents of two U.S. cities. *Archives of Environmental Contamination and Toxicology* **26**: 47–59.

Wolff, M. S. 1999. Twenty-five years of surveillance for contaminants in human breast milk. (Letter) *Archives of Environmental Contamination and Toxicology* **36**:504.

Wolff, M. S., Berkowitz, G. S., Brower, S., Senie, R., Bleiweiss, I. J., Tartter, P., Pace, B., Roy, N., Wallenstein, S., and Weston, A. 2000a. Organochlorine exposures and breast cancer risk in New York City women. *Environmental Research*, **84**:151–61

Wolff, M. S., and Toniolo, P. G. 1995. Environmental organochlorine exposure as a potential etiologic factor in breast cancer. *Environmental Health Perspectives***103** (suppl. 7): 141–5.

Wolff, M. S., Zeleniuch-Jacquotte, A., Dubin, N., and Toniolo, P. 2000b. Risk of breast cancer and organochlorine exposure. *Cancer Epidemiology, Biomarkers and Prevention* **9**:271–7.

Wright, C., Leidy, R., and Dupree, H. J. 1994. Chlorpyrifos in the air and soil of houses eight years after its application for termite control. *Bulletin of Environmental Contamination and Toxicology* **52**:131–4.

Zheng, T., Holford, T. R., Tessari, J., Mayne, S. T., Owens, P. H., Ward, B., Carter, D., Boyle, P., Dubrow, R., Archibeque-Engle, S., and Zahm, S. H. 2000. Breast cancer risk associated with congeners of polychlorinated biphenyls. *American Journal of Epidemiology* **152**:50–8.

29 Impacts of Piers on Juvenile Fishes in the Lower Hudson River

Kenneth W. Able and
Janet T. Duffy-Anderson

ABSTRACT We examined the impacts of man-made structures, especially large piers, on fishes in the lower Hudson River, USA over a number of years. We used a multifaceted approach, and evaluated: 1) the distribution and abundance of fishes under piers, at pier edges, in pile fields, and in open water areas, 2) feeding and growth of young-of-the-year fishes (winter flounder, tautog, and Atlantic tomcod) under and around piers, and 3) availability of benthic prey for fishes under and adjacent to large piers. A review of our studies suggests that species diversity and species abundance were depressed under piers relative to nearby habitats. The only species that were routinely collected from under piers were those that do not appear to solely rely on the use of vision to forage (American eel, naked goby, Atlantic tomcod). Results from studies of the distribution of benthic invertebrate prey for fishes around piers suggest that prey abundances under piers are more than sufficient to support fish growth, however, results of directed growth studies indicate that feeding and growth rates of visually-feeding fish species (winter flounder, tautog) are negative under piers (that is, fish lose weight). It is not likely that factors associated with pier pilings, such as reduced flow or sedimentation, affect feeding, since studies of fish growth in pile fields (piers without the decking) indicate that fish grow well in that habitat. Rather, it appears that the decking associated with piers creates conditions of intense shading that impede foraging activities. We propose that under-pier areas, and potentially any areas that significantly reduce light penetration to depth in near shore areas, are poor habitats for fishes, and we urge careful consideration of shading effects prior to the construction, restoration, or renovation of overwater structures.

Introduction

The reshaping of New York Harbor by European settlers first occurred in the mid 1600s with the construction of two small, wooden piers along the East River to accommodate shipping and trade (Buttenwieser, 1987). From this modest start, the East River became an active seaport by the 1700s and efforts then were already underway to reshape its shoreline and construct larger piers in its waters. In contrast, waterfront development in the lower Hudson River lagged behind because the hard, rocky bottom of the Battery Park area tended to make pier building difficult (Buttenwieser, 1987). Eventually, the development of powerful pile-driving machinery overcame this obstacle and by the late 1800s the Hudson River supported hundreds of piers and docks.

Many eighteenth and nineteenth century piers were built upon filled, closed bases and were often situated in parallel and in close proximity to one another. These designs made piers more stable and capable of servicing larger ships, but they also obstructed water flow (Bone, 1997). Other early piers were made of wood and floated on the surface of the water in closed squares or rectangles, also restricting flow and allowing the buildup of stagnant water and refuse. In 1870, health concerns prompted open hearings held by the Department of Docks (1870–1942) where the construction of open-piling finger piers was suggested (Buttenwieser, 1987). This form, piers built on open piling bases and at right angles to the shoreline, is now common in New York Harbor.

The goal of the Department of Docks was to modernize the harbor for commercial shipping and they oversaw the construction of stone, iron, and concrete finger piers on a massive scale. Environmental impacts were largely ignored in favor of expanding trade capacity (Bone, 1997). During this era, Chelsea Piers were created as were numerous ferry terminals, warehouses, and immense stone and iron piers. In addition, the Department radically transformed the geography of Manhattan's waterfront, straightening the natural contours, dredging, and constructing an extensive system of riverwalls and bulkheads (Betts, 1997). Yet in spite of these efforts, the decline of New York Harbor as a commercial port was evident by the 1920s. Noncommercial interests along the Upper West Side had already defeated measures to commercialize the principally residential neighborhoods and pushed instead to develop open, recreational spaces. The creation of Riverside Park and the later construction of recreational piers and athletic facilities effectively halted maritime commercial activity on the West Side. The continued decline of major shipping in New York Harbor came in the 1960s when commerce relocated to New Jersey's Elizabeth Seaport (Buttenwieser, 1987).

Today much of the New York Harbor waterfront stands in disuse and disrepair. There is a strong interest in revitalizing the city's waterfront including construction of the Hudson River Park (www.hudsonriverpark.org). When completed, this park will be a five-mile-long public walkway along the Hudson River stretching from Battery Place to 59th Street, and its development includes the restoration of thirteen preexisting piers (Wise, Woods, and Bone, 1997). Other plans for the waterfront include Trump Place on the Hudson River front between 59th and 72nd streets. Though the city is in need of more open space, there are apprehensions about the impacts of pier restoration and construction activity on the surprisingly resilient biological resources of the Hudson River Estuary (Able and Duffy-Anderson, 2005).

The concern for the Hudson River Estuary ecosystem is not misplaced. The progressive transformation of the Hudson River has taken its toll on near-shore habitats. Over the years, the practices of dredging, filling, and bulkheading have eliminated the naturally sloping land-sea interfaces of tidal marshes and beaches (Squires, 1992). Nearly 50,000 acres of tidal wetlands have been lost in New York Harbor, and over 20 percent of that loss has occurred recently, between 1950 and 1970 (Bone, 1997). Landfill and piers have been pushed out farther and farther into the Hudson River channel and have gradually created a passageway that is considerably more narrow than its pre-European state. These changes have likely affected local circulation patterns, water velocity, and bottom topography.

In spite of these perturbations, the Hudson River and its estuary are functional ecosystems that support a complex mosaic of animal life in their waters. Biological productivity is high and a variety of species of zooplankton (Stepien, Malone,

and Chervin, 1981; Pace, Findlay, and Lints, 1992), deposit feeders (Rice et al., 1995), and suspension feeders (Strayer et al., 1994) are supported. An array of larger invertebrate organisms such as sevenspine bay shrimp (*Crangon septemspinosa*), daggerblade grass shrimp (*Palaemonetes pugio*), blue crabs (*Callinectes sapidus*), and a variety of molluscs are also common (Stanne, Panetta, and Forist, 1996), and many of these serve as prey for economically valuable species including Atlantic sturgeon (*Acipenser oxyrinchus*) (Dovel and Berggren, 1983; Van Eenennaam et al., 1996), shortnose sturgeon (*Acipenser brevirostrum*) (Hoff, Klauda, and Young, 1988), American shad (*Alosa sapidissima*) (Smith, 1985), striped bass (*Morone saxatilis*) (Waldman et al., 1990), and blue crabs (Wilson and Able, 1992). The estuary also provides critical spawning and juvenile habitat for a variety of ecologically important fish species such as Atlantic tomcod (*Microgadus tomcod*) (Dew and Hecht, 1994a; 1994b), winter flounder (*Pseudopleuronectes americanus*) (Able, Manderson, and Studholme, 1998), bluefish (*Pomatomus saltatrix*) (Chiarella and Conover, 1990), alewife (*Alosa pseudoharengus*) (Dovel, 1981), and bay anchovy (*Anchoa mitchilli*) (Dovel, 1981), among a variety of others (Able and Fahay, 1998). Finally, the Hudson River Estuary is an important migratory pathway for striped bass (Secor and Piccoli, 1996) and shad (Limburg, 1996), and provides important overwintering grounds for striped bass as well (Hurst and Conover, 1998).

The Hudson River Estuary is resilient but its aquatic species assemblage continues to be vulnerable to anthropogenic stress. Factors that degrade water quality such as chemical pollution, industrial discharge, municipal runoff, and sewage effluents compete with biological uses of the estuary. Efforts have been made to improve water and sediment quality in the lower Hudson River (Brosnan and O'Shea, 1996; O'Connor, Ranasinghe, and Adams, 1998), but there has been little effort to remedy the effects of centuries of shorezone modifications.

There have only been a few studies that examined the impact of man-made structures on estuarine fauna (Cantelmo and Wahtola, 1992; Stoecker, Collura, and Fallon, 1992) and as a result, we were interested in determining the impacts of man-made structures, especially large piers, on

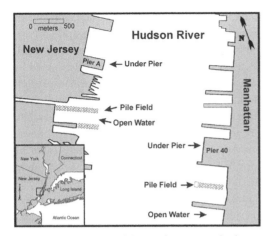

Figure 29.1. Location of the study areas in the lower Hudson River. Adapted from Able et al. (1998).

fishes in the lower Hudson River. In this chapter, we focus on the lower Hudson River and synthesize the results of our efforts from 1993 to 1999 to assess the effects of large municipal piers on juvenile fishes and selected invertebrates. Results of these studies may be representative of the effects of piers in general and could be of considerable interest to managers, developers, and conservationists working in the Hudson River Estuary and in other urban estuaries.

Studying the Effects of Piers

STUDY AREA

The study area was located in the lower Hudson River (New York Harbor), 3 km north of the Battery and 14 km south of the George Washington Bridge. Two concrete municipal piers, Port Authority Pier A (213 × 100 m), located in New Jersey, and Marine and Aviation Pier 40 (351 × 255 m), located in Manhattan, were selected as the target study sites (Fig. 29.1). We used a comparative approach and established four representative habitats associated with piers, including underneath piers, pier edges, pile fields, and open water. Under-pier sites were established under the platform decks of piers, edge sites were established at the light-shade interface between the edge of the pier and the water beyond, open water areas were located immediately adjacent to the piers (20–40 m beyond the pier edges), and pile field sites were established in areas consisting of pilings (after the deck tops of the piers

had been removed). Pile fields were situated approximately 300 m south of Pier 40 in New York and approximately 450 m south of Pier A in New Jersey.

The study area has been highly modified from its original, pre-European contours and as a result virtually no natural, shallow-water habitat remains. Concrete bulkheads predominate on both sides of the Hudson River and make the transition from the street to the water level abrupt; depths at the water line average 3–5 m (Duffy-Anderson, personal observation). In addition, much of the Harbor bottom is dredged so there is a marked vertical drop off toward the channel (from 3 m to 16 m). The lower Harbor is tidally flushed so that, like other estuaries with extensive freshwater input, the zone undergoes dramatic changes in salinity over a single tidal cycle, as much as 7–21‰ (Duffy-Anderson, personal observation), though average ranges over one tidal cycle are approximately 5–10‰. In mid August, salinities can be as high as 28‰. Temperatures during the spring, summer, and fall sampling periods (May/June–September/October, 1993–99) generally ranged from 14–26 °C and levels of dissolved oxygen during the same period generally ranged from 3–8 mg l^{-1}. Photic depths in the summer range from 3–6 m depending on sediment loading and phytoplankton growth (Stross and Sokol, 1989). Average light intensities in open water areas are considerably higher (10–50 μE^{-2} s^{-1}, depths 2–5 m) than light levels underneath large piers with solid concrete tops (0–0.02 μE^{-2} s^{-1}, depths 2–3 m) (Able et al., 1998; Duffy-Anderson and Able, 1999).

HABITAT QUALITY ASSESSMENT TECHNIQUES

Our assessment strategy was consistent with the guidelines established by the National Marine Fisheries Service for fish habitat evaluation on Essential Fish Habitat (EFH) (Schreiber and Gill, 1995; Minello, 1999). EFH defines four levels of evaluation, ranging from the most basic, initial fish presence-absence characterization (Level 1) to the most sophisticated, estimates of fish production (Level 4) (Able, 1999). We used this multilevel approach to assess the impacts of piers on fishes in the Hudson River. First, we employed Level 1 and 2 approaches, and estimated distribution (Level 1) and abundance (Level 2) of fishes around piers and in other adjacent habitats to rank their habitat value relative to one another. Next we used estimates of feeding and growth (Level 3) to quantify the habitat value of each of those areas. We have not attempted to employ a Level 4 approach, estimating fish production, as this method requires additional estimates of population size, rates of natural mortality, and fish immigration and emigration that are currently unavailable. Nonetheless, by using the first three levels of assessment we have provided a layered, multidimensional, and independent assessment of the habitat value of piers for fishes.

Responses of Fishes to Piers

DISTRIBUTION AND ABUNDANCE

We examined the spatial distribution (Level 1) and abundance (Level 2) of fishes under piers, at pier edges, in pile fields, and in open water in 1993, 1994, and 1996 (see Able et al., 1998 for a more complete description) to assess their value as habitat. Unbaited traps were deployed on the bottom at each of the study sites where they remained submerged for 24 h and were recovered on the following day. All captured fishes were measured and catch data were standardized to catch per unit effort (CPUE, expressed as individuals trap^{-1} day^{-1}).

As a result of the above efforts, we collected 1,756 individual fish of thirty different species in three years of sampling across all habitat types. Most of the fishes were young-of-the-year (YOY) individuals (see Able et al., 1998; Duffy-Anderson, Manderson, and Able, 2003), though large American eels (*Anguilla rostrata*) were common. The most abundant fish species was the striped bass, which made up 23 percent of the total catch. Atlantic tomcod, American eel, black sea bass (*Centropristis striata*), and cunner (*Tautogolabrus adspersus*) also constituted large portions of the fish catch, comprising 17 percent, 12 percent, 10 percent, and 7 percent, respectively. There were variations in abundance of individual species among years, with large numbers of certain species occurring in some years and not in others. For example, black sea bass were collected in high numbers in 1994 but in 1993 and 1996 they were very rare. Similarly, spotted hake (*Urophycis regia*) were collected in abundance in 1996 but were infrequent in 1993 and 1994. Finally,

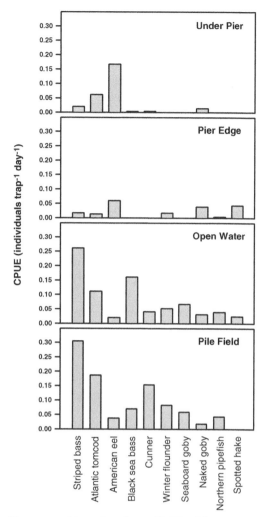

Figure 29.2. Mean abundance (CPUE) of the 10 most abundant fish species under piers, at pier edges, in open water, and in pile fields based on data collected in 1993, 1994, and 1996.

cunner were very abundant in 1993 and 1994, but were completely absent from collections in 1996.

There were marked dissimilarities in fish distribution in different habitats. Mean fish abundance (CPUE) was consistently lower under piers (though variability was high) compared to open water, pile field, or edge habitats. Only one species, the American eel, was ever collected from under-pier areas more frequently than in any other habitat (Fig. 29.2). Atlantic tomcod and naked goby (*Gobiosoma bosc*) were not uncommon in under-pier traps but they were collected in higher numbers at other sites. In addition, the total number of species collected from under piers was lower (n = 16 species) than the total number collected in pile fields (n = 21 species) or in open water (n = 27 species). Many of the species collected from under-pier habitats were only collected once and were never observed under piers again during the three year sampling survey. In contrast, many of the species found in the other habitat types were observed there on more than just one occasion and some, such as spotted hake, tautog (*Tautoga onitis*), and northern pipefish (*Syngnathus fuscus*), were collected repeatedly (Able et al., 1998). It should be noted that the traps used in this study were designed specifically to sample small, young-of-the-year, benthic fishes. As such, other fish species that are common to the Hudson River may not have been effectively sampled, especially pelagic fishes that occur higher in the water column. Still, our data suggest that fish abundance is consistently depressed under piers over multiple years, indicating that piers are lower-quality habitats for fishes relative to edges, pile fields, or open water (Able et al., 1998; Duffy-Anderson and Able, 1999; Able, Manderson, and Studholme, 1999; Duffy-Anderson et al., 2003).

Interestingly, the three fish species collected under piers (American eels, Atlantic tomcod, and naked goby) and the decapod species (Able and Duffy-Anderson, 2005) collected share a common characteristic; they do not rely strictly on the use of vision to forage; rather, they demonstrate various abilities to utilize alternative sensory systems to locate and capture prey. For example, American eels and Atlantic tomcod can detect chemicals in solution (Herrick, 1904; Teichmann, 1954; Silver, 1979). Some gobies have been shown to have a similar ability to detect chemicals (Utne and Bacchi, 1997), though it has also been demonstrated that their reactive distance to predators declines with decreasing light intensity (Aksnes and Utne, 1997), suggesting that vision is still an important component of the overall sensory behavior of the animals. Intense shading from the solid decks of the piers examined in our study drastically reduced light penetration to the waters below. Light levels under piers were approximately 4–5 orders of magnitude lower than outside of piers (0.001–0.02 $\mu E^{-2}\ s^{-1}$ under piers versus 20–60 $\mu E^{-1}\ s^{-1}$ outside of piers, Duffy-Anderson and Able, 1999).

Occasionally the levels were so low that they were below the detection of our light meters. Light is a limiting factor that affects the ability of visually-foraging fish to search for prey (Boeuf and Le Bail, 1999). At low light intensities, important factors associated with prey recognition, such as prey contrast and hue, are reduced (Gerking, 1994) limiting the ability of fish to identify prey items. Similarly, reactive distance, the maximum distance at which visual predators can detect their prey (Vinyard and O'Brien, 1976) declines with declining light intensities (O'Brien, 1979), reducing the search volume of visually feeding fish. Thus, visually foraging fishes may not occur under piers because conditions of intense shading interfere with one or more of the steps in the predation cycle. We therefore speculate that under-pier areas may only serve as functional habitat for a few select species, perhaps only those with supplementary sensory systems that allow them to forage more effectively in darkness, while simultaneously being inhospitable to a variety of other estuarine species.

GROWTH OF SELECTED FISHES
If certain species are better able to forage under piers than others, that ability should be reflected as a difference in growth rate. Therefore, we designed a series of experiments to determine differences in growth rates between fishes more frequently collected under piers and those that were infrequently found in under-pier habitats. We hypothesized that species collected under piers would have higher growth rates in under-pier habitats than species that occurred there less often. These studies would not only reveal more about differences in pier habitat use among fishes, but they would also provide a more quantitative measure of pier habitat quality (Level 3) that could augment our initial observations.

Based on abundances estimated from the trapping experiments, we chose two fish species that were uncommon in our under-pier collections, winter flounder and tautog, and one species that was collected from beneath piers more regularly, the Atlantic tomcod, as our target species for growth experiments. Young-of-the-year fish of a single species were confined to benthic cages deployed to open water, pile fields, under piers, and at pier edges for ten day periods and changes in fish weight (that is, growth rate in weight) were determined. Randomly chosen specimens also served as controls, which were kept in the laboratory for ten days without food. Growth experiments occurred in 1994, 1996, 1997, and 1998 (see Duffy-Anderson and Able, 1999; Able et al., 1999; and Metzger, Duffy-Anderson, and Able, 2001 for more complete descriptions).

As a result of these experiments over four years, we observed variations in growth rate among habitat types and between the three test species. Young-of-the-year winter flounder had negative growth rates (that is, they experienced weight loss) when they were caged under piers, indicating that the fish had fed poorly (Fig. 29.3). In fact, weight loss under piers was strikingly similar to weight loss among control individuals, the fish that were intentionally starved in the laboratory for ten day periods. In contrast, winter flounder grew well in open water habitats adjacent to piers and in pile fields. Individuals also grew at pier edges but rates in that habitat were generally lower than in pile fields or open water (approximately 40 percent less).

Growth rates among caged YOY tautog followed similar patterns, though variability was somewhat higher (Fig. 29.3). Tautog caged under piers also lost weight at rates comparable to laboratory-starved control fish. In contrast, tautog caged at pier edges, in pile fields, and in open water grew rapidly with several individuals actually doubling their body weight over the course of the ten day experiments.

Results with Atlantic tomcod yielded somewhat different results. In contrast to the YOY winter flounder and tautog, two species that lost weight under piers, YOY Atlantic tomcod gained weight when caged in under-pier habitats, though weight gain under piers was not as rapid as weight gain at edges or in open water (Fig. 29.3). In fact, though growth under the pier was positive, it occurred at nearly half the rate as growth at pier edges or outside of the pier, a substantial discrepancy that could have important impacts on the overall recruitment success of juveniles to the adult population (Sogard, 1997; Beck et al., 2001).

The general outcome of the growth experiments followed hypothesized patterns. Fishes that were more frequently collected from under piers should be better able to utilize those habitats than fishes

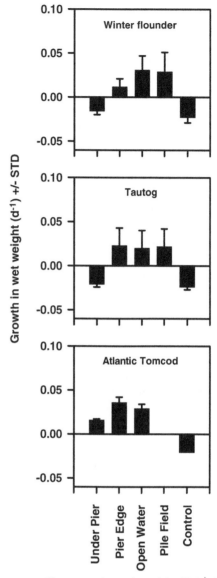

Figure 29.3. Mean growth rate in weight $(G_W) \pm$ STD of young-of-the-year winter flounder, tautog, and Atlantic tomcod caged under piers and in adjacent habitats in the lower Hudson River based on data collected in 1994, 1996, 1997, and 1998.

that occur there less frequently, and indeed, growth observations supported that theory. However, the data also suggested that while YOY Atlantic tomcod could grow in under-pier habitats, growth was lower than at edges or in open water. Therefore, we concluded that under-pier areas were unsuitable habitats for YOY winter flounder and tautog, and low-quality habitats for Atlantic tomcod relative to edges or open water. It was still not clear why piers had these negative effects, but it seemed unlikely that factors associated with pilings themselves were responsible because growth rates in pile fields (pilings without decking) were similar to growth rates in open water.

Why could Atlantic tomcod grow better under piers than winter flounder or tautog? We formulated two hypotheses to address this question: 1) Atlantic tomcod were better able to forage in low light and therefore could locate more food than winter flounder or tautog, or, 2) Atlantic tomcod consumed a different food source than the other two species. Winter flounder and tautog consume primarily benthic organisms as prey (Pearcy, 1962; Grover, 1982) but previous work on juvenile Atlantic tomcod suggested that individuals <90 mm TL consumed primarily planktonic prey types (Grabe, 1978). The Atlantic tomcod used in these experiments were in this size range (44–91 mm TL), therefore, the hypothesis that they utilized a different food source seemed likely. We examined the stomach contents of the caged fish to determine whether the diets among the three test species were dissimilar. We also used the data to compare the feeding habits of each species under, at the edge, and outside of the pier.

FEEDING

The stomachs from YOY winter flounder, tautog, and Atlantic tomcod used in several of the caging growth experiments (1996, 1997, 1998) were removed and the contents were identified. Afterwards, the contents were dried and weighed to examine stomach fullness. This procedure only revealed the diet of fishes at the end of the experiment but it probably represented the diet of the fishes during the entire ten day feeding experiments.

The types of prey consumed by winter flounder caged under piers, at pier edges, and in open water were similar and benthic organisms comprised the majority of the stomach contents. Interestingly, winter flounder caged under piers had some food in their stomachs but growth under piers was negative. Thus, it seemed that their restricted energy intake was not sufficient to meet their metabolic expenditures. Principal prey items of winter flounder caged at all locations were harpacticoid copepods and gammarid amphipods.

Polychaetes, isopods, barnacles, ostracods, and brachiopods were also found in the stomachs of some fish caged at edges and in open water, but were absent from the stomachs of under-pier fish. Mean stomach content dry weights were generally lower under piers ($\bar{x} = 0.07$ mg $\pm$ 0.13) than in open water ($\bar{x} = 0.34$ mg $\pm$ 0.46), which is consistent with lower growth under piers compared to edges or outside.

Results were similar among caged tautog. Tautog also consumed primarily benthic organisms, though identification of stomach contents in this species was more difficult due to the grinding of food items with the pharyngeal teeth (Olla et al., 1974). Most of the contents appeared to be harpacticoid copepods and mysids, though amphipods were occasionally found in the stomachs of fishes caged outside of the pier. Tautog caged outside of the pier generally had higher stomach content dry weights ($\bar{x} = 0.24$ mg $\pm$ 0.54) than of those caged under the pier ($\bar{x} = 0.06$ mg $\pm$ 0.12) and lower stomach weights were probably directly related to poor growth of tautog under piers.

The diets of caged Atlantic tomcod were very similar to those of caged winter flounder and tautog; Atlantic tomcod consumed benthic prey organisms (see Metzger et al., 2001 for a more complete description). In fact, we did not find a single planktonic prey item in the stomachs of the dissected fish even though this has been reported in other studies (Grabe, 1978). Principal prey items for caged tomcod were harpacticoid copepods and amphipods, though we also found isopods, nematodes, invertebrate eggs, saltwater mites, and a polychaete. Like winter flounder and tautog, Atlantic tomcod caged under the pier had a lower mean stomach content dry weight ($\bar{x} = 0.34$ mg $\pm$ 0.77) than fish caged at the edge ($\bar{x} = 0.99$ mg $\pm$ 1.3) or outside of the pier ($\bar{x} = 1.01$ mg $\pm$ 1.13), again probably contributing to observed lower growth rates. It appeared that growth of Atlantic tomcod under piers was not explained by differences in diet. It seemed more likely that our first hypothesis, that Atlantic tomcod could forage more efficiently in low light than winter flounder or tautog, was correct.

Recall that at the conclusion of the growth experiments we determined that the growth rates of all three test species, winter flounder, tautog, and Atlantic tomcod were depressed under piers relative to edges or open water. Since the above experiments revealed that all three of these species exploited the same food source, it could be that the general depression in growth rates under piers was due to lower abundances of benthic prey under piers compared to edges or outside. Since this hypothesis remained untested, we attempted to quantify the benthic prey organisms in the sediments around a pier to determine whether prey levels under piers were depressed.

PREY AVAILABILITY

We examined the availability of benthic prey for YOY fishes caged around a municipal pier by coring the sediments around Pier 40 during the summers of 1998 and 1999 (June–July). Four replicate samples (3.0 cm diameter, 2.0 cm depth) were collected under, at the edge, and outside of the pier. Samples were returned to the laboratory where the contents were sorted, identified, and enumerated (see Duffy-Anderson and Able, 2001 for a complete description).

The benthos was dominated by nematodes and foraminifera (98 percent), though invertebrate eggs, polychaetes (capitellids and nereids), and copepods also made up a portion of the assemblage. Previous work indicated that nematoda and foraminifera did not make up a significant portion of the diet of YOY winter flounder, tautog, or Atlantic tomcod (Grabe, 1978; Klein-MacPhee, 1978; Sogard, 1992; Stehlik and Meise, 2000; Vivian et al., 2000; Metzger et al., 2001). As such, more appropriate estimates of prey availability for these fishes excluded nematodes and foraminifera from the analyses. Interestingly, when these two taxa were eliminated, significantly higher fish prey abundances were noted under the pier compared to outside in both years, though there were no significant differences in prey dry weight across the transect (Duffy-Anderson and Able, 2001). Previous findings at a nearby pier (Pier 76) in the lower Hudson River (Stoecker et al., 1992) found overall invertebrate abundances were higher under the pier than outside. It is currently not known if the apparent lower prey availability in open water is a function of grazing by perhaps, more abundant fishes, and higher

availability under the pier is due to reduced grazing under piers caused by a depression in fish abundance. It is important to note that benthic prey appeared to be available in sufficient quantities for feeding of fish caged underneath municipal piers. Therefore, the hypothesis of limited prey availability under piers seemed an unlikely explanation for lower growth rates under piers as determined in the caging experiments. With this hypothesis eliminated, the issue of low light availability under piers seemed to take on even more significance.

Discussion

The potential value of man-made structures as habitats for fishes is of considerable interest and may be especially relevant in urban estuaries like New York Harbor where little natural habitat remains in shallow, nearshore waters. We have shown that at least one type of man-made structure, large piers, do not afford suitable habitat to a number of fish species in the lower Hudson River. This conclusion is based on three of the four levels of habitat evaluation, distribution (Level 1), abundance (Level 2), and feeding and growth (Level 3), as previously outlined (Schreiber and Gill, 1995; Able, 1999; Minello, 1999). We conclude that under-pier areas are poor-quality habitats because they support low fish abundances, inhibit feeding, and suppress growth. We believe that low light levels under piers (as measured over several years of study) are directly related to their lower habitat value relative to other areas (Table 29.1) and several lines of evidence support this view. First, the few species that are more commonly collected from beneath piers (American eels, Atlantic tomcod, naked goby, decapod crustaceans) share an ability to capitalize on sensory systems other than vision (chemoreception, mechanoreception) to locate prey in conditions of near-darkness. Visually feeding fishes generally do not occur under piers, probably because the low-light conditions there interfere with their ability to feed. Second, two fish species that use visual foraging mechanisms, winter flounder and tautog, show reductions in food intake and poor growth under piers, in spite of having more than sufficient numbers of prey available for consumption. Third, these same two species of fish grow

Table 29.1. Habitat values of pier-related habitats in the lower Hudson River based on estimates of distribution, abundance, feeding, and growth of young-of-the-year fishes in New York Harbor

Habitat	Level 1 (Distribution)	Level 2 (Abundance)	Level 3 (Feeding and Growth)	Level 4 (Fish Production)
Under pier	–	–	–	N/A
Pier edge	++	++	++	N/A
Pile field	+++	+++	+++	N/A
Open water	+++	+++	+++	N/A

N/A indicates data not available.

well in pile fields, which are areas that are virtually identical in structure to piers themselves but lack the decking that reduce light levels in the water below. Finally, a species of fish that can utilize alternative prey detection mechanisms, the Atlantic tomcod, can grow under piers, albeit at reduced rates compared to other habitats. Considered collectively, these findings indicate that under-pier habitats are not utilized by many fish species because foraging is impeded by conditions of intense shading. The consequences of shading may not be solely restricted to piers, as other large objects casting substantial shadows may have similar effects. Such items could include, but are not limited to, permanently moored vessels, floating platforms, and large docks.

Management Considerations

An important consideration for proposed developments in New York Harbor is whether the effects of piers can be mitigated through structural modifications. We did not attempt to compare various pier characteristics in our studies, however, others have identified several key features of man-made structures that affect growth of adjacent vegetation and it may be that some of those factors are important for fishes and invertebrates as well. For example, dock height (distance from the water's surface) has been shown to be an important factor affecting growth of vegetation (Kearney, Segal, and Lefor, 1983; Burdick and Short, 1999). It follows that structures that float directly on the water's surface would allow the least amount of light penetration below and may, in fact, be a worst-case scenario for visual feeders. Similarly, pier width could have

an affect on light penetration. The piers examined in our studies were extremely wide and covered in asphalt, allowing no light penetration immediately beneath their surfaces. Future pier construction efforts could consider a light-penetrable design. Artificial lighting beneath piers is probably not as efficient as allowing incident sunlight to pass through because fishes are sensitive to the characteristics of the light spectrum as well as to its absolute light intensity (Fernald, 1993). Finally, piers that are built in a north-south direction tend to support greater densities of eelgrass than piers that run east-west (Burdick and Short, 1998) because an east-west configuration follows the daily path of the sun and results in continuous shading beneath the pier.

It is currently not known whether the effects of piers can be reduced with nominal structural revisions or whether more drastic remedies are required. Studies that more closely examine the effects of edges may provide some answers. Fish abundances are higher at edges than under piers (Duffy-Anderson et al., 2003) and growth can occur at edges even among fish species that show negative growth under piers (Duffy-Anderson and Able, 1999). Pier edges have the potential to modify the intensity of shading by diffusing the pier shadow (Burdick and Short, 1998) and the duration of shading by refracting incident light. Our results suggest that some easing of shade effects occurs around edges so pier designs that allow greater edge-to-surface ratios may be preferable.

Future work should be conducted to determine how broadly applicable our observations of pier impacts are. The studies discussed in this chapter were conducted underneath very large piers but marinas, fishing piers, and individual boat docks all have the capacity to shade potential fish habitat. Shade-related impacts in these systems may be of even greater concern as many of these smaller piers are often constructed in natural, shallow-water areas that provide important habitat for young-of-the-year fishes (Able and Fahay, 1998; Minello, 1999). The effects of piers in oceanic environments has not been well studied. Oceanic piers exist in many coastal communities but their effects on fishes are still unknown. Examples of ocean-side structures that could have shade-related impacts include beach-side homes, condominiums and hotels, and large, public piers. Studies that examine the impacts of piers in these environments are much needed and could provide important information on habitat use, growth, survival, and recruitment.

Conclusions

New York Harbor is home to a variety of marine and estuarine species that depend on informed and responsible management practices. Recognition of the important ecological role this system plays is critical to the overall health of the estuary. Development projects that would reduce species abundance, limit diversity, inhibit feeding, and lower growth should be avoided. We have demonstrated that municipal piers in the lower Hudson River have these consequences, and our studies suggest that shading is responsible. We support efforts to reduce the duration, intensity, and area of shading in existing and future pier development projects. The lower Hudson River continues to be important spawning and juvenile fish habitat for a host of commercially and recreationally important species so new development projects that have the potential to shade open, shallow-water (<5 m) areas in this system should be carefully evaluated prior to approval.

Acknowledgments

We gratefully acknowledge the support of the Hudson River Foundation, whose continued interest in our ideas has made the work presented in this chapter possible. Special thanks is due to many individuals who assisted in this effort, especially J. Manderson, D. Vivian, and C. Metzger. The National Marine Fisheries Service at Sandy Hook, the U.S. Army Corps of Engineers at Caven Point, The River Project, the Borough of Rumson, and Liberty State Park all generously provided access to their facilities. M. Ludwig provided comments on an earlier version of this chapter. This is Rutgers University, Institute of Marine and Coastal Sciences Contribution 2004–05. This is FOCI Contribution Number 0440.

REFERENCES

Able, K. W. 1999. Measures of juvenile fish habitat quality: examples from a National Estuarine Research Reserve, in Benaka, L. R. (ed.), *Fish Habitat: Essential Fish Habitat and Rehabilitation*. American Fisheries Society Special Symposium 22, Bethesda, MD, pp. 134–47.

Able, K. W., and Duffy-Anderson, J. T. 2005. *A Synthesis of Impacts of Piers on Juvenile Fishes and Selected Invertebrates in the Lower Hudson River*. Rutgers University, Institute of Marine and Coastal Sciences Technical Report #2005–13, New Brunswick, NJ.

Able, K. W., and Fahay, M. P. 1998. The First Year in the Life of Estuarine Fishes in the Middle Atlantic Bight. New Brunswick, NJ: Rutgers University Press.

Able, K. W., Manderson, J. P., and Studholme, A. L. 1998. The distribution of shallow water juvenile fishes in an urban estuary: the effects of man-made structures in the lower Hudson River. *Estuaries* 21(4b):731–44.

1999. Habitat quality for shallow water fishes in an urban estuary: The effects of manmade structures on growth. *Marine Ecology Progress Series* 187:227–35.

Aksnes, D. L., and Utne, A. C. W. 1997. A revised model of visual range in fish. *Sarsia* 82:137–47.

Beck, M. W., Heck, Jr., K. L., Able, K. W., Childers, D., Eggleston, D., Gillanders, B. M., Halpern, B., Hays, C., Hoshino, K., Minello, T., Orth, R., Sheridan, P., and Weinstein, M. 2001. The identification, conservation, and management of estuarine and marine nurseries for fish and invertebrates. *Bioscience* 51:633–41.

Betts, M. B. 1997. Masterplanning: Municipal support of maritime transport and commerce 1870–1930s, in Bone, K. (ed.), *The New York Waterfront: Evolution and Building Culture of the Port and Harbor*. New York: Monacelli Press Inc., pp. 39–83.

Boeuf, G., and Le Bail, P. Y. 1999. Does light have an influence on fish growth? *Aquaculture* **177**(1–4): 129–52.

Bone, K. 1997. Horizontal city: Architecture and construction in the port of New York, in Bone, K. (ed.), *The New York Waterfront: Evolution and Building Culture of the Port and Harbor*. New York: Monacelli Press Inc., pp. 87–151.

Brosnan, T. M., and O'Shea, M. L. 1996. Long-term improvements in water quality due to sewage abatement in the lower Hudson River. *Estuaries* **19**:890–900.

Burdick, D. M., and Short, F. T. 1998. *Dock Design with the Environment in Mind: Minimizing Dock Impacts to Eelgrass Habitats. An Interactive CD-ROM*. Durham, NH: University of New Hampshire.

1999. The effects of boat docks on eelgrass in coastal waters of Massachusetts. *Environmental Management* **23**:231–40.

Buttenwieser, A. L. 1987. *Manhattan Water-Bound: Planning and Developing Manhattan's Waterfront from the Seventeenth Century to the Present*. New York: New York University Press.

Cantelmo, F. R., and Wahtola, Jr., C. H. 1992. Aquatic habitat impacts of pile-supported and other structures in the lower Hudson River, in Wise, W., D. J. Suszkowski, and J. R. Waldman (eds.), *Proceedings: Conference on the Impacts of New York Harbor Development on Aquatic Resources*. New York: Hudson River Foundation, pp. 59–75.

Chiarella, L. A., and Conover, D. O. 1990. Spawning season and first-year growth of adult bluefish from the New York Bight. *Transactions of the American Fisheries Society* **119**:455–62.

Dew, C. B., and Hecht, J. H. 1994a. Hatching, estuarine transport, and distribution of larval and early juvenile Atlantic tomcod, *Microgadus tomcod*, in the Hudson River. *Estuaries* **17**:472–88.

1994b. Recruitment, growth, mortality, and biomass production of larval and early juvenile Atlantic tomcod in the Hudson River Estuary. *Transactions of the American Fisheries Society* **123**: 681–702.

Dovel, W. L. 1981. Ichthyoplankton of the lower Hudson Estuary, New York. *New York Fish and Game Journal* **28**:21–39.

Dovel, W. L., and Berggren, T. J. 1983. Atlantic sturgeon of the Hudson estuary. *New York Fish and Game Journal* **30**:140–72.

Duffy-Anderson, J. T., and Able, K. W. 1999. Effects of municipal piers on the growth of juvenile fish in the Hudson River estuary: a study across a pier edge. *Marine Biology* **133**:409–418.

2001. An assessment of the feeding success of young-of-the-year winter flounder (*Pseudopleuronectes americanus*) near a municipal pier in the Hudson River estuary, U.S.A. *Estuaries* **24**:430–40.

Duffy-Anderson, J. T., Manderson, J. P., and Able, K. W. 2003. A characterization of juvenile fish assemblages around man-made structure in the New York-New Jersey harbor estuary, U.S.A. *Bulletin of Marine Science* **72**:877–89.

Fernald, R. D. 1993. Vision, in Evans, D. H. (ed.), *The Physiology of Fishes*. Boca Raton, FL: CRC Press, pp. 161–89.

Gerking, S. D. 1994. *Feeding Ecology of Fish*. New York: Academic Press.

Grabe, S. A. 1978. Food and feeding habits of juvenile Atlantic tomcod, *Microgadus tomcod*, from Haverstraw Bay, Hudson River. *Fishery Bulletin* U.S. **76**:89–94.

Grover, J. J. 1982. "The comparative feeding ecology of five inshore, marine fishes off Long Island, New York." Ph.D. Dissertation, Rutgers, The State University of New Jersey.

Herrick, C. J. 1904. The organ and sense of taste in fishes. *Bulletin of the United States Fish Commission* **22**:239–72.

Hoff, T. B., Klauda, R. J., and Young, J. R. 1988. Contribution to the biology of shortnose sturgeon in the Hudson River Estuary, in Smith, C. L. (ed.), *Fisheries Research in the Hudson River*. Albany, NY: State University of New York Press, pp. 171–89.

Hurst, T. P., and Conover, D. O. 1998. Winter mortally of young-of-the-year Hudson River striped bass (*Morone saxatilis*): size-dependent patterns and effects on recruitment. *Canadian Journal of Fisheries and Aquatic Sciences* **55**: 1122–30.

Kearney, V., Segal, Y., and Lefor, M. 1983. The effects of docks on salt marsh vegetation. Connecticut State Department of Environmental Protection.

Klein-MacPhee, G. 1978. Synopsis of biological data for the winter flounder, *Pseudopleuronectes americanus* (Walbaum). *FAO Fisheries Synopses* **117**: 1–43.

Limburg, K. E. 1996. Growth and migration of 0-year American shad (*Alosa sapidissima*) in the Hudson River estuary: otolith microstructural analysis. *Canadian Journal of Fisheries and Aquatic Sciences* **53**:220–38.

Metzger, C. V., Duffy-Anderson, J. T., and Able, K. W. 2001. Effects of a municipal pier on growth of young-of-the year Atlantic tomcod (*Microgadus tomcod*): A study in the Hudson River estuary. *Bulletin of the New Jersey Academy of Science* **46**(1):5–10.

Minello, T. J. 1999. Nekton densities in shallow estuarine habitats of Texas and Louisiana and the identification of Essential Fish Habitat, in Benaka, L. R. (ed.), *Fish Habitat: Essential Fish Habitat and Rehabilitation*. American Fisheries Society, Special Symposium 22, Bethesda, MD, pp. 43–75.

O'Brien, W. J. 1979. The predator-prey interaction of planktivorous fish and zooplankton. *American Scientist* **67**:572–581.

O'Connor, J. S., Ranasinghe, J. A., and Adams, D. A. 1998. Temporal change in sediment quality of the New York Harbor area. *Bulletin of the New Jersey Academy of Sciences* **432**:1–6.

Olla, B. L., Bejda, A. L., and Martin, A. D. 1974. Daily activity, movements, feeding, and seasonal occurrence in the tautog, *Tautoga onitis*. *Fishery Bulletin*. **72**:27–35.

Pace, M. L., Findlay, S. E., and Lints, D. 1992. Zooplankton in advective environments: the Hudson River community and a comparative analysis. *Canadian Journal of Fisheries and Aquatic Sciences* **49**:1060–9.

Pearcy, W. G. 1962. Ecology of an estuarine population of winter flounder *Pseudopleuronectes americanus* (Walbaum). *Bulletin of the Bingham Oceanographic Collections* **18**:1–78.

Rice, C. A., Plesha, P. D., Casillas, E., Misitano, D. A., and Meador, J. P. 1995. Growth and survival of three marine invertebrate species in sediments from the Hudson-Raritan Estuary, New York. *Environmental Toxicology and Chemistry* **14**:1931–40.

Schreiber, R. A., and Gill, T. A. 1995. *Identification and Mapping of Essential Fish Habitat: An Approach to Assessment and Protection*. Habitat Policy and Management Division, NMFS; and Strategic Environmental Assessments Division, NOS, NOAA.

Secor, D. H., and Piccoli, P. M. 1996. Age- and sex-dependent migrations of striped bass in the Hudson River as determined by chemical microanalysis of otoliths. *Estuaries* **19**:778–93.

Silver, W. L. 1979. "Electrophysiological responses from the olfactory system of the American eel." Ph.D. Dissertation. Florida State University, Tallahassee, FL.

Smith, C. L. 1985. *The Inland Fishes of New York State*. Albany, NY: NY State Department of Environmental Conservation.

Sogard, S. M. 1992. Variability in growth rates of juvenile fishes in different estuarine habitats. *Marine Ecology Progress Series* **85**:35–53.

   1997. Size-selective mortality in the juvenile stage of teleost fishes: a review. *Bulletin of Marine Science* **60**:1129–57.

Squires, D. F. 1992. Quantifying anthropogenic shoreline modification of the Hudson River and Estuary from European contact to modern time. *Coastal Management* **20**:343–54.

Stanne, S. P., Panetta, R. G., and Forist, B. E. 1996. *The Hudson: An Illustrated Guide to the Living River*. New Brunswick, NJ: Rutgers University Press.

Stehlik, L. L., and Meise, C. J. 2000. Diet of winter flounder in a New Jersey estuary: ontogenetic change and spatial variation. *Estuaries* **23**:381–91.

Stepien, J. C., Malone, T. C., and Chervin, M. B. 1981. Copepod communities in the estuary and coastal plume of the Hudson River. *Estuarine, Coastal, and Shelf Science* **13**:185–95.

Stoecker, R. R., Collura, J., and Fallon, Jr., P. J. 1992. Aquatic studies at the Hudson River Center Site, in Smith, C. L. (ed.), *Estuarine Research in the 1980s. The Hudson River Environmental Society Seventh Symposium on Hudson River Ecology*. Albany, NY: State University of New York Press, pp. 407–27.

Strayer, D. L., Hunter, C. C., Smith, C. L., and Borg, C. K. 1994. Distribution, abundance, and roles of freshwater clams (Bivalvia: Unionidae) in the freshwater tidal Hudson River. *Freshwater Biology* **31**:239–48.

Stross, R. G., and Sokol, R. C. 1989. Runoff and flocculation modify underwater light environment of the Hudson River Estuary. *Estuarine, Coastal and Shelf Science* **29**:305–316.

Teichmann, H. 1954. Vergleichende Untersuchugen an der Nase der Fische. Zeitschrift für Morphologie der Tiere **43**:171–212.

Utne, A. C. W., and Bacchi, B. 1997. The influence of visual and chemical stimuli from cod (*Gadus morhua*) on the distribution of two-spotted goby *Gobiusculus flavescens* (Fabricius). *Sarsia* **82**:129–35.

Van Eenennaam, J. P., Dorashov, S. I., Moberg, G. P., Watson, J. G., Moore, D. S., and Linares, J. 1996. Reproductive conditions of the Atlantic sturgeon (*Acipenser oxyrinchus*) in the Hudson River. *Estuaries* **19**:769–77.

Vinyard, G. L., and O'Brien, W. J. 1976. Effects of light and turbidity on the reactive distance of bluegill (*Lepomis macrochirus*). *Journal of the Fisheries Research Board of the Canada* **29**:1193–1201.

Vivian, D. N., Duffy-Anderson, J. T., Arndt, R. G., and Able, K. W. 2000. Feeding habits of young-of-the year winter flounder, *Pseudopleuronectes americanus*, in the Hudson River estuary, U.S.A. *Bulletin of the New Jersey Academy of Sciences* **45**:1–6.

Waldman, J. R., Dunning, D. J., Ross, Q. E., and Mattson, M. T. 1990. Range dynamics of Hudson River striped bass along the Atlantic coast. *Transactions of the American Fisheries Society* **119**: 910–91.

Wilson, K. A., and Able, K. W. 1992. *Blue crab (Callinectes sapidus) habitat utilization and survival in the Hudson River.* New Brunswick,

NJ: Rutgers University, Institute of Marine and Coastal Sciences, Technical Report. 92–49.

Wise, M. Z., Woods, W., and Bone, E. 1997. Evolving purposes: The case of the Hudson River waterfront, in Bone, K. (ed.), *The New York Waterfront: Evolution and Building Culture of the Port and Harbor.* New York: Monacelli Press Inc., pp. 193–233.

30 Physiological and Genetic Aspects of Toxicity in Hudson River Species

Isaac Wirgin, Judith S. Weis,
and Anne E. McElroy

ABSTRACT The Hudson River Estuary has been polluted for many decades with organic contaminants including PCBs, dioxins/furans, PAHs, pesticides, and a variety of toxic metals, including cadmium and mercury. Most of these toxicants are poorly metabolized, highly persistent, bioaccumulative, and biomagnify in Hudson River populations, sometimes to record high levels. Many surveys have quantified tissue levels of these contaminants in resource species, but despite public concern and a need to evaluate toxicities for regulatory actions, few studies have directly addressed their biological impacts on Hudson River populations. With several notable exceptions, toxicant-induced perturbations are not frequently observed in Hudson River populations, even those for which high levels of exposure have been documented. This may have resulted from the ability of populations to acquire resistance to high levels of contaminants, either through genetic adaptations or compensatory physiological acclimation responses. While offering short-term benefits to impacted populations, resistance may be associated with evolutionary costs to populations and may compromise the viability of affected communities. Ideally, in the future, contaminant studies should focus on those species for which toxic alterations have been observed which may impact population viability, their levels of contamination should be quantified, and controlled laboratory experiments should be conducted to confirm that the contaminants of concern are able to induce these toxic manifestations in the affected taxon.

The Problem: Assessment of Toxicity of Hudson River-borne Pollutants

There is a need for government agencies to evaluate the toxic impacts of contaminants on the Hudson River (HR) biota to determine if damage to its populations has occurred and to guide remediation efforts. Surveys have quantified the concentrations of these xenobiotics in HR environmental matrices including water, sediment, and biota. The ability of many of these contaminants to bioaccumulate, and for the lipophilic, poorly or non-metabolizable pollutants, to biomagnify in the upper trophic levels of the Hudson River food chain has been documented. Far fewer studies have evaluated toxic effects of these contaminants on Hudson River populations.

Because of its history as a sink for extraordinarily high levels of contaminants, four locales in the HR Estuary (Foundry Cove, New York, river miles (RM) 0 to RM 197 of the main stem HR, the Passaic River, New Jersey, and Berry's Creek, New Jersey), have been designated as U.S. Federal Superfund sites (Fig. 30.1). For some pollutants and exposed taxa, sediment concentrations and tissue burdens of contaminants were among the highest ever observed worldwide. Contamination of the Newark Bay complex in the lower estuary with dioxins/furans (PCDD/Fs) is extensive because of their release from an industrial facility along the tributary Passaic River, which for decades manufactured phenoxy herbicides and DDT. A 197-mile reach of the HR is designated a Superfund Site, the largest in the country, because up to 1.3 million pounds of PCBs were released from two electrical capacitor manufacturing facilities at RM 195 and RM 197. Sediments in Berry's Creek, New Jersey, which drains into the Hackensack River, contained among the highest mercury (Hg) levels known in freshwater ecosystems nationwide.

Populations in the HR Estuary have been exposed to levels of many contaminants that elicit toxic effects in laboratory animals. However, intrinsic compensatory mechanisms may ameliorate the toxic effects of many of these contaminants. Exposure to contaminants does not necessarily mean that they bioaccumulate to toxic levels. Decreased

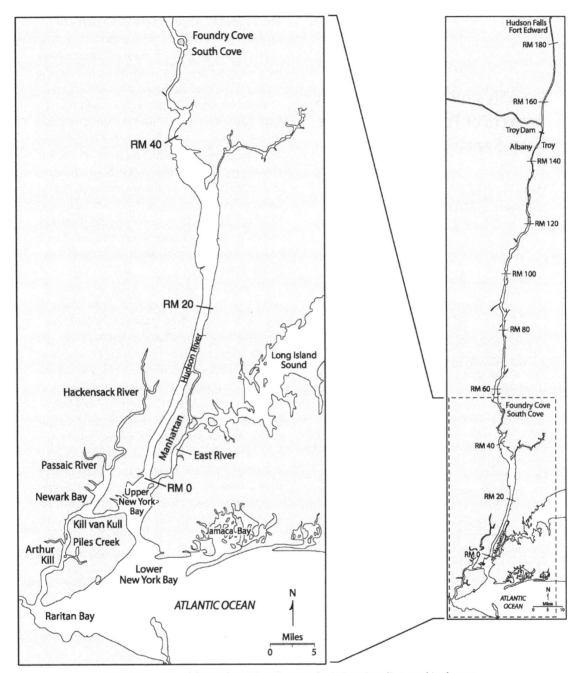

Figure 30.1. Map of the Hudson River Estuary depicting sites discussed in the text.

uptake and increased efflux are two possible strategies that have evolved to decrease bioaccumulation of toxicants. Furthermore, bioaccumulation does not always translate into toxicity at the cellular, organismic, or population levels. Genetic adaptations and mechanisms of physiological acclimation exist that may modulate the toxicities of environmental pollutants. Strong selective pressure for genetic variants in the structure or expression of enzymes that metabolize contaminants or repair damaged deoxyribonucleic acid (DNA) may decrease toxicities. Similarly, exposure-induced alterations in the expression of receptor or other signal transduction pathway molecules or the intracellular sequestration of toxicants are physiological mechanisms that may modulate toxicity.

The aim of this chapter is to present and evaluate those studies that investigated the toxic effects of HR-borne organic and metals pollutants on its invertebrate and vertebrate populations. Compared to the numerous studies that have documented tissue burdens of HR contaminants in a variety of taxa, far fewer investigations have addressed the ecological effects of these pollutants.

Toxicities of Metals to Populations in the Hudson River Estuary

METALS CONTAMINATION IS HIGH IN THE LOWER HUDSON RIVER ESTUARY

Numerous surveys have demonstrated elevated levels of metals in sediments and organisms in different parts of the lower HR and particularly the Newark Bay complex. Metal contamination is associated with municipal wastewater treatment plants, urban runoff, combined sewer overflows, automobile emissions, metals-based industries, effluents from chemical manufacturing plants, and atmospheric deposition (Williams et al., 1978; Meyerson et al., 1981). A comprehensive survey of water quality in the lower HR estuary demonstrated few exceedances of water quality criteria for metals, with the exception of Hg (Great Lakes Environmental Center, 1996). However, sediments often accumulate the metals that enter the aquatic environment. Metals can bind to sediment particles to varying degrees, are released into interstitial water, and exert harmful effects on biota.

Surveys done in the 1990s at locales around Newark Bay demonstrated that surficial sediments from the lower Passaic River and the Arthur Kill had the highest levels of contamination in the area; concentrations of As, Cd, Cu, Hg, Ni, Pb and Zn exceeded several benchmark sediment quality values (Bonnevie et al., 1994). Many of the sediment samples from the lower Passaic River had metals (Cu, Pb, Hg, Ni, Zn) at concentrations that greatly exceeded the Long and Morgan (1991) Effects Range- Low (ER-L) and Effects Range – Medium (ER-M) values. In general, metal concentrations at these sites were lower at the surface, reflecting decline of new inputs after environmental regulations

took effect and high sedimentation rates. The highest amounts of metals were deposited in the 1950s and 1960s, followed by a subsequent decline (Wenning, Bonnevie, and Huntley, 1994).

BIOACCUMULATION OF METALS

Bioaccumulation and toxicity of metals is influenced by physical and chemical factors and is dependent on the speciation of the metal. Bioavailability of metals can be affected by sediment characteristics such as pH, redox potential, organic content and the presence of acid volatile sulfides (Di Toro, 1992). In many cases, it is the free ion that is responsible for accumulation (Zamuda and Sunda, 1982). The salinity of the water is a critical factor, and generally uptake is inversely proportional to salinity. This may also relate to the amount of free ion available (Sunda, Engel, and Thuotte, 1978). Dissolved organic matter may bind metals and make them less bioavailable (Zamuda and Sunda, 1982). Organisms in areas with higher dissolved organic matter will have relatively less bioaccumulation. Organisms also derive their metal body burden from food, and organisms at higher trophic levels derive a greater amount of their body burden from food than from water.

Despite elevated levels of some metals in sediments, bioaccumulation does not always occur in fish from even the most contaminated areas in the estuary. Fish from Berry's Creek (a Hg Superfund site) and the nearby Passaic River had mean body burdens of Hg that were well below 1 μg g^{-1}, the U.S. Food and Drug Administration (FDA) action level (Santoro and Koepp, 1986). However, the mean level alone does not demonstrate that individual specimens of striped bass *Morone saxatilis*, American eel *Anguilla rostrata* and sunfish *Lepomis* sp. from these sites had 1–2 μg g^{-1} Hg. Bioavailability of Hg in Berry's Creek was low, probably in part because Hg in the Creek is not methylated perhaps due to the high sulfur levels in the sediments that inhibit methylation by bacteria (Berman and Bartha, 1986).

In contrast, organisms in Foundry Cove, a Superfund site off the main stem HR with Cd levels in the sediments of up to 10,000 μg g^{-1} did bioaccumulate Cd. Analysis of Cd in the macrobenthos in Foundry Cove indicated that Cd was bioavailable and accumulated in striped killifish

Fundulus diaphanus and cattails *Typha angustifolia* (Hazenand Kneip, 1980). Consumption of contaminated blue crabs *Callinectes sapidus*, appeared to be a potential source of Cd exposure to humans (Kneip and Hazen, 1979).

Many have noted, however, that populations from contaminated sites tend to accumulate proportionately lower amounts of metals in relation to sediment levels than populations from cleaner sites (Khan, Weis, and D'Andrea, 1989; Khan and Weis, 1993a). This may be due to enhanced excretion or reduced uptake, either of which can result in enhanced tolerance in organisms from polluted environments (Foster, 1977).

TOXICITY OF METALS

While some metals, such as Cu and Zn are biologically essential at trace levels, others such as Cd, Hg, Ni, and Pb do not play any normal biological role, and are toxic at low concentrations. Since the estuary is highly contaminated with many organic contaminants as well as metals, it is difficult to point to a particular pollutant or pollutants as being primarily responsible for a given problem. Long et al. (1996) examined the spatial extent of sediment toxicity in major U.S. estuaries using three standard toxicity tests: the 10-day amphipod survival test with bulk sediments, the 5-minute microbial bioluminescence test, and either the 1-hour sea urchin fertilization or 48-hour mollusk embryo tests with pore water. Amphipod tests indicated that toxicity was most widespread in Newark Bay (85 percent of the area), as well as in other parts of the Hudson-Raritan estuary (38 percent). When spatial patterns of toxicity were compared with the distribution of toxic chemicals, the results suggested that metals were generally not the cause of the observed toxicity, with the possible exception of mercury (Wolfe, Long, and Thursby, 1996).

Resistance: A Population Strategy to Cope with Contaminants

On occasion, populations, such as lake trout *Salvelinus namaycus* in Lake Ontario are extirpated by chronic exposure to chemical contaminants (Cook et al., 2003). Alternatively, populations may develop resistance (increased tolerance) when exposed to chemical contaminants as a result of genetic adaptation or physiological acclimation. However, the acquisition of resistance is not a predictable consequence of exposure to metals, aromatic hydrocarbons, or other toxicants. Ecosystem-specific exposure conditions and life history characteristics of challenged populations probably determine whether acute toxicities occur or resistance develops (Wirgin and Waldman, 2004). Physiological acclimation develops when resistance in an individual is increased after exposure to low levels of a toxicant and will disappear after it is returned to clean environments. In contrast, genetically-based adaptation results from selection pressure on populations in polluted environments and will persist (at least for several generations) after the organisms are placed in clean water. Selection occurs on preexisting polymorphisms at genes that may ameliorate the effects of toxicant exposure. The existence of genetic resistance in a population is evidence that the toxicant is exerting effects on the population level (Luoma, 1977). Resistance may also have deleterious effects on the community level by increasing the bioavailability of contaminants to higher levels in the food chain. Individuals in a population will vary in their resistance (Courtenay et al., 1994; Nacci et al., 2002a), and the population tolerance distribution in an impacted population can be shifted toward increased resistance, since those individuals have the highest fitness in such an environment. Although there have been many reports of resistant populations from polluted sites around the world, in most cases, a distinction between physiological acclimation or genetic adaptation was not made.

RESISTANCE OF WORMS IN FOUNDRY COVE TO METALS

Some relatively clear examples of effects of metals on populations are the development of resistance to particular metals. Studies have focused on two sites: Foundry Cove (FC) off the main stem HR (color plate 3) with Cd, and Piles Creek, New Jersey, (off the Arthur Kill) with many contaminants, including Hg. Klerks and Levinton (1989a) found that the oligochaete worm *Limnodrilus hoffmeisteri*, an abundant species at Cd-Ni contaminated FC, had increased tolerance to Cd (and to combinations of Cd, Ni, and Co) compared to worms from a nearby reference site in South Cove. The resistance was not due to reduced uptake of metal; instead, worms from FC had a higher uptake of Cd from metals-rich sediments than worms from the reference site. Descendants of the FC population that were born and raised in the laboratory also exhibited tolerance, though they were slightly less tolerant than those from FC, indicating that resistance had a largely genetic basis. The authors suggested that resistant individuals have a reduced fitness relative to non-resistant ones in a clean environment.

In selection experiments with reference worms, levels of resistance comparable to those observed in FC worms were attained in one to four generations (Klerks and Levinton, 1989b). FC worms had elevated levels of a metallothionein-like metal binding protein, although this was never identified. Metal binding proteins such as metallothioneins are a common mechanism of metal detoxification in plants and animals. Tolerance of high Cd was shown to be genetically determined (Klerks and Bartholomew, 1991) and subsequent genetic analysis indicated that a single gene may be responsible for resistance in the FC population (Martinez and Levinton, 1996). The absence of tolerant worms at the South Cove reference site suggested that there was a cost associated with the Cd-resistance in these worms, and that tolerance would disappear shortly after remediation of FC (which occurred in 1994). Some decrease in resistance was seen in 1997 at some sites, but the distribution indicated an initial mixing of previously resistant and non-resistant populations within FC, rather than costs associated with resistance causing a decline in resistance (Levinton et al., 1999). As of 2002, the resistance of Foundry Cove worms has converged with those at unpolluted sites (Levinton et al., 2003).

In addition to the metal-binding protein, FC worms also sequestered a considerable amount of their Cd burden in metal-rich granules (MRGs), another widespread detoxification mechanism. Electron microprobe analysis revealed that these granules had equal amounts of Cd and S, suggesting that they may be cadmium sulfide (Klerks and Bartholomew, 1991). The storage of Cd in granules has potential effects on the trophic transfer of metals from the worms to their consumers since MRGs are less easily assimilated than dissolved material (Wallace, Lopez, and Levinton 1998).

RESISTANCE TO MERCURY IN CRABS AND SHRIMP FROM PILES CREEK

Sediments from Piles Creek (PC) have elevated levels of many metals and organic contaminants that were derived from industrial sources. In the 1980s, Hg levels in the sediments were 10–20 ppm, but they have declined in recent years. Fiddler crabs *Uca pugnax* from this site are more tolerant to methylmercury (meHg) than conspecifics from reference sites. Because tolerance could not be induced by preexposure of reference site crabs, it appears to have a genetic basis (Callahan and Weis, 1983). Likewise, grass shrimp *Palaemonetes pugio* larvae from PC were more tolerant than those from reference sites to meHg, but not more tolerant to inorganic Hg. Adult shrimp from PC, however, were more tolerant to both inorganic and organic forms of Hg (Kraus, Weis, and Weis, 1988; Kraus and Weis, 1988). Metallothioneins were present in greater amounts in the adult PC than the reference shrimp, and these may have been responsible for their tolerance to inorganic Hg, which was not present in larvae. These data suggested that tolerance to inorganic Hg was acquired after exposure (acclimation), whereas the tolerance to meHg was genetic and present in the larvae as well as adults.

RESISTANCE TO MERCURY IN KILLIFISH FROM PILES CREEK

Resistance to Hg in the Piles Creek (PC) killifish population is much more complicated. It was initially found that the embryos from females from reference sites were highly variable in their response to meHg, that is, some females produced eggs that were very resistant to teratogenic effects, others produced eggs that were susceptible, and others produced eggs of intermediate susceptibility (Weis, Weis, and Heber, 1982a).

In contrast, killifish from PC produced almost all resistant embryos (Weis et al., 1981); eggs and sperm also tolerate meHg (Khan and Weis, 1987). Part of the resistance was due to reduced uptake of Hg through the chorion, a trait associated with the female. Batches of eggs that were tolerant of meHg were not necessarily tolerant of other toxicants. In fact, PC embryos were more susceptible to inorganic Hg than embryos from reference populations (Weis et al., 1982). Therefore general chorionic impermeability is not the mechanism of resistance to Hg. Another potential mechanism of tolerance is more rapid development, which would allow the embryos to pass through sensitive critical early life stages more quickly (Toppin et al., 1987). Newly fertilized eggs do not express the protein (Weis, 1984).

PC eggs do not fertilize successfully in full strength seawater, whereas eggs and sperm from reference populations fertilized successfully in a wide variety of salinities (Bush and Weis, 1983). This reduced salinity tolerance may be a "cost" associated with Hg tolerance in the PC population. The high variability of susceptibility within reference populations may allow them to withstand episodic influxes of contamination.

Despite resistance in PC gametes and embryos, it was not seen in larvae or adults (Weis et al., 1985; 1987). If chorionic permeability and developmental time are the major contributors to the embryonic tolerance, these are irrelevant after hatching. Sensitivities of larvae to acute exposures were comparable in PC and reference populations. Subsequent studies on sublethal effects revealed that PC larvae were less able to depurate Hg than larvae from the reference population and were less resistant to behavioral effects of meHg (Zhou and Weis, 1998). Larval exposure increased susceptibility to predation to a greater degree in PC larvae than in reference larvae (Zhou and Weis, 1998).

PC adults showed increased signs of stress, slower growth, shorter life span, and decreased tolerance than reference adults (Toppin et al., 1987). However, they became reproductive at a smaller size and younger age similar to metal-adapted populations of the isopod *Porcellio scaber* (Donker, Zonneveld, and van Stralen, 1993). Subsequent studies revealed that the PC fish had abnormal behavior – they were sluggish and poor at capturing prey and avoiding predation (Smith and Weis, 1997). Field-collected specimens had a diet comprised largely of detritus, rather than live food. Detritus provides little food value for killifish, which may account for their slower growth and reduced lifespan. While the abnormal behavior was correlated with brain Hg, it may be a result of overall contaminant loads rather than any specific chemical. The abnormal behavior is associated with reduced serotonin in the brains of the adults (Smith et al., 1995) as well as altered thyroid status (Zhou

et al., 1999). Clearly, PC fish demonstrate a number of pollution-related problems and abnormalities, as well as the life stage-specific tolerance.

Toxicities of Organic Contaminants to Invertebrates in the Hudson River

LEVELS OF ORGANIC CONTAMINANTS IN INVERTEBRATES FROM THE HUDSON RIVER ESTUARY

Few studies have quantified organic pollution levels in invertebrates in the HR ecosystem. The New York State Department of Environmental Conservation (NYSDEC) maintains a database on a suite of organic and inorganic contaminants analyzed in fish and wildlife tissues from the 1970s to the present. Entries for invertebrates in the HR are limited, with PCBs being the only contaminant consistently detected. Total PCBs in samples of aquatic insects collected in 1999 above Hudson Falls generally ranged from 1 to 10 ppm. Levels of PCBs in crayfish and physid snails collected from the same locations had lower PCB concentrations, ranging from 0.1 to 6 ppm, with PCB concentrations in grass shrimp collected downriver near Yonkers ranging from 0.3 to 0.5 ppm. Although data are limited, invertebrates, particularly those found in the upper reaches of the river, may still serve as a significant source of PCBs to the HR food web.

In 1993, NYSDEC conducted a large survey of contaminant levels in finfish, bivalves, crustaceans, and one squid species from different regions of the New York Harbor (Skinner et al., 1997). Levels of total PCBs in softshell clams *Mya arenaria* were generally low, averaging from <0.03 to 0.32 ppm. In lobster *Homarus americanus* and blue crabs PCB levels in muscle tissues were also low, averaging 0.03 to 0.07 ppm, but levels in hepatopancreas were much higher, averaging 6.6 to 13.2 ppm and were similar to levels reported in an earlier survey in 1982 and 1983 (Belton et al., 1985). Organisms collected from the upper Harbor region (which includes the portion of the HR below the George Washington Bridge) tended to show the highest body burdens. Body burdens of total DDT and chlordane were lower with average concentrations even in hepatopancreas being less than 1 ppm in blue crabs and lobster.

In 1998 and 1999, NYSDEC conducted studies on the health of benthic invertebrate communities in thirty-two tributaries of the HR from RM 18 to RM 150 to identify those that are major sources of contaminants to the main stem river (Bode et al., 2001a). Invertebrates, including caddisflies, crayfish, and helgrammites, from roughly 50 percent of the streams exceeded state levels of biological concern for PAHs, metals, or pesticides while only 15 percent showed exceedances for PCBs. In thirteen tributaries studies in more detail, total PCBs exceeded 1 ppm only at one locale, but almost all sites exceeded state levels of concern (Bode et al., 2001b).

Populations of marine bivalves at almost 300 sites nationwide have been used as integrators of environmental chemical contamination in a variety of federal programs collectively termed Mussel Watch. In 1986 and 1987 sampling, some of the highest PAH concentrations nationwide were reported for mussels *Mytilus edulis* collected from the Hudson/Raritan Estuary (3 of 3 sites exceeded 5 μg/gdw). PCB levels in mussels were also high, but lower than those in Buzzards Bay, and comparable to those in Boston Harbor. Total DDTs were also highest at one of the Hudson/Raritan sites, 550 ng/gdw, with levels at other Hudson/Raritan sites comparable to those observed in other urban estuaries (Boehm et al., 1988).

A number of new organic compounds, mostly newer pesticides and chlorinated benzene were added in the 1990s to the Mussel Watch analyte list (Wade et al., 1998). One of these, chlorpyrifos, was detected in mussels from two of the Hudson/Raritan sites at concentrations exceeding 10 ng/gdw ranking well above the nintieth percentile of all measurements made. Given the high levels of nonylphenol ethoxylate metabolites recently measured in some portions of the lower HR estuary, consideration should be given to their inclusion in the Mussel Watch program.

ASSESSMENTS OF TOXICITY FROM HUDSON/RARITAN SEDIMENTS

A variety of measures were used in a national ranking of sediment toxicity. Sites in the Hudson/Raritan Estuary and the upper East River ranked 1, 3, 5, and 7 nationally in toxic potential (Long and Morgan, 1991). In response, a large survey was conducted in 1991 in which the toxic potential of sediments collected from the Hudson/Raritan Estuary was measured directly by a number of different tests (Long et al., 1995; 1996). In the 1991 assessment, sediments from 69 percent of the stations were toxic in at least one test. Toxicity tests with the amphipod *Ampelisca abdita* indicated that 46 percent of sediments were toxic, while 41 percent of sites were classified as toxic using the Microtox bioluminescent bacterial assay, and only 27 percent of sediments inhibited survival or growth of bivalve embryos. Toxicity was most directly correlated with sediment PAH concentrations. In a later focused survey of Newark Bay, 84 percent of sediments were toxic to *Ampelisca abdita* and toxicity was more directly correlated with sediment concentrations of chlorinated hydrocarbons.

Gardinalia and Wade (1998) reevaluated national Mussel Watch results from 1994 through 1997 using a biomarker perspective. Using data on the relative abilities of individual PAHs, PCBs, and PCDDs to induce cytochrome P4501A (CYP1A) enzyme activity in rat liver hepatocytes, they calculated total induction equivalents (ΣIEs) for the body burdens of these contaminants measured in indigenous mussels. Despite their low induction equivalency factors, PAHs, because of their high concentrations comprised 95 to 99 percent of the total ΣIEs for all sites in the Hudson/Raritan Estuary (Table 30.1) and greater than 90 percent for the majority of sites around the country.

Beginning in 1993, the U.S. Environmental Protection Agency (USEPA) conducted another large assessment of the Hudson/Raritan Estuary through 1994 in their R-EMAP study (Adams, O'Connor, and Weisberg, 1998). This program was intended to evaluate long-term trends in the spatial patterns of sediment quality in the Harbor Estuary system. In addition to sediment chemistry and toxicity tests, this study also computed a Benthic Index of Biotic Integrity (B-IBI), based on benthic community structure. Sediments from half of the sites had at least one contaminant at levels that exceeded Long and Morgan's (1991) Effects Range Median (ER-M) values. Total PCBs, DDT, and Hg were the only toxicants whose average concentrations exceeded ER-M values. Degraded B-IBIs were also highly correlated with chemicals. Combining

Table 30.1. Contribution of PAHs, PCBs, and Dioxins/Furans (PCDD/PCDFs) to total induction equivalents in bivalves collected from the New York/New Jersey Harbor Estuary as part of the National Status and Trends Surveys 1994–1997

Location	NS&T ID	pg/g ΣEIs	% Contribution		
			PCBs	PCDD/Fs	PAHs
Raritan Bay	HRRB	552	3	2	96
Lower Bay	HRLB	986	3	2	95
Upper Bay	HRUB	2,140	1	0	99
Jamaica Bay	HRJB	669	2	1	98
Throgs Neck Br.	LITN	644	3	1	96

Adapted from Gardinali and Wade (1998).
pg/g ΣEIs calculated as the sum of measured concentrations of 4 PCDD/Fs, 5 PCBs, and 7 PAHs times their respective induction equivalency factor (as compared to 2,3,7,8-TCDD).

sediment contaminant levels, B-IBI indices, and *Ampelisca* toxicity test results, Newark Bay and the Upper New York Harbor showed the most impairment, with Jamaica Bay ranking third. Despite differences in the extent and magnitude of sediment toxicity reported by Long et al. (1995) and Adams et al. (1998), both studies concluded that a significant percentage of the area in the Harbor Estuary has the potential to cause adverse impacts on aquatic invertebrates.

Few studies have assessed the effects of organic contaminants in the Hudson/Raritan Estuary on physiology or reproduction in invertebrates. Rice et al. (1995) conducted three different invertebrate toxicity tests on sediments from seventeen depositional areas in the Hudson/Raritan Estuary. They compared a ten-day acute toxicity test to chronic tests examining mortality and growth in three Pacific Coast invertebrate species. Polychaete growth was the most sensitive parameter, with sediments from 65 percent of sites causing significant reductions, whereas amphipod mortality was the least sensitive measure. These results indicated that there is widespread potential for physiologic affects from contaminated sediments on invertebrate populations from throughout the HR Estuary.

McElroy, Elskus, and Fay (2000) used selective techniques to isolate different classes of organic contaminants and then conducted toxicity tests using these fractions to determine which contributed most to the toxicity in New York Harbor sediments. Easily desorbable organic contaminants were isolated as extracts from sediments, which were then partitioned into fractions enriched in alkanes and aliphatic material, PCBs, PAHs, and polar organics and amended separately to a reference sediment. Only the sediments amended with the PAH fraction were toxic, which corroborates earlier conclusions that organic contaminants such as PAHs are responsible for toxicity observed in sediments from around much of the HR Estuary.

RESISTANCE OF INVERTEBRATES TO ORGANIC CONTAMINANTS

Evaluation of the toxicity of sediment samples taken from the HR Estuary have routinely been conducted using native amphipods such as *A. abdita* collected from Rhode Island (RI) or occasionally a Pacific Coast species. These tests use *A. abdita* as a surrogate for native species, but the question remains as to whether indigenous amphipods are more tolerant to contaminants in polluted natural environments than the test organisms used. This was addressed when side-by-side tests compared survival between *A. abdita* collected from RI and from Jamaica Bay (JB) (Serbst et al., 2001). *A. abdita* from both populations showed good survival in reference sediment but JB amphipods showed lower mortality in JB sediments and contaminated New Bedford Harbor, Massachusetts sediments, suggesting that they had developed resistance.

Much work still needs to be done to understand how invertebrates are responding and adapting to contaminants in their environment. Given the high levels of contamination in parts of the HR Estuary, the well-studied examples of resistance in several fish and one invertebrate species to organic and inorganic contaminants, the HR represents an excellent study site from which to address this issue. This and the study of potential trophic transfer of persistent contaminants from the benthos, through aquatic food chains to top predators and to humans remain important questions that need to be addressed to understand both the risks of these contaminants and the mechanisms of resiliency of indigenous populations.

Toxicities of Organic Contaminants to Vertebrates in the Hudson River

THE ROLE OF TOXICANTS IN POPULATION DECLINES OF STRIPED BASS

Striped bass abundance coastwide during the late 1970s and early 1980s was at or near record low levels and several studies attempted to identify the causes of these declines. Some of these focused on the possible role of toxicants. Initially, Mehrle et al. (1982) reported that vertebrae of striped bass collected in 1978 from the HR had less strength and stiffness, and ruptured at lower forces than in those from three other estuaries, perhaps due to elevated levels of contaminants. Burdens of contaminants in different life stages of striped bass from the HR were not dramatically higher than those from other estuaries, with the exception of three Aroclor PCB mixtures (Mehrle and Ludke, 1983). Although extensive congener specific analyses were not conducted, these authors cautioned that PCDD/Fs, and non-ortho substituted PCBs levels in striped bass from the HR were sufficiently high to warrant concern.

Striped bass larvae were exposed at different salinities to graded doses of a mixture of inorganic and organic (including PCBs) contaminants that reflected their concentrations and profiles in water and striped bass from several spawning rivers. Survivorship of larvae was significantly reduced by the contaminant mixture, but results were highly dependent on salinity – mortality was more pronounced at lower salinities. Larvae exposed to the mixture were significantly impaired in swimming capacity and predation-induced mortality compared to controls. Tissue residues of contaminants in larvae that had been exposed to the mixture

were "within the range of what young-of-the-year striped bass could be exposed to in their natural habitats," suggesting that contaminant exposure might be contributing to decreased recruitment to natural populations.

The effects of PCBs and other contaminants on early life-stage and reproductive success was experimentally addressed. Larvae from striped bass females from the HR were fed *Artemia nauplii* from two sources; one contaminated with PCBs and the second cleaner (Westin et al., 1983). No effect on survivorship or growth was observed after feeding on PCBs-contaminated diet. However, while embryos and early larvae from untreated mothers had higher concentrations of PCBs than larvae from the same mothers that had been feeding on the contaminated shrimp, there was considerable variation among the mothers in the burdens of PCBs that they off-loaded to their eggs, and it was noted that contaminant burdens in the earliest life stages were diluted by growth during larval development.

In a second study, striped bass eggs were obtained from females from three hatcheries including one from the HR (Westin et al., 1985). Total PCBs levels in the unfertilized eggs of HR females were high and exceeded those from Chesapeake Bay and SC females. A significant inverse relationship was found between the concentrations of four chlorinated hydrocarbons in unfertilized eggs; PCBs, DDTs, hexachlorobenzenes, and chlordanes, and median mortality time in starved larvae from the three locales. The effect of chlorinated hydrocarbons-contaminated diet on the bioaccumulation of these four xenobiotics and their toxicity in post yolk sac larvae was evaluated. Maternally, rather than dietary-contributed contaminants, had the most impact on survival of larvae even after feeding for twenty days on contaminated prey. These results highlight the importance of maternal transfer of contaminants on early life-stage success in fish.

White perch *Morone americana*, which is closely related to striped bass, was used as a surrogate in studies in which both genders were treated with environmentally relevant PCB77 (Monosson, Fleming, and Sullivan, 1994). Neither sex exhibited reductions in plasma concentrations of estradiol, testosterone, or vitellogenin. But, the highest dose of PCB77 significantly delayed and suppressed ovarian growth and maturation, reduced oocyte diameter, and decreased survival of larvae. The investigators suggested that PCBs may compromise reproductive function in HR fish populations.

In summary, although striped bass from the HR may exhibit higher levels of PCBs and other toxicants compared to conspecifics from elsewhere, there is little empirical evidence to suggest that their population declines could be attributed to toxicant exposure. In fact, retrospective analysis of PCB concentrations in adult females from 1976–97 and estimates of abundance of eggs, larvae, and juveniles found no relationship between PCB exposure and any measures of abundance (Barnthouse, Glaser, and Young, 2003). The imposition of severe management restrictions in the 1980s coastwide to limit or ban fisheries resulted in a rapid and massive resurgence of abundance of the coastal migratory stock of striped bass suggesting that overfishing was the primary reason for declines.

LESIONS IN BROWN BULLHEAD FROM THE HUDSON RIVER

Brown bullhead *Ictalurus nebulosus* from industrialized locales are often susceptible to environmentally-induced liver (hepatic and biliary) and skin neoplasms probably from exposure to PAHs (Baumann, 1998). Histopathological studies were conducted on brown bullhead that were collected in the mid 1980s from sites above and below the major sources of PCBs to the upper HR (Kim et al., 1989). As expected, mean concentrations of total PCBs in muscle were more than sixty-fold higher in bullhead collected from locales downstream of the PCB sources. However, there was no significant difference in the prevalence of gross abnormalities between the two exposure groups. Although tumors were absent in both groups, the prevalence of several histopathologic lesions suggestive of contaminant exposure was elevated in the PCB-contaminated group. The prevalences of histopathologies in liver, spleen, and kidney exceeded 75 percent in fish from the downriver site, compared to 2–13 percent in bullhead from the upriver reference site. While the absence of neoplasms

in bullhead from the HR may be surprising given the vulnerability of bullhead to environmentally-induced carcinogenesis, PCBs usually do not induce DNA damage and perhaps the PAHs required to initiate DNA lesions may be in insufficient concentrations at these HR locales.

LIVER CANCER AND A TRUNCATED AGE STRUCTURE OF ATLANTIC TOMCOD FROM THE HUDSON RIVER

Atlantic tomcod *Microgadus tomcod* is an abundant anadromous species in the HR and other estuaries north to southern Labrador. The HR estuary supports their southernmost spawning population and summertime temperatures may present thermal stress. Although tomcod move seasonally within estuaries, they do not coastally migrate; their entire life cycles are spent within natal estuaries making them effective sentinels of environmental degradation. Tomcod are benthic, have lipid-rich livers, and tend to bioaccumulate high levels of lipophilic contaminants. Tomcod are the only wintertime spawners in the Estuary making their young life stages important prey to HR resource and other species (R. C. Chambers, National Marine Fisheries Service, personal communication). Historical data from the HR utilities have demonstrated an overall downward trend in the abundance of adult tomcod in the HR over the past decades suggesting recruitment impairment (Anonymous 1999).

Tomcod collected during spawning in the HR from the mid 1970s to the early 1980s exhibited high prevalences of gross liver tumors that were later histologically defined as hepatocellular carcinomas (Smith et al., 1979). More than 50 percent of one-year-old and 90 percent of two-year-old HR tomcod exhibited hepatic tumors compared to prevalences of 0–10 percent in tomcod from cleaner estuaries in New England (Cormier and Racine, 1990). Concurrently, tomcod from the HR exhibited a truncated age structure compared to tomcod from elsewhere (Dey et al., 1993). More than 97 percent of the HR spawners were one-year-olds, less than 3 percent were two-year-olds and three-year-olds were almost absent. In comparison, spawning aggregations in Canadian rivers were comprised primarily of three and four-year-olds and tomcod up to seven years of age were regularly observed.

INVESTIGATIONS ON THE ETIOLOGY OF CANCER IN THE HUDSON RIVER TOMCOD POPULATION

Studies were initiated to determine the etiology of the elevated prevalence of hepatic tumors and pre-neoplastic lesions in the HR population driven by the hypothesis that the epizootic resulted from exposure to chemical contaminants. Initially, no relationship was found between the prevalence or size of lesions and levels of total PCBs, pesticides, or selected heavy metals (Smith et al., 1979; Dey et al., 1993). Unfortunately, levels of these toxicants were not compared between tomcod from the HR and cleaner rivers.

The prevalence of tumors was compared between tomcod from the HR and the cleaner Sheepscot River, Maine, that were collected in June as juveniles and reared under controlled laboratory conditions to December (spawning time) of that year (Cormier and Racine, 1990). This study was based on the assumption that early life stages in fish are most sensitive to the carcinogenic effects of contaminants and that critical exposures to cancer-causing contaminants had occurred by June in the environment. In December, tumors and other hepatic lesions were absent in tomcod from both populations and therefore no insights were gained into the etiology of neoplasia. These results were consistent with almost all other attempts to induce tumors under controlled laboratory conditions in fish from natural populations that exhibit epizootic episodes of neoplasia and suggested that other approaches were needed to identify the cause of disease.

USE OF BIOMARKERS TO DETERMINE THE ETIOLOGY OF CANCER IN TOMCOD

Biomarkers provide an indirect approach to address the etiology of perturbations in natural populations. Biomarkers are quantitative endpoints, usually measured in sentinel species, of exposure to and biological effects of stressors. If significantly induced biomarker responses occur at mechanistically linked hierarchical steps of biological organization, a weight of evidence approach may be used to infer cause of perturbations at the organismic, population, or community levels. Thus, the objective of biomarker studies is to demonstrate significant responses in ecosystems at endpoints from the molecular through the population/community levels. Molecular biomarkers can provide a direct link between exposure and effects but may be of low ecological relevance, whereas it is more difficult to establish cause and effect relationships between exposure and responses at the population/community levels but alterations are of high ecological importance. A biomarker approach was used to explain the high prevalence of tumors in tomcod from the HR.

Tomcod from the HR are exposed to much higher levels of classes of xenobiotics that initiate and promote chemically-induced neoplasia than tomcod from elsewhere. Metabolites of PAHs "initiate" chemical carcinogenesis by inducing DNA lesions and signature mutations at sensitive oncogenes and tumor suppressor genes. It is difficult to directly measure PAH levels in fish tissues because of their rapid metabolism. However, a quantitative, indirect measure of exposure to high molecular weight PAHs, fluorescent aromatic compounds (metabolites of PAHs) (FACs) in bile, was developed. Adult and juvenile tomcod from the HR exhibited six to eight-fold higher levels of FACs than tomcod from four cleaner estuaries confirming the bioavailability of PAHs to the HR population and their metabolism (Wirgin et al., 1994).

PCBs and PCDD/Fs "promote" chemical carcinogenesis by enhancing the growth of cells with damaged DNA at the expense of nearby normal cells that are more sensitive to the toxicity of these compounds. Unfertilized eggs (Roy et al., 2001) and livers of juvenile (Yuan et al., 2001) and adult (Courtenay et al., 1999) tomcod from the HR estuary exhibit much higher levels of these contaminants than tomcod from elsewhere, sometimes at world-record levels. For example, hepatic burdens of the most toxic dioxin congener, TCDD, in six-month old tomcod from the Newark Bay complex ranged between 897 and 655 ng/kg body wt (Yuan et al., 2001) indicating that the population is exposed at early, presumably sensitive life stages. These levels of TCDD were 10 to 500-fold higher than in matched tomcod from the cleanest river tested, the Margaree River in Nova Scotia. Similarly, wet weight levels of toxic coplanar PCBs were 40 to 100-fold higher in tomcod from the

HR, compared to those from two cleaner rivers in Canada (Courtenay et al., 1999).

HEPATIC CYP1A1 EXPRESSION AND HEPATIC DNA DAMAGE IN TOMCOD FROM THE HUDSON RIVER

The presence of xenobiotics within tissues does not necessarily mean that they are biologically active. To address this issue, hepatic levels of CYP1A1 mRNA were compared between adult tomcod from the HR and four cleaner Atlantic Coast rivers. CYP1A1 expression is a widely used biomarker of exposure and early effect in fish because it is dose-responsively induced (increased) by exposure to environmentally relevant concentrations of PCDD/Fs, coplanar PCBs, and PAHs, and its encoded enzyme activities convert environmental PAHs to their active DNA-damaging metabolites. Also, the persistent induction of CYP1A1 by poorly metabolized PCDD/Fs/furans and PCBs generates reactive oxygen species which also damage DNA by generating modified bases (Schlezinger, White, and Stegeman, 1999). CYP1A1 expression may also be a biomarker of susceptibility to damage because of interindividual and interpopulation variation in its gene structure (Roy et al., 1995) and expression (Courtenay et al., 1994). CYP1A1 transcription is mediated through the aryl hydrocarbon receptor (AHR) – a signal transduction pathway whose activation mediates most, if not all, toxic responses to aromatic hydrocarbons in fishes (Hahn, 1998). Thus, induction of CYP1A1 serves as an easily quantifiable surrogate for complex toxic responses mediated by the AHR.

Hepatic CYP1A1 mRNA levels in adult tomcod from the HR were fifteen to twenty-two-fold higher than in those from the cleanest river tested (Wirgin et al., 1994). Additionally, environmentally exposed or chemically treated tomcod from the HR showed much higher levels of CYP1A mRNA expression than three other common anadromous HR species (Wirgin et al., 1996), a result that was consistent with the high prevalence of neoplasms in tomcod and their absence in the other species.

While induced levels of hepatic CYP1A1 are indicative of exposure to and bioactivity of PAHs, it may not always be predictive of increased hepatic DNA damage. To address this issue, the ^{32}P postlabeling assay, a measure of DNA adducts levels, was used to compare hepatic DNA damage in adult tomcod from the HR and four cleaner estuaries. DNA adducts result from the binding of the reactive metabolites of PAHs and some other compounds to DNA. Levels of hepatic DNA adducts were approximately forty-fold higher in tomcod from the HR than in tomcod from the cleanest rivers tested (Wirgin et al., 1994) demonstrating that environmental agents, probably PAHs, were in fact incurring hepatic DNA damage to the HR population.

REDUCED CYP1A1 INDUCIBILITY IN TOMCOD FROM THE HR

Controlled laboratory experiments were conducted in which adult tomcod were collected from the HR or Miramichi River (MR) and treated with graded doses of TCDD, coplanar PCBs, and PAHs. High levels of hepatic CYP1A1 mRNA expression were observed with all chemicals in tomcod from the MR – maximal levels of gene induction ranged between 50 and 460-fold (Courtenay et al., 1999; Yuan, 2003). Surprisingly, tomcod from the HR responded very differently than those from the MR to treatments with TCDD and four coplanar PCBs, but not to B[a]P and a second PAH. Much higher treatment doses of PCBs or TCDD were needed to induce significant CYP1A1 expression in tomcod from the HR, although maximum levels of gene induction for each compound were similar for the two populations (Fig. 30.2).

Genetic polymorphisms were reported in the coding regions of *CYP1A1* (Roy et al., 1995) and *AHR* (Roy and Wirgin, 1997) among tomcod populations. For both genes, tomcod from the HR exhibited genotypes that were absent in tomcod from elsewhere. It is tempting to speculate that these polymorphisms contribute to the reduced inducibility of CYP1A1, however empirical evaluations of the functional importance of the variant alleles have yet to be conducted.

HERITABILITY OF REDUCED CYP1A1 INDUCIBILITY AND ITS PREVALENCE IN THE HR POPULATION

CYP1A1 mRNA expression was significantly lower in larval offspring of HR parents compared to those of MR descent for both compounds, indicating that genetic differences in CYP1A1 inducibility exist between the two populations. However, significant

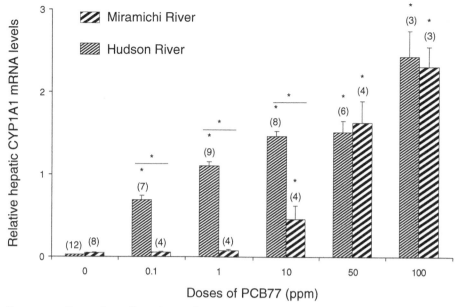

Figure 30.2. Comparison of hepatic cytochrome P450 1A1 mRNA expression levels in adult Atlantic tomcod from the Hudson River and the Miramichi River (MR) i.p. injected with graded doses of coplanar PCB77. Data are expressed as means ± standard errors. Sample sizes are in parentheses over error bars. * Indicates significant ($P < 0.001$) induction of CYP1A1 compared to corn oil-treated controls.

induction of CYP1A1 was observed in PCB77 exposed larvae from HR parents, suggesting that a single-generational physiological acclimation response also contributed to decreased CYP1A1 inducibility in tomcod from the HR population.

CORRESPONDENCE BETWEEN HEPATIC CYP1A1 AND TOXICANT LEVELS IN HUDSON RIVER TOMCOD

Congener-specific hepatic levels of PCDD/Fs and PCBs were also compared among samples of YOY tomcod from multiple sites in the HR estuary extending from RM 1 to RM 120, including Newark Bay (Yuan et al., 2001; Ikonomou et al., 2004). YOY fish (4–7 months old) were used with the anticipation that their vagility was less than that of adults, their hepatic contaminant and CYP1A1 mRNA levels would reflect localized conditions, and congener-specific signatures could be used to micro-map bioavailable pollutant levels and perhaps identify their sources.

The expectation of a gradient from upriver sources to New York City in hepatic PCB levels in tomcod from the main stem HR was not observed. The lowest levels of PCBs were observed at the most upriver sites and the highest levels at RM 37 (Ikonomou et al., 2004). Surprisingly, levels of PCBs at sites within Newark Bay were as high as those at the most contaminated site in the main stem HR and congener patterns were similar to those in the main stem HR.

Hepatic levels of PCDD/Fs were highest in tomcod from two sites in the Newark Bay complex, almost certainly resulting from their transport from the single herbicide manufacturing facility on the lower Passaic River. Ratios of total PCDDs to total PCDFs and congener-specific analyses of both indicated that there are different sources in the main stem HR compared to Newark Bay and the likely absence of exchange of tomcod between the two waterways.

Levels of CYP1A1 mRNA expression were also quantified in YOY tomcod from forty sites in the HR estuary to evaluate the correspondence between hepatic CYP1A1 and hepatic concentrations of PCBs, PCDD/Fs and to determine the utility of gene expression in evaluating the microgeographic distribution of contaminants within the estuary (Yuan et al., 2001). Significant spatial heterogeneity in CYP1A1 mRNA levels was observed among

A.

B.

C.

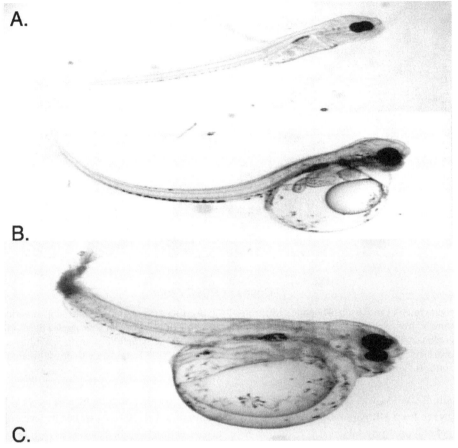

Figure 30.3. Photograph of Atlantic tomcod larval offspring of Miramichi River broodstock that were waterborne exposed to; a) solvent vehicle, b) 1 ppm B[a]P, and c) 1 ppm PCB77.

sites with levels of gene expression differing maximally by twenty-three to thirty-four-fold. Although levels of PCBs and PCDD/Fs and CYP1A1 mRNA were highest in tomcod from the Newark Bay complex, there was little relationship between hepatic contaminants and hepatic CYP1A1 mRNA in tomcod from sites in the main stem HR. Based on these results and controlled laboratory experiments which demonstrated impaired CYP1A1 inducibility by PCBs and TCDD, it was hypothesized that high levels of CYP1A1 in environmentally exposed tomcod from the HR is due to PAHs or other contaminants not measured.

RESPONSE OF TOMCOD TO MIXTURES
OF CONTAMINANTS

Industrial and municipal waterbodies are almost always polluted with complex mixtures of contam-inants, yet little is known of their toxic interactions. Studies investigated the effects of coexposure to metals (As, Cd, Cr, and Ni) and PCB77 or B[a]P on CYP1A1 inducibility and early life-stage toxicities in tomcod. In adult tomcod, all four metals significantly decreased induction of hepatic CYP1A1 by PCB77 or B[a]P, suggesting that environmental mixtures containing metals may alter toxic responses mediated through the AHR. Studies also demonstrated that PCB77 and B[a]P evoked similar AHR-mediated early life stage toxicities in tomcod (embryo mortality, accelerated time to hatching, pericardial and yolk sac edema, cranial malformations) as previously seen in TCDD or coplanar PCB-treated freshwater fish (Fig. 30.3). Coexposure of tomcod embryos to B[a]P and Cr (and to a lesser extent As) ameliorated two of these toxicities: embryo mortality and reduced time to hatching. Similarly,

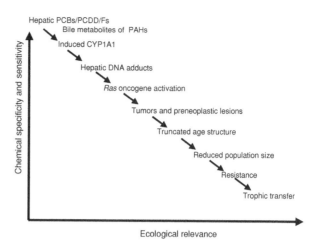

Figure 30.4. Schematic of biomarkers at different hierarchical levels of biological organization from exposure through the community level that are altered in Atlantic tomcod from the Hudson River.

tomcod embryos coexposed to Cr and B[a]P exhibited significantly lower levels of DNA adducts than embryos exposed to B[a]P alone (Sorrentino et al., 2004). These results suggest that coexposures to environmental mixtures result in significantly different toxicities than predicted based on experiments with single chemicals.

RESISTANCE OF HUDSON RIVER TOMCOD TO PCBS AND TCDD INDUCED EARLY LIFE-STAGE TOXICITY

Early life-stage toxicity is a sensitive response of fishes to coplanar PCBs, PCDD/Fs and PAHs. In controlled laboratory experiments, environmentally-relevant profiles and concentrations of coplanar PCBs and TCDD were tested for their abilities to induce early life-stage toxic responses in F_1 and F_2 tomcod of HR and MR ancestry (R. C. Chambers and I. Wirgin, unpublished data). Toxic effects were evaluated by means of lethal (hatchability, yolk-sac larval lifespan) and sublethal (morphometry, behavior, growth) responses of tomcod offspring from the two source populations. HR embryos had a high percentage of embryos hatching at all doses whereas survival of MR young life stages decreased with increasing dose. A multivariate set of fourteen morphometric characters were unresponsive in HR tomcod to PCBs or TCDD dose, whereas twelve of these characters were modified by dose among the MR treatment groups. In all responses, young life stages of MR descent displayed effects at doses equivalent to burdens of

PCBs and TCDD found in livers of environmentally exposed HR tomcod. These results show that early life stages of tomcod from unimpacted populations are sensitive to PCBs/TCDD, that these two populations differ dramatically in their sensitivities to these chemicals, and are consistent with HR population having undergone significant evolutionary change perhaps due to chronic exposure to these pollutants.

In summary, tomcod from the HR exhibit biomarker alterations at a variety of mechanistically linked hierarchical steps of biological organization from exposure through the community levels (Fig. 30.4). This is suggestive of a chemical etiology to cancer and perhaps reduced size of the HR population.

RESISTANCE TO TCDD AND PCBS IN KILLIFISH FROM THE HUDSON RIVER ESTUARY

Killifish (mummichog) *Fundulus heteroclitus* is a very common, benthic species with a restricted home range, but a wide distribution in estuaries of eastern North America. Prince and Cooper (1995a,b) compared the sensitivity of killifish from Newark Bay to those from cleaner Tuckerton Harbor, New Jersey, to TCDD-caused lethality and induction of CYP1A expression. Killifish embryos and adults from the reference site were significantly more sensitive to lethality of waterborne and dermally applied TCDD than those from Newark Bay. In embryos and adults, there were no differences in TCDD absorption

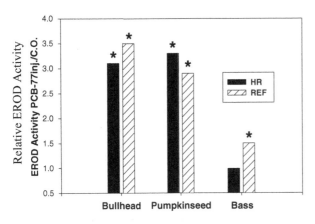

Figure 30.5. Relative response to induction 7 days after i.p. injection of PCB-77 (1.0 mg/kg) in three species of Hudson River (HR) fish collected near Poughkeepsie, NY, or from a hatchery (REF). EROD activity in PCB treated fish is expressed relative to control fish from the same sites injected with corn oil (C.O.) alone. * Indicates significantly different ($P < 0.05$) from control response.

between the two populations, suggesting that mechanisms other than differential uptake or efflux were responsible for variable susceptibilities. Furthermore, CYP1A-encoded ethoxyresorufin O-deethylase (EROD) activity was not significantly inducible by dermal administration of TCDD in adult killifish from Newark Bay. In contrast, dose-responsive induction of EROD activity, up to thirty-fold, was observed in killifish from Tuckerton Harbor.

Resistance to PCBs was also observed in killifish from Newark Bay and two sites in the main stem HR (Elskus et al., 1999). Environmentally-exposed adult killifish from Newark Bay and the HR exhibited ten-fold higher levels of total PCBs than those from reference sites. However, there were no site-related differences in measures of reproductive success including number of eggs deposited, embryo and larval survival, and larval length. Treatment of depurated adults from Newark Bay and a reference site with medium and high doses of an environmentally relevant mixture of PCBs did not result in site-or dose-related differences in hatching success, larval growth, or larval mortality. However, hepatic CYP1A expression was not inducible in adult fish from Newark Bay, but was not inducible in adults from the reference site. Furthermore, hepatic, gill, gut, and heart CYP1A expression was induced in larval offspring of reference site parents, but not in those of Newark Bay parents. This demonstrated that the resistant phenotype in killifish from Newark Bay was heritable to at least the F_1 generation and that modulated gene inducibility was not tissue-specific. Resistance to

overt toxicity and CYP1A expression from PCBs and PAHs has also been observed in killifish from two other highly polluted locales, New Bedford Harbor, Massachusetts, (PCBs) (Nacci et al., 1999), and the Elizabeth River, Virginia (PAHs) (Meyer and Di Giulio, 2002), suggesting that resistance in fish may be a common occurrence in chronically exposed populations.

RESISTANCE OF OTHER FISH POPULATIONS IN THE HUDSON RIVER

Is resistance common in other resident species in the HR? Brown bullhead, pumpkinseed *Lepomis gibbosus*, and largemouth bass *Micropterus salmoides* collected near Poughkeepsie, New York, and matched reference fish from a hatchery were treated with PCB77 and EROD activity was measured. EROD was induced in all three species of hatchery origin and in pumpkinseed and bullhead, but not in bass from the HR, indicating that resistance had developed in only one of three co-occurring species (Zielinski, 2001) (Fig. 30.5). Additional studies of largemouth bass demonstrated that although CYP1A was not induced by PCB77, it was by B[a]P. Although exposure to B[a]P increased EROD similarly in bass from the HR and hatchery, HR bass formed 60 percent fewer B[a]P-DNA adducts than the hatchery bass (Zielinski, 2001). Nacci et al. (2002) also reported reduced levels of B[a]P-DNA adducts in resistant killifish from New Bedford Harbor, however these fish also were less responsive to induction of EROD activity by B[a]P.

Response of Hudson River Fish to Endocrine Disrupting Chemicals

Endocrine disrupting chemicals (EDCs) are exogenous synthetic and natural compounds or their metabolites that alter endocrine function and cause deleterious effects at the level of the organism, its progeny, and/or populations. The adverse effects of EDCs probably result from their ability to mimic the structure and elicit the biological activities of natural hormones, often estradiol (E_2). A wide variety of synthetic chemicals found in municipal, industrial, and agricultural effluents including alkyl phenol ethoxylates, PCBs, dioxins, pesticides, and PAHs, and others have been found to induce strong estrogenic activities in vertebrate animals, most often fishes.

Exposure of fish populations to EDCs may result in reproductive impairment and histological pathologies. In situ exposure of fish to effluents from sewage treatment plants alters sex ratios, induces hermaphroditism, and impairs kidney function. Controlled laboratory experiments have demonstrated that some EDCs can reduce the fertilization rate of sperm from exposed males and the survivorship of larval offspring of crosses with exposed males. Therefore, environmental exposure to suites of EDCs can compromise recruitment success of impacted populations.

Biomarkers have been developed to allow for rapid and sensitive assessments of exposure of fishes to EDCs. Expression of biomolecules, including steroids and vitellogenin (Vtg), may be altered by exposure to EDCs. Vtg is an egg-yolk precursor protein that is normally synthesized in the liver of reproductively active females and is transported via the bloodstream to the developing oocytes where it serves as a nutritional source. Expression of Vtg is normally high in reproductively mature females and is much lower in males and reproductively immature females. The gene encoding for Vtg is present in males and immature females-it just is not active.

A limited survey of gene expression in native YOY striped bass collected at HR RM20 and in adult male killifish collected from Newark Bay failed to detect Vtg while female and male killifish injected with E_2 did (McArdle, McElroy, and Elskus, 2004). Studies comparing Vtg expression and levels of circulat-

ing male and female specific hormones in winter flounder *Pleuronectes americanus* from two sites in Jamaica Bay and a reference site showed only minor evidence of endocrine disruption (McElroy et al., 2004). These data suggest that endocrine disruption is not widespread in resident fish in the Harbor Estuary. Correlations between induced Vtg and higher level effects in HR populations' reproductive impairment or histological alterations have not yet been conducted. Also, the abundance of striped bass and recruitment to the HR population are at or near historical peaks, suggesting that reproductive impairment from EDCs may not be a problem for HR fishes.

HR MINK: BIOACCUMULATION AND TOXICITY OF PCBS

Mink *Mustela vison* is very sensitive to reproductive disorders induced by coplanar PCBs including reduced early life survivorship, kit weight, and litter size (Wren, 1991). Controlled feeding studies, including some with PCBs-contaminated fish from the Great Lakes (Aulerich, Ringer, and Iwamoto, 1973), demonstrated the toxicological effects of environmental mixtures of PCBs on mink reproduction (Jensen et al., 1977). Because these toxicities were related to chemical structure and varied greatly among structural classes of PCBs (Tillitt et al., 1996), it is likely that these responses are mediated through the AHR pathway.

Analyses of a small number of mink and river otter *Lontra canadensis* collected in 1982 and 1984 from locales adjacent to the HR revealed elevated burdens of PCBs; concentrations that exceeded those that cause reproductive disorders in ranched mink (Foley et al., 1988). NYSDEC news releases indicated that livers from mink and river otter collected near the HR between 1998 and 2000 near Hudson Falls and Troy, NY, exhibited fourteen-fold higher levels of PCBs than mink collected from sites more distant from the river (NYSDEC, 2001). The mean level of PCBs in mink collected within 1 km of the river exceeded the EC_{90}-effect level for health impairment (Smit et al., 1996).

A NYSDEC trapping survey compared the status of mink populations in close proximity and more distant from PCB-contaminated HR locales based on the fact that mink populations exhibit very limited home ranges and thus toxicological effects from contaminants would be spatially restricted. The survey suggests that mink populations are reduced in size near the PCB-contaminated section of the HR compared to those at reference sites.

TREE SWALLOWS, PCB CONTAMINATION, AND REPRODUCTIVE DISORDERS

Tree swallow *Tachycineta bicolor* is a common migratory and breeding species along the HR corridor and is predatory on emergent aquatic insects. Tissue burdens of PCBs and their effects on reproductive success were analyzed in tree swallows that occupied artificial nest boxes constructed at three sites downstream of the most PCB-contaminated section of the HR and at control sites that were upriver (Champlain Canal) of the point sources or in Ithaca, New York, a locale distant from the HR.

Despite high tissue burdens in specimens at the Champlain Canal (probably due to their migrations through the PCB contaminated HR corridor), total PCBs and TEQ burdens were still higher in eggs and nestlings from the three HR locales downriver of the PCB hotspots (Secord et al., 1999). Nestlings at the most contaminated sites exhibited two to four times greater concentrations of PCBs than the eggs from the same sites, suggesting that their diets were contaminated with PCBs. The PCB homologue pattern in insects from the HR was similar to that in the tree swallows, suggesting that prey from the HR was the primary source of contamination to the nestlings. TCDD TEQs from PCBs in tree swallows from two of the downstream sites were among the highest ever reported in the avian literature, exceeding those TCDD TEQs linked to adverse health effects in a number of bird species including total reproductive failure (Ludwig et al., 1993).

Nests built along the HR were significantly lighter and had fewer feathers than those at reference sites, indicating their lower quality. Furthermore, the number of fledglings produced was significantly correlated with the number of feathers in nests at the onset of egg-laying. This is among the first evidence of behavioral abnormalities in populations of passerines associated with exposure to PCBs. Nest abandonment and hatchability of eggs differed significantly between the contaminated and control sites resulting in significantly lower fledgling production at the contaminated sites for one of the two years of the study. Laboratory experiments would have predicted 100 percent embryo mortality in the field, which clearly is not the case. Tree swallows may be particularly resistant to PCB-induced toxicity or that individuals in the HR population may have developed tolerance to these chronically high exposures (McCarty and Secord, 1999a,b).

Stapleton et al. (2001) used DNA fingerprinting to compare mutation rates in tree swallows from two contaminated HR sites to those in cleaner populations. Mutation rate was calculated based on the number of DNA fragments in the fingerprinting patterns of nestlings that did not match those in their parents. Mutation rates were very similar at the contaminated and cleaner sites despite a 182-fold difference in tissue burdens of total PCBs in nestlings. It is likely that the higher chlorinated PCB homologues present in the HR biota are not highly mutagenic.

Management Implications

Toxic responses that are meaningful at the organismic/population/community levels are only beginning to be evaluated in HR taxa. For example, despite their exposure to and bioaccumulation of cancer-causing toxicants, high prevalence of liver neoplasms, and a truncated age structure, laboratory studies have yet to be conducted in which the role of specific contaminants such as PCBs in inducing tumors is investigated in Atlantic tomcod. Early life-stage toxicities are very sensitive and population-relevant outcomes in fish from exposures to PCDD/Fs and coplanar PCBs. The likelihood of these compounds in eliciting these early life-stage effects in HR fish is only beginning to be explored. Similarly, fish are highly sensitive to EDCs, yet only recently have studies been initiated to evaluate these responses in fish exposed to HR contaminants.

One conclusion from the studies conducted to date is the unexpectedly small number of gross toxicities observed in HR populations despite their exposure to, and bioaccumulation of, high levels of contaminants. In part, this results from the ability of chronically exposed populations to acquire resistance to toxicants through genetic adaptation, physiological acclimation, or a combination of both. The development of resistance may be common in fish populations from highly impacted ecosystems such as the HR. Although evolutionary change is typically viewed as a lengthy process, selection pressure in highly polluted environments may be so intense such that change occurs more rapidly than originally thought possible. This has been empirically demonstrated in oligochaete worms which under controlled laboratory conditions acquired resistance in only a very few generations and perhaps in PCB-exposed killifish. What are the life history characteristics that allow some species to acquire resistance and others not? In rodent models, mechanisms have been elucidated that may provide physiologically-based tolerance of PCDD/Fs and PCBs and the applicability of this and other potential mechanisms of acclimation of natural populations should be explored.

While resistance may provide short-term benefits to populations in the face of insult from individual or single classes of toxicants, they probably do not come without associated costs. These may include enhanced sensitivities to other stressors or decreased physiological performance in the absence of toxicants in remediated environments. Also, the presence of resistant populations increases the likelihood of transfer of contaminants to higher trophic levels in food chains. Furthermore, the widespread occurrence of resistance in challenged populations may compromise the use of biomarker approaches, in that false negative responses may be observed. Mechanistic studies on the bases of resistance may provide insights into their attendant costs and likely persistence in remediated environments and molecular tools are under development in aquatic taxa to address this question.

Another problem in evaluating the toxicity of individual or classes of contaminants to HR populations is their exposure to complex mixtures of chemicals in combination with physical stressors. Even in well-defined rodent model systems, there is much uncertainty regarding the toxic effects of mixtures of chemicals and the mechanistic bases of their actions. Preliminary results with fish suggest that the toxic effects of exposure of adults and young life stages to mixtures of metals and PCBs or PAHs may be profound. Even within individual classes of xenobiotics, such as PCBs, interactive effects among different forms of a single toxicant class may be other than additive and significantly affect toxicity.

Another problem in assessing the toxicity of individual or classes of contaminants is that the extent of interindividual, interpopulation, and interspecific variation in response to environmental exposure is large, making statistical interpretation of results from these studies difficult. For example, should highly sensitive or more tolerant species be used as sentinels? The use of feral animals in laboratory studies introduces difficulties not encountered in typical toxicological experiments.

For the future, investigations are needed which combine field observations of adverse effects at the organismic level that may be detrimental to population/community viability with controlled laboratory studies in which similar alterations are induced in the same species with environmentally realistic levels of model contaminants. Furthermore, studies in which the mechanistic bases of these toxicities are identified may in the future allow for the application of relatively simple molecular assays in environmental risk assessment. But, successful adoption of this strategy requires long-term commitments on the part of the investigator and funding agencies.

Acknowledgments

IW acknowledges support of NIEHS SBRP Grant ES10344 and Center Grant ES00260.

REFERENCES

Adams, D. A., O'Connor, J. S., and Weisberg, S. B. 1998. Final Report Sediment Quality of the NY/NJ Harbor System. EPA/902-R-98-001.

Aulerich, R. J., Ringer, R. K., and Iwamoto, S. 1973. Reproductive failure and mortality in mink fed on Great Lakes fish. *Journal of Reproduction and Fertility* (Suppl.) **19**:365–76.

Barnthouse, L. W., Glaser, D., and Young, J. 2003. Effects of historic PCB exposures on the reproductive success of the Hudson River striped bass population. *Environmental Science and Technology* **37**:223–8.

Baumann, P. C. 1998. Epizootics of cancer in fish associated with genotoxins in sediment and water. *Mutation Research* **411**:227–33.

Belton, T., Ruppel, B., Lockwood, K., Shiboski, S., Bukowski, G., Roundy, R., Weinstein, N., and Whelan, H. 1985. *A Study of Toxic Hazards to Urban Recreational Fishermen and Crabbers.* Office of Science and Research. New Jersey Department of Environmental Protection, Trenton, NJ.

Berman, M., and Bartha, R. 1986. Control of the methylation process in a mercury-polluted aquatic sediment. *Environmental Pollution Series B* **11**:41–53.

Bode, R. W., Novak, M. A., Abele, L. E., and Heitzman, D. I. 2001a. *Biological assessment of tributaries of the Lower HR.* New York State Department of Environmental Conservation, Albany, New York.

2001b. *Biological assessment of tributaries of the Lower Hudson River II. Targeted studies of stressed streams.* New York State Department of Environmental Conservation, Albany, New York.

Boehm, P. D., and 19 coauthors. 1988. R. *Phase 2 Final Report on National Status and Trends Mussel Watch Program Collection of Bivalves and Surficial Sediments form Coastal U.S. Atlantic and Pacific Locations and Analysis for Organic Chemicals and Trace Elements.* Battelle Ocean Sciences, Battelle Pacific Northwest, Science Applications International Corp, San Diego, CA.

Bonnevie, N. L., Huntley, S. L., Found, B. W., and Wenning, R. J. 1994. Trace metal contamination in surficial sediments from Newark Bay, New Jersey. *Science of the Total Environment* **144**:1–16.

Bush, C. P., and Weis, J. S. 1983. Effects of salinity on fertilization success in two populations of killifish, *Fundulus heteroclitus. Biological Bulletin* **164**:406–417.

Callahan, P., and Weis, J. S. 1983. Methylmercury effects on regeneration and ecdysis in fiddler crabs, (*Uca pugilator, Uca pugnax*) after short-term and chronic pre-exposure. *Archives of Environmental Contamination & Toxicology* **12**:707–714.

Cook, P. M., Robbins, J. A., Endicott, D. D., Lodge, K. B., Guiney, P. D., Walker, M. K., Zabel, E. W., and Peterson, R. D. 2003. Effects of aryl hydrocarbon receptor-mediated early life stage toxicity on lake trout populations in Lake Ontario during the 20th century. *Environmental Science and Technology* **37**:3864–77.

Cormier, S. M., and Racine, R. N. 1990. Histopathology of Atlantic tomcod: A possible monitor of xenobiotics in northeast tidal rivers and estuaries, in J. F. McCarthy and L. R. Shugart (eds.). *Biomarkers of Environmental Contamination*.Boca Raton, FL: Lewis Publishers, pp. 59–71.

Courtenay, S. C., Grunwald, C. M., Kreamer, G.-L., Fairchild, W. L., Arsenault, J. T., Ikonomou, M., and Wirgin, I. I. 1999. A comparison of the dose and time response of CYP1A1 mRNA induction in chemically treated Atlantic tomcod from two populations. *Aquatic Toxicology* **47**:43–69.

Courtenay, S., Williams, P. J., Grunwald, C., Ong, T.-L., Konkle, B., and Wirgin, I. I. 1994. An assessment of within group variation in CYP1A1 mRNA inducibility in Atlantic tomcod. *Environmental Health Perspectives* **102**(Supplement 12):85–90.

Dey, W. P., Peck, T. H., Smith, C. E., and Kreamer, G.-L. 1993. Epizoology of hepatic neoplasia in Atlantic tomcod (*Microgadus tomcod*) from the Hudson River estuary. *Canadian Journal of Fisheries and Aquatic Sciences* **50**:1897–1907.

Donker, M. H., Zonneveld, C., and van Stralen, N. M. 1993. Early reproduction and increased reproductive allocation in metal-adapted populations of the terrestrial isopod, *Porcellio scaber. Oecologia* **96**:316–323.

Elskus, A. A., Monosson, E., McElroy, A. E., Stegeman, J. J., and Woltering, D. S. 1999. Altered CYP1A expression in *Fundulus heteroclitus* adults and larvae: a sign of pollutant resistance. *Aquatic Toxicology* **45**:99–113.

Ferguson, P. L., Iden, C. R., and Brownawell, B. J. 2001. Distribution and fate of neutral alkylphenol ethoxylate metabolites in a sewage-impacted urban estuary. *Environmental Science and Technology*, **35**:2428–35.

Foley, R. E., Jackling, S. J., Sloan, R. J., and Brown, M. K. 1988. Organochlorine and mercury residues in wild mink and otter: comparison with fish. *Environmental Toxicology and Chemistry* **7**: 363–74.

Foster, P. L. 1977. Copper exclusion as a mechanism of heavy metal tolerance in a green alga. *Nature* **269**:322–3.

Gardinali, P. R., and Wade, T. L. 1998. Contribution of PAHs, PCBs, and PCDD/PCDFs to the total induction equivalents (ΣIEs) in mollusks. *Marine Pollution Bulletin* **37**:27–31.

Great Lakes Environmental Center. 1996. *Summary of the Phase I metals sampling and analysis program for the NJ component of the NY/NJ Harbor estuary program.* Prepared for the NJ Harbor Dischargers Group, Little Ferry, NJ.

Hahn, M. E. 1998. The aryl hydrocarbon receptor: a comparative perspective. *Comparative Biochemistry and Physiology* Part C: **121**:23–53.

Hazen, R. E., and Kneip, T. J. 1980. Biogeochemical cycling of cadmium in a marsh ecosystem, in J. Nriagu (ed.), *Cadmium in the environment. Part 1. Ecological cycling.* New York: John Wiley & Sons, pp. 399–424.

Ikonomou, M., Fernandez, M., Courtenay, S. C., and Wirgin, I. I. 2004. Spatial variation and source prediction of PCBs and PCDD/Fs among young-of-the-year and adult tomcod (*Microgadus tomcod*) in the Hudson River Estuary. *Environmental Science and Technology* **38**:976–83.

Jensen, S., Kihlstrom, J. E., Olsson, M., Lundberg, C., and Orberg, J. 1977. Effects of PCBs and DDT on mink (*Mustela vison*) during the reproductive season. *Ambio* **6**(4):239.

Khan, A. T., and Weis, J. S. 1987. Effects of methylmercury on sperm and eggs viability in two populations of killifish, *Fundulus heteroclitus*. *Archives of Environmental Contamination and Toxicology* **16**:499–505.

1993a. Bioaccumulation of heavy metals in two populations of mummichog (*Fundulus heteroclitus*). *Bulletin of Environmental Contamination and Toxicology* **51**:1–5.

1993b. Differential effects of organic and inorganic mercury on the micropyle of the eggs of *Fundulus heteroclitus*. *Environmental Biology of Fishes* **37**:323–7.

Khan, A. T., Weis, J. S., and D'Andrea, L. 1989. Bioaccumulation of four heavy metals in two populations of grass shrimp, *Palaemonetes pugio*. *Bulletin of Environmental Contamination and Toxicology* **42**:339–43.

Kim, J. C. S., Chao, E. S., Brown, M. P., and Sloan, R. 1989. Pathology of brown bullhead, *Ictalurus nebulosus*, from highly contaminated and relatively clean sections of the Hudson River. *Bulletin of Environmental Contamination and Toxicology* **43**:144–50.

Klerks, P. L., and Bartholomew, P. R. 1991. Cadmium accumulation and detoxification in a Cd resistant population of the oligochaete *Limnodrilus hoffmeisteri*. *Aquatic Toxicology* **19**:97–112.

Klerks, P. L., and Levinton, J. S. 1989a. Effects of heavy metals in a polluted aquatic system, in S. A. Levin, S. A. and M. A. Harwell (eds.), *Ecotoxicology: Problems and Approaches*. New York: Springer-Verlag, pp. 41–67.

1989b. Rapid evolution of metal resistance in a benthic oligochaete inhabiting a metal-polluted site. *The Biological Bulletin* **176**:13–141.

Kneip, T. J., and Hazen, R. E. 1979. Deposit and mobility of cadmium in a marsh cove ecosystem and the relation to cadmium concentration in biota. *Environmental Health Perspectives* **28**:67–73.

Kraus, M. L., and Weis, J. S. 1988. Differences in the effects of mercury on telson regeneration in two populations of the grass shrimp, *Palaemonetes pugio*. *Archives of Environmental Contamination and Toxicology* **17**:115–120.

Kraus, M. L., Weis, J. S., and Weis, P. 1988. Effects of mercury on larval and adult grass shrimp (*Palaemonetes pugio*). *Archives of Environmental Contamination and Toxicology* **17**:355–63.

Levinton, J. S., Klerks, P., Martinez, D. E., Montero, C., Sturmbauer, C., Suatoni, L., and Wallace, W. 1999. Running the gauntlet: pollution, evolution and reclamation of an estuarine bay, in M. Whitfield, J. Matthews and C. Reynolds (eds.), *Aquatic Life Cycles Strategies: Survival in a Variable Environment*. Plymouth, UK: Marine Biological Association of the United Kingdom, pp. 125–38.

Levinton, J. S., Suatoni, E., Wallace, W., Junkins, R., Kelaher, B., and Allen, B. 2003. *Rapid Loss of Genetically Based Resistance to Metals after the Cleanup of a Superfund Site*. Washington, DC: Proceedings of the National Academy of Sciences **100**:9889–91.

Long, E. R., and Morgan, L. G. 1991. *The Potential for Biological Effects of Sediment-sorbed Contaminants Tested in the National Status and Trends Program*. NOAA Office of Coastal and Estuarine Assessment, Seattle, WA.

Long, E. R., Robertson, A., Wolfe, D. A., Hameedi, J., and Sloane, G. M. 1996. Estimates of the spatial extent of sediment toxicity in major US estuaries. *Environmental Science and Technology* **30**:3585–92.

Long, E. R., Wolfe, D. A., Scott, J., Thursby, G. B., Stern, E. A., Peven, C., and Schwartz, T. 1995. *Magnitude and Extent of Sediment Toxicity in the Hudson-Raritan Estuary*. NOAA Tech. Mem. NOS ORCA 88.

Ludwig, J. P. et al. 1993. Caspian tern reproduction in the Saginaw Bay ecosystem following a 100-year flood event. *Journal of Great Lakes Research* **19**:96–108.

Luoma, S. 1977. Detection of trace contaminant effects in aquatic ecosystems. *Journal of the Fisheries Research Board of Canada* **34**:436–9.

Martinez, D. E., and Levinton, J. 1996. Adaptation to heavy metals in the aquatic oligochaete *Limnodrilus hoffmeisteri*: evidence for control by one gene. *Evolution* **50**:1339–43.

McArdle, M., McElroy, A. E., and Elskus, A. A.. 2004. Enzymatic and estrogenic responses in fish exposed to organic pollutants in the New York-New Jersey (USA) Harbor Complex. *Environmental Toxicology and Chemistry* **23**:953–9.

McCarty, J. P., and Secord, A. L. 1999a. Nest-building behavior in PCB-contaminated tree swallows. *The Auk* **116**:55–63.

1999b. Reproductive ecology of tree swallow (*Tachycineta bicolor*) with high levels of polychlorinated biphenyl contamination. *Environmental Toxicology and Chemistry* **18**:1433–9.

McElroy, A. E., Elskus, A. A., and Fay, A. A. 2000. New approaches for toxicity identification: evaluation of hydrophobic organic contaminants in sediments, in F. T. Price, K. V. Brix, and N. K. Lanes (eds.), *Environmental Toxicology and Risk Assessment. Recent Achievements in Environmental Fate and Transport: Ninth Volume ASTM STP1381*. West Conshohocken, PA: American Society for Testing and Materials, pp. 239–55.

McElroy, A. E., Mena, L., Magliulo-Cepraino, L., Schreibman, M., and Denslow, N. Submitted. Limited evidence of endocrine disruption in adult winter flounder living in Jamaica Bay, NY, a sewage-impacted estuary. *Marine Environmental Research*.

Mehrle, P. M., Haines, T. A., Hamilton, S., Ludke, J. L., Mayer, F. L., and Ribick, M. A. 1982. Relationship between body contaminants and bone development in East-Coast striped bass. *Transactions of the American Fisheries Society* **111**:231–41.

Mehrle, P., and Ludke, L. 1983. *Impacts of Contaminants on Early Life Stages of Striped Bass*. Progress Report 1980–1983. Columbia National Fisheries Research Laboratory, Fish and Wildlife Service, U.S. Department of the Interior, Columbia, Missouri.

Meyer, J., and Di Giulio, R. 2002. Patterns of heritability of decreased EROD activity and resistance to PCB 126-induced teratogenesis in laboratory-reared offspring of killifish (*Fundulus heteroclitus*) from a creosote-contaminated site in the Elizabeth River, VA, USA. *Marine Environmental Research* **54**:1–6.

Meyerson, A. L., Luther, G. W., Krajewski, J., and Hires, R. I. 1981. Heavy metal distribution in Newark Bay sediments. *Marine Pollution Bulletin* **12**:244–50.

Monosson, E., Fleming, W. J., and Sullivan, C. V. 1994. Effects of the planar polychlorinated biphenyl 3,3′,4,4′-tetrachlorobiphenyl on ovarian development, plasma levels of sex steroid hormones and vitellogenin in the white perch (*Morone americana*). *Aquatic Toxicology* **29**:1–19.

Nacci, D. E., Champlin, D., Coiroo, L., McKinney, R., and Jayarman, S. 2002. Predicting the occurrence of genetic adaptation to dioxinlike compounds in populations of the estuarine fish *Fundulus heteroclitus*. *Environmental Toxicology and Chemistry* **21**:1525–32.

Nacci, D., Coiro, L., Champlin, D., Jayaraman, S., McKinney, R., Gleason, T. R., Munns, Jr., W. R., Specker, J. L., and Cooper K. R. 1999. Adaptations of wild populations of the estuarine fish *Fundulus heteroclitus* to persistent environmental contaminants. *Marine Biology* **134**:9–17.

NYSDEC. 2001. *Hudson River PCB Biota Database*. Bureau of Habitat, Division of Fish, Wildlife and Marine Resources, Albany, NY. Updated March 13, 2001.

Prince, R., and Cooper, K. R. 1995a. Comparisons of the effects of 2,3,7,8-tetrachlordibenzo-*p*-dioxin on chemically impacted and nonimpacted subpopulations of *Fundulus heteroclitus*. I. TCDD toxicity. *Environmental Toxicology and Chemistry* **14**:579–88.

1995b. Comparisons of the effects of 2,3,7,8-tetrachlorodibenzo-*p*-dioxin on chemically impacted and nonimpacted subpopulations of *Fundulus heteroclitus*. II. Metabolic considerations. *Environmental Toxicology and Chemistry* **14**:589–96.

Rice, C. A., Plesha, P. D., Casilas, E., Mistano, D. A., and Meador, J. P. 1995. Growth and survival of three marine invertebrate species in sediments from the Hudson-Raritan Estuary, New York, *Environmental Toxicology and Chemistry* **14**:1931–40.

Roy, N. K., Kreamer, G.-L., Konkle, B., Grunwald, C., and Wirgin, I. 1995. Characterization and prevalence of a polymorphism in the 3′ untranslated region of cytochrome P4501A1 in cancer prone Atlantic tomcod. *Archives of Biochemistry and Biophysics* **322**:204–213.

Roy, N. K., and Wirgin, I. 1997. Characterization of the aromatic hydrocarbon receptor gene and its expression in Atlantic tomcod. *Archives of Biochemistry and Biophysics* **344**:373–86.

Santoro, E. D., and Koepp, S. J. 1986. Mercury levels in organisms in proximity to an old chemical Site (Berrys Creek, Hackensack Meadowland, New Jersey, USA). *Marine Pollution Bulletin* **17**:219–24.

Schlezinger, J. J., White, R. D., and Stegeman, J. J. 1999. Oxidative inactivation of cytochrome P4501A stimulated by 3,3′4,4′-tetrachlorobiphenyl: production of reactive oxygen by vertebrate CYP1As. *Molecular Pharmacology* **56**:588–97.

Secord, A. L., McCarty, J. P., Echols, K. R., Meadows, J. C., Gale, R. W., and Tillit, D. E. 1999. Polychlorinated biphenyls and 2,3,7,8-tetrachlorodibenzo-p-dioxin equivalents in tree swallow from the upper Hudson River, New York State, USA. *Environmental Toxicology and Chemistry* **18**:2519–25.

Serbst, J. R., Kuhn, A., Tagliabue, M., and Ringenary, M. 2001. Differences in stressor sensitivity in geographically distinct populations of *Ampelisca abdita*. *SETAC* 2001. p. 169.

Skinner, L. C., Prince, R., Waldman, J., Newell, A. J., and Shastay, Jr., J. 1997. *Chemical Residues in Fish, Bivalves, Crustaceans and a Cephalopod from the New York-New Jersey Harbor Estuary: Dioxins and*

Furans. New York State Department of Environmental Conservation, Division of Fish, Wildlife and Marine Resources, Albany, New York.

Smit, M. D., Leonards, P. E. G., Murk, A. J., de Jongh, A. W. J. J., and van Hattum, B. 1996. *Development of otter-based quality objectives for PCBs.* Institute for Environmental Studies. Vrije Universiteit, Amsterdam. p. 129.

Smith, C. E., Peck, T. H., Klauda, R. J., and McLaren, J. B. 1979. Hepatomas in Atlantic tomcod *Microgadus tomcod* (Walbaum) collected in the Hudson River estuary in New York. *Journal of Fish Diseases* 2:313–319.

Smith, G. M., Khan, A. T., Weis, J. S., and Weis, P. 1995. Behavior and brain chemistry correlates in mummichogs (*Fundulus heteroclitus*) from polluted and unpolluted environments. *Marine Environmental Research* 39:329–33.

Smith, G. M., and Weis, J. S. 1997. Predator-prey relationships in mummichogs (*Fundulus heteroclitus*): effects of living in a polluted environment. *Journal of Experimental Marine Biology and Ecology* 209:75–87.

Stapleton, M., Dunn, P. O., McCarty, J., Secord, A., and Whittingham, L. A. 2001. Polychlorinated biphenyl contamination and minisatellite DNA mutation rates of tree swallows. *Environmental Toxicology and Chemistry* 20:2263–7.

Sunda, W. G., Engel, D. W., and Thuotte, R. M. 1978. Effects of chemical speciation on the toxicity of cadmium to the grass shrimp *Palaemonetes pugio*: importance of free cadmium ion. *Environmental Science and Technology* 12(4):409–413.

Tillitt, D. E., Gale, R. W., Meadows, J. C., Zajicek, J. L., Peterman, P. H., Heaton, S. N., Jones, P. D., Bursian, S. J., Kubiak, T. J., Giesy, J. P., and Aulerich, R. J. 1996. Dietary exposure of mink to carp from Saginaw Bay. 3. Characterization of dietary exposure to planar halogenated hydrocarbons, dioxin equivalents, and biomagnification. *Environmental Science and Technology* 30:283–91.

Toppin, S. V., Heber, M., Weis, J. S., and Weis, P. 1987. Changes in reproductive biology and life history in *Fundulus heteroclitus* in a polluted environment, in W. Vernberg, A. Calabrese, F. Thurberg, and F. J. Vernberg (eds.). *Pollution Physiology of Estuarine Organisms.* Columbia, SC: University of South Carolina Press, pp. 171–84.

Wade, T. L., Sericano, J. L., Gardinali, P. R., Wolff, G., and Chambers, L. 1998. NOAA's 'Mussel Watch' project: current use organic compounds in bivalves. *Marine Pollution Bulletin* 37:20–6.

Wallace, W. G., Lopez, G. R., and Levinton, J. S. 1998. Cadmium resistance in an oligochaete and its effects on cadmium trophic transfer to an omnivorous shrimp. *Marine Ecology Progress Series* 172:225–37.

Weis, J. S., Renna, M., Vaidya, S., and Weis, P. 1987. Mercury tolerance in killifish: a stage-specific phenomenon, in J. Capuzzo and D. Kester (eds.).*Oceanic Processes in Marine Pollution 1. Biological Processes and Wastes in the Ocean.* Malabar, L: Krieger Publ. Co., pp. 31–6.

Weis, J. S., and Weis, P. 1984. A rapid change in methylmercury tolerance in a population of killifish, *Fundulus heteroclitus*, from a golf course pond. *Marine Environmental Research* 13:231–45.

Weis, J. S., Weis, P., and Heber, M. 1982. Variation in response to methylmercury by killifish (*Fundulus heteroclitus*) embryos, in J. G. Pearson, R. Foster and W. Bishop (eds.). *Aquatic Toxicology and Hazard Assessment, Fifth Conference.* ASTM STP 766. American Society for Testing and Materials, Philadelphia, Pennsylvania, pp.109–119.

Weis, J. S., Weis, P., Heber, M., and Vaidya, S. 1981. Methylmercury tolerance of killifish (*Fundulus heteroclitus*) embryos from a polluted vs non-polluted environment. *Marine Biology* 65:283–7.

Weis, J. S., Weis, P., Heber, M., and Vaidya, S. 1982. Investigations into mechanisms of methylmercury tolerance in killifish (*Fundulus heteroclitus*) embryos, in W. Vernberg, A. Calabrese, F. Thurberg, and F. J. Vernberg (eds.). *Physiological Mechanisms of Marine Pollutant Toxicity.* New York: Academic Press, pp. 311–30.

Weis, J. S., Weis, P., Renna, M., and Vaidya, S. 1985. Search for a physiological component of methylmercury tolerance in the mummichog, *Fundulus heteroclitus*, in F. J. Vernberg, F. Thurberg, A. Calabrese, and W. B. Vernberg (eds.), *Marine Pollution and Physiology: Recent Advances* Columbia, SC: University of South Carolina Press, pp. 309–26.

Weis, P. 1984. Metallothionein and mercury tolerance in the killifish, *Fundulus heteroclitus. Marine Environmental Research* 14:153–66.

Wenning, R. J., Bonnevie, N. L., and Huntley, S. L. 1994. Accumulation of metals, polychlorinated biphenyls, and polycyclic aromatic hydrocarbons in sediments from the lower Passaic River, New Jersey. *Archives of Environmental Contamination and Toxicology* 27:64–81.

Westin, D. T., Olney, C. E., and Rogers, B. A. 1983. Effects of parental and dietary PCBs on survival, growth, and body burdens of larval striped bass. *Bulletin of Environmental Contamination and Toxicology* 30:50–7.

1985. Effects of parental and dietary organochlorines on survival and body burdens of striped bass larvae. *Transactions of the American Fisheries Society* **114**:125–36.

Williams, S. C., Simpson, H. J., Olsen, C. R., and Bopp, R. F. 1978. Sources of heavy metals in sediments of the Hudson River estuary. *Marine Chemistry* **6**:195–213.

Wirgin, I. I., Grunwald, C., Courtenay, S., Kreamer, G.-L., Reichert, W. L., and Stein, J. E. 1994. A biomarker approach to assessing xenobiotic exposure in Atlantic tomcod from the North American Atlantic coast. *Environmental Health Perspectives* **102**:764–70.

Wirgin, I. I., Konkle, B., Pedersen, M., Grunwald, C., Williams, P. J., and Courtenay, S. 1996. Interspecific differences in cytochrome P4501A mRNA inducibility in four species of Atlantic coast anadromous fishes. *Estuaries* **19**:913–22.

Wirgin, I. I., Kreamer, G.-L., Grunwald, C., Squibb, K., Garte, S. J., and Courtenay, S. 1992. Effects of prior exposure history on cytochrome P450IA mRNA induction by PCB congener 77 in Atlantic tomcod. *Marine Environmental Research* **34**:103–8.

Wirgin, I., and Waldman, J. R. 1998. Altered gene expression and genetic damage in North American fish populations. *Mutation Research* **399**: 193–219.

———. 2004. Resistance to contaminants in North American fish populations. *Mutation Research* **552**:73–100.

Wolfe, D. A., Long, E. R., and Thursby, G. B. 1996. Sediment toxicity in the Hudson-Raritan Estuary: Distribution and correlations with chemical contamination. *Estuaries* **19**:901–912.

Wren, C. D. 1991. Cause-effect linkages between chemicals and populations of mink (*Mustela vison*) and otter (*Lutra canadensis*) in the Great Lakes basin. *Journal of Toxicology and Environmental Health* **33**:549–85.

Yuan, Z., Wirgin, M., Courtenay, S., Ikonomou, M., and Wirgin, I. 2001. Is hepatic cytochrome P4501A1 expression predictive of dioxins, furans, and PCB burdens in Atlantic tomcod from the Hudson River estuary? *Aquatic Toxicology* **54**:217–30.

Zamuda, C. D., and Sunda, W. G. 1982. Bioavailability of dissolved copper to the American oyster *Crassostrea virginica* I. Importance of chemical speciation. *Marine Biology* **66**:77–82.

Zhou, T., John-Alder, H., Weis, P., and Weis, J. S. 1999. Thyroidal status of mummichogs (*Fundulus heteroclitus*) from a polluted versus a reference habitat. *Environmental Toxicology and Chemistry* **18**:2817–23.

Zhou, T., and Weis, J. S. 1998. Swimming behavior and predator avoidance in three populations of *Fundulus heteroclitus* larvae after embryonic and/or larval exposure to methylmercury. *Aquatic Toxicology* **43**:131–48.

Zhou, T., Weis, P., and Weis, J. S. 1998. Mercury burden in two populations of *Fundulus heteroclitus* after sublethal methylmercury exposure. *Aquatic Toxicology* **42**:37–47.

Zielinski, J. 2001. "Responsiveness of Hudson River Fish to Cytochrome P4501A Inducers and its Relationship to Genotoxicity." MS Thesis, Marine Sciences Research Center, State University of New York, Stony Brook, Stony Brook, NY.

Index

Lightning Source UK Ltd.
Milton Keynes UK
UKOW06f1621040914

238059UK00007B/350/P

DATE DUE
